German Studies in the United States

German Studies
in the
United States

A Historical Handbook

Edited by

PETER UWE HOHENDAHL

THE MODERN LANGUAGE ASSOCIATION OF AMERICA
NEW YORK   2003

© 2003 by The Modern Language Association of America
All rights reserved
Printed in the United States of America

For information about obtaining permission to reprint material from MLA book
publications, send your request by mail (see address below), e-mail (permissions@
mla.org), or fax (646 458-0030).

LIBRARY OF CONGRESS CATALOGING-IN-PUBLICATION DATA

German studies in the United States : a historical handbook / edited by Peter Uwe
Hohendahl.
   p. cm.
Includes bibliographical references and index.
  ISBN 0-87352-988-X (hardcover : alk. paper)—ISBN 0-87352-989-8
(pbk. : alk. paper)
  1. German philology—Study and teaching (Higher)—United States.
2. Civilization, Germanic—Study and teaching (Higher)—United States.
I. Hohendahl, Peter Uwe.
  PF3068.U6G38 2003
430'.71'173—dc22   2003018165

Printed on recycled paper

Published by The Modern Language Association of America
26 Broadway, New York, New York 10004-1789
www.mla.org

CONTENTS

1

The German Faculty: Organization and Experience
EDITED BY PATRICIA HERMINGHOUSE

2

Instruction
EDITED BY FRANK TROMMLER

3

Approaches and Methods
EDITED BY PETER UWE HOHENDAHL

4

Research in Historical Perspective
EDITED BY JOHN A. MCCARTHY

German Studies in the United States

A General Introduction

PETER UWE HOHENDAHL

The Project

This volume offers a history of German studies in the United States. Writing the history of an academic discipline, whether located in the sciences or in the humanities, is no longer a new idea. In recent years, the history of English studies in England and the United States has received a great deal of attention (Graff; Scholes). Similarly, in Germany, the history of German studies (*Germanistik*) has played a significant role in the definition of the field as a way of coming to terms with the field's interesting but also complex past (Fohrmann, *Das Projekt*; Weimar). The same cannot be said about the evolution of German studies in the United States. Although American Germanists have occasionally scrutinized their past in order to understand their present situation, a comprehensive study has been lacking (Benseler, Lohnes, and Nollendorfs; Trommler, *Germanistik in den USA*). It seems that practitioners of Germanics in this country have been interested more in solving immediate problems in their discipline than in analyzing their history. But since the present outlook of the field is not overly promising in terms of enrollments and available faculty positions, such analysis is needed. Germanics, like many other disciplines in the humanities, must cope with drastic changes in the university as well as with outside pressures that have undermined the self-understanding of Germanists in this country and raised the question of the discipline's identity. In the essays in this volume, the term *Germanics* is used exclusively for the

American institution of teaching German language, literature, and culture; *Germanistik* is used exclusively for the profession in Germany. *German studies* is used for a broader view of the profession, a view that transcends language and literature. *Germanist* is used for both German and American members of the profession.

Today German studies finds itself at a crossroads, faced with an uncertain future in an academic environment where neither the traditional liberal arts college nor the research university that dominated the twentieth century can be taken for granted any longer. It is appropriate under such circumstances to take stock and reflect on the development of a professional discipline that can trace its beginnings back to the late nineteenth century and may have reached its postwar peak in the decade between 1958 and 1968, when federal support through the programs of the National Defense Education Act gave German studies a national visibility. That the powerful response of the United States government to the Sputnik crisis benefited all foreign language programs demonstrates that the development of German studies cannot be studied and grasped as a merely internal scholarly and pedagogical evolution. More than once, political and social factors influenced its course.

For this reason the project of this volume could not be carried out along the lines of a strictly intrinsic history of science, focusing on the construction of paradigms and paradigm shifts as a mode of understanding the evolution of a particular discipline. Instead, the history of Germanics, as it is presented here, deliberately foregrounds various aspects that a methodology-oriented approach would consider extrinsic. For lack of a better term, our history might be called institutional, exploring multiple, sometimes heterogeneous aspects of German as a professional discipline. The contributors often did research in uncharted territories without the assurance that there would be a definable and rewarding result. While questions of methodology and theory have received extensive treatment, they have been juxtaposed with less familiar questions, such as the composition of the professoriat, employment patterns, and the impact of foreign cultural politics. This broader and more varied outlook has altered the nature of the project as well: instead of a disciplinary history, the volume presents the history of an academic profession. To accomplish this goal, the organization of the work had to be adjusted. We abandoned the narrative and chronological approach in favor of articles that cover specific topics, thereby offering a kaleidoscope of perspectives that complement one another. Our project is significantly different from recent German research that also widens the definition of the history of *Germanistik* without presenting a systematic approach (Fohrmann and Voßkamp): it has increased the use of empirical and statistical research as a tool in the analysis of problems for which a narrative approach is less suited.

An institutional history of German studies in the United States cannot treat the discipline as an isolated phenomenon. There is not only the environment of the American university and the impact of changing social and political factors to be considered but also the relevance of neighboring fields such as English, French, philosophy, and history. Moreover, since its inception, German studies in North America had to respond to the development of philological and literary studies in Germany, which had already established themselves in the early nineteenth century. From the German point of view, American and other foreign attempts to develop a discipline of German literary studies were viewed as a variant of *Auslandsgermanistik* ("Germanics in foreign countries") that would be expected to follow the natural lead of the mother country. This expectation has played a discernible role in the development of American German studies, although more in the consciousness of the participants than in the actual structure of the profession. Therefore, neither in its location in the university or college nor in its place in the field of academic professions can German studies be constructed in isolation. During its history, the discipline has shared important features with other disciplines: like English and French, it struggled for recognition as a serious scholarly field in the late nineteenth century, and with other foreign language departments it shared the threat of falling enrollments after the abolition of college foreign language requirements in the early 1970s. At different times, methodological and theoretical considerations created links between German studies and history, philosophy, and anthropology. Finally, budgetary concerns in the university frequently grouped German studies with other humanities departments. The professional autonomy of Germanics may have increased during the last thirty years, as indicated by the various new professional organizations in the field, but the discipline has also become more integrated into the American mainstream and, by the same token, more dependent on neighboring disciplines. Whether this process can be adequately described as Americanization depends on what one wants to foreground. While Americanization seems to have taken place in terms of professional organization, in terms of methodology and theory it would be more appropriate to speak of an internationalization that has defined literary studies since the 1970s. The New Criticism may well have been the last specifically American approach in literary criticism. Subsequent debates in theory have been characterized by an increasing degree of international exchange in which the question of national origin has become less and less meaningful. Instead, high-profile academic institutions and centers on both sides of the Atlantic have become the crucial places for transfer and appropriation. A more interesting question is how German studies has participated in this process.

Our project differs from an intrinsic history of the discipline in several ways. First of all, it is not a history of famous scholars and their influence on one another. Neither is it limited to a history of literary theory—that is, a history of approaches in German studies—that would trace the development of theoretical and methodological positions from the nineteenth century to the present. It is problematic anyway that such a development can be constructed as a teleological evolution from inferior beginnings to more truthful positions in the present, although an increase in complexity cannot be denied. Instead, the volume contains a broad array of materials that illustrate various aspects of the profession. Part 1, "The German Faculty," explores the organization and professional awareness of the German faculty in the American academy by examining problems of professional identity, employment patterns, and the change of academic values in the profession. The structure of teaching receives a more extensive and systematic treatment than customary in part 2, "Instruction." Some essays deal with the history of the German undergraduate and graduate program; others focus on the development of the canon of German literature taught in the classroom and the training of language teachers. The volume differentiates between the discipline of German studies and the profession. While part 5, "Organizing the Profession," examines the emergence of professional organizations and the history of professional journals, part 6 deals exclusively with the changing profile of the professoriat. Part 7 carries this broader treatment a step further by exploring the cultural, social, and ethnic context of German studies in the United States. The essays in this part analyze the impact of German immigration, the influence of the German government on the definition of the discipline, and the influence of German cultural organizations on the self-understanding of the profession. Parts 3 and 4 examine the development of theory, methodology, and the changing configuration of scholarship.

The Parameters of the Project

Before turning to an outline of the history of Germanics, the question of the boundaries and the stakes must be addressed. Where was the discipline located in the academy and what were its goals? The assessment of a century of German studies in the United States provides a chance to examine past achievements and future opportunities. To some extent the present work means to do this. Yet such an approach could easily underestimate the shifts in the institutional environment that in the 1990s and early twenty-first century have tended to subvert conventional definitions of disciplines. The American research university, the place where German studies as well as other foreign literatures and English studies developed and flourished, is in the midst of major restructuring. The distinction between the academic world and the world of business, between the sphere of ideas and theories and the sphere of commercial enterprises, is no longer clear. After the end of the cold war the American research university found itself in a new and challenging environment in which traditional patterns of research, especially in the natural sciences, became more difficult to uphold, because the federal government, which had previously focused its attention on defense research, was less interested in funding basic research. At the same time, private industry increasingly encouraged joint projects in which the division between basic theoretical and applied research was less clearly drawn (Slaughter and Leslie). In a recent assessment of the epistemological foundations of research, Michael Gibbons and his research group observe that the assumed priority of theoretical projects over applied research no longer describes the actual development of the 1980s and 1990s. They also note that this shift is by no means limited to the natural sciences but has major ramifications for the social sciences and the humanities as well (Gibbons, Limoges, Nowotny, Schwarzman, Scott, and Throw). Research and scholarship in German studies will therefore be affected by the self-understanding of a restructured American research university. A definition of the university's corporate goals in terms of excellence without much regard to the specific content of its disciplines will also affect German departments. Dereferentialization undercuts the aesthetic and moral value of the literary canon and thereby the mission of *Bildung* ("self-improvement"). More broadly, it redefines the relation between scholarship and educational services.

Not only are the boundaries of Germanics as a discipline currently blurry; the professional stakes are also high. The uncertain future of the humanities, and German studies among them, makes difficult an examination of the past. It undercuts the perception of disciplines as natural phenomena whose growth the historian can trace from modest beginnings to preordained ends. Instead, it underlines the historical character of academic disciplines and the fact that they owe their existence to specific cultural and social conditions in the past and have been shaped by changing needs in the university as well as by a variety of outside factors. In German studies a crucial factor was the creation of the American research university in the 1870s; the founding of Johns Hopkins (1876) and the University of Chicago (1891) are important examples (Geiger). That the new university was modeled on the German university as a place for the conception of independent research and scholarship would apply to many disciplines, but for German studies in particular it was the locus for an approach to literary criticism and linguistics that could be adopted. Briefly stated, the formation of the research university redefined the teaching of German in the United States. While the Anglo-American college system had room for language instruction and some teaching of German literature (as a form of moral and aesthetic appreciation), it was only with the development of graduate programs and specifically with the introduction of the PhD degree that the German language and German literature became the focus of autonomous disciplinary research in which methodological concerns played a major role. The much discussed German connection contained two separate moments: on the one hand, the influence of specific research methods that dominated literary studies in Germany during the later nineteenth century—that is, historical positivism—and, on the other, the more fundamental appropriation of the university as an autonomous institution devoted to learning and research. The autonomy turned out to be much more important for the history of German studies in the United States than did historical positivism, which was limited to a fairly short period.

It would be a serious mistake, however, to see the development of German studies exclusively in the light of the research university. Even those scholars who strongly encouraged the new research paradigm around 1900, among them Marion Dexter Learned, Kuno Francke, Julius Goebel, and Albert B. Faust, never thought of German exclusively in terms of *Wissenschaft* ("scholarship"). There were other equally important considerations, among them the significance of the German ethnic community in this country—that is, the fact that between 1850 and 1900 more than four million Germans had come to the United States—as well as the importance of German high culture for the educated American elite. While the German background of many Americans did not play a major role in the development of German studies after World War II, it was a discernible factor in the late nineteenth century, when German was still used in ethnic communities, where German schools competed with English ones, religious services were conducted in German, and German newspapers created a public sphere in which the German language was the medium of communication. The presence of these German immigrants, especially in areas where they had formed larger settlements, set the stage for the rise of German studies in the United States. But the growth of German as an academic discipline at the university cannot be derived simply from the existence of ethnic German culture in North America. Although some Germanists, most notably Goebel, attempted to create a direct link between the ethnic Germans and the discipline, the interests and cultural orientations of these groups were more distant than is commonly assumed (see Peterson in this volume). The study of German classicism, which defined literary studies during the late nineteenth century (see Hermand in this volume), was hardly central to most of the German ethnic community. When one looks more closely at the projects of the leading Germanists before 1914, it turns out that many of their concerns were related more immediately to an older interest in German idealism expressed by the American transcendentalists than to the conservative religious orientation of ethnic German culture. The relation between the field of German studies and the German community, therefore, was complex. The most persistent and effective connection between the two was the teaching of the German language at the secondary level, which served as an entry requirement for academic studies. For this reason high school enrollments have always played an important role in the national assessment of German studies in this country. The dominance of German as the first foreign language before World War I and the disastrous decline in enrollments during the war because of anti-German sentiments left their mark in the collective memory of the discipline. The decline was perceived as a fundamental threat to the existence of German studies. For Germanists like Alexander R. Hohlfeld, German culture in the United States was not a foreign culture but an indigenous regional culture that should be preserved at all costs. This protectiveness blinded Germanists to some extent to the actual needs of academic German departments, which were not as closely tied to the German cause as they thought.

The adverse fate of German during and after World War I is only one example of the relevance of the larger social and political context for German studies in the United States—obviously an extreme one, because the existence of the discipline was at stake. One could investigate the impact of major po-litical events and trends on the definition of the academic goals of German studies, but that approach occludes important elements of continuity and fails to acknowledge breaks that do not coincide with political configurations. Still, there is an obvious logic to seeing American Germanics as an expression of German-American foreign relations. More than once Germanists in the United States were invested in promoting cultural and political goals that were closely related to national politics, either on the German or the American side. Even the attempts to remain apolitical in this country, for instance during the early years of National Socialism, at least indirectly reflected a political position. The importance of political history for the fate of German studies is reinforced by the impact of political institutions on the German side. The significance of *Kulturpolitik*—that is, the cultural policies of the German government—should not be underestimated. Beginning with the first decade of the twentieth cen-tury, close ties between American Germanists and the Prussian government played a role in the shaping of German studies (see Seeba in this volume). The impact of these state interventions is difficult to measure in quantitative terms, because they occurred at different levels, but they have been a continuous element in the history of German studies. It is worth noting that the most successful collaboration occurred from the 1970s on, when American German-ists began to distance themselves from their colleagues in Germany. While during the 1930s German state intervention was characterized by the desire to manipulate German studies in this country in accordance with the ideological goals of National Socialism, after World War II West German agencies such as the Goethe Institut and the German Academic Exchange Service (DAAD, Deutscher Akademischer Austauschdienst) demonstrated considerably more sensitivity in dealing with American universities and the specific needs of German studies. They were increasingly more interested in cooperation with American institutions than in merely presenting a positive image of Germany. This cooperation resulted in a paradoxical situation: the trend toward an

Americanization of German studies in this country went hand in hand with increased collaboration between the institutions carrying out German policies and American colleges and universities.

By comparison the much discussed influence of German *Germanistik* appears to be a minor feature. While it participated in shaping German studies before World War I through graduate training, textbooks (language and literary history), and personal contacts, that influence in later phases should not be overrated. For one thing, the genteel Anglo-American tradition of literary studies, which had also modeled literary studies in the German form before the rise of professionalism in the late nineteenth century, continued to be present as a vital element of college education (Graff). Its proponents, who were particularly vocal in English departments, flatly denied the value of scientific studies and focused the attention on moral and aesthetic questions instead. The fairly narrow emphasis on German classicism, which characterized both teaching and research in American German departments before World War I, was the result of two converging tendencies: on the one hand, the persistent interest of the genteel tradition in moral and aesthetic values, for which authors such as Goethe, Schiller, and Lessing could provide the best examples, and, on the other, the impact of German *Literaturwissenschaft* ("literary scholarship"), which equally foregrounded German classicism. For this reason two leading scholars of Germanics, the German-born Francke, of Harvard, and the American-born Learned, of the University of Pennsylvania, could fundamentally agree on the task of German studies in the United States, namely, its cultural mission. The logical extension of this basic agreement was the idea of faculty exchanges between Germany and the United States, a project in which Francke was involved before the outbreak of the war. With the support of the Prussian state, a broad transdisciplinary exchange program was set up that included literary historians, philosophers, and historians (see Seeba in this volume).

After World War I the partial identity of German studies in the United States and Germany (it was never more than a partial identity) gave way to a more distanced relation. While German literary criticism went through a phase of theoretical and methodological controversy in which *Geistesgeschichte* ("history of ideas") emerged as the hegemonic force, for a number of reasons American Germanists were less involved in these debates (see Hohendahl in this volume, "From Philology to the New Criticism"). First of all, the disastrous decline in enrollments urged them to focus their attention on the undergraduate program, especially on language instruction. Second, American criticism, as it was practiced in English departments, showed little interest in the philosophical turn of German criticism during the 1920s; it was considered too abstract for the analysis of literature. It is possible that this pressure from the English departments created an intellectual barrier between American criticism and German criticism. With the rise of the New Criticism in the 1930s and

1940s and its concomitant importance in English departments, this distance could only widen. It is not accidental that in 1945 even a German-born scholar like Karl Viëtor, who had been a practitioner of *Geistesgeschichte* in Germany before he came to Harvard, advised his American colleagues to steer away from a philosophical approach that in his opinion was not only vague and lofty but also ethically problematic. But this advice overlooked the fact that *Geistesgeschichte* had never exerted a major influence on American Germanics.

Essentially the discipline of Germanics in the United States emerged as a hybrid with Anglo-American and German features in the setting of the American university, an institutional factor that ultimately determined the acceptable degree of German influences. World War I demonstrated that American public opinion could shape the course of the discipline when its German partiality was seen as hostile to American interests (see Hoecherl-Alden in this volume). Although the hybrid nature of German studies did not disappear after World War I, its configuration and balance changed, because the German ethnic element no longer played a significant role in the profession and the missionary approach had lost much of its purchasing power after the vilification of German culture during the war. The phenomenon of hybridity after World War II can best be defined either as a symbiosis of the American New Criticism and the German "werkimmanente Interpretation" ("intrinsic criticism") inaugurated by Wolfgang Kayser and the Swiss critic Emil Staiger during the 1940s and 1950s or as a form of international cooperation of the American New Left and its West German counterpart during the 1970s and 1980s. In either kind of cooperation, however, there were forces in the profession that disagreed—sometimes strongly—on how to understand the common project. They would denounce it as foreign or at least as outside the proper scope of American criticism. While more conservative American Germanists tended to perceive radical forms of political criticism as a dangerous German element, American liberals of the 1970s could understand versions of close reading as part of a problematic, conservative German heritage. Finally, even the American turn of the late 1980s and 1990s under the auspices of German studies as cultural studies did not really eliminate the hybrid character of the discipline, since the new paradigm drew on a variety of theoretical and methodological positions, some of which were indebted to German theory. Yet it is also apparent that this new form of hybridity has a much stronger international flavor than earlier versions; therefore, it would not be very helpful to define its nature in terms of national traditions.

The Phases of German Studies in the United States

The history of Germanics in the United States is marked by a number of turning points that have conveniently served as guideposts, among them World War I and the end of World War II. Obviously these markers refer to important political and military events that also affected the development of the profession. The result is by now a familiar narrative about the ups and downs of German studies in the United States. But does this approach do justice to the development of the profession from the late nineteenth century to the present? As soon as one examines more specific factors such as the methodology of language teaching or the composition of the professoriat, the customary political dates begin to lose their relevance. Some of the essays in this volume look at continuities and breaks in the history of Germanics that do not coincide with the political narrative. The following sketch uses the conventional framework, but with the understanding that not all elements fit into it.

The foundation of the Nationaler Deutschamerikanischer Lehrerbund in 1870 may be considered the inception of professionalized German studies in this country, yet in the broader context of the humanities, the foundation of the Modern Language Association in 1883 serves as an equally important event (see Bernd in this volume). Still, these dates only approximate the rapid but uneven formation of modern German departments at American universities and colleges. By 1900 German as a professional discipline was in clear evidence at major American research universities such as Cornell, Harvard, Chicago, and the University of Pennsylvania. These institutions, beginning in the 1880s, first developed PhD programs and correspondingly a strong emphasis on research among their faculty members. What must not be forgotten, however, is that they continued to be involved in undergraduate education, which included instruction in modern languages and literatures. As a result, modern foreign language departments, among them German departments, developed as two-tiered operations. In most instances, the increasingly professionalized faculty served in both the undergraduate and the graduate program, participating in various degrees in language teaching, undergraduate literature and culture courses, and the training of graduate students. These new departments had to deal with emerging tensions between the traditional mission of the undergraduate program and the professional needs of graduate students, who were expected to join the profession after receiving the PhD (see Berman in this volume).

While the undergraduate program continued to emphasize humanistic values that could be exemplified through major literary texts, the rise of graduate programs called for the development of scientific methods and theoretical reflection, which were basically imported from the German university. Hence around 1900, in the wake of Wilhelm Scherer (the most influential German academic critic of his time) and his school, philology and historical positivism became the methodological basis of the German graduate program. Yet in this shared frame American Germanists began to develop their own research projects, which reflected indigenous interests. Unlike their German colleagues, they could not overlook the fact that they served at academic institutions that continued to focus a large part of their energy on the undergraduate program. At the level of the graduate program, this emphasis also reinforced a strong interest in German classicism (Lessing, Goethe, Schiller), since future faculty members had to be prepared to serve the needs of the undergraduate program (see Richter in this volume).

However, that American graduate students, even those from a German ethnic background, experienced the German literary tradition as part of a foreign culture suggested the need for an awareness of cultural difference. This awareness could not be transferred to the students by simply appropriating the standards of late-nineteenth-century German literary criticism. One can observe the consciousness of cultural difference in the projects of Learned and Francke, who were both convinced of the importance of German high culture for the future of the United States. While Learned explored the culture of the German ethnic community (with emphasis on Pennsylvania) and considered its link with German elite culture, Francke, originally trained in Germany as a medievalist, became increasingly convinced of the need for a literary history written especially for an American audience. In his *Social Forces in German Literature* (1896) he emphasized the social and cultural context of German literature precisely because he believed that only this approach would enable American students to understand fully the evolution of the German mind.

The pedagogical link between the undergraduate and the graduate program in the German department of the late nineteenth century would extend into the twentieth century as well. It has characterized the history of German studies in the United States, including the inevitable tensions between undergraduate instruction and graduate training, that is, between the importance of research and the value of a general liberal education. These tensions have marked all language departments as well as English studies, but in German they were underscored because German-born and German-trained faculty members appeared to embody the spirit of research while American pragmatism supported the needs of the undergraduate program. These stereotypes have endured in the history of German studies. They returned in the critique of *Geistesgeschichte* during the 1950s and in a different version in the theoretical debates of the 1970s. Advocates of undergraduate education have typically underlined the special mission of the undergraduate program and warned against overemphasis on research (associated with the German university) as too specialized and too removed from the needs of the college.

The growth of German departments came to a sudden halt when the United States entered the war against Germany in World War I. The severe official measures against the use of the German language and against the dissemination of German culture created the first serious crisis for the profession, not only because of dropping enrollments but also because the profession seemed to have lost its mission, which had been associated with the transfer of German high culture. There can be little doubt that the first phase of Germanics came to an end in 1917. Yet the basic features and elements of German studies, which had evolved over a period of forty years, survived the crisis, largely because of the structure of postsecondary education in the United States, in which foreign languages occupied a relatively secure place in the humanities. If German lost its privileged position, it could still function under the umbrella of the foreign languages and their professional organization, the Modern Language Association. German departments could legitimize themselves in pragmatic terms by focusing on language teaching and general information about German life and culture. Graduate programs participated less in the theoretical debates, although the number of completed dissertations increased again. In this context, the American Association of Teachers of German (AATG), founded in 1926, played an important role (see Herminghouse in this volume, "History of the AATG"). Whereas some United States Germanists took part in the lively German theory discussion of the 1920s, it is apparent that this discourse was not at the center of their professional identity. The American discussion was less intense and less controversial. When following it in such professional journals as *Germanic Review* or the *German Quarterly*, one gets the impression of individual contributions that were not sufficiently interconnected: open questions found no resolutions, a hypothesis or suggestion was not necessarily picked up by a later contribution. The discussion of language teaching, however, remained a central part of the professional discourse (see Schulz in this volume, "Teacher Development at the Beginning of the Twentieth Century"). In short, in terms of literary theory the interwar years were characterized by low participation and a lack of clear orientation. With respect to matters of approach, one can possibly speak of a growing rift between German and American Germanists, insofar as the American side never made a strong effort to follow the new German paradigm by appropriating *Geistesgeschichte*, but there was also no definitive shift to another paradigm before the impact of the New Criticism in the 1950s. A possible exception might be the attitude toward *völkisch* and fascist criticism that entered the American discussion during the 1930s. But even there, as has been noted by more than one observer, German studies in this country avoided a clear commitment (see Hohendahl in this volume, "From Philology to the New Criticism"). The debate about the significance and merit of National Socialism was, for the most part, carried out in professional rather than theoretical and political terms. Public statements tried to avert damage to the German profession.

Despite the harsh setbacks of 1917, Germanics as a profession could continue its work and eventually recover, since there was enough continuity in most of the areas that defined the discipline. Neither the goals and methods of language instruction nor the conceptions of literature and aesthetic values were seriously affected by the war. Whether the old-fashioned grammar-and-translation approach was to be replaced by the natural or the direct method was a question debated among a highly specialized group of professionals within the modern languages (see Schulz in this volume, "Pedagogical Issues in German-Language Teaching"). While an argument could be made for or against creating a German atmosphere in the classroom, such an argument would refer to the success of language instruction rather than to the promotion of a particular image of German culture. By the same token, discussions about reading lists and a definition of the German literary canon did not show an immediate and serious break with the prewar tradition, which was largely fixated on German classicism augmented by Romantic authors (Kleist, E. T. A. Hoffmann, Heine) and had little regard for realism and a certain amount of hostility toward German modernism. If there was a shift around 1920, it had more to do with the legitimacy of the known canon than with its radical revision (see Blackwell in this volume). The canon's patriotic component was no longer a selling point at American universities in the postwar period. There was some acknowledgment that the prewar focus had been too narrow and should be broadened to include more nineteenth-century authors. This lack of radical measures should not surprise the historian, since the composition of the professoriat did not change significantly. By and large, the faculty consisted of the same members who had been involved in the political struggles of the war years. In short, the profession followed a strategy of assimilation rather than radical reform (see Hoecherl-Alden in this volume). This reform was postponed until the end of World War II, when a new generation of Germanists, among them a number of refugees from Nazi Germany, defined and propagated a new project.

For many reasons, the end of World War II was a turning point for Germanics. Unlike as in World War I, in 1942 American Germanists fully supported the war efforts of the Allies and thereby protected the profession from anti-German sentiment. Toward the end of the war, leading Germanists began to think about rebuilding the profession with a stronger emphasis on language teaching, because this service might be in demand with the increased global visibility of the United States. Some expected financial support and larger enrollments because of the numerous returning soldiers. But, in theoretical and methodological terms, 1945 marks a break if not a turn. The separation between the German discourse and the American discussion that began to emerge during the 1920s and 1930s was reinforced by the defeat of Nazi Germany. Not only German politics but also German scholarship had lost its credibility. In the internal American debate German *Geistesgeschichte* was held responsible in part for the errors of the German mind. This shift was also strongly supported by German refugees, some of whom, in earlier phases of their careers, had been indebted to this approach. The perceived theoretical vacuum strengthened the position of such American scholars as Hermann Weigand and Walter Silz, who had already developed a different approach during the 1930s and encouraged the appropriation of the New Criticism in the following decade. The emphasis on close reading in the study of literature and the belief in the primary importance of aesthetic and moral values determined the cultural side of the German undergraduate and graduate program of the 1950s and 1960s, while a more pragmatic attitude defined the approach to language teaching. Its methods were no longer oriented toward the reception of literature. Increasingly one has to speak of two professions under the roof of the German department, a development that was officially acknowledged in 1970 with the founding of *Die Unterrichtspraxis*, a journal devoted to the teaching of the German language. The next logical step would have been the complete separation of language instruction and the teaching of literature and culture, as indeed occurred at Cornell University. Yet most American German departments resisted this step and defended the traditional notion of a unity of language and literature— even after 1980, when the shift toward cultural studies increased the tension between the two conceptions of German studies.

The extent to which the foreign languages, German among them, had depended on government funding became clear in the late 1960s when National Defense Education Act (NDEA) money was running out and when, at more or less the same time, language requirements were abolished at many colleges. The sudden drop in enrollments in language classes, on which German departments relied for their graduate programs, coincided with what became the most consequential revision of the German program in its history. To a large degree this reform was motivated by concerns over enrollments. The institution of film and culture courses and the infusion of an interdisciplinary consciousness that would in the long run change the outlook of the profession was a pragmatic response to the perceived threat that German departments might lose their secure place in the humanities. In charting a new course, however, American Germanists realized that they could rely on remarkable new theoretical resources on both sides of the Atlantic. The involvement in various forms of Marxist theory (Frankfurt school, British cultural Marxism, French structuralist Marxism) as well as the appropriation of feminist theory, in both its American and its French version, changed the character of the German program during the 1970s and 1980s (see Lennox in this volume). The pressure to improve enrollments and the desire to reinvent German studies went hand in hand. The increased presence of women's studies and feminist theory in German departments also reflected a changed composition of the faculty. What has been called the feminization of the profession took place roughly between 1971 and the end of the cold war. While Germanics was still functioning as a profession that relied on the conventions of an old-boys network during the early postwar decades, the 1970s and 1980s, aided by affirmative action programs, witnessed the increase of women in the German profession from 23% to 40% (see Teraoka in this volume).

The sense of crisis that has characterized the mentality of German studies since the early 1970s has also stimulated theoretical and methodological discussion, a fact that was reflected in the formation of new professional organizations such as the German Studies Association and the Lessing Society. They provided an institutional basis for new ideas and practices in the same way that new journals like *New German Critique* and *German Studies Review* provided a forum for the revision of Germanics. The formation of German studies as opposed to German literature and language was the result of this challenge that the profession was facing. The formation included the new historicism, colonial and postcolonial studies, gender studies, and post-Freudian psychoanalysis (see Kacandes in this volume).

These methods and fields of inquiry not only transformed the outlook of German studies but also underscored its proximity to neighboring literature and language departments. The sense of national particularity, which used to include a certain indebtedness to the self-understanding of the national culture that one studied, diminished in comparison with the significance of the theoretical concepts applied to the material. The term *Americanization*, which has been used in the professional discussion to denote this shift, does not adequately describe the transformation of the discipline, since it focuses too much on the growing distance between *Germanistik* in Germany and German studies in the United States. Its true character became fully apparent only after 1990, when the globalization of cultural theory undermined national traditions altogether. The German profession in this country has been drawn more into this new orbit than has German *Germanistik*, which retains a stronger sense of a national project (of *Bildung*).

Since 1920 the teaching of German literature in the United States has evolved in ways that have not been compatible with German *Germanistik*. As we have seen, the American profession hardly participated in the practice of the various strands of *Geistes-* and *Ideengeschichte* ("history of ideas") proposed by German Germanists. In terms of methodology and theory a rapprochement between *Germanistik* and Germanics occurred only after World War II, under the aegis of intrinsic criticism. In the discussion of the 1950s and 1960s the proximity of the New Criticism and German *Werkimmanenz* was frequently mentioned, mostly as a positive sign that the isolation of German criticism had been overcome. That leading American proponents of close reading and stylistic analysis such as René Wellek and Leo Spitzer were affiliated with comparative literature encouraged the notion of an international rather than a national project, with contributions from many sources (Russian formalism, Czech and French structuralism, German phenomenology). One of the most prominent émigrés, Spitzer, strongly advised American Germanists as early as

1945 to discard the national project in favor of a European understanding of literary criticism.

From about 1950 until 1970, American and German literary criticism followed a similar though by no means identical path, a fact that was acknowledged on both sides of the Atlantic. The decades after 1970, however, were again characterized by a growing distance. Especially on the American side, younger Germanists voiced reservations about what they believed to be the hegemony of *Germanistik*. Their resistance was directed primarily against the politicization of German literary studies with strong Marxist overtones, while the other dominant theoretical trend of German criticism—that is, *Rezeptionsästhetik* (Constance school of reception aesthetics)—was rarely mentioned (Holub, *Reception Theory*). This silence is surprising, because during the 1970s a similar approach became prominent in the United States under the term *reader-response criticism* (David Bleich, Jonathan Culler, Stanley Fish, Norman Holland). Yet the Constance school (Wolfgang Iser, Hans Robert Jauss) had only a limited impact on American criticism, and it withered away after 1990. In short, reception theory did not become the common project of the 1970s and 1980s. *Germanistik* emphasized the importance of social history for the interpretation of literature, while American Germanists either continued to practice some version of intrinsic criticism or began to pick up the language of poststructuralist theory, as it was received by way of French and comparative literature departments. As a result, between 1970 and 1990 American Germanists were divided among three different models of criticism. Mainstream Germanists favored a continuation of American textual criticism, possibly enriched by a deeper appreciation of cultural and social history. The New Left endorsed critical theory (Frankfurt school) for its project of political and social criticism and supported alliances with the New Left in West Germany and other European countries. Finally, poststructuralist theory was adopted by a relatively small number of critics, mainly at elite institutions. But if American Germanists did not speak with a common voice, Germanists in Germany also did not agree on a single paradigm. Similar theoretical divisions characterized the development of criticism in West Germany, especially during the 1980s, when French theory (Foucault, Derrida, Lacan) began to influence literary studies and Niklas Luhmann's systems theory emerged as a new sociological model that could be applied to literary studies as well. Under these circumstances the distance between Americans and Germans appeared to be growing. The more recent emphasis on cultural studies in American German studies (as distinguished from literary criticism in the narrow sense), which drew on various American and European theoretical traditions, only underlined the difference.

Although the contrast between German studies in the United States and *Germanistik* in Germany has been described here mostly in methodological and theoretical terms, it has at least as much to do with the organization and the self-image of the profession. From the very beginning, American German departments looked different from German *Seminare*. Two features in particular marked the development of American departments that were missing in Germany: the centrality of language instruction as a basic service to the college and the strict division between the undergraduate and the graduate program. That American colleges usually do not have graduate programs heavily involved in research further emphasized the difference. At the college level, teaching of the German language and German literature was part of a general liberal arts education. In structural terms, only the German departments at research universities became comparable with the professional organization of *Germanistik* as it evolved in Germany during the second half of the nineteenth century. To put it differently, American German departments were to a large extent service departments, taking care of the needs of other disciplines and the general public. This functional purpose also determined the composition of the faculty: the distinction between professional and nonprofessional faculty members was expressed, for example, in the hierarchy of professors over lecturers. Language teaching was the place where women first entered the profession before they began to make an impact on literary criticism, mostly after 1970. As has been noted by more than one observer, the feminization of the American profession during the last decades of the twentieth century had no parallel in *Germanistik*, which for a number of reasons remained male-dominated. The successful history of the organization Women in German, which was founded in 1974 and began with more than six hundred members, demonstrates not only the growing influence of feminism in American German studies but also a shift in the composition of the profession that is largely absent in Germany (see both Lennox and Friedrichsmeyer in this volume).

The hybrid nature of the American German department has itself changed during the history of the profession. The second half of the twentieth century, especially the final three decades, was marked by an accelerating trend toward research and scholarship. Faculty members were also expected to be productive scholars. Of course, the German profession was not unique in this respect. The new trend found its organizational equivalent in the foundation of new professional organizations such as the Lessing Society, the Goethe Society, the Brecht Society, and the North American Heine Society as well as in the fast rise of the German Studies Association during the 1980s and 1990s (see Friedrichsmeyer in this volume). For Germanists who entered the profession after 1970 this new development led to a different outlook. The expectations of the home institution had to be balanced against the increasing demands of the profession. The ethos of teaching and service had to be connected with the role of the scholar and public critic who regularly attended conferences and other professional events away from his or her home campus. As some commentators have observed, the 1970s witnessed the rise of the professor as an academic entrepreneur—with both positive and negative consequences for the ethics of the profession (see Tatlock in this volume).

The Present Outlook

The paradox of the recent past of German studies in the United States has been the contrast between the vibrant professional activities of the faculty in the area of research and scholarship and the fact that the basic enrollments of German departments have been continually threatened by larger and mostly uncontrollable forces in the academic and social environment. The situation is, to be sure, similar in French studies, where enrollments have also been sluggish. The professional response to the predicament of German studies has been a collective effort to treat it as a challenge. Repeated laments about lost ground in enrollments have not stopped the professoriat from developing new strategies to cope with unexpected shifts in the structure of the university and higher education in general as well as with the pressures of social forces from the outside. A remarkable feature has been the reaffirmation of the importance of language instruction for the fate of the German department. While the 1980s witnessed the transition from a literature-oriented to a broader, culture-focused German program (see Kacandes in this volume), with a tendency to de-emphasize the use of German in the classroom, the 1990s saw not only a significant revival of the discussion of language teaching but also innovative attempts to intertwine the appropriation of language and culture (Kramsch, *Language*). This strategy challenges the potential administrative separation of language and culture in the corporate university, where language instruction could be outsourced as an essentially technical skill and the teaching of foreign literature and culture merged with general cultural studies departments. First and foremost, these intertwining efforts intend to rescue the particularity of a foreign culture threatened by the homogenizing tendencies of the corporate university (where "diversity" is only a slogan); they attempt to save a critical project of *Bildung* by amalgamating language instruction with the study of cultural artifacts. This struggle is being carried out mostly in the undergraduate program. Only the future will show whether this defense of the German department can succeed, whether its faculty can persuade the academic environment of the benefits of this mission. The stakes are high: they concern the future of the discipline in an environment in which a traditional national focus has lost much of its former purchasing power. Again, this apprehension is shared by other foreign languages—notably French, Russian, and Italian (M. Green).

In recent discussions, two opposing positions have emerged. On the one hand, Martha Nussbaum strongly defends a project of *Bildung* through the classical humanities. She has tried to demonstrate not only the feasibility of such a program but also the need, in both moral and political terms, for a new liberal education that would be based on critical self-examination in the philosophical sense. This program is not limited to traditional Western culture; non-Western languages and cultures would be part of a project that rethinks liberal education in global terms. On the other hand, both Bill Readings and John Guillory, working with a sociological assessment of the contemporary American university, have developed a considerably more pessimistic outlook. They interpret the present restructuring of the American university as the end of the classical liberal program of *Bildung*, which was supported by a social class willing to invest in a liberal education as a form of cultural capital. In this view the study of German high culture will be severely affected, since it depends on the interest of students and their parents in investing in a strenuous and expensive learning process without immediate usefulness.

These two scenarios project decidedly different futures for German studies. In Nussbaum's assessment of present needs and tasks, German studies is an essential part of the education; in Readings's and in Guillory's analyses there may be some persuasive arguments for the usefulness of learning the German language and possibly a justification for acquiring some general knowledge about the German-speaking countries but hardly a strong reason for an intensive study of German high culture. It appears that at present American German departments are preparing themselves for both alternatives.

Note

Throughout this volume, the English translations of German quotations are provided by the authors of the essays, unless otherwise indicated.

1

The German Faculty

Organization and Experience

Edited by
PATRICIA HERMINGHOUSE

Introduction

Historically, the changing of convictions about what constitutes the mission of the German department has been a hallmark of the profession. While some nineteenth-century departments saw themselves in the service of cultural maintenance for the large German immigrant population and their descendants, others argued that their function was to provide students with access to great texts of the humanistic heritage. During World War II and in the immediate post-Sputnik era, arguments about strategic national interests held sway. In what is sometimes described as the postnational era of globalization and transdisciplinarity, rethinking the mission of the German department is, in many places and kinds of institutions, once again the order of the day.

On many campuses, as a result of increased centralized administrative control and the widespread move of faculty members to interdisciplinary activity, the department as such may be losing its dominance. Larger departments often forfeit much of their former unitary self-understanding as they evolve into conglomerates of highly specialized scholars, who are linked more closely to their peers in distant institutions than to one another. A century after what John McCarthy describes in this section as the "departmentalization of knowledge" in the nineteenth century, centers (with a capital *c*) have been emerging in many institutions as the preferred locus for much teaching and research. The effect on traditional language departments can be disorienting: the competing demands for faculty service and administration in such centers, the threat of having bread-and-butter service courses moved into language centers, the need to support staffing budgets with large-enrollment courses taught in English—all make it difficult to maintain the nucleus of national literature courses that long were at the core of the departmental mission described by McCarthy. Unsurprisingly, scholars who stray beyond departmental boundaries into such centers risk being suspected of lack of focus and commitment to their disciplinary home.

Another challenge to this traditional identity increasingly occurs when small departments are integrated, often against their will, into larger multi-language units, typically departments of foreign or modern languages. Such consolidation is usually an administrative measure to effect greater financial efficiency or, less commonly, a response to departments' inadequacies in running their own programs. The success of these arrangements depends on whether the various national language sections are able to maintain their individual disciplinary profiles without becoming pitted against one another in competition for scarce resources and on whether the consolidated department is able to utilize its size to position itself more favorably in institutional structures.

Regardless of how they function, departments remain the critical link between the individual scholar, in this case the Germanist, and the institution, which provides one's public professional identity ("Professor Wise, Bookmore University"). This identity, however, is established and sustained in the departmental context: hiring, tenure, promotion, and salary decisions; course assignments and committee service; and a certain level of research support all represent ways in which the individual career is determined by the department. However, as some of the contributors to this section note, there are often inherent tensions between activities that promote individual careers (frequently referred to as "my work") and the quotidian needs of a department. These tensions are usually resolved, or at least addressed, in the larger context of institutional priorities, which themselves respond to changes in the political and economic environment. Inevitably the well-being of a department depends on how successfully it mediates between these institutional priorities and the interests of its members over the course of time. The complex and sometimes conflicting value systems of the constellations that shape the priorities of individual academics are described in this section by Jeffrey L. Sammons in terms of the "constituencies" to which they are obligated.

The change from the gentlemen's club atmosphere of the early departments to the highly administered corporate environment in which present-day departments must operate has generally not benefited German departments, despite the good news that initially seemed implicit in recent administrative talk of globalizing the curriculum. On the one hand, these changes are reflected in the allocation of resources and assessment of institutional returns on investment in academic programs: forms of bean counting that establish metrics based on numbers of credit hours generated, majors and minors serviced, grants awarded, and research citations as indices of excellence.[1] With the insistence on measurable outcomes has come the language of *brand values, right-sizing, pricing strategies, outsourcing, market analyses of potential student consumers and competitors.*

When it is based on a competitive model of autonomous, entrepreneurial production of knowledge, documented in single-author publications and independently taught courses, the academic reward system can work against departmental cooperation and contribute to fragmentation. Despite the increasing professionalization of language instruction, newly hired junior faculty members, who are frequently responsible for overseeing the language curriculum and developing instructional technologies, are soon confronted with institutional reluctance to accord such labor-intensive assignments due recognition in a research-oriented environment.[2] Yet another effect bears mentioning here, at least in passing: the hardening of professional class lines that separate a privileged academic elite from the academic underclass whose labors keep the enterprise going. Increasingly, the division that Gerhard Weiss refers to as a "schism" between language and literature teaching has come to be less the traditional one between senior faculty members teaching advanced courses and seminars and junior faculty members teaching heavier loads, mostly at the lower end of the curriculum. Rather, the schism is between tenure-track faculty members, who enjoy a particular set of privileges and rights, and the growing ranks of adjunct and part-time faculty members, usually with PhDs, who teach the so-called service courses, often for less pay than graduate students.

In this difficult environment, it falls to the department chair to navigate a course through the shoals of increased bureaucracy on behalf of both the visions of colleagues and the needs of the discipline. Whether appointed or elected, chairs face pressures to accomplish ever more administrative tasks while simultaneously experiencing significant reductions in the autonomy with which they can proceed. The formalization of hiring and tenure procedures that were implemented to open access to the profession to formerly excluded constituencies, for example, together with expanding measures of accountability and assessment that seek to improve responsiveness to the student constituency, is manifested in the huge piles of paper that clutter most chairs' offices. Nonetheless, with astute management and cultivated contacts with peers in the institution and across the country,[3] many chairs do succeed in leading their departments to develop vibrant programs that take maximum advantage of what is possible and appropriate in their particular situation.

Lynne Tatlock's in-depth survey of the value systems of full professors (some now retired), aged 45 to 85, whose careers began in the decades from the 1930s to the 1980s, provides insight into how "the shift from professing values to producing knowledge" has been experienced by the most senior members of the profession. In their relatively satisfied comments on the course of their careers she finds considerable evidence that most members of this cohort have maintained their fairly strong communitarian values while managing to negotiate the competing demands of their various constituencies over time. But while their perceptive remarks demonstrate that the split between the production of knowledge (research) and its dissemination (teaching) is not as recent as one generally assumes, they also indicate the consensus that extends from graduate students to emeriti about the detrimental effects of increased pressures for professionalization. Complaints about escalating requirements not only for promotion and tenure but also for job entry reflect the fear that an increase in the quantity and quality of publications may be occurring at the expense of personal, political, and pedagogical values, what Tatlock, mindful of the star system, describes as "a shift from the profession as calling to the profession as performance." If, as Tatlock suggests, professors are increasingly disinclined to serve the needs of their institution and their profession as they pursue their individual careers through research and prolific publication, the department may cease to be a bulwark of faculty autonomy and intellectual exchange. Yet, in an interesting dialectic—or vicious circle, depending on one's location in the system—such achievement of outside visibility, the profiling described by John McCarthy in the first essay of this section, is necessary to secure the department's competitive position in the environment of its current constituencies.

Notes

1 In a much-cited 1996 study *The University in Ruins*, Bill Readings denounced the deleterious effect of attempts to create the "university of excellence" with such strategies.

2 A lively debate about this academic division of labor followed on the publication of Dorothy James's controversial 1997 article "Bypassing the Traditional Leadership: Who's Minding the Store?"

3 Such contacts among department chairs in all types of higher education institutions, from community college through PhD-granting university are facilitated at the national level by the Association of Departments of Foreign Languages (ADFL) and the Association of Departments of English (ADE), organizations of department chairs affiliated with the Modern Language Association. Their helpful journals, the *ADFL Bulletin* and the *ADE Bulletin*, are available by subscription to any MLA member.

The History of the Organization
of German Departments
in the United States

JOHN A. MCCARTHY

At 125 years, the German department as an academic unit is not very old. More frequently than not, it was and is a hybrid form. The hybridity makes it more difficult to assess both the influence of the department's structure on the fulfillment of its mission and the effect of that mission on its organization. To be sure, the changing shape of the German department is tied to structural transformations in institutions of higher learning. Those institutions in turn are tied to broader political and economic conditions outside the academy. While not always mutually supportive or even acknowledged, interaction between town and gown has existed since the inception of the profession. That interaction assumes various shapes, including direct outreach efforts by a university and the incorporation of emergent social values in a community into a department's curriculum. The discipline of Germanics and its social environment are nonetheless separate entities, each driven by its own dynamics. The interpretation of what is occurring outside the confined institutional space can lead to different approaches to fulfill the departmental mission. A key to understanding these relations is the self-understanding of Germanists both as intellectuals in a broader sense and as providers of specific services in the home institution. Sometimes convergent, sometimes divergent, those identities influence the shape of the undergraduate major and the graduate degrees. Frequently, those identities translate into committee assignments with a broader or narrower focus; they imply responsibilities, not only at the departmental, college, and university level (depending on the kind of institution involved) but also beyond the institution itself. Self-perception does matter.

In tracing the history of structural developments in the German department, therefore, it is important to maintain a double focus: one on metadiscourse (that is, on the debates that range beyond an institutional identity) and another on the institutional identity (that is, on the daily activities on campus, in and outside the classroom). In the first area, Germanists have historically assumed various guises as proponents of a national philology, purveyors of a humanistic canon, practitioners of an American *Germanistik*, and most recently participants in literary and critical theory (New Criticism, new historicism, deconstruction, Marxist criticism, reception aesthetics, gender and queer studies, cultural studies, film studies). The badge of metadiscursiveness is displayed in journals, at conferences, and in advanced undergraduate and graduate courses. When a new metadiscourse begins to emerge, it is usually without a place in the existent departmental structure, but if it elicits a popular enough response, it can eventually contribute to a restructuring of the faculty and its (departmental) responsibilities, thereby altering external perceptions of the department. On campus, a Germanist shares a global intellectual identity with another identity, that of local provider of language instruction and other service courses dictated by the home institution's general education and graduation requirements. These latter sets of requirements mirror the nonacademic world and tend to shape curricular offerings. If departments do not adapt to changing external values, they lose out in the total economy of intellectual life.

Critical in any examination of the history of German departments is the issue of whether the organizational structure is reactive or proactive. That structure varies synchronically among different institutional types. In other words, one must ask whether a department is part of a national or regional institution, a private or public liberal arts college, a private or public research university, a religious or secular institution, a comprehensive four-year regional university or a two-year community college. The structure can also vary diachronically in the same institution. German departments initially emerged from historically amorphous groupings of several academic units. Many that did achieve individual departmental status were later reintegrated into departments of modern languages and literatures, of Germanic and Slavic languages, of German and Russian, and so on. To be sure, the departments that experienced such transformations are in the minority nationally. The vast majority of the German programs listed in the 2000 Monatshefte / *Max Kade Institute Directory of German Studies*, for example, never attained independent, departmental status. Clearly, size and the fourfold mission of a department—major and minor curriculum, service, liberal education, and research—directly affect the organization of its faculty. Yet another factor seems important: perceptions of territorial threat. In the 1960s and 1970s German departments responded to courses on Goethe and Thomas Mann offered in translation by English departments by developing their own courses in translation; in the 1980s and 1990s the pattern of reaction was repeated when German departments began to offer cultural studies courses, in part to underscore the need to go beyond the monolingualism of many cultural studies initiatives.

Finally, we must consider whether the chief executive officer of the department is an appointed head with broad discretionary powers or an elected chair serving for a specified term and held accountable to departmental colleagues. Whether chairs have real power, professional stature, and refined interpersonal skills is a major factor in their ability to use institutional structures for the good of the department.

My essay discusses some of the factors that have influenced the organization of German departments in the past and continue to influence it in the present. It examines both how that organization enabled Germanics to evolve and how it hindered disciplinary development. Finally, I look at the prospects for the future.

The changing structure of the German department clearly reflects the history of the Germanics profession as well as the department's relation to other units in the institution (Hohendahl, "Nationale Ausdifferenzierungen" 360, 375). Thus there is some overlap between my essay and others in this volume. It is not possible to offer here more than a cursory overview of the questions that need to be asked in assessing the relation between the institutional structure of the profession and its changing profile. The history of Germanics rendered in the manner of Gerald Graff's *Professing Literature: An Institutional History* has yet to be written.[1] In the main, then, Graff's study, James M. McGlathery's monograph *German and Scandinavian at Illinois: A History*, and materials I have unearthed at the University of Pennsylvania serve as a guide in the following.[2] Only the general contours of the still unwritten history of the organization of German departments in colleges and universities emerge here. In large measure I compare the development of the departments at the University of Pennsylvania and the University of Illinois, Urbana. I chose them for modeling because their histories are representative of their peer group, because statistical data for both institutions have been analyzed, and because their departmental histories can be traced back to the origins of professionalization around 1868. Other institutions, such as Michigan and Indiana or Columbia and Harvard, could serve the same purpose.

For several reasons, the Universities of Pennsylvania and Illinois can be considered representative of the major research and teaching universities, which tend to dominate in a history of departments. One institution is private, the other public. One is an East Coast, urban establishment with roots reaching back to Benjamin Franklin's Charter School in the mid-1750s, the other is a rural midwestern institution created by the Morrill Land Grant Act of 1862 to promote instruction in agriculture and the technical arts. Yet both evolved into strong and influential centers for Germanics, even if they were not consistently numbered among the elite programs in the nation.[3] Moreover, they housed two of the most influential journals of the profession, especially during the first decades: *Americana Germanica* (1897–1902; then *German American Annals*, 1903–19) at Penn, and the *Journal of English and Germanic Philology* (1897–) at Illinois. But perhaps their representative value lies most in that they were neither at the top nor at the bottom of their peer group in terms of size or PhD production, although each definitely could boast highly profiled professionals at various times in its history.

National rankings based on quantitative (NB: not qualitative) measures shed some light on the situation. Eighty institutions responded to a survey of doctorates awarded in German during the years 1965–89. The survey made clear that the distribution is uneven among the reporting institutions, which fall into five categories: (1) those awarding more than 3 degrees per year (10 universities), (2) those averaging 2–3 degrees per year (12), (3) those averaging 1–2 degrees per year (18), (4) those awarding fewer than 1 PhD per year (25), and (5) those with fewer than 10 doctorates in 25 years (15). The first category accounts for almost half the total doctorates awarded in the time span. With 71 and 67 doctorates respectively, the Universities of Illinois and Pennsylvania fall into the second category, in places 13 and 14 overall.[4] In the 1997 survey of degrees granted between 1985 and 1994, Penn was in place 11 with 16 doctorates awarded and Illinois was in place 19 with 11 PhDs, in a total field of 20 institutions.[5] To compare these figures with those of their earlier history, note that between 1891 (when it awarded its first doctorate in German) and 1918 Penn produced 45 PhDs, while Illinois awarded 16 between 1908 (when it awarded 3) and 1920. (For about a decade after World War I there was a hiatus in PhD production across the nation.) Penn and Illinois, therefore, ranked in the top quarter of all doctoral programs. Yet it may not be wise to attach too much significance to these numbers. For one thing, there is no way of knowing how accurate the surveys are.

The history of departmental organization seems to accord with several general phases of unequal length, largely influenced by external historical and social forces. They are preceded by a long incubation period from the mid–eighteenth century to the 1860s. In the following discussion I label those phases of development as:

Professionalization and Expansion: From the Civil War to World War I, 1861–1917

Contraction and Renewal: The Interwar Period, 1917–42

Ivory Tower Stability: From World War II to Sputnik, 1942–57

Explosive Growth, Expanding Views: From Sputnik to the End of the Cold
   War, 1957–90
Conclusion: Past and Future, 1990–

This chronology of transformation roughly corresponds to McGlathery's
schematization.[6] My division is not intended to capture all the nuances of
events and their significance for higher education. Rather, it represents a working hypothesis designed to stimulate reflection on the kinds of interactions
that affected the organization of German faculty in their institutions. Very
useful in fleshing out the portrait are the numerous reports on the state of the
profession appearing since the 1920s in *Monatshefte*, the *German Quarterly*, the
Modern Language Journal, and *Modern Language Notes*. *PMLA* and, later, the *ADFL
Bulletin* and *Profession* also provide valuable materials. These reports and studies
detail faculty appointments, departmental size, enrollment figures, changing
requirements, curricular innovation, outreach efforts, visiting professors, internal institutional priorities, the influx of nontraditional students, research initiatives, external funding opportunities, study-abroad programs, faculty and
student exchanges, conference activity, the impact of state and federal regu-
lations, unionization, equal opportunity directives, concerns about economic
downturns, transatlantic relations, and ideological debate on the role of
German. From start to finish, departmental identity has been frequently conflicted by changing conceptions of the department's mission, both in the institution and in society at large (e.g., see ADFL's revised "Checklist for Self-Study
for Departments of Foreign Languages and Literatures"). Factors extraneous to
a specific disciplinary mission have often proved crucial.

Professionalization and Expansion: From the
Civil War to World War I, 1861–1917

Although Karl Follen set the tone for the study of German in the United States
when, as professor of church history and ethics, he introduced a course of
study in German at Harvard in 1825 and even called for the establishment of
a German American university, the professionalization of Germanics did not
occur until after the Civil War. Simply put, the foundation for a departmental
structure was absent—namely, the teaching and researching of *German* philology and literature (cf. Trommler, "Germanistik nicht als Nationalphilologie"
877). Until the 1880s a significant amount of support for the study of German
in higher education came from outside the academy, specifically from popular
print media such as the *Dial* and the *Atlantic Monthly*. Collectively, these journals, magazines, and newspapers formed a kind of college without walls (Rowland; Trommler 869). Only after the founding of the MLA in 1883 did
Germanists (along with the other national philologists) have a public forum

for the advancement of their particular disciplines and a means to bolster their efforts locally. The MLA, along with state associations of teachers of German, provided a locus for isolated Germanists to marshal support for the organization of their discipline into a departmental presence on campus.

The usual arguments for the establishment of German as a separate discipline and department were twofold. First, knowledge of German was deemed necessary for access to important scientific debates and findings emanating from a number of disciplines in Germany and Austria. Second, the call to legitimize the study of modern foreign languages and cultures alongside classical Greek and Roman cultures became ever more vocal in the course of the nineteenth century. The debate on legitimacy continued into the early twentieth century, prompting a rethinking of college entrance and exit requirements. Ultimately, the modern languages replaced the traditional humanistic languages of Greek and Latin as major cultural forces in the academy. The introduction of these new language requirements clearly paved the way for the growth of departmental structures.

The early academic success of German was partly due to the importance of practical knowledge and skills to American culture. Paradoxically, it also derived from efforts to nurture a more intellectual strain in American culture. As seen from the European and specifically German perspective, a confluence of German and American culture promised to bring American culture to full flower (McCarthy, "Indigenous . . . Plant" 151–52; Blackwell, "Control-Alt-Delete" 196). That ambition had begun with the transcendental movement in New England in the 1830s (Margaret Fuller, Ralph Waldo Emerson) and continued with Henry Wadsworth Longfellow and James Russell Lowell.

In the university setting, Penn appointed Oswald Seidensticker as university professor of the German language and literature in 1867; he served in that position until his death in 1893. Seidensticker's efforts were aimed primarily at undergraduate language and literature teaching as well as at bridging the gap between town and gown. As a one-man department, he could not think of empire building, but he did succeed in advancing the view that German and American culture could interact productively. It should be noted that *philology* in this early phase connoted a broadly humanistic interest in grammar, morphology, etymology, criticism, geology, political history, customs, art, architecture, and mythology along with literature proper; it was a discipline intent on disclosing the soul of a people through the expressions of its culture and civilization. Everything could be read as a semiotic sign of the distinctive national quality. Based on theories of race, the rise of philology as the distinctive disciplinary quality should not be underestimated as a determining factor in the formation of language and literature departments in the late nineteenth century (cf. Graff 70). That broad philological agenda marked public pronouncements around 1900 by such Germanists as Henry Wood (Johns Hopkins), Marion Dexter Learned (Penn), Albert B. Faust (Cornell), Calvin Thomas (Columbia), and Alexander Hohlfeld (Wisconsin).

Not until the last quarter of the nineteenth century did departments of language and literature (English, German, French, etc.) emerge. Penn established such departments in 1851, Harvard in 1872, Johns Hopkins in 1876, Chicago in 1892, Cincinnati in 1900, and Penn State in 1901 (see Graff 66; Schade).[7] Wisconsin, too, can date its origins to 1901, when Hohlfeld arrived from Vanderbilt to develop the department. However, the establishment of a graduate school and a graduate program did not necessarily translate into a department of German. Princeton University, which began offering German in 1831, had two professors of German as early as 1877, but one was housed in the School of Arts, the other in the School of Sciences. In the 1880s German at Princeton was housed in the Department of Languages and Literatures, which included Greek, Latin, English, rhetoric, and oratory as well as French and German. Not until 1891 did German begin to emerge as a distinct program at Princeton, with the designation of language groups; it was finally identified as the Germanic and Romanic Section of the newly reorganized Department of Modern Languages (Bottigheimer, "One Hundred" 86–88). That was typical of the pattern.

Particularly noteworthy is the origin of the department at Penn. As early as 1792, Penn had established the position of professor of German and Oriental languages, one of six professorships in the newly formed Faculty in the Arts; it was appointed to Justus Heinrich Christian Helmuth, DD. However, in the ensuing, difficult years at the university the rank was lowered to instructor of German. In response to continued disciplinary growth Penn announced in 1851 major structural changes in order to compete better with the 130–40 colleges extant in the United States at the time for a limited pool of college-bound youth. That plan provided for seven academic departments: "of Ancient Languages, Mathematics, Natural Philosophy and Chemistry, Intellectual and Moral Philosophy, English Literature, Modern Languages, and of Physiology and Natural History." In essence, Penn created one of the first departments of modern languages and literatures in the nation, if not the first. Courses in five of these departments were required for graduation. A "School of Arts, Mines and Manufactures" was also established, which contained its own Department of German and French Languages (McCarthy, "Indigenous . . . Plant" 154). In 1857 Penn named the Reverend Charles C. Shaeffer the first professor of German language. He was followed in 1867 by Seidensticker as "Professor of the German Language and Literature." Both Schaeffer and Seidensticker were appointed to the Academic Department, which had been established in addition to the Faculty of Arts. To assess the chronological significance of Penn's actions, we should note that the Deutsches Seminar at Rostock dates from 1858, a year after Schaeffer was appointed, and that Seidensticker's appointment coincided with the creation of the Deutsches Seminar at the Universität Tübingen in 1867.

By 1893 Penn had organized itself into a College Department, teaching 2,066 students from 44 states and territories and 77 foreign countries, offering 329 courses by 255 instructors grouped under 33 heads and falling roughly into 7 divisions: the arts, the sciences, the Wharton School, the School of American History, biology, architecture, and music. The graduate school was known as the Department of Philosophy and enrolled 117 students of the above-mentioned total. Noteworthy is that one-fifth of the library holdings of 110,000 bound volumes dealt with modern languages and criticism. When he died in 1916, Learned (PhD at Johns Hopkins in 1893) held the title of "Professor of the Germanic Languages and Literatures," while his colleague Daniel Bussier Shumway was "Professor of Germanic Philology" and Edward Charles Wesselhoeft was simply "Professor of German." The academic titles reflect the growing professionalization of the faculty. Additionally, there were 5 instructors in German, 1 instructor in German and Scandinavian languages, and 1 assistant in German, for a departmental total of 10 members in 1915–16. During Learned's stewardship (1895–1916) the graduate program in German grew from 2 to 12 students with several on scholarship. (In 1915–16 the overall graduate student body numbered 669; it decreased to 335 in 1918–19.)

While the catalog of the University of Illinois (est. 1867) for its second year of operation contains an entry for a "Department of German Language and Literature," the designation is misleading, for there was only one German instructor during the university's first decade of existence. Moreover, the term *department*—as at Penn—referred initially to a larger academic unit, such as a faculty, college, or school. By the late 1880s German was offered in a School of English and Modern Languages, which was located in a College of Literature and Science. German was offered since 1868 by Captain Eduard Snyder (born Schneider, 1835–1903); this one-man German faculty (1868–96) was first appointed as "Assistant Professor of Book Keeping and German," listed the following year as "Professor of Book-keeping and Military Tactics, and Instructor in German," and promoted in 1892 to "Professor of German Language and Literature." Snyder also served as dean of the College of Literature (in 1874), then of the later College of Literature and Science. For most of his tenure he was, in fact, only part-time in German (McGlathery, *German* 5, 9–11). Snyder was succeeded in 1896 by Lewis Addison Rhoades, assistant professor of German, who had been formally trained in Germanics (BA and MA from Michigan in 1884 and 1886 respectively, Dr. phil. from Göttingen in 1892). Rhoades brought in two instructors of German the following year to deal with rising enrollment: Chester Harvey Rowell and George Henry Meyer. Meyer was promoted to "Assistant Professor of German Language and Literature" in 1900 (22). Rowell was replaced in 1898 by Neil Conwell Brooks, the first faculty member in German at Illinois to have an American doctorate (Harvard, 1898).

In 1902 Brooks was promoted to assistant professor, later assuming duties as curator of the Museum of European Culture, which opened in 1913 and was ostensibly modeled on Kuno Francke's Germanic Museum at Harvard (22). Brooks became acting interim head of German after Rhoades left Illinois to become head and professor of German at Ohio State.

In 1906, Gustav E. Karsten moved to Illinois from Indiana as professor of German and head of the newly consolidated Department of Modern Languages (in 1905) until his death in January 1908. He brought with him the *Journal of English and Germanic Philology*. Julius Goebel joined the faculty as professor of German in 1908, serving as head until 1926. His appointment coincided with a restructuring of the modern languages into separate departments; he was head of Germanic and Romance languages. By 1916–17 the faculty consisted of 6 professors and 6 instructors; the department had only 1 graduate assistant. Between 1893, when the graduate school was established at Illinois, and 1918, Illinois produced, as mentioned, 15 PhDs (the first 3 in 1908) along with 40 MAs. By 1942 Illinois had produced 50 PhDs (McGlathery 56, 83).[8]

Of particular importance is that Goebel was hired to head a department for which Otto Eduard Lessing, George Henry Meyer, and Neil Conwell Brooks had served as interim heads. Based on that history, the feeling arose for the first time that all permanent members of the department should be given a say in the running of it. Departmental policy could no longer be determined by one individual; the opinions of colleagues with comparable experience and academic stature would have to be heeded. At Illinois the traditional model of a senior professor assisted by several junior colleagues had given way rather quickly to the more modern model of a group of several scholars of equally high standing. Autocratic rule—typical of the one-full-professor and headship models—became questionable as the appropriate means of governance (see McGlathery 46). That is also what happened at Penn (and of course elsewhere), albeit later, during the 1930s and 1940s.

Moreover, the presence of two or more high-profile scholars in the department led to the idea that productive senior scholars might better serve the institution by devoting their time to writing and research than by tending to administrative chores. This idea set the tone for the later establishment of research professorships and endowed chairs with reduced teaching loads, which had the (unintended) effect of creating a competing structural model in democratically run departments, especially in the last third of the twentieth century.[9] Then too, the presence of a supporting staff of untenured instructors and assistant professors (most recently TAs and adjuncts) translated into high teaching loads of four to five courses per term for full-time personnel, even at the major research institutions. Compounding the trend was the lack of a voice for this staff in departmental affairs. Typically, voting was (and in certain instances, such as promotion decisions, still is) according to rank.

These developments, along with the establishment of new institutions, frequently based on the German model, were part of a larger process of professionalization between 1865 and 1917. These institutions came into being simultaneously with a new professional-managerial class, which had specific needs and expectations (e.g., the Wharton School of the University of Pennsylvania, which was founded in 1883). Some that were already established reorganized themselves in response to industrial and social changes following the Civil War, which placed ever greater emphasis on professional expertise. Land-grant institutions were, of course, commissioned to favor the applied sciences. In sum, these forces worked to set new priorities in higher education in the United States, accentuating differences between the time-honored mission of liberal arts colleges (originally founded by religious groups) and that of the modern research university. Changes in higher education mirrored the rise of professionalism in the sciences, medicine, law, and commerce outside the walls of the academy. The example of the successful grocery merchant in Baltimore who endowed Johns Hopkins was emulated by captains of industry well into the twentieth century: for example, Commodore Cornelius Vanderbilt, Ezra Cornell, John D. Rockefeller (Chicago), Leland Stanford, Washington Duke. In turn, the academy felt pressure to compartmentalize knowledge and expertise in order to achieve greater efficiency. Of course, the range of knowledge was expanding exponentially as well. And that knowledge, especially in the natural sciences and technical arts, increasingly required access through a foreign language. Thus even before 1900 reading courses were established in the natural sciences, the forerunners of what today are called service courses: German for engineers, German for chemists, business German, and so on. The undergraduate and graduate curricula established at Penn and Illinois in the first phase of development remained largely intact well after 1950. Interestingly, by 2000 specialized courses began to emerge as semiautonomous concentrations (e.g., German for engineers at Rhode Island and Minnesota; language across the curriculum).

Johns Hopkins is frequently cited as the model of higher education that changed the academic landscape in dramatic fashion. That change involved a movement away from the dilettante to the specialist, and it opposed the teacher-generalist model with that of the publisher-scholar, whose purpose was to advance the frontiers of knowledge and not simply to preserve the canon. The new model sought to promote the new sciences for a new world and a new era without neglecting the value of traditional culture (compare Francke, Hohlfeld, and Learned; see McCarthy, "Indigenous . . . Plant" 149–52; C. Nollendorfs, "First World War"). Saliently, the new institutions were generally unimpeded by inherited local traditions. The intellectual goal was no longer merely to preserve but also to extend knowledge in discrete increments, to report on those gains in precise language, and to share the results of groundbreaking work with colleagues beyond one's own institution. The professionalization of knowledge influenced the hiring of new faculty members and their internal organization. In many instances the success (or failure) of a department was due to the vision (or its lack) of the chair. In other words, the question of who was hired when acquired great importance.

It is here that a diachronic analysis of an institution seems instructive. It therefore becomes a sine qua non to know who served when as chair (or head). The sequence of chairs at Penn is: Seidensticker (1865–93), Learned (1895–1916), Shumway (1916–36), Ernst Jockers (1936–44), Alfred Senn (1944–46), Otto Springer (1946–62), André von Gronicka (1962–72), Albert Lloyd (1972–78), von Gronicka (1978–79), Frank Trommler (1979–85), Horst S. Daemmrich (1985–97), Trommler (1997–98), Simon Richter (1998–). At Illinois the sequence is: Snyder (1868–96), Rhoades (1896–1903), Karsten (1906–08), Goebel (1908–26), Albert William Aron (1926–45), Helmut Rehder (1946–55), Frank Banta (1955–67), Harry G. Haile (1967–73), Elmer H. Antonsen (1973–82), Herbert Knust (1982–85), James McGlathery (1985–91), Marianne Kalinke (1991–2000), U. Henry Gerlach (2000–).

The general procedure was for the dean to hire a research-oriented professor to meet the overall mission of the institution. The new hire was expected to be not only adept at transmitting new knowledge to advanced students in the classroom but also able to transmit that knowledge to a wider audience. This person was frequently hired to head the department and held that position until retirement, death, or departure. The so-called mandarins of the era (Learned, White, Francke, Wood, Faust, Goebel, et al.) were one-man operations; they generated excitement and research agendas through their own work, the establishment of scholarly journals, the placement of their students, and the growth of their departments. That individual-centered model was not unlike the self-made man ideal of the era. Today, it survives in truncated form as the celebrated superstar, made possible in part by universities flush with money and driven by a commodity-market or Madison Avenue mentality. The present-day chair, by contrast, is inundated in an endless stream of paperwork due more to state and federal mandates and to fact-finding initiatives than to any intellectual or disciplinary objective. The litigious nature of contemporary society, aimed at preserving the rights of individuals, has increasingly transformed the academy and influenced how chairs function and departments operate. A century after the first major initiatives to professionalize higher education, grievances against chairs and professors for a perceived lack of professional behavior are not uncommon. This state of affairs is not quite what the early mandarins envisioned. It is a development with such profound consequences for the organization of the department as to deserve separate treatment.

When Learned assumed the reins at Penn in 1895, he found a mere skeleton of a department. Charged with changing that situation, he added new faculty members, beginning immediately with Shumway, who had studied in

Göttingen and came to Germanics from English philology. Learned then established a long-lived journal, *Americana Germanica*; organized outreach efforts to include the high schools and the local German-heritage community; prioritized a vital research agenda (including comparative studies); introduced a lecture series and the seminar method of teaching; organized a German conversation group for students; and attracted top graduate applicants from around the nation and abroad. When he died in 1916, the department had grown to occupy a dominant position in the nascent discipline. What Learned succeeded in doing at Penn, others accomplished at Harvard (Francke), Wisconsin (Hohlfeld), Columbia (Calvin Thomas), Cornell (Horatio S. White, Albert B. Faust), Michigan (George A. Hench), and Illinois (Goebel).

The curriculum had been expanded to include offerings on Gothic, Old Saxon, Old High German, Middle High German, *Nibelungenlied*, Walter von der Vogelweide, sixteenth-century literature, literature from Opitz to Klopstock, Lessing, Goethe, Schiller, Grillparzer, Kleist, Heine, history of the German novel, novelle, Hauptmann, and so on. This list mirrors exact course titles and is very similar to curricular offerings at Illinois in the first decade of the twentieth century (which held sway into the 1960s; see McGlathery 43). When I began my own career at Penn in 1972 as an assistant professor, that standard curriculum was still in place, augmented by courses on twentieth-century literary developments (see also the curricula, e.g., in "Personalia—1938–1939"). Thus, by 1916, the German department had become a well-established, freestanding unit at a number of research institutions across the continent.

An illuminating assessment of the mission of undergraduate and graduate education is offered by the brochure produced under Karsten's brief tenure as chair to mark the new, combined department, *The Study of Modern Languages at the University of Illinois, 1906–07*. Under five headings the brochure lists the objectives of undergraduate German studies. *In nuce* they are: (1) immediate serviceableness: reading knowledge for scientific study or facility in speaking and writing for travel or business; (2) literary study as access to the traditions, culture, and values of another people; (3) professional teacher preparation; (4) disciplinary training for graduate work in literature and philology; (5) mental discipline or the development of critical thinking (qtd. in McGlathery 40–41). These objectives are, of course, very similar to current expectations in the undergraduate mission. Graduate work entailed a minimum of one year for the MA, three years for the PhD. A striking feature of both the graduate study and the thesis is the frequently comparative nature of the work.

Contraction and Renewal: The Interwar Period, 1918–42

The devastating impact of the Great War and of anti-German sentiment on the young profession is well documented and does not require reiteration here.

However, the size of the change does, especially in the connection between high school and college German programs: high school enrollment in German fell by 95% between 1915 and 1922. While 316,000 high school students enrolled in German before the war, only 14,000 were enrolled five years after its end (Zeydel, "Teaching . . . to the Present" 361–62). The Wall Street Crash of 1929 and the Great Depression complicated matters further. The sudden loss of enrollment at all instructional levels and economic difficulties occasioned a reduction in staff, increased teaching loads, and prompted the elimination of small sections. With the survival of German endangered, more attention had to be shifted to first- and second-year language courses. Anne Bodensieck Tyre summarized the dilemma when she queried in her 1934 assessment "The Status of German in Some Universities, Colleges, and High Schools," "How can a department exist, progress, or accomplish anything with merely first year work?" (Bodensieck Tyre 109). General cultural courses (*Landeskunde*) and more service courses were introduced to keep hands busy and make the learning of German meaningful beyond elementary courses. Courses already in place before the war—German for chemists, German for engineers, German for business— were taught by senior faculty members.[10] Nonetheless, many Germanists had to seek alternative employment. For example, all but eight of the twenty-five faculty members at Wisconsin had to be let go (C. Nollendorfs, "First World War" 178). The loss of teaching opportunities translated into problems in attracting and placing qualified graduate students. Departments had to define a new mission and function in the institutions, while department heads had to be creative in increasing enrollment.

The profession fought back. A survey of German enrollment in American colleges and universities in 1933 sponsored by the Carl Schurz Memorial Foundation ("German Enrollment" [1934]) showed 67,318 total enrollments in the 395 colleges and universities that replied to the survey; an additional 2,501 students were enrolled in 39 normal schools and teachers colleges, and 5,555 were reported in 86 junior colleges. (Those figures compare very favorably with enrollment data 66 years later, when some 96,000 students were taking German at more than 3,000 institutions of higher learning [Brod and Welles 23, 26]!) Of the twenty-three explanations for the increases, the most common were: (1) interest in a natural science requiring knowledge of German, (2) general interest in things German, (3) a larger incoming class, (4) premedical requirements, and (5) the importance of German for graduate or professional studies ("German Enrollment" [1934] 129). Of the seventeen reasons explaining decreases in enrollment, the most common were: (1) adverse economic conditions, (2) unfavorable reaction to the political situation in Germany, (3) perception of German as a difficult language, and (4) scarcity of teaching positions (130). Obviously, conditions external to the structure of American institutions of higher education were critical to German enrollments.

To stimulate and reward interest, scholarships were endowed (e.g., at Illinois and Wisconsin), prizes for undergraduate and graduate work and book prizes were introduced (e.g., at Penn the Carl F. Lauber Prize was introduced in 1928, the Edward B. Ziegler Davis Prize in 1935, and the Daniel B. Shumway Prize for an undergraduate woman in 1937). The German honor society Delta Phi Alpha was established, and chapters sprang up around the nation. Three of the oldest are at Penn, Rutgers, and Vanderbilt (all dating from 1930). Delta Phi Alpha has continued to be a major focus of student-oriented activity at these institutions and elsewhere. Theater productions at Penn and picnics at Illinois also became part of official departmental activities (continued today, e.g., at Rutgers, Texas, and Wisconsin). Departmental involvement in the efforts of local chapters of the AATG (est. in 1926) rose and fell as the need for outreach was felt.

In addition to innovation in language instruction, literature and cultural offerings expanded into the nascent field of comparative literature. Efforts were made to teach German literature in the context of European culture (Daemmrich 316). Judging by the dissertations produced, research topics remained essentially unchanged at places like Penn and Illinois. It should be noted that comparative studies had already been part of Germanics as philology broadly defined. Even more important was the Germanist's role as mediator of the foreign culture in the United States during the 1920s and 1930s, when the need for transatlantic understanding was especially acute. The influx of highly educated exiles from National Socialist Germany toward the end of this period definitely advanced the contextualization of German culture in a larger framework (Sammons, "Die amerikanische Germanistik" 115–16).

Through the intense public relations efforts and the help of such organizations as the Carl Schurz Memorial Foundation, enrollments gradually began to climb again in the 1920s and 1930s. The foundation played a role in the 1920s and 1930s, not unlike that of the DAAD (German Academic Exchange Service [Deutscher Akademischer Austauschdienst]) in recent decades. The "Personalia" report in *Monatshefte* for 1938–39 lists data for 29 departments (as compared with 396 departments listed in 1997). A few figures should suffice to indicate the size of some programs. Berkeley employed 11 full-time faculty members and 7 assistants to teach 1,735 undergraduate and 36 graduate students. Perhaps most notable among the faculty were Lawrence M. Price and Franz Schneider ("Personalia 1938–39" 396). Having by far the largest graduate program at the time, Columbia enrolled 120 graduate students in German along with 713 undergraduates. The faculty consisted of 11 full-timers and 13 part-timers (R. H. Fife and F. W. J. Heuser were among the best-known professors there). Cornell's program was of moderate size in both faculty (3 full professors, 2 assistant professors, and 2 instructors) and enrollment (just 4 graduate students). Albert B. Faust had just retired, and Victor Lange was newly arrived from Toronto. Harvard's large faculty of 17 full-time members and 4 part-time teaching assistants taught a total of 856 students during the academic year (there is no indication of how many of those were graduate students). Most notable of the 2 full professors was Karl Viëtor; of the 2 associate professors, Taylor Starck, who later chaired the department; of the 4 assistant professors, F. O. Nolte; and among the 9 instructors I. S. Stamm. The German faculty at Illinois consisted of 9 full-time faculty members (2 full, 2 associate, and 2 assistant professors, 3 instructors), and 10 part-timers. A total of 1,129 undergraduates and 42 graduate students were enrolled there in 1938–39. That Albert W. Aron was head although Herbert Penzl (recently arrived from Michigan) was the better-known scholar suggests that administrative function and academic stature were no longer necessarily bound together. Johns Hopkins had 3 full professors (E. Feise, W. Kurrelmeyer, R. Roulston) together with 2 part-time instructors and taught 200 undergraduates and 10 graduate students.

Penn had 10 full-time faculty members, 670 undergraduates and about 50 graduate students enrolled in German (a respectable number but still down from the 99 registrations in graduate courses in 1932–33) ("German Enrollment" [1934] 131). Ernst Jockers and Alfred Senn were the two most prominent of the 4 full professors. Adolf Klarmann was an assistant professor, later rising through the ranks to full professor and a position of prominence in the discipline during the 1950s and 1960s. Adolph Gorr, first as instructor and then as assistant professor, served continuously at Penn until his death in 1972. Of moderate size with 7 full-time faculty members and 4 part-time teaching assistants, Stanford University enrolled 494 undergraduates and 6 graduates in 1938–39. Bayard Quincy Morgan (full), Kurt F. Reinhardt (associate), and F. W. Struthmann (associate) were on the faculty. Finally, Yale employed 12 full-time faculty members. Most notable among the 4 full professors was Hermann J. Weigand, who was designated director of graduate studies (the only such designation for any school in the data for 1938–39). W. G. Moulton went on to a distinguished career at Princeton. There were 687 undergraduates and 14 graduates enrolled. At this time, Bryn Mawr, Princeton, and Smith enrolled 2 graduate students each in their programs. Judging by the courses offered, Bryn Mawr emphasized philology, while Smith College clearly favored literature, although it did offer a seminar on Old Norse. We should bear in mind that several members of the faculty in each of the larger programs were experts on Scandinavian and Dutch as well as linguists, so that the actual number of Germanists is lower. Obviously, a department the size of Wisconsin (21 full-time, 15 part-time teaching assistants), with its wealth of noted scholars (Frederick Bruns, W. Freeman Twaddell, Helmut Rehder, A. R. Hohlfeld, Senn), could not be managed like a more modestly sized program such as the one at the University of North Carolina, Chapel Hill, with its 5 professors (of whom only Assistant Professor Werner P. Friedrich is remembered today) and 5 part-time teaching assistants. Moreover, going by the detailed lists of advanced literature and philology courses included in the "Personalia" for 1938–39—which seem to mark the increasing professionalization of the discipline—we might expect the more advanced professors in a large department to be ever less involved in language instruction. Yet speculation about how a department was governed (by fiat, by committee) and how courses were assigned (by individual choice, by prerogative of the chair) needs to be analyzed on a case-by-case basis. Such information can be found only in directives from a dean and reports from a faculty.

Ivory Tower Stability: From World War II to Sputnik, 1942–57

The academic pattern was established by the early 1940s and continued after the war, with one salient exception: the introduction of the Army Specialized Training Program (ASTP) at all major universities across the country. To meet the wartime need for fluent speakers of German, faculties redirected their attention to innovative language teaching, especially the method of total immersion. The intensity of the programs and the need to devise up-to-date instructional materials on the fly is well documented for both private (Penn) and public (Illinois) institutions. Faculty members at all levels were involved in this effort, which often meant teaching overloads. John Frey at Illinois, for example, doubled his load from seventeen to thirty-four credit hours during the war years, and Henri Stegemeier, who had been hired to assist Frey, took on the responsibility for grading the correspondence courses offered via the Extension Division to GIs during the war years without extra compensation. The correspondence courses offered were the first five semesters of German (McGlathery 86–88). At the University of Pennsylvania, Adolph Gorr functioned similarly, assisted by Adolf Klarmann. They were, of course, also driven by a sense of patriotic duty.

The war had an additional impact on the structure of departments: many tenured and nontenured faculty members were called to military service. They were often especially prized for their native or near-native fluency (e.g., Otto Springer was in military intelligence during the mid-1940s, and Henry Remak served in the censorship office). The ASTP programs sent thousands of military personnel to campuses nationwide. Some returned to pursue their graduate studies after the war (among them were Max Dufner, who returned to Illinois to study with Rehder, and Remak, who received his PhD at Chicago in 1947). Many returning GIs took advantage of the GI Bill to get an undergraduate education. Having had firsthand language experience in Germany, many were interested in the study of German. As long as United States occupational forces were stationed in Germany (through the 1980s), Germany remained in the forefront of American consciousness. Returning GIs and their families raised the possibility of higher enrollment in German classes, especially at institutions located near large army bases. The impact of a military presence on the structure of a department deserves to be explored at such regional institutions as Austin Peay University in Clarksville, Tennessee, which is in easy reach of sprawling Fort Campbell. Similar situations existed, for example, in North Carolina, Texas, Colorado, and California. One might also wish to examine the potential influence of ROTC programs on the shape of departments (see Nickisch).

Like other institutions, Illinois and Penn experienced a postwar surge in enrollment due to the GI Bill. In 1946–47 the resident enrollment in German at Illinois was 2,724, virtually all of it in basic language courses. This increase, of course, put pressure on the department to meet those needs with faculty resources. One result was the enhanced use of teaching assistants as regular teachers. By contrast, in 1946–47 there were only 71 advanced undergraduate and graduate registrations. Helmut Rehder, who had taken over as head of the department in 1946, marshaled a teaching force of 18 (by comparison, it was 30 in the 1980s; see McGlathery 90–91). In 1955, Rehder left Illinois to accept the headship at the University of Texas, where he transformed the German department over the next twenty years, helping it obtain a dominant position in the field, vying with Indiana as the largest German department in the 1960s. At Penn it was Otto Springer as chair who oversaw the growth in enrollment, which increased from about 670 in 1939 to 1,220 by 1947 and grew again in 1947 to 1,437. However, enrollment at Cornell, Emory, Harvard, Mount Holyoke, Muhlenberg, Princeton, Rice, Swarthmore, and Yale remained essentially unchanged in the years immediately after the war. Whereas some midwestern institutions showed a clear decrease (Indiana, Minnesota, Oberlin, Ohio State, Wisconsin), private institutions like Columbia, Northwestern, Notre Dame, Stanford, Vanderbilt, Villanova, and Washington University posted gains. What caused these differences in growth rates is a topic for future investigation.

In fall 1947, the faculty at Penn had grown to 13 full-time members (3 full, 1 associate, 1 assistant professor, 7 instructors, 1 lecturer) and 6 assistants. But by fall 1957 there were only 9 full-timers: Springer, Klarmann, Detlev Schumann, and Senn as full professors, Gorr as the lone assistant professor, and 4 instructors. There were 7 assistants. In fall 1957 Illinois also had 9 full-time members (up from 7 in 1947): 2 full professors (Stegemeier, Friedrich W. Kaufmann), 3 associate professors (M. I. Jehle, F. J. Nock, Frank G. Banta), and 4 instructors. While there is no entry for teaching assistants in 1957, Illinois had indicated 11 ten years earlier. Columbia had 19 full-time faculty members in 1957 (7 at senior rank), including Carl F. Bayerschmidt, Walter Silz, André von Gronicka, William T. H. Jackson, Jack M. Stein, Walter H. Sokel, and Inge Halpert. That same year Harvard retained 14 part-time assistants and 9 full-time faculty members. Among the full-timers were the 3 full professors: Stuart Atkins, Bernhard Blume, and Henry C. Hatfield. Princeton, now with Victor Lange as chair, had grown to 11 members, but 8 had junior rank. There were 5 teaching assistants. Like Columbia and Harvard, Yale had a strong faculty: 11 with 12 teaching assistants. Heinz Bluhm was chair, and his fellow full professors were Curt von Faber du Faur, Heinrich E. K. Henel, K. Reichardt, and H. J. Weigand. Among the junior faculty were Christoph E. Schweitzer (later UNC Chapel Hill), Peter Demetz, and Theodore S. Ziolkowski (later Princeton). Washington University in Saint Louis employed Fred O. Nolte, Raymond Immerwahr (later Univ. of Washington, then Univ. of Western Ontario), Liselotte Dieckmann, James W. Marchand (later Illinois), and Ernst Loeb (later Kingston Univ.), with Erich P. Hofacker as chair. They had 3 teaching assistants. To learn how these various departments were organized—in particular, how hiring and promotion were handled—requires detailed investigation. Also of interest is the question of whether one German department consciously imitated the structure and activities of other German departments in friendly rivalry or whether it pursued individual disciplinary objectives.

Explosive Growth, Expanding Views: From Sputnik to the End of the Cold War, 1957–90

The first expansion in graduate education before World War I was repeated in equally dramatic fashion during the decade 1957–67, which has been labeled "the fat decade" (Alter 9). The Sputnik shock that caused Americans to reevaluate educational institutions led to the National Defense Education Act of 1958 and a huge investment of federal dollars in higher education; 50,000 fellowship holders poured into graduate programs (Ziolkowski, "Seventies" 246). Coupled with an increase in the number of college-bound youth in general, pressure to expand mounted. State systems opened new campuses—for example, Illinois at Chicago Circle; Indiana at Indianapolis; Massachusetts at Boston Harbor; New York at Buffalo and Stony Brook; California at Davis, Irvine, and La Jolla. Each branch campus began to vie for its own graduate programs. Other universities added to their faculty rosters. Truly phenomenal was the Modern Language Department at the University of Maryland, which had 140 faculty members worldwide in 1960. The unusual number of faculty members in German was surely inflated by Maryland's satellite campuses serving armed forces overseas. Some new institutions such as the University of California, San Diego, opted to group all the modern literatures together, while others such as the State University of New York, Buffalo, chose the freestanding departmental model with the full range of required courses.

To obtain the faculty members needed to meet the rapid expansion, startups were forced to draw them from existing programs. Buffalo, for example, lured Peter Heller from Massachusetts at Amherst and Peter Boerner from Wisconsin. The newcomers arrived full of ideas about how to organize a new program. SUNY Buffalo also entertained a lively succession of visiting scholars (Michael Hamburger, Katharina Mommsen and Momme Mommsen, Heinz Moenkemeyer) to augment the standing faculty. In the 1960s Stuart Atkins left Harvard for UC Santa Barbara, Heinz Politzer moved from Oberlin College to Berkeley, Herbert Penzl moved from Michigan to Berkeley, von Gronicka moved from Columbia to Penn, and Wolfgang Paulsen moved from Connecticut to Massachusetts. All these departures and arrivals happened in the 1960s, but similar moves continued over the next two decades. In most cases, the professor moved to lead an expanding department, to shape the discipline through new hires and the implementation of a competitive curriculum. Last but not least, young talented scholars from Europe were attracted in droves, enriching and altering the way business was done in American German departments: Katharina Mommsen, Reinhold Grimm, Peter Uwe Hohendahl, Walter Hinderer, Frank Trommler, Paul Michael Lützeler, Andreas Huyssen, Wulf Koepke, and many others joined Karl S. Guthke and Jost Hermand, who had ventured across the Atlantic in the late 1950s. It has become a commonplace to note the influence of these scholars on the intellectual shape of the profession, but their influence on the structure of departments, on daily operations, on hiring and promotion practices, and on curricular matters requires closer scrutiny.

Despite the high demand for qualified personnel to cover more sections of courses, the contrary move of reducing teaching loads was introduced in order to attract new faculty members. The need was so acute in the 1960s that many graduate students received offers to teach without having completed the dissertation. Their departures made it difficult for some home graduate institutions to cover courses by using them as teaching assistants and to reduce teaching loads. Banta, who took over as chair at Illinois after Rehder left for Texas, nonetheless succeeded in reducing the load for both teaching assistants and full-time faculty members. Eighty-five percent of the teaching in the early 1960s was devoted, we should note, to elementary work. That disproportion was due in large part to the language requirement at the university and, as Banta remarked, to the poor quality of elementary language instruction in the high schools. Students had to repeat elementary courses on entering college. Banta suggested in the early 1960s a number of steps to improve the situation: (1) closer ties between the university and the high schools, (2) the appointment of a second language acquisition expert to coordinate language instruction and monitor the quality of instruction, (3) an increase in foreign language entrance requirements, (4) strengthening the teacher-training programs, and (5) a state law requiring teachers to major in a subject rather than in educational theory (McGlathery 108). The proposal echoed Learned's support of a similar plan around 1900 in Pennsylvania.

All these laudable proposals reemerged in a national debate in the 1980s. For example, Herbert Knust (head at Illinois 1982–85) in fall 1984 appointed the first faculty member with a research commitment specifically to second language pedagogy: John F. Lalande II. Penn did the same with the appointment of Karl F. Otto, also in the mid-1980s. Until then, the junior faculty (along with Albert L. Lloyd) took responsibility for the departmental Language Teaching Seminar, which met three to four times per semester and served as a clearinghouse for pedagogical issues encountered in the coordination of first- and second-year German. Faculty members were also charged with classroom visitation. However, with the appointment of Otto (who had come from the Univ. of Illinois, Chicago) Penn wished to combine traditional research interests with the new demand for second language acquisition (SLA) theory. The appointment of a faculty line specifically to pedagogy and SLA theory was a major step in the professionalization of graduate student training. Similar expertise was stressed elsewhere: Claire Kramsch at Berkeley, Heidi Byrnes at Georgetown, Dorothy James at Hunter College, Renate Schulz at Arizona, Janet Swaffar at Texas. Most major departments now have such an expert. The student unrest of the late 1960s and early 1970s had radically altered the playing field shortly after graduate programs had geared up to meet the instructional demands of the Sputnik era.[11]

Another issue was the teaching load. At Penn the normal teaching load for assistant professors in the 1960s and 1970s was six courses a year, and teaching assistants were responsible for three courses a year. The load for assistant professors was reduced in the mid-1970s, not by any fiat from above but by the fact that the assistant professors who served as undergraduate chair, and thus essentially had responsibility for scheduling and curricular development, determined that the course load could be lowered by one course a year without detracting from the overall undergraduate program. In doing so, the teaching load was brought into line with assistant professors in classics, English, French, and philosophy. A fait accompli was hard to change. The course reduction at Illinois had occurred already in the 1960s for senior professors, who taught four courses a year. McGlathery reports that in 1990 he was still trying to achieve a reduction for associate and assistant professors at Illinois to two courses per semester (*German* 140). Of course, private institutions are not subject to state mandates on teaching, which affect the organization of departments at public institutions. What happened at Penn would have been unlikely at Illinois.

Course assignments were another matter. Having gone through an era when junior faculty taught mostly language courses, senior faculty looked on graduate seminars and upper-division literature courses as an earned right, one the next generation had to earn as well. Assistant professors had to content themselves with an occasional advanced course, often waiting until promotion to associate professor to teach a graduate seminar. Or they sought an outlet for their literary and critical ambitions by teaching in other programs such as general literature, humanities programs, honors courses, first-year writing courses (since the 1970s), literature in translation, women's studies (since the late 1970s), critical theory (since the 1970s). Such was the case, at least, at Penn and Illinois. Now colleagues seek active involvement in extradepartmental programs in order to realize their interdisciplinary aspirations, to enhance their promotion chances, or (in some smaller programs) simply to have something to teach.

Given the steady increase in faculty and enrollment numbers through the 1960s and especially the rapid expansion of graduate programs to accommodate the perceived need for teachers in colleges and high schools, competition among the schools intensified. Some newcomers sought to rival the traditional stalwarts for visibility by organizing annual conferences and developing new thematic emphases (Univ. of Massachusetts, SUNY Albany, Univ. of Wisconsin, Washington Univ.). In the 1980s, graduate student conferences began at Berkeley and Cincinnati and proliferated rapidly. Continuing the tradition, Rutgers held its first annual graduate student conference in February 2001. Some departments (e.g., UC Irvine, Illinois) established a tradition of hosting a cash-bar reception at the MLA Annual Convention. Aside from providing a welcome venue for Germanists to mingle, the affair also highlights the hosting department. UC Irvine has been particularly successful in consistently organizing such an event.

Study-abroad and exchange programs were also initiated and expanded, at both the student and faculty level. The Junior Year in Munich and Junior Year in Freiburg im Breisgau are among the oldest. Vanderbilt's exchange program with Regensburg for undergraduate and graduate students was established in the late 1960s, for graduate students to the Freie Universität Berlin a little later. The University of California has a long-standing study-abroad program at Göttingen. Smith College and the University of Cincinnati have programs in Hamburg. Smaller liberal arts colleges such as Muhlenberg, Calvin College, and Wheaton College send students to Germany on interim or summer programs. Often these programs are the single most important source for keeping up enrollments in upper-division courses (see Ziefle 180). Faculty exchanges with German and Austrian universities have also become commonplace; writers-in-residence programs have sprung up, supported by the Max Kade Foundation and other sponsors. Max Kade began to support departmental efforts by funding fellowships, residence houses, and cultural centers designed to advance the study of things German. It has played a role in the post-Sputnik era comparable to that of the Carl Schurz Foundation before World War II.

The atmosphere of a gentleman's society gradually gave way to a more diversified, perhaps even a plebeian atmosphere, especially after the democratic and liberalizing thrust of 1968.[12] The shift in tenor had to do with the entrance of large numbers of first-generation and nontraditional college students. An ethnically more diverse student population, including greater numbers of women in the academy, was the result. Moreover, faculty members began to organize into bargaining units, which transformed the nature of the relation between faculty and administration (e.g., Oakland Univ. in 1969). A generation later, graduate students also unionized or tried to do so (e.g., New York Univ., Rutgers, Temple, Yale). The trend toward collective bargaining and its significance for the structure of departments deserves special analysis to determine what effect it has on the discipline.

The curricular development in the 1980s proved to be a movement toward German studies (Indiana led the way in the mid-1970s), cultural studies, and critical theory. In the 1990s postcolonial interests were added to the mix.[13] As a consequence of altered expectations, the writing of textbooks for language and culture instruction—which used to be viewed approvingly in the pre-1960s era and were even penned by more-traditional scholars such as von Gronicka and Stuart Atkins—fell into disfavor, often not counting in tenure and promotion decisions.

These transformations and new expectations of the faculty prompted changes in how departments were organized. Into the 1960s it was still commonplace to appoint a head of the department, who had the autonomy to govern according to his (rarely her) own best ideas. A head had the authority to make all teaching assignments, to set schedules, to assign office space, to approve special acquisition and travel requests, and to organize a lecture series. Yet, increasingly from the 1960s on, the head was replaced by a chair with a fixed term, who was approved by the faculty and appointed by the dean. The chair's responsibilities became somewhat clouded: does he (increasingly since the 1980s, she) primarily serve the interests of the faculty or those of the administration? Departmental committees shared responsibility for much of the organizational work previously assigned to the chair. The expansion of the undergraduate and graduate programs in the 1960s had residual effects long after the growth had ceased. In part because of the institutional momentum gained and the desire for greater professionalization of the discipline since the 1970s, it proved necessary to appoint a director of undergraduate studies and a director of graduate studies (at Vanderbilt, Penn, etc.). In the largest programs, a director of language studies and teacher training was also named. In some cases even a director of the language laboratory—now of the media center— proved necessary (e.g., American Univ., Delaware). Committees were formed to cull through graduate applications; other committees established to oversee curricular reform; still others to review promotion and tenure cases; still others to search for new faculty members and, once hired, to mentor them. Visiting Max Kade professors and DAAD lecturers had to be identified and integrated. Someone had to be involved in undergraduate recruitment and advising, with responsibility for such activities as the German club, Delta Phi Alpha, the annual Oktoberfest, and film series. Graduate student representatives joined standing faculty committees. State and federal directives regarding equal opportunity and concerns about sexual harassment reshaped the workplace environment. Sunshine laws were enacted to help ensure that business was conducted openly (at least at public institutions). What used to be a club atmosphere evolved into the semblance of a public enterprise with an emphasis on collective equality and personal accountability.

Today, most chairs complain about the lack of authority to accomplish any truly meaningful change; they have seen the position reduced to that of a paper pusher dependent on the dean of the college, who controls the purse strings (or maybe not!).

The transformations noted above must be factored into an assessment of how the organization of the German department responded to external pressures and how it realized intellectual objectives. As always we need to ask the perennial questions: To whom and to what end do we teach German? (C. Nollendorfs, "Special Survey"). Is it possible, Cora Lee Nollendorfs (Kluge) asks, that the restructuring of departments into high-powered graduate programs has cost us the benefits of a good undergraduate program at the larger institutions (391)? Strikingly, E. H. Magill, a French philologist at Swarthmore, asked a very similar question a hundred years earlier, in 1892, even though Swarthmore was (is) small and had no graduate program. If the most one can hope for is that 5% of the undergraduates in your classroom will pursue graduate studies in the subject, "What are you going to do with the other 95 percent?" (qtd. in Graff 77). The more things change, the more they stay the same, it seems. Moreover, when it comes to academic jobs for the 5% who do pursue graduate study in Germanics, most will not likely be to train graduate students.

Conclusion: Past and Future, 1990–

All the growth did not endure. SUNY Buffalo's dramatic growth dissipated within twenty years; by 1990 the German department there had lost its independent status and was integrated with other modern languages and literatures. Recently, it discontinued its undergraduate major. Between the mid-1970s and mid-1990s, Stanford's German department shrank in size by three-quarters. Bryn Mawr, Boston University, Catholic University, Colorado, Kentucky, Smith, Tufts, Tulane, and other institutions lost their doctoral programs. Large midwestern state universities experienced downsizing. Penn State's doctoral program was threatened with cancellation in the late 1990s; the department was eventually amalgamated with other languages and comparative literature in 1998. How did these events affect departmental structures? Oakland University in Rochester, Michigan, went from 6 faculty members for German in a literature department to 2 Germanists by the mid-1980s.

Muhlenberg College, which had a contingent of 7 faculty members for German in 1947 and 6 in 1967, now has but 1.5 German faculty members. In 1970 Calvin College had 7.5 faculty full-time equivalents but saw that figure decline to 2.5 by 1997. Oberlin College, Lehigh University, and Lafayette College experienced a similar downward trend. That development was repeated more or less dramatically at all kinds of institutions across the nation. Yet the question of whether the losses of faculty full-time equivalents necessarily translate into fewer majors and minors requires closer scrutiny (see Ziefle 179–81).

To talk about transformation in departmental size, organization, and function is a slippery business. We cannot simply assume that the college model of American education forfeited its role to the rival model of graduate education with its penchant for professionalization and advocacy of research agenda. We cannot simply assume that the tension between literature and philology (or later between language and literature) was of no consequence for the way departments organized and understood themselves. We cannot simply assume that the cultural divide between Germans and Americans had no impact on the functioning of departments even during their heyday. Tensions between the core college mission and the professionalization of training at graduate institutions remained. In fact, for most of the history of departments, it was a matter of adding to existing core curricula, of expanding into newly discovered areas relevant to survival and thrival. A new layer of professional expectation was placed on the traditional role of teacher-educator. In many instances, it signaled a transformation of the undergraduate college into one academic unit in a diversified graduate institution (e.g., Columbia, Harvard, Yale, Princeton). Yet not all colleges underwent such a structural transformation: Amherst, Carleton, Hamilton, Oberlin, Sewanee, Swarthmore, and Wheaton, for example, retained their undergraduate character and ethos. The fact of only a partial shift in institutional structure—in no way a universalizing movement—will have to figure prominently in a detailed study of German departments and their self-organization.

Certainly, methodological approaches to the discipline must also figure into the history of departmental structures. Philology played a key role in the initial professionalization of the discipline, establishing the study of language and literature as a rigorous, objective science. While increased challenges to the hegemony of philological studies were evident from the 1930s on, literature did not really rise to the fore until the 1940s and 1950s, when it was influenced by a politically unfavorable climate and supported by the Agrarians in the South (esp. Vanderbilt) and New Criticism in the Northeast (esp. Yale). Close reading or *werkimmanente Kritik* began to transform the structure of many departments, because literary training had to be offered as rigorously as courses in Gothic and the history of the German language. More hires were made after 1968 in twentieth-century German literary studies. Literary study was further augmented by historical perspectives and an emphasis on cross-disciplinary expertise. These altered expectations prompted changes in the graduate mission of departments, the shape of the curriculum, and connections to other departments. With every new research perspective, pressure to professionalize the training was felt anew. Thus, the calls by early Germanists for rigorous pursuit of knowledge were echoed later by advocates of expanding fields of knowledge: comparative literature (Henry Remak, Victor Lange, Erich Heller, Heinz Politzer), Marxist-leaning criticism (Reinhold Grimm, Jost Hermand, Jack Zipes), feminist studies (Ruth Klüger, Ruth-Ellen Boetcher Joeres, Susan Cocalis, Patricia Herminghouse), and more recently German cultural studies (Irene Kacandes, Sara Lennox, Jeff Peck).

And what of the future? Will German departments exist as independent units, or will they be grouped with other languages, as at Delaware, Penn State, and Rutgers? Will language instruction continue to be spun off to independent units, as it was suggested at Penn, instituted and recently rejected at Cornell, and newly introduced at Stanford? Will German departments be subsumed under the aegis of English or literature departments, as at UC San Diego or the University of Tennessee? They might even be integrated into history departments, or they might hire historians (as at Michigan), musicologists (as at Wisconsin), and art historians. If we excel in cross-disciplinary endeavors and in investigating every cultural fact as a symbol, that possibility is not unimaginable. Of course, this speculation applies only to the larger, advanced-degree-granting institutions, not the colleges where as a rule German is housed with other languages.

The future structure of German departments is likely to be a mixture of the old and the new. Whatever the solution at a local institution, it seems clear that repeated calls for an action agenda will be heeded and acted on. Every so often an agenda for the twenty-first century is promulgated that seems to have roots in the efforts of earlier Germanists like Learned at Penn around 1900 and Hohlfeld at Wisconsin after World War I. Occasionally reform efforts take on a larger, programmatic status; examples are Bayard Quincy Morgan's (Stanford) 1944 call to arms "After the War: A Blueprint for Action," Barbara Elling's 1976 "Career Alternatives for Students of German" (esp. 244–46), and Heidi Byrnes's 1996 "An Action Agenda for German Studies in the Twenty-First Century." An AATG committee on articulation K-16 has provided the most recent data (2002) on motivation for studying German at the high school and college levels. Its findings and recommendations are important for the (re-)structuring of German departments in colleges and universities (Andress et al.). (See also Trommler, "Updating.")

What each of these action agendas has in common is the desire to maximize departmental structure to realize one or both of these objectives: to ensure that Germanics be a part of the general humanistic curriculum of American higher education; to emphasize the practical value of the German language for careers in science, technology, commerce, and international relations. These two goals are also present in *A User's Guide to German Cultural Studies* (1997) edited by Scott Denham, Irene Kacandes, and Jonathan Petropoulos. A primary purpose of that handbook is to provide a practical guide to the teaching of culture in its various representations (text, film, architecture, music, etc.). In her introduction to the volume Kacandes firmly emphasizes the theoretical and interdisciplinary character of German studies as cultural studies, so that two contending models evolve: practical applications of German language competency and the integration of German studies in the discourses of cultural studies, where English departments are clearly dominant.

The models, agendas, and (re)conceptualizations of the future mission of German studies will succeed or fail depending on how Germanics is organized institutionally, how involved the faculty is in long-range strategic planning, how generous deans are in assigning new (joint) lines, and how adept Germanists are in maintaining an identity distinct from monolingual cultural historians and in articulating language instruction K-16. If we fail to meet these perceived needs, the structure of the German department as a distinct unit will likely dissolve into large units entrusted with language instruction across the board and cultural studies under the aegis of English departments, which are dominant, having more students, more faculty lines, and greater momentum. Clearly, ours is a period of transition. But every period has been.

Notes

1 Hidden treasures of information, which could lend that history exceptional detail, await discovery at all kinds of institutions across the United States. For example, the home page of the National Union Catalog lists oral-history resources and other archival material with a bearing on the changing profile of various departments (see lcweb.loc.gov/coll/nucmc). To facilitate research, a representative selection of these documents should be published in a volume similar to Gerald Graff and Michael Warner's *The Origins of Literary Studies in America: A Documentary Anthology*. Graff and Warner document developments for English departments primarily for the period 1874–1917. One would of course require a multivolume anthology of reports to cover developments after 1917. A research group at the Deutsches Literaturarchiv Marbach under the direction of Christoph König and in the capable hands of Hanne Knickmann has compiled a biographic directory of Germanists around the world, which should prove to be immensely useful to future studies. More recently the group has begun to assemble chronicles of American as well as German departments. I am indebted to Knickmann of the *Internationales Germanistenlexikon* for sharing information.

2 See Bayerschmidt; Bottigheimer, "One Hundred and Fifty Years"; J. Hatfield; Mueller-Vollmer, "Differenzierung"; Nikisch; C. Nollendorfs, "First World War"; Prokop; Schade; Scheck; and Ziefle.

3 By comparison, the University of California, Berkeley, a longtime leader in the field, did not really get started until after the turn of the century (although it had been

granted a charter earlier). And its "southern" campus in Los Angeles, UCLA, was not even established until 1919.

4 Immediately preceding them in places 11 and 12 were Michigan (78 doctorates awarded) and Ohio State (72). Immediately following were Cornell (61) and North Carolina (61) tied in place 15 and Johns Hopkins in 17 (60) (Sander, "Doctorates" 322). For the fifteen years 1965–79, Volkmar Sander lists Princeton, Penn, and Illinois as having awarded 50 doctorates each. Stanford and Indiana produced the most PhDs, 97 and 84 respectively, while UCLA and Johns Hopkins awarded 49 and 45 respectively (compare the tables in "Doctorates" 320–21).

5 Wisconsin had the most with 36, then Berkeley with 32, Texas 24, Princeton 23, Harvard 22, Yale 21, and Cornell 20. Between Penn and Illinois we find Washington University with 15 PhDs, Michigan 14, Stanford 14, University of Washington 13, University of North Carolina 12, Ohio State 12, and Virginia 12 (C. Nollendorfs, "Special Survey").

6 Graff's units of division correspond more closely to the themes and tenor of historical and critical studies dominant at a given time rather than to the organization of English departments themselves (see his table of contents and chapter introductions). Schade follows a tripartite scheme in charting the department's genesis at Cincinnati: "*Gründerzeit* (1900–34), consolidation (1934–61), and outreach (1961–2000)" (299).

7 I am grateful to Ernst Schürer, who is writing a history of his department, for the information on Penn State.

8 To better judge the significance of these accomplishments, one should note that in 1898–99 the total graduate enrollment in all disciplines at Michigan was 77 graduate students, at Indiana 71, at Minnesota 132, at Kansas 42, and at Illinois 31 (McGlathery, *German* 24). However, in fall 1910 graduate enrollment in German at Illinois had reached 48, and the total graduate student enrollment at Illinois in 1913–14 stood at 375, including 75 women (50, 85–86). At Wisconsin in 1916–17 the German department had 25 faculty members who taught 1,400 students (C. Nollendorfs, "First World War" 178).

9 The rise of the mandarin model was clearly intended from the outset. In 1874, at the first appearance of a professional profile, James Morgan Hart commented: "The German professor is not a teacher in the English sense of the term; he is a specialist. He is not responsible for the success of his hearers. He is responsible only for the quality of his instruction. His duty begins and ends with himself" (264). And Hermann C. G. Brandt, a professor of German at Hamilton College, asserted at the inaugural meeting of the MLA in 1883: "Teachers of modern languages . . . do not realize that their department is a science" and must be conducted accordingly, because "a scientific basis dignifies our profession. . . . By introducing scientific methods, we shall show before long . . . that the teacher must be as specially and scientifically trained for his work in our department as well as in any other" (57–60; qtd. in Graff 68–69). Both calls for professional independence and disciplinary training resonated throughout the ensuing 125 years of professional transformations. The image of the self-sufficient researcher was, to be sure, challenged dramatically by the sixty-eighters, who brought about a new reorganization of departments (of course, always in confluence with other factors).

10 Adolf Klarmann (PhD at Penn, 1931) told me in the early 1970s that new reading courses were designed to make up for the lack of enrollment in the traditional courses.

11 For example, I graduated from high school in 1960, took my BA in 1964, earned my MA in 1967, and completed the PhD in February 1972. But I had already secured a full-time teaching position in fall 1969, moving to Penn in fall 1972. By then the bottom had begun to fall out of the market. I was lucky.

12 This democratization process became manifest especially when departments ballooned in the 1970s: Berkeley expanded to 18 faculty members and 36 graduate

students on fellowship, Illinois to 18 faculty members and 28 TAs, Indiana to 22 and 32 respectively, Michigan to 22 and 34 respectively, Ohio State to 20 faculty members and 28 funded students, Stanford grew to 16 full-time faculty members and 9 funded students, Virginia to 20 faculty members and 12 TAs, Wisconsin to 21 faculty members and 30 TAs. Of course, the actual number of graduate students is larger than the funded positions reported in the survey. McGlathery reports that Illinois had 73 graduate students in 1966–67. Three years earlier the number was 39, and a quarter century later it was again at that level: 38 in 1989–90 (137).

13 Peck, "British"; most recently Hohendahl, "Nationale Ausdifferenzierungen"; McCarthy, "Was heißt es"; Trommler, "Germanistik nicht als Nationalphilologie."

The Constituencies of Academics and the Priorities of Germanists

JEFFREY L. SAMMONS

The academic scholar and teacher has obligations to several constituencies that certainly overlap but may be heuristically distinguished from one another. The first of these is students, in the majority: undergraduates. Advanced students are an ancillary constituency, although one quite demanding of time. A second is collegial: disciplinary and interdisciplinary, in one's own department and institution as well as nationally and, especially in our field, internationally. A third is constituted by the larger intellectual community, comprising other academics, especially in the humanities, along with writers, public intellectuals, and the media in which their interests and concerns are articulated. A fourth is a vertical constituency that I will call governance; it begins at the lowest level with chairpersons, deans, provosts, and in some cases institutional presidents and ascends to boards of trustees, state legislatures, and national policy makers. Finally, there is a fifth environmental constituency of the larger community, diverse, amorphous, and uncertainly ascertainable in its level of interest and relevance. A subset of it is elementary and secondary education. The foreign languages are among the fields relevant to this segment, although their circumstances are almost entirely regulated by the vertical constituency.

By and large, society perceives only the first and fourth of these constituencies. This is why academics, who often feel that they are working themselves ragged, that practically every hour they are not in class they must make a choice as to which task has the highest priority, find themselves accused of loafing at society's expense while not teaching enough or attentively enough or not working relevantly enough for public purposes. The labor of mentoring advanced students is generally invisible, and research and scholarship are regarded with several kinds of suspicion—partly because much scholarship is unintelligible to the uninitiated and can be made by the ill-intentioned to sound like jabberwocky or trivia; partly because research is suspected of being a self-indulgent boondoggle that distracts from teaching, especially as there are fleeting clues that scholars enjoy doing it; and partly because of an inchoate fear that scholarship in the humanities may be subversive or, in the curious political vocabulary of our curious land, "liberal." The role of the vertical constituency is often to require conformity with received opinion and support for the virtues and discipline alleged to ensure that social institutions and practices remain unaltered. Thus the persistent threat of censorship and control, not infrequently in the form of, or masquerading as, assaults on tenure.

The different constituencies can have a shifting relation to academic priorities and to one another; there can be harmonies and congruencies or incompatibilities and antitheses in various constellations. Furthermore, in my opinion these constellations are to a very large extent historically and socially determined, thus relatively resistant to decisionistic exertions by academics, individually or collectively: that is, it is unlikely that academics set the priorities, even if their rhetoric persuades them that they must. Much of the current discourse of assessing blame and demanding change may therefore be ineffectual. As far as the Germanic field is concerned, the most imaginable compatibility among the constituencies is visible in the much maligned first phases of the discipline in the nineteenth century. The reasons for this are the intimate German American cultural symbiosis that evolved during the century and the high regard in which German culture was held among educated people. A contributing though not defining strength in the environmental constituency was the large, vigorous, and articulate German American community. The field was rather easily able to insert itself into this situation as, in some considerable part, a service discipline. First of all, there was the need for anyone with aspirations, not just to higher culture but to higher education, to learn German, which became by a wide margin the leading foreign language in the United States. Beyond this need there developed a widespread confidence in the elevating, civilizing, and emancipatory potential in German culture of immediate, even practical relevance for America. All five of the constituencies described here participated in this superintending discourse.

We have come to look on this history with a jaundiced eye. A characteristic example of the attitude we have developed is Richard Spuler's well-informed and instructive, if rather belligerent, study of the use made of the *Goethezeit* classics in the constitution of the Germanic field (*Germanistik*). In such exercises of purgation it is sometimes forgotten that the prestige of German culture in the nineteenth century was a massive social fact and not an imposition of academics besotted with the cult of Goethe and German nationalism. It is, of course, well known that the American university raised itself to modern scholarly standards on German models (see Veysey, esp. 125–33). Sometimes the development tends to be presented as a loss of innocence, a seduction into the disciplinary boundaries and preoccupation with research that are alleged to burden our institutions today. But there is considerable evidence that American universities were in a distinctly inferior condition. One witness is Charles Godfrey Leland, the future translator of Heine's prose works, who was a student at Princeton in the early 1840s. Having had an extensive reading habit since boyhood, he regarded himself as considerably more learned than his professors and found the institution "entirely in the hands of the strictest of 'Old School' Presbyterian theologians," where no German was taught, as it was the language of the devil, and French was banned as irreligious. In retrospect he regarded Princeton as his "Mala Mater" (Leland 84; Pennell 1: 40). He escaped to picture-book student life in Heidelberg and Munich, where he felt emancipated.

In the urge to indict our past we have lost track of this not only elevating but liberating promise of German culture that many felt and experienced. Beyond the arts and sciences, educational practice, and religion—especially biblical criticism—that culture strongly influenced American writers. William Dean Howells, for example, declared that he owed to Heine, then regarded in America as part of German culture rather than in exile from it, "my literary liberation"; "he undid my hands, which I had taken so much pains to tie behind my back" (125). The prestige was widely distributed; from New England transcendentalists to Saint Louis Hegelians, Germany was the model and the cynosure. "Germans allegedly had high standards of education, superior intelligence, and deep moral earnestness—in the words of Gustav Koerner, 'the most humane, the most just, the most genial and noble of all peoples.' Germany was 'the guide of civilization, the modern Hellas of art and science' " (Rippley, "German Assimilation" 129). In 1891, Josiah Royce remembered "a generation that dreamed of nothing but the German university. . . . German scholarship was our master and our guide" (Veysey 129–30). There is a good deal of evidence, although not systematically studied to my knowledge, that this prestige was internationally shared. It surely accounts for the momentum of German Jewish assimilation, also today more maligned than understood. Matthew Arnold wrote in 1868: "It is in science that we have most need to borrow from the German universities. The French universities have no liberty, and the English universities have no science; the German universities have both" (Farrer 192n29). Even Spuler's point (*Germanistik* 77) that American histories of German literature in the nineteenth century tended to be "small and unscholarly volumes," sacrificing "thoroughness and comprehensiveness to pragmatism and leisurely appreciation" (which corresponds to my own observations), might well point to the domestication of the German literary and cultural heritage in the environmental constituency—that is, might be a sign of strength. From this point of view, the propagation and valorization of German culture in the evolving Germanic field seems not only natural but required by the imperatives of the time, a duty to the vertical and environmental constituencies of just the sort that today's academics are charged with neglecting.

Exactly how this congruence of constituencies began to crumble is not entirely clear. Even if one acknowledges some justification for the elevated prestige of German culture in the nineteenth century, there can come a point in such matters, to borrow the vocabulary of French imagologists, where *image* becomes *mirage*. The concept of the "land of poets and thinkers," the slogan reformulated from Mme de Staël's "la patrie de la pensée" (43), survived in the minds of many even after the Franco-Prussian War, Bismarck's regime of blood and iron, and Germany's brief but sufficiently atrocious colonial record into a time when it was becoming increasingly illusory. However, it is not obvious that historical changes directly affect national images, which often exhibit a remarkable tenacity over time. It may be, rather, that the harmonious congruence was something of an optical illusion to begin with or came to be so, that the environmental and, ultimately, the governance constituencies were never so completely with the program as the keepers of the grail in their elitism may have supposed. In any case, the whole constellation collapsed with stunning rapidity at the time of World War I (see Hoecherl-Alden in this volume). This event is well known and has been much studied and analyzed (see, e.g., C. Nollendorfs, "Deutschunterricht" and "First World War"; Kirschbaum; Trommler, "Inventing"). It is not clear to me, however, that it has yet been fully understood, perhaps because it is overdetermined. The entry of the United States into the war aroused a militant patriotism that speedily replaced the isolationism that had preceded it; a saturation of the labor market previously filled by immigrants had motivated a new nativism; the prohibition movement came to be directly hostile to the German Americans, who liked to drink beer on Sunday afternoons, who had been complaining for decades about American blue laws, and whose organizations came to be financially sponsored by the big breweries. None of these pressures seem quite sufficient to have terminated the broad and deep German American symbiosis; nevertheless, the evanescence of the constituencies was dramatic. Nothing discloses the radicality of the breach more than the bald statistic reflecting the near disappearance of the educational segment of the environmental constituency: between 1915 and 1922 the number of American schoolchildren learning German fell by 96%. Even with some recovery, German as a foreign language had fallen to its now permanent position well below French and Spanish (see Benseler in this volume; Zeydel, "Teaching . . . to the Present" 361–62).

Everyone who has any knowledge of the history of the Germanic field is aware of this episode. But I have been arguing for some years that we chronically underestimate its consequences down to the present day, that we have not always acknowledged the extent to which it has continued to resist the pursuit of priorities. Not only were the environmental and, with it, the student constituency devastated; drawn into the black hole with them, in the course of time, was the academic, intellectual, and literary constituency. Colleagues in the other literary disciplines, including the comparatists, with few exceptions know vanishingly little about the German tradition outside of certain privileged provinces such as Romantic theory, Nietzsche, or Benjamin. The occasional writer with any relation to the German canon, such as the (incidentally) Canadian-born Saul Bellow, acquires thereby the reputation of uncommon erudition. Evidence of this vacuum can be extracted from the public discourse virtually daily. A notorious example some years ago was E. L. Doctorow's *Ragtime*, which was in the public eye for months before anyone noticed that it was modeled on Kleist's *Michael Kohlhaas*, not in an esoterically allusive way but quite obviously on the surface; and even then, six years later, the critic Gene Siskel, after interviewing the director of the film version, Milos Forman, reported that the book was inspired by "Frederick Kleist's short novel, 'My Coal House' " (16).

As I have noted at intervals, the *New York Times* is an inexhaustible source of such solecisms. I restrict myself to those that came to hand in a single month. An article on Berlin restaurants mentions the "reincarnation of Lutter & Wegner [sic] . . . on the site of the house of E. T. A. Hoffmann, the 19th-century artist, writer and wastrel" (Apple; 29 July 1998)—this of one of the hardest-working and most conscientious personalities in the history of German letters. As background information for a summer theater revival of Thornton Wilder's *The Matchmaker* we are informed: "Before 'Hello, Dolly!,' of course, there was the play it was based on, Thornton Wilder's winsome, all-American farce" (Marks; 15 July 1998). That the "all-American farce" was in turn based on Nestroy's all-Austrian farce, *Einen Jux will er sich machen*, is known, of course, to experts on Wilder but apparently not to the fact checkers of the *Times*, if there are any. But the mistake that nearly sent me to the keyboard for yet another letter to the editor appeared in an article on an elaborate Spanish commemoration of the four-hundredth anniversary of the death of Philip II, in which it was remarked that he "bore a potential heir, Don Carlos, later the subject of the Verdi opera that bears his name" (Goodman; 1 July 1998). No educated American would have written such a phrase in the decades before World War I.

Fussing about such things may seem petty and parochial. But I insist that they are symptoms of an environmental situation that makes the perpetual intradisciplinary contention about priorities to some extent unavailing. The crisis at the time of World War I eradicated constituencies but most seriously, in my opinion, the intellectual and literary. There is no echo of that loss—and also no monitoring of the ignorant nonsense about German arts and letters of the past that sometimes enters the public sphere—because there are no gate-keepers. This tabula rasa in the academic constituency at least partly accounts for the fact that a book like Daniel Jonah Goldhagen's *Hitler's Willing Executioners* could not only be published but also, more distressingly, be passed by Harvard's political scientists as a dissertation and given prizes.

There was, of course, some recovery from the rock bottom of World War I. Positive efforts were made to restore contact with German letters by the *Nation* and the *New Republic*, which made a point of giving attention to contemporary writers such as Rilke, Hauptmann, Wassermann, Feuchtwanger, Werfel, and Thomas Mann, along with a number of others (Köpke, "Lifting"). But a concentration on contemporary writing, exclusively mediated by translation, as worthwhile as it may now appear compared to the near silence in our time, cannot substitute for a knowledge of the tradition. Another crisis-born initiative was the founding of the American Association of Teachers of German in 1926 (Weiss, "From New York"). The focus of the AATG was naturally on the propagation of German as a foreign language. Here lay the beginning of a long series of exhortations in various formats to the environmental constituency, sometimes with attempts to channel them through the vertical constituency, with the purpose of persuading people of the value of learning German. Obviously this is a necessary and unceasing task, but there is something irredeemably melancholy about it, because it was at one time not necessary—should not be necessary, one might think, in a rationally ordered world. And it is a confession of weakness, obliging us to pragmatic arguments, a sacrifice of *Bildung* to *Ausbildung*, a consequence that worries some of us more than others.

The enfeebled literary discipline, I believe an eventual history of American *Germanistik* would show, began to adapt to the revolution in literary studies spreading through American universities in the 1930s that has come to be known, not always with precision, as the New Criticism. Thus the German field ventured to establish a renewed consonance with the lateral academic constituency. In this connection I often think of one of my teachers, Hermann J. Weigand, a casualty of the World War I devastation, who initially had to find his way back into the academy as a Scandinavianist. While I know of no evidence that he ever paid any attention to the New Criticism or any literary-theoretical discourse, objectively his techniques of exceptionally precise close reading, along with his developing interest in psychoanalytic interpretation, made him one of those who elevated criticism in our field to a standard that ought to have been acknowledged by our sister disciplines. The potential continued to be unrealized as the Germanic field, which had lost nearly a generation of scholars, came to be replenished with exiles from Nazism. On the one hand, many of them brought traditions of German hermeneutics and interpretive practices in descent from Russian formalists and Czech and Polish structuralists that were not wholly incompatible with the intrinsic methods becoming dominant in the Anglo-American literary disciplines. That the key figure in the formation of comparative literature in the United States, René Wellek, had come from the Prague school was of signal importance for the success of the endeavor in the American context.

On the other hand, the priorities of many of these welcome guests, who greatly enriched the quality of scholarship in the Germanic field, tended to be oriented, unremarkably, on constituencies in Germany and Central Europe. It has been regularly pointed out of the literary exiles that they showed relatively little interest in their American environment (e.g., Pfanner 85; Ott 278–79). There developed a tendency to write largely if not exclusively in German, to hold conferences exclusively in German, to publish abroad, and to relate more to colleagues in German-speaking countries than to those in their own institutions. But it must be remembered that the American colleagues may not have encouraged dialogue, a barrier on which I can remember bitter complaint from my elders in my student days. In any case, this tendency was reinforced by the need for the still undermanned field to recruit a younger generation of scholars from abroad during the post-Sputnik expansion. One sometimes got the feeling that the Germanic field in America was functioning as a branch of the German-Austrian-Swiss university system only accidentally located in this country. American-born scholars sometimes were treated as foreigners in their own departments, some of which recruited many of their graduate students from abroad, making American students feel unwelcome and subaltern. Thus the breach from the national intellectual and academic constituency—instigated, to be sure, by others—was in a sense institutionalized. I was one of those who complained about this breach ("Some Considerations"). But the complaint may already have been becoming obsolete at the time that I made it. American Germanists were writing more in English and participating more in their own institutions and on the national level. If I may cite a kind of recantation I offered a dozen years later:

> We have deans, vice-chancellors, leaders in all manner of activities and organizations. We have supplied three of the last eight presidents of the Modern Language Association; the three preceding from our field were scattered among twenty presidents. In some areas it looks as though we are recovering the leadership in foreign language pedagogy that our field held a generation ago. ("*Germanistik* in the Academy" 13)

In the meantime, a new priority had supervened, and this truly was a case of imposition from a force quite outside the collective will of the Germanic field. Here the constituency was quite massively that of governance. I refer, of course, to the effect of the National Defense Education Act of 1958 in the wake of the Sputnik crisis of the preceding year. We emerged from the ghetto, lusting for assimilation. An academic labor shortage developed, which we were only too happy to relieve; graduate programs burgeoned; undergraduate German courses were full of students. I might remark parenthetically that this was the atmosphere in which I was socialized as a scholar and teacher, and I have come to think that its determination of consciousness greatly interferes with my competence for judging and advising in the current situation. At the time it seemed like only justice. We, along with the other humanistic disciplines, did not do the arithmetic that would have indicated that the rate of expansion at that time would mean that at some time in the future every American adult would be a university professor. Probably those who governed us were not impelled by a need to finance profounder inquiries into *Minnesang, Die Wahl-verwandtschaften,* or *Der Zauberberg,* although that is what we wanted to do. Perhaps it was not unfair that, after we had eloquently defended the pragmatic value of learning the German language, teaching it was expected of us. Only an occasional wise person—I remember one, Dieter Cunz—recognized that the commitment to the governance constituency was a Faustian bargain, in the traditional, not the Goethean sense.

The rebuilding of a humanistic discipline under the aegis of national defense was a misfortune. There is a lack of respect or at least a lack of understanding on the part of the governance constituency for what a humanistic discipline actually does, which is quite irrelevant to national defense. Perhaps in a modest way the learning of a foreign language and of something about its culture might in principle be of some value to policy considerations, if there were any indication that the governance constituency had any desire or motivation to make use of it. But most of the evidence and experience of people in a field like ours runs the other way. Recently we were told that many a CIA country specialist has never visited the country for which he or she is responsible and does not know its language. That the foreign language fields bought into the post-Sputnik boom is understandable, indeed inevitable, but the underlying irrelevance made the bargain fragile, as became apparent as early as the mid-1970s, with much disruption and disappointment to many capable and highly trained people—a human waste that, as we know, continues to the present day.

All the activity, all the achievement, all the students in the classrooms did not alter the Germanic field's relation to the constellation in any enduring way. The field recovered no detectable prestige in the environmental constituency; in its educational segment and in the student constituency we have been witnessing, after a period of improvement, a steady decline in numbers. The invincible lack of interest in Germanic matters in the other literary disciplines and in comparative literature, given its preoccupation with the French fireworks, continues unabated. In some places, deans and provosts have begun to find the Germanic field altogether dispensable. It is not surprising that the field is now struggling to revise its priorities. The options are limited, however, and appear to be at present mainly two.

The discipline's lack of echo in the local academic constituency is to be dealt with by occupying that constituency's ground. This is the meaning, I believe, of the immense amount of virtue that has accrued to the shibboleth of interdisciplinarity in recent times. We are to become not only comparatists— which in truth we always were—but also semioticians, historians, social scientists, psychologists if not psychoanalysts, and whatnot. Perhaps I am overly skeptical about this movement, but so far I have seen a clear gain only in feminism, because of its potential for opening the constricted Germanistic literary canon. It is not clear to me that we will be welcomed in dialogue by other disciplines, and we may sometimes be lacking in an adequate sense of their standards, as appeared in a recent foray into historiography that turned out to be an embarrassment (Sammons, "Were German-Americans Interned"). The rhetoric about interdisciplinarity is related to the other option, an effort to deal with the preoccupation of the lower end of the governance constituency with student enrollments: to develop curricular offerings of maximum attractiveness. Logically this strategy means that the curriculum will be defined not by the discipline but by the undergraduate constituency. Given that constituency's low level of previous knowledge and expectations, the definition it imposes has become very constrictive: in many cases to the twentieth century, to Weimar, the Holocaust, the Wall, unification, and gender. It leads to the sacrifice of literary study to pragmatic purposes, of *Bildung* to *Ausbildung*; to a decoupling of the field from its international constituency, specifically the Germanic field in the German-speaking countries; and, in some cases, to the notion that these pedagogical purposes can dispense with a knowledge of the German language.

We are making a serious and conscientious endeavor to deal with a historically and sociologically determined situation over which the discipline itself has little leverage. But the sense of panic that lies behind that endeavor sometimes affects the discourse. In 1991 a symposium of California graduate students and their mentors ascribed an extraordinary list of crimes to the German literary canon: departmental and professional tyranny, frustration of initiative and interdisciplinarity, suppression of the Third World, articulation of social and political power, marginalization of women and reinforcement of phallocentric gender oppositions, denial of history, imposition of judgment, repression of subjectivity, declaring works to be classics that are lucky survivors of an anecdotal process (Bledsoe, Estabrook, Federle, Henschel, Miller, and Polster). In view of the established literary-sociological results of the minor importance of literature, especially canonical literature, for society at large and for the determination of consciousness, one wonders whether all this is not a little hysterical. Only one contributor to the volume pointed out, to be sure with regret, that the German canon reform of the 1960s and 1970s turned out to be "epiphenomenal" without effecting deeper political change (Holub, "Rewriting" 24).

My postulate that the establishment of priorities is motivated by determinants largely beyond our control suggests that, as the Borg say in *Star Trek*, resistance is futile. Still, I think much of the current thrashing around takes place in an atmosphere of crisis that gives little opportunity for assessing the cost of emergency procedures. We might assess it in the interest of another constituency, perhaps a virtual one: that of posterity. Before we determine completely to dismantle the traditional Germanic field, we might consider that it has been responsible for a thousand years of language and literature in fourteen ancient and modern languages in what are now at least ten countries. No one else in the academy will protect and preserve this vast and variegated heritage, certainly not the comparatists. While it does not look as though there is any way that the field can fully maintain itself as one of the sister disciplines in language and literature, it is worth asking whether it is a service to the future to allow that priority to drift into oblivion.

How Split Were Our Values?

The Well-Lived Life of the German Professor in American Academe, 1938–99

LYNNE TATLOCK

What values—institutional and professional—shaped the lives of professors of German in the United States who have been recognized for their professional achievements? To offer a partial answer to this question, I conducted 31 telephone interviews and one in-person interview, each from one to two and a half hours in length. The professors ranged in age from 45 to 85 (the oldest woman was 75); 18 were retired or semiretired. These interviews took place between 26 August and 31 October 1999. While all the interviewed had done research and published on German literature, language, culture, or pedagogy, 4 had PhDs in comparative literature. The oldest among the interviewed acquired a PhD in 1938 at the age of 24, the youngest in 1984 at the age of 29. One entered the profession with a position at an American institution with possibility for promotion in the 1930s, 1 in the 1940s, 9 in the 1950s, 12 in the 1960s, 7 in the 1970s, and 2 in the 1980s. The median age for completion of the PhD and entry into the field in the United States with a tenured or tenure-track appointment was 30; the extremes were 24 and 40.[1] Of the interviewed, 21 were men and 11 women—a gender imbalance dictated by patterns of employment and promotion in the profession and one that will presumably diminish for a similar sampling twenty years from now, given the increased prominence of women in the field since the commencement of affirmative action in 1965. All but 2 of the women I interviewed acquired their first tenure-track position after 1965. Of the interviewed, 14 were European-born and 5 had taken PhDs at foreign universities (1 European PhD was American-born);

of the European-born professors, 5 came from Jewish families fleeing Nazi persecution.

My selection was limited to full professors at institutions requiring research and publication for tenure and promotion. Taken as a whole, this sample offers a diverse palette of professional achievement—indeed, sometimes such diversity can be found in the curriculum vitae of a single individual—that includes teaching; service to the local academic community and to the profession at large; administration; and publication in academic specialties like pedagogy, translation, linguistics, as well as literary and cultural studies that address a range of historical periods and employ a variety of critical approaches. Although some of them might dispute the adequacy of their rewards, these professors constitute a group that has indeed been rewarded by the profession at large and by their home institution—with tenure, promotion, critical acclaim, teaching awards, offices in professional organizations, editorships or positions on editorial boards, named professorships, internal and external grants and fellowships, research accounts, special privileges such as reduced teaching loads or secretarial support, and finally the sheer prominence and respect that accompany frequent publication. My account does not examine the values of those who did not succeed in this professional context and therefore does not attempt to investigate whether such lack of success correlates with differing personal principles. The values of academics at institutions where publication was not expected for advancement and the values of those whose professional life occurred adjacent to the tenure system—for example, lecturers—are also not considered.

This sample does not, of course, offer a profile of the field as it is constituted at the turn of the twenty-first century; instead it offers snapshots of the profession over several decades and is weighted toward professors who completed their degrees and began full-time employment in the 1960s, professors now retired or nearing retirement. It concentrates on persons over 55, although not exclusively, in order to gain a longer view of the profession—that is, to acquire a sense of the changes in values and rewards during the decades following World War II, when institutions of higher learning experienced radical shifts: the postwar increase in college enrollments, the boom of the post-Sputnik years, the Equal Opportunity Employment Act in 1972, the fall of the Berlin wall in 1989, and the aftermath of the cold war in the 1990s.

Historians have often told the story of the development of American academe as a profession after the first academic revolution in the late nineteenth century, when "the status conferred upon research-oriented professors came to exceed that accorded those committed to undergraduate instruction" (McCaughey 23). This development, so the story goes, created a split in values between the production of knowledge and the transmission of knowledge. As a result of the professionalization of the production of knowledge in academe, it was assumed "that intellectual activity was primarily if not exclusively the business of universities and those employed therein" (24). This statement suggests that the professionalization of academe conforms to the well-known pattern of specialization and the concomitant creation of monopolies that regulate credentials and fees.[2]

The founding of Johns Hopkins University in 1876 as an institution devoted to graduate studies following the German model harbingered the future of academe in America, in which the research professor would reign supreme. Robert McCaughey characterizes this change as

> the transformation of academic life from a selfless but marginal calling—one that appealed to the bashful 'and the beaten—to a rewarding but demanding profession capable of attracting, in [Yale] President Eliot's words, "men of capacity and ambition." (32)

Not everyone encouraged the shift from professing values to producing knowledge, nor did it occur overnight. In 1908, Irving Babbitt (1865–1933), professor of French at Harvard, protested the growing emphasis on the generation of knowledge as antithetical to the mission of the humanities to teach values:

> The philologists are better organized than the dilettantes, and command the approaches to the higher positions through their control of the machinery of the doctor's degree. . . . Yet it is this acceptance of the doctor's degree as proof of fitness for a chair of literature that is doing more than any one thing to dehumanize literary study and fix on our colleges a philological despotism. The degree as now administered puts a premium, not on the man who has read widely and thought maturely, but on the man who has shown proficiency in research. (131–32)

Protesting such developments and speaking of a professoriat assumed to be male, Babbitt sarcastically suggested that those who taught literature had to prove their manliness through philological research modeled on the sciences, since

> in the educational institutions, especially the large universities of the Middle West, the men flock into the courses on science, the women elect the courses in literature. The literature courses, indeed, are known in some of these institutions as "sissy" courses. The man who took literature too seriously would be suspected of effeminacy. The only really virile thing is to be an electrical engineer. (118–19)

Already in 1908, Babbitt anticipated, in his own way, what we now recognize as the late-twentieth-century feminization of the humanities in a culture in which the sciences, perceived as masculine, dominate.

Babbitt could not know that women would not only study literature but also teach it as tenured members of the professoriat. Nor could he know that the entry of women into the professoriat would go hand in hand with feminism and change the shape of knowledge throughout the university. In fact, a man interviewed for this project cited hiring and promoting women as one of his most important contributions to the field.[3]

After 1890, universities committed themselves to research as an institutional goal and vied with one another for the prestige based on it. Nevertheless, even as they promoted research, they sought to "instill both liberal culture and modern science, to pursue both disinterested learning and practical knowledge, and to graduate bachelors of arts, aspiring professionals, and doctors of philosophy" (Geiger 15). As Robert Geiger explains, "administrators who spoke for the institution as a whole grew adept at invoking whichever university ideal best fit the occasion and the audience. Faculty and students pursued their particular tasks largely oblivious to the other facets of the enterprise." Thus, he concludes, "the twentieth-century research university came to exist on the basis of the 'patterned isolation of its component parts' " (16).

In individual disciplines this oppositional tug of teaching and research made itself known early in the century, but, as Geiger points out, teaching itself was not professionalized until research disciplines had been established (20). However, when the Modern Language Association was founded in 1883 by college teachers of French and German "who wanted their subjects recognized as appropriate for advanced university study," the tension between pedagogy and research was already pronounced. Although language teaching occupied a prominent place on the agenda of the early MLA, it was secondary to other concerns in the struggle for legitimacy and professionalism; these goals, it was thought, "could be attained only through the development of recognized scholarship in these subjects" (25).

The dual commitment to undergraduate teaching and scholarship prompted the division into teaching faculty and research faculty. As early as 1910, Yale president Arthur T. Hadley warned against such splitting: departments might, as a result, maintain a teaching force of "reasonably good instructors" of only moderate ability, inadvertently keeping out "men of less [teaching] experience but more promise" (qtd. in Geiger 75). By the 1920s, the tenure system was in place at major research institutions, demanding research and publication alongside teaching. At ambitious institutions, junior faculty members had to toe the line and publish or leave the university altogether; they could not simply teach well (75).

While Babbitt lamented the changing valuation of the humanities, particularly in the study of language and literature, his contemporary in German, who lived out his professional life at an institution more modest than Harvard, did not fear that the humanities exposed him to emasculation. In 1892

German-born Otto Heller (1863–1941) began teaching at Washington University in Saint Louis, where the first ten years of his salary had been guaranteed by the beer magnate Adolphus Busch (Morrow 188–89). His career as a professor of German effortlessly straddled the split between transmitting and producing knowledge.[4] Heller aspired to a life in academe as the proverbial Renaissance man. He regularly taught courses in elementary German grammar along with two instructors who made up the rest of the tiny department. He styled himself simply as a literary critic—both a specialist and a generalist—a critic who spoke and published on Pushkin, Shaw, Ibsen, and Maeterlinck, not to mention an array of German writers from relatively obscure women authors to Goethe. In the first half of the nineteenth century, his department was too small and the demand for German language instruction too great for there to be a hierarchy in which some were excused from language teaching. Departmental and disciplinary divisions at Washington University then were porous, and individual professors not only were close to the centers of power but also had a good understanding of the entire organization. They could play many roles simultaneously, including that of the public intellectual. With multiple contacts to cultural organizations in the surrounding community, Heller was often called on locally to give public performances, both in person and on the radio. He also served for several years as the editor of the book section of the premier newspaper of Saint Louis, the *Post-Dispatch*. In this case, a tenured professorship in the humanities meant a fully realized "masculine" career: a life of debating, deliberating, and doing, a career supplemented by rich meals and fragrant with the spice of his ubiquitous cigar.

By referencing Heller's life, I do not intend to evoke nostalgia for the days of cigar-puffing martinets or for the dilettantish gentlemen scholars whose passing Babbitt lamented; instead, my purpose is to suggest that the values espoused by the German professoriat in America (1945–99) have not been as narrowly defined as some observers of American academe maintain and, further, that the very autonomy granted by tenure has enabled leading professors to pursue a variety of activities. As one interviewee put it, "Once you've reached full professor, you really can't expect to get any higher. So you can pursue what you think is important." In short, for the Germanists interviewed, long-term professional success and career satisfaction have meant creative activity in a mesh of personal values and institutional pressures more often than mere frenetic publication as evidence of knowledge production. Their pursuit of success in the profession has led to a negotiation of competing demands that transform over time, demands determined by the institution, the profession at large, the changing character of the students, and the economy and the purposes for which these students are being educated. Commitment to these competing demands has varied over time according to a professor's stage of life. Not every person interviewed enjoyed the variety of activity and the degree of local influence of Otto Heller, but many came close and some even surpassed him.

Germanics in America has not developed apart from the increasingly professionalized academic world and has inevitably been shaped by it. This situation was firmly established by the time the 32 practitioners interviewed entered the profession. Nevertheless, the interviews suggest that the prestige accorded publication and specialization did not deter successful professionals in the discipline from adhering to communitarian values that demand significant commitment to activities other than publication. These professors did not see teaching, service, and scholarship as a set of irreconcilable demands but as interesting features of the profession. They acted, perhaps atavistically, as if a career in academe were a calling, one requiring personal sacrifice and service to the community. They made that sacrifice freely.

"*Germanistik* in America in those days [the 1940s and 1950s] . . . was a vocation, not a profession. You were a secular priest . . . a missionary with a sacred task of educating America's youth," an octogenarian explained. His formulation suggests that he also believes this notion to belong to the past. He may not be right about that. A well-published interviewee with a PhD from the mid-1980s asserted that "serving as a role model, providing women students with models of someone who could handle professional and private life, modeling the pleasure of being an intellectual" was the most important thing she had accomplished in her career. Although somewhat more epicurean, this assertion harmonizes better with the older professor's notion of "secular priests" and a life devoted to duty than with the idea of scholarly publication as supreme achievement.

Intellectual zeal; deep commitment to a critical brand of liberalism thought to be institutionalized in the university, specifically in the practice of teaching; and a sense of a cultural mission surfaced repeatedly in the interviews. Notably, two interviewees mentioned having flirted with a religious calling before embarking on a career in academe, and two women cited the importance of previous activity in their respective churches. An American-born professor described the decision to pursue a PhD as a quest for fulfillment, to do something that mattered. Several women described themselves as feminists pursuing a political mission in academe. Some interviewees spoke of their academic work as tied to other kinds of political activism, and some mentioned their successful mission to shift the orientation of the field from belletristic literature toward broader cultural debates and problems under the rubric "German studies." In nearly every case, these professors tied scholarship and publication to the pursuit of these missions. One remarked ruefully that his rate of publication had slowed down once he became less interested in ideological criticism—that is, after he had fulfilled what he had once seen as his cultural mission. A European-born interviewee from a Jewish background described his deep need to heal what had been torn asunder by the Nazis, World War II, and the Holocaust.

Several professors said that their enjoyment of reading, their wish to capitalize on their ability to write, and a compelling love of literature diverted them from another career path to the study of German. One decided to pursue a career in academe when he discovered that he could be paid for his personal avocation—reading and writing. Interviewees frequently described falling in love with German literature in college. One who did not build his career on literary scholarship per se maintained that Lessing's *Minna von Barnhelm* sold him on German as an undergraduate even as he was planning to attend medical school. Another recounted how, as a young recruit in the army, he discovered a talent for languages that pushed him toward academe. Most stressed their liking of the work required by academe and pointed out the importance of understanding this work as its own reward. This understanding led most to put in long hours; one woman characterized a mentor as working "like a demon," a pattern that she herself followed.

The attitude toward work described by many of these interviewees reflects what Magali Sarfatti Larson has characterized as typical of those professions where the idea of a calling plays a central role: "Because their [professional] choice was relatively free and their work is relatively interesting and creative, they maintain alive the idea that work may have an *intrinsic* value . . ." (61). In my interviews some contradictions emerged between what the professors said about their work and what they had actually done; that is, even as most stressed the intrinsic value of their work, a certain spirit of entrepreneurship appears to have shaped the lives of many. Their lack of awareness of their own entrepreneurial instincts can perhaps be explained in part by the discrepancy between the tangible material rewards and the long hours they devoted to their work, as compared with more lucrative professions such as law or medicine: it was an entrepreneurship with limited financial return.

They certainly took pride in uncompensated service. They maintained that they put in long hours serving the university (with, e.g., committee work) as well as the profession (by, e.g., writing book reviews) even when such effort did not lead directly to salary increases and promotion. Three interviewees who reviewed books regularly, though the reviewing was in their opinion not explicitly rewarded, spoke of their delight at perfecting an art form and their appreciation of the forced opportunity to engage intellectually with an author. Most, however, did not believe the intrinsic reward of reviewing books sufficiently compensated them for the time involved. If they reviewed books at all, most did so out of sense of duty to the profession or of obligation to colleagues.

Some found even committee work rewarding. One woman noted that "the tricks of the trade" came to her through committee work and that opportunities arose—even job offers—as a result of contacts made through it. Several, both women and men, cited the importance of committee work for enabling them to understand not only their home institution but the profession at large.

A well-published professor who entered the profession in the late 1970s remarked that even today he takes pleasure in small things, like a well-taught class or a well-received talk. Another recounted the advice given him by a colleague practically on his deathbed: "Bear in mind that institutions have no memory or conscience, that they are inherently ungrateful. Don't expect the institution to reward you. Your reward is the thing itself." Beyond the joy in the thing itself, for most interviewees, honor in the form of public recognition or simply the respect of one's colleagues served more as a reward than any hope of monetary compensation, though in some rare cases there was such compensation.

One intrinsic reward of the profession is a degree of autonomy. Yet the historian Samuel Haber sees a professor's independence as limited, as "exercised from a position of subordination." Professors issue the most important commands that they must obey, but these commands come not from their will or from the organization of which they are a part but from "exalted values beyond the reach of both"; professors are "largely self-directed and at the same time, responsible" (293). Haber emphasizes the limits placed on professorial autonomy; those interviewed tended, in contrast, to stress the importance and positive good of this delicate balance between autonomy and responsibility. They insisted that with the autonomy comes an obligation to the collective and that professors ignore communal responsibilities at their peril. An interviewee pointed out that over the past decades paradoxically the "professional character [of academe] has been professionalized out of existence," that is, it has shifted toward what he termed a "corporate model" according to which the administration is ever more intrusive and professors have less control. Their abdication of responsibility is in part to blame for this development, he maintained: "The professor on his high horse who refuses to care about the department" puts faculty governance at risk. Many others expressed the fear that subsequent generations would not be willing to serve their community and that young professors are not developing institutional loyalty. One professor said that for a short period her institution relieved assistant professors from service but then discovered that it "sent the wrong message." Two interviewees noted, in fact, that their universities had of late begun to seek ways of rewarding service and that promotion to full professor required a record of service.

Many declared that they remained devoted to undergraduate teaching even when they also taught in lively and demanding graduate programs. A German-born professor spoke of her love of American undergraduate students in the 1960s: "They were so interested and worked so hard." Several interviewees described how much they enjoyed discussing issues with undergraduates. Two of the retirees interviewed, a septuagenarian and an octogenarian, continue to teach undergraduates.

When asked about mentoring, most characterized it simply as one of the many duties that must be their own reward. Some of the male professors understood the query about mentoring as referring only to advising students about their doctoral work, but the majority of interviewees understood mentoring more broadly, as including undergraduates as well. Many stressed their love of mentoring, and a few went so far as to say that mentoring was one of their most important professional obligations, although they believed it unlikely that people would be rewarded or even become known beyond their departments for that work. Many noted that of late mentoring has become mandated at their institutions and thus more formalized. One felt that this trend may not necessarily be a good thing. In his opinion such formalization reveals the increased dependency of junior colleagues on senior colleagues and of students on professors that has resulted from the tight academic job market and increasing expectations for promotion and tenure. This dependency, he asserted, diminishes the possibility for free intellectual exchange. Most said that they themselves had received practically no formal mentoring, often not even much advice on their dissertations, and that in fact they had not particularly wanted it. When pressed, however, most could point to several older colleagues or peers who had served as role models or offered them concrete help or advice at key points in their careers.

While most interviewees had received grants from their home institutions as well as from outside agencies, nearly all said that at some point they decided to use their private means to help cover research expenses and that lack of funding did not necessarily mean that they would drop a research project. These professors did not characterize themselves as having spent large amounts of time and emotional energy worrying about grants, although most did note that their institution encouraged faculty members to seek outside funding. They observed that the honor of receiving a grant could be nearly as important as the money. One interviewee from a research university explained that since his teaching load of two courses a semester was probably half of what was a normal load for a professor at another kind of institution, he figured that half of his salary was for research. "I tried to live up to that; my very generous salary could go partly toward financing that research." He further expressed his dislike of the attitude of some colleagues in the humanities who, he believed, felt that their research should always be financed in addition to and on top of their salary. "You do research for the honor, for your own feeling about the thing," he asserted.

Older practitioners who lived a portion of their professional lives in a time of boom—and these were all my subjects over the age of 55; they had completed their PhDs and entered the job market by the mid, even late, 1960s—seemed on the whole not to have suffered from the tension between the production of knowledge and the transmission of knowledge to undergraduates. They claimed that they had little trouble finding jobs—one was offered a job, which he did not take, on an elevator at an MLA convention. They repeatedly said that as assistant professors they were scarcely aware of what tenure was, that they were not instructed as to what it took to acquire it, that it was even conferred on them without their knowing that they were under consideration for it. Getting tenure was not the focus of their lives as assistant professors, and they felt none of the anxiety that fills assistant professors at the turn of the twenty-first century. As one colleague noted, you could always go someplace else.

But few indicated a lack of awareness about the necessity or importance of publishing, although for some this awareness came slowly. One interviewee began his career at a four-year college with a heavy teaching load in the 1950s; he realized early on that he had to write his way out of that position if he hoped ever to have what he considered a full-fledged career—that is, one in which he received recognition and exercised influence beyond the boundaries of his home institution. On the whole, professors who had secured posts at research institutions and who had published from the beginning of those appointments seemed to consider it simply part of the job and not a life-or-death matter. Furthermore, they generally enjoyed it, since they had entered the profession in order to exercise certain talents, writing being one of them. Scholarship could be taken up or put down as projects developed or as other obligations at the university demanded their attention. The oldest person interviewed, a man who had spent most of his career at a premier university, described a well-tempered attitude to research and publication:

> I never felt under great pressure to publish. I published because I had things to say . . . just enough to keep me going. Sometimes there would be two to three years when I didn't have anything to say, but then I would have a batch of ideas. No one ever pressured me in between. I was always doing what I wanted to do: teaching. . . . [When I published] I always had the student in mind.

But three of the German-born interviewees, who acquired posts at American universities in the late 1960s and the 1970s, maintained that their familiarity with the German university system, which demands publication, had pushed them from the start to publish heavily; one of them said that publishing in Germany secured him entry into the profession in America. Yet even as some stressed the value of publishing inculcated in them by the German system, all the German-born professors interviewed characterized their experience as professionals in America as offering them enormous latitude, both in professional activities and in choice of scholarly investigation. A European-born professor who was once torn between journalism and academe managed in the context of American academe to address intellectual questions that crossed the boundary between the two careers.

Since all regarded publication as an important source of satisfaction and prestige, the value of various kinds of publication concerned many. Two professors, distinguished for their expertise in translation, for example, expressed diverging views of the rewards translation brought. One had experienced it as an exciting connection to contemporary culture, which at times inspired an entrepreneurial approach. He believes that translation has become more acceptable as an academic exercise. The other retains a keen sense that while German professors acknowledge the importance of translation, they see it as a mere convenience to their teaching and condescend to those who do it. Most academics, this interviewee maintained, have a poor understanding of the nature of translation, which, relying heavily on intuition, falls somewhere "between scholarship and art."

Several professors who had published on a wide range of authors, issues, or periods in Germanics conceded that they made a strategic error by not specializing more narrowly—that is, they recognized that their disregard of the ethos of specialization characteristic of modern professionalization in the West was disadvantageous. They thought they might have been rewarded with outside offers or enhanced professional status had their work been more specialized. Yet it is not clear that they were *not* rewarded precisely for their breadth and versatility. Indeed, possibly the most privileged of the professors interviewed can by no means be seen as a specialist; he has published on cultural figures whose works span two centuries and several disciplines. In the American context the relatively small size of departments and the concomitant need to teach a broad array of courses appear to have created significant latitude for diversified scholarship for those with the energy to pursue it.

All, including those who saw themselves more as comparatists than Germanists, taught German-language courses at some point in their career. Without exception, none of those trained in the United States resented doing so at the beginning of their career. Those trained in Germany, however, spoke of the burden of teaching language courses without training or experience of American institutions, and one noted the added difficulty of simultaneously acquiring English skills. Older colleagues who began teaching in the 1950s and 1960s, even in prestigious departments, reported loads of three to four courses a semester that consisted largely of language teaching. Several, who had not taught language courses for years, noted that they disagreed with the practice of their home department in which professors did not teach language courses, but they also asserted either that their efforts to change this practice had been unsuccessful or that they had not tried particularly hard to change it. All seemed aware of the professional denigration of language instruction, but initially they had not necessarily expected to be excused altogether from language teaching, and some did not expect to be excused now. Many simply considered it one of the service components of the profession. Others spoke of anticipating that heavy teaching loads in language at the beginning of their careers would be gradually replaced by undergraduate content courses (usually literature) and graduate courses in their specialties. Because of heavy enrollments in German in the 1960s, however, some found themselves teaching graduate courses in their first three years. The large size of departments, and in particular graduate programs, made feasible hierarchies of course assignments and patterns of advancement based on them. Several retirees noted that they had found these hierarchies comfortable, because they offered clear-cut patterns of advancement and because each stage brought with it a defined set of expectations.

Those who entered the profession before the 1960s initially had modest expectations: they reckoned on low pay, heavy teaching loads, and uncertainty of employment. Unlike those who entered the profession after the mid-1960s, the oldest colleagues spoke of beginning their careers with lectureships that eventually turned into assistant professorships with the possibility of tenure. That things turned out differently, that they received frequent job offers over the course of their careers, lighter teaching loads, and salary increases, seems to have left at least some of them with a permanent sense of well-being in the profession. One emeritus septuagenarian spoke of the thrill of learning how to play the professional game and reaping the accompanying rewards. Another professor recalled the wildly expanding "seller's market" and the acquisition of entrepreneurial habits in the boom years: "My generation was the entrepreneurial generation. We realized fairly early on that we could turn our qualifications and achievements into commodities." This was a time "when you could easily and frequently get offers and parlay them into better salaries. This made us independent entrepreneurs. Some have maintained that attitude to the extreme—the pursuit of one's own career."

Those whose careers began in what one interviewee described as "wealthy sylvan postwar America" had high expectations and then suffered the contraction of the field and the reduction of opportunities, especially at their home institution. Not surprisingly, many expressed less satisfaction than did those of an older cohort; two had retired early, and others spoke of doing so. As one put it, "I chose German because it seemed to me at the center of things; [after the war and on through the cold war] Germany was on everyone's lips." This, he went on, was no longer the case. When asked about the difference between them and colleagues in other areas of the humanities, several expressed their frustration at having to explain themselves, to defend the field, to justify what they were doing to uncomprehending faculty members in other fields in the humanities. They had the feeling that no matter what they achieved, they would still be viewed as marginal by colleagues in the next building.

Those older interviewees who were not yet retired and who expressed relatively unabated satisfaction with their professional lives generally had positioned themselves well at their universities early in their careers—with reduced teaching loads, good staff support, research accounts, and the like—and were shielded from the vicissitudes of the profession and the university. But even those favorably positioned were by no means impervious to changes at the university. One spoke, for example, of a sense of loss during the last decade, of feeling that critical debates carried on in Germanics no longer generated the interest outside the field that they once had.

The development of connections to colleagues, disciplines, and programs beyond one's own department appears to have been of key importance to long-term satisfaction. Nearly everyone interviewed pointed readily to such personal, intellectual, and professional contacts and such transdisciplinary activity, although the importance of it varied from person to person.

Adaptive behavior also seems to have contributed to long-term satisfaction. Two who had chosen early retirement, in part because of their dissatisfaction with their universities, had over the years involved themselves in such significant professional activities—perhaps in part as compensation for the unsatisfactory situation at their home institutions—that retirement scarcely meant a decrease in professional activity. They could continue to enjoy the aspects of academe that they valued without the daily misery of dealing with the aspects they deplored.

Those who had entered the profession before 1970 spoke of frequent job offers over the course of their careers, but 15 had remained for their entire career (to date) at the same institution. Two had had tenure-track or tenured appointments at 6 different institutions. The median number of tenure-track positions for the group was 2, the mean 2.1. Gender plays a role here: of the 11 women, 3 had taught at 2 institutions and the other 8 had remained (to date) at the same institution where they began their career—that is, 73% as compared with 33% of the men. The 4 professors—all male—who changed jobs most often had entered the profession before 1970, 3 of them before 1960. In other words, practitioners did not appear to change jobs for the sake of changing jobs; they made a move only when it brought significant improvements with it. Interviewees spoke most often of moving to assume or give up an administrative position (usually the position of department chair) while saving face at their home institution. Of the 32 professors interviewed, 21 had served or were serving as chairs. Of the 11 who had not chaired a German department, 2 had had substantial administrative duties outside their primary department, and a handful of those interviewed had served both in the central administration of their university and as a department chair.

How did the chairs view their task? Some spoke of an eagerness to assume this responsibility and then of an inability to do the job well. Others who began as reluctant chairs came to view it as critical to their understanding of the profession. Some nostalgically recalled the days when chairs had a freer hand and resources were more plentiful. Not surprisingly those who accepted a chair with a specific mission fared better than those who were forced simply to serve as caretakers or to participate in the downsizing of a department. Many felt that chairs had an increasingly difficult task as a result of the bureaucratization of the university and the increasingly litigious nature of society in general; they lamented the burgeoning committee work and paperwork that robbed them of time.

Interviewees were asked whether the work demanded of them as professors of German put them out of step with their university's system of rewards or whether it required commitments of them that differed from those required of faculty members in other disciplines. Some failed initially to understand the question and even after prompting still answered negatively. Yet even when they did not say yes, many did eventually express the feeling that their career had been unlike that of others.

Several noted that early in their career they had to teach more courses than did their colleagues in English; others pointed out that while German certainly demanded a great deal of its professors, colleagues in other fields had many more students. Having fewer students offset the greater workload. One interviewee stated unequivocally that declining enrollments in German and his own talent for reversing this trend on a local level had shaped his career from beginning to end. This activity, he stressed, would not have been necessary in other disciplines in the humanities or, for that matter, in other commonly taught languages.

Some American-born interviewees cited the learning and maintaining of foreign language skills and foreign cultural behaviors as a special and sometimes tedious demand of the discipline. They also spoke of laboring under the perception that they were required to measure up to standards and codes set by native speakers even while teaching in the American context. "I was the token American," one remarked. "My colleagues were native Germans, and those who could function and compete with native Germans were preferred." Three women interviewed noted that they initially felt compelled to imitate the model of the male native speaker, which had caused them discomfort. Some American-born colleagues felt that this demand was a burden less on their practices as scholars than on their teaching; one recalled a professor who quipped as he left for class, "I'm off to impersonate a German." The younger American-born interviewees tended to place a higher value on passing as Germans by speaking unaccented German. One believed that she owed certain successes to her ability to speak nonaccented German; it had helped her land her first job. On the whole, the older professors had a more relaxed attitude toward passing. This difference may result in part from shifts in teaching methods during the 1960s that increasingly stressed oral proficiency; possibly it results also from new standards set by the influx of native-speaking students and colleagues from Europe after the war. Many older interviewees, including a European-born one, tended to feel that the language of instruction in a literature class should be English. One older German-born colleague reported that when she first came to the United States in the late 1950s, she was told that she had to do everything in English; it was not until nearly a decade later that she was encouraged to teach in German. Another retired colleague, also European-born, asserted that she preferred teaching in English, because she "liked to teach in the language in which the [American] students think."

When asked about conflicts between their personal values and those of the profession or home institution, the interviewees expressed little dissatisfaction. They tended to see their work as a calling; as Wilbert E. Moore explains, "Commitment to a calling involves acceptance of the appropriate norms and standards, and identification with professional peers and the profession as a collectivity" (8). One professor did note that his experience with the dishonesty of several of his colleagues had caused him distress, put him at odds with the departmental culture, and eventually led him to seek employment elsewhere. Another mentioned that in retrospect he felt that the long hours he had worked were stolen from his family, but at the time he had not given it much thought: "It was a matter of course; it was part of the culture." Yet another said that in working for the profession he had neglected his private life and his health. But few male interviewees addressed the neglect of one's private or family life spontaneously; most spoke instead of their need to get a job to support their wives and families, of the pressure to complete their graduate degrees because they were living a hand-to-mouth existence as graduate students even as their families expanded.

The women I interviewed experienced family pressures differently. Most of the women who had been married, particularly those with children, repeatedly suffered tension between career and family. In their younger years they often chose family over career because of social pressure. One of the married women, however, noted that she prided herself on her ability to demonstrate to her students the possibility of having a private and a professional life simultaneously.

Of the 11 women I interviewed, 9 were or had been married; 8 were significantly delayed in their career by family demands. One woman took herself off the tenure track to rear several children. Another was on a half-time appointment for nearly 10 years. Two women followed their husbands when their husbands secured their first academic position. One of these quit her PhD program and began anew elsewhere a few years later; the other interrupted her studies for a considerable time when she got pregnant and thus did not complete her PhD until she was 40. One of the retired women maintained that her experience in the 1960s showed that "if you were a woman, you were supposed to be single" to be considered for a tenure-track position. This same woman asserted that she had finally resumed her career, against these odds, because she felt it increasingly as a calling.

When asked how things had changed in the profession, many felt that the professional values they espoused were not in harmony with recent trends. Some of this disharmony has been noted above, but there are additional tensions.

Those interviewees who worked in the orbit of German studies felt that recent changes in the field met their own interests and fit better with their cultural values; indeed, they often regarded this shift as marking their own professional achievement. Similarly, several women who identified themselves as feminists asserted with satisfaction that the field had changed during the span of their career: they had moved from the margin to the inside, where they felt they now exercised authority.

Those interviewees who identified themselves primarily as scholars of belletristic literature spoke of a sense of loss and, in some cases, of relief that they had retired "just in time." Two professors noted their dismay at the influx of high theory into literary studies in the 1970s, a trend they felt diverted scholarly attention from or obscured the cultural artifact itself. One interviewee pointed to his feeling that the field had once been more unified, that one had known not only who the influential people in the profession were but also had had a good overview of the central issues in the field; people in different branches could talk to one another more easily. In his view, people were now going their own way. "Of course," he added, this "may be more democratic."

Changing methods and theories and increasing specialization affected not only professors' feelings about their practice of literary and cultural studies. One interviewee, who gave up teaching beginning German in the early 1980s, noted that the teaching methodologies employed in these courses at his institution had become so technical that the courses were no longer enjoyable to teach, nor did he feel qualified to teach them. He regretted the gap between language teaching and instruction in literature and culture at universities, a gap that, he felt, was widening as a result of increasing specialization on both sides. Linguists of an older school also noted the shift of the field around them; one had all but dropped German to devote himself to information technology, which continues to occupy him in his retirement.

An octogenarian observed, "My colleagues of twenty years younger seem not to be happy. They are very distinguished, well known, have high salaries, and yet they don't seem to enjoy their teaching anymore." They seemed to him not to find the enterprise as rewarding as he had, even though on the surface of it they had been richly rewarded. Something was changing generally at the university, he mused. Attitudes of students were different, and the importance of the subject matter was diminishing. His remarks were well observed, for his younger colleagues did indeed repeatedly express their unhappiness about the loss in prestige of the humanities in general and Germanics in particular as well as about the changing interests of students.

Many of those interviewed coupled increased publication requirements for promotion and tenure with an increased professionalization that they viewed negatively. One well-published professor observed that in some sense increased professionalization had improved the quality of publications, but that at the same time younger colleagues were following "the dictates of the profession rather than their own intellectual agendas." The oldest person interviewed summed up his view of professionalization with a statement about the present-day absurdity of conferences: "Now you go to a conference and don't have time to talk to people." Another elderly professor stated his feeling that younger colleagues were not as interested in politics and social questions as they once were; they were simply interested in being professionals, in publishing for the sake of publishing. In short, these professors were describing a shift from the profession as calling to the profession as performance.

Several believed that increased professionalization resulted from demands for knowledge production, which paradoxically brought about a loss of intellectual community in departments. One person pointed out that his colleagues' focus had shifted from their department to the profession at large; his colleagues were either working in isolation on their "own work" or e-mailing colleagues at other institutions and not talking to their colleagues at their home institution. Such unintended fragmentation precludes the formulation and realization of coherent programs and projects at home, several interviewees argued. But then, some had already seen this fragmentation during the entrepreneurial 1960s, and some saw the obliviousness of earlier generations to communal needs as contributing to the woes of the present.

Professionalization as described above suggests a profession in danger of losing its soul—a fate that those at the beginning of the twentieth century feared would befall the profession well before the persons interviewed even entered it. Of course the very notion that the profession has a soul suggests that the understanding of the profession as a calling is still alive and well among this group. And at least some entering the profession at the turn of the new century have a sense of calling. Given that their elders cannot offer the hope of "sylvan postwar America" or even promise them a job, they must surely be propelled in part by idealism.

In sum, these 32 interviews indicate that over the period 1938–99, and particularly in the boom years of the 1960s, academe in America has offered a rich and diverse area of activity for those professors of German and comparative literature who were able to identify and reap its rewards. Moreover, these rewards—many intangible in the first place—were not linked only to specialization or shaped only by the publish-or-perish dictum. The interviews do reveal the perception that broader possibilities have diminished in recent years as the humanities and Germanics have become more marginalized in academe. They also reveal the fear that as a result of increased emphasis on publication for tenure, the university will find itself tenuring a disaffected generation of professors reluctant to serve it and the profession because they have been trained to think of their careers largely in individualist terms of research and publication. In the view of the interviewees, the possibility grows for still greater loss of faculty autonomy and of intellectual exchange at the university.

Notes

1 The 4 German-born professors with PhDs from German institutions experienced delays between the completion of their degrees and securing tenure-track or tenured appointments in the United States of 1, 3, 6, and 6 years. Despite these delays, the median age remains 30. For interviewees who entered the field when it was standard practice for new PhDs to start out in lectureships that could be converted to tenure-track appointments, I understand these lectureships to constitute entry into the tenure system.

2 Of course, in American academe, largely institutions and not individual practitioners impose and collect these fees; in their specific work at the university, professors are therefore several steps removed from the exercising of the financial privileges of monopoly, except in the case of outside consulting, an activity that is seldom lucrative for the Germanist.

3 Many of the interviewed pointed to women's greater presence and enhanced status at the university as one of the most important changes that occurred during their time in academe.

4 My characterization of Heller derives from Jean Heller's tribute to her husband, which includes letters, essays, newspaper articles, and panegyrics by his colleagues; Washington University course catalogs; a list of Heller's publications held by Olin Library at Washington University; and oral recollections of a former dean of the graduate school, Edward N. Wilson, who did not know Heller personally but has known people who did.

Changing Employment Patterns
in German Studies

GERHARD WEISS

The Changing Job Market

In the American educational system, German studies—that is, the study of the language, literature, thought, history, and culture (in the broadest sense) of the German-speaking countries—has traditionally been considered part of the humanities, with no expectation for practical career applications outside the field of self-perpetuation, which is teaching. The questions Why study German? and What are you going to do with it? have confronted students majoring in the subject since it became an academic discipline in the nineteenth century, and those questions continue to challenge their teachers to defend the importance and value of this endeavor. The questions have been posed at least since the inauguration of the first professor of German language and literature at Harvard University, Charles Follen. His "Inaugural Discourse," delivered on 3 September 1831, offers an eloquent apologia for the study of German, pointing to the growing importance of German literature, philosophy, theology, and science (*Works* 132).

To introduce the American public to the riches of the German language that Follen proclaimed, one needed professional teachers. Thus, teaching at the secondary and postsecondary levels has always been the primary career field for those engaged in German studies. Teaching has traditionally been a volatile commodity in the United States, and the availability of positions for teachers of German has fluctuated greatly over time. On the secondary school level, it reached its peak shortly before World War I and its nadir at the end of the war and in the years immediately thereafter, when instruction in German was removed from the curriculum of many high schools or even forbidden outright by state law. Since then, German has recovered somewhat but continues to maintain its (sometimes distant) third place among foreign languages taught in the United States.

In the pre–World War I period, the teaching of German on the secondary school level depended heavily on the immigrant community—with German schools in existence in Milwaukee, Cincinnati, Saint Louis, and other places. Teachers usually came from these communities and often were members of religious orders. Most were immigrants themselves. On the postsecondary level, German-born and German-trained instructors were also very much in evidence, although there was always a sprinkling of Americans without any ethnic link to Germany. Important, however, is that a large number of instructors, even on the postsecondary level, were expected to teach other subjects in addition to German. A review of the list of German faculty members in the Modern Language Association *Proceedings* of 29–30 December 1884 shows that almost one half of all teachers taught Latin, Greek, French, music, and—in two cases— even bookkeeping in addition to their German assignments ("List"). German instructors at all levels were, in those days, primarily language teachers (see also Peterson in this volume).

As the field became more sophisticated, the number of graduate programs increased, as did the number of PhDs teaching in colleges and universities (in 1884, only a little over 10% of the professoriat teaching German is listed as holding the PhD degree ["List"]). Today, of course, the PhD is a sine qua non for any college job in German, and the master's degree is a highly desirable credential at the high school level (see Schulz in this volume, "Teacher Development").

The job description of those teaching German at any level has changed considerably over the years. While for many generations the emphasis was on grammar, vocabulary, translation, and reading traditional literature or scientific journals, from the 1920s on we witness an increasing interest in communication and practical applications. In a 1928 survey conducted by the AATG, its results summarized in "Shall German Be Taught in Our High Schools?," Frederick W. J. Heuser of Columbia University asked "a select number of prominent Americans in all walks of life . . . for a frank expression of opinion" (52). Among the very supportive responses to the survey, we find that in addition to the expected need of German for future scientists, the value of the language for America's trade relations is frequently stressed.

The need for instructors able to teach practical German reached a peak during World War II; the United States War Department established total immersion and area studies courses. This war effort created changes in teaching methods and goals that have left their mark on the instruction of German to this day. After World War II, it was expected that a teacher at any level would have a good, active command of the language, which led to the current job requirement on the postsecondary level of near-native fluency. Furthermore, since the 1960s, a broader concept of German studies has prevailed, which entails knowledge of history, current politics, and social aspects. For many secondary school teachers, this new approach has meant a need for retooling, for participating in workshops and summer seminars. For college faculty members it has opened new fields of interdisciplinary research, but it has also raised the expectation of ancillary competencies beyond one's field of specialization. Totally new graduate studies concentrations have developed in recent years, exploring areas such as culture studies, gender studies, and film.

The increased professionalization and orientation toward research in German departments at major universities since the 1960s have led to a schism between language and literature teaching, so that today most instructors of professorial rank will not be found in the beginning language classroom. In the past, even the most senior faculty members were involved in language instruction in addition to their teaching specialty. Even though academic prestige today is weighted heavily in favor of teaching subject courses, there is a growing recognition that language teaching itself can be a research-oriented discipline and not just the cash cow for enrollment-starved departments. Prospective college instructors are well advised to be aware of current trends in language pedagogy in addition to their field of literary specialization, in order to be competitive for a good job. Being able to teach business German; serve as language coordinator; develop proficiency testing; and, last but not least, establish computer programs are bread-and-butter skills for those entering the field at the beginning of the twenty-first century. Much has changed since Follen became professor at Harvard in 1831—the gender distribution in the profession as well. While in the early days college teaching of German was a man's job (the 1884 MLA *Proceedings* indicate that just a little over 11% of the instructors were female, and only 3 women held professorial rank ["List"]), in 1999 the number of women in the profession reached 43%, with 33% in upper professorial ranks and an increasing percentage serving as department chairs ("Statistical Retrospective" 538; see also Teraoka in this volume).

Types of Jobs

The types of teaching positions available in German have not changed much over the years, but the requirements have. The number of undergraduate majors in college who plan on a career teaching high school German has declined since the late 1960s, because many high schools have responded to demographic and global developments by emphasizing Spanish rather than German.

Teachers who can offer both languages still have a good chance of employment. Today, anyone hoping to become a German teacher should seriously consider having a second field for which there is greater demand (frequent combinations are German and English as a second language, German and remedial reading, German and coaching, etc.).

On the postsecondary level, the number of positions is small and the competition great, particularly for PhDs in twentieth-century German literature. The advertised job descriptions have often become so demanding they are a source of frustration for applicants. Typically candidates for beginning assistant professor positions are expected to have demonstrable excellence in undergraduate language teaching, to show commitment to scholarship and research, and certainly to possess native or near-native fluency in German. Experience with grant applications (a very important skill at the present time) is a significant additional qualification. Tenure-track positions are scarce (as they have often been in the history of the profession), but in recent years an increasing number of adjunct or temporary academic appointments have become available. These positions usually are limited to language teaching and involve heavy teaching loads but no research expectations. Jobs in this category are relatively plentiful, especially at larger universities. This development may be a boon for some, as it certainly is for college administrators who seek to reduce instructional costs and increase staffing flexibility. Most, however, see it as a form of exploitation and an erosion of the tenure system, as a bane.[1] Since the adjunct-temporary category of academic professionals is rapidly growing, the people in it are now represented by their own special-interest delegates in the Delegate Assembly of the Modern Language Association. Junior and community colleges also offer a limited number of positions for language teachers, but they usually do not grant tenure.

The whole process of finding academic employment has greatly changed during the last thirty years. In the "good old days" the old-boys network was the primary conduit for job seekers; today positions must be clearly advertised in appropriate venues, the most important of which is the MLA *Job Information List*, published since 1971 and issued four times during the academic year in print and now available online. Search requirements are now based on stringent rules backed by federal law. A search has become a legal process, requiring careful planning and detailed accounting of every action taken and of every choice made. The profession has turned professional to a fault: the fewer positions there are, the greater the academic requirements and expectations have become. To be sure, many departments have taken steps to prepare their students for the highly competitive and stressful process of job interviews (which usually take place at the MLA Annual Convention) by establishing support groups, organizing mock interviews, and rendering whatever other assistance might be needed.

Alternative Career Paths

Since the number of PhDs in German graduating from American universities continues to exceed the academic positions available, serious consideration must be given to an alternative career. This is not an easy task. While a Germanist in Germany may find employment in a publishing house or as a journalist, an American graduate has a more difficult time finding a meaningful position outside academe. But difficult does not mean hopeless. There will always be a small number who find employment in such places as government, library, research centers, or academic administration (see Karell). Coupled with other skills, a degree in German may open up opportunities in business, international finance, or law.[2] It must be clearly understood, however, that any alternative career path requires additional expertise. Just having a degree in German will rarely qualify one for a position outside teaching. The search for a meaningful career outside academe for holders of a PhD in any field of the humanities continues to be a critical point of discussion, as reflected in MLA committees, Woodrow Wilson Foundation conferences, and assorted guidebooks.[3] It is also a topic addressed with increasing frequency by some of the major PhD-conferring graduate programs, which invite former students who have succeeded on an alternative career path to speak about their experiences.

Workloads and Leave Policies

With the increased emphasis on professionalism, work conditions have improved and opportunities for academic growth and development have greatly increased. On the secondary school level, workshops and even sabbaticals have become available to many teachers, something unheard of before World War II. In the early 1960s, following the passage of the National Defense Education Act (NDEA), summer and yearlong institutes offered (paid) opportunities for high school teachers not only to familiarize themselves with new concepts of German studies and language teaching but also to spend an extended time in Germany (e.g., at the Stanford Univ. Second Level NDEA Institutes in Bad Boll; see Weiss and Lohnes). Since the early 1970s, the Goethe Institute, often in conjunction with the AATG, has become an active partner in preparing German teachers for the shift in curricular emphasis to the broader field of German studies, offering weekend language and German studies seminars, which focus on information gathering, the interpretation of current events, and new approaches in second language acquisition. The number of school partnerships and exchanges (practically nonexistent before World War II) continues to increase, and today it is rare that an American high school teacher of German has not visited a country where the language is spoken.

On the postsecondary level, the increased emphasis on research and publication at most institutions has led to a general lowering of faculty teaching loads—from up to eight courses per year (and sometimes even more) to the current average of four to six. Sabbaticals and research semesters have become more readily available, and access to funds for travel to conferences or to Europe for research are innovations that faculty members have come to enjoy only since the 1960s. The number of grants available to the professoriat has greatly increased. While the Guggenheim (a highly competitive plum) dates back to 1925, many opportunities have evolved only since the end of World War II. Most notable among these are the various Fulbright grants, the stipends offered through the German Academic Exchange Service (DAAD) (see Littmann), the Alexander von Humboldt Stiftung (founded in 1860 and originally limited to the sciences but now also open to the humanities), and the National Endowment for the Humanities (NEH).

Indeed, working conditions for faculty members have greatly improved since German became an academic discipline at American universities and colleges in the early nineteenth century. And so have the expectations. The publish-or-perish syndrome is very much alive at most institutions. Young faculty members entering the profession may be given all kinds of incentives—a new computer, course reductions, research leaves—but with the gift comes the pressure to produce, to make it through the tenure review in their sixth year of probationary service. The criteria for tenure and promotion continue to become more stringent, and many a person who was promoted to full professor a few decades ago might have trouble gaining tenure today.

The field of German studies has never been in the mainstream of American education. Its history shows occasional moments of glory and a great deal of benign neglect. For much of the time, German departments at the college or university level were quite small—certainly smaller than many are today—and relatively few of them offered doctoral programs. But from the latter part of the nineteenth century to World War I, German maintained a prominent place in the curriculum of American secondary schools, assuring employment for many teachers. In the 1920s and 1930s, German held its own in colleges and high schools, with a limited number of positions available at both levels. A radical change occurred during the Sputnik era of the early 1960s, when German benefited from the sudden surge of interest in foreign languages and cultures as a matter of national security. Funding through the NDEA led to rapid growth of German departments and an overproduction of PhDs. In 1968 the dropping of language requirements at many colleges created a serious reduction in enrollment and a cutting of positions, resulting in a major job crisis for graduates. Since the 1980s, German at the postsecondary level has stabilized but on a much smaller scale than during the heyday of the 1960s. Even now, the number of PhDs entering the job market is greater than the positions available, although projected retirements raise hope for employment of those currently completing their degrees. On the secondary level, the situation currently is bleak.

Career opportunities and employment patterns in German studies remain volatile. It is not a field for the masses. What will be the future? If the past is any indication, we can respond, More of the same.

Notes

1 For a discussion of the role of adjunct faculty members, see Sullivan.

2 A survey of departments conducted by *Monatshefte* in 1979 yielded the following list of nonacademic jobs obtained (number of mentions given in parentheses). *Education:* administration (8), high school teaching (7), historian (2), library or archive work (13). *Public service:* armed forces (2), foundation work (1), German government agencies in the United States (3), government service (4). *Communications:* broadcasting (2), editorial and publishing (8), newspaper (1), translation (5). *Business:* accounting and bookkeeping (2), banking (1), building trades (2), independent business (5), interior decorating (1), international business (1), managerial (6), real estate (1), repairs (2), restaurant (1), sales (6), secretarial (3), stockbroking (1). *Other:* computers (3), laboratory technician (1), legal or paralegal (1), psychotherapy (1), ranching (1). This list does not claim to be complete, but it does reflect the broad range of alternative careers, especially in the areas of education, government service, and publishing ("Placements").

3 The following titles are offered as a sample: Barbara Elling, "Career Alternatives for Students of German"; Sandra Gilbert, *Final Report of the MLA Committee on Professional Employment*; Lucille Honig and Richard Brod, *Foreign Languages and Careers*; *MLA Guide to the Job Search* (since 1997, this guide has a special chapter on career opportunities outside higher education for PhDs in the humanities); Nancy A. Risser et al., *Humanities PhDs and Non-academic Careers: A Guide for Faculty Advisers*; Samia L. Spencer, *Foreign Languages and International Trade: A Global Perspective*; Robert Weisbuch, *The Humanities Ph.D. and Careers outside the Academy* and *Unleashing the Humanities: The Doctorate beyond the Academy*.

2

Instruction

~

Edited by
FRANK TROMMLER

Introduction

The contributors in part 2 illuminate the everyday reality of the discipline as it unfolds in the classroom with the interaction of teachers and students, drawing on many tools that have been shaped by the profession and are in constant need of rethinking and updating. Though challenged by new electronic devices that create virtual learning situations, classroom interaction is still the core of foreign language instruction and its curricular and pedagogical institutionalization. This centrality is highlighted by a focus primarily on undergraduate instruction in the following articles, which provide depth and reflection on teacher training, enrollments, textbooks, and the reading canon. Part 2 also includes an overview of graduate education and a programmatic piece on the significance of interdisciplinarity for the concept of German studies, which has substantially changed the approach to the discipline in the last two decades of the twentieth century.

That graduate education figures less centrally in this overview might be construed as a reflection of its current ranking in academe. Indeed, as Russell Berman indicates in his comprehensive assessment of undergraduate education since the nineteenth century, the trend to downscale graduate programs has taken on new momentum with the end of the cold war, which was the best period ever for the American research university. Graduate education is expensive but usually justified by the research agenda of the individual department; it is also dependent on budgetary factors that may replace research with instruction, so that graduate students have to take over senior faculty teaching.

In the light of this lopsided division of labor, a more extended discussion on instruction would have to focus on graduate students not only as learners but also as teachers. In many research universities, basic instruction of foreign languages is still the domain of teaching assistants. Their role does not say anything about their effectiveness in conveying the language and culture. Their effectiveness might often be higher than that of the faculty, but there is growing concern that the professionalization of language instruction can only progress at the expense of scholarly accomplishments—and vice versa. Graduate students are in danger of compromising their rights as learners and apprentices.

It should not be forgotten that it was the installation of graduate programs that gave the instruction in foreign languages and literatures a boost more than a hundred years ago. When in 1908 the MLA president Oliver Farrar Emerson reflected on the progress that the introduction of modern languages in lieu of Greek and Latin represented, he took up Charles Francis Adams's then famous verdict of "The College Fetish" as the epitome of mindless antiquarianism in nineteenth-century college education. Emerson was enamored with what he called "the new investigative spirit," the source of which he considered to be the German seminar room:

> Before that time it had usually been enough for a teacher to present the facts embodied in a text-book of the subject. He usually made little attempt to keep up with the latest results of research. Many of these results he did not appreciate, or know how to apply. Not an investigator himself, he could scarcely correlate the new knowledge with that which he had come to regard as fixed and unchangeable. All this was radically altered by the new investigative spirit. Those training in the graduate school there learned what research really meant, and how it could be applied in their several fields. The teacher became an investigator as well, and thus added to his function of imparting knowledge that of extending the boundaries of what is known. (lxxx)

Emerson's enthusiasm reflects the best of the Humboldtian link between *Forschung und Lehre* ("scholarship and teaching"), research and instruction, a combination that has been called obsolete and yet is alive and well in classrooms, tutorials, and seminars—*if* teacher and students join together and the subject allows it. Generally it did not carry far into the undergraduate classroom, and graduate education remained a rather hierarchical knowledge transfer, where the professor handed down the wisdom. In his concise overview, Simon Richter leaves little doubt that graduate study hardly liberated itself from the traditional knowledge transfer until the 1970s.

The recent surge of instant information on the Internet, information that was once hard to obtain, could extend the spirit of investigation in new ways, especially when directed toward interdisciplinary German studies. Doubtless the material will have to be screened vis-à-vis the means of established and footnoted scholarship. As the growing interest in interdisciplinarity—a pre-requisite for the extension of the linguistic and literary orientation of Germanics toward German studies—empowers the new investigative spirit, a balance will have to be struck between the pedagogical benefits of this empowerment and the slide into dilettantism while dealing with previously inaccessible materials. Wolfgang Natter's essay provides important arguments for such an empowerment.

Many factors seem to warrant the conclusion that the two-tier instructional setup in German and other foreign language departments—separating language from philology and literature instruction—that dominated the decades after World War II has been disintegrating. The distribution of teaching assignments reflected a two-class system. Now, the increasing professionalization of language pedagogy that gave applied linguistics and second language acquisition a higher profile as well as other status- and curriculum-based transformations challenge this setup and this system. The division between tenure-track and non-tenure-track faculty that Patricia Herminghouse mentions in her introduction to the previous section is clearly characteristic of the present situation; it is being most hotly contested in English and Spanish departments, given their strong need for teaching personnel. However, one cannot apply the fusion of language and literature teaching in German without qualifications. As a result of the scarce resources of departments, non-tenure-track faculty members are often asked to teach surveys on culture or literature while tenured faculty, observant of the attention to language pedagogy, are learning to maintain a tight grip on language courses that represent the backbone for healthy enrollments.

As Renate Schulz shows in her analysis of teacher development since the early twentieth century, Germanists, reflecting the German pedagogical tradition and its strong impact on nineteenth-century American education, seem to have been more committed to providing good training for teachers than were other foreign language specialists. On the whole, however, a dearth of good teachers has plagued the discipline during the twentieth century, at least since World War I, as most sources confirm. That a constant influx of German-born teachers—among them many women at the high school level whose husbands taught at colleges—helped overcome the lack of qualified American-born teachers does not necessarily indicate a higher quality of teaching. Notwithstanding the great contribution of German-born teachers to the survival of German in American classrooms, which can be traced from the beginnings in the eighteenth century to the present, the flaws and peculiarities of their teaching, epitomized in the image of the German instructor as the guardian of grammar-based drills, should not be overlooked in a historical assessment of everyday instruction. The reforms of language pedagogy that reached the field of German in the 1980s and found a remarkably strong response can be understood as a definitive shift away from the native-speaker paradigm toward a specifically American approach to the four skills. Schulz's other, longer essay on the developments in methodology in this volume, "Pedagogical Issues in German-Language Teaching," provides further insights into the precarious balance between skills and grammatical accuracy on the one hand and communication strategies on the other, which has been at the center of never-ending controversies and attempted reforms.

The contributions to part 2 on enrollments, textbooks, and the literary canon are also diachronic. David Benseler provides an extremely helpful contextualization of the long-term slide of German enrollments with the developments of the first half of the twentieth century. Jeannine Blackwell's statistics-based overview of the canonical use of authors other than Goethe and Schiller and her special tabulation of women authors are indispensable for an informed discussion of literature, which has been the key to a broader involvement with German culture. The realm of textbooks, to which Cora Lee Kluge offers access through thorough investigation of the German textbook collection at the University of Wisconsin, has been the least explored so far. Generally, the importance of textbooks and writing of textbooks cannot be overstated. This investigation provides a close link between an earlier concept of scholarship, which accorded the writing of textbooks—not articles—the most respect, and the everyday conduct of classes in colleges and universities. Kluge's findings about the pastoral image of Germany conveyed in most textbooks until the 1960s corresponds with Blackwell's statistics. Whatever the instructional value of this romantic view of Germany, it has been persistent and obviously highly successful, while the reality of the industrial, urban, and militaristic Germany remained confined to the realm of politics. Any deeper understanding of the dynamics of instruction in German language and literature during the period of the two World Wars will have to be based on a thorough investigation of this spirit of educational shelter.

In keeping with this reflection of the still unexplored intercultural encounter in everyday instruction, one other component should be mentioned, as it represents the most basic yet most evasive part of instruction (a kind of anthropology of the profession): the mentality and cultural equipment of the American student in the classroom and the various strategies of teachers to gain access to this mentality in order to draw students into learning one of the more difficult languages and entering one of the more complex and controversial literary and cultural terrains. The much debated opposition between utilitarian and educational justification for learning German fades when evidence is given that German language teachers succeeded in teaching the students something about themselves, transforming intercultural stereotypes into more complex understandings of identity and difference.

The Undergraduate Program

RUSSELL A. BERMAN

The roots of today's undergraduate programs in German can be traced back to the colonial period. Instruction in the German language began as early as the 1680s, in the school curriculum for children of immigrants in the Germantown colony; an all-German primer prepared by the leader of the colony, Franz Daniel Pastorius, was in widespread use by 1702. While German schools also developed in the Mennonite and Moravian communities, the genuine forebear of college-level German was the Academy of Philadelphia, founded in 1749 through the initiative of Benjamin Franklin and the American Philosophical Society. Its charter refers specifically to the teaching of French, Spanish, and German. In 1755, the academy became a degree-granting college, and in 1779 it was transformed into the University of Pennsylvania, an institution that reflected Franklin's experience visiting the University of Göttingen in 1766.

Tracing the origins of undergraduate programs to the (relatively) distant past of colonial Philadelphia can serve to legitimate the study of German as deeply rooted in the traditions of American higher education. Yet this genealogy also exposes features that are endemic to the study of German in the United States, recurring in varying configurations during the subsequent centuries. German programs carry a double mission of instructing American students in German language while also cultivating an interest in German intellectual life. Those goals sometimes come into conflict, but they remain inextricably linked. In many periods, moreover, the relation between German in American colleges and the interests of the German American ethnic population colored the discussion of German instruction. Similarly the articulation between precollege and college language instruction remains an abiding concern. Finally, the evidence of the Philadelphia academy displays the status of German as one of several foreign languages—that is, the vicissitudes of German programs are obviously part of the larger history of foreign language instruction in the United States.

Anxieties regarding the rationale for foreign language study were already present at the Philadelphia academy: Franklin recommended modern languages for "merchants," foreshadowing programs of business German and linkages between language study and vocational plans. Moreover, the study of foreign languages at the academy was to be restricted to "leisure hours" (Zeydel, "Teaching . . . through World War I" 24). It was not until more than a century later that foreign language programs overcame this marginalization through full integration into the curriculum. Nonetheless, throughout the history of American higher education, undergraduate instruction in German and the other foreign languages has faced doubts regarding the academic seriousness of second language acquisition. While foreign language study ceased to be a matter relegated to leisure hours, American colleges and universities generally do not accord to foreign languages, especially modern foreign languages, either the resources or the prestige accorded to the core humanities fields, such as English, history, and philosophy. This hesitation regarding languages has two main sources. First, the study of any single language and culture is necessarily particularistic and therefore at odds with the tendency in modern scholarship toward general or universal formulations. The study of a foreign language is rarely concerned with language in general, and institutional efforts to integrate foreign language study into a department of linguistics, such as at Cornell in the late twentieth century, have not been successful. Second, this tension between foreign language programs and the inner logic of the university is compounded by the character of American national culture, which, reflecting the tendency of an immigrant society oriented toward integration and assimilation, has not placed a premium on proficiency in foreign languages.

During the American Revolution and its immediate aftermath, instruction in German declined, which has sometimes been attributed to a reaction against the role of Hessian and Hanoverian mercenaries among the British forces. "Not World War I, but the Revolutionary War was the first historical event of this nature that dealt a blow to the status of German in the US" (Hugo Schmidt 3) This hypothesis reveals another constant in the discourse on German: an implicit if shifting political frame surrounds German instruction in the United States nearly from the start. The renewed interest in German after 1815 reflected the rise of a generation that had not lived through the revolution as well as the vigorous reception of German literature and philosophy in New England intellectual life. A German tutor, Meno Poehls, taught at Harvard in 1816, although only for one year. In 1817 George Ticknor was appointed as professor of French and Spanish, and his influence elicited greater interest in modern languages in general. That interest led, in 1825, to the appointment of Charles Follen, a political refugee from Germany, who had been recommended by Lafayette.

Teaching at Harvard, Follen developed textbooks of considerable influence as interest in German grew, and college instruction in German language and literature became increasingly institutionalized. Nevertheless, in 1836, Follen's contract was not renewed, a decision that has been explained as a result of his outspoken opposition to slavery and his advocacy for free speech. Whatever the reason, Andrew P. Peabody, one of the students in his first class, describes the deep impact of the course and the power of Follen's engagement:

> [The course reader] contained choice extracts in prose, all from writers that still hold an unchallenged place in the hierarchy of Genius, and poems from Schiller, Goethe, Herder, and several other poets of kindred, if inferior, fame. But in the entire volume Dr. Follen rejoiced especially in several battle poems from Körner, the soldier and martyr of liberty. I have never heard recitations which impressed me so strongly as the reading of those pieces by Dr. Follen, who would put into them all of the heart and soul that made him too much a lover of his country to be suffered to dwell in it. (Zeydel, "Teaching . . . through World War I" 30)

Peabody's testimony demonstrates the capacity of instruction in a foreign language and literature to inspire an American undergraduate through the encounter with a distant problematic, which nevertheless resonated with values of the American republic. In addition, the abolitionist Follen must certainly be seen as an heir of Pastorius, who had participated in the first public protest against slavery by a nonslave in the United States. The undergraduate German program emerges as a two-way street in which alternative cultural specificities coincide and values undergo critical examination and transformation. Yielding much more than the mastery of particular skills or the transmission of a literary taste, the study of a foreign culture bears within it the possibility of reflection and criticism. For Peabody at least, the undergraduate program in German at Harvard was not only about a canon of German literature, it was also about liberty and its dialectics in a complex network of political asylum, immigration, and aesthetic experience.

Appointed to Ticknor's position in 1836, Henry Wadsworth Longfellow taught at Harvard for two decades, and his lectures on Goethe were popular and influential in spreading interest in German culture. Meanwhile German instruction was incorporated into the curriculum at a number of other colleges and universities, including Bowdoin, Amherst, and the University of Virginia, and it continued to spread during the nineteenth century, because of immigration, the rising prestige of German scholarship, and the growing importance of Germany in international affairs. Nevertheless, the substance of this instruction was typically limited to acquisition of reading knowledge, while skills in speaking and writing were treated as, at best, secondary. As German and the other modern foreign languages gradually displaced first Greek and then Latin, instructional practice in the modern languages frequently entailed little more than an adoption of the methods of teaching associated with the classical languages. The predominance of a grammar-translation model of instruction was modified only mildly in new textbooks of the 1860s; a full-scale modernization of language instruction did not take place until the mid–twentieth century.

American higher education underwent dramatic changes in the decades after the Civil War in ways that still structure contemporary debates with regard to the curricular structure, vocational specialization, and disciplinary specialization. In general, mid-nineteenth-century college curricula were rigid and highly prescriptive, often explicitly linked to the specific denominational mission of an individual institution. However, this system was challenged and fundamentally revised by Charles William Eliot, who during his long tenure as president of Harvard from 1869 to 1909, introduced the free elective system that allowed students a heretofore unheard-of degree of freedom in choosing their courses. Liberal education, Eliot argued, necessitated granting students the responsibility of choice, a strategy that appealed to American secularist tastes for a cultural antidogmatism while also responding to the explosion of knowledge in the late nineteenth century. Meanwhile, the size of both the course catalog and the faculty burgeoned. The corollary to free electives was, however, specialization in an area of concentration or a major field. Henceforth, undergraduate programs would be concerned with providing instruction both for generalist students (interested in basic language learning as well as introductory courses on literature and culture) and for those students choosing to major in German, requiring more-advanced instruction.

Basic foreign language instruction, in fact, remained one of the few pockets of required instruction in Eliot's system, surviving to the present as the foreign language requirement in some institutions. Meanwhile, his critics, notably James McCosh, president of Princeton, accused him of nothing less than undermining the viability of liberal education precisely by denying students the guidance they needed to navigate successfully through the growing fields of scholarship. The alternative to free electives emerged as the prescription to study the several branches of knowledge, which later came to be designated as distribution requirements. The fundamental criticism of Eliot's liberalization of education, however, remained that a largely unstructured course of study would lack a core and that students would therefore lose their way among dispersed specializations in the increasingly rigid division of intellectual labor among disciplines.

Eventually, courses providing overarching perspectives on culture and civilization were developed. A century of debates in American higher education has revolved around the nature of such core courses in the humanities. In 1919, Columbia led the way with the introduction of the Contemporary Civilization course, driven in part by the interest in articulating a cultural mission for the United States as it assumed a leadership role in international affairs in the wake of World War I. The University of Chicago followed suit in 1931 with the Great Books course. Similarly, Stanford initiated a Western Civilization course in 1935, which, undergoing complex permutations over subsequent decades, became a topic of national controversy during the so-called culture wars of the 1980s (Lindenberger, *History* 152; Allardyce et al.). In these courses, faculty members from various departments, but especially history and literature (including modern foreign literatures), came to play important roles, by teaching outside narrowly disciplinary or departmental structures. Through such courses, undergraduates have often been introduced to German figures like Luther, Goethe, Kant, Marx, Nietzsche, Freud, Kafka, and Mann in an interdisciplinary and, of course, international framework. But undergraduate German programs also have their own long history of offering comparable culture courses, presenting literature, art, and philosophy in translation.

Thus the topic of undergraduate instruction in German culture points to two salient and fairly constant features: a curriculum that includes considerable material that is not narrowly literary but rather integrates figures such as Kant, Marx, and Freud into the teaching agenda; some competition over which unit in the college or university can lay claim to the German material for instructional purposes. The interdisciplinary culture courses of the twentieth century highlight the possibility that the German intellectual tradition can be addressed outside a departmental curriculum.

As college offerings expanded and student choice grew, the possibility of a career-oriented specialization emerged as a challenge to liberal arts education. While Franklin had recommended learning languages for business purposes, the overwhelming rationales for any language study (modern or ancient) in undergraduate programs remained cultural enrichment and personal growth. The option to select courses primarily in terms of job preparation ran counter to fundamental assumptions of American college education. Such preprofessionalism in college education remains a large concern at the beginning of the twenty-first century. Around 1900 the issue erupted poignantly in debates among African American leaders. Booker T. Washington, highly celebrated by the white political establishment, argued for the benefits of a restrictively vocational training for black students. This conservative stance represented a pragmatic compromise with the realities of racial segregation. His eloquent opponent, W. E. B. Du Bois, denounced Washington's quietistic refusal to countenance the notion of African American students studying foreign languages because of the presumed irrelevance of those languages to vocational goals:

> . . . so thoroughly did [Washington] learn the speech and thought of triumphant commercialism, and the ideals of material prosperity, that the picture of a lone black boy poring over a French grammar amid the weeds and dirt of a neglected home soon seemed to him the acme of absurdities. One wonders what Socrates and St. Francis of Assisi would say to this. (45)

Arguing fully in the spirit of liberal education, Du Bois located the justification for language study in the access to intellectual traditions, philosophical aspirations, and emancipatory values; whether foreign language learning had a commercial value was irrelevant. Consequently, while at the University of Berlin in 1893, he wrote back to the newspaper at his alma mater, Fisk, that the college students should study Goethe "for the rise of the negro people" (Lewis 139). Du Bois clearly imputed a critical substance to the project of cultural transfer inherent in the undergraduate study of foreign literature. (Returning from Berlin, he taught German briefly at Wilberforce.)

Worries about the viability of a liberal arts agenda for undergraduate education stemmed, additionally, from another version of specialization: the accelerated strengthening of the disciplinary basis of scholarship associated with the emergence of the modern research university in the 1870s. Yale awarded its first PhD in 1861. Johns Hopkins was founded in 1876, specifically with a research agenda borrowed from the contemporary German university. Other American universities, such as Columbia, Cornell, Michigan, and Pennsylvania, followed suit, developing graduate programs devoted to systematic and original scholarship and increasingly distinct from undergraduate programs. Undergraduate programs undoubtedly benefited from this transition in the institutionalization of knowledge, with its increased rigor and spirit of scientific progress. In the same period, the foundation of the Modern Language Association in 1883 marked the growing professionalization of scholarship in the research university and led to concerted advocacy for the systematic integration of languages into the curriculum, in contrast to their earlier status as largely marginal tutorials. Indeed the MLA, initially concerned centrally with foreign language pedagogy, played a key role in the undermining of the hegemony of the classical languages in American higher education. German, with its high enrollments, was frequently seen as likely to displace Ancient Greek in instructional programs. Meanwhile the emergence of specialized graduate training and the growing prestige of research inexorably shifted attention and resources away from undergraduate education, even in those colleges that were separate from formal research enterprises, since their faculty members too were ultimately held to the same professional standards as colleagues at universities. Undergraduate programs reflected this reorientation insofar as preparation for graduate study became an additional, indeed sometimes implicitly primary goal of the curriculum.

With regard to both language and literature, undergraduate education came to stand increasingly in the shadow of the graduate and research undertaking. There was, however, vocal opposition to this primacy of research: advocates of undergraduate education repeatedly called for specific attention to undergraduate needs, viewed as distinct from the graduate project of scholarly professionalization. Writing in 1928, Lilian L. Stroebe commented:

> The modern college student does not yearn for book learning or abstract ideas. What he yearns for is "life," and if the instructor can show that Goethe and Schiller wrote their immortal works as interpreters of life (and not for scholars to edit with introductions and notes), half the battle is won. The students must feel the reality of the subject, and of course they will never feel it, unless the instructor is convinced of it and is able to transmit his conviction to his students. (125)

The comment reflects the competition between alternative goals: on the one hand, the preparation of scholars, associated with preparing editions and footnotes; on the other, the education of lay readers, with an interest in the existential significance of literature to life. While this emphatic appeal to the relevance of literature echoes the cultural and ideological predispositions of the post–World War I era, it is in fact symptomatic of the more general tension inherent in modern higher education between the demands of rigorous scholarship and the interests of undergraduate education. An undergraduate program oriented primarily toward professional research would run the risk of appearing irrelevant and unappealing to students not pursuing an academic career. Thus Stroebe's comments anticipate remarks by Robert Spaethling who, a half century later, in 1976, insisted that "underneath our Germanist cloaks, there must be available and accessible, the educator" (174). The choice between being a Germanist and being an educator sets in stark contrast the competing desiderata of research and undergraduate education in the twentieth-century university.

At the beginning of the twentieth century, undergraduate German instruction at the college level was largely a matter of reading skills, focused on Lessing, Goethe, and Schiller and a slowly expanding group of more recent authors. World War I and the isolationism that followed reduced interest in foreign languages in general, although for none as dramatically as for German, partly because of the anti-German sentiment that swept the country in 1917. However, it is also true that German instruction before World War I was sometimes implicated in an uncritical admiration of the Wilhelmine Empire, which in turn made German programs all the more likely targets in the contest of war-time passions.

In an interesting contrast to the retreat from international involvements after World War I, World War II led to a revival of interest in language learning due to the military need to train foreign language speakers and a widespread public acceptance of American leadership in global politics. The cold war and the Sputnik scare similarly magnified the importance of foreign language study, with important consequences for the character of undergraduate programs, especially language programs that underwent a profound modernization. Research in second language acquisition accelerated, resulting in innovative teaching strategies that finally overcame the nineteenth-century grammar-translation methods. The National Defense Education Act of 1958 (and other legislation) provided funding for foreign language learning, just as demographic trends swelled the ranks of students entering college (in fact, higher education had begun to expand significantly after World War II, as colleges and universities were opened to returning GIs). German enrollments grew enormously, from 110,000 in 1959 to nearly 214,000 in 1965, representing 22.5% of foreign language enrollment (in contrast to 39% for French and 32.6% for Spanish) (Hugo Schmidt 7).

Yet these robust enrollments concealed underlying problems. Because the metamorphosis of German programs involved a redefined understanding of second language acquisition, one aimed more at contemporary linguistic usage than at the understanding of classical texts, the inherited literary curriculum had to surrender its centrality. Language learning alone, however, was hardly a plausible definition of a college major, and departments have consistently resisted becoming mere service departments that exist solely to provide language instruction. Efforts to present canonic literature as somehow relevant represented at best a stopgap measure. An alternative program would eventually emerge in the interdisciplinarity of the German studies movement of the late twentieth century.

Meanwhile, the enormous growth in enrollments entailed a demographic democratization of the college experience, opened to a less elite population. This social transformation carried with it an increased attention to the vocational opportunities associated with college education. While the liberal arts model invoked a notion of autonomous culture, valuable for its own sake and as a vehicle for personal growth, college education came to be viewed more in terms of postgraduate job opportunities. This issue had been thrashed out long before, but the reification of higher education underwent a quantum leap after 1968. German programs, like all majors, were increasingly forced to argue their vocational relevance for students.

During the last third of the century, enrollments dropped again, approximately to the levels of the late 1950s. To some extent, this decline can be attributed to the abolition or dilution of college foreign language requirements, although in this shrinking pool of modern foreign language enrollments a dramatic redistribution has also taken place: Spanish enrollments have grown rapidly, to more than 50%, while German hovers around 10%. The new foreign language profile in American higher education reflects both a greater awareness of multicultural linguistic diversity in the United States and the critique of Eurocentrism in cultural debates. It is also certainly a result of the shrinking of high school–level German programs: by 1980 only 2% of high school students studied German (Sander, "Figures" 236). For college programs this drop in turn implies that nearly all students of German begin at college from the start instead of entering directly into intermediate courses. The ensuing challenge is to find ways to introduce substantial cultural and literary material earlier in the undergraduate curriculum than was previously done. The redesign of the language program at Stanford, in the mid-1990s, for example, involved a systematic presentation of German cultural history in first-year courses and opportunities for intensive work with literature in the second year rather than in the third (Berman and Bernhardt-Kamil 22).

In the light of the methodological and theoretical debates in literary studies in both the United States and the Federal Republic of Germany, undergraduate programs underwent considerable revision. In many instances, interdisciplinary German studies tracks have been introduced as an alternative to the more traditional study of German literature. In other cases, the curriculum as a whole has become more diverse, replacing the earlier focus on classical and modernist literature with a range of topics reflecting contemporary research interests: German film, feminism, intellectual history, critical theory, postcolonial approaches to minorities in Germany, and cultural studies. Contemporary undergraduate programs are conceived less as an insular study of a limited set of canonic literary masterpieces, more as an interdisciplinary inquiry into the various questions that concern the field and that interact with scholarship on German society and culture in other disciplines. This interdisciplinarity has brought new enthusiasm and energy to many programs. At the same time, it runs the risk of shifting student interest and faculty loyalty to units outside the German department (McVeigh 58).

The decline in overall enrollments in German has cast a pall over undergraduate programs (and perhaps even more so over graduate programs, where future teachers of undergraduates are trained). Whether the post-1989 processes of European unification and economic modernization will lead to greater or less interest in Germany and German programs is unclear; the moment of unification itself did produce increased interest, but only briefly. In any case, it is useful to remember that the declining number of bachelor's degrees granted in the foreign languages corresponds to comparable and sometimes larger declines in other humanities fields, including English and history. The very nature of college education has shifted toward the social sciences and preprofessional opportunities. The German field has responded by attempting to reinvent its programs with a greater focus on the study of Germany as a society and culture than on Germany's literary tradition.

The new century brings a mix of challenges and opportunities for all languages, German among them. The argument for vocational language study has never been particularly compelling, at least not in mainstream liberal arts college education. If preprofessionalism—choosing courses in terms of career plans—continues to grow, the status of language learning may become even more threatened. The profession's curricular self-scrutiny, which began in response to enrollment declines in the 1970s, will surely continue and lead to further adaptions of the undergraduate program—all the more so, given a growing public emphasis on the quality of undergraduate education and calls for a reinvigoration of a culture of inquiry for undergraduates. The era of the clear priority of graduate education and research may have come to an end. German programs can respond to the contemporary interest in processes of cultural transfer in globalization, while a larger reinvention of the humanities invites undergraduate German programs to participate more centrally in college education in new and complex ways.

Finding Students

Toward a History of
Germanics in the United States

DAVID BENSELER

Enrollment and curriculum drive most determinations regarding individual departments in American higher education. They interact both antagonistically and supportively. They can cause or merely reflect changing institutional priorities, yet they may function as absolutes in the hiring and permanent retention of faculty members. Because other articles have dwelt on the nature of a revitalized discipline's curriculum and content (see, e.g., Hohendahl, "Fate" and "How to Read"; Trommler, "Recovering"; Benseler, "Upper Division Curriculum") and on how the delivery of that content might be improved and made more visible (Byrnes, "How Visible?"; Sammons, "Germanistik im Niemandsland"; Schulz et al.), my observations here focus on enrollments, their promise or their reality, as a historically key factor to departmental establishment and growth, to survival and revitalization. Enrollments are but one of a multitude of factors and considerations regarding the relative health of a discipline or department. Nevertheless, they are the currency of productivity-driven institutions, where productivity is defined as the number of students enrolled in courses taught by a particular unit—be that head count; student credit hours taught (the number of students registered for credit in the course multiplied by the number of credits for the course); or the number of majors, number of minors, or number of students completing both undergraduate and graduate programs. Some private colleges and universities also record the number of inquiries about, expressions of interest in, or written mentions of a department or unit by potential students.

In short, enrollments are, as Henry Schmidt once wrote, the capital of the academic enterprise of Germanics in the United States, subject to the competition of the free market. The failure to grow—to show a profit, as it were—indicates that departments and programs "are in danger of devaluation or dissolution in times of economic crises" ("Wissenschaft" 67). The capital thus provided by enrollments affects institutions from top to bottom, from the president's office to individual departments, including language sections within multilanguage departments.

Enrollment growth and size led to the initial formation of academic departments (Rudolph 399–400). John Brubacher and Willis Rudy echo Frederick Rudolph's focus on overall enrollment:

> The structure of the institutions began to change. The larger the college grew, especially the larger its faculty grew, the more it became necessary to specialize and to delegate duties . . . faculties began to subdivide themselves into departments of instruction. (367)

Bruce Kelley's history of Yale does not chronicle the establishment and growth of the institution's German department, but it does note how student demand, under President Jeremiah Day (1817–47), moved modern languages from the area of a subject matter offered by private tutors employed at the expense of interested students to the status of an optional subject taught by an individual instructor employed by the university. French was added because of student demand in 1825, German in 1831, Spanish in 1841 (165). Kelley also describes briefly German's rise to the status of a regularly offered subject, the hiring of Julius Petersen (330), and German as a required subject under the 1917 curriculum reform (347).

Academics and nonacademics alike outside the discipline have only sporadically regarded the teaching and study of foreign languages as important or essential. Just when knowledge of German might have benefited the populace the most, as the United States entered World War I, several American states banned and continued to forbid the speaking and teaching of it.[1]

The federal government and national initiatives have also aided enrollments or focused attention on them, although not without some—charitably—direction and focus provided by the profession. Foreign language professionals commonly regard the passage of the 1958 National Defense Education Act (NDEA), the establishment of the President's Commission on Foreign Language and International Studies (1978), and the recent inclusion of a mention of the discipline in the core curriculum for the schools as accomplishments demonstrating public awareness of the growing importance of language and literature studies in modern American life. Indeed, for Germanists, NDEA programs turned out to be especially beneficial, renewing teachers' enthusiasm, improving their teaching, and drawing doctoral students to the discipline (Weiss and

Lohnes). But foreign language professionals seem largely unaware of the battles that the profession's various organizations fought in order for languages to be included in the national effort. The NDEA was originally designed and intended only for mathematics and the sciences. The president's commission and its report initially concentrated on international studies to the exclusion of foreign languages (Twarog). The original concept of both programs succumbed to intense lobbying by an energized foreign language profession. Finally, it took spirited and remarkably tenacious involvement by the Joint National Committee for Languages and numerous allied professional organizations for foreign language study to be mentioned even tangentially during the recent discussions in this country regarding the core curriculum for the schools—a curriculum that still does not really include foreign languages and, in essence, exiles their study to a position among other marginalized curricular offerings (Edwards; Strolle).

Materials written by Germanists for professional journals portray the history of the discipline in the United States in terms of an ongoing concern for survival, of efforts to attract enrollments sufficient to prove demand, and of attempts to spur continuing interest in a subject matter that nearly died out during and after World War I (see esp. Zeydel, "Teaching . . . through World War I"; Seidlin, "History"). German again declined precipitously during and after the war in Vietnam as faculties canceled numerous college and university requirements and allowed electives designed by and based on student wishes to take their place.[2]

This historical concern with enrollments appears at the founding of the American Association of Teachers of German (AATG). In his opening statement in the *German Quarterly* on the formation of the AATG, the president of the organization, Camillo von Klenze, wrote that in the face of steady but nevertheless weak recovery from the steep enrollment decline caused by American reaction to the war, "it becomes imperative for us teachers of German to use every legitimate means of improving the position of German in our schools, colleges, and universities" (3). The first article other than the president's statement, Robert Fife's "Some New Paths in Teaching German," discusses little other than enrollments. The "Notes and News" section contains a table of enrollments of all foreign languages taught in the schools of the major cities of the nation (150–52). The preoccupation with enrollments continues unabated in "Notes and News"; indeed, it spreads by 1933 from a primarily eastern focus to include a close look at the topic in the Midwest, possibly because of the growth of AATG chapters there (188–91).

In 1934, the *German Quarterly* presented the results of a national survey of higher education German enrollments conducted by the Carl Schurz Memorial Foundation based on survey responses from 431 colleges and universities, 131 normal schools and teachers' colleges, and 171 junior colleges

("German Enrollments" [1934]). By the next year concern seems to have abated somewhat; included is only a report (Gruenberg) on the status of German in Missouri. However, by 1938 the foundation was again expressing concern, lamenting the absence of what should be a symbiotic relation between school and college German programs:

> The growth of German enrollment, at one time rapid, but now very slight, has stopped far short of its pre-war position. . . . But the future is doubtful, and unless much greater strides are taken in reinstating German in the high schools there can be little hope of its gaining further ground in colleges and universities. ("German Enrollments" [1938] 9)[3]

Concerns expressed by some immediately outside the profession of Germanics continued in 1939 in a report prepared by the publisher Crofts and reprinted from that company's own earlier publication, the *German Quarterly*, so that it would not escape the attention of Germanists ("German Enrollments" [1939]).

Enrollment surveys disappear from the pages of the *German Quarterly* during the war years. One can assume, given the Army Specialized Training Program (ASTP), that the statistic had become superfluous, temporarily at least. One can also speculate that the number of Americans studying German in the ASTP was one the American government did not wish to disseminate. By 1944, Bayard Quincy Morgan was already speculating in print about ways and means of raising enrollments in the postwar years, thereby expressing his concern at the possibility of a return to the status quo. He bases his recommended actions on three assumptions: "modern foreign languages will hold an increased amount of public attention; foreign relations . . . will be stressed and cultivated; speaking knowledge of foreign languages will be generally recognized as important" ("After the War" 241).

Morgan's first recommendation for action, which indicates he was thinking in terms of marketing and enrollments, could have been written in and for virtually any decade from 1945 to the present (with the possible exception of the 1960–69 heyday of the NDEA). He asserts that the profession will need to "improve and promote public relations" and goes on to say that it should "collect and/or secure significant utterances in favor of foreign language study by prominent citizens other than language teachers" and ready "carefully worded statements" for school officials, the PTA, and "all other bodies concerned with public education." He recommends the formation of a "pressure group" to advocate foreign language and German study (241).

Initially in articles (e.g., Tyre; Purin, "German"), then in the annual "Personalia" compilations, the periodical *Monatshefte* has provided a regular focus on enrollment patterns and statistics since about 1930, also providing regular information about individual Germanists, individual Germans, and news of matters important to the general well-being of German and German American life in the United States. *Monatshefte*'s "Personalia" is first mentioned as a part of "Berichte" in volume 29 (1937). Volume 27 (1935) had already begun publishing a list (by institution) of faculty members visiting in the United States from Germany. The "Personalia" segments then began including graduate and undergraduate enrollment data regarding German. The periodical continues to gather annually, by institution, information on the number of both graduate and undergraduate majors and minors in German.

The preoccupation with enrollments and survival is reflected clearly in other professional organs and forums (see, e.g., Moore and Benseler ["Enrollments," "Rationales"]). No matter how much we dislike numerical portrayals as a primary means of assessing success or perceived quality, the ability to attract enrollments is widely used as a criterion in program or department evaluation. The strength or weakness of the local demand for the product usually dominates a large portion of the visits of evaluation teams to individual campuses. Numbers are frequently discussed in professional symposia and meetings, especially in the context of positions lost or gained because of enrollments. Recently, indeed, an entire book (Van Cleve and Willson) and a published collection of symposium papers given at Vanderbilt University (McCarthy and Schneider) were dedicated to concern at the decline and marginalization of the discipline. Since their own well-being hinges largely on the continuing success of the disciplines they represent, professional organizations as well have exhibited a preoccupation with enrollments. The importance of numbers is manifested in periodic surveys done by the MLA and its affiliated Association of Departments of Foreign Languages.[4]

Each year department heads in Big Ten universities gather by discipline (in this case by language group) for a discussion of professional issues as they affect departments.[5] These discussions, held under the aegis of the Committee on Institutional Cooperation (CIC), take place only after the chairs have completed a lengthy form detailing all statistical matters of comparative importance pertaining to each department. All matters from faculty and TA salaries to the number of hours taught by faculty members and by TAs are detailed. On their return home, participants use the information gained for a variety of purposes: improving working conditions in their departments, gaining additional funds for salaries, lobbying for additional staffing, and so on. Predictably, the CIC form and subsequent discussions of it at the chairs' gatherings are dominated by enrollment figures.

Like Edwin Zeydel's history of the teaching of German in the United States ("Teaching of German . . . through World War I" and "Teaching of German . . . to the Present"), those few departmental histories that are available show that we have become aware of the need for and desirability of understanding our professional roots. Public expression of this need started in this country with a book of nearly thirty essays on the profession edited by Walter Lohnes and

Valters Nollendorfs (*German Studies in the United States*); it was followed in relatively short order by dissertations and books by Richard Spuler (*Germanistik in America*), Magda Lauwers-Rech (*Nazi Germany and the American Germanists*), Ellen Nagy (*Women in Germanics*), and Gisela Hoecherl-Alden ("Germanisten in 'Niemandsland' "). Publications not rooted in doctoral dissertations began to look even more closely at our professional history. Including the present volume, at least eight books or compilations examining our development have appeared since 1988 or will shortly (Benseler, Nickisch, and Nollendorfs; Timm; McCarthy and Schneider; McGlathery, *German*; Lauwers-Rech; Nagy, *Women*; Roche and Salumets; Van Cleve and Willson). Since its decline during World War I (before that time, McCarthy believes; see "Indigenous . . . Plant" 146–47), Germanics has been a lighthouse ("Leuchtturm" [147]) for other disciplines (esp. at Penn). The discipline, in the form of German departments or German sections of foreign language departments, has struggled to seem more than merely peripheral to American higher education (Lange, "History" 13; Henry Schmidt, "Rhetoric"). Peter Uwe Hohendahl expresses similar concerns. "Obviously, our more recent interest in the history of German studies in America," he writes, "has been closely related to the current struggle to keep our discipline alive and vital during a period of budget cuts and the ongoing process of restructuring in the American university" ("How to Read" 3–4).

Departmental and disciplinary histories (Bottigheimer, "Hundred and Fifty Years"; Doherty; McCarthy, "Indigenous . . . Plant"; McGlathery, *German*; Nickisch; Seidlin, "History"; Zeydel, "Teaching of German . . . through World War I" and "Teaching of German . . . to the Present") help us begin to understand the evolution of the profession. In his history of the teaching of German in the United States, Zeydel describes the impact of World War I on German study in this country almost entirely in terms of enrollments.

Of the works tracing the development of individual departments, the earliest is Oskar Seidlin's 1969 study of German at Ohio State ("History"). Part of a larger work by many hands commemorating the university's centennial, his history is nearly fifty-eight double-spaced typescript pages. Seidlin focuses on accomplishments during the stewardship of successive chairs, from the first, Joseph Millikin, through the fifth, Dieter Cunz. He notes that German was introduced at Ohio State for practical reasons (so future students and graduates could stay abreast of events in agriculture, science, and the mechanical arts), that it benefited from the high regard of this nation for things German before World War I, and that it suffered then the same misfortunes as the rest of the discipline following that turmoil (1–2). This last point he drives home with considerable force, noting that in 1914–15 Ohio State University had a German enrollment of 2,291 students out of a total university student body of 4,597— that is, 50%. He continues:

But the outbreak of World War I was to inflict a blow from which the department did not recover for many years. The enrollment figures speak a language whose clarity leaves nothing to be desired:

1914–15	2,291 students
1915–16	1,583 students
1916–17	654 students
1917–18	149 students (12)

In his first twenty-four pages, Seidlin chronicles the establishment of the department, its growth, and the impact of World War I on it. He portrays some of the scholarship and intellectual interests of some members of the department and notes the unit's growth after the war, especially in philology and linguistics. He measures relative success in its mission by again pointing to enrollments: in 1945–46 a total of 1,703 students registered for German. Because of the GI Bill, the following year saw a total enrollment in German of 3,218 students. The figure tapered off to a steady 1,400 per year until 1956 (28).

Craig Nickisch provides a glimpse into the slow establishment and gradual development of the discipline and its initial German enrollments at the United States Military Academy, where curricular change literally required an act of Congress. First suggested as an addition to the curriculum in 1808, again in 1872—in the aftermath of recent Prussian successes—then again in 1917 and 1939, German instruction finally began at West Point in 1942 with the enrollment of 112 cadets (76–79).

Ruth Bottigheimer's observations about the German department at Princeton ("Hundred and Fifty Years"), together with John McCarthy's about the one at the University of Pennsylvania ("Indigenous . . . Plant"), reflect moments of early professional unease and vacillation. The history of Germanics at Princeton, Bottigheimer observes,

> demonstrates a fluctuating sense of German as a discipline, a gradually shifting perception of the scholars who taught German language and literature, as well as a later slow decline of the proud self-confidence the discipline seemed to enjoy when German science and technology reigned supreme in the nineteenth century. (83)

McCarthy notes that his

> main focus is on the shaping of Germanics in the late nineteenth and early twentieth century at the University of Pennsylvania . . . because the early phase of Germanics in the USA at Penn represents an Americanized version of *Germanistik* which proved decisive in its critical approach, its thematic

preferences, and its admiring yet not uncritical reception of *Germanistik* even during the so-called "period of contentment from 1900 to 1915" (Rippley, "Ameliorated Americanization" 221, qtd. on 146)

He mentions early enrollment problems at Penn, the difficulty of attracting people to the discipline, and notes that the discipline's problem with popularity was not restricted to students: "even among American intellectuals there was no real willingness to learn a modern foreign language." He points out as well that while "demographic shifts can partially explain the lack of interest in Germanics approaching the year 2000, some of the earlier reasons still obtain" (148).

James McGlathery's book *German and Scandinavian at Illinois* contains plentiful detail about faculty, enrollments, scholarship, and teaching methodologies in that department's development—thanks, in part, to well-preserved departmental records and solid archival collections (e.g., the department's first ten serious students of German are named and an outline given of what became of eight of them [10–11]). This history utilizes a wide variety of material, including deans' reports, and provides ample evidence of the symbiotic relation between positive enrollments and faculty growth and rewards. For example, David Kinley, then dean of literature and arts (1895–96), points out in his report that "the German department shows a larger increase of students than any other in the college (having risen 115 students). . . . A third instructor is, in my judgment, imperatively necessary" (qtd. in McGlathery 18).

McGlathery also chronicles the same enrollment concerns that others had, especially during the years of World War I when his German department lost over 40% of its students from 1916–17 through 1917–18 (59). Interestingly enough, he reports the initiation of substantial training for TAs very early (academic year 1929–30) under the headship of Albert William Aron (1927–45). Aron was among the earliest Germanists to recognize a need for the training regarded as essential today.

Americans' sudden aversion to things German during World War I cost thousands of students and hundreds of teaching jobs, but by World War II the public was able to see that speakers of German were needed for the war effort, and many Germanists not in uniform were able to remain employed, judging from the faculty listings in *Monatshefte* during the war years. Many university programs remained basically intact by teaching uniformed personnel under the auspices of the ASTP. Other contributions of Germanists to the war effort are brought into sharp relief in Hoecherl-Alden's "Cloaks and Gowns." She notes that for reasons of "patriotism and issues of job security," Germanists were brought to "jump on the bandwagon and invest their energies" in helping American service personnel learn the language (144).

The desire for renewal prompted a symposium sponsored by the DAAD (the German Academic Exchange Service [Deutscher Akademischer Austausch-dienst]), the University of Delaware, and Vanderbilt University in October 1994 (McCarthy and Schneider). While most of the proposals coming from the symposium, to the credit of its organizers and participants, relate to curriculum, professional content, and policy matters, the first recommendation for post-symposium action is: "Broaden the potential student population whom German studies might serve by recognizing that our content pertains to all disciplines" (162).

Focusing on graduate education, Robert Holub points to the negative effect of some numbers on the profession. He maintains that German departments in the United States are graduating far too many new holders of the doctorate and asserts bluntly that the profession should

> make every effort to bring the number of PhDs in line with the number of new positions available, by (a) eliminating, combining, and reducing graduate programs, and (b) curtailing the hiring of foreign-trained scholars and the training for foreign students. ("Graduate Education" 35)

In the mid-1970s, Renate Schulz won an NEH grant to determine why certain undergraduate foreign language programs in the United States were successful. She defined success as enrollment-driven: "Since enrollment figures were the only objective measure available from a large number of institutions, the initial criterion for success was stated in terms of enrollment increases between the fall terms of 1972 and 1976" (*Options* 10). Schulz, whose report was published as a book by the MLA, surveyed more than 3,000 institutions, most of them twice; 693 departments returned her survey during one of the two mailings. A large number of departments did not return the form, she surmises, because they considered their curriculum "unsuccessful in generating student interest" (i.e., they had nothing positive to report). In the reporting departments, German was the language that suffered the largest drop (18.5%) in enrollments (1). In the chapter "Factors Influencing Enrollment Growth," she notes that these factors are instructional quality; nontraditional options courses and program diversification; intensive courses; course credit options; special methodological approaches; out-of-class activities; recruiting, publicizing, advising (13–29). Departments indicated they had reacted to the crisis (enrollment decline) in a variety of ways, the most common of which was to alter the curriculum. Schulz notes that the "693 departments responding to the questionnaire reported almost 1,800 new courses developed between 1972 and 1976" (3) and provides a lengthy list of those courses (3–8).

Schulz's work was followed nearly twenty years later by John Van Cleve and A. Leslie Willson's even louder alarm. If the title of the book, *Remarks on the Needed Reform of German Studies in the United States*, does not convey the authors' point of view directly enough, the first sentence of the foreword erases all possible doubt:

> This book arose from its authors' conviction that their profession is sliding silently toward oblivion. . . . We hold that the metaphor of a silent slide is deadly accurate. Not only has Germanics been losing tens of thousands of students for the past twenty-five years . . . , if the slide and the silence [of Germanists] continue, the field will die. (ix)

The first printed page (vii) after the table of contents presents a full-page graph: "Enrollments in the Six 'Major Languages' at US Institutions of Higher Education, 1968–1990." Reflecting the enrollment data published in MLA enrollment surveys, the graph portrays clearly the continuing decline of German. From 1968 to 1990, German enrollments in colleges and universities in the United States fell 92,000, from 225,000 to about 133,000 students. Pulling no punches, the authors continue: "Decay is usually a complex process, and the circumstances surrounding the decay of German study are many and varied. There is a host of causes, but of the symptoms one is particularly frightening. We have lost tens of thousands of students" (1; see Van Cleve and Willson for a discussion of enrollments not continued here).

The latest published enrollment figures available to the profession (Brod and Welles) for the first half of the 1990s are supplemented with the winter 1999 *MLA Newsletter* ("MLA's Fall 1998 Survey"). German enrollments in American colleges and universities continued to decline steeply from 1990 to 1995: actual enrollments reported fell from 133,348 (1990) to 96,263 (1995)—a decline of 28%. The bad news does not end there. They fell by another 7,200 students from 1995 to 1999, thus yielding a total decline for the decade of approximately 33%. Neither a business nor a discipline can tolerate losses of that magnitude for very long. A 7% decline may be an improvement over the losses of the first half decade, but the decline nevertheless continues. Helene Zimmer-Loew portrays German enrollments for 1960–98, using data gathered by the MLA and by ACTFL.

No matter what one thinks about the administrative use of enrollments in higher education, they are and doubtless will continue to be used in a wide variety of contexts. Positive enrollment trends generally provide larger budgets for staffing, research, collegial travel, and other faculty needs. That enrollments have both influenced and reflected the state of Germanics in the United States is nothing new. But, if tomorrow's faculty members in Germanics are not provided some solid packaging and marketing techniques for their subject matter and some practical experience in public relations techniques as part of today's graduate programs, it is entirely possible that Germanics as such will continue to lose its audience and eventually fade away. Van Cleve and Willson observed in 1993 that "pragmatism is alien to the preparation offered most PhD candidates in American Germanics. . . . The transition from graduate study to professional duties is so abrupt as to be debilitating" (32).

Hohendahl points clearly to the possibility of the disappearance of the discipline and stresses the notion that subject-matter excellence is not enough. He writes:

> As part of the humanities, German departments have been targeted for downsizing or even elimination. . . . [S]mall language departments are costly and not productive enough, . . . quality and sophistication are not a guarantee for institutional success. ("How to Read" 4)

During the slightly more than one hundred years since the discipline was formed in this country, it has gone from option to requirement, from banishment during World War I to rejuvenation and subsequent decline, from elective requirement to its present marginalized status. Geoffrey Chaucer recorded the concepts I have discussed here—and the inevitable result of not addressing them directly, of not paying heed—some six hundred years ago in the prologue to the "Nun's Priest's Tale." Like Chaucer's Knight, I too

> . . . take great displeasure
> In tales of those who once knew wealth and leisure
> And then are felled by some unlucky hit.
> But it's a joy to hear the opposite.
> . . .
> Your story then would have been told in vain,
> For, quoting the authorities again,
> "When lecturers find their audiences decrease,
> It does them little good to say their piece." (2771–74, 2799–802)

We have had the enrollment problems presented here on and off for eighty years now. Surely history must teach us that our usual approach of Band-Aids and ointment will no longer suffice—if it ever did. We should have long since fully understood Chaucer's meaning.

Notes

1 See, for example, Clifford Bernd's graphic description of actions against German, Germans, Germany, and German Americans in the state of Ohio during the last years of the Great War. See also the letters from United States Commissioner of Education P. P. Claxon to Robert Slagle, then president of the University of South Dakota (McGlathery, *German* 61–63).

2 The most recent example of such awareness may be found in Simon Richter's editorial in the *Chronicle of Higher Education*, noteworthy because he spells out what he would and would not do to raise enrollments ("Help").

3 Anxiety, even fear, about high school enrollment was expressed more than sixty years later on the AATG online chat site. This statement is not atypical: "I received

a desperate phone call from a teacher in my state asking if the number of students in German is rising, declining, or stabilizing. . . . She told me (her) principal is going to cut the German program in the future because he heard at a principals' conference that the number of students learning German is declining so much as to make it a 'dead' language."

4 See Brod, *Survey* [1974] and *Survey* [1996]; Brod and Huber, "Foreign Language Enrollments" [1992] and "Foreign Language Enrollments" [1997]; Brod and Welles.

5 Illinois (Urbana), Illinois (Chicago), Indiana, Iowa, Michigan, Michigan State, Minnesota, Northwestern, Ohio State, Penn State, Purdue, and Wisconsin compose the educational institutions of the Big Ten. In reality, given the attendance of the University of Chicago, representatives of thirteen institutions normally attend these meetings.

Teacher Development at the Beginning of the Twentieth Century

RENATE A. SCHULZ

A brief look at prevalent modes of preparation and the qualifications of German teachers in the early years of the twentieth century is useful in understanding the problems faced by the profession at that time. For a more thorough review of foreign language (FL) teacher development during the past century, see my essay "Foreign Language Teacher Development."

Numerous articles decried the lack of trained German teachers and the quality of teachers in the field (Broemel; Hepp; Fick, "Erfolgreicher Deutschunterricht"; Busse, "Die Lehrerbildung"). Formal training for German teachers in the schools had been available since 1878, when the Nationales Deutschamerikanisches Lehrerseminar was established by the Lehrerbund in Milwaukee. While J. Eiselmeier reported in 1918 the existence of a number of church-sponsored teacher seminaries during the nineteenth century ("Ein Beitrag"), the Lehrerseminar was the first effort to train bilingual (German-English) teachers for the public schools. Based largely on German models of teacher preparation, the Lehrerseminar offered a four-year curriculum for students who entered the program at the age of sixteen. High school graduates enrolled in a three-year course. An announcement in *Monatshefte* in 1901 informs us that learning how to teach German and English was not the only objective of the Lehrerseminar. It stated that to facilitate the prospective German teachers' assignment, the teacher training curriculum also included physical education ("eine gediegene turnerische Ausbildung"), which would enable the teachers to teach gymnastics according to the German system ("Nationales Deutschamerikanisches Lehrerseminar" 252). We are also told that the connection of the Lehrerseminar with the teacher training institution of the North American Athletics Association (Turnerbund) facilitated this task.

The minutes of the twenty-ninth annual meeting of the Lehrerbund ("Verhandlungen") provide insight into the assessment procedures used to certify prospective German teachers after the three-year curriculum of the Lehrerseminar. The written part of the exit examination consisted of a German essay, a test of German literature, an English essay, and a test of English literature and mathematics. Unspecified oral tests were administered in physiology, biology, geometry, psychology, pedagogy, history of pedagogy, world history, and German and English grammar. Students apparently also had to present a lesson in the Musterschule, attached to the Lehrerseminar, to demonstrate their teaching ability, but pedagogical or general professional knowledge was not tested. The various assessments were administered and evaluated by a committee of representatives of the Lehrerbund. The 1899 minutes noted that 17 of the 19 students who presented themselves for the exam received their *Lehrerzeugnis* ("teacher certificate"), including three teachers for the kindergarten level. Graduation from the institution was considered by several states as equivalent preparation to graduation from a normal school. The Lehrerseminar did not have large enrollments, however, and was far from able to meet the demand for qualified German teachers for American schools. During World War I, the Lehrerseminar was renamed the National Teachers Seminary, but it closed its doors in 1919.

With the notable exception of training provided by the Lehrerseminar, the general state of teacher development around the turn of the twentieth century is summarized by Eiselmeier, who in 1902 remarked that in the field of American education at large there was no area that demonstrated more chaotic conditions than teacher training ("Der amerikanische Volksschullehrerstand" 224). John Weigel noted as late as 1916, "One of the most obvious defects in American education is the lack of proper agencies for the training and equipment of teachers" (16). Using statistics of the National Education Association for 1900, Eiselmeier pointed out that the 306 teacher training colleges (normal schools) that existed during that year together with "normal departments" (i.e., education departments) in other postsecondary institutions were far from able to fill the nation's demand for qualified teachers. He estimated that 75% of entering teachers came without any professional training. He also estimated that the average elementary and middle school teacher stayed in the profession for only 3.5 years, mainly because of low salaries, lack of social benefits, and lack of security of employment. The average annual salary for the seven-month-long school year in 1890 was $332.59 for male teachers and $281.68 for female teachers—considerably less than the pay for laborers in factories or individuals practicing a trade and also less than teachers were paid in Germany or Great

Britain. Since teaching did not pay enough to support a family, the large majority (70%) of teachers were women. A report of the test results of the 1904 graduating class of the Lehrerseminar ("26. Generalversammlung" 222) noted regretfully the sparse representation of males among its graduates. B. Kuttner explained why women, moreover, did not last long in the teaching profession:

> Under normal circumstances, it cannot be a woman's goal or wish to raise, forever, the children of strangers. Nature has predetermined her for other accomplishments. It gave her the role of loving wife, advisor to her husband, tender mother, and teacher *of her own* children. If she is offered the opportunity to follow the man of her choice, she willingly flees the scene of activity she dislikes, and finds more satisfaction in the new sphere of life, if harmony of the heart blesses their union, than the chalk dust of the classroom could ever offer her. ("Die berufliche . . . Stellung" 90–91)

The MLA's Committee of Twelve had already in 1898 provided some guidelines for the preparation of FL teachers (Rosenstengel). But these specified only their desired linguistic and literary knowledge and made no mention of pedagogical training. Eiselmeier insisted that the training of German teachers must include "methods of teaching modern languages, and a sufficient amount of practice teaching." He also felt the need for a certain amount of "Germanization," by which he apparently meant "a sympathetic attitude which enables [the teacher] to appreciate the valuable cultural elements which German possesses. Antagonistic and critical inclinations toward German life must be eliminated" ("Training" 6).

In those states that had some form of teacher licensing, blanket licensing was customary—that is, teachers were expected to be able to teach any subject for which there was need. Being of German heritage or knowing German (either because one had native-speaker competence or because one had studied the language in some way) was often a sufficient qualification for being hired as a German teacher in the schools. In 1909, H. H. Fick described the hiring process of German teachers in Erie, Pennsylvania, as follows: "When a new German teacher is needed, some one with a German name is chosen and sent to some of the best German teachers with the instruction to observe their methods of teaching" ("Erfolgreicher Deutschunterricht" 236). Ten years earlier, G. F. Broemel indicated that even language competence was not always a prerequisite for being hired, if the candidate for the teaching position was "a client of a man whose political influence [was] great" (16) or if the candidate was a friend or relative of a member of the school board.

Robert Di Donato, who described FL teacher training around the turn of the century, pointed out that teachers of modern languages were constantly criticized for incompetence but that little was done to improve their training.

Already in 1900 Joseph Krug tried to refute the apparently common accusation of teacher incompetence, explaining that teachers (at least in Cleveland) were practically all graduates from a two-to-four-year curriculum in a normal college and that the admissions criteria of normal colleges were generally stricter than those of liberal arts colleges. Discussing the urgent need for continuing in-service development, he criticized the fact that FL teachers in secondary schools usually had to teach two other subject areas and that, because of low salaries, male teachers in particular were forced to give private lessons to ensure their families' material survival.

In 1916, Weigel described efforts at the Universities of Wisconsin, Texas, and Chicago, as well as at Columbia University, to develop teacher-training curricula, which start to resemble those offered today, including language-specific methods instruction, directed observation, and practice teaching. His description of a German methods course listed many components that are used today. His report that a course entitled The Teaching of German in Secondary Schools attracted 57 teachers during the summer of 1915 indicates that teachers certainly saw a need for in-service development. Strikingly, predating by seventy years recommendations made by the Holmes Group (*Tomorrow's Teachers*), Weigel proposed a fifth-year graduate teacher-training program for certification.

A report of a national survey conducted in the spring of 1916 gives an overview of the state of German teacher preparation in the United States (Jenny). The survey aimed to discover the number of German teachers in high schools, the teachers' cultural and linguistic heritage, their academic training, and how many of them had studied abroad. Of the 764 schools contacted, 586 (77%) responded, providing information on 1,464 teachers of German. Although the results of the survey differed widely depending on geographic region, an overall summary of the results indicated that 12% of the teachers were German-born, 41% were of German heritage, 85% held the BA degree, 19% had been trained in normal schools, 13% had both college and normal training, 20% held advanced (mostly master's) degrees, and 30% had studied in Germany, with 12.5% having spent at least one year in that country.

Only one contribution in the early years of *Monatshefte* addressed the preparation of college teachers. Stating that teachers needed to be prepared to teach everything that contributes to the understanding of German life, H. C. G. von Jagemann provided an early definition of what in the 1970s was to become German studies. Among the academic qualifications he listed a high degree of literary knowledge, language competence, and such well-developed translation skills that a translated version of a text would elicit the identical thoughts and feelings as the original. In addition, he included in his qualifications familiarity with children's and popular literature and a thorough exposure to German cultural history and *Landeskunde* (knowledge about everyday behavioral patterns). He also prescribed a lengthy stay in Germany, at least for the American-born teacher.

If the general state of FL teacher education at the beginning of the twentieth century sounds dismal, it appears that German teachers were, however, among the better trained. In 1920, W. R. Price commented regretfully on the loss of many German teachers due to the practical elimination of German in American high schools during World War I. He maintained that before the war, 75% of New York secondary students had studied German and that "German was the best taught of all foreign languages in the State of New York" (346). After World War I, when German was reintroduced in the schools, German teachers had apparently lost their lead in superior qualifications. A 1935 survey, conducted by Clifford Parker in New Hampshire, revealed that German teachers reported an average number of only 2.6 years of language study. The only group of teachers reporting fewer years of study were Spanish teachers, with an average of 1.87 years.

The Modern Foreign Language Study, which was started in 1924, investigated the status of FL teacher preparation, including entry-level requirements, required courses, and available diplomas, as well as state and city requirements governing the hiring of teachers. It also looked at years of teaching experience and the percentage of teachers who had resided abroad. The 1929 report of the study, *The Training of Teachers in the Modern Foreign Languages* (Purin) "revealed conditions nothing less than shocking" (Freeman, "What Constitutes" 294).

Neither the National Defense Education Act, which supported "the greatest mass re-training of language teachers in the history of American education" (Cioffari 62) during the 1960s, nor the President's Commission on Foreign Language and International Studies (*Strength through Wisdom*), which determined in 1979 that "the decline in foreign language enrollments is in large measure a response to poor instruction" (13), led to lasting, large-scale improvements in FL teacher preparation and certification.

Teacher development remains a crucial area of concern. FL teacher development and certification procedures are far from unified (Kleinsasser; Schulz, "Foreign Language Teacher Development"), and many of the issues discussed earlier still plague us today. Part of the problem is that too many teachers of German have only a minor in the language, that too many need to teach subjects other than German to stay employed (Schulz, "Profile") and thus simply do not have the time to stay current in language and cultural developments. Also, the move to German studies, and the laudable intent to make departmental courses more accessible to a broader audience by teaching courses in English, may exacerbate the problem, as it limits the opportunities of prospective German teachers to hone their language skills. The importance of extensive language practice is brought home by the results of a study of prospective Spanish teachers; the study showed that those students who indicated that all or most of their courses had been taught in Spanish showed higher success rates on an oral proficiency test than those who indicated that many of their courses were taught in English (Pino).

Although the training of high-quality teachers is an essential strategy for professional survival, few university German departments consider teacher development a priority. Even though a number of survey studies demonstrate that FL teachers prefer courses in language and culture to general education courses for in-service development, few departments make such in-service development options available. While the efforts at setting standards for both learners (*Standards* [1996]) and teachers (Schulz et al.) are to be welcomed, their impact is as yet uncertain, particularly since they are not mandatory and the profession is reluctant to assess formally whether the recommended standards are being met. German departments, and FL departments in general, are reluctant to certify the language competence of prospective FL teachers through any formal evaluation procedures, be they locally developed or standardized, since rigorous standards or rigorous assessment may hurt enrollments and further discourage people from selecting the study of German as major field or teaching as a career option.

Textbooks

CORA LEE KLUGE

An inquiry into American textbooks for the teaching of German language, literature, and culture is an essential part of any investigation into German studies in the United States. These texts reflect pedagogical fashions and practices in American education. Their nature has been dictated, at least to some extent, by the existing structures of German studies curricula, and they, in turn, have played a role in defining courses, course sequences, and even entire programs. In addition, they reveal fluctuations and vicissitudes in the field of German studies, such as those caused by the political situation of the United States vis-à-vis Germany, and they show how Germanists attempted to secure and preserve their position in the American educational system. Beyond this, one hopes that the textbooks reflect literary and cultural traditions in Germany. They have helped mediate perceptions of Germany and its traditions and people to Americans, and they provide one of the essential keys to any analysis of the changing image of Germany in this country. Therefore, textbook writers, editors, and publishers, for better or for worse, have played a major role that goes beyond educational practices or shaping American Germanics into what it is today.

When this report refers to German textbooks, it means those texts intended for teaching German as a foreign language. It attempts to exclude texts used in schools where the language of instruction was German, though admittedly many such books were published in America through the years. Pupils or students enrolled in these schools presumably came from German or German

American backgrounds and were not attempting to learn the language beginning with the basics.

It is not easy to investigate German textbooks, as only scattered information exists. The primary materials on which such an investigation could be based have not even been assembled. There is no complete list of the texts, and there is no depository with a complete inventory. The only attempt to gather such materials is the Frances Ellis Collection of North American German Textbooks, housed in the Special Collections of the Memorial Library at the University of Wisconsin, Madison. The approximately 440 volumes that made up the core of the collection came to Wisconsin after the death in 1981 of its original assembler, Frances H. Ellis (PhD, Univ. of Wisconsin, 1940, and long-time professor of German at Indiana University, Bloomington). Since then the number of textbooks has grown, largely through private and departmental donations; the collection now numbers over 1,100 cataloged items, some 850 of which are listed in a preliminary catalog published in 1998 (Dillon, Hinrichsen, and Lindquist); more still have not been cataloged. This report relies heavily on the materials and data available in the Ellis Collection.

First, a word of caution: the Ellis Collection has shortcomings beyond its incompleteness, and the picture that emerges is thus unavoidably skewed. A disproportionate number of the texts included in the collection are those published by large national publishers, and the writers and editors of these texts were often educators at American colleges or universities. No effort was made to exclude other texts; rather, the predominance of these texts probably results from the simple fact that more of them were printed and sold. In all likelihood, they had greater and more widespread influence. Nevertheless, there were large numbers of texts published by local publishers for use in a particular state or even community, and many of the writers and editors were high school rather than college teachers. One such text that did find its way to the collection illustrates how interesting these local texts can be because of their particularity. Entitled *Buchstabir- und Lesebuch: Zum ersten Unterricht der Kinder* and printed in 1872 "in Amana im St. Iowa," it indicates what kind of elementary instruction in German was given to Amana children of that time. Incidentally, this text was meant for pupils with some native knowledge of the German language. An inkling of the quantity and type of materials that are not adequately represented in the Ellis Collection—but that were an important part of the German textbook scene—can be found by checking *Monatshefte*, particularly in the years before 1928, when it appeared under the auspices of the teachers academy known as the Nationales Deutschamerikanisches Lehrerseminar in Milwaukee, Wisconsin, first under the title *Pädagogische Monatshefte* and later under the title *Monatshefte für deutsche Sprache und Pädagogik*. Advertisements and book reviews published there mention many textbooks prepared by schoolteachers for use in their local elementary and high school classes.

The focus of the Ellis Collection is on North American imprints prior to 1970. Different editions of what is basically the same text as well as variant states of the same edition are included in the collection. The statistical data given here may be affected by this redundancy, despite attempts to avoid misleading statements. The oldest texts listed in the preliminary catalog are two from the 1850s; the most recent are two from the 1970s. For all practical purposes, the collection has not yet been cataloged beyond the year 1970. Fully 75% of the texts in the published catalog were published between 1900 and 1949, just over 8% were published in the 1890s, and just over 8% were published in the 1950s. The number of texts published in the various decades reflects more what has been donated than what was actually published, to be sure; still, these numbers are of interest and may give some indication of what was available. For example, we note the following distribution for the decades of the first half of the twentieth century: 169 texts in the 1900s, 132 in the 1910s, 56 in the 1920s, 179 in the 1930s, 99 in the 1940s. There are few texts from the 1920s in comparison with the other decades; furthermore, 40 (nearly three-fourths) of those from the 1920s were published in the final three years of the decade, 6 of them reprintings of texts with earlier copyrights. These numbers reflect what is known about the crippling, nearly fatal blows dealt German programs in the years following World War I and their only gradually successful efforts at rebuilding.

The earliest texts for learning German in America were published in Europe. These include Benedictus Beiler's *A New German Grammar, to Which Are Added Some Useful and Familiar Dialogues* (London, 1731), Bachmair's *A Complete German Grammar* (England, ca. 1750); Christian Ludwig's *Dictionary of High Dutch and English* (originally published in Leipzig in 1745); and George H. Nöhden's grammar text and reader, commonly used in England and mentioned in the United States in the 1820s. Charles (Karl) Follen, who taught German at Harvard beginning in 1825, compiled a *Deutsches Lesebuch für Anfänger* (1826) and wrote a *Practical Grammar of the German Language* (1828) for his students. These texts, possibly the first American imprints among German textbooks, were followed by two works put together by Hermann Bokum: *An Introduction to the Study of the German Language* and *Bernays' Compendious German Grammar*, both published in Philadelphia in 1832. The 1850s saw the appearance of Heinrich Gottfried Ollendorff's *Grammar and Exercises* and *Reader*, Bernard Rölker's *Reader*, Emil Otto's *Conversational Grammar*, and Franz Ahn's *Complete Method of the German Language*.[1]

An investigation of the early textbooks confirms our ideas, long acknowledged, about how German was taught in this period. Grammar was basic, translation exercises were mandatory, and the goal of the program was to learn to read. This standard grammar-translation method, no matter what its specific twists (described in introductions to various texts from the period as the analytic, synthetic, deductive, inductive, verb-key, and writing-reading [*schreib-lese*] methods), depended on "theoretical" grammar descriptions and then application of the theory to the "practical" task of reading German texts. Success in reading was demonstrated by the ability to translate into English. Traditionally, and not only in this earliest period, college German programs prescribed a basic grounding in grammar in the first year, followed by second-year and third-year reading courses. High school programs were structured the same way but proceeded at a slower pace.

Early beginning texts tried to be all-inclusive and to facilitate rapid progress. Thus the oldest text in the Ellis Collection, W. H. Woodbury's *A New Method of Learning the German Language: Embracing Both the Analytic and Synthetic Modes of Instruction: Being a Plain and Practical Way of Acquiring the Art of Reading, Speaking, and Composing German* (New York: Ivison, Blakeman, and Co., 1855), presents grammar paradigms, translation exercises from German to English and vice versa, reading exercises, and a vocabulary section. The "speaking" part of the program would not result in anything approaching conversational fluency. This text was to be followed by his *Elementary German Reader*, whose third edition is in the Ellis Collection (New York: Ivison and Phinney [and numerous other publishers], 1857 [c. 1853]). The reader contains short selections from "the best sources," texts that would be far too difficult for students at this stage of their career, including pieces from Goethe's *Wilhelm Meister*, Humboldt's *Kosmos*, and Kant's *Allgemeine Naturgeschichte*. To assist the student, there are a full vocabulary in the back of the book and a profusion of footnoted references throughout to sections of the grammar text (20–30 such references on a typical page); notes and aids for practically every word abound and, according to the author of the text, "almost every kind of grammatical difficulty is obviated" (p. 3). Similarly, Franz Ahn's *New Practical and Easy Method of Learning the German Language: With Pronunciation by J. C. Oehlschlager* (rev. ed., New York: E. Steiger, 1869) contains a practical part, consisting of translation exercises from German to English and English to German and a German reader (which includes a Grimm fairy tale, poetry, and a scene from Schiller's *Wilhelm Tell*), followed by a theoretical part, consisting of grammar paradigms.

At the beginning of the twentieth century, another important beginning text appeared—one that spawned a number of books of exercises designed to be used with it. This was B. J. Vos's *Essentials of German* (New York: Henry Holt, 1903), the fourth, revised edition of which (1914) is in the Ellis Collection. Vos's lessons contained grammar explanations, vocabulary, German text(s) with questions, a drill exercise, and English sentences to translate into German. As a professor of German (at Johns Hopkins and later Indiana University), Vos was concerned with pedagogical questions: in the preface to the fourth edition he states that beginning lessons have been shortened, that less is taken for granted in the way of grammar terminology, and that the lesson on the strong verb has been delayed until after the treatment of the adjective. Since that time, the order of presentation of material has of course continued to be a matter of debate.

The largest category of textbooks in the Ellis Collection—approximately 60%—is literary texts intended for the purpose of teaching reading skills and German literature. It is difficult to distinguish between the various levels for which the texts were meant, but some books contain more assistance, such as vocabulary lists or exercises, and are obviously directed toward students and their teachers who are proceeding at a slower pace, while others merely provide introductions to the literary works themselves.

There were educators who made a career of writing and editing such texts, a champion among whom was Wilhelm Bernhardt, longtime teacher and director of German instruction in the high schools of Washington, DC; 23 editions of his can be found in the collection. But it should be noted that a number of the leading American Germanists of the twentieth century also devoted time to the preparation of reading texts: Karl J. R. Arndt (Louisiana State, Clark), William Herbert Carruth (Kansas, later president of Stanford), A. R. Hohlfeld (Vanderbilt, Wisconsin), Victor Lange (Princeton), B. Q. Morgan (Wisconsin, Stanford), Eduard Prokosch (Texas, Wisconsin, Yale), Walter Silz (Ohio State), and others. In addition, members of the German Department at the University of Wisconsin worked together to produce aids for teaching German literature, such as the *Wortindex zu Goethes* Faust by A. R. Hohlfeld, Martin Joos, and W. F. Twaddell (Madison: U of Wisconsin, 1940) and the *German-English Vocabulary to Lessing's* Emilia Galotti (Madison: U of Wisconsin, 1941).

The textbook authors and editors were not in agreement on what kinds of texts would best serve their students' needs: entire short texts or selections from longer ones? easier texts, which could be read in quantity, or more difficult ones, which could be studied in depth? Often enough, however, it seems that neither the importance of the author and work involved nor pedagogical considerations carried the most weight when editors chose what to present; rather, it was a text's real or supposed popularity with students. Thus a strange and eclectic group of texts became available in one edition after another. Arranged in order of quantity in the Ellis Collection, works by Goethe are at the top of the list (with a total of 35), followed by Schiller (33), Theodor Storm (26), Paul Heyse (19), Gustav Freytag (17), Wilhelm Hauff (13), Gotthold Ephraim Lessing (11), Gottfried Keller and Ernst von Wildenbruch (each with 10), and Rudolf Baumbach and Friedrich Gerstäcker (each with 9). *Hermann und Dorothea* is Goethe's most frequently named work, while *Wilhelm Tell* is Schiller's. By far the most frequently represented among all works of German literature is Storm's sentimental *Immensee;* the collection contains 16 copies of this work, at least 12 of which were prepared by separate editors or editorial partnerships. The next two works in popularity are Gerstäcker's *Germelshausen* and Heyse's love story *L'Arrabbiata*. Surprisingly, the appeal of these three texts was not a passing fashion: textbook editions of *Immensee* appeared with great regularity at the rate of about two editions per decade between 1890 and 1947, while new editions of *Germelshausen* appeared from 1900 to 1947 and of *L'Arrabbiata* from 1896 to 1933. *Germelshausen*, virtually unknown in Germany, made its way into popular American culture, inspiring the musical *Brigadoon*, the first big hit of Frederick Loewe and Alan Jay Lerner, which opened in 1947 and was followed by a film version in 1954.

The image of Germany that long prevailed (and perhaps still prevails) in America was part of the legacy of these German readers. This image is often that of the fairy-tale landscape. Traditional as well as modern fairy tales are frequently the fare (including those of the Grimm Brothers and a number by Rudolf Baumbach and Ernst von Wildenbruch). The Black Forest (in stories by Emil Frommel), the Thuringian Forest (in stories by Baumbach), and the mountains of Austria's Styria (in stories by P. K. Rosegger) are the settings in one reader after another. Clair Hayden Bell's edition of Felix Salten's *Bambi: Eine Lebensgeschichte aus dem Walde*, with illustrations by Kurt Wiese (Boston: D. C. Heath and Co., 1932)—undoubtedly the major source for Walt Disney's movie by the same title—is moralistic, woodsy, and typical of many of the texts beginning German students were reading.

Beginning in the late 1920s, however, a new group of textbooks came onto the market containing selections from more recent literature. These included William Diamond and Frank H. Reinsch's *Nachlese: Easy Short Stories from Contemporary German Literature* (New York: Henry Holt, 1927), William Diamond and Bernhard A. Uhlendorf's *Mitten im Leben: Short Stories from Contemporary German Literature* (New York: Henry Holt, 1928), C. H. Handschin's *Elf neue Erzählungen* (New York: Prentice Hall, 1930), Ewald Paul Appelt and Erich Funke's *Modern German Prose: Short Stories by Ten Representative Authors* (Boston: D. C. Heath, 1936), Ernst R. Dodge and Margaret H. Viereck's *Etwas Neues* (New York: American Book, 1936), Margaret Jeffrey and Johanna E. Volbehr's *Zwölf Dichter der Gegenwart* (New York: Henry Holt, 1937), and Ruth Buka's *Learning German from Modern Authors* (New York: Macmillan, 1939). Some of the authors represented were Hermann Bahr, Hans Carossa, Marie von Ebner-Eschenbach, Gerhart Hauptmann, Thomas Mann, Rainer Maria Rilke, Arthur Schnitzler, Hermann Sudermann, and Ludwig Thoma. Not all these texts contained selections of literary value; in fact, Charles Handschin even states that one of the authors is of "no significance as a literary man," but he argues that "it is believed that greater amounts should be read than was formerly the practice in this country" (*Elf* v). These texts nevertheless went a long way toward correcting the image of Germany presented earlier, by adding a more modern dimension.

Though far fewer in number than the literary reading texts in the Ellis Collection and constituting just less than 5% of the total, an interesting group that could be classified as texts for the study of culture or *Landeskunde* (all cultural, social, political, and economic aspects of a nation) follows a similar historical development. Earlier examples of this category present descriptions and photographs of the Rhine River, medieval castles, folk costumes, and picturesque farmhouses, without balancing this view with other realities of modern Germany. These books include texts such as Paul Valentine Bacon's *Im Vaterland* (Boston: Allyn and Bacon, 1910) and Philip Schuyler Allen's *An den Ufern des Rheins: Vom Bodensee bis zu den Niederlanden* (New York: Henry Holt, 1917). In the 1930s, new texts began to present a more modern perspective. Ernest R. Dodge and Margaret H. Viereck's *Stimmen aus Deutschland* (New York: Henry Holt, 1934), for example, contains the sections "Das Deutsche Museum in München" and "Neuere deutsche Baukunst"; and Gerhard Baerg's *Deutschland: Kulturlesebuch mit Übungen* (New York: Henry Holt, 1938) emphasizes the power and modernity of the German transportation system and has photographs of buildings such as the Reichsgericht and the Deutsche Bücherei in Leipzig.

Writers of culture texts were aware that Germany's rapidly changing political situation might quickly render their offerings dated, and they employed various means to deal with the problem. One method was to concentrate on older periods or even on ancient German culture, beginning with the Germanic tribes and the Germanic gods, and more or less to ignore the current situation. Otto Siegfried Fleissner and Else Mentz Fleissner's *Deutschland von heute und gestern: Ein Lesebuch der deutschen Volkskunde* (New York: F. S. Crofts, 1934 [c. 1930]), for example, deals with the land, the sagas, and customs and traditions, among other things, mentioning Hitler only briefly at the end of a chapter entitled "Vom Kaiserreich zur Republik." Similarly, Emil L. Jordan's *Deutsche Kulturgeschichte im Abriß* (New York: Appleton-Century-Crofts, 1937, 2nd printing 1940), ends with 1933, since, as the author states, "the political, economic, and cultural development of central Europe is far from settled" (p. vi), and Walter Gehl's *Lebensbilder aus der deutschen Geschichte* (ed. Paul H. Curts [New York: Harper and Brothers, 1939]) concludes for all practical purposes with the beginning of rebuilding after World War I.

There were texts that went a little further in dealing with recent events. Handschin, in his *Introduction to German Civilization: An Outline* (New York: Prentice Hall, 1937), involves himself with current issues, in one section defending the Nazi Party against recent charges that it is "antagonistic to the Church and devoted to a new pagan cult" (p. 121). William Hubben, Wilhelm R. Gaede, and Karl Reuning take on another current topic in their text *Die deutsche Jugendbewegung* (New York: Cordon, 1937), namely, the development and nature of the Hitler Youth.

Historically oriented works of the 1930s, such as Handschin's English-language *Introduction to German Civilization* (mentioned above), which was intended as a supplement to German courses to correct a "defect in much

modern language instruction," namely, "that it affords no systematic knowledge of foreign civilizations" (n.p.), led to a new category of more-com-
prehensive texts for studying literature and culture that flourished after the
end of World War II. Thus Robert Lohan, dissatisfied with his students' erron-
eous notion "that German literature has reached its peak in *Immensee . . . L'Arrabiata* [sic] . . . and perhaps Mr. Slezak's *Sämtliche Werke*" (p. 5), presented his
Living German Literature (vol. 1, 3rd ed. [New York: Frederick Unger, 1946]), a
history of German literature in German containing selections of major texts
and marginal notes, with chapters on the Middle High German period, the
sixteenth century, the seventeenth century, and the *Blütezeit* ("the flowering,"
Klopstock through Schiller). These texts foreshadowed later and even more
comprehensive collections such as Kurt F. Reinhardt's two-volume *Germany:
2000 Years* (New York: Frederick Ungar, 1950, 2nd ed. 1961).

World War II had one major impact on the teaching of German as a foreign
language in America. Aware of a need for people who could communicate orally
in foreign languages, the United States in 1942 established the Army Specialized
Training Program and began training both military and civilian students in
intensive courses. In this program, linguists, whose challenge was to teach their
students to speak, employed methods very different from those in traditional
grammar texts, which had been used primarily to help students learn to read.
The irony, incidentally, of America's needing speakers of German in World War
II, less than a quarter of a century after America did all it could to prohibit
the German language at the time of World War I, should not escape even casual
observers.

This new emphasis on oral work was quickly reflected in textbooks available for general use. One such text is *Spoken German* by Jenni Karding Moulton
and William G. Moulton (Linguistic Soc. of Amer., 1944, republished by Henry
Holt, 1948) and another is Helmut Rehder and Freeman Twaddell's *German*
(New York: Henry Holt, 1947). The mimicry-memorizing (mim-mem) method
quickly became the rage; conversation was the basis of the program, and students were urged not to let the printed word get in the way of their learning.
Since that time, spoken German has remained an unquestioned and integral
part of the language instruction program, and the grammar-translation method
has been put aside for all but those students who desire only a reading
knowledge.

A number of cultural texts from the years immediately following World
War II fail entirely to reflect the realities of the new European situation, perhaps
because of uncertainty about the long-range stability of the postwar status quo.
Instead, these texts present a Germany of the past and thus seem oddly dated,
at least in hindsight. Josef K. L. Bihl's *German One: A Cultural Approach* (Boston:
Houghton Mifflin, 1949), for example, features a map in its frontispiece that
shows none of the new borders. Indeed, in a conversation in lesson 4 of this

textbook, the teacher explains the difference between *Deutschland*, which is termed "der geographische Namen," and *das Deutsche Reich* [!], which is termed "der politische Namen" (p. 35). Worse yet is Bihl's *In deutschen Landen* (Boston: Houghton Mifflin, 1953), which, despite its publication date and although it purports to be a "cultural geography primer" (p. v), with information about areas such as Thuringia, Saxony, and even Silesia, contains no mention of the postwar situation, including the existence of the German Democratic Republic—except in a table in the back (p. 202).

Similarly, reading texts from the period immediately after World War II tend to present only prewar selections, thereby avoiding fascism, the war experience, and other problems of recent history. For example, *Allerlei Menschen*, edited by Paul H. Curts and Frank H. Reinsch (New York: Henry Holt, 1949), a collection picked as being "best suited for classroom use" (n.p.), includes works by Ludwig Thoma, Herrmann Bahr, Peter Rosegger, Marie von Ebner-Eschenbach, and Jakob Wassermann. A refreshingly different approach was taken by *Deutsche erleben die Zeit*, by Hanna Hafkesbrink and Rosemary Park (Boston: Houghton Mifflin, 1949, 2nd ed. 1956); supported by a grant from the Rockefeller Foundation, it contains authentic German texts dealing with the political situation in Germany, the two World Wars, the resistance movement, and so on, all of which were written between 1928 and 1946. Even more successful in modernizing the reading fare, at least in terms of sheer numbers, was *Aus unserer Zeit* by Ian C. Loram and Leland Phelps (New York: Norton, 1956, 1965, 1972, 1988), whose stories representing "writers and literary trends of twentieth-century German literature" (from the preface to the first edition) were read by many generations of students.

Financial aspects of the textbook industry are a fascinating part of this topic and worthy of further study. The publishers whose texts are most numerous in the Ellis Collection are, in descending order: Heath, Henry Holt (later Holt, Rinehart and Winston), Ginn, the American Book Company, Crofts, Oxford University Press, Prentice Hall, and Macmillan. To learn which publishers realized large profits from the sale of textbooks for German, one would have to access their business records—no easy task. Another part of this picture, of course, is the additional earnings available to teachers of German through sales of successful texts. Without a doubt, this source of income could be significant in individual cases.

By the late 1960s, the number of American textbooks for the study of German had begun to decrease, at least in part because of the widespread availability of textbooks published in Germany for the study of German by foreigners. The Max Hueber Verlag of Munich with its series Sprachen der Welt was well represented in the American market, with titles such as *Deutsche Sprachlehre für Ausländer*, by Heinz Griesbach and Dora Schulz (1955, 1967); the two-volume collection *Deutsche Erzählungen*, edited by Linde Klier and Uwe Martin (vol. 1, 1963; vol. 2, 1965); and the ten volumes of *Geschäfts- und Verhand-lungssprache Deutsch*, by Hans Wolfgang Wolff (1974–77), which were designed specifically for business German courses. One must mention also the publications of the Langenscheidt Verlag (Berlin, Munich, Vienna, Zürich, and New York), the Klett Verlag with its series Klett Edition Deutsch, and the publications of InterNationes.

A reduction in foreign language requirements and thus a decline in enrollments have become a fact of life in recent years, and since the mid-1970s at the very latest, publishers have foreseen a lack of profitability and therefore shown little interest in German texts for any level beyond the first or second year. This lack of interest has led to a deplorable shortage of texts for upper-level students and majors. Teachers must now prepare the kinds of questions, footnotes, handouts, and assignments for their classes that used to be readily available in good textbooks. At the same time, the availability of photocopy machines and, more recently, the Internet has had an effect that goes beyond the scope of this article, and it will continue to alter the situation in ways that teachers of this generation cannot fathom.

There exists no corpus of secondary literature on the topic of American textbooks for the study of German. Further information on very limited parts of this topic is available in articles published in *Teaching German in America: Prolegomena to a History* (Benseler, Lohnes, and Nollendorfs). Renate A. Schulz's contribution to that volume describes historical developments in foreign language pedagogy that support and parallel portions of my account (see her "Methods").

Note

1 See Zeydel's "The Teaching of German in the United States from Colonial Times through World War I." Originally part of *Reports of Surveys and Studies in the Teaching of Modern Foreign Languages*, published by the MLA in 1961, it was reprinted in the *German Quarterly* in 1964 and again in *Teaching German in America: Prolegomena to a History* (Benseler, Lohnes, Nollendorfs).

American Graduate Studies in German

SIMON RICHTER

Formal graduate studies in the United States date back to 1870 and the inauguration of Harvard's graduate school and to Johns Hopkins University, founded in 1876. The first PhD in Germanic languages and literatures was conferred in 1879 by Cornell, to Waterman T. Hewett ("The Frisian Language and Literature"), and in German literature proper in 1886 by Columbia, to Hugo J. Walther ("The Syntax of Cases in Walther von der Vogelweide") (Rosenberg 35). The first Hopkins doctorate in German was granted to Marion Dexter Learned, later professor of the University of Pennsylvania, in 1887 for a study on Pennsylvania German (Zeydel, "Teaching . . . through World War I" 45), although John Dewey's 1884 dissertation "The Psychology of Kant" (Rosenberg 35) narrowly predates that of Learned and already raises the question of the definition of German studies that has preoccupied American Germanists for the last thirty years.

A historical investigation of graduate studies in German (Germanics, *Germanistik*, or German studies) at American universities might proceed from a variety of documentary sources. Statistical breakdowns of dissertation titles by topic, university, and sex of the author yield interesting insights into scholarly trends and social factors. Analysis of graduate course offerings culled from university bulletins illustrates curricular and academic priorities. The individual recollections of retired and senior professors lend important detail and color. Indeed, since the 1970s American Germanists have been attempting to come to terms with the discipline's history and particularly its relation to German

Germanistik, largely along the lines of intellectual and institutional history (e.g., Benseler, Lohnes, and Nollendorfs; Lohnes and Nollendorfs; Trommler, "Germanistik nicht als Nationalphilologie"). None of these means, however, conveys a sense of the lived experience of graduate studies in German during the last 125 years.

Like childhood, graduate study is both an institution, whose culture changes and varies in response to determining conditions, and a temporary phase, through which thousands have passed, retaining some memories, repressing others. At once a privilege and a period of measured indignity, graduate study has long been a peculiar locus of deferred autonomy, protracted financial and intellectual dependence, and disciplinary submission. The life of graduate students in the field of German has been compounded by the long-standing cultural and intellectual dependence of American *Germanistik* on its German prototype (Lange, "Thoughts" 10 and "History" 10). Even if a history of graduate studies in German cannot directly access this lost experience, questions such as the following should inform any perspective: How did the German cult of the professor ordinarius determine and constrain the social and intellectual life of graduate students? When did graduate students in numbers attain the right to select their own dissertation topics and become proprietors of their ideas? How did women and other minorities in the profession cope in a pervasively white male milieu? In what ways did graduate students come to identify with and perpetuate the authority of their discipline? In what ways did they resist that authority and reshape their discipline?

Graduate study in every discipline in the United States shares a common origin in the German university. The nineteenth-century German university represented the pinnacle of advanced research; its principles of *Lern- and Lehrfreiheit* ("academic freedom") were revolutionary. Between 1815 and 1914 more than ten thousand Americans studied at universities in Berlin, Leipzig, Heidelberg, Halle, Bonn, Munich, and Göttingen, the vast majority in the period after 1850 (Brubacher and Rudy 175). They were attracted by the instructional techniques—the seminar, the lecture, and the laboratory—and the international preeminence of German learning. Among the American students were men such as Daniel C. Gilman, the founder and first president of Johns Hopkins, and Frederick A. P. Barnard, president of Columbia (178). American graduate schools, either newly founded or grafted onto existing universities, were structurally and organizationally modeled on the German university, particularly the one in Berlin, and committed to research in a manner heretofore unknown in the United States. The Johns Hopkins University is the premier example. It "fixed an indelible image of a research-oriented Germany" and "symbolized German research" (Veysey 129).

American emulation of the idea of the German university, however, was not slavish. It tended to be pragmatic and dispensed with the idealist overlay that held sway in Germany. Indeed, a sort of misprision that still attends the unresolvable difference between *Wissenschaft* (a capacious concept almost synonymous with knowledge itself) and *science* (understood as research) allowed Americans to translate an idea of the research university back to the United States that did not strictly correspond to the reality of the German university (125–33). It would remain for American graduate programs in German to cling to the nationalist and ideological elements of German *Wissenschaft*. For much of their history, American graduate programs in German would be the true believers in the methodological and cultural superiority of German *Germanistik*.

In the nineteenth century, the prevailing intellectual model for German studies in Germany and the United States was philology. In the first twenty-five years of graduate studies in the States, an almost equal number of dissertations were written in philology (23) and literature (26), although literature, too, was most frequently approached in a broadly philological manner (Rosenberg 37). In the 1880s, Princeton, for example, had two professors of German, one who taught philology in the School of Arts and a second who taught literature in the School of Sciences. Literature courses gravitated toward the undergraduate curriculum, while philology made up the bulk of graduate studies. In 1912, literature was reincorporated into the graduate curriculum at Princeton (Bottigheimer, "One Hundred and Fifty Years" 86). Despite an even beginning, literary topics continually increased, so that in the period 1931–40 in the United States 276 dissertations were written in literature and 55 in philology (Rosenberg 37). This trend has never been reversed. Philology, for its part, gave way to linguistics in the 1970s (a process that began earlier [Lange, "History" 5]) and in the 1990s also to applied linguistics and second language acquisition.

Of the dissertations in German or Germanic literature recorded between 1873 and 1949 (Rosenberg), 53 focused on the Middle Ages, Reformation, and baroque, with a clear preference for the Middle Ages. Dissertations on the classical literature of the eighteenth century predominated, totaling 153. Eighty-two were written on Goethe, 25 on Schiller, 16 on Herder, 15 on Lessing, 12 on Kleist, and 11 on Wieland. These statistics correspond to the curricular and ideological priorities that prevailed through most of this period. There were 12 dissertations on Tieck and 16 on Heine. Particularly striking for the first half of the twentieth century is the popularity of Hauptmann, with 22 dissertations. The first of these was completed by Martin Schütze in 1899 at the University of Pennsylvania (Rosenberg 40), when Hauptmann was still alive, and may be attributable to Learned's commitment to contemporary literature. But the exception proves the rule for this period—the studied commitment to historical distance and the avoidance of living authors—and Schütze's dissertation must be regarded as an anomaly. As late as 1936, the Indiana University literature curriculum stopped in the mid-nineteenth century with Hebbel and Storm (Remak 176).

The emphasis on Goethe and Schiller in teaching and research dates back to the beginnings of graduate studies in the United States. The curricula at Hopkins and other prominent universities at the turn of the century (Cornell, Harvard, Northwestern, and Wisconsin) focused disproportionately on German classicism (Spuler, *Germanistik* 47–48). As Richard Spuler puts it:

> Classicism was . . . fundamentally construed as the realization of an ideal humanity, of a specifically Germanic *harmonia*. . . . The perceived attributes of German Classicism operated as value-giving norms demanding universal validity—Goethe and Schiller took on superhuman dimensions, and the heritage was mythologized. (150)

But the emphasis on Goethe and Schiller would not hold. Even if graduate curricula themselves remained largely unchanged, reflecting faculty priorities (or intransigence), the 1950s saw a clear shift in the selection of dissertation topics toward the twentieth century. In 1957, 10 dissertations focused on the twentieth century in contrast to 5 for the Enlightenment, classicism, and Romanticism together. In 1968, the ratio was 40:25; in 1978, 30:18; in 1998, 31:16. Students may not in all cases have been autonomous in selecting their precise topic, but they were certainly increasingly able to choose their period and in doing so exerted a slow influence on the graduate curriculum.[1]

Although statistical analyses of dissertation topics reveal largely glacial changes, the graduate curriculum itself may have been even slower to change in its more than 125-year history (Ryder 121–22). For decades a cautious German professoriat clung to works that were considered safe and inoffensive— the two World Wars taught many to tread softly. Generally speaking, curricular transformation and innovation were more likely to be found at the undergraduate level, where the following combination of circumstances prevailed: concerns about enrollment, the desire to respond to nonliterary interests and needs of students, and perhaps the deployment of junior faculty members. At the graduate level, in the period beginning after the World War II, comparative literature departments and other departments regularly laid claim to aspects of German studies that had been gladly relinquished by departments of German (Nietzsche, Freud, Marx, Heidegger, critical theory, hermeneutics, gender studies, and film studies; see Gillespie). By the same token, departments of German resolutely resisted French-inflected American literary, cultural, and feminist theory. Certainly, single graduate programs can be identified that succeeded in integrating these elements into their curriculum and cultivated a cordial relation with comparative literature (e.g., Hopkins, Indiana, Stanford, Wisconsin), often thanks to the stubborn and risk-taking efforts of individual professors.

For the most part, however, change was resisted. The graduate curriculum has also only very slowly and reluctantly given way on the inclusion of women writers in the canon (see Blackwell in this volume). In this instance, individual (women) professors were joined in their efforts by (women) graduate students and aided by the solidarity that expressed itself in the formation of Women in German in 1974.

The sole and partial exception to resistance to curricular change has been the relatively long and vexed engagement with what is variously called German studies, German culture studies, or cultural studies. (One could argue that German film studies has been a part of this complex [see Kaes, "New Historicism"]). Russell Berman states that culture already belonged to the repertoire of Germanists in the late nineteenth and early twentieth centuries ("Concept" 242). As early as 1916, Columbia offered a course in German civilization and culture, and others soon followed. Something akin to *Landeskunde* (area studies) has often been taught as a part of the undergraduate German curriculum. When World War I began, Princeton, for instance, offered the course Study of German Institutions and the course Military German. Ever since the first enrollment debacle resulting from repressive United States anti-German language policies during the period of World War I (to the point of outlawing the teaching and even speaking of German [Zeydel, "Teaching . . . through World War I" 48; C. Nollendorfs, "First World War"]), faculty members have responded in differing degrees to student needs. Since the 1960s and more intensely since the 1970s, many German departments have instituted German studies majors for their undergraduates. A series of individual faculty voices and even whole departments (e.g., Indiana) have called attention to the now well-established lack of coherence between undergraduate curriculum demands and graduate training.

Efforts to modify the graduate curriculum were and continue to be halting, despite the status of some of the faculty publicly calling for change. Faculty members at the University of Wisconsin in conjunction with their long-standing publication of *Monatshefte* have been instrumental in enabling the public discussion. The hesitation may have been due in part to the lack of a compelling intellectual rationale for the study of culture in departments of German. Practical opportunism on the undergraduate level does not justify a wholesale revamping of a time-honored literary graduate curriculum. Literary scholars of a New Critical or philological stamp, already assailed by deconstruction and literary theory generally, did not embrace the "Bloomington model" of German studies as culture studies instituted in the early 1970s (Helbig, "German Studies"). Nonetheless, persistent efforts by scholars, the increasing prominence of the German Studies Association in the mid-1980s, the influence of cultural studies in the United States (linked to Stephen Greenblatt and the new historicism [Kaes, "New Historicism"]) and the United Kingdom (the Birmingham school), as well as the university-wide tendency to think in terms of interdisciplinary fields of study (women's studies, gay and lesbian studies, area studies, etc.) led to a variety of models for graduate programs in German, ranging from the modest incorporation of single courses into the curriculum to complete overhauls. After a century and more of almost total uniformity in the course offerings of graduate programs in the United States, it is refreshing to see some departments willing to take considerable risks in elaborating their versions of a German studies program—two recent examples are Chicago and Michigan. Whether these ventures will succeed is another question. In any case, the prospective graduate student who surfs the World Wide Web in search of suitable graduate programs now encounters a greater diversity of programs and course offerings than ever before.

It was only in the late 1990s that a significant though still not over-whelming number of dissertations were being written in German studies. Basic trends (from an analysis of 1998 and 1999 dissertations in *Monatshefte* 90 [1998] and 91 [1999]) show a continued preference for the twentieth century and especially the first half. Many dissertations are literary in nature but include aspects of cultural studies (race, gender, class) or are interdisciplinary. There is a slight increase in multiple-author studies, though single-author dissertations continue to prevail. In 1999 there was not a single dissertation concerned with Goethe or Schiller. Few dissertations on German film were written in either 1998 or 1999. It is reasonable to assume that the effects of recent programmatic and curricular change will appear more noticeably in the first decade of the twenty-first century.[2]

If there ever was a sea change in graduate German studies, it was in the numbers of women graduate students, the influence of feminism, and the ac-tivism of Women in German. Since the mid-1970s women have formed the majority of graduate students in German (Blackwell, "Turf Management" 273). In 1968, 102 men completed dissertations compared with 30 by women, a ratio of more than 3:1. Ten years later, 50 women took their PhD compared with 43 men. In 1988, the ratio was approximately the same (40 women and 36 men). By 1998, however, the trend had clearly taken hold: 58 women were granted their degrees compared with 36 men. Approximately the same ratio obtains for 1998: 44 women and 30 men. For many of these women, especially in the 1970s and 1980s, graduate study in German entailed confrontation with a patriarchal culture still marked by the ethos of its beginnings. When moral and intellectual support in the departments themselves was in short supply, the newly formed organization Women in German helped foster a strong fem-inist consciousness. From its inception in 1974, Women in German was unique in breaking down the barrier between graduate students and faculty members and was instrumental in transforming the student-professor relationship. As more and more young female PhDs became professors, many departments rewrote their graduate reading lists and revised their curricula to include more women writers (see Blackwell in this volume).

Graduate student matriculations tend to ebb and flow and are often linked to the peaks and valleys of demographic trends (e.g., the baby boom). The Sputnik shock of the 1960s gave a dramatic impulse to graduate studies across the board. German departments, expanding, had to cope with a dearth of young PhDs. In 1961, Edwin Zeydel reported that "larger universities grant, on the average, two or more doctorates each year in Germanics, not enough to satisfy the demand without recourse to Europe" ("Teaching . . . through World War I" 45). But in the last quarter century, the academic job market generally and in German specifically has been depressed with only intermittent flurries of hiring. From time to time, discussions arise concerning the ethics and economics of accepting graduate students in the face of diminished job opportunities. Certainly one of the effects of these public discussions (in the period 1975–85 [Haenicke 258] and again in the second half of the 1990s [see Holub, "Graduate Education"]) has been to decrease further the pool of potential graduate students. In 1979, according to Theodore Ziolkowski's calculations, there were only "68 students who could be said to constitute a truly national applicant pool for Germanics" ("Seventies" 248). Anecdotal evidence from the most recent round of recruiting (for 2000–01) indicates that this worrisome trend continues.

At the beginning of the twenty-first century, graduate students in German enjoy a greater autonomy than at any point in the history of graduate studies in German. The cult of the professor has largely been jettisoned, but so too has the mystique of a lifetime devoted to literature. An honesty-in-advertising approach on the part of recruiting departments usually informs the students of the vicissitudes of an academic career. Competition among universities over the best applicants to graduate school is beginning to resemble the negotiations of a tenure-track job search. The debate continues regarding the status of graduate students: Are they professors in training or employees of the university? The IRS watches with interest because of the tax consequences. Although graduate students in German departments have not been at the forefront of efforts of graduate students (i.e., teaching assistants) at large to affiliate themselves with unions at major state and private universities, they have necessarily been affected by the decisions in individual cases as well as by the discourse.

In the 1990s increasing numbers of students organized graduate student conferences at their institutions, to the point that it became difficult to find a weekend during spring semester when there was not a conference. In the same vein, two significant graduate student publications exist (*Focus on German Studies* at the University of Cincinnati and *New German Review* at UCLA). The ideal curriculum vitae of a recent PhD includes one or two articles, several scholarly presentations, and certification in a supporting area (e.g., women's studies, film studies, second language acquisition, computer instructional technology). In sum, contemporary graduate students are engaged in a process of preprofessionalization. The culture of graduate studies has changed accordingly and differs now, more than ever, from that of its long history.

Notes

1 "Dissertations in Progress" [1949]; "Dissertations in Progress" [1966]; "Doctoral Dissertations, 1977–78"; "Doctoral Dissertations" [1988]; "Doctoral Dissertations" [1998 and 1999].

2 All these statistics have been taken from the "Personalia" issues of *Monatshefte* 1998 and 1999. Analysis of the data (sex of author and dissertation topic) was done as carefully as possible, though there may be a slight margin of error—for example, because of names that are not gender-specific.

German Literary History and the Canon in the United States

JEANNINE BLACKWELL

Most American teachers of German since the 1820s have grappled with finding level-appropriate German classroom texts whose themes and characters present the German national character and culture in a positive, thought-provoking light. Yet deciding which texts meet those social and moral criteria and at the same time meet prevailing aesthetic norms has not been easy. Every decade new texts have been tried, most discarded, a few retained; texts deleted under one set of political circumstances are often reinstated when times change. As the data given in tables 1 and 2 in the appendix show, the publicly presented German canon in America has shifted greatly from about 1820 to 1948 and beyond. It moved from a narrow use of contemporary texts sympathetic to Anglo-American transcendentalism and educational utopianism (c. 1830–80) to a near replication of anthologized texts from the German secondary school system by a growing German American community, 1880–1914 (Zeydel, "Teaching . . . through World War I"; *Report* 618–22). The changes in the canon after 1914 are documented elsewhere in this volume (see the essays by Sammons, Tatlock, Werner): from 1914 to 1945 the canon was subject to the unstable political situation; from 1945 to 1976 texts of traditional *Germanistik*, combined with rediscovered works of the early twentieth century and the Gruppe 47, dominated American reading lists. Since the 1970s, the canon has expanded so drastically that it has atomized, and an established canon no longer exists except in certain "closed" periods like the early medieval and in specialized eras or topics (such as expressionism). Today's academic conferences and much of academic graduate course work feature previously ignored literary constituencies: writers of the former GDR, proletarian and revolutionary authors, women, German Jews, multicultural German writers, gays and lesbians. Also favored are the genres of the popular press, film, song, theater, and critical theory. Many graduate programs, faced with a proliferation of possibilities and new constituencies among their students and faculties, have stopped issuing standardized graduate reading lists altogether.

By compiling a master list from published and unpublished reading lists, proposals from national organizations, and conference proceedings from 1880–1914, 1948, 1983, and 1993, I attempt to quantify which works have actually constituted a German literary canon in America in different epochs. The lists before 1914 are taken from seminaries, advanced high schools, and normal colleges rather than from university graduate reading lists, because these advanced secondary lists were the basis of teacher training in many normal schools and contributed substantially to the German reading canon of the American public and private universities by 1950. Graduate research study in Germanics began in America only after the 1880s and then only for a small part of the German literary audience in America. To highlight certain shifts of text canonization in the post-1945 period, I use reading lists from two sample years in American graduate programs in German.

The first organized classes in German literature, beginning around 1820 to 1830, reflected the tastes and influences of English Romanticism (Coleridge, Carlyle, Sir Walter Scott) and transcendental thought in New England (Margaret Fuller and others) rather than the influence of historical philology in German universities (*Report* 614–15). The interest of the transcendentalists in the sublime and ineffable led them, via Mme de Staël and the English poets, to appreciate fairly modern works by Herder, Goethe, Schlegel, Kant, and certain German Romantics. At the same time, the political republicanism of certain key teachers such as George Ticknor and Karl Follen dictated that idealistic patriotic works by Körner and Schiller should be classroom fare and their own reading canon. The interests of both these groups—the transcendentalists and political republicans—combined for those New Englanders who began to adapt the institutions established by German and Swiss idealistic educators like Emmanuel de Fellenberg, Johann Heinrich Pestalozzi, and later Friedrich Fröbel. The utopian, nature-based education ideal, firmly grounded in Rousseau's and Schiller's writings, found resonance in New England and then elsewhere. Many influential intellectuals made the pilgrimage to see these German and Swiss educational institutions in situ; they visited Göttingen and Weimar as well, establishing Goethe and Schiller by the 1840s as the core of the German intellectual canon in America and the bildungsroman as its privileged genre.

The mass of German political exiles and economic immigrants from 1848 to the 1890s took up the works of Schiller and the patriotic nationalist Romantics as their favored texts as immigration spread west. Simultaneously, the normal schools, land-grant colleges, and seminaries of the Midwest were established and to some extent served the educated members of the emerging immigrant communities. Readings at these schools, which eventually became dominant in German higher education in America, were based on the textbooks and prescribed reading lists of the "Prussian" *Realschule* and *Gymnasium* and the officially approved textbooks of the Second Reich (Dillon, Hinrichsen, and Lindquist; Alwall; for an evaluation of anthologies, see Hohlfeld, "Anthologien"). Although there was some overlap in these Second Reich selected readings with the texts appreciated by the transcendentalists (such as Schiller's *Wallenstein* and Goethe's *Faust*), many Second Reich anthologies were demonstrably more national-patriotic in content than the earlier collections of Follen for his Harvard students. An American controversy from the 1880s to the 1910s related to these two different visions of the German canon: Was the American version of it to be a pedagogical tool for training young readers, many of German heritage, in moral rectitude and German patriotism inspired by German idealism, or should the American canon be an intense intellectual exercise in the sublime in literature, philosophy, and art for an Anglo-American educated elite?

Among the many Germanists who addressed these questions early in the profession were the influential scholars Julius Goebel, Kuno Francke, Alexander Hohlfeld, and Marion D. Learned. For Goebel, German poets of the previous century—that is, since the 1780s, developed "a distinctly modern human ideal, an ideal of culture, which can be made the basis of our higher education" ("German Classics" 158). Learned, president of the MLA in 1910, said the aim of language study was "to inform, inspire, and adapt the technique of the masters to the literary conditions of our land and time for the creation of a lasting immortal literary form"; the teacher's task was to "rear a new race of poets," to create a new "*ars poetica Americana*" ("President's Address" lix). In contrast with this grandiose pedagogical aim, Hohlfeld criticizes the Germans, and the German anthologies he is reviewing in 1912, for their pitiful attempts to claim as great literature "the so-called literary revolution of the 1880s" ("Anthologien" 200), from which anthologizers seek to slap together a modern national aesthetics. For scholars like Hohlfeld, the older works of the de Staël tradition were the heart of the canon, not to be replaced with modernist texts.

Juxtaposed to these opinions of major scholars at the university level stood the assessments of high school and college teachers, many from the Midwest, who considered several canonical German texts inappropriate for American conditions: linguistically too challenging, aesthetically too intricate, and of dubious political or moral worth for younger students. Many of these teachers advocated the careful choice of teachable-length classics, while they insisted on eliminating such perceived trash as the works of Roderich Benedix, Viktor

Blüthgen, Wilhelmine von Hillern, Gustav von Moser, and Heinrich Zschokke (Hänssler 140–41; J. Jones 175–76; cf. Winter 182–83 for a less critical view). Such texts had become part of reading lists because of their inclusion in anthologies for the *Realschule* and *Gymnasium* classroom, but also because of shifts in popular reading tastes among Germans and German American immigrants.

Of greatest concern to most teachers was finding level-appropriate German texts that displayed the Germans positively. *Monatshefte* tried to meet this need by instituting regular features in its "Vermischtes" column for locating such texts (see, e.g., "Was in den Volksbibliotheken") and by listing cheap texts available for the German classroom (see, e.g., "Klassenbibliothek"). Certain issues, displayed in key texts and genres, served as a flashpoint for this debate. Among these are, first, the place of fairy tales, other children's literature, romance, and German stereotypes in the American classroom; second, the purpose of reading classical German texts; and third, the problem of immorality and violence in high art forms, which might also be called grappling with the sublime, with immature readers in mind. One thematic issue continues over these hundred years: What aspects of the true Germany should we, as the purveyors of German culture in America, display, advocate, or criticize?

A gathering of seven nationally published reading lists from 1884 to 1911 shows the shift from the high artistic aim of the earlier nineteenth century to the pragmatics of textbooks. With one notable exception, Horatio S. White's at Cornell, all proposed reading lists dealt with works after 1750 (plus an occasional listing of Opitz and Gottsched). Where Gottsched, Goethe, Grillparzer, Herder, Klopstock, Lessing, Opitz, and Schiller held sway in 1884 and the bildungsroman dominated as a form for emulation, other writers and genres loom large by 1899, when a national reading list in the foreign languages was promulgated by the MLA: Gustav Freytag, Friedrich Gerstäcker, Heinrich Heine (his patriotic or regionalist works only), E. T. A. Hoffmann's historical stories, Kleist's *Prinz Friedrich von Homburg*, Gustav Moser, Ernst von Wildenbruch, and Schiller's "Lied von der Glocke" become dominant authors and texts. The "easier" genres of anecdote, historical fiction, *Heimat* literature, novella, and animal tale become more frequent on American reading lists by 1911. There is nearly complete overlap between the authors listed in table 1 in corresponding years and those anthologized in approved schoolbooks of the Second (and later Third) Reich (Alwall). At the same time, there was in the American lists more stress on the freedom-fighting or exiled poets of the 1848 generation, such as Georg Herwegh, Ferdinand Freiligrath, Carl Schurz, and Heine, and, most noteworthy, on the more activist Sturm und Drang plays of Schiller. A certain schizophrenia emerges here: Can one be a pro-1848 revolutionary exile and pro–Second Reich pedagogue simultaneously? Given America's special status as immigrant land, where these different time strata coexisted in the German American community, such creative dissonance was indeed possible, and even desirable, in order to unite the various reading constituencies: the Anglo-American elite who learned German as a second language for intellectual purposes and for the grand tour, the acclimatized émigré political liberals who saw their role in continued republican civic virtue, and the economic immigrants after 1860 who wanted their children to remember the patriotic heritage and regional landscapes of the homeland's past. The focus of the multiple aims of the German American community was the public commemoration of Schiller, a gesture that embodied the popularity of this conflicted poet, celebrated as a philosopher, utopian, revolutionary, Swabian hero, and author of "Lied von der Glocke." This was the heyday of Schiller's popularity on American reading lists.

The first instabilities in the ever-growing canonical list came when the MLA instituted a national reading list in the foreign languages in 1896, published in 1899. The list proposed by the MLA Committee of Twelve, purportedly designed for public school instruction but actually more similar to a contemporary college reading list (Mensel 163–66), was influential but received strong criticism from a number of teachers who were opposed to a list of textbooks or any list whatever (Loiseaux xii-xiii). Arthur Kiefer, a high school teacher from Piqua, Ohio, voiced concerns about the domination of "Idealien" over "Realien" in the classroom, stating that students might be introduced to the literature of the German people but do not learn much of their life ("Report" 137). Kiefer wanted to delete from this MLA list all fairy tales; sentimental stories like *Immensee*; stories about young children, physical intimacy, wine consumption; and stories with a "sexual undercurrent," even those in the best works. He advocated removing those works "von Schlafrock, Pantoffeln, Zipfelmütze, zerstreutem Professor oder ähnlichen Grossmutterscherzen" ("about robes, slippers, nightcaps, absentminded professors, or similar fuddy-duddy jokes") and advocated using modern texts, not those of much older epochs ("Der deutsche Unterricht" 108). In effect, his program would have eliminated much literature of the "Max und Moritz" (violent children's humor) and *Heimat* type and rendered the list less regional and popular. Above all, he questioned the viability of jumping in one semester straight to *Faust, Wallenstein*, or *Maria Stuart*. Marion D. Learned at the University of Pennsylvania, in contrast to Kiefer, thought that the reading materials, particularly novellas, were much too easy and that the public had been dumbed down by journalistic writing and materialism. A return to a Schillerian classical education was needed for students from kindergarten up, in his opinion ("Germanistik" 105–07).

By 1911, the time of the report of the MLA Committee of Fifteen, the sequel to the Committee of Twelve, the PhD in Germanics with training in philology and the literary-historical method had become established at private research universities. Public school teacher training was becoming more specialized, and the reading lists now proposed centered solely on the secondary school classroom. The Committee of Fifteen made it distinctly understood that "the lists herewith given do not make the least claim to canonical authority" but were merely representative of types of texts (Loiseaux xiii). The fairy tales, children's stories, novellas, animal stories remained; a large selection of patriotic-military stories were retained; a few works with "sexual undercurrents," such as *Emilia Galotti*, were included. *Faust*, however, was omitted, and the 1911 list was indeed easier, as it reflected the growing chasm between literary research scholarship and public school instruction (Henry Schmidt, "Rhetoric" 170–71).

This last attempt by the MLA to establish a German literary canon preceded the abrupt halt in Germanics in North America during and after World War I (C. Nollendorfs, "First World War"; Henry Schmidt, "Rhetoric"; Zeydel, "Teaching . . . through World War I"). Indeed, other than the influence of European modernism among the cultural elites of America, as documented in the literary reviews of nearly seven hundred German books by Gabriele Reuter in the *New York Times Book Review* from 1923 to 1939, the German literary canon in the public schools and in the public sphere was in a state of abeyance until 1945 (Tatlock, Introduction). Although German exiles certainly enriched American literary life, those fleeing the Third Reich were likely to gain a foothold more in the film industry than in popular publication in the American literary market. The notable exceptions—Franz Werfel, Bertolt Brecht, and Thomas Mann—stand in contrast to the many exiled authors who regained neither popular nor canonical status, such as Lion Feuchtwanger, Jakob Wassermann, Felix Salten, and Vicki Baum.

After 1945, the academic and literary landscape changed drastically in the United States with the massive expansion of public universities to incorporate students of the GI Bill. A sizable number of those students had experience of Germany and Germans as well as an acquaintance with its popularized *Heimat* culture through the United States Army and its educational and recreational programs in the American zone. At the same time, graduate programs grew substantially to meet the demands of National Defense Education Act language initiatives. The texts chosen for such an expanded program at Rutgers University beginning in 1943, run for training members of the United States Armed Forces STAR (Selection, Training, and Replacement) unit, was reported in 1948 (Holzmann). The reading list for this program constituted a partial reinstatement of the pre-1914 mix of texts, minus the politically patriotic: the aesthetic education model of high literature (Goethe, Schiller), *Heimat* stories (by Gottfried Keller, Clara Viebig, and Theodor Storm), children's and animal stories (Berthold Auerbach, Waldemar Bonsels, Marie von Ebner-Eschenbach, and Wilhelm Busch), a flirtation with modernism and expressionism (Nietzsche, Brecht's *Trommeln in der Nacht*, Ludwig Renn, Hofmannsthal, Döblin, Hesse), and a few older *Soldatenstücke* ("military pieces") such as *Minna von Barnhelm* and *Prinz Friedrich von Homburg*. For the first time, German Jewish issues were visible on an American reading list: the first inclusion of Droste-Hülshoff's "Die Judenbuche" and several texts by German Jewish writers (Bruno Frank, Leonhard Frank, and Karl Franzos). Reflections of the recent political past are also included on this list: Hans Grimm's *Volk ohne Raum*, Hermann Löns's *Der Werwolf*, and works by Ina Seidel. Yet the Rutgers faculty members also kept the old since-forgotten favorites of previous lists: Otto J. Bierbaum, Peter Rosegger, and Ernst von Wildenbruch. They showed a new interest in the authors Fontane, Hesse, Hauptmann; included for the first time Jean Paul and the fantastic tales of E. T. A. Hoffmann; and had a predilection for autobiography and autobiographical fiction. They understood that their trainees were not students of literature but were assigned to the program to gain oral fluency in German and understanding of German history, geography, and institutions.

This incipient reconstitution and expansion of the old canon lasted long enough for the wartime and immediate post-1945 generation of scholars to establish an American canon along the lines laid out by the Rutgers group; that canon was manifest in a variety of anthologies of the 1950s and 1960s (see Feise and Steinhauer, *German Literature . . . Liberal Age* and *German Literature . . . Age of Crisis*; Gaede and Coogan; Liptzin, *From Novalis*). American anthologies of the late 1960s (immediately before the canon began to unravel) by Reginald Phelps and Jack Stein, Peter Heller and Edith Ehrlich, and Peter Demetz and W. T. H. Jackson are virtually identical to the postwar *Germanistik* lists by Karl Conrady, Wulf Segebrecht, and Mathias Bertram. These anthologies reflect the growing collaboration of German *Germanistik* and German scholars in America in the 1960s.

The powerful disorientation caused by the fall of *Germanistik* in fascism, the absence of a new canonical thrust from German academe until the 1960s student movement, and the discontinuity of the tradition of *Dichter und Denker* ("poets and thinkers") after Auschwitz meant that America would have to go elsewhere for new German literary impetus. As in the 1820s and 1830s, literary events outside academe helped shape the new American canon: Gruppe 47, the Oberhausen Manifesto filmmakers, GDR cultural politics, and social movements of previously marginalized groups who took theory for their own all contributed to the postwar German canon, particularly in America.

A prime example of a postwar social movement having a profound influence on reading habits and canonical choices is the women's movement. This movement generated major changes in the graduate reading lists of Germanics in America and elsewhere. Table 2 compares women writers on MA reading lists from graduate German programs in America from 1983 and 1993. Several trends emerge from these data. First, the number of graduate schools that reported offering a standardized reading list declined from 73 graduate institutions in 1983 to 42 in 1993, taken from the same pool of programs (the

Monatshefte directory of programs designated "graduate"). A typical response from the reporting schools was that their programs had moved to individually designed reading lists based on student interest or course work. This trend away from a rigorously inculcated literary canon indicates the growing lack of consensus about which German literary works should be read.

Yet even with this decline in the number of programs dictating a standard list, the number of individual works on the 1993 reading lists increased almost exponentially. Women writers on these lists show where much growth took place: their number increased by 45%, a formidable change over a ten-year period. Moreover, the number of women's texts cited increased by 118%. In 1983, 35 authors were represented by 77 works; in 1993, 51 authors tallied up 168 works listed. The massive expansion of the number of authors and works contains an interesting mix of women authors: the transcendentalist, Romantic tradition and after (Karoline von Günderrode, Bettina von Arnim, the Schlegel women, and Droste-Hülshoff; Droste-Hülshoff's entry into the canon has been firmly established [see table 2]); a very few authors from the older philological tradition, who are gradually being eliminated from these lists (Roswitha, Hildegard, Mechthild von Magdeburg, Catharina von Greiffenberg); a substantial number of late-nineteenth-century rediscovered realist, neo-Romantic authors (Ebner-Eschenbach, Reuter, Huch, Andreas-Salomé); and a very much larger number of twentieth-century authors, most of them post-1970. This variety means that there is not yet an established canon of postwar German women authors to be included in the literary canon beyond Christa Wolf. The same trend toward atomization is to be found among male authors on these MA lists, where Günter Grass emerges as the only clear modern winner.

Texts from what used to be the cultural margins—films; works by women, gays and lesbians, Germans of non-German heritage, and Holocaust survivors—have come to prevail in discussions of modern German literature in America. Literary anthologizing has become issue-driven, thematically specialized, and ever more interdisciplinary, most often edited by scholars focused on marginalized constituencies. The number of graduate institutions offering a standardized list is rapidly declining, and those who do retain lists use ever more contemporary works by an ever larger number of authors from more widely dispersed social and ethnic groups. Ideological criticism in and surrounding the texts has begun to play a primary role in their function in the classroom and the conference.

The predominantly twentieth-century master list of authors and works presented at the Kentucky Foreign Language Conference from 1948 to 1999 (*Programs*; see Friedrichsmeyer in this volume ["Role"]) and the shifts in North American graduate reading lists from 1983 to 1993 stand in profound contrast to the list advocated in 1994 by Wulf Segebrecht (*Was sollen Germanisten lesen?*) and the list of texts included in *Deutsche Literatur von Lessing bis Kafka*, by

Mathias Bertram. The difference between the informally established North American list and the published *Germanistik* lists lies in the North American list's predominant contemporaneity, its far-flung inclusiveness of noncanonical works, and its footloose attitude toward generic boundaries of literature.

While a master list of great German books still exists in North America, it is very much contested and has been shunted off and surpassed by postmodern popular and critical cultural production. As in the 1880s, creative dissonance in the American Germanics canon is still the order of the day. This apparent schizophrenia is even desirable, in order to unite the various reading constituencies: the Anglo-American elite who are learning German as a second language for intellectual purposes and for the grand tour; the acclimatized political and economic émigrés after 1945 who want to keep parts of the *Germanistik* tradition alive; and a new audience receptive to multicultural, gendered, and politicized texts. It is not surprising that the focus of the multiple aims in the canon of North American Germanics is on Christa Wolf and Günter Grass, who embody these contradictory impulses: their works are linguistically challenging, aesthetically intricate, and display conflicted political aims; they are reflective of, yet critical toward, the canonical tradition. It is not Daddy's canon anymore.

Appendix

Table 1
Proposed German Reading Lists in America, 1880–1948

Sources

a. 1884: Goebel, "German Classics"
b. 1898: "Report of the Committee of Twelve"
c. 1901: Wolf, "Lehrplan"
d. 1903: Bahlsen
e. 1906: "Report of the Committee on a Four Years' Course"
f. 1910: Winter
g. 1911: Hänssler
h. 1948: Holzmann

x = recommended
0 = cited for omission

Author and Work	1884 (a)	1898 (b) intermed.	1898 (b) advanced	1901 (c) 9th	1901 (c) 10th	1901 (c) 11th	1901 (c) 12th	1903 (d) 2nd yr.	1906 (e) 3rd yr.	1906 (e) 4th yr.	1910 (f) 2nd yr.	1910 (f) 3rd yr.	1910 (f) 4th yr.	1910 (f) 5th yr.	1911 (g)	1948 (h)
Andersen, H. C.																
general works								0			x		x			
Anzengruber, Ludwig																
general works															x	
Arndt, Ernst Moritz																
Des Deutschen Vaterland				x												
Arnold, Hans (Babette von Bülow)																
general works											x					
Fritz auf Ferien																
Auerbach, Berthold																
Barfüßele																x
Baumbach, Rudolf																
general works								x			x					
Im Zwielicht			x					x								
Waldnovellen								x								
Der Schwiegersohn								x							0	

Author and Work	1884 (a)	intermed. 1898 (b)	advanced	1901 (c)	9th	10th	11th	12th	1903 (d)	2nd yr.	1906 (e)	3rd yr.	4th yr.	1910 (f)	2nd yr.	3rd yr.	4th yr.	5th yr.	1911 (g)	1948 (h)
Benedix, Roderich																				
general works																			0	
Benzmann, Hans, ed.																				
general works																			x	
Bernhardt, Wilhelm, ed.																				
Novellettenbibliothek				x																
Aus Herz und Welt									x		x									
Bierbaum, Otto Julius																				
general works																			x	
Stilpe																				x
Bismarck, Otto von																				
Reden																			x	
Bloem, Walter																				
Der krasse Fuchs																				x
Blüthgen, Viktor																				
general works																			x	
Bonsels, Waldemar																				
Die Biene Maja																				x
Brecht, Bertolt																				
Trommeln in der Nacht																				x
Brentano, Clemens																				
Kasperl und Annerl																				x
Bruns, Friedrich																				
Die Lese der deutschen Lyrik																				x
Bürger, Gottfried August																				
Das Lied vom braven Manne				x																
Busch, Wilhelm																				
Max und Moritz																				x
Carossa, Hans																				
Eine Kindheit																				x
Verwandlungen einer Jugend																				x
Chamisso, Adalbert von																				
general works															x					
Peter Schlemihl									x											x
Die Sonne bringt es an den Tag				x																

Table 1 (cont.)

Author and Work	1884 (a)	intermed. 1898 (b)	advanced	9th / 1901 (c)	10th	11th	12th	2nd yr. / 1903 (d)	3rd yr. / 1906 (e)	4th yr.	2nd yr. / 1910 (f)	3rd yr.	4th yr.	5th yr.	1911 (g)	1948 (h)
Dehmel, Richard																
general works															x	
Döblin, Alfred																
Berlin Alexanderplatz																x
Droste-Hülshoff, Annette von																
general works															x	
Der Knabe im Moor			x													
Der Brief aus der Heimat				x												
Die Judenbuche																x
Ebner-Eschenbach, Marie von																
general works															x	
Die Freiherren von Gemperlein	x															
Krambambuli											x					x
Eichendorff, Josef von																
Aus dem Leben eines Taugenichts								x			x					x
Elz, Alexander																
Er ist nicht eifersüchtig															0	
Ernst, Otto																
general works															x	
Ernst, Paul																
Der Schatz in Morgenbrotstal																x
Falke, Konrad																
general works															x	
Fischer, Johann Georg																
general works															x	
Fontane, Theodor																
general works															x	x
Wanderungen durch die Mark								x							x	
Frau Jenny Treibel																x
Die Poggenpuhls																x
Fouque, Friedrich de la Motte																
Undine		x	x								x					x
François, Louise von																
Die letzte Reckenburgerin																x
Frank, Bruno																
Trenck																x

Author and Work	1884 (a)	intermed. 1898 (b)	advanced	1901 (c)	9th	10th	11th	12th	1903 (d) 2nd yr.	1906 (e) 3rd yr.	4th yr.	1910 (f) 2nd yr.	3rd yr.	4th yr.	1911 (g) 5th yr.	1948 (h)
Frank, Leonhard																
Das Ochsenfurter Männerquartett																x
Franzos, Karl																
Die Juden von Barnow																x
Freiligrath, Ferdinand																
Prinz Eugen, der edle Ritter				x												
Die Trompete von Vionville					x											
Die Auswanderer						x										
Gesicht des Reisenden					x											
Frenssen, Georg																
Jörn Uhl												x				x
Freytag, Gustav																
general works									x			x			x	
Soll und Haben		x	x									x				x
Die Journalisten		x														x
Bilder aus der deutschen Vergangenheit		x														
Aus dem Staat Friedrichs des Grossen										x						
Fulda, Ludwig																
general works									x				x			
Der Talisman			x													
Unter vier Augen										x						
Geibel, Emanuel																
Meister Andrea									x							
Morgenwanderung						x										
Gerstäcker, Friedrich									0							
general works												x				
Irrfahrten		x							x							
Germelshausen									x						0	
Goethe, J. W. von																x
general works (not *Faust*)	x	x							x				x	x	x	
"Der Sänger"			x													
Aus meinem Leben				x												

Table 1 (cont.)

Author and Work	1884 (a)	intermed. 1898 (b)	advanced	9th 1901 (c)	10th	11th	12th	2nd yr. 1903 (d)	3rd yr. 1906 (e)	4th yr.	2nd yr. 1910 (f)	3rd yr.	4th yr.	5th yr.	1911 (g)	1948 (h)
Goethe (cont.)																
Hermann und Dorothea	x			x				x			x		x			
"Der Erlkönig"				x		x										
Egmont							x	x	x				x			
Iphigenie	x							x		x						
Torquato Tasso								x					x			
Werther		x														x
Dichtung und Wahrheit		x						x								
Götz von Berlichingen								x					x			x
Faust								x								x
Balladen										x						
"Sesenheim"								x								
"Napoleon I."													x			
Gotthelf, Jeremias																
general works												x				
Uli der Knecht																x
Gottsched, Johann Christoph																x
general works	x															
Graf, Oskar Maria																
Anton Sittinger																x
Greif, Martin																
general works															x	
Grillparzer, Franz																
general works														x	x	
Die Ahnfrau	x															
Der Traum ein Leben			x													
Weh dem, der lügt															x	x
Der arme Spielmann																x
König Ottokars Glück und Ende																x
Grimm, Hans																
Volk ohne Raum																x
Grimms, Jakob und Wilhelm																
Märchen								x			x					
Groller, Balduin																
general works															x	

Author and Work	1884 (a)	1898 (b)		1901 (c)				1903 (d)	1906 (e)			1910 (f)				1911 (g)	1948 (h)
		intermed.	advanced	9th	10th	11th	12th		2nd yr.	3rd yr.	4th yr.	2nd yr.	3rd yr.	4th yr.	5th yr.		
Groth, Klaus																	
general works																x	
Hauff, Wilhelm																	
general works								x				x					
Lichtenstein		x						x	x								x
Hauptmann, Gerhard																	
general works												x				x	
Bahnwärter Thiel																	x
Der Biberpelz																	x
Der Ketzer von Soana																	x
Die versunkene Glocke																	x
Die Weber																	x
Hebbel, Friedrich																	x
general works																x	
Agnes Bernauer																	x
Heine, Heinrich																	
general works		x														x	
Reisebilder		x						x									
"Die Grenadiere"			x														
"Die Harzreise"																	x
Über Deutschland			x														
Henckell, Karl Friedrich																	
general works																x	
Herder, Johann Gottfried																	x
general works	x							x									
Hermann, Georg																	
Jettchen Gebert																	x
Hesse, Hermann																	
Knulp																	x
Peter Camenzind																	x
Schön ist die Jugend																	x
Heyse, Paul																	
general works								x				x				x	
Colberg								x									
Hillern, Wilhelmine von																	
Höher als die Kirche								0				x				0	

Table 1 (cont.)

Author and Work	1884 (a)	intermed. 1898 (b)	advanced	1901 (c)	9th	10th	11th	12th	1903 (d)	1906 (e)	2nd yr.	3rd yr.	4th yr.	1910 (f)	2nd yr.	3rd yr.	4th yr.	5th yr.	1911 (g)	1948 (h)
Hoffmann, E. T. A.																				x
general works														x						
Historische Erzählungen		x		x																
Meister Martin der Küfer																				x
Der goldene Topf																				x
Hoffmann von Fallersleben, A. H. von																				x
"Das Lied der Deutschen"				x																
Hofmannsthal, Hugo von																				
general works																			x	
Der Tor und der Tod																				x
Holz, Arno																				x
general works																			x	
Huch, Ricarda																				
general works																			x	
Erinnerungen von Ludolf Ursleu, dem jüngeren																				x
Jensen, Wilhelm																				
general works														x						
Jordan, Wilhelm																				
Durchs Ohr									x											
Keller, Gottfried																				x
Novellen														x					x	
Kleider machen Leute											x									
Das Fähnlein der sieben Aufrechten																				x
Romeo und Julia auf dem Dorfe																				x
Kerner, Justinus																				
Der reiche Fürst				x																
Kleist, Heinrich von																				
general works									x										x	
Prinz Friedrich von Homburg			x																	x
Michael Kohlhaas									x										x	
Klopstock, Friedrich Gottlieb																				
general works	x								x											

Author and Work	1884 (a)	intermed. 1898 (b)	advanced 1901 (c)	9th	10th	11th	12th	1903 (d) 2nd yr.	1906 (e) 3rd yr.	4th yr.	1910 (f) 2nd yr.	3rd yr.	4th yr.	5th yr.	1911 (g)	1948 (h)
Körner, Theodor																
general works															x	
Zriny	x							x								
Vetter aus Bremen								x								
Nachtwächter								x								
Kotzebue, August von																
Die deutschen Kleinstädter																x
Kröger, Timm																
Um den Wegzoll																x
Kurz, Isolde																
general works															x	
Lenau, Nicolaus																x
Der Postillon			x													
Lersch, Heinrich																
Hammerschläge																x
Lessing, G. E.																
general works	x	x											x	x		
Minna von Barnhelm		x			x			0			x	x				x
Emilia Galotti			x			x										
Nathan der Weise								x								
Lienhard, Friedrich																
general works															x	
Liliencron, Detlev von																x
general works															x	
Anno 1870																
Kriegsnovellen															x	
Lingg, Hermann																
general works															x	
Löns, Hermann																
Der Werwolf																x
Mann, Heinrich																
Der Untertan																x
Mann, Thomas																
Brief an den Dekan der Universität Bonn																x
Die Buddenbrooks																x

Table 1 (cont.)

Author and Work	1884 (a)	intermed. 1898 (b)	advanced	1901 (c)	9th	10th	11th	12th	1903 (d)	1906 (e)	2nd yr.	3rd yr.	4th yr.	1910 (f)	2nd yr.	3rd yr.	4th yr.	5th yr.	1911 (g)	1948 (h)
Mann, Thomas (cont.)																				
Unordnung und frühes Leid																				x
Der Zauberberg																				x
Mechow, Karl Benno von																				
Das Abenteuer																				x
Meissner, Marie																				
general works														x						
Meyer, C. F.																				
general works																			x	
Gustav Adolfs Page	x																			x
Der Schuß von der Kanzel																				x
Jürg Jenatsch																				x
Meyer-Förster, Wilhelm																				
Karl Heinrich											x									
Miegel, Agnes																				
general works																			x	
Geschichten aus Alt-Preussen																				x
Mörike, Eduard																				
general works																			x	
Mozart auf der Reise nach Prag																				x
Mosen, Julius																				
Andreas Hofer (Lied)			x																	
Moser, Gustav von																				
general works																	x			
Der Bibliothekar	x																		0	
Der Schimmel																			0	
Mueller, F. Max, ed.																				
Der Glockenguß zu Breslau			x																	
Deutsche Gedichte												x								
Muenchhausen, Börries von																				
general works																			x	
Nestroy, Johann Nepomuk																				
Einen Jux will er sich machen																				x
Nietzsche, Friedrich																				
Die fröhliche Wissenschaft																				x

Author and Work	1884 (a)	intermed. 1898 (b)	advanced	1901 (c)	9th	10th	11th	12th	1903 (d) 2nd yr.	1906 (e) 3rd yr.	4th yr.	1910 (f) 2nd yr.	3rd yr.	4th yr.	5th yr.	1911 (g)	1948 (h)
Opitz, Martin																	
general works	x																
Paul, Jean (Friedrich Richter)																	
Dr. Katzenbergers Badereise																	x
Platen, August Graf von																	
Das Grab am Busento				x													
Presber, Rudolf																	
Die bunte Kuh																	x
Raabe, Wilhelm																	
general works																x	
Die Chronik der Sperlingsgasse																	x
Raimund, Ferdinand																	
Der Bauer als Millionär																	x
Ranke, Leopold von																	
Karl V.												x					
Renn, Ludwig																	
Krieg																	x
Riehl, Wilhelm Heinrich																	
Novellen	x								x							x	
Das Spielmannskind										x							
Der stumme Ratsherr										x							
Die sieben Nothelfer												x					
Rosegger, Peter																	
general works												x				x	
Waldheimat	x																
Die Schriften des Waldschulmeisters																	x
Rückert, Friedrich																	
Barbarossa				x	x												
Schanz, Frida																	
general works																x	
Scheffel, Viktor von																	
general works														x			
Der Trompeter von Säckingen	x																
Ekkehard		x															x

Table 1 (*cont.*)

Author and Work	1884 (a)	intermed. 1898 (b)	advanced	1901 (c)	9th	10th	11th	12th	1903 (d) 2nd yr.	1906 (e) 3rd yr.	4th yr.	1910 (f) 2nd yr.	3rd yr.	4th yr.	5th yr.	1911 (g)	1948 (h)
Schenkendorf, Max von																	
Die deutschen Ströme				x													
Schiller, Friedrich																	x
general works	x	x							x			x	x			x	
"Der Alpenjäger"			x														
"Der Graf von Habsburg"			x														
"Die Bürgschaft"			x														
Der Neffe als Onkel	x	x							x								
"Lied von der Glocke"	x	x		x					x	x			x				
Balladen	x	x															
Wilhelm Tell	x			x					x	x			x				x
"Der Ring des Polykrates"				x													
"Die Kraniche des Ibykus"				x													
Maria Stuart		x		x					0				x				
Jungfrau von Orleans	x			x	x												
"Der Taucher"				x													
Wallenstein		x							x		x		x				x
Der Geisterseher	x								x								
Die Braut von Messina		x															
"Gustav Adolph in Deutschland"										x							
Schönaich-Carolath, Emil																	
general works																x	
Schönherr, Karl																	
Der Armendoktor																	x
Scholz, Wilhelm von																	
Das Buch des Lachens																	x
Schrakamp, Josepha																	
Erzählungen aus der deutschen Geschichte					x		x										
Schüler, Gustav																	
general works																x	
Schurz, Carl																	
Reden									x								
Lebenserinnerungen																	x

Author and Work	1884 (a)	intermed. 1898 (b)	advanced	1901 (c)	9th	10th	11th	12th	1903 (d) 2nd yr.	1906 (e) 3rd yr.	4th yr.	1910 (f) 2nd yr.	3rd yr.	4th yr.	5th yr.	1911 (g)	1948 (h)
Schwab, Gustav																	
Sagen									x								
Seidel, Heinrich																	
general works									x								
Leberecht Hühnchen											x	x					
Herr Omnia												x					
Seidel, Ina																	
Lennacker																	x
Das Wunschkind																	x
Slezak, Leo																	
Meine sämtlichen Werke																	x
Speyer, Wilhelm																	
Der Kampf der Tertia																	x
Spyri, Johanna																	
Moni der Geißbub										x							
Stifter, Adalbert																	x
general works											x			x			
Studien														x			
Storm, Theodor																	x
general works									x					x			
Immensee										x		x					x
Der Schimmelreiter																x	x
St. Juergen														x			
Pole Popenspäler														x			
Strachwitz, Moritz Graf von																	
general works														x			
Strauss-Torney, Lulu von																	
general works														x			
Sudermann, Hermann																	x
general works													x				
Johannes			x														
Frau Sorge																	x
Heimat																	x
Sybel, Heinrich von																	
general works													x				

Table 1 (cont.)

Author and Work	1884 (a)	1898 (b)		1901 (c)				1903 (d)	1906 (e)			1910 (f)				1911 (g)	1948 (h)
		intermed.	advanced	9th	10th	11th	12th		2nd yr.	3rd yr.	4th yr.	2nd yr.	3rd yr.	4th yr.	5th yr.		
Thiess, Frank																	
Der Abschied vom Paradies																	x
Die Tor zur Welt																	x
Thoma, Ludwig																	
Lausbubengeschichten																	x
Thomas, Adrienne																	
Die Katrin wird Soldat																	x
Tieck, Ludwig																	
Genoveva			x														
Trinius, August																	
travel stories								x									
Uhland, Ludwig																	
general works		x										x					
Des Sängers Fluch				x													
Schwäbische Kunde					x												
Viebig, Clara																	
Das Weiberdorf																	x
Töchter der Hekuba																	x
Volkmann-Leander, Richard von																	
general works								x	x			x					
Wagner, Richard																	x
Die Meistersänger													x				
Wassermann, Jakob																	
Das Gänsemännchen																	x
Weber, Carl Maria von																	
Feldmusik und Waldmusik				x												x	
Werfel, Franz																	
Der Abituriententag																	x
Wiechert, Ernst																	
general works												x					
An der Majorsecke															0		
Die Majorin																	x
Wieland, Christoph Martin																	
general works								x									

Author and Work	1884 (a)	intermed. 1898 (b)	advanced 1901 (c)	9th	10th	11th	12th	1903 (d)	2nd yr. 1906 (e)	3rd yr.	4th yr.	2nd yr. 1910 (f)	3rd yr.	4th yr.	5th yr.	1911 (g)	1948 (h)
Wilbrandt, Adolf																	
Jugendliebe								x									
Wildenbruch, Ernst von																	
general works												x				x	
Das edle Blut	x							x	x							x	x
Heinrich		x															
Neid								x								x	
Mennoniten								x									
Väter und Söhne								x				x					
Der Letzte																x	
Das Orakel																x	
Wilhelmi, Alexander																	
Einer muß heiraten																0	
Zschokke, Heinrich																	
Der zerbrochene Krug								0				x				0	
Zweig, Arnold																	
Der Streit um den Sergeanten Grischa																	x

Table 2
Women Writers on MA Reading Lists

1983: 73 reported lists, out of 118 inquiries to graduate programs

1993: 42 reported lists, out of 73 inquiries to graduate programs

List is arranged chronologically to 1945; postwar listing is alphabetical. X = one citation; number of multiple citations is given after X in parentheses for Droste-Hülshoff only.

Number of Lists Including Author and Work

Author and Work	1983				1993			
	20+	10–19	3–9	1–2	20+	10–19	3–9	1–2
BEFORE WORLD WAR II								
Hroswitha von Gandersheim								
Abraham		X						X
Calimachus				X				
Dulcitius		X						X
Selected play								X
Vorrede zum 2. Buch				X				
Brief an die Gönner				X				
Hildegard von Bingen								
Selections								X
Scivias				X				X
Mechthild von Magdeburg								
"Swester Mehthilt"								X
"O du brennender berg"								X
"Du solt minnen das niht"								X
"Were alle die welt min"								X
Das fließende Licht der Gottheit								X
Selected works				X			X	
Liederbuch der Klara Hätzlerin				X				
Elisabeth von Nassau-Saarbrücken								
Hug Schapler				X				
Eleonore von Österreich								
Pontus und Sidonie				X				

Number of Lists Including Author and Work

Author and Work	1983 20+	1983 10–19	1983 3–9	1983 1–2	1993 20+	1993 10–19	1993 3–9	1993 1–2
Catharina von Greiffenberg								
"In äußerster Widerwärtigkeit"				X				X
"Auf meinen bestuermeten Lebens-Lauff"								X
"Gott-lobende Fruehlings-Lust"								X
"Über das unaussprechliche H. Geistes-Eingeben"			X					X
Selected poems			X				X	
Geistliche Sonnette				X				
Hoyers, Anna								
Selected poems (Gedichte des Barock)				X				
Zeidler, Susanna Elisabeth								
"Begläubigung der Jungfer Poeterey"								X
Gottsched, Luise								
Die Pietisterey im Fischbeinrocke				X				X
Karsch, Anna Luisa								
"Das Harz-Moos"								X
"Lob der schwarzen Kirschen"								X
"An den Domherrn von Rochow"								X
Briefe an Gleim								X
Selected poems								X
LaRoche, Sophie von								
Geschichte des Fräuleins von Sternheim			X				X	
Arnim, Bettina von								
Die Günderode (selections)								X
Dies Buch gehört dem König								X

Table 2 (cont.)

Number of Lists Including Author and Work

Author and Work	1983 20+	1983 10–19	1983 3–9	1983 1–2	1993 20+	1993 10–19	1993 3–9	1993 1–2
Arnim (cont.)								
"Wer sich der Einsamkeit ergibt"								X
Prose selections								X
Goethes Briefwechsel mit einem Kinde				X				
Günderrode, Caroline von								
Selected poems								X
"Der Nil"								X
"Die eine Klage"								X
"Der Kuß im Traume"								X
"Liebe"								X
"Adriadne auf Naxos"								X
Mereau-Brentano, Sophie								
"Durch Wälder und Felder"								X
Varnhagen, Rahel								
Ein Buch des Andenkens								X
Briefe								X
Chezy, Helmine von								
"Ich bin so reich in deinem Andenken"								X
"Ach, wie wär's möglich dann"								X
Droste-Hülshoff, A. von								
Die Judenbuche	X (39)				X (19)			
Selected poems	X (20)					X (9)		
"Die ächzende Kreatur"								X (1)
"Am Turme"		X (4)				X (7)		
"Durchwachte Nacht"			X (1)					X (1)
"Im Grase"		X (3)				X (5)		
"Im Moose"			X (1)			X (3)		
"Der Knabe im Moor"		X (3)				X (3)		
"Lebt wohl"								X (1)
"Letzte Worte"			X (1)					
"Mondesaufgang"			X (1)					X (2)
"Spätes Erwachen"								X

Number of Lists Including Author and Work

Author and Work	1983 20+	1983 10–19	1983 3–9	1983 1–2	1993 20+	1993 10–19	1993 3–9	1993 1–2
Droste-Hülshoff (*cont.*)								
"Das Spiegelbild"				X (2)		X (8)		
"Pfingstmontag"								X
"Der Heidemann"								X
Das öde Haus								X
"Die Taxuswand"								X
"Der Weiher"				X (2)				X (2)
Hensel, Luise								
"Abendlied"								X
Lewald, Fanny								
"Beim Lesen der Heiligen Schrift"								X
Jenny								X
Ebner-Eschenbach, Marie von								
Das Gemeindekind								X
Er läßt die Hand küssen								X
Božena								X
Huch, Ricarda								
Erinnerungen von Ludolf Ursleu dem Jüngeren			X					X
"Liebe"								X
Lasker-Schüler, Else								
Selected poems			X				X	
"Ein alter Tibet Teppich"				X				X
"Gebet"								X
"Heimweh"								X
"Mein blaues Klavier"				X				X
"Senna Hoy"								X
"Weltende"								X
Langgässer, Elisabeth								
Die Bootstaufe								X
Das unauslöschliche Siegel				X				
Untergetaucht				X				
Seidel, Ina								
Lennacker				X				

Table 2 (cont.)

Number of Lists Including Author and Work

Author and Work	1983				1993			
	20+	10–19	3–9	1–2	20+	10–19	3–9	1–2
Seghers, Anna								
Agathe Schweigert				X				
Aufstand der Fischer von St. Barbara				X				X
Ausflug der toten Mädchen				X			X	
Das Schilfrohr								X
Das siebte Kreuz			X				X	
Transit				X				X
AFTER WORLD WAR II								
Aichinger, Ilse								
Selected works			X					X
Abgezählt								X
Der Gefesselte			X				X	
Knöpfe								X
Spiegelgeschichte			X				X	
"Winterantwort"				X				
Arendt, Hannah								
Selected works				X				
Eichmann in Jerusalem								X
Bachmann, Ingeborg								
Selected novel								X
Selection of poems	X				X			
Alle Tage								X
Alles							X	
"An die Sonne"				X				
"Anrufung des Großen Bären"			X				X	
"Erklär mir, Liebe"				X				
"Fall ab, mein Herz"				X				
"Mein Vogel"				X				
Undine geht (3)							X	
Das dreißigste Jahr				X				X
Die gestundete Zeit			X					X
Der gute Gott von Manhattan				X				X
Drei Wege zum See								X

Number of Lists Including Author and Work

Author and Work	1983 20+	1983 10–19	1983 3–9	1983 1–2	1993 20+	1993 10–19	1993 3–9	1993 1–2
Bachmann (*cont.*)								
Jugend in einer österreichischen Stadt								X
Malina						X		
Der Fall Franza								X
Borchers, Elisabeth								
"Immer ein anderes"				X				
"Jemand schweigt"				X				
Domin, Hilde								
Selected poems								X
Drewitz, Ingeborg								
Selected novel								X
Im Zeichen der Wölfe (sel)								X
Elsner, Gisela								
Selected prose				X				
Frischmuth, Barbara								
Die Klosterschule								X
Selected work				X				X
Rückkehr zum vorläufigen Ausgangspunkt								X
Bindungen								X
Jelinek, Elfriede								
Selected novel								X
Flugasche								X
Die Klavierspielerin							X	
Kaschnitz, Marie Luise								
Selection of poems			X			X		
Zuende							X	
Das Haus der Kindheit							X	
Kirsch, Sarah								
Selected poems				X			X	
"Breughel-Bild"				X				
"Dieser Abend, Bettina . . ."								X
"Der Droste würde ich gern Wasser reichen"								X

Table 2 (cont.)

Number of Lists Including Author and Work

Author and Work	1983				1993			
	20 +	10–19	3–9	1–2	20 +	10–19	3–9	1–2
Kirsch (cont.)								
"Ende Mai"								X
Blitz aus heiterem Himmel								X
Rückenwind								X
Katzenkopfpflaster								X
Königsdorf, Helga								
Bolero								X
Lavant, Christine								
Selected poems								X
Kreuzzertretung								X
Auf allen Stufen meines Leibes								X
Leutenegger, Gertrud								
Das verlorene Monument								X
Maron, Monika								
Selected novel								X
Flugasche								X
Mayröcker, Friederike								
Selected poems								X
Mechtel, Angelika								
Die Träume der Füchsin			X					
Mitgutsch, Waltraud								
Selected novel								X
Morgenstern, Beate								
Im Spreekahn								X
Morgner, Irmtraud								
Selected work			X					
Die Heiratsschwindlerin								X
Drei Variationen über meine Großmutter								X
Gute Botschaft der Valeska in 73 Strophen								X
Novak, Helga								
Brief an Medea (1)								X
Lagebericht (1)								X
Eis (1)								X

Number of Lists Including Author and Work

	1983				1993			
Author and Work	20 +	10–19	3–9	1–2	20 +	10–19	3–9	1–2
Özakin, Aysel								
Aus: Du bist willkommen: Gedichte								X
Türkische Frauen lernen lesen und schreiben								X
Kultur								X
Unterschied								X
Wie lernt man . . . Türkin kennen?								X
Rasp, Renate								
Selected prose				X				
Rehmann, Ruth								
Der Mann auf der Kanzel								X
Reimann, Brigitte								
Selected works				X				
Reinig, Christa								
Selected poems				X				X
"Entmannung"				X				
Skorpion								X
Rinser, Luise								
Selected works				X				X
Gefängnistagebuch								X
Den Wolf umarmen								X
Runge, Erika								
Frauen: Versuche zur Emanzipation								X
Sachs, Nelly								
Selected poems			X				X	
"An euch, die das neue Haus bauen"								X
"Chor der Geretteten"								X
"Einsamkeit"								X
"Erde, Planetengreis"								X
"O die Schornsteine"								X
"O der weinenden Kinder Nacht"								X
"Schmetterling"								X

Table 2 (*cont.*)

Number of Lists Including Author and Work

Author and Work	1983				1993			
	20 +	10–19	3–9	1–2	20 +	10–19	3–9	1–2
Schubert, Helga								
Mondstein								X
Struck, Karin								
Selected prose				X				
Wander, Maxie								
Selected prose				X				
Protokoll Erika D.								X
Wohmann, Gabriele								
Selected works				X				X
"Ach wie gut, daß niemand weiß"				X				
"Ich bin kein Insekt"								X
"Übeltäter"								X
"Wieder ist alles gut gegangen"								X
"Verjährt"								X
"Ernste Absicht"								X
Ausflug mit der Mutter								X
Wolf, Christa								
Selected works		X						X
Kein Ort, Nirgends				X				
Nachdenken über Christa T.		X				X		
Der Schatten eines Traumes								X
Nun ja! Das nächste Leben								X
Kindheitsmuster						X		
Kassandra						X		
Störfall								X
Der geteilte Himmel		X				X		
Wolter, Christine								
Ich habe wieder geheiratet						X		
Zeller, Eva								
Eine Seele von Mensch						X		

Practicing Disciplinarity and Interdisciplinarity in German Studies

How Much and What Kind?

WOLFGANG NATTER

This essay focuses on interdisciplinarity, German studies, and German Studies in the United States as institutionalized forms of knowledge production, professionalization, and training. The essay presupposes a view of both disciplinary structures and the curriculum they underwrite as theoretical and applied instruments. Like a book, these instruments are not simply reducible to the material object one holds in one's hands but also the point of interface for various support systems that enable them to be produced, disseminated, consumed, and critiqued. Further, the increasingly porous distinction between German studies, as the study of German language, literature, and culture in departments of German, and German Studies, as the study of "things German" pursued as a transdisciplinary, nondepartmentally based form of inquiry, organizes the present essay as it does the recent history of interdisciplinary German studies. Throughout, the comparatively decentralized character of the university system in the United States is also presupposed, as are differences in resource allocation for such study in the contexts of North America and the Federal Republic of Germany. The essay addresses what the recent past suggests about interdisciplinarity; views German studies and German Studies as a participant in this general process; reflects on the specific present character and operations of German Studies both inside and outside departments of German language, literature, and culture; and concludes with a list of pragmatic suggestions.

Where Is German Studies in the Academic Landscape?

The proliferation of interdisciplinary programs reflects notable shifts in thinking about disciplinarity and interdisciplinarity. Indeed, some commentators have suggested that the proliferation of interdisciplinary areas—in 1987 one reputable source listed some 8,500 definable knowledge fields—substantiates the advent of a postdisciplinary epoch.[1] Recent reformations of various geographically defined "area studies" contribute to this evidence, a tendency particularly notable where their reformation exceeds the premise of regionally centered exceptionalism embedded in earlier institutional emplacements.

The relations between bounded notions of place and the study of culture have received renewed attention in the light of the historical and contemporary globalization of economic activity; of the emergence of new technologies and infrastructures; and of transitions in social, political, and cultural networks. The variable history of attempts to locate Germany with respect to Western, Central, and Eastern Europe has likewise received attention. The study of "things German" has been affected by this change, like other geographically encapsulated interdisciplinary fields—for example, American studies and African studies.[2]

For scholars of German language, literature, and culture, assumptions about the nation-state as the logical and inevitable frame of analysis for these objects of study; about the epistemologies and methodologies that the category has authorized; and about the sometimes too seamless articulation of dominant and subaltern identities in presumed representational texts, events, and processes have received ever greater scrutiny in the light of the insights of the Frankfurt school and poststructural, deconstructive, feminist, postcolonial, queer, post-Marxist, and transnational studies. Each of those social epistemologies has invited practitioners to call into question the processes of identity formation that have fixed identity boundaries within and across the scales contained by categories denoting the individual, the region, the nation, the canon, text-context relations, popular and elite culture, gender, class, race, sexuality, and ethnicity.

Equally important has been an epistemological gaze directed at the character of the disciplinary spaces accorded such study in the organization of the university. That organization has generally constituted disciplines through processes of boundary formation that delimit areas and identities "as ones set apart."[3] The intellectual and scholarly promise of interdisciplinary German studies has therefore required discovering and nurturing institutional spaces in which practitioners from different disciplines can assemble and reflect both on things German and on their methodologies, cognizant that no single discipline has exclusive purchase on the research object. German Studies (at least hitherto) for the most part functions both as a specific form of transdisciplinarity—with crucial institutional spaces sustained by organizations such as the German Studies Association, by its annual meetings, by a number of journals, and in multiple disciplinary-based local college and university contexts, where the pursuit of things German may appear either as one of a discipline's subdisciplines (as with history, political science, or geography) or (increasingly reflected in many former German language and literature departments) as the central designation lending identity to a discipline's departmental mission (i.e., German studies). At present, German studies and German Studies are a field of knowledge as well as the organization of the field in both disciplinary and nondisciplinary ways that stand in determinate and mediated relations to the history, culture, and social organization of Germany and other nations and regions where the German language and culture have found expression in the material, institutional, and cultural landscape.[4]

Frank Trommler observed over a decade ago, "There is hardly an academic program in German (in the US) that does not reflect the spread of this concept [interdisciplinarity] either in its institutional setup or in the intellectual orientation of its courses."[5] Of course, the precise character and attributes of this reflection have varied, depending on the inclinations and range of expertise of faculty members as well as on local administrative support. As Trommler suggested, pragmatic initiatives rather than theoretical grounding have generally been the major stimulus for this development. At the same time, theory has been the means to explore meaningful dialogue across the disciplines and divisions of the university in the 1980s and 1990s. Theory played a considerable role in giving practitioners of interdisciplinary German studies an informed sense of why interdisciplinarity may or may not be so hard to practice—for example, by providing the conceptual tools needed to grasp more fully disciplinary developments and their entwinement with other cognate fields and how these developments have both enabled and inhibited disciplinary/ interdisciplinary pursuits. Throughout, the disposition or *Haltung* required of participants and institutions to pursue collaborative multidisciplinary research and teaching has been recognized as an extremely important factor in ensuring the success of that pursuit, whether motivated pragmatically or theoretically.

German Studies—a Discipline?

German studies and German Studies today are the product of substantial efforts to promote interdisciplinarity over the past three decades. What is perhaps less obvious is how it is also the beneficiary of a sustained discipline-based form of interdisciplinarity. Contributing disciplines, including Germanics, have never been so monolithic or unidimensional as their hagiographic histories sometimes suggest. Most disciplines, not only in the humanities, have taken recourse to some version of a golden age as part of their ongoing narrative of self-legitimation (Graff; S. Weber) or have monumentalized a sense of long duration in order to camouflage the appearance of being contingent or all too novel. Such attempts mask the demonstrable fact that disciplines are products of our modern, disciplinary age and that their past and present have generally been shaped by contention, disagreement, and renegotiations about what ought to constitute their core and periphery.

In thinking about the place of German studies in interdisciplinarity, one should also ask, What are disciplines and what functions do they perform for their members? Briefly, summarizing some of the literature: Disciplines are diffuse types of social organizations for the production of particular knowledge. They differ in size, goal, and structure. They are constantly changing kaleidoscopes of smaller components, varied in form but still related through a general process of specialization.[6] Their scope is not anchored by a prediscursive teleology inscribed in them. Further, changes in a discipline are regularly spurred by contacts with adjoining fields as much as by a centered logic of immanent disciplinary development. Disciplines are not only intellectual but also social structures, organizations made up of social agents with interests and networks that affect their development. Boundaries within and among disciplines shift and overlap, because ideas, techniques, and the researchers who create them do not remain in fixed intellectual places. Such a dynamic perspective offers a view of disciplines as fissured sites influenced by other disciplines, as heterogeneous practices, as hybrid activities.

Organizationally, however, disciplines, like the curricula they authorize, also function as an interface between knowledge production and knowledge markets—patrons as well as clients. The inception of the corporate model in academia in the 1990s confirms the relation in its multiple prior articulations, including ones that vouchsafed Germanics under the sign of the New Criticism (Hohendahl, "Fate"). Further, in a disciplinary age, disciplinarity effects a measure of standardization and is to a great extent about the ways and means of identity and exchange. With respect to exchange, a discipline may be thought of as a protectionist device responding to the alteration of the market by the actions of both the discipline's members and others. Fully fledged disciplines are "systems of multi-generational, multilateral exchange—that is to say internal, partly protected markets" (Turner). They promise professional assurance that the departments belonging to the same discipline in different university settings are more or less interchangeable with one another, a principle that is implicit in the mechanisms of peer review that oversee the regulation of employment, tenure, teaching, and bestowal of degrees. While such interchangeability also allows considerable latitude for productive discussion regarding the knowledge contents inscribed in formulations of the canon and the curriculum, the exchange mechanism is itself a prime factor in the persistence of certain disciplinary arrangements in the universe of knowledge.

The 1980s and the 1990s have witnessed a significant maturation of the intellectual scope and practices of interdisciplinary German Studies, but in an organizational sense German Studies can hardly at present be identified as a discipline. Should it become one? Will departments of German studies (or others) offer further institutional spaces for its multidisciplinary emplacement, or will developments lead to other institutional arrangements in support of interdisciplinary German Studies? Continued reflection on the practices of interdisciplinary study, appropriate curricular resolutions, and a professional culture to sustain them will doubtless remain on the agenda of Germanists, whatever their disciplinary stripe. The broader literature on interdisciplinarity, however, does not suggest that its current pursuit can or ought to be guided by the utopian hope of a total, synthesizing capacity or a universal interdisciplinary language. Instead, interdisciplinarity should be considered as a matter of practices and *Haltung* for both individuals and the institutions that assemble them. A set of signposts follow, anticipating the further development of these practices.

Practical Suggestions

While it is not true that there are as many kinds of interdisciplinarity as there are interdisciplinary practitioners of German studies or German Studies, the range of subdisciplinary and disciplinary interfaces is quite broad. No one person can give voice to the range of experience already explored. Perhaps contributions of short pieces (500–1,000 words) to a collection about the opportunities, definitions, and constraints bearing on interdisciplinary German studies could attempt this articulation (see "Forum"). Such a collection would reveal many disciplinary affiliations and make visible the varied settings from elementary school to university levels where German studies or German Studies operate.

Curricular requirements at colleges or universities should be carefully scrutinized for their potential to enable multidisciplinary and interdisciplinary work that substantially involves aspects of German studies. Courses might range from team-taught seminars with colleagues in other fields at the undergraduate or graduate levels to courses or course sequences that fulfill introductory and general-level undergraduate requirements. Certificate minor and major programs might be institutionalized. These requirements, commensurate with a broader rethinking of area studies, need not entail the encirclement of the field's expertise specifically in a course setting that announces Germany as the topic.[7]

As noted in a report published in 1997 by *Monatshefte*, many undergraduate majors in German are double majors in another discipline, such as political science, history, English, international relations, business, or economics. The report suggests an existing base of client interest for continued curricular developments of interdisciplinary German studies. The actual interests and expertise possessed by faculty members in any given local context will doubtless influence the efficacy of pursuing a particular interdisciplinary direction, but one can imagine a leading and active role for German studies scholars and teachers that would widen, enrich, and institutionalize evolving interdisciplinary fields—and perhaps disciplines. An openness to this world of possibilities requires abandoning a posture that frequently has made some German departments self-enclosed and insular.

In pursuit of interdisciplinary German studies, involvement in the professional life of another discipline needs to be considered part of one's professional commitment. A scholar of German literature and culture should consider attending not only MLA, German Studies Association (GSA), or Women in German annual meetings but also those of professional associations in a related field. In North America, some associations might be the American Historical Association, American Philosophical Association, American Association of Geographers, American Sociological Association, and the Interdisciplinary Social Theory Consortium. Although financial considerations may curtail such attendance, it is crucial for gaining a differentiated understanding of the present, past, and future states of the disciplines with which scholars of German studies might commune and for relaying to colleagues in those other areas the sorts of issues, methodologies, and epistemologies that are addressed by German studies and that might be useful for those colleagues addressing related research problems. Such participation over time affords a nuanced perception of the debates and fault lines that operate across many disciplinary fields, limits disciplinary caricature of the other, enhances recognition of a similar bundling of elements at play in one's home discipline, and leads to a greater recognition of the value of literary and cultural German studies in the eyes of other disciplines. In general, a marker of success will be the extent to which colleagues located in related disciplines actually cite work from German studies when addressing research topics that have a cross-disciplinary scope. At present, there is quite a way to go.

For interdisciplinarity to thrive, a professional culture needs to be cultivated that encourages and rewards faculty members and students for publishing in research outlets outside the primary disciplinary field and that continues to support those publication organs that have historically pursued interdisciplinary research. Literary Germanists, for example, can contribute to a broader recognition of the value of close reading; aesthetic, literary, and cultural theory; as well as the sorts of evidentiary procedures and functions (production, reception, critique) that literature itself offers in explaining cultural, social, and political processes. The maxim that good teaching is informed by good research follows too for interdisciplinary work.

Letters from colleagues from related disciplines that can demonstrate the value of interdisciplinarity should be accepted and encouraged at the crucial institutional times of passage (hiring, tenure, and promotion). Where interdisciplinarity is not yet practiced, German studies departments could develop a culture in which German Studies faculty members located in other disciplines are welcomed to participate as full members of students' committees. Thesis and exam committees play an important role in establishing the understanding crucial to interdisciplinary pursuits.

The GSA should consider formalizing a more subtle set of subdisciplinary categories to describe the work of its members. Beyond a chronological and disciplinary description and organization of the fields, the GSA could offer participation in substantive and theoretical areas of interest that are inherently multidisciplinary. Historians of science have stressed that specialization and the call for interdisciplinarity go hand in hand; they are not antinomies. At the very least, such a compilation would contribute to further self- and external understanding of the association's scholarly trajectories and enable the association to exercise some leadership in encouraging interdisciplinary research outcomes.

The GSA might begin planning to facilitate the production and delivery of Web-based materials solicited from its membership. Once the efforts were in place, they would result in a wide offering of usable classroom material. The impulse is a practical one, its aim to overcome a primary obstacle in establishing German Studies in many local contexts, yet careful planning is necessary here.

Lastly, as humanists in particular are aware, the discourse of interdisciplinarity prior to and under the corporate model does not translate evenly into support structures available to all faculty or departments. Interdisciplinarity in itself does not cancel, annul, or sublate the history of North American higher education since the cold war era; it does not change the distribution of resources, which are embedded in the academic structures that predate, negotiate, and administer our fields. Interdisciplinary or multidisciplinary studies will entail risk (Hohendahl, "Fate"): there is a danger that contemporary administrative advocacy of interdisciplinary study under the corporate model may portend organizational streamlining, academic Taylorism, and a deepening of the principles of self-exploitation and surplus extraction. It behooves local constituencies to insist on institutional recognition for engaging and redefining interdisciplinary programs of teaching and research devoted to things German. Here too the GSA may play a role in encouraging such recognition.

Such engagement offers considerable intellectual pleasures of discovery, but extending the purview of teaching and research from previous understandings and expectations requires work and time. Much depends on the local contexts, on the level of administrative support, on faculty and student interests.

For better or worse, disciplines are unlikely to be replaced as the dominant in the immediate future by another organizational matrix for teaching and research. But disciplines will doubtless continue to reflect the widening competition and differentiation likely to occur under emerging forms of client-patron knowledge production and dissemination. For German studies in North America, the cogency of debates centered on Germany and Central Europe, as compared with those dealing with the Pacific Rim, Latin America, and postcolonial Africa, will need to be argued, not assumed, even given the powerful traditions of thinking written in German on the relations between aesthetics and politics, social movements, cultural history, public memory, civil society, and the constitution of the public sphere. Arguably, the continued articulation of German studies will also need to occur in the context of a truly international understanding, not merely interdisciplinary and not merely containable by a gaze informed by the North Atlantic Alliance.

The script of globalization, to use a shorthand term for diverse processes that develop with frequent repetition, albeit unevenly in various locales, does suggest similar stories being written in many different places, with the same distribution of benefits and burdens, the same flows of cause and effect, and all tending to diminish claims for a delimited, exceptionalist understanding of place. Recent theories of globalization in area studies have stressed the need for place-based objects of study to be rethought in both historical and contemporary contexts. This work registers a more sophisticated understanding of the center-periphery phenomenon both "in" a "home" area and in relation to the edges of the process, and thus it registers an increased recognition of the importance of transnational considerations in defining relations between center and periphery whether from "above" or "below." This work also lends support to the view that globalization must "take place," that it must occur on the ground of multiple and simultaneous sites (best recognizable in conditions of transformation and restructuring) (Natter, "Über Identität"). It is only on the basis of such grounded work that these broader commonalities can be established.[8] There are excellent reasons, beyond protectionism, why place-based German studies ought to continue to receive a good share of support in such a comparative approach, but with the caveat that German studies must also continue the work of offering arguments for its value in global-regionally defined American and German contexts.

German studies and German Studies are but one instance of a very broad recasting of the procedures, contents, and practices affecting and responding to the organization of knowledge production in research and teaching. This broader scope may or may not be comforting to one who is asking when enough (interdisciplinarity) is enough. A great deal of evidence and reflection about present and past states of disciplinarity and interdisciplinarity suggest nonetheless that we are past the point of pondering the pros and cons, the epistemological virtue or impossibility of interdisciplinarity. The process is being driven not only by student enthusiasm, well-meaning educators, and administrators mediating the corporate model of the university but also by the persistent development of research and the teaching of it. It is less a question of whether and more a question of how much and what kind of interdisciplinary German studies will be fostered in the next years and what sorts of practices umbrella organizations can sustain or develop on its behalf.

Notes

1 For example, Gibbons, Limoges, Nowotny, Schwarzman, Scott, and Throw; Newell; Weingart and Stehr, esp. the introduction (xi–xvi); and the bibliographies given in all three books. See also Crane and Small, cited by Klein 16.

2 For American studies, see Wiegman. Historical depth is offered in Maddox. For African studies, see P. Stone; Watts; Makins; Prewitt. For Germany's emplacement in Europe, see Schultz and Natter.

3 Natter; McCarthy and Schneider. See too the annotated bibliography of relevant conferences from the 1980s and 1990s, journal issues, and books, many financially supported by the German Academic Exchange Service (DAAD), in Denham, Kacandes, and Petropoulos.

4 See *Guidelines for Curricula*, whose differences in emphasis from its earlier version (*Guidelines for Curricular Organization*) bespeak a noteworthy maturation of the idea and institutional practices of nondisciplinary German Studies.

5 "Future" 201. I am also indebted to the author's foregrounding and embodiment of the idea of interdisciplinary *Haltung* ("posture").

6 In Weingart and Stehr, see particularly Klein and the introduction (xi–xvi); Weingart; and Hollingsworth and Hollingsworth. See also Rheinberger.

7 Several of the syllabi assembled in the *User's Guide to German Studies* (Denham, Kacandes, and Petropoulos), notably those situated at Stanford, and the anthropology-history seminar at University of Chicago offer models of these sorts of initiatives. At the University of Kentucky, the graduate seminar in German Studies I organized also led to the institutionalization of a graduate-level certificate in German Studies. Collegial thanks to the faculty members in Lexington, who have supported this effort, particularly my fellow instructors of that pilot seminar: Dan Breazeale (philosophy), Wallis Miller (architecture), John Pickles (geography), and Jeremy Popkin (history). Thanks as well to the German Academic Exchange Service and the College of Arts and Sciences at the university for generously supporting it, a workshop, and a follow-up seminar. Finally, it is a pleasure to express my admiration and thanks to the editors of the present volume for providing an ongoing source of inspiration in my own professional undertakings.

8 The literature on globalization is of course global, but no current list would be complete without Held et al.; Castells; Gibson-Graham; Lefebvre; and Beck.

3

Approaches and Methods

❧

Edited by
PETER UWE HOHENDAHL

Introduction

Part 3 explores questions of methodology and theory in the field of language teaching on the one hand and literary and cultural studies on the other. Although the authors and the recipients of theoretical and methodological work were housed in the same department and shared larger professional concerns, theoretical writing on language teaching and the discourse on literature and culture developed for the most part separately. Occasional overlaps notwithstanding, each side insisted on the particular requirements in its area of specialization and frequently paid little or no attention to the concerns of the other side. The exception may have been the very early years of the profession, when the relevance and pedagogical value of the modern languages had not yet been fully established in the American academy. Yet, by 1900 the differentiation had already occurred. The discussion about the proper construction of German literary history or the correct selection of German authors to be read in the classroom was no longer connected to the heated discussion about language requirements in high school. By the same token, the teaching of German as a foreign language in the United States defined itself in the context of linguistics, psychology, and education theory rather than literary theory. This schism has persisted until recently, when outside pressures encouraged both sides to seek a rapprochement. In this effort the work of Claire Kramsch has played an important role. Between 1900 and 1990, however, the history of methodology in the field of Germanics was divided into two separate strands, each with its own set of particular concepts, authorities, and traditions. It could be argued that language teachers and instructors of literature and culture were part of two distinctive disciplines although members of the same profession (i.e., Germanics). Whereas language teachers looked to linguistics and psychology for guidance, professors of literature were more likely to engage in a dialogue with other national literatures or with history and philosophy. Only on a metatheoretical level could these different outlooks merge again. The question of teaching objectives, for instance, could bring both sides together to consider the issue of utilitarian purposes versus a general development of the mind (*Bildung*).

The discourse on language instruction by and large remained more closely connected to pragmatic classroom issues, while literary and cultural theory were more influenced by scholarly concerns that touched the classroom less directly. It is not accidental that the acceleration of theoretical discourse—that is, the rise of theory as such, as it occurred after 1970—corresponded to an increase in research-oriented professorial activities. While Renate Schulz underlines the similarities of the problems addressed in language pedagogy today with those mentioned around 1900, Sara Lennox and Irene Kacandes strongly emphasize the shift in focus after 1970. In fact, Kacandes suggests that the theoretical discourse has changed so much that one may well speak of a new disciplinary identity. Seen in the larger context of theory formation, the German department of the late twentieth century became more interconnected with discussions in neighboring fields. These trends might eventually lead to a dissolution of Germanics as a separate profession, were it not for the interest in teaching a particular language, namely German. While literary studies, and especially cultural studies, have more recently diffused the conventional contours of the German department, the field of language teaching has tended to reinforce these boundaries, even when the locus of theoretical work was not exclusively or not even primarily the German language. Moreover, the noted difference between language theory and literary and cultural theory was intensified by the existence of two distinctive professional cultures. In the field of language pedagogy, theory was mostly perceived as a tool for classroom practice. By contrast, literary and cultural theory, especially after 1970, aspired to a more autonomous status. Theoretical work became a value in itself. It is, as Schulz notes, only very recently that a similar tendency can be observed in foreign language acquisition.

Given the separation of the two fields, we cannot expect to find common patterns of development. Still, we can recognize a number of similarities—for example, the dependence of American scholars on German models in the early phase of the profession, especially before 1900. Both fields show a significant shift in orientation during the 1920s and again around 1970. But the remarkable turn in literary studies after 1945, caused by the rise of the New Criticism in American German departments, seems to have no parallel in the theory of foreign language acquisition. While the theoretical discussion of literary studies appears to have been uneven and relatively unfocused during the interwar years, the foreign language discourse, including the approach to German, seems to have been stronger and more centered. According to Schulz, the theoretical discussion demonstrated continuity from the 1920s to the 1960s; the paradigm shift occurring around 1970 coincided with the shift in literary theory observed by Hohendahl, Lennox, and Kacandes. Still, what literary critics have called the linguistic turn takes on a more specialized meaning in language pedagogy. Here we observe the impact of first language acquisition theory on the conception of foreign language learning.

On the whole, it is safe to assert that from 1880 to the present, literary and cultural theory have been produced primarily at research universities, typically in conjunction with PhD programs, while German departments at the college level have been on the receiving end and much less involved in the use of theory. The acceleration in the production of theoretical knowledge during the last three decades has definitely left its permanent imprint on the training of graduate students in German. Graduate students' familiarity with the current theoretical discussion is taken for granted by leading United States German departments. What is remarkable about the development of the late twentieth century is the increasing internationalization of the theoretical debate. In the field of Germanics this internationalization has sometimes been described as Americanization, a term that would be misleading if one looked exclusively at the cultural origins of individual theories; yet it would be appropriate if one considered the coexistence of those theories in the American academy. This institutional coexistence has put increasing pressure on the theoretical autonomy of national literature departments, including English departments. Where one could discern entrenched national traditions before 1970, the international circulation of theories has increasingly eroded such enclaves, imposing instead a new standard of familiarity with the latest international development. In this context the insistence on the privileged position of a specific German, English, or French tradition has become outdated, although the object of study—namely, German, English, or French literature and culture—retains its particularity. The emergence of theory *tout court* has slowly diminished the intellectual autonomy of national literature departments and at the same time brought their theoretical efforts into closer proximity. That proximity is especially evident in the most recent developments in queer theory and postcolonial theory, which have moved across traditional departmental boundaries and in fact eroded conventional notions of literary studies. The contemporary controversy about the definition and function of cultural studies is just as heated in French departments as in German departments, as can be gleaned from Sandy Petrey's (French) polemic against Russell Berman's proposal for a (German) cultural studies curriculum (Petrey). Whether the same equalization holds for the discourse on language teaching is another question. It seems that the dialogue among language teachers is more based on theories and methodologies developed and applied in the United States. In part, this situation may be the result of American dominance in the field of linguistics; in part, it may be simply the result of the stronger classroom orientation of the discipline—its specific grounding in the broader American education system, where the larger financial and organizational resources of the research university are needed as much for the production and dissemination of theoretical knowledge.

Pedagogical Issues in German-Language Teaching

A Retrospective

~

RENATE A. SCHULZ

The teaching of German as a foreign language (FL) in the United States has been influenced by developments in linguistics, psychology, and education as well as by political, economic, demographic, and technological changes. The latter changes affect directly the complex issues of curriculum development, including selection of content, instructional objectives, recruitment and placement of students, sequencing of instruction (i.e., time available for instruction as well as articulation between instructional levels), materials development, and approaches to teaching and assessment. Sociopolitical and economic determinants have influenced definitions of the field, public attitudes toward it, and enrollment patterns. The following review is limited to general pedagogical concerns, changes in theoretical assumptions underlying prevalent teaching methods, instructional objectives, and approaches to teaching and assessment.

Teaching German, 1899 to 1918

Pedagogical issues in FL teaching are seldom language-specific. Methods used to teach and test German in the United States reflect curricular practices and trends in modern FL teaching in general, particularly after the turn of the century. One can assume from early issues of the *Pädagogische Monatshefte* (*Monatshefte*) that before the turn of the twentieth century, American German teachers looked to the German Reich for guidance rather than to teachers of other modern languages in American schools and universities. Many of the early pedagogical discussions do not differentiate between German instruction for Anglo-Americans (i.e., German as a FL) and instruction for German Americans (i.e., German as a heritage language). Philipp Huber expresses his frustration with this lack of differentiation, calling it the main obstacle to pedagogical progress (76).

With the publication of the influential report of the MLA's Committee of Twelve in 1898—described by Rosenstengel in 1900 as by far the best treatise on FL instruction published in the United States ([1.4] 12)—and aided by *Monatshefte* and the *Modern Language Journal (MLJ)*, which began publication in 1899 and 1916 respectively, German teachers started to consider more broadly their role in the American context of FL education. It is noteworthy that the report of the Committee of Twelve addressed only the teaching of French and German. Since most of the FL examples provided in the report are in German, one can assume that German teachers had a strong hand in formulating the committee's recommendations. Spanish at that time was apparently not considered among the languages spoken by "the great makers of European civilization" (Rosenstengel 10).

Early volumes of *Monatshefte* provide some indication of the burning issues at the beginning of the twentieth century. First was competition with the classical languages and the fight for academic credibility. An editorial written under the pseudonym "Pencil Vania" estimated that there were about 6,000 German teachers in the United States in 1901. Presumably, these teachers taught in schools heavily populated by German immigrants. The membership of the Nationaler Deutschamerikanischer Lehrerbund (NDL), founded in 1870, consisted of barely 600 members at the turn of the century, and only 100 of them attended the organization's annual meeting in 1900. German as an academic subject and modern languages in general were clearly still fighting for credibility. Emil Dapprich's conviction, expressed in 1899, that one year of instruction in a modern language with a modern method had more educational value than three years of traditional instruction in Latin was apparently not shared by many educational leaders at the time. Even in 1914, Ernst Mensel talks of "the manifest discrimination . . . against foreign modern languages in favor of the classics" (166).

Second, there was the issue of teaching approaches. The early professional literature mentions an overabundance of ill-defined methods (Hepp; Fröhlicher; Kenngott). Richard Wischkaemper even refers to a prevailing "Methodenwut" ("methods fury") and "Methodenekstase" ("methods ecstasy") (130, 134). Ted Frank, Janet Hildebrand, and Renate Schulz ("Methods") all provide an overview of American teaching methods used in both schools and colleges during that time.

Third was a lack of consensus regarding instructional objectives. The professional literature at the beginning of the twentieth century reflects growing disagreement as to whether German should be taught to develop general mental faculties or competence for utilitarian purposes.

Fourth was the lack of agreement regarding the role of grammar. Both Louis Kelly and Diane Musumeci have documented the long controversy regarding the role of explicit grammar instruction in FL learning. Around 1900 there were passionate debates about the need for grammatical analysis, rule learning, and grammar as content of FL instruction.

Fifth, numerous articles decried the state of teacher preparation and the lack of trained teachers, particularly for teaching German at the elementary school level (Fick, "Erfolgreicher Deutschunterricht"; Broemel; Hepp; Busse, "Die Lehrerbildung"). (See "Teacher Development at the Beginning of the Twentieth Century" in this volume.)

Sixth, instructional time frames were perceived to be unrealistic. The two-year FL curriculum that had apparently become the standard by 1900 was recognized as totally inadequate for developing meaningful language skills (Rosenstengel; C. Krause, "What Prominence"). In 1905 Alexander Hohlfeld criticized the practice of limiting German instruction to the last two years of high school. Advocating a four-year sequence, as was the practice in Latin, he optimistically predicted that the extension of the prevailing two-year language course would be only a question of time. He felt that this issue would be resolved through purely pedagogical considerations and would be hindered more than advanced by an emphasis on specifically German American interests ("Die Zukunft").

Seventh, although the Committee of Twelve in 1898 saw no value in including FL in the curriculum of the primary grades, German instruction in the elementary schools had numerous advocates. Hohlfeld conceded, however, that it would be impossible to include German in the primary grades in public schools where German Americans were not heavily represented ("Die Zukunft"). H. H. Fick reported that by 1870 German was taught in the elementary schools of 24 American cities (partly in FL and partly in early versions of bilingual programs) ("Erfolgreicher Deutschunterricht"). One reason for offering German early on was that barely a quarter of the children stayed in school after the fifth grade.

Eighth, lack of academic standards and attrition between instructional levels also concerned the profession (Broemel). Several authors blamed the recently instituted open admission to high schools for a drop in the general academic ability of students and for the high attrition rates in German after the first year. Without doubt, the grammar-translation approach, widely used in FL teaching at the time, required relatively high academic ability, as well as high motivation and was not suitable for mass education. The inadequate preparation in English grammar of students entering German classes was also of concern.

Ninth, problems in sequencing instruction to facilitate transition from high school to college were also mentioned (Mensel). Hohlfeld expressed concern over the particular difficulties in articulating elementary-level courses taught by the direct method with subsequent instruction in literature courses ("Die direkte Methode"). According to Carl Krause, "the too hasty striving after the classics" was an abomination and the basic mistake of all American FL instruction ("Teaching" 184).

Tenth, Mark Twain's ruminations on "the awful German language" were not the only attestation that German was considered difficult (U. Thomas). Although it was widely taught—often, of course, to what would now be called heritage learners—German already was perceived to be more difficult to learn than other modern languages taught in American schools and colleges. This perception was strengthened by the prevalent printing convention using Gothic script rather than the Latinized print (Silberberg). The MLA's Committee of Twelve also pointed out "that the German grammatical terms are rather difficult to learn" (Rosenstengel [1.5] 27), and E. W. Bagster-Collins ("Beobachtungen") and Bayard Quincy Morgan ("In Defense") agreed that learning German was "an arduous affair."[1]

Eleventh, already in 1900, an editorial introduction in *Monatshefte* (1.4, p. 1) reported on cutbacks in German instruction due to budgetary constraints (see also Kuttner, "Wertschätzung"). One reason for the cutbacks must have been that the large German immigrant population that had arrived during the second half of the nineteenth century was assimilating with the American-born population. No one could foresee the catastrophe that was to beset German-language teaching because of World War I.

Additional concerns referred to overly large classes (Rosenstengel), to the lack of differentiation in methods and materials between high school and college German instruction (Bagster-Collins, "Beobachtungen"), and to an overemphasis in the professional literature on elementary language instruction, neglecting the development of approaches and materials for advanced German instruction (Hohlfeld, "Die direkte Methode").

Theories of Language Learning and Teaching
at the Beginning of the Twentieth Century

Teaching a language presumes that those engaged in that venture have certain beliefs regarding the nature of language and how languages other than the mother tongue are acquired. These beliefs consciously or subconsciously guide teachers' instructional practices.

Dapprich gave some insights into emerging theories of language and language learning and teaching in 1899. He stated that language was a product of the mind and that its development was governed by the same laws of all organic things. He saw imitation, extensive drill (33; "eine lange Reihe von Uebungen der Sprachgymnastik"), and natural language learning talent as most important for language learning but admitted that planned and systematic pedagogical procedures could considerably accelerate language acquisition. Dapprich called for the scientific study of second language (L2) development. He also expressed his conviction that L2 learning benefited the development of the mother tongue. Further, he recognized the importance of motivation in L2 learning and advocated that instructional techniques be adapted to the level and interests of the learners. Sounding surprisingly modern, he recommended that language instruction be embedded in content instruction and expressed strong criticism of then prevalent instructional practices:

> I consider the memorizing of isolated words, the reciting of disconnected sentences, the translating of phrases back and forth from one language into the other utter nonsense; at best, such practices create language acrobats and chatterboxes [*Schwätzer*] who talk for the sake of talking; in most cases such practices create deadly boredom, which is the enemy of all true learning. (35)

Dapprich posited ten guidelines for teaching. Among them are that neither grammar instruction nor translation are appropriate in the beginning FL classroom; that oral skills development should precede reading and writing; and that FL instruction should begin in kindergarten, with a minimum of one instructional hour each day. In elementary school, FL instruction was to be given by the grade-level teacher, at the high school level by teachers trained as content area specialists. For reading material he advocated texts by the best authors of a language. While the Committee of Twelve had maintained that "memorizing of poetry is not of sufficient importance to deserve a place in the course" (Rosenstengel 27), Dapprich was convinced that memorizing and reciting the best poems and singing the best folk songs were powerful means of creating interest (36).

Starr Cutting also called for a theoretical foundation for language teaching and pointed to several "Grundwahrheiten" ("basic truths"), which he believed to be based on the nature of language and on the makeup of the human brain. He proposed that human language was essentially an oral phenomenon and that the true essence of a people's mentality was not in poetic language but in colloquial speech used in the family, at the marketplace, and in social gatherings. Echoing the members of the Committee of Twelve, he considered the sentence as the basic unit of a language. While he saw language learning as mainly habit formation, he also alluded to the role of creativity in language use and concluded that language use was first and foremost an art and not a science ("Einige Prinzipien"). Almost a century before empirical research indicated that beginning learners have difficulty focusing simultaneously on the form and the message of an utterance (VanPatten), Cutting stated that attempts to teach simultaneously the art of using a language and the science of language development were doomed to failure. Recognizing the role of motivation in language learning, he advocated inductive learning of grammar, limiting translation to rendering texts from the mother tongue into the FL, and using any pedagogical means that aroused the interest of the learner. He also mentioned the role of active and passive memory, differentiating between what has more recently been called procedural and declarative knowledge (J. Anderson). He asserted the need for recycling, the role of reading in providing comprehensible input, and the role of intensive versus extensive reading in vocabulary building. There were even isolated voices pleading for learner-centered instruction. Werner Spanhoofd, for instance, reminded his peers that the individual learner, not the teacher, was the most important factor in the learning process.

Many of the seeds of current theories of learning and teaching had already been sown early in the century. For example, P. R. Radosavljevich presented a cogent discussion of the importance of "Lernmethoden," now known as learning styles. Generally speaking, the emerging fields of linguistics (through insights into the nature of language) and of experimental psychology (through insights into learners and learning) started to reshape the field and helped solidify the place of modern languages in the school curriculum. By 1915 discussions in modern language teaching were even beginning to influence the teaching of Latin (Almstedt).

Instructional Objectives and Pedagogical Approaches before 1925

The early years of the twentieth century were marked by disagreements between proponents of language learning for the cultivation of the mind (mostly but not exclusively representatives from the postsecondary level) and advocates of modern languages as vehicles for communication. The report of the MLA's Committee of Twelve clearly had not considered the utilitarian value of language learning to be central.

Generally, practical four-skills objectives slowly gained acceptance in the schools. According to Hermann Woldmann, speaking was the last in the recommended sequence of skills, preceded by reading, writing, and understanding. At the postsecondary level, developing mental discipline through grammatical analysis and reading remained the prevalent objective of FL study until the beginning of World War II, when national need related to the war effort and the Army Specialized Training Programs moved the development of oral competency into the limelight of pedagogical attention.

The first quarter of the twentieth century marks a slow transition from dominant objectives and approaches practiced for centuries in teaching the classical languages to an elite group of students to those objectives and approaches appropriate for teaching living languages and for the needs and abilities of an average population of learners. This transition, however, did not take place without strident rhetorical battles between traditionalists and reformists. Despite Cutting's recognition of language as primarily an oral phenomenon ("Some Defects"), it was generally accepted "that the High Schools and Colleges have not the necessary time to teach both literature and language, and are obliged to neglect the practical acquisition of the living tongue for the literature" (Learned, "When" 89).

German was taught predominantly by analyzing sentences, by memorizing grammatical rules and vocabulary lists, and by reading aloud and translating literary texts. Although teaching was mostly in the grammar-translation mode, the report of the Committee of Twelve maintained already in 1898 that "the day of the pure grammar-method is past" (Rosenstengel [1.4] 11) and discussed the natural method, the psychological method, the phonetic method, and the reading method in terms of their potential value to FL teaching.

The natural approach, a nontraditional method, attracted considerable attention. It was also referred to as the conversational method, new method, reform method, concrete method, question-answer or Socratic method, or the Berlitz method. Jean Hepp traced the historical development of the natural method and stated its essential characteristic to be the exclusive use of the target language in the classroom. The basic tenet was that pupils should learn a FL as children learn their mother tongue. But the principles of first language (L1) acquisition, as then understood, were not elaborated. The major objection of traditionalists was that advocates of the natural approach argued (in varying degrees) against formal grammar teaching and translation as mainstays of language instruction. M. D. Learned, for instance, referred to "the abuses connected with the so-called natural method," asserting that "it is a well established fact in the experience of the best teachers that language must be taught and learned with systematic reference to rules of construction" ("When" 89).

Arthur Altschul perceptively pointed out that the apparently chaotic array of methods could be divided into two categories [*Hauptmethoden*]: the formal, abstract, and analytic approach (e.g., the grammar-translation method) and the direct, imitative, concrete, or synthetic approach (e.g., the natural method). A strong advocate of the natural approach, he recommended conversation practice as a valuable component of all language instruction, regardless of objective or method ("Über die natürliche Methode").

A teaching sample (*Lehrprobe*) offered by Altschul shows that natural approaches did not require exclusive use of the target language for classroom communication. The classroom protocol demonstrating his "concrete method" (basically a stream-of-consciousness, teacher-centered, question-answer approach) shows that German is reserved exclusively for the exercises while English is used for all other classroom communication ("Lehrproben").

By the 1930s, apparently encouraged by Charles Handschin's *Methods of*

Teaching Modern Languages as well as by the so-called Walter method (an adaptation of the direct method advocated by Max Walter and used at the Musterschule in Frankfurt am Main, Germany), teachers began to favor the direct
method over the natural approach. While some authors attributed the origin
of the direct method to Wilhelm Viëtor's *Der Sprachunterricht muß umkehren*,
published under the pseudonym Q(uosque) T(andem), both the direct and
natural approaches date back to long before the twentieth century (Kelly; Musumeci). Hermann Almstedt defined the direct method as "the direct mode of
learning a foreign language, without the intervention of the vernacular" (82).
The language-learning sequence proceeded from listening to speaking to reading. German was to be used orally by teacher and students, and the textbook
was to be entirely in German as well. Grammar teaching did have a recognized
place in the direct method, although "grammar should be studied inductively;
i.e., that the living reading-text should yield the grammatical abstractions
which we usually call rules" (84). Almstedt assured his colleagues that "accuracy,
systematic and orderly procedure, drill, reviews etc., etc., are not given up"
(84). He also pointed out that "the demands made upon the teacher by the
Direct Method are greater than those made upon him by the old time grammar-
translation procedure" but that "it creates a living interest, through the psychological process of holding the attention and urging visualization" (86–87).
The growing popularity of the direct method also brought with it a need for
realia—or *Anschauungsunterricht* to illustrate language and cultural phenomena
through multisensory involvement. Students were to be surrounded to the
extent possible by a "German atmosphere," and newly learned words were to
be mentally connected to their visual representation (Kenngott; Wolf,
"Hilfsmittel").

As early as A. M. Kenngott and William Cooper maintained that the direct
method was used in many high schools and colleges, its acclaim was far from
unanimous. Wischkaemper, for instance, declared that the really great accomplishments of language teaching and learning were made during the heyday
of the grammar-translation method (131). Complaining that the attention to
training the ear had resulted in the loss of any sense for the systematicity of
language and development of actual mastery, he felt that the direct approach
subjected learners to a disordered wilderness of random, sensual impressions
and that America was the only country in which physical and mental neglect
and softening threatened to become a serious national problem. Other critics
stated that reading materials used in direct-method instruction made "strong
concessions to triviality" (Grumann 281).

As early as 1916 Max Griebsch called for a principled eclecticism in language teaching, recognizing that one single method could not possibly be appropriate for all learners and contexts ("Warum"). To what extent
nontraditional approaches could be used at all depended, of course, on the

oral language competence of the teacher. In 1907, the editor of *Monatshefte* declared that the most important question facing the profession was whether a German teacher should be able to speak the language (Griebsch, Editorial [1907]). The use of German in the classroom—the role of translation, grammar teaching, and actual conversation practice—remained controversial throughout the first half of the twentieth century.

Interestingly, the demise of both the natural and direct methods was attributed to the widespread reduction of German-language teaching during World War I (see Price; "Notes and News" [*MLJ*]).

Assessment Practices before 1925

Several authors mentioned the use of entrance examinations and the (New York) Regents Exams (Bagster-Collins, "Beobachtungen"), but procedures used to assess students' achievement were not described in detail in any of the publications aimed at German teachers. Krause complained that prevalent evaluation practices did not test "pupil's knowledge of language and *Sprachgefühl*" ["a sensitivity for language"] ("Discussion" 309). He provided sample test items that support the impression that tests required mainly translations and grammatical manipulations. Ernst Mensel pleaded for the inclusion of an oral test as part of the college admission exam. Despite an MLA resolution passed in 1908 to support "a test in pronunciation and ability to understand the foreign language" (165), oral exams had not yet become common practice. Cooper reported that prevalent testing practices using mainly translation formed "a still unsurmountable barrier" (244) to broad use of the direct method in the schools.

German Teaching in the United States between 1928 and 1970

Despite the cessation of *Monatshefte* in 1918, German-specific issues continued to be discussed during the later war and early postwar years. For instance, the *Modern Language Journal* published 33 articles between 1916 and 1928 dealing specifically with German-language teaching. Pedagogical discussions resumed full force in 1928 with the resumption of *Monatshefte* and the start of the *German Quarterly (GQ)*.

Of the estimated 784,352 students of FL in public schools in 1925, French accounted for about 56%, Spanish 39%, and German—the most commonly taught language before 1915—4.4%. Twelve states offered no German whatsoever, while 15 states offered German in only one or two schools (Fife, "Some New Paths"). Issues raised after World War I hardly differed from those discussed earlier, with the exception that the teaching of Gothic script was by now considered "rank nonsense" (Hagboldt 42). None of the other pedagogical concerns raised during the first quarter of the twentieth century had been resolved. Clearly, the most important issue for the German teaching profession was to recover a place in the school curriculum. Also, the lack of public appreciation for FL learning in general was of concern. While other university departments were frequently called on for public service and information, "foreign languages have received [only] an occasional call from some woman's literary or travel club of the so-called cultural type" (Spiker 65). More than fifty years before the President's Commission on Foreign Language and International Studies and Paul Simon's *The Tongue-Tied American*, Claude Spiker maintained that we can "no longer . . . afford to wait at home for the foreign purchaser: we must go to him . . . dealing with him in his own *milieu*" (68). He urged FL teachers to assist in helping America connect with other peoples and cultures, "for it is only through the medium of its language that one enters sympathetically into a foreign civilization" (70).

The general trend away from the nineteenth-century view of education as developing mental discipline to the social functionalism of the early 1920s was also reflected in discussions about FL teaching (Weisert). Matthew Willing called for limited objectives geared to reflect "the trend toward a more explicit, a more idealistic, and a more comprehensive social functionalism" (278). He also reported on trends toward greater individualization in instruction to accommodate different learning rates, interests, and modes of self-expression, recognizing "that we learn by doing rather than by what is done to us" (282).

The decline of educational standards continued to preoccupy a number of German educators. They bemoaned the fact "that the entire curriculum has been made easier, that standards of scholarship have been lowered, and that the content of the 'difficult' subjects has been adulterated" (Huebener, "Will Our Educational Standards" 1). The role of grammar also remained in the center of pedagogical discussion (Heffner). Curtis Vail commented in 1948 that "we have gone from method to method, with each succeeding one trying in vain to dethrone grammar" ("Language Learning" 145).

German in the elementary schools had been a dormant subject for many years but resurfaced in the mid-1950s, to gain increasing attention during the post-Sputnik years, supported by the National Defense Education Act (Beerbaum; Krauss).

Among newly emerging trends and issues were considerations of the use of technology in FL teaching (Appelt; Whyte, "On the Use"). Serious discussions about the use of television started in the 1950s (Bourgeois; Reichert, "Conventional Textbooks"), but Siegfried Müller reported that teaching FL by TV dated back to 1947 and that by 1955 seven American cities offered German-language programs on TV. There was debate on the use and misuse of the language laboratory and the tape recorder (Logan). George Scherer predicted in 1965 that "the electronic classroom . . . may become the predominant language teaching aid in the future" (344). In 1968 we find the first discussion of computer-assisted instruction (Ruplin and Russell). But several authors expressed disappointment that many of the early promises of technology had not materialized (Appelt; Scherer).

Given that FL study was considered by many an appropriate field of study only for the academically talented, ability grouping became popular. So did exploratory language courses. Their primary purpose was to determine the learners' probable chance of success in the actual study of a FL, "in order to avoid the lamentable waste involved in having our language classes cluttered up with the unfit and the uninterested" (Blancké 73). Also, such courses were to give students some basis for choosing a particular language for in-depth study later on. Wilton Blancké concluded, however, that exploratory courses were inefficient predictors of FL aptitude, a waste of time, and without inherent educational value.

Kulturkunde ("the study of culture") also received increasing attention. A survey by J. Alan Pfeffer in 1937 of 109 postsecondary institutions with an enrollment of more than 1,000 students revealed that 73% of German programs offered no courses in *Kulturkunde* and that only about 5% combined courses on literature and civilization. As to the definition of culture and the content of existing culture courses, Pfeffer reported a state of chaos.[2]

Other topics of concern were underenrolled upper-level courses and the problem of having to combine third- and fourth-year students in smaller colleges (John Hess, "Problem"), dissatisfaction with university language requirements ("Values"), meaningless credit hour requirements (Piel), and hostility of colleges toward high school instruction (Buchwalter).

Three events occurred during the fifty years following World War I that gave rise to increasing public awareness about the role, place, and problems of American FL education: (1) the Modern Foreign Language (MFL) Study conducted during the late 1920s, which provided evidence of the dire situation in FL education, including teacher training (Purin, "Training" and *Training*); (2) the Army Specialized Training Programs (ASTP) created during World War II; and (3) the National Defense Education Act (NDEA), which invested massive federal funds during the 1960s to improve American education.

The MFL Study, initiated in 1924, commissioned a number of research studies to examine the field of FL education in the United States and was instrumental in encouraging more scientific observation of language learning and teaching. According to Bagster-Collins, the MFL Study concluded that the profession was endeavoring to do too much and did none of it well ("Underlying Principles"). Given that the standard high school course was only of two years' duration, the MFL Study recommended teaching only reading skills (Coleman). This reading focus gave rise to vocabulary frequency studies and the creation of a *Minimum Standard German Vocabulary* (Wadepuhl and Morgan), the development of graded readers, and extensive test development, including the beginning of standardized achievement tests (Morgan, "New Hope").

In the early 1940s the professional literature started to describe war-related efforts in language instruction. While World War I had negative effects on American FL education in general, World War II increased the interest in FL learning. The war effort gave rise to the ASTP and to courses in scientific German, medical German, translation (particularly in women's colleges), and to conversational courses. A survey of wartime German courses found that "with regard to changes in the aim of instruction the impact of the war is truly epoch-making" ("Adjustment" 116). However, the report noted with regret that none of the survey respondents had increased the time allocated to FL learning, although less than fifteen years earlier, the Coleman Report maintained that useful oral competence could not be developed in the traditional two-year sequence (Coleman).

In 1944, an entire issue of the *German Quarterly* was devoted to the Army Specialized Training Program (*Army*). The prevalent objective of ASTP intensive courses for "student soldiers" was to develop oral abilities. Instruction was generally delivered in daily, large-group "presentation sessions" conducted by "linguistic scientists" and lengthy, small-group, drill and recitation sessions conducted by "native informants." The fundamental idea behind the ASTP approach was that "language learning is basically physiological, mechanistic— not intellectual" (Ittner 180). The accepted framework for ASTP courses was apparently Leonard Bloomfield's *Outline Guide for the Practical Study of Foreign Languages*. The concentrated war effort involving linguists, psychologists, and language teachers led to a "revival of methodological theorizing" (Springer 224) and laid the foundation for the audiolingual method, which was widely used during the 1950s and 1960s. But Bayard Quincy Morgan ("Memorandum") dismissed the "extravagant claims" for the "Army Method," maintaining that the success of the ASTP was due not to a new language-learning principle but rather to the increased teaching and learning time available. Although the ASTP was short-lived, intensive courses did not cease at the end of the war. A 1946 issue of the *German Quarterly* focused on postwar efforts in higher education to make intensive instruction part of the regular FL curriculum (*Symposium*).

The NDEA was passed in 1958 in response to the Soviet Union's launching of the world's first space satellite, *Sputnik I*, a technological feat that motivated the United States government to invest millions in an attempt to improve education, particularly in math, sciences, and FL, in the cold-war competition for technological superiority. The NDEA supported hundreds of summer institutes for teachers in the United States and abroad—among them many exclusively for German teachers—aimed at improving American teachers' language and professional competence. It also supported materials and test development. This support resulted in the development of the MLA Foreign Language Proficiency Tests for Teachers and Advanced Students, an ambitious, seven-part test battery, evaluating competence in the four language skills, linguistics, civilization, and professional preparation. Kenneth Mildenberger called the NDEA impact on FL instruction one of "truly epic proportions" (350). NDEA funds also supported research efforts to determine the superiority of the audiolingual method over more traditional teaching approaches. But research did not support audiolingualism's claim to superiority for long (Scherer and Wertheimer; Smith).

By the late 1960s, NDEA efforts in the area of FLs started to wane, but the frantic activities of the preceding decade and the national attention gained for FLs had some lasting benefits. For instance, 1967 witnessed the founding of the American Council on the Teaching of Foreign Languages (ACTFL), and in 1968 the AATG, with the generous support of the Volkswagen Foundation, founded *Die Unterrichtspraxis*, a pedagogical journal explicitly devoted to improving and promoting the teaching of German in the United States at all instructional levels. This golden age of American FL education also led to the publication of a large anthology entitled *The Teaching of German: Problems and Methods* (Reichmann). The volume was intended as a comprehensive handbook for German teachers; more than any other single publication of the time, it reflects the state of the field at the end of the 1960s. Although Hugo Schmidt stated that methodological eclecticism was the prevailing teaching practice, and although a number of contributing authors questioned the theoretical underpinnings of audiolingualism, the practical guidelines were still strongly anchored in that approach. Other publications influenced by the emerging fields of applied linguistics and contrastive linguistics were William Moulton's *The Sounds of English and German* and *A Linguistic Guide to Language Learning*, Herbert Kufner's *The Grammatical Structures of English and German*, and Robert Politzer's *Teaching German: A Linguistic Orientation*. Unfortunately, the valiant efforts in teacher development during the 1960s were only remedial. They led neither to measurable improvements in students' language competence nor to meaningful change in FL teacher certification, which had been suggested by Lohnes ("Training").

Instructional Objectives and Pedagogical Approaches, 1925–70

Instructional objectives ranged from an exclusive focus on reading, as was advocated by Algernon Coleman, to the predominantly conversational objectives of the ASTP and the development of all four language skills and of insights into everyday cultural patterns advocated by audiolingualism during the 1960s. Without doubt, a large number of teachers continued to focus on the development of the mind through the study of grammar and practice in translating literary works.

Max Griebsch's seven-part series, entitled "Zur Methodik des deutschen Unterrichts," published in *Monatshefte* between 1930 and 1934, is an indicator of the state of the art in methods of teaching German at the time. Griebsch made recommendations and gave examples of how the direct method should be used in teaching speaking, reading, and grammar. In 1937, however, Pfeffer informed us that the American enthusiasm for the direct method had begun to wane and that teaching practice had become eclectic.

The Coleman Report stimulated much discussion about new approaches (e.g., Neuse; Koischwitz and Hurd; Coenen; Heffner), but no cohesive approach to developing reading skills emerged. H. A. Basilius defined "the reading method" as "that heterogeneous assortment of devices, good, bad, and indifferent, which have at various times been advocated and used to realize the reading objective" (179). What was to be read remained controversial as well. Hess warned that "if we go on feeding our students on a diet of [Erich] Kästner books . . . , we make it almost impossible to do worthwhile work in the third year" ("Problem" 121). For many, the only worthwhile texts remained the established literary canon. Finally, while reading seemed appropriate to many for two- or three-semester requirement courses at the college level, an exclusive reading objective was considered inappropriate for those students who intended to major or minor in a FL.

It is uncertain how many language programs actually adopted a reading objective. Herbert Schueler claimed that few institutions actually used the reading objective and that the majority of FL classes still were taught with a grammar-translation focus ("Foreign Language Teaching"). Herbert Reichert wrote that "the grammar-translation method is at present quietly reestablishing its position, under the claim of meeting the reading objective best" ("Translation" 175). However, an AATG Committee Report ("Values") stated in 1948 that reading knowledge had become the general goal for a two-year college program and pleaded for "an eventual acceptance of a standardized curriculum" (207) for that purpose. It defined reading ability "as the skill required to understand correctly and quickly without translation the material on the printed page, in the same way which one reads English" (204–05).

Apart from the direct method, the only approach touted that could lay claim to the label "method" was audiolingualism. Numerous descriptions of that method are available (e.g., Benseler and Schulz, "Methodological Trends"; Schulz, "Methods"). Suffice it to say that the stimulus-response-reinforcement model of behaviorist psychology, combined with the discrete-point focus of structural linguists, became *the* American method. Form-focused pattern drills, immediate error correction, and mimicry and memorization of dialogues held sway well into the 1980s.

Assessment Practices, 1925–70

By 1925, assessment practices in FLs—influenced by psychometric theories and assessment techniques in vogue in the social sciences—began to change from the predominantly open-ended, subjective assessments (e.g., compositions and translations) to "new-type" objective tests, usually time-restricted, discrete-point tests of grammar or vocabulary. Objective testing permitted comparisons of achievement of learners in different groups and at various stages of language study, ushering in the practice of standardized testing. W. C. Decker reported that the New York Regents Exam for high school graduation consisted exclusively of multiple-choice, true-false, and completion items that tested vocabulary, grammar, and reading comprehension and complained about both the quality of assessment and low standards. Referring to a 1927 report by the Carnegie Foundation on the state of American education, he maintained that "the pupils and students in our American schools and colleges are the most examined and the poorest educated in the world" (74). He also mentioned the availability of prognostic tests to determine language-learning ability and efforts to develop scales for composition grading. As stated by Bagster-Collins, "the MFL Study did much to bring the new type of test to the attention of teachers and gave the impetus to experimental work and to further study" (Rev. 45). The American Council Alpha German Test, for instance, was used to establish achievement norms; however, those were "depressingly low" (Hagboldt 42). Willing alluded to the use of comprehensive or proficiency tests but did not further describe such assessments. The use of objective tests also encouraged the movement to formulate discrete-point learning objectives, since multiple-choice testing required that a representative sampling of knowledge and skills taught be assessed (Grueningen).

Growing German enrollments during the early 1960s, particularly in upper-level courses, led to increased use of the College Board's advanced placement exams in language and literature. Subsequent losses in German enrollment led to the elimination of the German AP literature exam in 1982. Of historical interest are publications, such as the September 1965 issue of the *German Quarterly* or the 1969 fall issue of *Die Unterrichtspraxis*, that devoted intensive discussion to AP concerns and that predicted that the AP exams would become the leading means of articulation between high school and college-level instruction and establish national standards for college-level work to be offered in high schools (Lohnes, "Advanced Placement").

The teaching of FLs became the subject of intensive theoretical speculation and research efforts following quasi-scientific designs. In the first issue of *Die Unterrichtspraxis*, Eberhard Reichmann complained that since the mid-1940s the professional literature was dominated by "theoretical study, scientifically controlled experiment and pure research" and that "practical and experience-tempered pedagogy takes a poor second place in the professional teaching literature" ("Introducing" 1). The same issue included a position statement drafted by a National Symposium on the Advancement of the Teaching of German in the United States ("National Symposium"). A number of the forward-looking recommendations (e.g., to develop four-to-nine-year instructional sequences or to measure achievement in terms of proficiency levels) still have not been widely implemented.

German Teaching in the United States, 1970 to the Present

The 1970s brought a paradigm shift in linguistic and language acquisition theories as well as in pedagogical approaches influenced by first language acquisition theories, which viewed language learning as innate. Further impetus for change came from insights gained from discourse and speech-act theory that language use was determined as much by sociocultural as by grammatical rules (Hymes), as well as by Stephen Krashen's monitor model. Teaching approaches began to stress the importance of comprehensible input, a low affective filter, and communicative interaction over rote memorization, pattern drilling, and emphasis on automatizing grammatical structures in noncontextualized language practice. Language was now seen as speech-act- or discourse-based rather than sentence-based.

In Krashen and Tracy Terrell's 1983 version of the natural approach, L2 learners need only large amounts of appropriate, contextually bound input. Neither formal grammar instruction nor error correction are deemed essential or even useful for language learning to occur, since errors are a natural part of language development. Communicative and proficiency-oriented approaches, which started to gain popularity in the early 1970s, saw purposeful interaction and negotiation of meaning as equally important as comprehensible input (Omaggio Hadley). Pedagogical recommendations stressed creative language use, participatory and collaborative learning, and an emphasis on language meaning over language form.

During the 1970s, the study of second language acquisition (SLA), defined as denoting "an interdisciplinary approach to [the study of] language learning phenomena . . . that combines study in cognitive science, linguistics and psycholinguistics" (Rankin 23), gained recognition as a research discipline and occasioned a growing focus on concerns and methods of inquiry in the field of applied linguistics that were teaching-related. One finds, however, few contributions during the early years of Die Unterrichtspraxis that tied theoretical or research developments in the emergent field of SLA to pedagogical implications for the teaching of German in the United States. The journal featured a broad spectrum of teaching-related concerns, course descriptions, and teaching tips for discrete phonological or grammatical structures or literary selections. A 1977 issue (10.2) focused on the need for incorporating career education into FL instruction.

During the past twenty years, focus issues in *Die Unterrichtspraxis* have dealt with research in SLA (14.2 [1981]), applications of technology (17.1 [1984], 30.2 [1997]), the move to proficiency-based instruction (17.2 [1984], 23.2 [1990]), and the need for promoting diversity in German instruction (25.2 [1990]). The need for promoting German study (23.1 [1990]) continues to occupy the profession, particularly in view of the declining enrollments after the short-lived growth spurt caused by the reunification of Germany. Additional concerns of a general pedagogical nature are also reflected in individual articles or reports dealing with programmed instruction, the quality of multisection courses, aptitude testing, placement and articulation between high school and college, the college FL requirement, FLES (foreign language in the elementary schools), intensive and total immersion instruction, competency-based education, study abroad, testing, FL exploratory programs, business German, and professional standards for teachers.

German teachers apparently did not join the frenzy of methodological innovation reported in the professional literature of the 1970s and early 1980s (see Benseler and Schulz, "Methodological Trends"). A special focus issue of *Die Unterrichtspraxis* "Developing Communication Skills" (16.2 [1983]) shows, however, that communicative language teaching made inroads in the German classroom as well. In a survey of teaching methods used in beginning German courses at the college level, Richard Helt and David Woloshin found that 10.2% of the respondents checked a communicative-competence oriented approach as their preferred teaching method. The largest number of respondents (61.8%) professed practicing an eclectic approach; an equal number of teachers (7.6%) stated a preference for the audiolingual and traditional methods. Unfortunately, the survey was flawed, given that the various methods mentioned were not clearly defined. It is interesting to note that as much as 40% of respondents listed grammatical knowledge as their first priority among the instructional objectives. Among the four language skills, speaking was considered most important, followed by listening. Cultural awareness played a relatively minor role. Helt and Woloshin point out that the dual focus on grammatical knowledge and speaking skills was somewhat incongruent in a communication-oriented approach to teaching.

Communicative language teaching advocates exclusive target-language use and authentic language input. It emphasizes language as a means of communication, and it values interaction, negotiation of meaning, and comprehensibility over grammatical accuracy. The approach seeks to reduce learner anxiety through group activities and an avoidance of direct and immediate error correction that was the vogue during audiolingualism. The basic problem with all communicative approaches, which seek to replicate conditions of natural child language learning, is that the conditions of L1 acquisition are impossible to replicate in large-group, formal educational settings, particularly for adolescents and adults. Formal disciplinary instruction, by definition, has explicit, measurable objectives; a specified content and method(s) for its analysis, organization, and presentation; and recommended strategies for practice. In essence, the target language and its literature are no longer the defined objects of study, as they were in most previous approaches. As advocated in content-based instruction, the language becomes mainly the delivery system for other disciplinary knowledge or for interpersonal communication. This change in focus from teaching comparative insights into language systems to developing functional survival skills with undefined contents may weaken the place of FL instruction in the discipline-based system of traditional education. Given the fact that the ACTFL performance guidelines for K-12 learners indicate that even learners who studied a FL for twelve years can be expected to reach a rating of only Intermediate-Mid for speaking (Swender and Duncan),[3] critics of FL education may ask whether the required commitment of time and resources is not too costly simply to develop survival skills in a language, especially since those skills are probably maintained for only a short time if the language is not used on a regular basis.

German Teaching in the United States at the Turn of the Twenty-First Century: Where Are We Now?

It is difficult to find many defining moments in the history of German-language teaching in the United States. Certainly, World War I was such a moment, since it changed the place of German in the school curriculum for the remainder of the century. On the positive side, one might mention the NDEA period, but its impact did not last long.

Crisis has been a high-frequency word in American education in general and in FL education in particular throughout the twentieth century. Decreasing enrollments, low levels of achievement, and public indifference to FL learning have been lamented for at least the past hundred years. While in most applied fields, such as medicine, engineering, or agriculture, new approaches advanced the field and remedied weaknesses of the past, newly proclaimed methodological innovations in FL teaching did not necessarily correct the problems of earlier approaches. What, then, are the burning pedagogical issues that confront the teaching of German in United States schools and colleges at the turn of the twenty-first century?

First must be mentioned the relatively low enrollments and the elimination of German programs (at all levels) for budgetary reasons or because of a lack of qualified teachers. The growing status of English as a world language, the diminishing immigration from German-speaking Europe, and the lessened strategic importance of Germany due to the end of the cold war (when up to half a million US military personnel were stationed in Germany, and quite a number of them decided to actually learn German after they returned home) have greatly lessened the demand for German-language instruction. The role that was played by German-speaking immigrants in encouraging bilingual instruction at the turn of the last century has now been assumed by Spanish-speaking immigrants who insist that their heritage language not be left to die.

A second issue is the lack of lengthy, articulated instructional sequences that can lead to meaningful language proficiency. According to Roger Minert, of the small number of students who study German in high school (less than 7% of all students enrolled in public schools), only about 28% continue German study in a third-year course (173–74). Given demands by competing areas in the curriculum, it is unlikely that large numbers of students will stay in the classroom long enough to actually develop a usable and lasting competence in German. Teacher development is another crucial area of concern (see Schulz, in this volume, "Teacher Development").

Elizabeth Bernhardt notes that language teaching has been slowly decoupling itself from literature study and identifying more closely with applied linguistics. While the interdisciplinarity of FL learning and teaching is now broadly recognized, university German departments have only reluctantly permitted their doctoral candidates to abandon the exclusive focus on literary analysis and engage in interdisciplinary research related specifically to the learning and teaching of German in the American context.

The last thirty years of the twentieth century have witnessed much activity in theory building and research in SLA and teaching. A recent informal survey lists over two hundred journals alone that deal, at least in part, with issues of language analysis, language use, language learning, and language teaching. Research indicates that neither nativist nor cognitive theories or approaches fully explain the SLA process. Language is no longer viewed as predominantly a habit, though habit formation may play a role in L2 acquisition. It remains an open question to what extent child L1 acquisition processes also hold true in the learning of new languages for adolescents or adults in a classroom setting. There is emerging neurophysiological evidence that languages learned after puberty are not located in the same parts of the brain as is the mother tongue (Kim, Relkin, Lee, and Hirsch). In short, because of the complexity of language and the interaction of individual learner, sociocultural, and contextual factors that play a role in language learning, few definitive answers have emerged as to how foreign languages are learned and how they should be taught.

Generally speaking, at the turn of the twenty-first century, German-language teaching in the United States is broadly guided by convictions that language should be taught for communicative purposes rather than solely for linguistic or literary analysis and that the contents of instruction should draw on many knowledge bases in addition to that body of knowledge broadly defined as German studies. If there is one pedagogical rule, it is to maximize the language input, use, and interaction opportunities of the learner. The problem with communicative goals and approaches is that they necessitate long instructional sequences that are seldom available in the American educational context. We still have to define what lasting educational benefits are derived from one or two years or semesters of predominantly communicative German instruction focusing on oral skills development.

While the role of translation as a language-learning device is now seldom discussed, the role of grammar remains a popular topic. The basic question remains: Will FL learners of all ages and in all learning contexts acquire the language faster and more accurately if it is the object of study or if it is the medium of communication? The issue is no longer whether grammar should be taught but how grammar should be taught (Doughty and Williams; Lee and Valdman). Learner diversity and individual learner factors that may play a role in L2 learning, largely ignored during the first part of the century, are gaining increasing attention (Oxford and Ehrmann). Language assessment has moved from exclusively subjective procedures to exclusively "objective" ones, and today it grapples with finding valid measures of assessing communicative language use (i.e., so-called authentic or performance assessment) that can be used reliably for decision making (Liskin-Gasparro, "Assessment"; Wiggins). Evaluation with multiple measures has become the guiding principle for FL assessment.

Language teaching is no longer as dogmatic as it was during the first three quarters of the century, when specific methods were advocated, often with missionary zeal. As in any applied field, teaching included, methods must change and adapt as new knowledge evolves and circumstances change. We can only hope that the approaches of the future will correct the shortcomings of the methods of the past.

Notes

1 The reputation of German as a difficult language has a long history. Edwin Zeydel, for instance, reported that the Committee of Ten, established by the National Education Association in 1893 to determine the position of the modern languages in the precollegiate curriculum, recommended that only 200 pages of text be read during the first two years of high school German instruction. A comparable French course was to cover double that amount. During the third and fourth year of instruction, 700 text pages were recommended as a reasonable amount of reading material in German classes, compared with about 1,000 pages for French ("Teaching . . . through World War I").

The anecdotal evidence for the relative difficulty of German as a FL for native speakers of English was confirmed by the Foreign Service Institute's guidelines for instructional hours needed in various languages to achieve specific rating levels on the institute's Oral Proficiency Interview. While French and Spanish (together with

Afrikaans, Danish, Dutch, Haitian Creole, Italian, Norwegian, Portuguese, Romanian, Swahili, and Swedish) are rated as level 1 languages (i.e., taking less time to acquire for motivated adult American English speakers than level 2, 3, or 4 languages), German is listed among the level 2 languages (together with Bulgarian, Dari, Farsi, Greek, Hindi, Indonesian, Malay, and Urdu), necessitating generally a longer instructional sequence to reach the same levels of oral proficiency (Liskin-Gasparro, *ETS*).

2 About fifty years later, ACTFL similarly encountered difficulties defining culture. While the 1982 draft of the *ACTFL Proficiency Guidelines* included cultural knowledge and culture-specific behaviors as measurable goals of FL instruction, the 1986 and subsequent versions of the *Guidelines* omitted culture because of a lack of agreement in the profession on what cultural knowledge should consist of and because of problems in establishing hierarchies of cultural knowledge and understanding for the various proficiency levels.

3 The "ACTFL Proficiency Guidelines—Speaking," revised in 1999, states: "Speakers at the Intermediate-Mid level are able to handle successfully a variety of uncomplicated communicative tasks in straightforward social situations. Conversation is generally limited to those predictable and concrete exchanges necessary for survival in the target culture. . . . Because of inaccuracies in their vocabulary and/or pronunciation and/or grammar and/or syntax, misunderstandings can occur, but Intermediate-Mid speakers are generally understood by sympathetic interlocutors accustomed to dealing with non-natives" (Breiner-Sanders, Lowe, Miles, and Swender).

From Philology to the
New Criticism, 1880–1970

PETER UWE HOHENDAHL

The conception of a professional methodology in German linguistic and literary studies can be traced back to the 1880s. While various forms of literary appreciation already had their place in the American college in the earlier nineteenth century, the 1880s witnessed the demand for a scientific and self-reflective methodology. The foundation of research universities, such as John Hopkins and the University of Chicago, changed the forum and the audience for linguistic and literary studies. Whereas the traditional college had introduced the study of modern languages and literatures as a supplement to its curriculum, which had stressed the significance of the classics, the research universities, at least in theory, pushed the study of modern languages and literatures beyond the concern for the needs and interests of undergraduates. The investigation of these subjects became an end in itself, not needing to be justified through moral and aesthetic values. Under the model of the research university the most important form of legitimation was the scientific character of the enterprise, which could be demonstrated through the development of and the adherence to a scientific methodology. For this purpose a new discourse had to be created, namely a continuous discussion not only of the objects of study but also of the validity of the methods of study applied. The question of approach was moved from the focus on the beautiful and the good to scientific truth. In this respect the study of English, French, and German became comparable to the natural sciences.

The agents of this fairly rapid transformation of literary studies were a new breed of professors who saw themselves no longer primarily in the service of the college but rather as scientists who in their work responded less to their students than to their colleagues. Adopting a European model that was especially strong in Germany, they defined themselves as professionals in the service of scientific progress (Graff 55–80; Trommler, "Einleitung" 19–27). This new form of criticism cannot be understood without the professionalization of the American academy (Pan). For this reason the founding of the Modern Language Association in 1883 was a crucial marker for the development of literary studies in the United States. And the development of Germanics in the United States cannot be separated from the evolution of this influential professional organization, since it provided Germanists with a forum where they could share their professional concerns about German language and literature with colleagues in related European modern languages. Much of the early methodological debate appeared in the organization's journal, *PMLA*.

Although the early history of Germanics is closely connected with the emergence of the study of modern languages in general, one can make an argument for the special situation of the field of German. The methodology that was introduced in the 1880s was to a large extent imported from the German university system. Since the new American research university was modeled on the German university (on its ideal rather than on its reality), the study of language and literature was strongly influenced by the method of philology. This early dependence on German ideas marked American Germanics for almost a century, and in two ways. First, methodological reflections frequently developed in response to German debates. But this relation cannot be constructed, as some critics have done, as a form of colonial dependency. Rather, Germanics is different from English or Spanish because of its position as a field between research and theory in Germany, on the one hand, and criticism and theory in this country, on the other. Second, this special link has sometimes worked as a challenge. Professors of German in the United States have sometimes seen themselves in opposition to research and theory in Germany. Calls for an American approach have been part of the history of the discipline, beginning with the situation after World War I and still resonating in the call for cultural studies as a specifically American methodology in the 1990s. Of course, the link to the German discourse is only one pole. At the same time, one has to assess the methodological development of Germanics vis-à-vis American criticism as it has been articulated and disseminated primarily through English departments. The English connection turns out to be at least as powerful if not more important than the German link. This peculiar situation poses an interesting question: Has Germanics in the United States finally developed its own, autonomous methodology? The answer to this question remains open.

Philology and Positivism

Early discussion about the future of the modern languages in the United States
had a dual focus: it was concerned with the teaching of foreign languages
(German among them), but it also dealt with scholarly questions pertaining to
historical linguistics and the study of literature. In the early years of the MLA,
these practices were still intertwined, since they had not yet been established
as separate professional fields. German was no exception: its debate over linguistic and literary scholarship followed the general pattern emerging in the
association. Where German differentiated itself from the other languages was
the sphere of literary studies, but less for methodological or theoretical than
for cultural reasons. American Germanists, whether German- or American-born,
tended to claim for German literature a special value and status that they were
not ready to confer on Spanish or French literature (Henry Schmidt, "Rhetoric"). That similar claims were made for French classicism in French departments seems not to have influenced their way of thinking.

How, then, did the early Germanists define their task? How did they present
themselves in relation to the new university? In foreign languages, it was even
more important than in English to establish the field as a professional discipline
that could not be taught by anyone who could merely speak and write the
language without qualification in literature. Defining a method also established
professional boundaries in the research university. The vigor with which the
early Germanists took up the question of method tells us something about the
professional stakes. In this respect, the Americans could not help looking at
the German situation, where the professionalization of *Germanistik* had already
occurred in the early nineteenth century under scholars like Karl Lachmann
and the Brothers Grimm (Weimar 210–53; Meves). The professional success of
German *Germanistik* as a scientific discipline had occurred under the umbrella
of the philological method (which had favored the study of medieval literature).
This approach had marginalized the literary criticism of the Romantics as well
as the literary history of the Hegelians (Weimar 254–346; Fohrmann, *Das Projekt*
211–40). The victory of the philologists was the victory of specialization. By
the late nineteenth century the generalists had been driven out of the discipline
as ethically and epistemologically inferior. When American Germanics began
to constitute itself in the 1880s and looked to the German university for guidance, it found a highly developed and respected academic discipline that cov-
ered both linguistic and literary studies. Moreover, literary research was no
longer limited to medieval studies (Kruckis; Nutz). Modern literature from the
sixteenth to the nineteenth century had become a legitimate field of research
and teaching. The founding of chairs and seminars made it possible to organize
research as a collective task that transcended the motivation and knowledge

of the individual researcher. In particular, the philological method was seen as a safeguard for the production of objective and verifiable knowledge.

Among the most outspoken defenders of the new scientific approach to the modern languages was Hermann Brandt, who received his PhD in 1886 at Johns Hopkins University. At the 1883 meeting of the MLA he forcefully argued for the transformation of teaching (and, by implication, of research) to a scientific model. "I am ready to lay down and defend the following proposition: All teaching should start from a strictly scientific basis, and all aids in teaching, the textbooks, reference books, etc., should be constructed upon a strictly scientific basis" (29). The concept of science he invoked was adopted from the physical and biological sciences (e.g., Virchow, Darwin); correspondingly, the concept of a natural law serves as a basis for the evaluation of historical linguistics. Brandt perceives the study of literature as part of a larger linguistic enterprise, in which the examination of literary texts is not left to the fancy of the individual teacher but based on the same kind of rigorous analysis that has been applied to the history of language. Among other things, he calls for the syntactic analysis of Lessing's and Schiller's prose and the exact linguistic examination of Chaucer.

Philological investigations by themselves, as recommended by Brandt, could not replace classics as the leading discipline in the humanities, since these studies, precisely because of their scientific nature, did not touch on the crucial question of the moral and aesthetic value of literature. Like the English departments, which realized that the defense of their subject required a broader ideological and methodological framework, German departments were under pressure to prove the importance of their materials in the context of modern American culture. Germanists, in other words, were professionally in need of a mission. Such a purpose was found in an emphatic appreciation of the moral and aesthetic value of modern German literature, especially German classicism (Spuler, *Germanistik*). From the point of view of methodology, this project entailed a different approach from strict philology. The cultural mission that the American Germanists wanted to add to their program came into the foreground through the study of literary history. Here it was not scientific detachment from the literary text that was demanded but the opposite: a moment of empathy with the spirit of the other culture.

Literary History and the Historical Approach

When one surveys the scholarly work of the late nineteenth and early twentieth century, it becomes obvious that the influence of German positivism and its claim for scientific objectivity, as important as it was for the constitution of United States Germanics, was by no means the only force that shaped the

emerging discipline. The historical orientation of literary studies, which was a
common feature of the modern languages in the United States, could not be
pressed into the philological model to the same extent that philological tools
could be used for research in literary studies. There were two theoretical problems with which the discipline had to struggle: first, the conception of literary
development or evolution; second, the place of literature in the historical development at large. It is noteworthy that the historicity of literature was rarely
explored as a distinct epistemological problem. Instead, the discussion of the
late nineteenth century focused on the place of literature in the larger context
of social and cultural history. The call for a more rigorous and scholarly treatment of the history of German literature stressed the need for a more explicit
embedding of literature in the general historical evolution. In this respect American Germanists shared common historicist assumptions about evolutionary
processes. When they consulted the literary histories produced in Germany,
they encountered the historicist paradigm in its various formations from Georg
Gottfried Gervinus to Wilhelm Scherer. But the German examples could not
serve the needs of the American academy, since they were written by insiders
who were examining their own literature. In the American university the fundamental assumption was different: one had to describe a foreign literature for
an audience that was more familiar with the English literary tradition. Under
these conditions the mission of German literary history was to transform the
cultural self-understanding of the educated American. In other words, the problem of approach and method was closely linked to a specific cultural project
that meant to intertwine German literature and contemporary American culture. Broadly speaking, it was the concept of *Bildung* taken from the eighteenth
and nineteenth centuries that was expected to inform and improve the character of American culture.

This project had emerged as part of a cultural agenda earlier in the nineteenth century, when German philosophy and literature became significant for
American intellectual development (Trommler and McVeigh; Walz). In the literary histories of the 1870s and 1880s, the goal of familiarizing a general American audience with German high culture is implicitly and explicitly stated. The
authors of these works did not consider themselves researchers in the new sense.
Instead, the emphasis is placed on the cultural value of the German tradition.
Symptomatic is the title of Frederic Henry Hedge's work, which was based on
lectures he presented to Harvard undergraduates; *Hours with German Classics*
(1886) consists of twenty chapters that cover the history of German literature
from the Germanic period to the early nineteenth century. But there is no
serious attempt at historical periodization, nor does the author try to provide
his readers with an overview of the historical evolution of German literature.
Instead, he prefers individual authors or works that are deemed representative
of the spirit of German literature. Hedge defends the emphasis on individual

achievements—that is, masterpieces—rather than on historical movements or methodological considerations. He reminds his readers of the relative unfamiliarity of the English-speaking world with German literature, an unfamiliarity that only recently began to change. An American academic audience is still in need of a general introduction to the German tradition, an introduction that stresses its specifically German element to readers coming from the English or French tradition.

The popular literary histories of the 1870s and 1880s deliberately refrained from theoretical and methodological reflections, which their authors must have considered counterproductive. They were not interested in the application of the philological method hailed by the professionals in the MLA. The challenge to this mode of historiography came with the work of a younger generation of Germanists, who embraced the concept of literary studies as a science. The works of Kuno Francke, Marion D. Learned, and Julius Goebel, who shaped the profession in the 1890s and the first two decades of the twentieth century, exemplify the claim for a higher degree of scholarly rigor. Francke and Learned in particular exemplify the search for a new method for the conception of history. Informed about and clearly interested in research in Germany, these two scholars began to revise the design of literary history. But their methodological innovations were not exclusively motivated by theoretical interests in historiography. Rather, they were part of a larger cultural agenda that redefined the study of German literature and culture around the turn of the century. Without this context the methodological propensity of their historical work is difficult to judge.

Their research was driven and shaped by their understanding of the importance of the German cultural heritage for American culture. Because of this bias, they have been accused of a nationalist agenda by recent critics (Henry Schmidt, "Rhetoric"). This assessment is not without merit but misleading unless it is differentiated. In brief, the national mission that Francke, Goebel, and Learned assigned to German studies involved the role of German culture in the United States. The question that these authors posed again and again was, What is the contribution of German literature to the formation of the American mind (Francke, *Glimpses;* Goebel, *Das Deutschtum* and *Der Kampf*)? This question was posed not to stimulate analysis but to claim the importance of the German tradition for the building of American culture. This claim effected the revision of literary history. To put it differently, the methodological issue of historiography is to a large extent determined by a political concern that is rooted in German immigration and ethnic tensions between German Americans and Anglo-Americans.

It is vital to differentiate the agendas of these scholars. While they agreed on the eminence of German literature, they viewed the role of this tradition differently. For Goebel it was a matter of setting the record straight, of redressing an unfair treatment of German culture in the United States. As a spokesman of the Deutschamerikanische Nationalbund he stressed the need for a revision of the conception of American culture. In his volume of essays *Das Deutschtum in den Vereinigten Staaten von Nord-Amerika* (1904) he aggressively confronts the English bias of North American culture at the expense of other ethnic groups who also settled and cultivated the land.

Learned's program is similar to Goebel's agenda, but not only is its rhetoric dissimilar but also its political goal is seen in a different light. In his lecture "Germanistik und Schöne Litteratur in Amerika," Learned promotes the study of German literature as an important contribution to the development of a new American culture that will be founded on idealism rather than materialism. He strongly criticizes contemporary writers in the United States for their lack of familiarity with philology and the literary sciences (*Literaturwissenschaft*) and for their disinterest in the values of the humanities. He recommends improving the quality of American literature by following foreign models, among them German literature, especially German classicism (Goethe and Schiller). It is precisely this process of cultural transfer that Learned assigns to American *Germanistik*. He argues, "*Germanistik* offers a scientific method and a historical critique of literature, elements which have been almost absent among English and American scholars for a number of decades." The stress on methodological rigor refers to German philology as it was appropriated by American scholars such as George Ticknor and Edward Everett in the first half of the nineteenth century. To this program Learned adds another point, namely, the demand for "a cultural and historical conception of the synthesized material, for a conception of the literary moments of national history and the life of the people" (106). With this explicit interest in cultural history he moved beyond philology. For him, cultural history and, more specifically, ethnic history were particularly suited for the national mission of American Germanics.

Francke's shift to cultural history was motivated by similar concerns. While Learned saw himself as the teacher of a young and still immature American nation, the German-born and German-educated Francke, who came to Harvard as a young man, understood his role first and foremost as a mediator between the German cultural heritage and American democracy. That position became difficult to maintain during World War I, when this double identity became unacceptable to the American public. But before 1917 he used his prominent position as a professor of German at Harvard to promote the visibility of German literature and culture, not only in the academy but also in the larger public sphere.

For Francke cultural transfer was also a methodological problem. Among the Germanists of his generation he was possibly the most conversant in the German theoretical discourse of his time. In "The Evolutionary Trend of German Literary Criticism" he examines the development of German literary criticism under the influence of an evolutionary approach (*"German Ideals"* 129–89). While the historical part of this essay is not relevant in this context, some of his conclusions are. Francke sees his own generation as critics in the wake of Darwin, Wilhelm Riehl, Gustav Freytag, and Jacob Burckhardt. This odd blend reflects his dual concerns with the social and ethnic background of literature and his belief in values and ideas. Accordingly, he demonstrates a strong affinity to the historian Karl Lamprecht; the cultural historian Riehl; and, last but not least, the literary critic Herman Grimm. What can be learned from them, although in different ways, is an approach that stresses the embeddedness of a literary work in the larger sociohistorical context. Francke's admiration for Grimm at the same time indicates that Francke is less interested in the formulation of general laws (e.g., by Taine) than in the characterization of individual authors. His commitment to a social and cultural approach creates a certain distance from the philological model embraced by other Germanists. In fact, he underlines the limitations of a method that is in his eyes mostly analytic and mechanical.

Francke's *Social Forces in German Literature* states with great clarity that the author distances himself from two prevailing modes of literary studies: "The following attempt to define what seem to me the essential features of German literature is made from the point of view of the student of civilization rather than from that of the linguistic scholar or the literary critic" (v). His history is neither based on philology nor written in the vein of the older popular literary histories. Instead, it claims to "analyze the social, religious, and moral forces which determined the growth of German literature as a whole" (vi). Consequently, Francke pays much more attention to the social, political, and religious background of German literature than did Hedge or Bayard Taylor. The story is conceived as a master narrative consisting of multiple strands of forces that ultimately form a cultural unity. Despite its sociological aspirations, *Social Forces* is not deterministic, nor is it dialectically constructed. Francke keeps the narrative flexible enough to accommodate the various components that he wants to stress at a particular historical period. The difficulty, for which the author does not have a convincing solution, is the connection among the different strands—in other words, the link between the social and the literary, between the religious and the political. Therefore the attempted synthesis remained, as Francke himself conceded in the preface, incomplete. What has to be underscored, however, is the scholarly character of *Social Forces*: the book was not written for undergraduates or a general audience. Francke clearly set new standards.

Although Francke's approach was motivated by his sense of a cultural mission, the nationalist bias of this project is largely kept out of his scholarly work. More surprisingly, the same can be said about Goebel, whose aggressive ethnic nationalism clouded his judgment of German American relations. His early monograph *Über tragische Schuld und Sühne* (1884)—his dissertation—remains largely in the boundaries of the discourse of intellectual history. The study could be termed *Begriffsgeschichte* ("history of concepts"), since it sets out to follow the historical development of two key terms of modern drama theory ("tragische Schuld" is "tragic guilt," "Sühne" is "atonement"). The author's national agenda articulates itself primarily in the way in which the goal of the analysis is defined. For him, aesthetic theory as much as literary history has a national telos, which he clearly expresses. While the problem of positionality is undoubtedly stated, the following historical analysis fails to work it out. From a traditional German point of view the examination should have led to an affirmation of Goethe's and Schiller's position as the final word on tragedy. Yet Goebel seems to be critical of both authors. Consequently, the wished-for synthesis of the particular national tradition (the German) and the universal human perspective does not come about, leaving the reader uncertain where the author stands. This unresolved problem of positionality ultimately haunts this whole generation of scholars. Goebel's later essays on the history and role of the German Americans simply beg the question by claiming the superiority of German culture. In this respect Learned made a much more serious effort to combine cultural history and German Americans in his study *The Life of Francis Daniel Pastorius: The Founder of Germantown*, which deals with the early period of German settlement in Pennsylvania. Its detailed reconstruction of local ethnic culture in the United States demonstrates in concrete historical terms the German thread in the larger American text.

Gerald Graff has described the field of early English studies in America as a discipline in crisis from the very beginning (98–120). The same can be said about Germanics. The politics of cultural identity in which the Germanists took part in varying degrees affected their methodological reflections as well. The call for a scientific approach, which had dominated the early years of the MLA, could not answer the need for a method that would clarify the appropriation of German literature into the American cultural context. Cultural history seemed to offer the solution to this problem, since the cultural approach would address the national question in scholarly and scientific terms. But this redefinition of the project would only split the thorny question of the cultural identity of American Germanists into two parts: on the one hand, the German cultural heritage; on the other, its American reception and further development by German Americans.

Interest in the culture of the common people (Learned) and ethnicity (Goebel) correlates with some of the theoretical developments in Germany around the turn of the century. August Sauer's program and the work of Joseph Nadler, who emphasized ethnic roots as the ultimate ground of literary production, demonstrate a similar revision of the historical project, which had been closely connected with the idea of the nation-state (Hohendahl, "Bürgerliche Literaturgeschichte"; Fohrmann, "Von den deutschen Studien"; Dainat). While these names, and even that of the geographer Friedrich Ratzel, are occasionally mentioned in the American discussion, there seems to be no significant dialogue between the American and the German side on the question of influence. German influence remained largely limited to the positivist conception of literary studies as a unified science during the 1880s.

Similarly, the growing importance of *Geistesgeschichte* in Germany after the decline of the positivist model in the 1890s did not make itself felt in the United States before World War I and did not even become a major theoretical issue after the war despite Goebel's effort to transfer the new program to the United States. He contributed two essays to this debate: in 1918 he presented an introduction to the history and principles of hermeneutics, which was mostly based on the German tradition from Herder and Schleiermacher to Dilthey ("Notes"), and in 1926 he added a discussion of Dilthey's conception of literary history, an essay that continued to explore Dilthey's hermeneutics, especially his concept of *Erlebnis* ("experience") ("Wilhelm Dilthey"). At the end of the second essay Goebel steps out of his role as observer, presenting himself as a critic whose own work follows a similar path. Pointing to the writings of Ernst Cassirer, Fritz Strich, and Paul Kluckhohn, he proposes to adopt the new German model:

> The intense interest in the fundamental problems of philosophy which has developed in Germany since the war furnishes a strong impulse to studies investigating similar problems in the works of literature, mindful always of the vital difference between poetry and abstract philosophy. ("Wilhelm Dilthey" 156)

Again, this proposal did not stir a strong debate. Ernst Jockers's contribution of 1935 did not even mention Goebel.

The Search for a New Model

The growing dissatisfaction with the scientific model began to mark the American discourse already around the turn of the century, especially in English studies, where neohumanists such as Irving Babbitt launched a forceful counterattack that ridiculed mechanical and mindless research (Graff 81–97; Wellek, *Concepts* 256–81). In German criticism, the situation became even more complicated after World War I, because the nationalist project, which had been advanced by such leading scholars and teachers as Alexander R. Hohlfeld, Francke, and Goebel, lost support in the academy when the United States decided to enter the war on the side of the Entente. Subsequent public opinion branded not only the German government but also German culture as an expression of Prussian militarism (C. Nollendorfs, "First World War"). Because

of its close links to an ethnic definition of German studies, the project of
cultural history appears to have lost its legitimacy. Under these conditions both
language teaching and literary studies had to be revised. In his 1922–23 essay
"The Approach to the Study of German Literature," Lambert Shears pointed to
two stumbling blocks for revision: first, the narrow scope of positivist scholarship; second, the fixation of the older generation on German classicism.

From a theoretical perspective, the entire interwar period can be described
as a transitional phase during which some of the older historical work continued while a new generation began to rethink its methodological options. Neither positivism nor cultural nationalism offered a persuasive solution. But
unlike Germany, the American scene of the 1920s and 1930s was not characterized by fierce theoretical debates. The reason for this relative abstention
may have been that the efforts of American Germanists had to focus on institutional survival—that is, on enrollment problems in basic courses rather
than on advanced research. Also, the theoretical debates in neighboring literature departments, especially in English departments, made little impression
on the discourse of the discipline. But it has to be noted that they did not
represent any significant advancement over the older arguments. *Problems and
Methods of Literary History* by André Morize, for instance, written primarily for
students in French, merely rehearsed Gustave Lanson's positivism, while Edwin
Greenlaw's *The Province of Literary History* (1931) criticized the historical model
of positivism but ultimately failed to offer new arguments for the historical
project, since Greenlaw remained tied to a concept of history grounded in facts.
Thus he logically created a strict divide between literature and history.

The American attitude toward the turbulent theoretical debates in Germany was a position of interested detachment. One followed the discussion
without committing oneself to any of the conflicting models under discussion.
The *Journal of English and Germanic Philology* provided one of the best observation points; its reviews and review essays kept the American reader informed
about the German scene. But by 1920 this scene had become much more
foreign, a site that might be interesting and even instructive yet not by definition a part of the project of American Germanics. The essays of Shears, Werner
Leopold ("Polarity"), and Kurt Reinhardt, to mention a few examples, attempted to clarify the German debate and its relevance for the American discussion. Reinhardt's essay proceeds historically by reconstructing three phases
of literary criticism: the idealism of classicism and Romanticism; the positivistic
model of the later nineteenth century; and finally the new philosophical outlook of the present, which owed its initial force to the work of Dilthey. Reinhardt traces the new development back to the emergence of the
phenomenological movement (to Scheler, Geiger, Pfänder, and Heidegger),
which promises a new science that aspires to a synthesis of reason and life.

For an evaluation of the 1920s and 1930s, the distinction between self-conscious methodology and positivist methods is especially important, since much of the scholarship developed its approach through actual practice. Among the American scholars of the younger generation who began to make their mark in the 1920s, Walter Silz, a student of Francke, showed the closest affinity to German *Geistesgeschichte* in his early work. His study *Early German Romanticism* was an explicit dialogue with German scholarship. Silz understood his book as a critique of Fritz Strich's *Deutsche Klassik und Romantik* (1922), which he accused of creating artificial oppositions. However, Silz shared with the German practitioners of intellectual history a drive toward synthesis and a forceful rereading of the history of German literature from Sturm und Drang to the Romantics under overriding intellectual categories, which make possible broader philosophical comparisons where the older historical paradigm merely searched for influences and examined sources. This belief in the reality of concepts was clearly opposed by a critic like Hermann Weigand, for whom larger historical constructs had little attraction.

With his first book, *The Modern Ibsen*, Weigand distanced himself from established scholarly patterns. The study focused on Ibsen's plays, paying little attention to historical or biographical background. One might be tempted to call his method close reading, but that would be misleading, because the critic demonstrates no interest in the linguistic or formal structure of these plays. What fascinates the early Weigand is the psychology of Ibsen's characters, especially their ambiguous personalities. It is only in his second book, a study of Thomas Mann's *Der Zauberberg* (*Thomas Mann's Novel*) that Weigand broadened his approach to include thematic moments of the novel such as disease and metaphysical problems. While the examination of these themes in the novel brings the critic closer to the practices of *Problemgeschichte* ("history of problems"), the most innovative parts of the study are those concerned with structural and formal matters—for instance, the organization of the novel and the analysis of Mann's use of irony. Mann's departure from the realist tradition challenged Weigand: a new type of novel called for a new type of analysis. The appraisal of the novel needed to borrow from a variety of methods (narratology, history of ideas, and psychology [Freud]) to accomplish its task. This approach became the mark of the critic Weigand; for him, methods were tools to be used in specific situations rather than rigid and binding philosophical commitments.

While Weigand was consciously eclectic in theory and methodology, his preference for individual works or authors rather than larger historical constructs or strictly theoretical issues set the tone for much of the scholarly work of the coming decades. To some extent this preference would later mesh with the tenets of the New Criticism, although Weigand did not share the specific social and aesthetic ideology of New Critics. His strong and lasting interest in psychoanalysis, for example, set him apart from most of the critics of his generation.[1]

Dialogue and Confrontation with German Fascism

An inevitable question for the history of methodology is the significance of the rise to power of the National Socialists in 1933, an event that would strongly impact German *Germanistik*. Recent German scholarship has emphasized the continuity of *Germanistik* through the 1930s and 1940s, correcting the earlier assumption of a complete break in 1933 and 1945 (Barner; Dainat). While the American situation was different from the German in more than one respect, there were also parallels. Basically, there was a sense of continuity with respect to the definition of literary studies. At the same time, however, a discussion of the institutional as well as methodological changes in Germany could not be avoided, though most American Germanists showed initially little eagerness to come to terms with the influence of the new masters on the study of German culture.

While the impact of the Third Reich on American Germanics has received considerable critical attention (Pentlin; Salloch; Lauwers-Rech; Hoecherl-Alden, "Germanisten"), the response to the theoretical shifts in the German discourse deserves more scrutiny. The American profession was initially reluctant to confront the aggressive new paradigm in the light of the extremely negative experiences of World War I. A broader definition of German studies would include the cultural practices of the German people and would also encounter the ongoing political, legal, and social changes in Germany. In fact, older traditions of ethnically grounded cultural history that fell out of favor after 1917 could be invoked again. The even older project of German classicism could also be brought back into play as a form of resistance against the fascist ideology. Not only the German émigrés but also American-born Germanists who disagreed with racist theories employed the second strategy.

Affinities to the terms of *Nazi-Germanistik* slipped into the American discourse most easily through the interpretation of contemporary literature. Germanists who showed interest in the works of Hans Grimm, Wilhelm Schäfer, and Erwin Kolbenheyer were also likely to use the concepts of race, blood, and soil for their interpretations (Salloch). These essays tended to be hortatory rather than analytic. Germanists such as Selina Meyer, Shears, E. P. Appelt, and John R. Frey became particularly invested in the conservative or *völkisch* ideology of their authors, not always aware to what extent they also gave support to the Third Reich (Salloch). Jockers intervened more directly with his 1935 essay "Philosophie und Literaturwissenschaft," which argued in favor of a philosophical approach and more specifically recommended the concept of *Weltanschauungstypen* ("types of worldviews") for the study of German literature (175–77).[2] The more typical version of Nazi ideology is found in Lydia Roesch's article "Der völkische Dichter und seine nationale Sendung" (1937), which ends with the statement: "The new project consists therefore of a clear presentation of the German race and the German people, that is, of its deep and active grounding in nature" (158). This statement also evidences the antimodern investment of some American Germanists, which corresponded to the attitude of mainstream *Germanistik* in Germany.

This discourse was not supported by most American Germanists. Their resistance was expressed not only through explicit opposition but also through the choice of neutral or even antifascist writers (e.g., Thomas Mann, Ernst Toller, Franz Werfel) and the self-conscious retreat to the classical tradition. In fact, an explicit theoretically grounded critique of the *völkisch* and fascist concepts of literary criticism was the exception. More common was an implicit critique: values and principles marking the distance from the other side. Frequently, a critic would invoke the great literary tradition as a counterweight to the distortions of the present, sometimes without ever mentioning the National Socialists. A case in point is Oskar Seidlin's 1940 lecture "Das Humane und der Dichter," which defends Germany's humanism as a value that cannot be appropriated by fascism. The writings of Goethe are presented as a guide through dark times, when political extremes on the right and the left threaten to undermine universal human values. Henry Schmidt has rightly stressed the quasi-religious tone of this lecture, in which a literary work functions more like a religious than a literary text (Henry Schmidt, "What Is Oppositional Criticism?"). Seidlin would continue this value-focused approach after the war in his 1949 interpretation of Goethe's *Iphigenie*, in which the critic calls the heroine "the sister of man" (*Essays* 34) Not surprisingly, this reading promulgates the humanist credo as a network of eternal ideas without much regard for the problematic tensions of the drama. Ultimately, the critic delivers a message: "Through Iphigenia, a world, separated by hatred and suspicion, has become united" (43).

The emphatic turn to the literary work would also mark an increasing detachment from the paradigm of *Geistesgeschichte*. Karl Viëtor, since 1935 professor of German at Harvard University, declared in 1945, after an extensive survey of its methods, that this paradigm had come to an end. For Viëtor *Geistesgeschichte* had been devalued by its partial compromise with the ideology of the Third Reich ("Deutsche Literaturgeschichte"). While he argued for a renewal of literary studies through closer attention to the artwork, the Romanist Leo Spitzer, in a response to Viëtor, was even more critical of the nationalist tradition of German *Germanistik*. Spitzer favored a departure from literary nationalism altogether and proposed a comparative (European) model for the United States.[3]

The Rise of the Intrinsic Method in German

The end of the war marked a transition in the self-understanding of American Germanists but not a sudden emergence of a new theoretical model. While Viëtor's and Spitzer's critique of *Geistesgeschichte* became dogma after 1945,

Spitzer's recommendation to integrate German into comparative literature found only limited resonance in the discipline.

A younger generation of American Germanists found a new paradigm in a text-oriented approach. Although New Criticism had been quite visible as a critical movement outside the American academy (Wellek, *Concept* 5–7), it did not make a strong impact on German literary studies in the mid-1940s. At the center of the New Critical agenda stood the task of aesthetic and moral judgment of the artwork according to its language and composition. This anti-scientific credo fueled the movement and continued to resonate in its academic transformation. English academic criticism mediated the emergence of New Criticism as a dominant model in the following decades. In all likelihood Germanists became acquainted with it mostly through the academic version, as it was summarized in René Wellek and Austin Warren's *Theory of Literature*. As the authors note in their preface to the first edition, their work aimed at a synthesis of literary theory, scholarly methodology, and literary criticism, a thing unknown in Germany. This synthesis would redefine the boundaries of research not only in English studies but also in the foreign literatures. In the long run, the new and broadened concept of criticism would replace the concept of science (*Literaturwissenschaft*) that had characterized German *Germanistik* since the turn of the century. Still, *Theory of Literature* insisted on a well-defined methodology that was based on the difference between the literary work and literary criticism. For Wellek and Warren, criticism is relevant because of the work, but it follows its own rules. The authors are indebted to the New Criticism in the strict (rather, narrow) understanding of literature as "imaginative literature" (22), which they consider as an equivalent of *Wortkunstwerk*. The emphasis is placed on the special nature of literary language, specifically its ambiguity. Yet the insights of the New Critics are toned down and brought in touch with older scholarly traditions and concerns. The exceptional success of *Theory of Literature* as a textbook for several generations of graduate students can be explained by its synthetic approach, which includes areas of scholarship (literary history, sociology, psychology, etc.) for which the New Critics had little use. Hence one can speak of this work as a New Critical approach only in the sense that it invokes the aesthetics of the New Criticism as the unstated norm of criticism, in particular through the fundamental distinction between intrinsic and extrinsic criticism.[4]

When and how did the New Criticism begin to affect the study of German literature in the United States? This question is further complicated by the fact that American Germanists were exposed at the same time to the new German discussion focusing on the work of art—that is, "das sprachliche Kunstwerk" ("literary artwork") (Kayser; Staiger). The admixture of different elements and traditions in the theoretical and methodological discourse of the postwar decades is therefore difficult to assess, eluding a clear and easy definition. In German studies a serious theoretical discussion of the new paradigm did not occur before the 1950s, which does not prove that the new practice—that is, close reading—had not become part of research and teaching before that.

Ferdinand Gowa's 1953 review essay "Present Trends in American and German Criticism" provides a useful perspective on the theoretical discussion in the profession, since it situates American Germanics as participating in two distinct critical discourses. Gowa points to the New Criticism as the emerging American paradigm and alludes to the subsequent hostility of American critics toward German *Geistesgeschichte*; he also introduces new voices from Germany and Switzerland that seem to be more in tune with the emphasis on intrinsic criticism in the United States. Gowa stresses the similarities between Wolfgang Kayser's doctrine and the position of Wellek and Warren's *The Theory of Literature*. He highlights as common characteristics the special ontological status of the artwork, its exclusive aesthetic purpose, the emphasis on form/Gestalt, and the resistance to classifications of the literary work. But he does not stop there. His strategy is to push the arguments to the point where the position of the new theory has to be surpassed. In the end, he argues in favor of a new synthesis, one that would do justice to artistic qualities as well as to the social and philosophical problems contained in the text. In short, Gowa believes to detect almost a return to the criticism of the 1920s and 1930s "with the difference that they [the New Critics] emphasize more strongly the inclusion of an intrinsic analysis" (108).

Gowa perceived this new development as an advantage, a move beyond the narrow confines of national tradition. The internationalization of literary criticism is clearly seen as a desirable goal in the global context of the postwar era. Moreover, it relegitimates German criticism, which had been shunned after the war, and thereby sets up a new professional alliance between American and German theory—but now in the name of the artwork rather than the nation. His essay shares the epistemological horizon of the authors he reviews. Finally, he does not at any point compare the theoretical discourse with the actual scholarship done by American Germanists in the postwar years. It is also noteworthy that Gowa's intelligent and well-informed essay did not consider at all the historical conditions for the international success of the new intrinsic model.

Henry Hatfield's study *Thomas Mann: An Introduction to His Fiction*, published two years before Gowa's essay, might serve as an example of the attitude of postwar scholarship. The preface makes it clear that the author does not mean to follow the path of German scholarship, which in his opinion suffers from an overemphasis on ideological problems. While Hatfield subscribes to the timely emphasis on the literary text, the organization of his study does not reflect an exclusive concern with the individual artwork and its poetic language. Following Weigand, he organizes the chapters around larger themes; some titles are "The World of the Father," "Myth and Psychology," and "Exile's Return." Still, he presents himself more as a critic than a scholar. His discussion of *Doktor Faustus*, for instance, not only interprets the novel in terms of its composition and thematic structure but also judges its quality as a literary work. Hatfield doubts that the novel "is a satisfying aesthetic whole" (138). In a comparison with *Der Zauberberg, Doktor Faustus* is considered less successful in aesthetic terms. This conclusion is based on an organicist aesthetics, whose applicability to a modernist novel is never discussed.

By the early 1960s professional insiders like Wellek began to wonder about the fate of the New Criticism in the academic world; perhaps it had lost its vitality and was showing signs of mechanization and ossification (Graff 227). Its very professionalization in the English department—that is, its reduction to textual explication according to accepted rules and norms—endangered the core of aesthetic doctrine, namely, the autonomy and uniqueness of a work of art. A method that would repeatedly affirm the organic structure of a text under discussion failed to capture the very elements it tried to defend. In broader terms, the paradigm of intrinsic criticism had deliberately narrowed the range of legitimate questions to such an extent that it eventually created a zone of critical taboos that began to haunt the profession by the end of the 1960s, when urgent social and political questions infiltrated the American campus. At that historical moment the ritualistic quality of the paradigm became apparent. The protest of the New Left punctured the unspoken assumption that literary criticism could and should produce more readings for a (still) growing academic market.

On closer inspection, the crisis of intrinsic criticism can already be noticed during the 1960s when a new generation of critics came into its own. In the very attempt to follow the prescriptions of the New Criticism they discovered its limitations. Theodore Ziolkowski, for example, notes in *The Novels of Hermann Hesse* (1965) that his initial plan to emphasize the formal and structural aspects of the novels turned out to be unsatisfactory, because it excluded larger thematic questions that were essential to understanding Hesse. Consequently, he divides his study into a general thematic part and a second part dealing with Hesse's individual novels. Even in these readings much extrinsic historical material enters the discussion. Apart from specific intellectual and historical problems, Ziolkowski was interested in Hesse's position among modern European writers. A similar comparative interest can be detected in Walter Sokel's *The Writer in Extremis*, a study in which the deviation from New Critical thought is evident. For his assessment of German expressionism in the context of European modernism and the European avant-garde, Sokel had to historicize the modernist aesthetic principles that the New Critics had treated as a dogma.

What these attempts had in common was that they did not challenge the hegemonic paradigm. In particular, they did not openly disagree with the intrinsic-extrinsic dichotomy. The implicit search for a new model could be labeled a call for a new synthesis, as Gowa had already suggested in 1953. How welcome an open discussion of the problem was in the late 1960s can be seen from Jeffrey Sammons's largely positive review of Jost Hermand's *Synthetisches Interpretieren*. Although the study was written primarily for a German audience, Sammons acknowledges its larger implications for literary criticism in general, including the work of American Germanists. Like Hermand, he feels that German studies on both sides of the Atlantic is in need of a new approach. Thus he praises Hermand's outspoken and sometimes harsh criticism of German *Germanistik* and notes:

> The result is a survey of extraordinary felicity and exactness, and of greatest significance; I do not think it too much to say that the revitalization of our profession will be proportional to the extent which Hermand's account of the history of the discipline is grasped by those working in it. (99)

The review underscores the importance of a historical grounding of critical work, a move by which the reviewer distances himself from strictly formalist criticism, from existentialist criticism, and from variants of metaphysical criticism. Although he agrees with Hermand's low regard for ossified versions of *Werkimmanenz* and New Criticism, Sammons stresses the importance of modern hermeneutic techniques and the potential dangers of a sociology of literature without interpretative skills. His program seems to envision a synthesis of a sociohistorical and a hermeneutic approach that will break out of the cage of New Criticism the way Hermand showed the way for a break with German *Werkimmanenz*.

What distinguishes Hermand's analysis from the widespread call for a new synthesis is its rigorous questioning of the feasibility of such a model and the fear of remaining at the level of a mere combination of methods. He rightly focuses on the intrinsic-extrinsic opposition as a crucial stumbling block for methodological innovation (176–77) and points to the need for a reinterpretation of the concept of history before any explication of a literary work can succeed. For Hermand literary interpretation must be tied to a concept of historical progress that allows the critic to read and evaluate the artwork as part of the larger process of human emancipation. This call for a dialectical understanding of history moves him close to a Marxist position but not yet to a materialist stance. In this respect his study anticipates the debates of the 1970s.

Notes

1 His 1946 essay "Zu Otto Ludwigs *Zwischen Himmel und Erde,*" for instance, deliberately presses the psychological issue through the use of Freudian analysis. "What Ludwig

portrays in Appolonius is the classic characteristics of a neurosis with a split personality and severely weakened willpower. At the beginning we have the trauma, the psychological injury that is marked by a complex of specific symptoms" (130). As much as Weigand underscores the validity of his method here, he does not argue that psychoanalysis provides the final answer for the interpretation of the story. He points to another level where a number of accidental events begin to form a constellation that would doom the hero in any case. This argument reflects Weigand's general attitude vis-à-vis a literary text: it is ultimately the text that validates the method, not the method that enables the reading.

2 While Jockers considers the 1930s as a new phase in German literary criticism, his discussion very much continues the German tradition of *Geisteswissenschaften* ("humanities"), but then it claims to have found the appropriate category for the American situation in the concept of *Denkformen* ("modes of thought"). From his strong rejection of Adolf Bartels we may conclude that Jockers did not share the racism of the Third Reich. At the same time, his strident polemic against psychoanalysis (Freud rather than Jung) and his sympathies for Ludwig Klages, Julius Petersen, and Hans Leisegang suggest that he is at least open to more-intellectual versions of fascism. It was probably German (idealist) philosophy that attracted Jockers to these critics, not a commitment to Nazi Germany per se.

3 This plea was supported by Werner Richter in 1946, who also argued for a broadening of German studies in the direction of a general theory of literature. But this theory would include a number of different approaches, among them intellectual history. He explicitly disagrees with Wellek and defends the continued significance of *Geistesgeschichte* ("Strömungen" 108, 111, 112).

4 As late as 1986 Wellek was convinced of the basic thrust of the New Criticism and defended it against what he considered false accusations. Its principles are deemed to be valid "as long as people think about the nature and function of literature and poetry" (*American Criticism* 144).

Oppositional Criticism

Marxism and Feminism, 1970–80

SARA LENNOX

The Marxist and feminist approaches to German literature and culture that first emerged in the course of the 1970s can be understood only in the context of the political upheavals of the 1960s, though their relation to 1960s political movements in the United States is a complex one, modulated by the specific environments of American German departments. In contrast with West Germany, in America participation in the student movement was not predicated on adherence to Marxist or any other leftist principles. Nor could a young radical Germanist rely on the movement to learn the fundamentals of Marxism, since very many American radicals of the 1960s were earnest activists with little or no background in theory. Young leftists in Germanics could expect little help from other areas of literary studies in the United States, which were still enmeshed either in the formalism of the New Criticism, in which English professors had been trained, or in the more fashionable French structuralism of comparative literature departments. English-language Marxist literary analyses of the 1930s had scarcely risen above the level of a crude reflection theory deriving from the base-superstructure metaphor. Though the emergence in the 1970s of an oppositional criticism in Germanics is altogether unthinkable without the uprisings of the 1960s, the specific forms it assumed, the relatively unproblematic acceptance of a Marxist perspective (at least in comparison with the fate of that perspective in other national literature departments), and the tenacity of leftist (including left feminist) approaches in succeeding decades can be explained only by examining how those methods emerged from within (if sometimes also in reaction against) the United States German departments themselves.

First, unlike other departments of national literature, the German departments of the 1960s were strongly influenced by exiles—by the Germans from Hitler's Germany and their particular attitude toward the cultivation and dissemination of German culture. While those exiles have sometimes been accused of perpetuating a notion of German culture that is immune to or can inoculate against the vicissitudes of history (e.g., Henry Schmidt, "What Is Oppositional Criticism?"), other scholars have observed that the exiled Germanists impressed younger Germanists with a cosmopolitanism and verve not to be found in German *Germanistik* (see Trommler, *Germanistik*; Lämmert). In the 1950s and 1960s, the older generation of exiles was joined by younger German scholars who could not tolerate (or find academic jobs in) the stifling atmosphere of cold-war Germany. Though the political standpoints of the many refugees from the time of the economic miracle span a wide range of perspectives, a number of those political or economic exiles had engaged in or at least encouraged politicized literary scholarship even before the onset of the 1970s. Wolfgang Paulsen's third Amherst Colloquium in 1969 was titled "The Poet and His Age: Politics As Mirrored in Literature." At the University of Wisconsin, Jost Hermand was so active in reclaiming lost political texts that the *Times Literary Supplement* commented in 1971: "[S]o productive is he as editor and essayist at present that he almost seems a stage-army bravely fighting for the political view of literature in all parts of the field at once" ("Politics" 489). Indeed, in addition to his many other studies, Hermand, who came to Wisconsin in 1958 (with Reinhold Grimm, who joined him in Madison in 1969), exerted a significant influence on German literary studies in the Federal Republic of Germany (FRG) through Grimm's and his publication of *Basis: Jahrbuch für deutsche Gegenwartsliteratur* from 1970 to 1980 as well as the numerous papers presented at the Wisconsin Workshop, which was established in 1969. Several generations of young United States Germanists, who later became the discipline's Marxists (and sometimes even its feminists), found a safe haven for their political interests and encouragement for their new scholarly approaches among this older generation of German exiles. However, as many younger American Germanists have unhappily observed, numerous German-trained scholars in United States German departments in the 1950s and 1960s remained unable fully to cut the umbilical cord to the Federal Republic. As Frank Trommler has put it:

> [They] clearly tailored their activities for the discussions and publishing houses of the Federal Republic. That meant that American universities housed a German *Germanistik* whose intellectual orientation seldom broke out of the isolation of German departments and frequently intensified it. ("Einleitung" 30)

One startling example of this phenomenon is Hermand's own *Geschichte der Germanistik* (published in 1994!), which includes names of no United States–based scholar of non-German ethnicity except those of an American who co-edited a book with Hermand, a few scholars in Women in German, and David Wellbery. It treats all scholarship on German literature, including Hermand's own, as if it had been produced on German soil.

But the orientation of United States German departments of the 1960s toward the Federal Republic provided young Marxist Germanists with a further legitimation for their own political emphases. Since the 1966 Germanistentag (annual conference of Germanists) focused on the topic "Nationalism in *Germanistik* and Literature," West German *Germanistik* had also been a scene of turmoil, leading Michael Pehlke to remark in the programmatic volume *Ansichten einer künftigen Germanistik* (1969) that revolting German students were willing to entertain only two alternatives for the future of the discipline, its abolition or its radical transformation (20). To be sure, United States Germanics in the 1970s did not pursue the course taken by West German *Germanistik*, where, as Chryssoula Kambas describes, "since the early seventies the majority of professors and students had opted for an explicitly political self-conception" (58). Nor should it have taken the course of West German *Germanistik*, Walter Lohnes and Valters Nollendorfs argued in 1976: "German Studies, we think, are not and should not be *Germanistik*, even the *künftige Germanistik* discussed in the two pioneering Reihe Hanser volumes, which assess the situation in Germany" (Introduction 3). But the politicization of German literary studies and other areas of German life and thought from the mid-1960s on made it difficult to dismiss the nascent Marxism of graduate students who had recently returned from the Federal Republic.

Furthermore, German critical theory's highly sophisticated analysis of the culture of late capitalism made leftist approaches to culture legitimate—while simultaneously modeling a kind of armchair Marxism that could separate theory from praxis, carving out a space for Marxist-influenced criticism that did not entail career-destroying confrontations with older colleagues. Kurt Mueller-Vollmer quite correctly observes that the interest in critical theory began in the 1970s, with the translation of major texts by Adorno, Horkheimer, and Benjamin and the founding of the journals *Telos* (1971) and *New German Critique* (1974). Critical theory even motivated some students to enter the field of United States Germanics ("Differenzierung" 154). But David Bathrick points out that the appropriation of critical theory in the United States proceeded in the opposite direction from that of the FRG. It moved away from the optimistic interventionism of a Brecht or (in some of his incarnations) Benjamin to a focus on the more skeptical-pessimistic high theory of Adorno and another Benjamin variant ("Literaturkritik" 138). Whether the Frankfurt school and its associates should or should not be consigned to a Marxist camp depends, among other things, on how broadly the term *Marxism* is defined. In United States Germanics, perhaps in the United States academy as a whole, Frankfurt school critical theory moved young radicals toward Marxism in the late 1960s and early 1970s and (perhaps something like Hegel's owl of Minerva) steered them away from Marxism in a stricter sense, and from practice in general, as the 1970s wore on.

The final impetus propelling young Germanists toward Marxism in the early 1970s was the thaw that accompanied Erich Honecker's accession to power in the German Democratic Republic (GDR) in 1971. Honecker's proclamation of no taboos in GDR cultural production unloosed an outpouring of writing previously consigned to the bottoms of drawers. Young left-leaning scholars now found in GDR literature a new object of study that permitted, perhaps even necessitated, a Marxist approach allowing them to promote socialism with a human face without preventing them from making their way in the academy. Certainly, the focus of United States Germanics on East German literature still sometimes revealed a scholar's enthusiasm that was blind to the faults of the GDR and perhaps even of Marxism. It was often quipped that the enthusiasm in Germanics for the GDR was inversely proportional to one's distance from it. As Bathrick points out, critical theory could also perform the function of distancing scholars from positions taken in actually existing socialism through the theory's challenge to the orthodox or scientific Marxism of the Second International and of Eastern European Stalinism ("Literaturkritik" 141). At least some scholars of the GDR believed that they could find in the best GDR writing far-reaching critiques of the deformations occasioned by Stalinism that, unlike critical theory, were not prepared to relinquish a belief in the hope of realizing the utopias that Marxism envisioned. The best Marxist-influenced GDR scholarship of the 1970s approached its object of study from a position sympathetic to the ends of Marxism while distinctly critical of Marxism's execution in East Germany. Focusing their second number of *New German Critique* on the GDR, the journal's editors explained that their emphasis was an effort to open a (clearly Marxist-influenced) "discussion about the transition to socialism in an advanced industrial society." Feeling their way along a path full of ideological pitfalls, they remark that

> a critique of the GDR that does not make clear its anti-imperialist and anti-capitalist assumptions can easily fall into a legitimation of anti-communism in the West. At the same time, recognition of this fact does not imply that a critical approach to the GDR is rendered impossible. ("Editors' Introduction" 2–3)

Similarly, if more eloquently, Peter Uwe Hohendahl and Patricia Herminghouse, editors of *Literatur und Literaturtheorie in der DDR*, a collection of papers presented at the path-breaking GDR conference held at Washington University in April 1974, observe:

We make the provocative assumption that the current state of affairs in the GDR can be criticized because, despite the important accomplishments of the system, it represents only a preliminary stage of the social form that Marxist theory envisioned. (Foreword 8)

Of what, methodologically, did the Marxism of United States Germanics in the 1970s consist? Like the perspectives of the participants in the 1974 symposium on the GDR, the Marxisms of 1970s Germanists were likely to be as diverse as the practitioners themselves—and, as a consequence of the publication of increasing numbers of books on Marxist theory, the growing influence of poststructuralism toward the end of the decade, and the increasing acceptability of feminist approaches, also constantly changing. Nonetheless, a paper delivered by Bathrick, one of the founding editors of *New German Critique* and then a young faculty member at "red Wisconsin" (as it was termed in the 1970s), at an MLA forum in December 1975 captures some of the positions held by young United States Marxist Germanists at mid-decade. Though in its printed form Bathrick's talk was called "On Leaving Exile: American *Germanistik* in Its Social Context," the MLA talk was entitled "The New Left Perspective." It was one of four talks in a forum titled Other Perspectives on the Study and Profession of Germanics, sponsored by the Germanic Section, which was a clear acknowledgment from the discipline at large that the field was changing. As an alternative to traditional Germanics, Bathrick proposes an interdisciplinary method that would be based on

a dialectical materialist approach. By that I mean a method which sees the prevailing separation of our disciplines not as ontological givens but as another form of social fragmentation; one which would seek from within existing disciplines the methodological means by which to reintegrate one's understanding of a subject into a totalizing historical process.

The use of such a method would be premised on a new political engagement on the part of Germanists, a "commitment to engage oneself as teacher and scholar in the efforts of working people to eliminate the class, sex, and race-founded dominations upon which high culture rests and which have made us perforce purveyors of that culture" ("On Leaving" 256). Though Bathrick's call for an interdisciplinary, American-style German studies would meet an enthusiastic response in subsequent decades, his 1975 paper also reveals a variety of qualities that characterized Marxist Germanics at that time but have since passed into history. On the one hand, there is the embrace of a relatively orthodox approach to Marxism ("dialectical materialism," the Soviet term for its variant of a method Marx himself had called "historical materialism," the "totalizing historical process") that poststructuralism would soon draw into question; on the other, there is a commitment to Germanists' engagement in the democratic political struggles of working peoples, a call "to take sides," as Bathrick put it in his paper's final sentence (257). Even at the zenith of disciplinary politicization, that engagement was probably honored more often in the breach than in the observance. Because Marxism in Germanics was frequently an arcane theoretical posture and not an aggressive practical-political stance, battles could be fought, and often quite brilliantly, on journal pages rather than in the form of career-destroying bloodlettings in departmental hallways (let alone city streets). Heinz D. Osterle's observation of 1978 is cynical but quite savvy: "A position of ideological commitment is tenable and tenurable if it is expressed with caution and mental reservations" (15).

Until the late 1970s, when mainstream journals of United States Germanics began to accept Marxist contributions, *New German Critique* served as the primary publishing venue for United States Marxist Germanists as well as for scholars from other disciplines. Many of the scholars whose names appear in the earliest numbers of the journal are now established members of the field and seem to confirm Osterle's assertion that a commitment to Marxism did not necessarily damage one's career. Yet numerous graduate students who published reviews in *New German Critique* at that time and assisted in its production have, for a variety of reasons, since left the field: Marxism was certainly no guarantee of success. Among those who wrote for the journal in the 1970s, it is interesting to note that many cultivated those issues as focal points in their careers. Bathrick, Hermand, Alexander Stephan, Helen Fehervary, Carol Poore, Marc Silberman, and Jay Rosellini wrote on GDR culture; Jack Zipes, another of *New German Critique*'s founding editors, contributed a number of articles on children's education and children's literature and the politics of fairy tales and other texts for children; Andreas Huyssen, the associate editor, began his study of pop culture; together with Egon Schwarz, Russell Berman drew the Enlightenment's treatment of women, homosexuals, and Jews into question; Michael Jones dealt with neo-Marxist aesthetics; I looked at GDR literary theory; the late Henry Schmidt wrote on reception theory; and Hohendahl examined Adorno, Lukács, reception aesthetics, literary sociology, and the history of literary criticism. By the late 1970s many of the Marxist Germanists had attained faculty positions at prestigious United States institutions, and, to judge by their presence at national conferences, their variety of leftist Germanics had become not just acceptable but positively *en vogue*.

Bathrick's was not the only oppositional "other perspective" to be addressed at the 1975 MLA forum; along with "The American Perspective," presented by Jeffrey Sammons, and "The Comparative Perspective" of Herbert Lindenberger, Ruth Klüger Angress also presented "The Woman's Perspective." With incisive irony, Angress pointed out that it was as potentially exclusionary to speak of women's perspective on the field as to believe that, as a consequence of their Jewishness, all Jews would necessarily read literature the same way.

And yet, as a feminist Germanist herself, Angress maintained that women, like Jews, are better positioned to ask questions about unexamined assumptions and premises, literary or otherwise, that members of dominant groups might more easily overlook. Much work awaits those, she argued, who assume "the women's perspective": first, "to clean up or at least object audibly to the sexist inanities which riddle our secondary literature" and "our language textbooks, which are a sink of sexism"; then, and even more important, to elaborate a body of feminist criticism. Pointing to a range of unresolved gender-related issues from the *Nibelungenlied* to Brecht's *Mutter Courage*, Angress called on feminist scholars to forgo their "general cries of outrage" and take up the difficult tasks that await them:

> For while feminist criticism is regarded with suspicion in many quarters, we should not make it so easy for ourselves as to ascribe this suspicion solely to the entrenched male chauvinism of the profession. The truth is that we haven't even begun to do the job. (250)

Such feminist efforts were well under way in the field of Germanics. The 1974 Washington University conference on the GDR was path-breaking in another regard as well. Disciplinary legend suggests that it was at that conference reception, where male faculty members sat on chairs and female graduate students sat on the floor, that it all "clicked" (to use *Ms. Magazine*'s term) and the organization Women in German (WIG) was born. The new group put structures into place to support feminist scholarship, teaching, and survival in Germanics that were very pragmatic and very American. It was quite different from the relatively free-floating, mostly intellectual, and (despite Bathrick's appeal for solidarity with working people) predominantly European connections of Marxist Germanists.

The methodological directions pursued by members of WIG (to which many, if not most, established feminists in US Germanics belong, although they are not all active members) were also influenced by feminist literary scholarship in the United States far more than developments in Germany, where feminism had barely begun to make an impact. As in the earliest studies of Anglo-American feminism, feminist Germanists first focused, as Angress had proposed, on the genre of feminist analysis initiated by Kate Millett's *Sexual Politics* (1970), decrying the sexism of textbooks, scholarly studies, and primary literary texts themselves. (At this rather early period, sexism was understood to be at work when women were denigrated because of their sex, represented as less capable than men or as active only in realms stereotypically associated with women.) Thus WIG's first conference examined, among other topics, sex-role stereotyping in United States and GDR children's readers (Slepack) and cast "A Critical Look at *Brigitte*" (Wartenberg). The examination of sexism in literature slid easily into another familiar standby of feminist scholarship,

"Images of Women in the Works of . . . ," the second conference exploring the
woman question in the early work on Döblin (Tewarson), Volker Braun's
"Tinka" (Consetino), and "Women and the Aesthetic of the Positive Hero in
the GDR" (Fehervary). Because Germanists came somewhat late to feminist
scholarship, those early variants of feminist scholarship coexisted with approaches that were more fashionable at mid-decade. As Elaine Showalter observed in a 1975 review essay on feminist literary criticism:

> In the past five years, literary criticism concerned with women has gone well
> beyond sexual politics, to include the resurrection of lost women writers; the
> reinterpretation of well-known women writers; the utilization of material from
> linguistics, psychology, anthropology, art history, and social history; and the
> incorporation of methodologies from Marxist and structuralist criticism. (436)

Other papers at the first WIG conferences focused on women's historical accomplishments: literary salons in Berlin around 1800 (Hertz), revolutionary
women in imperial Germany (Pelz), women deputies in the Weimar Republic's
Reichstag (Fessenden). But, interestingly, *WIG Newsletter* 9 indicates that participants in the retreat segment of the first conference were somewhat baffled
about how to deal with the question of neglected women writers, the topic of
a Saturday evening discussion that focused on "the quantitative or bibliographic
problem of locating material about and by women writers and the much more
complex qualitative issue of which writers are worth dealing with from the
point of view of feminist values and/or literary merit." Patricia Herminghouse,
who summarized the discussion for the newsletter, reported: "All participants
agreed this [second] topic was far too profound to resolve without a great deal
of ground work, which would probably have to be undertaken by groups rather
than individuals." Doubtless the problem of literary evaluation was exacerbated
by the virtual lack of feminist literary theory until later in the decade. As
Showalter observed, "On the whole, feminist literary criticism and scholarship
have been stubbornly empirical; they have generated little theory and abstrac-
tion" ("Review Essay" 436).

   For Germanists, that problem began to be remedied by Silvia Bovenschen's
influential article of 1976, "Concerning the Question: Is There a Female Aesthetic?" ("Über die Frage"), and her book *Die imaginierte Weiblichkeit* (1979). By
the 1978 conference, too, WIG members were examining "The Women's Question and Aesthetics" and had begun their first discussions of French poststructuralist feminists like Hélène Cixous and Luce Irigaray. By the end of the
decade, under the influence of French theory as well as United States cultural
feminism and what Showalter later termed "gynocritics" ("Feminist Criticism"
248), the study of female writers alone, many WIG members, like other United
States (and West German) feminists, believed they knew the answer to Bovenschen's and many other questions about female specificity: women (*tout*

court!) were not only quite different from men (an assertion that would have horrified feminists in the 1960s) but quite probably also superior to them. The task of feminist scholars was to delineate that difference by retrieving and elaborating on an autonomous female subculture that patriarchal domination had hitherto obscured. Still, gynocritical studies like "Women Authors in the Nineteenth Century," "Contemporary Women's Culture," and "Integrating Women's Culture into the German Curriculum" continued to coexist alongside examinations of "Sexism in the German Language." That sea change could be observed in the quite different responses of WIG members to Christa Wolf's story "Selbstversuch" (1974). The 1975 newsletter was convinced that Wolf had succumbed to sexism:

> We feel that while Wolf is well aware of the effects of socialization on men and women, she nonetheless seems to accept the male assumption that biology determines one's emotional make-up. As a result, Wolf unwittingly supports the patriarchal view of women. ("Dialogue")

How to assess Wolf's story from a feminist perspective was also the subject of a quite heated exchange between Gisela Bahr and me at the 1977 Amherst Colloquium. Bahr asserted that Wolf's story was simply regressive, while I, with a number of caveats, nonetheless maintained, "For feminists the value of Christa Wolf's works consists in the recognition and articulation of these alternative forms of consciousness that she explicitly derives from her own experience as a woman" (Lennox, "Der Versuch" 221). By 1979 the problem of female difference seemed to be resolved in favor of difference, and the WIG session at the MLA addressed "Women's Letters, Diaries, and Autobiographies" in order to investigate the question of "a feminine or feminist aesthetic: are there specific ways in which women write differently than men, and if so, what do these differences mean?" (*WIG Newsletter* 16 [1979] 6). The 1979 conference focused for the first time on lesbian themes in German literature, a subject that accorded with the feminist theory of the time, which stressed the "lesbian continuum," as Adrienne Rich called it (648), binding together all women. The 1980 WIG conference, where the hitherto repressed issue of Jewish identity arose quite unexpectedly, presaged the debates around differences among women that would rend feminism in the 1980s and afterward.

In many ways, feminists in Germanics followed the course charted for them by the United States women's movement. They were also influenced by the specific conditions of United States German departments. As their presence at the 1974 Washington University conference on the GDR suggests, many early feminist Germanists had already aligned themselves with the new Marxist-influenced direction of United States Germanics, and their feminist scholarship in Germanics remained (and remains) more influenced by leftist perspectives than academic feminism elsewhere in the United States or in West Germany, where feminism was often considered a movement in opposition to the left rather than part of it. (See, e.g., the early, graphic feminist leaflet calling on women to relieve SDS's "socialist eminences" of their "bourgeois pricks" ["Die Anfänge" 17].) In their stirring foreword to *New German Critique*'s special 1978 feminist issue, Helen Fehervary, Renny Harrigan, and Nancy Vedder-Shults declared:

> Only when western Marxism begins to deal consciously with the material reality of half the human race will its analysis become truly concrete—a prerequisite for radical change. And only when feminism begins more consistently to formulate its ideas in a historical and materialist manner will its practice be capable of liberating all humanity. (3)

Many early members of WIG were attempting to elaborate such a Marxist feminist approach just as a flood of women's writing began to pour forth from the GDR, and those texts' approaches to the particulars of daily life in the framework of a commitment to socialism became a model for the kind of politics many members of WIG would pursue. With Wolf in the forefront, GDR women writers helped feminist Germanists envision utopian possibilities that far transcended the privatistic visions of much Western feminism and were premised on a far-reaching qualitative change in all society that would compel and enable the transformation of both men and women. At the very least, this commitment to a left feminist analysis spared Women in German the worst excesses of both radical and dress-for-success feminism; at the most, it may have inspired some of WIG members' best scholarly work.

WIG members were also affected to some degree by the isolation of German departments from a larger United States intellectual context. Certainly the attentiveness of feminist German studies to developments in United States feminist scholarship at large meant that WIG members were much more receptive to new theoretical approaches. It has been argued (Martin, "Zwischenbalanz"; Lennox, "Feminismus") that poststructuralism; the study of minority discourses in Germany; and, later, postcolonial theory entered German studies in good part as a consequence of feminist Germanists' efforts. But the failure of Germanics to engage with current theoretical currents has left its mark on feminists too, as Biddy Martin points out:

> To date women Germanists have been remarkably seldom represented in larger feminist discussions about the political implications of particular epistemological and critical strategies. Of course there are many reasons for this absence. Feminists in German literature were trained in German Departments in the US, many of which are more concerned with discussions in the Federal Republic than with debates in other fields here and which are well-known for

their resistance to Lacanian psychoanalysis, Derridian deconstruction, Althusserian Marxism, and Foucauldian discourse theory. (171)

Whether it is because of their United States Germanist training and connections, their Marxist (or empiricist) convictions, or (as Martin also suggests) their unwillingness to venture outside the secure confines of WIG, many feminist Germanists (like their male colleagues) are frequently not entirely au courant with recent theoretical developments. As a consequence, with a few striking exceptions like Martin herself, WIG members have not been leading participants in United States feminist debates.

Finally, because feminism was perceived as not just another theoretical perspective but also a standpoint with practical consequences for business as usual, the reception of feminist Germanists by the field at large has often been rockier and more uneven than the reception of Marxists. Like Marxism, feminism seemed to be accepted at the national level more swiftly than at the local level. By 1977 Women in German had become an allied organization of the MLA and was guaranteed its own sections at every MLA conference. WIG sessions at the AATG and the German Studies Association are not guaranteed, but those organizations have been generous about accommodating sessions officially sponsored by WIG. Paulsen devoted his Amherst Colloquium to the topic "Woman as Hero and Author" in 1977, the first conference of feminist German studies held anywhere, and *New German Critique* turned its entire thirteenth issue over to the feminists. But the editors of that issue explained in their foreword with some passion that the special issue was necessary because the journal's male editors took neither their female coworkers nor their female coworkers' feminist perspective seriously enough:

> Although several women worked intensively on the journal and participated in shaping its direction in the first years, the decisive conceptual work was carried out by the male editors and other men who served in an advisory capacity. Thus questions of social theory and culture were formulated primarily in terms of the critical Marxist tradition, and feminism, although it was considered a major political issue and a central problem of everyday life, was relegated to the periphery of discussion. (Fehervary, Harrigan, and Vedder-Shults 3)

At the departmental level, the climate for feminism was even worse, and in the early days of WIG some members reported that they kept their participation in the annual WIG conference a secret for fear of ridicule or worse from senior male members of their department. While such a response would be considered impossibly politically incorrect today, even at the beginning of the twenty-first century feminism has had less impact on German departments than on our colleagues in English, where a 1990 MLA survey reported 60.9% of the respondents (73% of the women, 55% of the men) said that feminism had influenced their teaching of English and American literature (Huber, "Today's Literature Classroom" 48). As late as 1992, Ruth-Ellen Boetcher Joeres, at the University of Minnesota in a department generally perceived to be quite friendly to feminism, observed:

> My present thinking is that *Germanistik* and feminism are reasonably unrelatable. *Germanistik* is a mostly male domain; feminism is mostly the province of females. Although that would not necessarily imply alienation, there seem to be very few connections. But it isn't even a matter of apples and oranges. It is more like elephants and parsley. (248)

Although men in American German studies have been slow to grant the advantages of feminist approaches and although feminist Germanists still complain about their marginalization (Fries), Valters Nollendorfs conceded in 1994 that, with the growing Americanization and feminization of German studies as a younger generation assumes control of the field, "a greater and more widespread acceptance and reception of German women writers is inevitable" ("Out of *Germanistik*" 7). If Nollendorfs is right, the prediction with which Ruth Klüger Angress ended her 1975 MLA address may yet become a reality:

> If feminist criticism will address itself to genuinely and generally interesting questions, it will soon cease to be peripheral. A "woman's perspective" will then become one of the Germanist's indispensable tools, whether that Germanist be male or female. (251)

From Deconstruction to Postcolonialism, 1980 to the Present

IRENE KACANDES

During the last twenty years "Germanics" has become "German studies." By German studies I mean the interdisciplinary study of events and cultural production occurring in German territories or involving Germanophone agents. It is not just that the training of many current faculty members took place in graduate programs as diverse as anthropology (e.g., Daphne Berdahl at Minnesota), comparative literature (e.g., Gerd Gemünden at Dartmouth), history (e.g., Peter Jelavich, previously chair at Texas, Austin), and political science (e.g., Andrei S. Markovits at Michigan) but, more significant, that the methodologies they—and many faculty members who have been trained in traditional German departments—employ in their current research and teaching do not necessarily develop out of the history of Germanics or follow theoretical paradigms from Germany. The walls of German departments have become porous as colleagues from outside disciplines introduce other methods and as Germanists develop dialogue down the hall rather than across the ocean. There no longer exists a "we" based on a common disciplinary orientation (philology) or a privileged object of study (the German literary canon). What needs to be addressed are the methods used by a diverse scholarly community interested in analyzing things German from multiple disciplinary perspectives. Because of the current "theoretical polyphony" (Hoesterey 594), what follows in this essay can make no claim to exhaustiveness, nor can it offer a chronological narrative. Rather, I present deconstruction, the new historicism, cultural studies, queer theory, and postcolonialism as approaches that have

243

become of interest to German studies scholars—in that order. Striking features of this polyphony include the primarily negative reactions of German historians to the so-called linguistic turn; German studies' embrace of cultural studies, particularly in the exploration of identity questions; the leading role of German studies scholars in queer theory; and finally their surprising but significant contribution to postcolonial studies.

Deconstruction

While the arbitrary and differential nature of the sign had been introduced by Saussure at the beginning of the twentieth century, the full implications of this idea found expression only decades later, with the so-called postmodernist, poststructuralist, or linguistic turn, the tenets of which entail that language can refer only to language and that there is no external, privileged position outside the instabilities of language from which to derive the truth. Contrary to popular opinion, these insights do not deny the existence of meaning; rather, they seek to expose "how each sign simultaneously *confers and derives meaning* with respect to other signs, so that any given sign is tacitly implied in another as a 'trace' or an effect of linguistic interdependence" (Kneale 187; my emphasis). Deconstruction, however, should be situated not only in relation to Saussure's insights about signs and signification but also in relation to Nietzsche, Freud, and Heidegger and their general decentering of our intellectual universe.[1] As an analytic method, deconstruction rethinks "both word and world from the point of view of textuality" (Kneale 188). More concretely, analyses often rely on etymology and rhetoric to show how words or figures deconstruct themselves. J. Hillis Miller has described deconstruction's method as simply good close reading (230).

One of the lasting positive legacies of deconstruction has been its intellectual rigor. Criticisms have included charges that deconstruction is "wilfully obscure" and that all deconstructionist readings sound alike (Guerin et al. 341, 342). But we could make the same charges from the deconstructionist perspective by pointing to the fact that "deconstruction is less an applied method than an intrinsic habit of language" and that therefore all texts can be deconstructed and indeed deconstruct themselves (Kneale 188). This answer will not likely satisfy all critics. As Barbara Johnson wrote in the wake of the de Man affair:

> What seems clearer than ever in the extreme violence and "glee" of the recent attacks on deconstruction is the extent to which any questioning of the reliability of language, any suggestion that meaning cannot be taken for granted, violates a powerful taboo in our culture. (xvii)

Deconstruction has been a boon to those Germanists who have published in a deconstructionist vein regularly for more than a decade. Werner Hamacher's essay "Das Beben der Darstellung" (in David Wellbery's widely used 1985 pedagogical volume *Positionen der Literaturwissenschaft*) introduced deconstructionist views to numerous Germanists in Germany and the United States. Although Hamacher insisted that those tenets do not constitute a method, he and Rainer Nägele have trained several generations of graduate students in the United States in "good close reading." Nägele justifies his regular return to certain authors like Hölderlin, Benjamin, Kafka, and Freud by explaining that their texts "have become for me testimonies of writing" (*Echoes* 5). The influence of Germanist deconstructionists beyond the sphere of German departments is demonstrated by Hamacher's coeditorship of the widely circulated volumes of Paul de Man's wartime journalism and of the responses to it (Hamacher, Hertz, and Keenan) as well as by the success of Eric Santner's deconstructionist-Lacanian study *Stranded Objects*, which put the subject of German postwar reactions to the Holocaust on the United States critical theory map. These contributions notwithstanding, deconstructive ways of reading have more frequently been rejected or ignored by scholars of German, in part because the issues raised preempt, overlap, or contradict existing intellectual traditions— for example, hermeneutics (Gemünden 191) and the work of Max Weber (Jelavich, "Contemporary Literary Theory" 374). Andreas Huyssen follows a similar logic in his influential study of postmodernism *After the Great Divide*, where he insists that poststructuralism really offers nothing new, being merely another variant of art for art's sake (208).

Historians of German have even expressed hostility toward deconstruction. Michael Geyer and Konrad Jarausch explain: "Losses of referentiality are frightening and make understandable the urge to hold on to and insist on realism in history which conflates text and reality" (247). Jelavich points specifically to the "horrors of the Nazi era," which he says

> hover over every conceptualization of the German past. Within that context, it is hard to avoid the conclusion that a denial of human agency exculpates the perpetrators of those deeds, while a denial of subjectivity amounts to silencing the voices of the murdered. ("Contemporary Literary Theory" 376)

In one of the least subtle versions of this line of reasoning, Kenneth Barkin argues, "The stakes are higher in German history; there is less room for French intellectual gymnastics" (246). While the obvious chauvinism and mischaracterization of intellectual work expressed here might make us want to dismiss this argument out of hand, deconstruction offers a direct response. As Johnson reasons:

> If idealism can turn out to be terroristic, if the defense of Western civilization can become the annihilation of otherness, and if the desire for a beautiful and orderly society should require the tidying action of cattle cars and gas chambers, it is not enough to decide that we now recognize evil in order to

locate ourselves comfortably in the good. In Nazi Germany, the seduction of an image of the good was precisely the road to evil. It is thus not out of "hostility" to the moral values of Western civilization that deconstruction has arisen, but out of a desire to understand how those values are potentially already different from *themselves*. (xvii)

Geyer and Jarausch come to a similar conclusion, suggesting that historians of German should devote attention to the historicity of signification—a subject that has "deeply concerned, even obsessed" German thinkers since the eighteenth century and yet is one about which "German History" has been "stunningly negligent" (248, 247). That such calls have been emerging increasingly from the historical profession (e.g., Crew 46) and that historians are joining German studies departments or programs where they are sure to encounter scholars who use the insights of deconstruction may lead to such work. Azade Seyhan's *Representation and Its Discontents* provides a good interdisciplinary model from a trained Germanist.

New Historicism

If in the age of German studies historians have increasingly been urged to take the linguistic turn, literary scholars have concomitantly been chided to take the historical turn. Although I agree that the new historicism is a "phrase without an adequate referent" (Veeser x), it illustrates the general changes described at the beginning of this essay. Anton Kaes is often credited for single-handedly bringing the new historicism to German studies (e.g., Berghahn, "New Historicism" 146). At the 1988 DAAD-sponsored conference on Germanics as German studies, Kaes pleaded:

> To put it provocatively, I regard New Historicism as a chance for the rejuvenation of our discipline: it offers us new questions, broadens our textual base, opens us to new archival sources, allows literary texts and other cultural representations to resonate more fully, and shows us new ways of writing about literature within larger networks of meaning. ("New Historicism" 211)

Kaes's own familiarity with the new historicism came from dialogue down the hall at UC Berkeley with its founding fathers, most notably Stephen Greenblatt. Only shortly after the DAAD conference, three United States–based Germanists (i.e., Kaes, Hohendahl, and Lützeler), without prior consultation, found themselves introducing the new historicism to Germanists in Germany. Though it was received there with much skepticism, the event is an example of another departure from the traditional pattern of methodological influence (see Berghahn's account 141–42; for the protocol of the conference, see Eggert, Profitlich, and Scherpe).

So what is the new historicism? The term itself suggests two ways that the approach presumably intends to replace or supersede: *new* historicism as opposed to *old* historicism and new *historicism* as opposed to new *criticism*. Both supporters and critics of the new historicism have suggested that it is best considered a set of reading practices (rather than a theory or a doctrine) that share hostility toward the objectivism and grand narratives of nineteenth-century forms of historicism, including Marxism (Brantlinger 46), as well as the notion of an autonomous text.[2] Greenblatt mobilized the term "cultural poetics" to get further away from grand narratives ("Towards a Poetics" 2). That term and his description of a work of art as "the product of a negotiation between a creator or class of creators, equipped with a complex, communally shared repertoire of conventions and the institutions and practices of society" (12) hint at the new historicism's debt to cultural anthropology (particularly Geertz's project of "thick description"). Louis Montrose's emphasis on textuality—Montrose coined the new-historicist chiastic slogan the "historicity of texts and the textuality of history" (23)—betrays a debt to structuralism and deconstruction, and his characterization of texts as socially produced and socially productive (23) gestures toward Foucault and particularly Foucauldian analyses of discourse and power.

The best work in the new historicism as in deconstruction has been praised for its sophisticated close readings. Typically two or more texts, one literary and one not, are juxtaposed and read for the way they inscribe the same historical moment. The nonliterary text is read not as background for the literary text but rather in a parallel fashion. New-historicist work is often launched with an attention-grabbing anecdote and includes self-reflexive, first-person gestures. Such procedures, it has been suggested, have rendered "the historical map . . . more interesting" (Hohendahl, "Return" 101) and have made a convincing case that scholars must study the links between writing and other social practices. Yet criticisms of the new historicism have been numerous. They extend from such diverse issues as the selection of materials, the focus of analysis, and the aims of such scholarship. Early charges that this approach was to only one period and one type of literature (Renaissance drama) have been met with a slew of new-historicist analyses of other periods and texts. Kaes himself made a huge contribution to the new historicism by applying its methods to filmic, not literary texts (*From Hitler to Heimat*, an adaptation of his earlier *Deutschlandbilder*). He writes, "I show how films of the New German Cinema have 'staged' existing discourses on the history and memory of the Third Reich. The films are analyzed as parts of larger discursive contexts within which they acquire multiple, often contradictory meanings" ("New Historicism" 218n24). Getting at "larger discursive contexts" for the Weimar period has been made easier for potential new historicists with the publication of *The Weimar Republic Sourcebook*, which Kaes edited with Martin Jay and Edward Dimendberg. Kaes made a further contribution to the new historicism by suggesting specific lines of inquiry (see his call for study of "the intermingling of larger discursive fields" [214]). The 1991 conference at the University of Wisconsin, Madison, organized by Klaus Berghahn addressed "the problem of how to transform [the new historicism's] synchronic approach to literature into the larger project of a diachronic reconstruction of literary history" (Berghahn, "New Historicism" 145).

Despite these expansions into new areas of inquiry, many criticisms persist. Patrick Brantlinger explains that the charges of "arbitrariness" relate to the (absent) theoretical framework: "Lacking the explanatory power that referring cultural phenomena to the material or economic base seems to afford, cultural poetics appears to grant its practitioners complete license to reconstruct any story about the past that they choose" (47). Feminists have objected to the new historicists' account of their method, which ignores the important repudiations through feminist theory and other oppositional criticisms of both new criticism and (old) historicism, without adding much to the analysis of gender relations (Newton; Lennox, "Feminism and New Historicism"; Friedrichsmeyer and Clausen). Hunter Cadzow laments:

> Despite the New Historicists' professed interest in cultural difference, many of them speak of societies as if they were monolithic entities and thereby suppress the fact that in a given political formation different paradigms for organizing economic or aesthetic activity exist simultaneously. (539)

This critique comes from the legitimate concern that the new historicism downgrades the aesthetic element altogether (Hohendahl, "Return" 103) and that it collapses " 'all levels of reality into one level of representation' and makes it difficult to talk about intentionality, causality, and change" (Jehlen qtd. in Lennox, "Feminism and New Historicism" 159). Attacks from the political and academic right and left (Veeser ix–xi) confirm just how difficult it is to pin down the new historicists' agenda (Hohendahl, "Return" 100). My contention is that nothing substantial differentiates new-historicist studies from work in cultural history (i.e., in the tradition of Schorske) or cultural studies, other than the scholar's decision to call it new historicist. With the notable exception of Kaes, most practitioners of German studies have in fact used these other labels.

Cultural Studies

Stuart Hall, who once proclaimed that "cultural studies is not one thing; it has never been one thing" ("Emergence" 11), has also asserted that "it does matter whether cultural studies is this or that. It can't be just any old thing which chooses to march under a particular banner. . . . [T]here is something *at stake*" ("Cultural Studies" 278). One of the ways in which cultural studies distinguishes itself is by showing precisely what is "at stake" in the world around us. It is this commitment to interrogating the structures of power (in addition to its constitutive interdisciplinarity) that made cultural studies the most popular paradigm for German studies in the 1990s (on cultural studies as dominant paradigm, see Weiner, "From the Editor" 5).

What then flies under the cultural studies banner? To quote a definition by the editors of the most influential compendium in the field to appear in the United States, cultural studies is

> an interdisciplinary, transdisciplinary, and sometimes counter-disciplinary field that operates in the tension between its tendencies to embrace both a broad, anthropological and a more narrowly humanistic conception of culture. Unlike traditional anthropology, however, it has grown out of analyses of modern industrial societies. It is typically interpretive and evaluative in its methodologies, but unlike traditional humanism it rejects the exclusive equation of culture with high culture and argues that all forms of cultural production need to be studied in relation to other cultural practices and to social and historical structures. Cultural studies is thus committed to the study of the entire range of a society's arts, beliefs, institutions, and communicative practices. (Nelson, Treichler, and Grossberg 4)

Like the new historicism, cultural studies aims to analyze cultural objects in relation to other social and historical structures. However, the objects typically studied are more diverse: everything from epistolary culture, sculpture (Weimar portrait busts), public buildings (the Neue Wache), and popular magazines (*Die Gartenlaube*) to Berlin cabaret, mass media, and the discourses of female asylum seekers and ethnic Germans—to cite just a few examples from German cultural studies (see S. Richter, "Ins and Outs"; MacLeod; W. Miller; Belgum; Jelavich, *Berlin Cabaret*; Lacey; Mueller, resp.). Aspects of colonial, postcolonial, and queer culture have also been examined under the rubric of cultural studies. In further contrast to the new historicism, work in cultural studies hardly has an identifiable methodology; indeed, practitioners pride themselves on drawing "from whatever fields are necessary to produce the knowledge required for a particular project" (Nelson, Treichler, and Grossberg 2; see also Gilman, "Why and How" 202).

As an academic endeavor, cultural studies derives inspiration from scholars as diverse as Richard Hoggart, Raymond Williams, Hall and his colleagues at the Birmingham Centre for Contemporary Cultural Studies; Theodor W. Adorno, Max Horkheimer, and the Frankfurt school; French theorists such as Roland Barthes, Michel Foucault, and Pierre Bourdieu; Marxists like Antonio Gramsci, Walter Benjamin, and Louis Althusser; and North American scholars like bell hooks, Janice Radway, and Andrew Ross, who have little more in common than the country in which they teach and an interest in identity politics and popular culture. This genealogy develops out of incompatible and even antithetical views about the nature of culture, its production, and its consumption. Yet this incompatibility has produced fascinating theoretical debates and laid the foundation for what may prove to be cultural studies' greatest legacy: the insistence on redefinitions of culture and on analyses of cultural consumers as also producers of culture. Criticisms of cultural studies have ranged from mockery of its goal (to describe the whole fabric of culture) to disapproval of its disregard of the canon, its lack of interest in premodern societies, and its lack of serious archival research and close reading (for refutation, see Kacandes, esp. 9–12, 18).

Even before the opening of the Iron Curtain and German unification transformed the cultures that German scholars studied, the late 1980s produced increasing calls for altered relations to discipline and to disciplines. The DAAD-sponsored conferences of 1988 and 1989 as well as their published proceedings (resp., *German Histories* and *DAAD Special Issue*) are filled with exhortations to interdisciplinarity. It is revealing that literary scholars, historians, and political scientists each conducted and published their discussions separately (Kacandes 14). The need to learn more about contemporary critical theory and to work more closely with colleagues from other disciplines led to the Cultural History Conference at the Center for European Studies at Harvard University in April 1994 (see Czaplicka, Huyssen, and Rabinbach), the German Studies as Cultural Studies conference at Davidson College in March 1995, and the *German Quarterly* special issue on culture studies in fall 1996 (*Special Issue*). The most crucial accomplishment of these discussions from the mid-1990s is the commitment to producing genuinely interdisciplinary—as opposed to multidisciplinary—work in the future (see Kacandes 15). Some new work resulted from the Davidson conference and appears in *A User's Guide to German Cultural Studies* (Denham, Kacandes, and Petropoulos). And some got its impetus through another channel, which I have been calling conversations with colleagues down the hall.

Around the same time that the specifically disciplinary discussions were taking place, Germanists took note of the increasing importance of minority studies in the United States and developed a powerful desire to investigate "the challenge to hegemonic cultural values" in German-speaking countries, past and present (Seyhan, Introduction 4–5). Indeed, the special issue of *New German Critique, Minorities in German Culture* (1989), is an institutional sign of the acceptance of truly different realms of investigation and heralds a whole series of lengthier studies on questions of cultural hegemony and constructions of identity (gender, ethnic, religious, national). To cite just a few that seem to have already left their mark: Leslie Adelson's *Making Bodies, Making History;* Russell Berman's *Cultural Studies of Modern Germany;* John Borneman and Jeffrey Peck's *Sojourners: The Return of German Jews and the Question of Identity;* Arlene

Teraoka's *East, West, and Others;* Erica Carter's *How German Is She?;* Alon Confino's *The Nation as a Local Metaphor;* Azade Seyhan's *Writing outside the Nation;* and the edited volumes *Gender and Germanness* (Herminghouse and Mueller) and *Unwrapping Goethe's Weimar* (Henke, Kord, and Richter). While there has been some concern in the German studies community that concentrating on questions of identity can "unwittingly reinforce our insular position in American academe by remaining German-focussed" (Kuzniar, "Cross-Gendered Cross-Cultural Studies" 122), these studies have built bridges between German studies and the cultural studies practiced in other departments. Alhough Marc Weiner fears that cultural studies has brought with it "cavalier textual interpretation based on ideological models more than on attention to semantic representation" ("From the Editor" viii), this charge is counterbalanced by the careful archival work and close reading in German cultural studies. Still, Weiner's query about the credibility of a discourse based on speaking from a "marginal" or nonhegemonic position as it becomes mainstream (vi-vii) is certainly worthy of further debate.

Queer Theory

Unlike any other approach considered in this overview, queer theory can be traced, at least partially, to concrete political action; it arose in response to the very real, very nonacademic AIDS crisis and to such mobilizing groups as ACT UP! and Queer Nation (see Case 164–65). The pejorative term *queer* is "construed as 'anti-normal,' in order to include a broad spectrum of ethnic, gender, and sexual practices, linking them one to the other under its umbrella term" (Case 166). Political and theoretical goals merge when Teresa de Lauretis wonders, "Can our queerness act as an agency of social change, and our theory construct another discursive horizon, another way of living the racial and the sexual?" (xi).

As an academic field, queer theory, also referred to as radical sexual theory, is unthinkable without the development of feminist theory. But its distinguishing features—such as the interrogation of the "stability and ineradicability of the hetero/homo hierarchy" (Fuss 1), the insistence on the cultural and historical variability of sexual practices, and the performance of gender—can be given additional lineages. Foucault's work on the history of sexuality, Lacan's revisionary reading of Freudian sexuality and ego development, and Goffman's notion of "dramaturgy" and "presentation of the self" can be cited as foundations for the anthropologist Gayle Rubin's description of the sex/gender system ("Thinking Sex" and "Traffic"); the philosopher Judith Butler's deconstruction of "woman" and her notion of the performance of gender ("Against Proper Objects," *Bodies,* and *Gender Trouble*); the science and cultural critic Donna Haraway's development of the idea of cyborgs and the reinvention of nature (*Primate Visions* and *Simians*); the literary scholar Eve Kosofsky Sedgwick's work on homosocial desire, the notion of closeting, and auto- and allo-identification (*Between Men*, *Epistemology*, and "Gender Criticism"); and the German studies scholar Biddy Martin's notion of the subject "beyond gender" (*Femininity*). These works are in turn the bedrock for queer studies.

The particularly close relation between queer theory and German studies can be traced through Martin's career development, from her active search for theoretical paradigms beyond Lukács and her discovery of Foucault in 1980 to her path-breaking series of articles in the 1980s and 1990s to her critique of and proposals for queer theory in *Femininity Played Straight: The Significance of Being Lesbian* (1996).[3] And yet, this relation is very old: "the discourse on homosexuality arose and continued for twenty years exclusively in a German context" in the 1870s and 1880s before being translated, literally and figuratively, into other languages (Kuzniar, Introduction 4–5). Why such discourse remained a German affair has yet to be addressed adequately, to my knowledge. Nonetheless, if Martin's articles from the 1980s lay a foundation for queer German studies in the United States, then the edifice begins to emerge at a well-attended 1992 MLA panel organized by Alice Kuzniar about reconsideration of the so-called age of Goethe through a queer lens. The fruits of the MLA panel appeared in *Outing Goethe and His Age*. Edited by Kuzniar, it presents queer research by a dozen different German studies scholars, including Simon Richter, Robert Tobin, and W. Daniel Wilson. Like Martin's *Femininity* and Kuzniar's anthology *Outing Goethe*, Sue-Ellen Case's *The Domain-Matrix: Performing Lesbian at the End of Print Culture* was published in 1996.

Martin offers insightful critical readings of Foucault and Lacan. She questions the specific mobilizations of anormativity and glorifications of "mobility, flux, destabilization and detachment" (28) that have been prevalent in queer studies to date. She makes a plea for "a queer studies that allows for attachments that are not necessarily politically consistent and acknowledges the incalculability of the subject" (14). The volume by Kuzniar contributes to the historicizing of queer theory by looking at a critical period in the "reconstruction of a gay archeology" before the homo/heterosexual opposition was firmly in place (Kuzniar, Introduction 32). Kuzniar corrects the story about one of the most canonically regarded periods in German and European literary history by pointing out that writers in the long eighteenth century themselves referred to the period as the century of Winckelmann and the century of Frederick the Great:

> This nominal dissimilarity hints at a certain denial among later generations of the potential importance of homosexuality, a situation that calls for re-reading the institution "*Goethezeit*" by resurrecting its own self-grounding in a gay-positiveness. (31)

Like Martin, Case has contributed to queer theory by critiquing the imperialism of *queer* and its "claim to all semiotic territories" (186). As her subtitle hints, she foregrounds her reconceptualization of queerness through cyberculture. She brings the work of German artists like the playwright Heiner Müller and the filmmakers Elfi Mikesch and Monika Treut to the attention of the queer scholarly community by exposing and exploring the imbrications of sexuality, commodity culture, and East-West politics (see esp. 127–87; on Mikesch and Treut, see also Kuzniar, *Queer German Cinema*). Martin, Kuzniar, and Case are noted as inspiring teachers whose students are in turn becoming teachers who shape German studies. For example, in April 1999 Katrin Sieg, a former student of Case and now associate professor of German studies at Georgetown University, guided the Northeast Workshop on Women's History and Culture (whose members include the longtime German studies practitioners Sara Lennox, Patricia Herminghouse, Renate Bridenthal, Mary Nolan, and Atina Grossman) in a weekend seminar on queer theory.

Postcolonial Criticism

While many believe postcolonial criticism was launched through the publication of Edward Said's *Orientalism* in 1978 (e.g., Williams and Chrisman 5), others indicate lack of agreement about its parameters (its object of study, methodology, political goals). Although it rarely figures in course or book titles, imperialism—"the extension or imposition of power, authority, or influence"— connects all these academic endeavors.[4] The field could be described as the wide-ranging critique of imperialist practices. In Homi K. Bhabha's formulation, "Postcolonial criticism bears witness to the unequal and uneven forces of cultural representation involved in the contest for political and social authority within the modern world order" ("Postcolonial Criticism" 437).

Said's book focused on colonial discourse and how those in power represented those whom they subjugated; specifically, it focused on the Occident's perception of the Orient. Bhabha suggested that work should also interrogate how the colonized were implicated in this relationship ("Of Mimicry" and "Postcolonial Criticism" 439). Scholars built on Said's (and Bhabha's) work by describing what the formerly colonized "wrote back," hence the title of one of the field's foundational volumes: *The Empire Writes Back* (Ashcroft, Griffiths, and Tiffin). By defining *postcolonial* as "all the culture affected by the imperial process from the moment of colonization to the present day" (2), the editors open up the field to the study of all majority and minority discourse.

Postcolonial criticism has contributed to transformations of the literary canon and to the concomitant subversion of the universalist claims once made on behalf of (Western) literature by (Western) liberal humanist critics (Barry 191). But even those who praise the field for such accomplishments point to what still needs to be done. The prefix *post-* is problematic because it can mean both "coming after" and "superseding" (Bennington 122; Baross 159). It has been argued, for example, that societies can experience a postcolonial phase only after a colonialist one, and yet it is generally premature to assign postimperialist status to any contemporary society (e.g., Williams and Chrisman 4). Anne McClintock suggests that the term *postcolonial* itself invites a reinstitution of the binary opposition that the field presumably sets about to deconstruct (colonial/postcolonial); the term thus hardly encourages consideration of multiplicity. She objects specifically to the way it obscures postcolonial relations not only between men and women but also among women ("Angel"). Along similar lines, critics have charged that the field has reinforced Eurocentrism by focusing exclusively on European colonization and decolonization. Jonathan Hart and Terry Goldie point out that Russian, Japanese, Chinese, and other colonizations have largely been ignored, as have indigenous languages and cultures (156).

Though Germany is part of Europe and cannot contribute to a correction of Eurocentrism, recent work in German studies should be cited for furthering our understanding of some of the problems just raised. The German case upsets the colonial/postcolonial binary opposition in a number of interesting ways because of the late acquisition and short life of actual German colonies, the method of decolonization, the relatively small number of former colonial subjects living in the nation-state of the colonizers, as well as the extraordinarily large number of Turks now living in Germany, whose presence cannot be situated in colonial history. One strand of German postcolonial investigation considers what mainstream white German authors have written about their travels into formerly colonized areas of the world (see Lützeler, *Der postkoloniale Blick*; see the essays that came out of a conference held at Washington University in March 1997 [Lützeler, *Schriftsteller*]). A different strand of investigation begins with Susanne Zantop's *Colonial Fantasies: Conquest, Family, and Nation in Precolonial Germany, 1770–1870*. Her study reveals the seductiveness for Germans of colonization, made noteworthy precisely because German powers did almost no colonizing before the late nineteenth century. In this sense, her work invites scholars of other cultures whose political states do not count as colonizers to consider what effect colonial discourse nevertheless had on those cultures. By reading a broad variety of texts (scientific articles, philosophical essays, political pamphlets, popular novels and plays, and travel literature), Zantop demonstrates the role that colonial fantasies played in shaping German national identity—an identity, she convincingly argues, that cannot be separated from racist and patriarchal ideology. The intertwining of nationalist fantasies with imperialist ones is further investigated in a volume edited by Sara Friedrichsmeyer, Sara Lennox, and Zantop, *The Imperialist Imagination: German Colonialism and Its Legacy*. This kind of work increases the understanding of how relations developed among European powers, since German fantasies betrayed the conviction that Germans would have been (and for a short time were) superior colonizers to the Spanish, French, and British (e.g., see 24).

Finally, the study of the process of unification of the former East and West German populations may well add yet another dimension to what the field wants to consider under its purview (see McFalls; Berdahl).

Approaches such as deconstruction and cultural studies could never have been developed without German thinkers such as Nietzsche, Freud, Heidegger, Adorno, and Horkheimer. Still, there is a widely held belief both within and outside German studies that Germanists have rarely played a leading role in developing these methodologies. While that may be true if one considers only the works that immediately launched those methodologies, it is false in the light of their subsequent development. Already in the mid-1980s, Sander Gilman's *Jewish Self-Hatred* and Andreas Huyssen's *After the Great Divide* made crucial interventions into national and international intellectual debates (on anti-Semitism and postmodernism, resp.). And, as I have pointed out, works like Santner's *Stranded Objects*, Adelson's *Making Bodies, Making History*, Martin's *Femininity Played Straight*, and Zantop's *Colonial Fantasies* contribute to theoretical discourses at large. While the identity of German departments has shifted, the identity of the addressees of work produced by those departments has shifted even more—and that bodes well for the future vitality of German studies.

Notes

1 One practical consequence of this heritage for German departments was that a certain number of students wanted to learn German in order to read these thinkers in the original. When deconstruction lost popularity, these students were lost to German departments as well (Kuzniar, "Cross-Gendered Cross-Cultural Studies" 123).

2 The relation between the new historicism and Marxism is particularly difficult to pin down. Most practitioners and critics would agree with Shea's assessment that on the one hand it rejects the base-superstructure model of vulgar Marxism and on the other it retains the Marxist notion that "human beings and their artifacts are 'constructed by social and historical forces' " (125). For further nuances, see Greenblatt, "Towards a Poetics" 2–8; Brantlinger 46–48; Gallagher.

3 Many of the essays in this book have been published previously; the introduction movingly summarizes how they fit together emotionally and intellectually.

4 Related adjectives, however, appear more frequently (e.g., McClintock, *Imperial Leather*; Friedrichsmeyer, Lennox, and Zantop).

4

Research in Historical Perspective

∽

Edited by
JOHN A. MCCARTHY

Introduction

The contributions to this section lend contour to the research profiles in Germanics since the establishment of graduate programs in the late nineteenth century. That study is, of course, a Sisyphean task. One must take a narrower rather than a broader view; otherwise, one could not construct a compelling narrative, provide stimulus for further reflection, or prompt discovery of untapped opportunities. The following explorations do just that for several areas of research in Germanics: literary history and theory, medieval studies, linguistics, German Jewish studies, and folklore. Preceding them is Jost Hermand's synoptic overview of developments in literary studies since their beginning. The contributors' conclusions seem to support Henry J. Schmidt's prognosis that "American Germanics is difficult to reduce to a common denominator because of its decentralization and heterogeneous membership" ("Wissenschaft" 77). This decentralization would appear to be a special mark of the developments after about 1970 as a result of the opening of the discipline to impulses emanating from GDR studies, folklore and fairy-tale studies, German Jewish studies, and women's studies.

In the early days of the discipline, the demarcation lines among literature, linguistics, and medieval history were not always clearly drawn because of the preeminence of philology in the nineteenth century. Derivative of classical philology, it is understood in the wide sense as "the study of language and literatures, arts and politics, religion and social customs" (Wellek and Warren 27). Hence philology extends beyond historical grammar, literary criticism and interpretation and includes the relation of literature to all kinds of knowledge (Thrall and Hibbard 351). In fact, in his symptomatic *Encyklopädie und Methodologie der philogischen Wissenschaften* (1877), Philip August Boeckh simply defined *philology* as the knowledge of the known. It is striking that Wellek and Warren's extraordinarily influential *Theory of Literature*, which prompted a renewal of literary criticism in the post-1945 period, draws so heavily on German scholarship, literary aesthetics, and forms. Indeed, the German distinction between *alter und neuer Philologie* ("old and new philology") is significant for the evolution of critical methodologies in German studies in the United States from its beginnings through the twentieth century.

It was not until the final third of the twentieth century that the significance of German philology began to wane in the classical sense as it had been popularized by the Brothers Grimm and mirrored in Boeckh's encyclopedia. It was broadly practiced in the nineteenth and twentieth centuries and exemplified by such notables in Germany as Karl Lachmann, Wilhelm Scherer, and Karl Bartsch and in the United States by Kuno Francke, Hermann Collitz, William Kurrelmeyer, Helene Adolph, Otto Springer, and George Schoolfield. "Old and new philology" had sought legitimization through adoption and adaptation by modern foreign language specialists of research techniques unique to the study of ancient Greek and Roman cultures. Greek and Latin were monolithic specialties entrenched in the schools and colleges; the modern foreign languages had to compete for a spot on the curriculum against their hegemony (Zeydel, "Teaching . . . through World War I" 41). In other words, modern foreign languages had to demonstrate that their methodologies were as rigorous and scientific as those of classical philology. Citing the practical value of knowing a second modern language in the contemporary world was not enough to legitimize its study. Hence a fruitful topic for further investigation is the essential tension that existed between philology in the older, narrower meaning (of the scientific study of language families, grammar, syntax and the relation between language and meaning—areas now absorbed into the more recent discipline of linguistics) and philology in the modern, more general connotation (literature, *Mediävistik* ["medieval studies"], and other disciplines). Just as the question of legitimization is central to the history of Germanics in the United States, the issue of authentication is seminal to the rise of various methodologies ranging from positivism to such movements as *Geistesgeschichte*, hermeneutics, literary sociology, structuralism, semiotics, deconstruction, reception theory, and postmodernism (see Maren-Grisebach; Nemec and Solms; Wellbery; Hohendahl, "How to Read").

Generally speaking, research foci in Germanics are like waves washing up on the shore: they rise to a crest, then come crashing down just to flatten out and listlessly ebb away. They come and go in erratic yet steady patterns. And they are dependent on external forces: wind, current, position of the moon, and so on. Although each cresting wave of formative energy eventually flattens out, it does succeed in redefining the coastline. The firmament remains stolidly resistant, but with time it looks different. The undulation of research waves is similar in its effect on the changing shape of Germanics and the idea of what is canonical. External mechanisms that determine which wave rises when in the history of literary criticism include the natural phenomenon of resistance to the reigning canon, departmental and organizational structures, funding opportunities, the proclivities of reviewing committees (hiring, tenure, editorial), the desire to engage North American academic debate, the indebtedness to German schools of critical thought, political and gender issues, and simple intellectual curiosity and refinement in a Kuhnean sense. These mechanisms also deserve closer scrutiny.

Not all research topics of interest to Germanists are encountered in the following pages. The Nietzschean narrowing of perspective ("Verengerung der Perspektive") as a life-advancing phenomenon is the operative principle in this section. Without that narrowing of vision, progress is less likely. Of course, there is blurring at the periphery. Jost Hermand, Francis Gentry, Orrin Robinson, Noah Isenberg, Donald Haase, and David Bathrick provide an initial mapping of the terrain, showing us the open plains, valleys, and multiple paths. The peaks and valleys require greater detailing, yet the roads of inquiry have been engineered.

How does one identify what research topics were preferred at various stages in the history of the profession? Of course, one could review the editorial comments and kinds of articles published in leading journals such as *PMLA, Monatshefte, MLN,* the *Germanic Review,* the *Journal of English and Germanic Philology,* the *German Quarterly*—all of which reach back into the earlier days of the discipline. For developments in the second half of the twentieth century, there are additional guides such as the *Lessing Yearbook, Women in German Yearbook, New German Critique, German Studies Review, Speculum, Journal of American Germanic Linguistics* (see the section "Organizing the Profession"). One could examine the conference programs for the MLA as well as its regional affiliates, the AATG, the German Studies Association, the Medieval Institute in Kalamazoo, and so on. One could evaluate the numerous symposia sponsored by the DAAD (the German Academic Exchange Service [Deutscher Akademischer Austauschdienst]) and the Max Kade Foundation over the past thirty years. One could scrutinize the lists of various publishing houses that have held (or hold) a position of prominence in German studies: the university presses of Cornell, Yale, Penn State, Nebraska, Minnesota, Johns Hopkins, Wayne State, Princeton, Cambridge, and Oxford. The Camden House, Continuum, Routledge, Rodopi, and Peter Lang presses could be used to round out the picture. Of particular interest would be topical monograph series and anthologies of fairy tales, German Jewish writers, women writers, and writers from the GDR.

For more recent years, one could look up the winners of the MLA Aldo and Jeanne Scaglione Prize for Studies in Germanic Languages and Literatures, the DAAD Book Prize of the GSA, the Max Kade Prize for the Best Article in the *German Quarterly*. Telling would be an assessment of grant applications to the Guggenheim Foundation, the American Council of Learned Societies, the American Philosophical Society, the Fulbright Foundation, and NEH, to determine how many German topics were represented and how the German proposals compared with non-German-focused proposals. And, of course, one could examine the topics of dissertations penned at various institutions and at various times in the history of the profession.

At this point the general contours of research interests in Germanics since the late nineteenth century seem to fall into these general eras: 1880–1900, 1900–17, 1918–45, 1945–75, then the 1980s and 1990s. These divisions are not hard and fast; many areas overlap, and the boundaries differ for linguistics and medieval studies. The waves of research may be distinct, but they do run into one another. The first PhDs awarded in North America reveal a clear penchant for philological studies. In 1879 Waterman T. Hewett took his doctorate from Cornell with a dissertation on the Frisian language and literature, while Hugo J. Walther received his doctorate in 1886 from Columbia with the thesis "Syntax of the Cases in Walther von der Vogelweide," and Marion Dexter Learned earned the first doctorate at Johns Hopkins in 1893 with a study of Pennsylvania Dutch. The first PhD in Germanics at Chicago was awarded to Francis A. Wood in 1895 for his examination "Verner's Law in Gothic and the Reduplicating Verbs in Germanic." The first PhD at Penn was awarded to Frederick W. Koenig in 1891 for his dissertation "Dativus Absolutus in Gothic." An apparent exception among these first studies was William J. Eckhoff's dissertation of 1891 at New York University on Goethe's educational views (Zeydel, "Teaching" . . . through World War I"; McCarthy, "Indigenous . . . Plant"). But the dissertation topics at Penn under the leadership of Learned between 1895 and 1915 reveal a rapid expansion into areas of philology in the broader sense. They mirror a growing interest in German American cultural influences and comparative studies. The year 1899 saw the dissertation "Gerhardt Hauptmann's Plays and Their Literary Relations" (Martin Schütze); in 1900 there was "Statistical History of German Drama in Philadelphia" (Orlando F. Lewis); in 1901, "Heinrich von Kleist and the Spanish Movement" (Glen L. Swiggett); in 1902, "Friedrich Schlegel's Relations with Reichardt and His Contributions to 'Deutschland' " (Samuel P. Capen); and in 1903 there were "The Harmony Society: A Chapter in German American Culture" (John A. Bole), "Translations of German Poetry in American Magazines" (Edward Ziegler Davis), and "Schiller in America" (Elwood C. Perry) (McCarthy, "Indigenous . . . Plant"; Trommler, "Recovering"). These kinds of German studies topics, interspersed with traditional philological studies, continued through the twentieth century. Of course they have been augmented by waves of new thematic, generic, and period foci such as women writers, fairy tales, GDR socialist literature, and transdisciplinary phenomena. Only a closer examination would reveal the peaks and valleys in the waxing and waning of local interest (see Daemmrich). Obviously, dissertations are of paramount importance in determining research "waves." The influence of scholars such as the historians George Mosse and Peter Gay, the literary scholar and folklorist Jack Zipes, the theater historian David Bathrick, or the feminist Ruth-Ellen Boetcher Joeres in charting new directions for German studies would offer an excellent opportunity for individual case studies.

A brief look at the volume of material devoted to Goethe in the pages of *MLN* between its founding in 1886 and the hundred-and-fiftieth anniversary of Goethe's death, for example, reveals both the continuity and divergence of research on a single author in a general-interest journal. A total of 149 articles and notes were published. Comparative studies of Goethe and Lenz, Goethe and Diderot, Goethe and Wordsworth along with examinations of the dating and origins of *Faust* dominated between 1886 and 1900 (31 essays). *Hermann and Dorothea* rose to the fore in the period 1900–17, accompanied by analyses of *Egmont* and Goethean poems and an occasional comparative study (Goethe and Goldsmith, Goethe and Schiller). (These titles are drawn from 28 essays). From 1918 to 1945 comparative studies took on greater importance (Goethe compared with Browning, Carlyle, Dante, Ibsen, Mme de Staël, Ovid, Poe, Pushkin, Rousseau) among the 36 articles published—no doubt because of the anti-German sentiment since the Great War. From 1945 to 1970 the comparative studies continued (Goethe compared with Gide, Heine, Longfellow, Shakespeare), while *Faust* studies tended to dominate among the 36 essays. This pattern continued through the 1980s, culminating in three relatively long works—Robert Heitner's "Goethe's Ailing Women" (*MLN* 95 [1980]: 497–515), Marc Shell's "Money and the Mind: The Economics of Translation in Goethe's *Faust*" (95 [1980]: 516–62), and Ralph Hexter's "Poetic Reclamation and Goethe's *Venetian Epigrams*" (96 [1981]: 526–55). Interspersed throughout the years are essays on Goethe's use of children's rhymes (1906), quotations (1909, 1910), word usage (1900, 1928), and proverbs (1955). Of course, this kind of approach to scholarship trends is selective and narrow. One journal and one author do not tell the whole story (see also Henry Schmidt, "Wissenschaft" 78–80).

Wilhelm Scherer's theory of the golden ages (*Blütezeitentheorie*), with cultural zeniths around 1200 (i.e., *Staufische Klassik*) and 1800 (i.e., *Weimarer Klassik*) (18–22), proved to be quite influential in determining research agendas from 1880 to 1980. Kuno Francke's *Social Forces in German Literature* (1896) helped draw attention to contemporary literature, promoting research agendas in graduate programs. Erich Heller's *Disinherited Mind* (1952), Walter Sokel's *Writer in Extremis* (1959), Jost Hermand's *Synthetisches Interpretieren* (1968), Jack

Zipes's *Breaking the Magic Spell* (1979), Sander Gilman's *Jewish Self-Hatred* (1986), and Azade Seyhan's *Writing outside the Nation* (2001) are markers of additional, more recent shifts in perspective. George A. Hench's 1893 edition of the Old High German *Isidor* translation and Eduard Prokosch's *A Comparative Germanic Grammar* (1939) represent turning points in *Altphilologie* ("classical philology").

What we find in this section's essays is a road map, which helps us chart the traversed territory more accurately, not only as we travel along the identified thoroughfares but also as we branch out into less-explored byways. Not evident from this review of major trends in the past, however, is what effect the opening up of Germanics to neighboring disciplines had on the self-definition of the discipline itself. By expanding into related areas such as film, politics, cultural history, mass culture, and transnational writing, we have moved away from a clear center of activity, from a focus on the literary text. Even when the text figures predominantly, the latest effort is frequently designed to deconstruct the myth of a monolithic German culture. To be sure, the early years of the profession were all about carving out territory and establishing German literature and culture as an independent field of inquiry. Having shored up that identity throughout the first half of the twentieth century, the middle years witnessed efforts to explore connections with other albeit more closely related disciplines such as comparative literature and history. Those outreach efforts may in fact mirror the Germanist's acculturation in the wider academic setting. The trend revealed a secure sense of self that allowed comparison without fear of losing one's own center. The outward transdisciplinary expansion accelerated after 1985, leading us far away from our home territory into diaspora studies, gender studies, queer theory, and postmodern inquiry. Instead of fearing a loss of center, we now experience a veritable fascination with the decentering of traditional scholarship. Worthy of special scrutiny in this connection is the question, How has the theoretical and thematic expansion of critical reflection affected the discipline's sense of autonomy? In other words, what constitutes the heart of Germanics at the beginning of the twenty-first century? The fear of disciplinary transmigration has been sounded in a series of articles published most notably in the *German Quarterly* (2000) and the *Jahrbuch der deutschen Schillergesellschaft* (1996–97).

We might also ask how American university presses view us today. How do publishing decisions affect the field of Germanics? What kinds of outlets continue to exist for centrist German studies among the university press group? There are clear indications that university presses are cutting back on their purely German lists, even canceling series. Increasingly, book series determine the marketability of monographs. Increasingly, presses are forced to make their decisions based on what sells rather than on the intellectual quality of a book's argument. Consequently, more and more Germanists are sending their work to foreign presses such as Niemeyer, Rodopi, and Königshausen and

Neumann. It would be useful to examine how often German articles get published in those journals that represent the expansion areas of the discipline: *Comparative Literature, Configurations, Eighteenth-Century Studies, PMLA, Philosophy and Literature.*

Finally, societies devoted to specifically German figures and topics have noted a decline in membership in recent years. Changing demographics seem in evidence everywhere. In sum, the phenomenon of the widening circle of research interests in Germanics from 1890 to 1990 and beyond offers us an opportunity not only to reassess the past research agendas in the field but also to determine its prospects for the future. The essays in this section hope to promote this process of reevaluation.

The Development of Research from 1880 to the Present

JOST HERMAND

1880–1917

As is well known, Wilhelmine Germany was held in high regard in the United States before World War I because of its economic strength, internationally recognized educational institutions, and cultural achievements. That respect provided the Germanists working at universities in this country with significant self-esteem, which was expressed in their teaching. Many scholars of German approached the supposedly intellectually "underdeveloped" Americans as cultural missionaries with the goal of leading them out of the uninspired Anglo-American materialism to the heights of German idealism. Most of their students, 25% of whom had already learned German in high school, were quite willing to follow them on this path.

As a result, these Germanists did not pursue research that was typical for literary studies in Germany in the 1880s and 1890s, which included the discovery of new sources, the production of critical editions of works, and the writing of biographical studies. Rather, they concentrated on extolling the impressive achievements of German literature. In doing so, they relied on Wilhelm Scherer's history about the golden ages of German literature (*Blütezeitentheorie*) and focused primarily on the works of the Hohenstaufen era and of Weimar classicism. They showed no interest in the so-called bizarre periods, such as the baroque or the early Romantic era, and paid equally scant attention to the literature of their own day.

This focus is particularly evident in the articles that appeared in the *Pädagogische Monatshefte*, an organ of the National German-American Teacher's Association (Nationaler Deutschamerikanischer Lehrerbund), which was founded in Milwaukee in 1897 by Max Griebsch. In addition to contributions concerning language pedagogy and philology, which were intended to strengthen and expand knowledge of the German language in the United States, this journal also published regular articles by leading Germanists such as Kuno Francke and Marion Dexter Learned. Again and again, they praised the classic German authors, who, they hoped, would exercise an aesthetic educational function as articulated by Friedrich Schiller in his letters *On the Aesthetic Education of Man*. By contrast, articles devoted to German literature in *PMLA* did not have such a pronounced nationalistic feel. In this journal, German was for a long time the only accepted academic language other than English. Still, there was little actual academic substance in the area of German studies; instead, specific authors were simply honored, particularly on the occasions of their anniversaries.

After 1900, this trend toward unquestioning praise became even stronger and pushed academic rigor further to the sidelines. During this time, German literary studies were undergoing a radical shift, moving from the strict methodological standards of positivism to a perspective more influenced by *Geistesgeschichte*. Most Germanists in the United States followed this trend. The entry of the United States into World War I against the German Reich was a tragedy for many of these scholars. After April 1917, when the first American troops were sent to the French front, American Germanists' efforts to impart a knowledge of the superiority of German culture came to a standstill. The *Pädagogische Monatshefte* ceased publication at this time, and American Germanists wrote almost exclusively about marginal, apolitical topics considered harmless in the remaining modern language journals.

1918–40

Immediately after World War I, German studies in America was characterized by a certain hesitancy. Up until 1917 many Germanists had enjoyed a great respect that reinforced their self-understanding as cultural emissaries; now they were confronted with an icy wind of hostility or outright hatred. In fact, some German departments, and the National Teachers' Seminary in Milwaukee, simply closed, leaving a number of German professors unemployed. Some could not even find work in high schools, because German instruction was for a time forbidden by law in many states.

The teaching of German literature ceased almost entirely for several years. Even for those who published books and essays on the subject, it was almost impossible to enter a career in German in the first half of the 1920s as a result of the strong aversion to everything German. This situation did not improve until the middle of the decade, when the Weimar Republic temporarily stabilized and America hoped for a growing democratization of Germany. Because of the prevailing conservative mood at that time, most American Germanists limited their study of German literature to the sacred, canonical texts of the Hohenstaufen and Weimar golden ages. They did, however, gradually begin to incorporate into their reading and teaching some works of the Romantic era as well as nationalistic conservative authors from the twentieth century. In this respect, they followed their colleagues in Germany, who still adhered to those authors included in the canon before 1914. But in their methodologies they moved further away from the once dominant *Geistesgeschichte* and turned to nationalistic-conservative (*völkisch*) or even prefascist approaches.

Thus the National Socialists' accession to power in 1933 did not signal a profound change for German studies in Germany or America. Fascist elements in German studies were considerably more pronounced in Germany than in the United States. Still, fascist tendencies cannot be overlooked in America, especially in the journal *Monatshefte*, which, with one brief exception, had not been published since 1917 and was reestablished in 1928. The main representatives of German studies in the United States during the early 1930s, such as Alexander Hohlfeld and Julius Goebel, were almost all Americans or German Americans who could not forget the shock of 1917. As a result, this group strove to avoid stirring up a new hatred of anything German. In addition to their continued consideration of the classic authors, they concentrated their essays primarily on modern nationalist-conservative writers such as Hans Grimm, Wilhelm Schäfer, Hermann Stehr, Paul Ernst, Erwin Guido Kolbenheyer, Gustav Frenssen, Hans Carossa, Agnes Miegel, and Karl Heinrich Waggerl. These contributions were not academic by today's standards of originality, critical incorporation of secondary literature, and methodological stringency. American Germanists of the 1930s did not conform to the thoroughness and rigor of German research methods. Instead, they sought to communicate in simplified form the cultural values of classical, Romantic, and nationalist-conservative works of literature, as emphasized in Germany, and to contribute to a general appreciation of this literature. Most of these essays are written in a tone of understanding praise. Critical elements, which would have entangled them in the troublesome issue of fascism, appear only in exceptional cases. The same is true for their reviews of studies appearing in Germany, which were rarely critical and generally passed over any fascist elements. But there were also those who sympathized with *völkisch* ideas, such as Otto Koischwitz, R. O. Roeseler, E. P. Appelt, and John R. Frey, who did not hestitate to introduce their convictions to a broader American public by emphasizing the heroic and Teutonic elements in the works under consideration.

1940–70

Only after 1941, when the United States entered World War II and the stream of exiled Germans and Austrians swelled, did a few liberal Germanists speak up in the modern language journals in the United States. They went outside the canon and introduced some works of German Jewish authors into the curriculum, especially after 1943–44. This change was made with extreme caution at first, without specifically antifascist or leftist tendencies. Thus, in the research focus of German studies in America toward the end of the war, the nationalist-conservative authors were gradually replaced with writers such as Hermann Broch, Hugo von Hofmannsthal, Arthur Schnitzler, Franz Kafka, and Franz Werfel. This replacement did not, however, call into question the canonical masterpieces of the Hohenstaufen era, the age of Goethe, the Romantic movement, or of poetic realism in any way. In fact, the emphasis on the classic authors actually grew even somewhat stronger, because of the influx of highly educated German and Austrian émigrés, who regarded America as a nation largely lacking in culture. As Germanists, their primary concern was the aesthetic education of those around them. Moreover, they were averse to anything political or social and preferred to keep a safe distance from such topics.

The exiled Germans and Austrians gradually moved into influential positions in American German departments since the late 1940s. Upon closer examination, they were not alone in avoiding politics. As a reaction to the social commitment of the "red decade" between 1929 and 1939 and shaped by the Great Depression, New Criticism had in the meantime established itself in English departments as the most prominent methodology in literary studies. This approach made a clear distinction between politics, history, and society on the one hand and supposedly autonomous great literature on the other. A clear symbiosis developed between the well-educated émigrés from Central Europe and those American scholars who haughtily looked down on mass media and its fixation on the entertainment industry. For example, the *Theory of Literature* (published in 1948 and frequently reprinted in the 1950s), was co-authored by the German-speaking Czech René Wellek and the American literary scholar Austin Warren but reads like a unified whole. The refugee from the Prague structuralist circle and the American committed to the formalism of New Criticism declared their opposition to any consideration of extrinsic values in the examination of literature. They focused almost exclusively on intrinsic values, such as language, style, rhythm, meter, metaphor, and symbol, which allegedly constituted the quality of all great literary works.

Though German studies publications in the United States during the 1950s and early 1960s maintained a number of aspects that were shaped by older traditions, their primary emphasis was on formal analysis, which was to prove the inner coherence of all great literary achievements. In addition to writing about Goethe, who was celebrated worldwide in 1949, and a few Romantics such as Novalis, Tieck, and Eichendorff, scholars of modern literature—such as Stuart Atkins, Bernhard Blume, André von Gronicka, Henry Hatfield, Heinrich Henel, Harold Jantz, Victor Lange, Herman Salinger, Walter Silz, and Hermann J. Weigand—began to delve into the works of Thomas Mann, Stefan George, Hugo von Hofmannsthal, Rainer Maria Rilke, Karl Kraus, and Franz Kafka. They mainly emphasized their apolitical, cosmopolitan traits as well as their formal literary qualities. In the early 1950s, at the apex of McCarthyism, there was a noticeable retreat into the realm of aesthetics. Even in the publications of German Jewish or Austrian Jewish Germanists, such as Peter Demetz, Heinz Politzer, Henry H. H. Remak, Egon Schwarz, Oskar Seidlin, Walter Sokel, and Werner Vordtriede, any sort of public coming to terms with the past (*Vergangenheitsbewältigung*) was largely absent, as it appeared too political and thus too risky.

As a result, research developed that was described at the same time by Germanists in West Germany as text-based (*werkimmanent*). Since German studies in America was still a rather small field, this research remained relatively marginal. Furthermore, the importance of academic publications was not emphasized by administrations, in deference to the concept of great teaching. It was not unusual for professors during this time to teach fourteen or sixteen hours a week. With the huge expansion of universities in the mid-1960s, the need for teachers became so great that even candidates who had just begun to write their dissertations received positions as assistant professors. Since the early 1960s many German departments in America hired young scholars from West Germany, such as Klaus L. Berghahn, Reinhold Grimm, Walter Hinderer, Peter Uwe Hohendahl, Anton Kaes, Ernst Schürer, Alexander Stephan, Frank Trommler, and me, which introduced completely new research interests into German studies in America. Among these academics from West Germany, some had been inspired by the liberal spirit of the post-Adenauer democratization movement after 1960, which culminated in a wave of student revolts between 1968 and 1973–74. This influx led to a considerable restructuring of teaching and research in the field of German studies.

Yet it was not only the new ideological impulses that prompted a clear shift from a rather conservative to a more liberal, even left-wing paradigm in the leading American German departments. The burgeoning financial support, which brought about a reduction of the teaching load, contributed to an entirely new research environment. While research had largely been an activity of individual professors interested in literature, who had occupied themselves in a highly personal way with a few of their favorite works, it now became more and more a vehicle for ideological debates. At times, the debates took on such a sharp tone that some of the older professors, who had until then dedicated themselves to the apolitical in the realm of New Criticism, felt provoked.

1970–85

Research in the early 1970s can hardly be compared with that of the preceding periods, because it stood in the shadow of the Vietnam War and the campus unrest caused by antiwar protests. Although political debates in the German departments in the United States were not carried out with the same intensity as in the *Germanistik* institutes of West Germany, a completely different climate developed with respect to research. Because of the rising scholarly interest in the division of Germany and its leftist traditions, the scope and the political relevance of publications assumed ever greater importance. German departments interested in improving their ranking organized academic conferences and attempted to increase the number of their MA and PhD candidates. They also expected their professors to distinguish themselves through major publications. Doctoral candidates, who had relied on local libraries for their research, had an increasing number of dissertation fellowships made available to them, so that they could conduct research in Germany, Austria, or Switzerland. They were also encouraged to make a name for themselves by giving lectures at the quickly multiplying sections of MLA conventions and international conferences.

The older Germanists, whether they were born in America or had emigrated from Europe, continued to focus their research primarily on the great masterworks of German literature from Goethe and Eichendorff to Stefan George, Thomas Mann, and Franz Kafka. The younger Germanists, however, developed after 1970 a sociohistorical point of view in opposition to the text-based approach. They no longer avoided second- or third-rate literary works or political and sociological texts. They were interested less in the aesthetically edifying function of literature than in its possibility for social, ideological, and political intervention. With the aim of attaining a better understanding of the historical development of literature, they considered everything written—including film scripts—to be literature or, more accurately, a literary document, regardless of its status as high or low in the older approach to German studies. When this group began its critical and ideological investigation of the previously sacrosanct Age of Goethe, as the Wisconsin Workshop of 1970 entitled Die Klassik-Legende (see Grimm and Hermand), many of the academics who had set the standards in the high culture of German studies in the United States, such as Oskar Seidlin, were deeply embittered.

Be that as it may, the practitioners of this new approach maintained a decidedly high-culture concept of literature, although it was understood more in political-educational terms and less in a formally aesthetic or existential manner. They did not want to demolish the older canon; instead they wanted to interpret it from a new, more critical point of view. Their sympathy lay above all with Lessing; the German Jacobins; Heine; the Young Germans; the forty-eighters; the naturalists; Heinrich Mann; and revolutionary expressionists such as Ernst Toller, as well as writers such as Lion Feuchtwanger, Bertolt Brecht, Anna Seghers, and Arnold Zweig. In short, they turned to those authors who had supported enlightened, left-wing (liberal or socialist) thought especially when confronting retrogressive or fascist forces. This group of scholars, including young Americans such as David Bathrick, Russell A. Berman, Helen Fehervary, Robert C. Holub, Sara Lennox, and Jack Zipes, also supported the study of leftist politicians, sociologists, historians, and psychoanalysts who had gone into exile—above all, Theodor W. Adorno, Walter Benjamin, Ernst Bloch, Magnus Hirschfeld, Max Horkheimer, Siegfried Kracauer, Leo Loewenthal, Georg Lukács, Herbert Marcuse, Hans Mayer, and Wilhelm Reich. The Germanists of the older generation, who were committed to the humanism of the Age of Goethe, had largely avoided these authors, because of ignorance, ideological aversion, or the pressures of the McCarthy era. These changes were made manifest at the conferences on exile literature held in 1971 in Madison and Saint Louis; in the creation of the International Bertolt Brecht Society in the same year; and in the founding in 1973 of the journal *New German Critique*, which dealt primarily with German antifascist authors and attempted to introduce their works into the discussions of politics and cultural theory in the American New Left.

That brought about definite ideological changes in the more liberal-minded German departments of the United States, which at that time included Columbia, Berkeley, Ohio State, Washington University, Wisconsin, and Cornell: there was a shift from rather conservative to more liberal authors and a change in the perceived social function of literature, which was now supposed to be accessible to all. A few representatives of the New Left almost went so far as to claim high literature, in the spirit of Bloch's "principle of hope," as one of the most important vehicles for the creation of individuals who are educated, enlightened, and thereby truly human. Accordingly this group, comprising young American Germanists drawn from the civil rights movement and the anti–Vietnam War protests as well as young Germanists who had emigrated from West Germany, did not hesitate to publish their works in the United States as well as in the Federal Republic, in the spirit of international solidarity characteristic of the New Left movement.

The tenor of these publications moved increasingly further away from purely Germanist subject matters and more toward cultural theory and political activism, which adopted the tone of antifascist writings from the leftists exiled between 1933 and 1945. These writings were, in the terminology of the day, as concrete as possible—that is, they were simultaneously sober and polemical. They subjected to harsh criticism all idealistic smoke screens and escapist maneuvers and supported their ideas with materialist theories built on the dialectical relation between the socioeconomic base and the cultural superstructure. A feeling of ideological solidarity resulted, which rendered differences between native-born Americans and native-born Germans unimportant. In a substantial number of cooperatively published works, various contributors translated one another's writings—in the proceedings of the Wisconsin Workshops, in the *Brecht Yearbook*, in the *Basis Yearbook*, and in *New German Critique*—to achieve as great an impact as possible.

This phase, however, did not last long. With the end of the Vietnam War, political activism in the United States declined as drastically as the West German student movement. Nevertheless, a number of new alliances developed shortly afterward in German studies in America, which were still sustained by a critical, emancipatory spirit although they grew increasingly subjective over time, in keeping with the new slogan "The personal is the political." The so-called second wave of feminism (Angelika Bammer, Evelyn T. Beck, Susan Cocalis, Patricia Herminghouse, Ruth-Ellen Boetcher Joeres, and Biddy Martin), the gay movement (Frank Hirschbach and James Steakley), and German Jewish studies (Amy Colin, Sander L. Gilman, and Liliane Weissberg) were the main trends involved in this shift. In opposition to the New Left movement, which had claimed relevance for society as a whole, these newer alliances emphasized minorities or the outsider. In academic publications, this emphasis was expressed in a careful reappraisal of the female, homosexual, or Jewish authors of the past who had been ignored in the dominant discourse of society; in an exact analysis of how the members of the dominant culture had portrayed representatives of the outsider group in their works; and in new attempts to develop the beginnings of a genuine female, gay, or Jewish aesthetic and self-awareness that would distinguish itself clearly from the dominant discourse.

Unlike the New Left practitioners, these groups were less likely to enlist German theories to support their ideas. Their publications appeared almost exclusively in English and at times—particularly when the topic dealt with Jewish phenomena—did not shrink from anti-German sentiments. Their academic tenor was generally just as polemical as the preceding New Left movement, but it started from a more subjective or group-oriented basis rather than from an orientation toward the whole of society. For this reason, some of these publications were read only in particular subgroups of American German studies, such as Women in German or the Gay and Lesbian Caucus of the MLA. There, however, they had quite an impact and triggered, at least temporarily, strong feelings of solidarity among the special groups they addressed.

1985 to the Present

Since the early 1980s, however, there has been no single theoretical paradigm that is recognized as the standard by the majority of Germanists in America. The concepts of postmodernism and the poststructuralism imported from France and modified in the United States have not changed the situation much in this respect, although they have been the subject of quite lively discussions. The term *postmodern* has proved to be far too diffuse and at the same time too sweeping to provide a new methodological anchor for literary theory. From the beginning, postmodernism was too splintered to be very useful, and it led to tangible results really only in the architecture debates of the 1980s. The discussions about poststructuralism, however, as advanced for instance by Werner Hamacher, Rainer Nägele, and David E. Wellbery, have left obvious marks on German departments in the United States, although less so than on French, English, and comparative literature departments. The result was a theory wave that made philosophy once again an important factor in German studies. As in the outsider or postmodernist discourses, the poststructuralism-influenced publications turned away from specifically German phenomena in favor of more abstract ontological and anthropological questions. Correspondingly, this area attracted little attention from those literary scholars who were more interested in the catastrophic course of political events in German history than in formal aesthetic or philosophical debates.

In contrast to poststructural discourses, German studies publications that profess to be a part of the cultural studies turn, oriented toward tangible historical facts, are often highly informative. Drawing on older German cultural history as well as American new historicism, these publications are of interest not only to Germanists but also to historians and scholars in disciplines related to history. For example, there have been many theoretical innovations and ideas since the early 1990s that have opened up entirely new fields of research as a result of the regular meetings of the German Studies Association and the conferences on cultural theory of some German departments. As long as interdisciplinarity does not degenerate into dilettantism and as long as the central focus on German literature and culture is retained, cultural studies research probably constitutes the most important trend in German studies in the United States at the moment. Through attempts to form new connections among literary, political, legal, medical, social, scientific, and gender-specific perspectives, this direction has created many new areas of research that the older German studies—particularly in its formal, aesthetic, genre-history or text-based approaches—could never have imagined.

—*Translated by Sara B. Young*

Medieval German Literary Research from the Late Nineteenth Century to the Present

FRANCIS G. GENTRY

Providing a brief history of medieval German literary research from the late nineteenth to the late twentieth century is not as straightforward a task as it might at first seem. In the first place the organization and mission of German programs and departments in the late 1800s and early 1900s in the United States were decidedly different from those in the 1950s or 1960s, when medieval literary research began to develop its own identity in German departments. Indeed, departmental thrust or action agendas of the twenty-first century more closely resemble those of our beginnings than of, let's say, 1985, and the position that medieval studies now occupies in the curriculum and strategic plans of German departments and programs is correspondingly modest.[1] With the exception of some departments at the more prestigious private and land-grant universities, medievalists who leave or retire are not being replaced by younger people in that specialty. Either lines are reallocated—if the department is fortunate—to other areas in the unit, for example, to pre-1750 cultural studies, or they are simply cut. Thus the following discussion does not provide suggestions about what can be done. It may be that there is little that can be done in the near future.[2] Nonetheless, medieval German philology has a long history behind it in the United States, and, just as in nineteenth-century Germany, it was the seedbed that allowed modern German studies to sprout and flourish. Although in the years prior to World War I—and well into the 1950s—medieval German literary scholarship in the United States made but a ripple in the small pond of German literary research in terms of quantity, it has in the last several years taken its rightful place in German literary studies both here and abroad. Indeed, medieval German studies in the United States became the forerunner of interdisciplinarity for the international area of *Altgermanistik* (the German term for "medieval German studies").

The story begins in the last two decades of the nineteenth century, when an interest began to take shape in the integration of modern foreign languages in the structure of American higher education as well as in the support of the research efforts of colleagues in those disciplines. Without doubt, the founding of the Modern Language Association in 1883 played a decisive role in this process. For with that founding the study of modern foreign languages, as well as English literature, began to take its place alongside the scholarly scrutiny and esteem enjoyed by classical Latin. This acceptance did not occur overnight, as Kemp Malone makes clear in his obituary of James Wilson Bright, English scholar, professor emeritus from the Johns Hopkins University, and longtime editor-in-chief of *Modern Language Notes* (1916–25). Malone writes with tongue in cheek of the popular perception of modern philology at the time of Bright's graduate career (1879–82): "Modern philology was still in leading strings, and was looked upon by the general public as a field meet for Continental refugees and broken-down clergymen rather than for men of science." Malone's observations about the disregard in which modern philology was held during those years may be quite true, but in a short time this attitude was to change. In 1884, Kuno Francke, then a researcher at the *Monumenta Germaniae Historica*, was appointed instructor of German at Harvard University, the first to hold a German position at Harvard since 1835, with the brief exception of the elderly Frederick Hedge (1805–90) for a few years in the early 1870s. Francke was an inspired appointment for Harvard in many ways. Not only was the long-vacant chair of German at America's oldest and most prestigious university finally occupied, it was held by an energetic and flexible young German academic who, although trained as a medievalist, embraced the open nature of his position.[3] In addition to extracurricular activities like evenings of literary readings for the public and the private reading of masterpieces of German literature with his better students, Francke lectured on the most varied topics in German literature and culture: German mysticism, German religious sculpture of the Middle Ages, German painting of the fifteenth century, German cultural history from Luther to Frederick the Great. Although he published much in the broad area of German studies, his *Social Forces in German Literature: A Study in the History of Civilization* must be viewed as his most important scholarly achievement. Equally as important is the fact that it was written in English. In the preface he notes:

> While there is no lack of works dealing with the history of German literature from the linguistic or the literary point of view, there seems to be a decided

need of a book which, based upon an original study of the sources, should give a coherent account of the great intellectual movements as expressed in literature. (v)

Literature, he goes on to say, "point[s] out the mutual relation of action and reaction between these movements and the social and political condition of the masses from which they sprang or which they affected" (v). His work enjoyed great popularity and went through several printings, but the socio-historical methodical direction he indicated was not followed and would not be encountered again until the last third of the twentieth century, more in Germany than in the United States. Nonetheless the lasting contributions of Francke to Harvard and to the discipline in general cannot be overestimated.

The Johns Hopkins University too played a formative role in the establishment of the new field. As a premier American institution organized for graduate education, it attracted some of the foremost philological scholars to its campus. In addition, *Modern Language Notes* (after 1963 simply *MLN*) was established there in 1886. The journal understood itself as providing for

> professors and teachers of the modern languages . . . a special organ of communication in which they might express their opinions and have the benefit of frank and unbiased criticism, with reference both to personal views on literary and scientific subjects, and to the numerous text-books and other works that are constantly appearing. . . . (Editor's Preface)

The thrust of the early articles and notes on German matters were by and large of a philological nature, and, as William McClain points out, they fall into three main categories: "morphological, syntactical, and semantic problems; textual editing; and lexicographical investigations" (McClain 421). If anything on medieval German literature appeared at all in the discussions, it was in the context of the canon. One of the great promoters of the canon, especially in the form derived from Wilhelm Scherer, was Julius Goebel, first German editor of the *Modern Language Notes* and later department head at the University of Illinois, Urbana. In his review of F. Max Müller's reader *The German Classics from the Fourth to the Nineteenth Century*, Goebel points out its relation to Scherer's literary history, in terms both of its emphases and of the personal contact between Müller and Scherer before the latter's death. Goebel, well known for his absolute dedication to mediating between Germany and the United States, the "two great Teutonic nations" (Rev. 166), and to furthering the study of German at American colleges and universities, viewed this reader, for example, not only as a collection of great literary works but also as a document illustrating the development of the German language. For Goebel and for so many like him at this early period, the language and its intricacies were inseparable from the literature. The literature possesses aesthetic appeal mainly because of the language in which it is written. At the end of his review Goebel makes this point absolutely clear (167). The view of literature primarily as philological documents reflecting language change predominated for many years and determined the scope and content of most scholarly research. And why was that so? Why was the German language elevated to an almost cultic significance in the minds of scholars teaching in America? The answer is both complex and simple: Viewed against the backdrop of the entire nineteenth century and the patriotic striving toward unification—from Grimms' *Wörter-buch* to the *Reichsgründung* ("founding of the Second Reich")—the German language was viewed as the glue that held Germans in the diaspora together, both before and after 1871, in that it provided a mirror of the nation and its culture. Thus teachers of German in the United States took upon themselves the added task of cultural mediation. Indeed, for many it became their main mission. Early scholars, whether of German birth like Goebel or Francke or of American birth like Marion Dexter Learned, claimed the greatness of German culture for America and sought tirelessly to promote its spread by the educated classes in both countries—and not to leave that mission to the uneducated and crude masses (Henry Schmidt, "Rhetoric"). In a tribute to Rudolf Hildebrand, Goebel expounds on his favorite theme of the sublimity of German culture and its rightness for the Anglo-Saxons:

> This [German] ideal [of humanity] is, however, not the exclusive possession of the Germans; it is, like the Greek ideal, an inheritance left for the whole human race. An especial claim on it have the nations of Germanic origin, the renaissance of whose antiquity, like that of the Anglo-Saxons, is also due to German philology. (175)

He provides an interesting if somewhat extreme example of the trans-plantation to America of the elitist attitudes of the nineteenth-century German professorial class. For Goebel—and for many others like him, who, it must be said, were all literary scholars of distinction—the teaching of the German language took on the mystique of a holy mission (McGlathery, *German* 45–66).

While literary research (meaning anything not medieval) was gradually able to emancipate itself from philological strictures, serious literary research on medieval German topics would have to wait until well after World War II. McClain cites the 1930s as the period when philology began to lose its stranglehold on academic scholarship, which in turn resulted in a

> perceptible weakening of one of the strongest ties between *Germanistik* in Germany and German studies in the United States. The sense of involvement in a collaborative effort, enjoyed by all scholars studying the history of the German language, constituted an important bond between American Germanists and their colleagues abroad; and that bond has never been as strong as in the heyday of philological studies. (421)

The situation in more-modern German studies is not all that bleak, however. Unlike General Douglas MacArthur's old soldiers, the philologists did not fade away but maintained their tenured positions for another generation. And while their influence on research in newer German literature was minimal, the same could not be said of their influence on medieval studies. Wolfgang Fleischhauer's 1954 review of Friedrich Maurer's pioneering book *Leid* may be taken as an example of this philological tenacity. Maurer's study came as a breath of fresh air in the area of medieval German studies, especially in *Nibelungenlied* research. While Maurer was a philologist of the first order, he thought it possible to grasp authorial intention in a medieval literary work and arrive at a consistent interpretation by utilizing the basic philological tool of the word study. To Fleischhauer, however, it appeared that Maurer was sacrificing his philological bona fides for the sake of a forced interpretation.[4]

Since the post–World War II years did not see an influx of Germans interested in medieval German studies to this country—prominent exceptions would be Julius Schwietering, who spent part of 1954 at the University of Chicago, and Joachim Bumke, who spent several years at Harvard in the 1960s—the comparable catalyst for much of the change in modern German studies research in the 1950s and 1960s was missing. Some German colleagues did, of course, come to America and enjoy a distinguished career—for example, Otto Springer (from Tübingen to Univ. of Pennsylvania), Michael Curschmann (from Munich to Princeton Univ.), and Ingeborg Glier (from Munich to Yale Univ.). These colleagues had something else in common: they all settled at prestigious private universities in the East. Ernst Dick (from Münster to Univ. of Kansas) is a notable exception to this trend. Their location at the beginning of this period should have guaranteed great influence, one would think. As we will see, however, the center of dramatic activity in the general area of Germanics and specifically in medieval German studies would shift to the large state universities, primarily in the Big Ten and on the West Coast. Until that shift took place, medieval German studies in the United States would mark time.

Dissertation topics, too, reflected the conservative nature of American German studies scholarship. The years 1886–1920 offer examples of clearly philological investigations like "Syntax of Cases in Walther von der Vogelweide" (Columbia, 1886), "The Compound Past Tenses, Active and Passive, in Middle High German as Represented by Heinrich von Veldeke, Gottfried von Strassburg, and Wolfram von Eschenbach" (Michigan, 1915); comparative studies like "The Relation of Wolfram von Eschenbach's 'Willehalm' to Its Old French Source 'Aliscans' " (Johns Hopkins, 1897); and what appears to be a socioliterary topic, "Expressions of German National Feeling in Historical and Poetical Literature from the Middle of the Tenth Century to the Time of Walther von der Vogelweide" (Harvard, 1893). Without doubt, the dissertation follows the lead set by Francke in his 1890 *PMLA* article and deals primarily with the Latin literature of the period. The years 1920–60 were essentially a mirror image of the earlier years, although gradually the number of unquestionably philological dissertations receded in favor of those with a literary thrust. But it is not yet possible to speak of definitive critical approaches or theoretical directions.

As the number and subject matter of the dissertations make clear, the period between 1886 and 1960 provides little evidence of significant activity in medieval German *literary* research. The same situation obtained in the area of book and article production. In fact, no book of seminal importance in medieval German literature was written by an American colleague during that period. The few essays that appeared during this time in such journals as *Modern Language Notes* or *Modern Language Quarterly* were straightforward philological articles that dealt with lexicographical or historical linguistic matters, or they were quasi-philological in substance and more concerned with the process of canon building and text reconstruction than with analysis. Two examples are H. M. Schmidt-Wartenberg's "Ein Tiroler Passionsspiel des Mittelalters" and Learned's book-length edition of the *Walthersage* in all its European variants.

The little that was written in the area of medieval literary studies was being undertaken by colleagues from other disciplines who drew German literary works into their comparative analyses. While Francke authored an article with the promising title "Modern Ideas in the Middle Ages?," in which he deals with some vernacular didactic poets of the thirteenth century and views their works as reform-minded and progressive, he quickly abandons them in favor of their Latin precursors as the decisive models for and true forerunners of humanism. He writes, "As historical documents they [the Latin documents] bear important witness to the growth in the twelfth and thirteenth centuries, of that spirit of individualism which is the soul of modern life" (184). This statement encapsulates the great obstacle that the study of medieval vernacular literature in general and of medieval German in particular had to overcome: it was not Latin literature—that is, it was not original.

The founding of the Medieval Academy of America (23 Dec. 1925) ex-emplifies this obstacle. The academy had its origins as a group of the MLA in 1921 with the topic "The Influence of Latin Culture on Mediaeval Literature" and later, simply, "Mediaeval Latin Studies" (Coffman 6; Wenger). The aims of the soon-to-be-established academy were drafted by a select group of men over dinner at the Harvard Club in Boston on 19 June 1925. Among the projects that these gentlemen envisaged for the new association was the "study of the relation of Mediaeval Latin to its Classical Background, to mediaeval vernacular literature, and to mediaeval and modern life and thought" (Coffman 14). Vernacular literature is mentioned only in the context of its relation to medieval Latin culture. While all literary studies of vernacular literature were theoretically affected, essays only on Old and Middle English as well as Old French literature were present from volume 1 on of *Speculum*. Articles on medieval German literature did not appear until around 1960. George Fenwick Jones's "The Function of Food in Medieval German Literature" seems to be the first devoted solely to German literature. Only since the mid-1970s have articles on medieval German topics been appearing in the pages of *Speculum*, although with no regularity. The same circumstance holds in other scholarly outlets. If before the mid-1960s articles on medieval German literature were uncommon, in the *MLN* for example, the situation improved after 1969, and the closer one comes to the 1990s, the more distinct the critical approaches are.

But it was in the 1960s and 1970s that the general area of medieval studies in the United States enjoyed a renaissance (Gentry and Kleinhenz). It was at this time, too, that medieval German studies began to seek a more appropriate role for itself in German departments. The evolution of medieval German studies as an acceptable graduate track in literature and the liberation of medieval German literature from philology was a protracted battle that could be felt in departments well into the late 1970s (e.g., in Wisconsin). In the mid-1960s in Indiana, where I received my graduate training, a clear line was drawn between specialists in medieval German literature and those in Germanic philology, which was understood as Germanic linguistics. Medieval literature was taught not as the handmaiden of philology but in its own right as literature. The impetus for change was sustained by the active involvement of faculty members and interested students from the department in the newly established Medieval Studies Program. The advantage to medievalists in German departments was clear: the participation in medieval studies programs removed both faculty members and students from the occasionally stifling if not hidebound atmosphere of more-traditional departments; exposed them to aspects of the larger discipline that would have been difficult to experience in the standard departmental structure; and opened up to them the grand parade of approaches to medieval literature, including medieval German literature. Obviously this process did not take place only at public universities, but because of the number of students involved in the 1960s and early 1970s—in 1968, Indiana University's German department had 120 graduate students—the influence of the breaking down of traditional departmental structures in favor of interdisciplinary approaches was more widely felt by the graduates of public institutions.

While all benefited from the exposure to other methods of approach and contact with colleagues from other disciplines, the training in German was still very much text-oriented; it was close reading, quite traditional. As a result, it would be difficult to point to any consistent theoretical-critical approach until the 1980s, because 1950 books, articles, and dissertations on medieval German literature far outnumbered philological studies. The sociohistorical approach, which gained a strong foothold in the United States in the 1970s, restricted itself by and large to postmedieval literature and was rarely found in medieval German literary studies, although this method was important among some

German *Altgermanisten*. Reception research, prominent in the United States in modern German literary studies and also in German-speaking Europe in medieval German studies, was successfully ignored by most American colleagues specializing in medieval German. In the United States, criticism remained primarily on the level of textual criticism, motif investigations, and influence studies. In other words, researchers on this side of the Atlantic were not accepting any impulses from their colleagues in Germany. Those Americans whose medieval scholarship involved either reception analysis or sociohistorical investigation were frequently viewed with suspicion by their colleagues. This situation did mirror somewhat the state of affairs in Germany, especially after 1968. In Germany, however, the differences fell generally along the fault line of age. In North America, in contrast, older colleagues were often more supportive of these new approaches than their protégés. The breach between German and American *Altgermanisten*, which had begun in the 1930s, seemed to have become fully realized in the 1970s and 1980s. Each side went about its business, benignly ignoring the other.

In the meantime, research in the United States gradually moved from an almost total reliance on textual criticism into the history of ideas and, finally in the 1990s, into theoretical analyses, gender criticism, queer studies, and consideration of the body. These approaches are all part and parcel of the critical apparatus of those of us who were in the first wave as students in the 1960s; we are now passing them on to our students. The new directions can be clearly seen in the titles of several recent dissertations: "The Concept of 'Reht' (Iustitia) in Early Middle High German Literature" (Wisconsin, 1991), "The Mirror and the Woman: Instruction for Religious Women and the Emergence of Secular Poetics, 1120–1250" (Princeton, 1997), "The Topography of Gender in Middle High German Arthurian Romance" (Penn State, 1995), "Courtly-Heroic-Fragmented: Bodies and Gestures in the *Nibelungenlied*" (Washington, 1998), "Kriemhild: Demon-Hero-Woman" (Washington, 1993), "Bodies at Court: Experiencing the Body in the Context of Minne and Chivalry in Wolfram von Eschenbach's *Parzival*" (Penn State, 1998). The extraordinary amount of contact between colleagues in the United States and Europe indicates that we have assumed an international leadership role. One has only to point to the annual meeting of the Medieval Institute in Kalamazoo, where for the past several years more than forty colleagues and students from Germany and Austria regularly attend and actively participate.

Medieval German studies in the United States had to travel a long road from its beginnings as a field in which only research into the structure of the language counted. By the late 1950s and early 1960s the discipline managed to free itself of its philological shackles, yet American medieval scholarship remained largely conservative and in many ways quite provincial. This state of affairs changed only with the scholarly activity of the first wave of trained medievalists from the 1960s and 1970s, all representing different methodological approaches. Certainly the mediating influence of German colleagues who came to this country in the 1950s, 1960s, and 1970s more than adequately provided bridges of contact with colleagues in Germany. Now their students, most American-born, are continuing and deepening these contacts to mutual benefit. It was this postwar generation of scholars that finally was successful in demonstrating to German colleagues that German studies and its practitioners in the United States deserved to be taken seriously.

As a postscript, I would add a few possibly provocative observations. The field of medieval literary studies became emancipated from its philological strictures but did not manage to escape the negative transference of unflattering attitudes toward philologists held by colleagues in postmedieval literature. In other words, neither our philological nor our literary colleagues accepted us. In the late 1970s, I was told by a Madison graduate student that I was "not bad, for a philologist," meaning he found the course on medieval literature that I was then teaching interesting for "someone in [postmedieval] literature." Then I chuckled, but now I do not, because it finally occurred to me that this attitude was not limited to Madison or to graduate students or, indeed, to the last century but was and is endemic to the profession. For some reason, colleagues in German departments found and still find it difficult to accept what colleagues in English and Romance languages departments have no trouble grasping— namely, that there is such a thing as medieval literature, that this literature makes similar kinds of aesthetic demands on a reader, and that medieval authors understood that they were doing something beyond providing interesting philological paradigms. The danger of not making an effort to view medieval studies as a part of the field as a whole results in the type of global and, unfortunately, quite inaccurate assessment of Frank Trommler from 1989, "Germanists have played scarcely any role in the recent revival of medieval studies in America" (*Germanistik in den USA* 36). Such comments from otherwise well-informed and respected colleagues bear eloquent witness to the rather dismal fact that medieval German literary research is simply not an accepted part of American German departments and programs.

It is ironic that medieval German studies in the United States should be experiencing newfound and well-deserved respect in the international community precisely when the discipline risks disappearing as an academic field except in a few large departments. Medievalists, like their colleagues in other areas, are still writing dissertations and ending up in positions where they seldom if ever teach in their chosen field, or they are forced to move from one temporary job to another. Paradoxically, as any year at Kalamazoo well demonstrates, there is a definite esprit among the practitioners of the art, a seriousness of purpose, and commitment to an area that seems only to grow in strength from year to year. If colleagues in other areas in German studies would finally support their local medievalist, this spirit would augur well not only for medieval German studies but also for the field as a whole in the United States.

Notes

1 In his brief memoir, *Deutsche Arbeit in Amerika*, Kuno Francke describes what his task was to be as the newly minted instructor in German at Harvard in 1884: "From the beginning it was left up to me to interpret the term 'German' in the widest possible sense, that is, to regard it as a collective term for political, social, intellectual, and artistic expressions of German history—essentially, in other words, to view my teaching activity as being in the service of German cultural history" (2).

2 Despite the spirited comments of the various contributors to Albrecht Classen's volume *Medieval German Voices in the Twenty-First Century*, it is clear that the field, as far as something desirable and desired in the American departmental structure, is on the downswing of Fortune's wheel—but, as is well known, what goes around comes around.

3 Although his teaching and research activities were broad-based, Francke remained at heart a medievalist, with his special interest in the late Middle Ages. In 1927, he was honored by the Mediaeval Academy of America and named a fellow of the academy.

4 Fleischhauer concludes his lengthy review as follows: "The justification for such a detailed review of Maurer's book does not lie merely in the necessity of refuting his very questionable results as such, but rather [in the necessity] of taking his claim seriously that even in literary and cultural matters the philologist has the right to make his voice heard. But we must not forget that he has to keep this right, by rigorously avoiding—whether in general or in specific details—detracting from the value of the facts by daring and occasionally arbitrary interpretations" (594).

Linguistics

ORRIN W. ROBINSON

In his 1979 contribution to a volume dealing with the European background of American linguistics, the eminent Berkeley Romanist Yakov Malkiel distinguishes among three historical stages in the aspirations of American linguists. In the first (late nineteenth and early twentieth century), research is seen as driven by the assumption that the initiative in linguistics lies with some other country, "usually with Germany." In the second, basically from the 1920s through the 1950s, we find a "strident, tumultuous search for identity and originality, occasionally accompanied by militant rejection of the European heritage." Commencing in the 1950s, American linguistics enters a period of "strong leadership devoid of any isolationist overtones" (107).

Given its subject matter—to wit, German and the Germanic languages generally—one might expect that American Germanic linguistics would stand as an exception to Malkiel's outline. If American linguistics in general could at one point change its focus from the historical description of Indo-European languages to the synchronic description of non–Indo-European (esp. Amerindian) languages, Germanic linguistics could not do so. And it is obviously quite difficult to assume "strong leadership" over a field that has many more practitioners in German-speaking countries than here. Nonetheless, Malkiel's characterization of American linguistics, while it must be tempered, is not totally inappropriate for American Germanic linguistics as well.

Germanic linguistics proper, of course, did not exist as such in the late nineteenth century. Rather, students of Germanics with an interest in language were part of the pack of German-influenced (or downright German) philologists who so dominated the literature departments of American colleges and universities in the late nineteenth century (see Graff, esp. 67–72). What precisely this thing called *philology* was, or is, is a notoriously unanswerable question:

> "Philology" is open to many misunderstandings. Historically it has been used to include not only all literary and linguistic studies but studies of all products of the human mind. . . . Today, because of its etymology and much of the actual work of specialists, philology is frequently understood to mean linguistics, especially historical grammar and the study of past forms of languages. Since the term has so many and such divergent meanings, it is best to abandon it. (Wellek and Warren 38)

Needless to say, the term has not been abandoned, at least not by scholars who feel they practice the discipline (see, e.g., R. Frank, "Unbearable Lightness"). One should perhaps add to the late-nineteenth-century (and present-day) understanding of *philology* an abiding concern not just with "past forms" but also, more narrowly, with older texts and their explication.

Among the first American journals devoted exclusively to Germanic philology, and certainly the most long-lived, was and is the *Journal of English and Germanic Philology*, published at the University of Illinois since 1906 but begun in Indiana in 1897 as the *Journal of Germanic Philology*. The founding editor, Gustaf E. Karsten, was a German professor of philology, and his editorial board consisted of a professor of English from Yale, a professor of German literature from Cornell, a professor of Germanic philology from the University of Michigan, and a coeditor from Leipzig. In that first issue, a relatively broad definition of *philology* is apparent. In addition to a number of articles devoted to historical English and Germanic linguistics ("The Voiced Spirants in Gothic," "Indo-European Root-Formation"), one finds quite a few dealing with more literary topics, even if the focus is on older texts ("Chaucer's Classicism," "Goethe and the Philosophy of Schopenhauer"). There is one article on the pedagogy of English. Articles are about evenly balanced between English and other Germanic topics.

Articles like the one on the voiced spirants of Gothic of course reflected a concern among nineteenth-century philologists with establishing, describing, and ordering the phonetic, phonological, and grammatical facts of all the older Germanic languages, related languages, and relevant protolanguages. But they frequently served as the building blocks for full-fledged grammars of those languages, which in turn served as the fodder for even more massive comparative Germanic and Indo-European grammars. Such grammars were always understood to be grounded in the concrete (i.e., written) products of speakers of the (primarily Indo-European) languages under study. Thus another of the proper tasks of philology was seen to be the production of careful editions of important older texts, accompanied by an appropriate, often quite detailed, technical apparatus. These editions, along with the comprehensive grammars of the various older (and newer) Germanic languages, the comparative grammars, and the individual articles and books on specific problems in older Germanic languages, were the main scholarly products of linguistically oriented Germanic philology before and after the turn of the century.

From the beginning of their existence in this country, American Germanic linguists have made their contributions to these tasks, and vital contributions at that. An example of an important early textual edition is the 1893 one of the Old High German *Isidor* translation and the Monsee Fragments, with accompanying grammar and glossary, by George A. Hench of the University of Michigan. A book on the Germanic weak preterite in 1912 by Hermann Collitz of Johns Hopkins (incidentally also the first president of the Linguistic Society of America) may serve as an example of foundational work in early Germanic grammar. The monumental 1905 *Grammar of the German Language* by George O. Curme of Northwestern (who also wrote a grammar of English that is still widely cited) illustrates the fact that Germanic philologists cared about modern German as well.

Such early foundational work perhaps reached its American apogee with the 1939 publication by the Yale professor Eduard Prokosch of his *Comparative Germanic Grammar*. This work, by an important Germanist who left his personal mark on a surprising number of later, more theoretically oriented American scholars (e.g., Bloomfield and Moulton), has not been superseded to this day.

As the names cited above indicate, many of the early practitioners of Germanic philology in America were Germans; even if they weren't, almost all of them had studied in places like Berlin, Heidelberg, and especially Leipzig. Even Leonard Bloomfield, an American product of Harvard, Wisconsin, and Chicago, was promoted from instructor in German to assistant professor of comparative philology and German at the University of Illinois only after fulfilling a more or less obligatory year of study in Leipzig in 1913–14 (R. Hall 13). Up to that point, American Germanic linguistics might indeed be seen as languishing at Malkiel's first stage, that of relative theoretical dependency on Europe.

Yet even if the initial impetus for doing foundational work came from nineteenth-century Germany, it can hardly be said that such work was neglected even after American linguistics began to establish its own distinctive identity. Given its date of publication, Prokosch's *Comparative Germanic Grammar* is a good example. American Germanists also continued to edit texts; one might mention here the post-1933 editions of the works of Notker the German by Taylor Starck of Harvard (in conjunction with the German scholar E. H. Sehrt [Sehrt and Starck, *Notkers des Deutschen Werke* and *Notker-Wortschatz*]) and

Starck's lexicographical works on the Old High German glosses and on Notker (see Starck and Wells). A more recent example is Robert L. Kyes's (University of Michigan) 1969 edition of the Old Low Franconian psalms and glosses.

While not ignoring the theoretical currents of the day, American Germanists (including many from Europe) to this day write grammars, carry out detailed studies of individual older texts, clarify grammatical issues pertaining to the Germanic languages and to German, and strive for a replacement to Prokosch's grammar. Reference grammars of older Germanic languages may be represented by Robert P. Ebert's (Princeton) coauthored *Frühneuhochdeutsche Grammatik* (1993) in an old and hallowed Niemeyer series (Ebert, Reichmann, and Wegera) or by Irmengard Rauch's 1993 *The Old Saxon Language*. My own *Clause Subordination and Verb Placement in the Old High German* Isidor *Translation* (1997) is an attempt to establish word-order facts in an important Old High German text (I like to think of this as my nineteenth-century book). Frans van Coetsem and Herbert Kufner's *Toward a Grammar of Proto-Germanic* (1972) takes a stab at outlining the important facts at all linguistic levels in the older Germanic languages, and a major project (led by Robert Howell and Joseph Salmons of the University of Wisconsin and Paul Roberge of the University of North Carolina) is presently under way to improve on, indeed supplant, Prokosch's synthesis after all these years, adding a significant sociolinguistic component to the more strictly grammatical discussions.

Yet with all this continuity there is no question that things have changed in Germanic linguistics as practiced in America. To get a feeling for this change, one might begin by comparing the first volume of the *Journal of English and Germanic Philology* with the 1997 centennial issue. The editors Achsah Guibbory and Marianne Kalinke stress the continuity of their journal and by implication of Germanic philology in general. The journal, they note, is international in its orientation and catholic in the range of its articles, which still, although they are responsive to contemporary perspectives and methodologies, pay "loving attentiveness to language and texts" (483). Yet there are in fact quite a few differences to be noted between the two volumes of the journal. Of its 19 (vs. the 1897 issue's 31) articles, the centennial issue devotes a full 12 to nonlinguistic English topics, 3 to post-1700 German literature, and 1 to the history of the journal. Even the article most devoted to a linguistic question deals primarily with *Beowulf*.

Does this difference reflect a change in the journal or in the field of Germanic philology? Both, but it stems primarily from developments in the field that have led many (though not all) of its practitioners to abandon the more humanistic tendencies of philology as understood by the journal in favor of a more strictly structural, language-internal approach.

Malkiel characterizes the middle period of American linguistics in general as involving "a switch from the precarious alliance with the humanities, characteristic of German scholarship ('*Geisteswissenschaften*'), to an equally delicate integration with the social sciences" (112). Partly because of the challenges facing them in the analysis of Native American languages, American linguists insisted that grammatical claims about individual languages had to be based on objectively determined data. Independent confirmation, not philological tradition or indeed humanistic speculation, was the name of the game.

This turn in American linguistics coincided with, and was certainly aided by, the foundation in 1924 of the Linguistic Society of America and the establishment of its journal, *Language*. For the first time, linguists in different subspecialties had a common forum in which they could achieve a more unified approach to the general study of language:

> The chance [was] given for the first time to linguistically-oriented classicists, Orientalists, medievalists, etc. to meet with one another rather than facing, as they had done for decades with frustrating results, other classicists, Orientalists, medievalists etc. indifferent or hostile to analysis of language. (Malkiel 115)

Germanic linguists were clearly included; they were in fact anything but peripheral players in this new trend. The man considered by many scholars to be the central figure in the formation of the Linguistic Society of America and in the movement known as American structuralism, Leonard Bloomfield, was trained as a Germanist, held several academic appointments in German linguistics and philology, and taught Germanic subjects most of his career. A brief glance at the list of the society's presidents over the years reveals many Germanic linguists with a high profile in the field as a whole.

In 1957, the Wisconsin Germanist Martin Joos published a volume of articles (written between 1925 and 1956) entitled *Readings in Linguistics*, and it unintentionally ended up being a summation of important work done in American structuralism (the Chomskyan revolution may be dated from that period). A brief glance at the volume's table of contents reveals the importance of contributions made by Germanic linguists: of the 43 articles, there are 9 such. Besides two by Joos himself, there are articles by Leonard Bloomfield, W. Freeman Twaddell, William Moulton, Werner Leopold, and Einar Haugen—all the authors arguably Germanic linguists, at least in part.

These qualifications, "arguably" and "at least in part," need to be made for several reasons. In the first place, from the very beginnings of Germanic philology, practitioners did not restrict themselves to the Germanic languages. The very nature of comparative philology as practiced in nineteenth-century Germany, and also in the United States, naturally drew scholars' attention back past Proto-Germanic to Proto-Indo-European and to such cognate language families as Celtic and Indo-Iranian. Did these scholars then cease to be Germanists and become Indo-Europeanists? Or were they both? The problem is illustrated in the person of the eminent early Yale linguist William Dwight Whitney (d. 1897), who published a frequently reprinted grammar of German along with his writings on the Indic languages and on the general science of language.

As this general science of language under the name *linguistics* assumed a more central role in the early and middle twentieth century in America, the disciplinary blurring only increased. Germanic linguists interested in the nature of language found themselves interested in languages that were only distantly, if at all, related to the Germanic family. Bloomfield, for example, did much of his important theoretical work on American Indian languages and languages of the Philippines. More recently, to name only two prominent Germanists, Herbert Penzl of UC Berkeley devoted much of his considerable linguistic insight to the Pashto language of Afghanistan, and Winfred P. Lehmann of the University of Texas (an Indo-Europeanist as well as a Germanist) has focused his attention on Japanese and Turkish, among other languages.

Returning to Joos's *Readings in Linguistics* volume, it should be pointed out that of the 9 articles by Germanists only 5 deal directly with Germanic topics, and all of those have a wider theoretical point to make. Furthermore, it seems unlikely that any of them would have fit comfortably in the pages of the *Journal of English and Germanic Philology*.

The disciplinary fluidity described above for the middle period of Germanic linguistics in America corresponded with a certain institutional fluidity as well. Winfred Lehmann's career at the University of Texas and indeed the entire history of the Germanic languages department there serve as excellent examples of this fluidity (Davis and O'Cain 186–88). Originally recruited by the classics department, Lehmann wound up being appointed to the Germanic languages department in 1949. He served there as a member of an interdepartmental committee planning a program in linguistics, which was finally established as a department in 1965 (with him as a professor in it). As for the Germanic languages department, it served as a springboard not only for the later linguistics department—Lehmann notes that "for a number of years linguists took their PhD degrees in Germanic languages, among them one who didn't know a word of German" (Davis and O'Cain 187)—but also for programs in Middle Eastern and South Asian languages. Lehmann's colleague Edgar Polomé, also originally recruited into the Germanic languages department, was the first chair of the Department of Oriental and African Languages and Literatures, which grew out of those programs.

Much of this institutional fluidity had to do with the fact that linguistics was establishing itself during this middle period as a separate discipline studied in a separate department—not only at Texas but all over the United States. Today linguistics is an established discipline in America. Malkiel is correct when he says that, because of a certain theoretical and methodological convergence between America and the rest of the world since the mid-1950s, American linguistics exercises "strong leadership devoid of any isolationist overtones." But what can we say about Germanic linguistics? If Germanic linguists are no longer leaders in the effort to establish a distinctively American approach to linguistics, what do they see themselves as doing?

First, American Germanists as a group never completely stopped doing full-fledged descriptive work on the Germanic languages. Furthermore, while the discussions are now more international, there are still theoretical battles to be waged. Researchers in Germanics are as welcome to join them as anyone else, and they have. Thus, while the impetus for generative grammar and later developments in theoretical phonology, morphology, and syntax may not have come from scholars whose primary interest was the Germanic languages (with the exception, of course, of Modern English and to a lesser extent other modern languages), Germanic scholars have frequently contributed insights that derived from their work with the Germanic languages to the refinement of the theories in question. Most, also, try to express their Germanic findings in a theoretically up-to-date way.

Because of the explosion of the field of linguistics proper, which is reflected in the number of its practitioners, in the number of languages studied by those practitioners, and in the kinds of linguistic issues raised by those languages, Germanic linguistics in America has gone from being a big fish in a small pond to being one fish among many in a pond that has reached the dimensions of a lake. To exemplify this, one might look at the titles of talks given at an annual meeting of the Linguistic Society of America. By my count, of the 269 talks given at the 1999 meeting in Los Angeles, precisely 5 dealt explicitly with Germanic material that was not Modern English (1 on historical German, 1 on Modern Norwegian, and 3 on modern German). Surely other talks dealt with Germanic material, but that material was part of other data making a more abstract, theoretical argument.

Despite these depressing numbers, there is no question that Germanic languages stand at the center of some hot topics in general linguistics. Germanic alliterative verse is central to a number of debates surrounding the right way to view metrical structure in general. The differential development of verb-second and related structures in Germanic languages out of a likely Indo-European verb-last pattern has fueled theoretical arguments concerning the abstract representation of syntactic structure. Yet these topics no longer belong exclusively to Germanists; the linguists discussing them frequently come from departments other than German. The topics are important precisely because they serve as data for a more theoretical discussion of the nature of human language.

One interesting consequence of this gradual marginalization of Germanic linguists in the Linguistic Society of America is that there has arisen the need for a forum where they can talk with one another and a journal where they can publish articles aimed at linguists with similar interests (shades of the creation of the society in the first place!).

At the present time, I count three reasonably large forums of this sort in North America and two journals (the *Journal of English and Germanic Philology*, which still publishes some linguistically oriented articles, would be a third). The oldest conference opportunity, as its name and its affiliation show, is surely the MLA Discussion Group for Germanic Philology. Although it is a small part of a much larger conference and organization, unlike the Linguistic Society of America it gives a time and a place for Germanic linguists to share their ideas with one another.

The annual meeting known alternately as the Berkeley-Michigan or Michigan-Berkeley Germanic Linguistics Roundtable, and now just the Berkeley Germanic Linguistics Roundtable, is another such place and time. As a multiday conference dedicated exclusively to Germanic linguistics, it offers more opportunities for professional interaction to more scholars than the discussion group can. A journal published by the roundtable organizers since 1996, the *Interdisciplinary Journal for Germanic Linguistics and Semiotic Analysis*, though not containing conference proceedings, nevertheless offers a publication outlet for many of the same scholars.

The largest of the venues for Germanic linguists, something of a spinoff of the Berkeley roundtable but hosted annually since 1995 by a variety of different universities in the United States and Canada, is the Germanic Linguistics Annual Conference. The sponsoring organization, founded in 1968 as the Society for Germanic Philology, characterizes itself on its Web page (www .germaniclinguistics.org) as being "the largest and most active organization in North America to serve the broad community of scholars teaching and researching in Germanic Linguistics and Philology" (*About the Society*).

The initial name of this organization suggests something of a return to the older view that Germanic linguists had of themselves as philologists. The suggestion might have been reinforced when the society commenced publication in 1989 of a journal entitled the *American Journal of Germanic Linguistics and Literatures*. The use of *American* may echo the separatist tendencies of American linguistics in general, but with its inclusion of *Literatures*, and given the name of the society itself, one might be forgiven the impression that this journal was likely to be in direct competition with the *Journal of English and Germanic Philology*.

This impression is contradicted by the name of the conference associated with the organization and even more by the subjects actually discussed at that conference. A glance at the titles of papers given at the most recent meeting (German Linguistics Annual Conference 9, in Buffalo, 25–27 Apr. 2003) confirms the almost exclusively linguistic (i.e., nonphilological) nature of the organization, with only a handful of 57 talks listed showing any sign of more than strictly linguistic interest.

Given the realities of the profession and the nature of most submissions to the journal, the society has in fact changed both its name and that of its journal. Since 2001, the organization has borne the name of the Society for Germanic Linguistics, and the journal, now published by Cambridge University Press, is called simply the *Journal of Germanic Linguistics*. Notable about this change is the abandonment not only of *Philology* and *Literatures* but also *American*. Indeed, on its Web page the society emphasizes the internationality both of its membership and of its conferences. In January 2003 it even held a joint conference, in London, with the *Forum for Germanic Language Studies*. More such overseas meetings are on the horizon.

American Germanic linguists today typically belong to a number of scholarly communities whose ends are often different. In the first place, most belong to German departments, and to a great extent prospects rise and fall with the health of those departments, even with the number of students taking the literature classes we do not teach. In the second place, many consider it important that linguists be not just Germanic linguists; one tries to keep up with and contribute to ongoing general theoretical discussions in fields such as phonology, syntax, and sociolinguistics. Finally, there is this unexplainable liking not just for language but for *Germanic* languages, which leads one to seek out like-minded souls both at home and abroad. Looked at closely, these three communities may be seen as a synchronic reflection of the diachronic progression of the discipline outlined here.

American Germanists and Research on Folklore and Fairy Tales from 1970 to the Present

DONALD HAASE

Folklore and fairy tale studies are closely tied to the history of German studies. Scholars describing the origins of *Volkskunde* ("folklore"), *Germanistik*, and the study of fairy tales typically credit Jacob and Wilhelm Grimm with laying the foundations for these fields (e.g., Bluhm v; Gerstner 129; Denecke, "Grimm" 186). Whether or not the Grimms deserve to be called the founders of folklore or "the fathers of *Germanistik*" (Denecke, *Jacob Grimm* 181), there is no doubt that their multifaceted philological scholarship helped shape these disciplines as they emerged in tandem during the nineteenth century. As the Grimms mined a broad range of cultural artifacts for their "etymological and linguistic truths," folklore and folktales—which they believed to be deeply rooted in oral tradition—assumed a central position in their philological project (Zipes, *Brothers Grimm* 10). Folklore and fairy tale studies have assumed a special place not only in the genesis of German studies but also in the United States over the last thirty years. It is particularly telling that contemporary debates about the future of German studies in the United States have been staged concomitantly with remarkably vigorous activity on the part of American Germanists conducting research on folklore and fairy tales.

Since the 1970s American Germanists have been engaged in a radical reexamination and revitalization of fairy tale studies that first began to take shape in postwar Germany. The German reassessment was both facilitated and complicated by the troubling role those studies had played in the national socialist past (Dow and Lixfeld; M. Stein, "Coming to Terms"; Zipes, "Struggle"). By the late 1960s, after two decades of postwar disengagement, German *Volkskunde* began to reverse its "sterile approach to the study of tradition" (Dow and Lixfeld 1), *Germanistik* moved away from *werkimmanente Interpretation* (a form of close reading akin to the practice of New Criticism), and both disciplines adopted critical methodologies that emphasized the sociohistorical and political forces informing folklore and literature. Implicated in the rise of German nationalism and tainted by their abuse in the hands of the National Socialists, fairy tales and the iconographic Brothers Grimm became the object of criticism and rehabilitation; they also became a magnet for scholars coming to grips with the past from across the political spectrum. Consequently, the next decade of fairy tale scholarship in Germany was momentous.

During this same period, the United States had also experienced a resurgent interest in fairy tales, sparked in no small part by the success of Bruno Bettelheim's book of 1976, *The Uses of Enchantment*. Along with the feminist critique of fairy tales, which gained momentum throughout the 1970s, Bettelheim's controversial psychoanalytic readings—which had a strong moral subtext—cast the classic fairy tale in a prominent role in America's culture wars (Haase, "German Fairy Tales"). Given the currency of the Grimms' stories in the American cultural canon, the genre became a perfect point of entry for socially and politically attuned American Germanists. While undergoing a methodological reorientation during the 1960s and 1970s, American Germanists generally declined to follow Bettelheim's morally conservative lead (Zipes, *Breaking* [1984] 160–82). Instead, they engaged with the new generation of German folklorists and literary scholars who were advocating sociohistorical approaches to the fairy tale. Three developments in German scholarship were especially important for the new wave of American fairy tale studies. One of these was the research produced by the team of scholars associated with the *Enzyklopädie des Märchens* (Ranke et al.), whose first volume appeared in 1975 and emphasized not only the comparative study of folktales in sociohistorical contexts but also the relation between oral narrative and literary traditions (see, e.g., Röhrich; Schenda). The second was the textual-philological research of Heinz Rölleke, whose illuminating studies and editorial work began to demystify the Grimms' *Kinder- und Hausmärchen* in the mid-1970s and paved the way for a better historical understanding of the tales. The third was the socially and politically critical approach that had begun to reevaluate the Grimms' tales as children's literature in the 1960s and 1970s. Utilizing Marxist ideas and critical theory, German scholars sought to reclaim the fairy tale's emancipatory potential by revealing the ideological underpinnings of the genre and exposing the Grimms' deliberate appropriation of traditional tales in the service of the socializing process (e.g., Bürger; Doderer; Richter and Merkel).

By the 1980s, American Germanists began to incorporate, modify, and go beyond these approaches. In 1979 Jack Zipes published a watershed book of

American fairy tale scholarship, *Breaking the Magic Spell: Radical Theories of Folk and Fairy Tales*. Zipes's influential study (which was republished in a revised and expanded edition in 2002) drew heavily on the work of the Frankfurt school, the philosophy of Ernst Bloch, and the ideological criticism practiced by Marxist fairy tale scholars in Germany. In the context of fairy tale studies, *Breaking the Magic Spell* is the first work to introduce American scholars at large to this radically new approach and its underlying critical German scholarship. Zipes's book demonstrates the vital role of fairy tale scholarship in the reorientation of Germanics. As a coeditor of *New German Critique*, a journal that reconceptualized the discipline, Zipes not only previewed his chapter on the politics of the fairy tales as an article in one of the journal's early issues ("Breaking"), he also characterized the book itself as "the product of the collaborative efforts of [his] friends and co-editors" at the journal (*Breaking* [1984] viii). Not only did the political thrust of Zipes's scholarship contribute to the development of fairy tale studies and to the revision of Germanics, but the scope of his book—which encompassed folktales *and* literary fairy tales and drew on texts by writers ranging from Grimm, Novalis, and Kästner to Oscar Wilde, Walt Disney, and J. R. R. Tolkien—extended well beyond the disciplinary boundaries of traditional *Germanistik*. *Breaking the Magic Spell* addressed a multidisciplinary audience and imported critical theory and German fairy tale scholarship into other disciplines; it also demonstrated the wide interdisciplinary potential of German studies and helped position fairy tale studies as an interdisciplinary project at the intersection of national literature and comparative cultural studies.

American Germanists continued to address multidisciplinary audiences and to change the direction of fairy tale studies in the United States by disseminating new German approaches to the genre. John Ellis's controversial monograph *One Fairy Story Too Many* did this in 1983 by using the research of Heinz Rölleke as a springboard for claiming that the Grimms had perpetrated a folklore fraud. While Ellis's sensational indictment rested on conclusions drawn from a misrepresentation of Rölleke's research, at the time of its publication his book had a broad reception among English-speaking readers and played an undeniable part in demythologizing the Grimms and their tales. Ellis's book received considerable attention in the 1980s not only because of its provocative claims but also because of its proximity to the Grimm bicentennial years of 1985–86. Partly inspired by those anniversaries, a series of conferences and seminars organized by American Germanists in the mid-1980s produced a number of essay collections that included research by German scholars in English and that were specifically intended, in the words of one editor, "to improve English-speakers' acquaintance with research being done by scholars writing in German" (McGlathery, *Brothers Grimm* vii–viii; see also Bottigheimer, *Fairy Tales*; Haase, *Reception*). But American Germanists were not simply engaged in missionary work for German *Volkskunde* and *Germanistik*. They also made their own mark on fairy tale studies, and they did so in ways that gave their research visibility beyond the discipline's usual territorial boundaries.

American Germanists have made particularly original and influential advances in feminist fairy tale studies (see Haase, "Feminist Fairy-Tale Scholarship" 23–28, 30–31). Building on the textual work of Heinz Rölleke, they produced important studies in the 1980s that demonstrated in detail how the depiction of women and the construction of gender in the *Kinder- und Hausmärchen* had been defined by the Grimms' practices and interventions as collectors and editors and how the Grimms' female informants had figured in the collection (see Bottigheimer, *Grimms' Bad Girls*; Tatar, *Hard Facts*). This widely read scholarship—which was grounded in textual history and sociohistorical contexts—changed the way fairy tale scholars in diverse disciplines understood and wrote about the Grimms' canonical collection, and it contributed to a new understanding of the complexity of the genre's relation to gender. Simultaneously, American Germanists were contributing to the recovery of an alternative fairy tale tradition by women (Blackwell, "Fractured Fairy Tales"; Jarvis). While some recovered texts were made available in German editions (by Jarvis; Arnim; Arnim and Arnim), more recently they have appeared in English translation—most notably in *The Queen's Mirror*, a pivotal anthology of tales edited and translated by Shawn Jarvis and Jeannine Blackwell that demonstrates the resonance of German studies across disciplines and helps shape the textual corpus and discourse of interdisciplinary fairy tale studies.

From its beginnings, folk-narrative research has had an international dimension, but since the 1970s the fairy tale scholarship of American Germanists (some of whom have doctoral degrees or appointments in comparative literature) has taken a pronounced turn toward comparative and extradisciplinary studies. From *Breaking the Magic Spell* to *The Oxford Companion to Fairy Tales* and beyond, Zipes has worked toward a comprehensive social history of the fairy tale in the West. Over time, the focus of his research, originally centered on German, American, and British contexts, has expanded to include French and Italian traditions (see "Bibliography"). This expansion is characteristic of the work by American Germanists. The first book-length comparison of three of the most widely recognized fairy tale collections—those by Grimm, Charles Perrault, and Giambattista Basile—was published in 1991 by an American Germanist (McGlathery, *Fairy Tale Romance*); and the first and only book-length study devoted to Giovan Francesco Straparola and his early collection of literary fairy tales—*Le piacevoli notti*—is the product of an American Germanist (Bottigheimer, *Fairy Godfather*). Since 1997, *Marvels and Tales: Journal of Fairy-Tale Studies*, which is international and interdisciplinary in scope, has been edited by an American Germanist, Donald Haase. Moreover, as editors and translators American Germanists have compiled widely read anthologies that have emphasized the fairy tale's cultural and generic variety (see Tatar, *Classic Fairy Tales*; Zipes, *Beauties, Great Fairy Tale Tradition, Trials, Victorian Fairy Tales*, and *Spells*). By drawing attention to alternate traditions, these anthologies have challenged the canonical status of Grimms' tales and encouraged readers to understand specific texts in historical and sociocultural contexts.

Unlike the impressive coverage of global cultures represented in the *Enzyklopädie des Märchens*, the fairy tale research of American Germanists has been less inclusive and largely Eurocentric. But by drawing on the methods of comparative literary studies and comparative folktale research, American Germanists have effectively bridged the gap between the study of oral narratives and literary fairy tales, and repositioned the classical tales of the West and the once privileged German *Kunstmärchen* in a tradition that is both geographically and generically much broader and more complex. Wolfgang Mieder's prolific work on the use of "folk literature" in poetry and in modern media such as cartoons, advertising, journalism, comic strips, and greeting cards has substantially enlarged the field (see *Disenchantments*, "Survival Forms," and *Tradition*), as has research on the fairy tale in visual media such as film and television (see Zipes, "Toward a Theory"; Haase, "Television").

In a way consistent with the trend toward cultural studies, American Germanists involved in fairy tale studies have been aggressively revising the canon, crossing disciplinary boundaries, and remapping the field. As a consequence, Germanics has not only played a leading role in the development of fairy tale studies as a transnational discipline, it has also intersected with folklore studies in ways that challenge, if not entirely erase, the boundaries separating folklorists from Germanists. The case of Mieder, a Germanist whose extensive work on folk literature and paroemiology ignores national boundaries and is embraced by folklorists, is representative. Similarly, Mary Beth Stein—a folklorist by training who has crossed into German departments ("How Big" 152)—has demonstrated through her scholarship how the two disciplines can benefit from critically acknowledging their historical bond and from forging new interdisciplinary connections (see esp. "How Big" and "Wilhelm Heinrich Riehl"). Instrumental in the evolution of *Germanistik*, folklore and fairy tale studies have been redefined in the context of cultural studies and once again are playing active roles as German studies reinvents itself in the twenty-first century.

Developments in
German Jewish Studies
from 1980 to the Present

NOAH ISENBERG

Like many other academic subfields, German Jewish studies has emerged from a range of different methodologies, scholarly disciplines, and general areas of inquiry that make its contours inherently multidisciplinary and relatively elusive of definition. The subfield has drawn considerable sustenance from established fields such as history, sociology, political science, and comparative literature; at the same time it has solicited significant insight from various theoretical enterprises, including feminism, Marxism, and cultural studies. Although there does not yet exist a single definitive core curriculum in German Jewish studies—and that is not necessarily a desirable or even a tenable objective—there are a number of important scholarly institutions (e.g., the Leo Baeck Institute, YIVO Institute, and the newly combined Center for Jewish History in New York) and academic journals that frequently publish work on German Jewish topics (e.g., *Leo Baeck Institute Year Book*, *New German Critique*, *History and Memory*). There are also a host of recent book publications, edited anthologies and single-authored monographs alike, that have contributed to a discernible turn in German studies over the past two decades. This essay outlines some of the broader tendencies in this subfield of German studies, noting the different directions it has taken. Given the transitional stage of the subject, my remarks are largely schematic and, at times, anecdotal in nature.

Today there seems to be no shortage of interest in German Jewish literary and cultural history in the American academy—both within and outside departments and programs in German studies. There are regular panels and special sessions at annual professional meetings, such as those of the German Studies Association; summer seminars sponsored by the Fulbright Commission and the German Academic Exchange Service; national and international academic conferences held at universities and colleges; and finally publication projects such as special issues of journals and university presses with specialized book series or general lists emphasizing this area of research. Without providing each and every example of what might broadly fall under the rubric of German Jewish studies—and given the diffuse and seemingly endless pool of examples, omission is inevitable—it may be possible to trace in rather broad brush strokes how the field has taken shape in the past two decades, in what kinds of settings developments have evolved, and which works and contributors have played a key role.

Scholarly Pioneers and Their Legacy

Until the late 1970s, German Jewish studies, if there was such a thing at that time, was pursued for the most part by professional historians, either in the pages of the *Leo Baeck Institute Year Book* (which began publication in 1953), in the institute's West German book series, or in independent monographs. George L. Mosse published his highly influential *Germans and Jews: The Right, the Left, and the Search for a "Third Force"* in 1970. As a professor of German and European history at the University of Wisconsin, Madison, his work in and out of the classroom affected an entire generation of young scholars—Steven Aschheim, Paul Breines, Anson Rabinbach, and others—who would go on to contribute to the general area of German Jewish studies. Mosse remained engaged in German Jewish scholarly debates throughout his extended career (see, e.g., *German Jews beyond Judaism* [1985] and *Confronting the Nation* [1993]). Several years after Mosse's initial work, the historian Peter Gay published *Freud, Jews, and Other Germans: Masters and Victims in Modernist Culture* (1978), a critical exploration of Jewish intellectual and cultural history before the rise of National Socialism. Together with his wife, the independent scholar Ruth Gay, he continued to record the history of German Jewry (see Ruth Gay, *Jews of Germany* [1992] and *Safe among the Germans* [2002]). Still, book publications among Germanists specializing in German Jewish studies were, with few exceptions (such as Zohn; Kahn), minimal throughout the first decades after the war. Not until 1979, when David Bronsen, a specialist on Joseph Roth, published (at a German publishing house, no less) an anthology of essays, *Jews and Germans from 1860 to 1933: The Problematic Symbiosis*, did Germanists in America begin to make a mark in this inchoate field.

New German Critique published three special issues dedicated to Germans and Jews (vols. 19, 20, 21; 1980–81), selections of which would later be included in the critical anthology *Germans and Jews since the Holocaust* (1986), edited by

Anson Rabinbach and Jack Zipes, two of the journal's founding editors. Like other such volumes (e.g., Reinharz and Schatzberg), *Germans and Jews* presented work by historians, political theorists, philosophers, and Germanists from the United States and abroad. Alongside contributions by veteran writers such as Jean Améry, Toni Oelsner, and Manès Sperber it gave voice to a new generation of critics and scholars, including Atina Grossmann, Moishe Postone, and Martin Jay, many of whom were weaned on the staples of the Frankfurt school and the teachings of the American New Left. To be sure, the critical legacy of the Institute for Social Research and its associates has served as an important scholarly touchstone, and although not fundamentally bound to German Jewish studies, it has left a serious impact on the field at large (see Jay, *Dialectical Imagination* and *Permanent Exiles*).

When Sander Gilman published his groundbreaking *Jewish Self-Hatred* in 1986, it followed the precedent that had been set by a handful of senior scholars—mostly historians—and was received in an academic climate increasingly attuned to identity politics and cultural studies. Drawing on a vast assortment of literary and nonliterary texts from the past several hundred years, Gilman offered a panoramic account of the diverse and sometimes contradictory dynamics of German Jewish identity formation. His approach was especially novel in that he devoted sustained attention to stereotypes, to the perceived otherness of the Jew, to the key tropes of German Jewish (as well as Yiddish and American Jewish) literature, and to the various kinds of cultural iconography invoked in such works. Like Aschheim's earlier *Brothers and Strangers*, *Jewish Self-Hatred* zeroed in on the intense interplay between German Jewish and East European Jewish culture, in particular the linguistic trappings of this relation. As Gilman asserts early in his study, "Jews were constantly being forced to define who they were in a language perceived not to be their native tongue. Here the world of myth led to certain basic conflicts within Jewish writers and thinkers, conflicts that served as the basis for self-hatred" (18). Gilman's work on racial stereotyping and cultural otherness proved instructive not only for German Jewish studies but for cultural studies in general, an area in which the German Jewish sphere may be seen as one among many spheres of inquiry (see Berman, *Cultural Studies*).

Anthologies and New Histories

One of the predominant tendencies in German Jewish studies has been the writing and rewriting of various strands of the larger history to ensure that Jewish writers, thinkers, and directors become—or, in some cases, become once again—a part of the German literary and cultural pantheon. This project began with the work of Bronsen and has continued to bear much fruit since the subsequent work of Rabinbach and Zipes. There have been an increasing number of anthologies focusing on German Jewish literature and culture, particularly since 1989. Consider Gilman and Karen Remmler's *Reemerging Jewish Culture in Germany: Life and Literature since 1989* (1994); Dagmar C. G. Lorenz and Gabriele Weinberger's *Insiders and Outsiders: Jewish and Gentile Culture in Germany and Austria* (1994); as well as the literary anthologies *Contemporary Jewish Writing in Austria* (1998), edited by Lorenz, and *Contemporary Jewish Writing in Germany* (2002), edited by Leslie Morris and Remmler. Some of these anthologies began as lectures delivered at academic conferences and appeared in print with the benefit of the thorough critical exchange among the participants. Recent volumes of this kind have attempted to forge new directions in scholarship, both in the period after 1945 (Morris and Zipes) and before (Brenner and Penslar). Finally, there have been ambitious survey histories produced by teams of scholars, such as Michael A. Mayer's four-volume *German-Jewish History in Modern Times* (1996–98).

Arguably the most monumental of these studies, both in terms of scope and level of scholarly collaboration, is the 1997 *Yale Companion to Jewish Writing and Thought in German Culture, 1096–1996*, edited by Gilman and Zipes. Contained in the nearly 900-page tome are substantive contributions from well over 100 scholars: historians, political scientists, sociologists, Germanists, art historians, and others—from the United States, Canada, France, England, Germany, Austria, and Israel. At the time, the editors of the volume sensed an urgency to produce such a collection. As they remark in their introduction, "To compile the first guide to Jewish writing in German at the end of the twentieth century is a clearly impossible yet absolutely necessary task, and we and our contributors have proposed to do both the impossible and the necessary" (xvii). Rather than attempt to write a continuous and seamless narrative overview of German Jewish literature and culture from the past millennium, the editors assembled an extensive series of essays that treat specific junctures in the grand sweep of history. Among the many contributions organized in a chronological fashion are: Arthur Tilo Alt on the medieval epic poem "Dukus Horant"; Liliane Weissberg on Salomon Maiomon's late-eighteenth-century autobiography; Michael Berkowitz on Herzl's *Judenstaat*; Amy Colin on Bertha Pappenheim; Anat Feinberg on Jewish theater after the Holocaust; Leslie Adelson on the work of American-born writer Jeannette Lander; and Robert Shandley on Peter Lilienthal's 1979 film *David*. In the end, as Gilman and Zipes envisage it, the volume "presents snapshots of moments and individuals in a changing culture and, through this kaleidoscope, affords the reader insight into the intricate transformations and contradictions of this culture" (xv).

German Jewish Studies versus Holocaust Studies

The vast scholarly and nonscholarly literature on the Holocaust experienced an enormous surge in the 1980s. Indeed, in the past two decades, the American audience at large has shown itself to be unusually receptive to—some might say obsessed with—books dealing with the Nazi genocide. As several critics have recently argued, with varying degrees of fervor and polemical edge (see Novick; Finkelstein), the study of the Holocaust has almost become an American pastime; certainly it has become a highly popular offering in the college and university curriculum. This development has served as a double-edged sword for German Jewish studies. On the one hand, it has piqued interest among students, scholars, and the general public in German history and culture from 1933 to 1945. On the other, it has tended to overshadow what preceded and followed these years. Put simply, for all too many students (and a disproportionate number of scholars as well), the history of German Jewry would seem to follow a rather straight path toward Auschwitz; whatever developed after 1945 is of little significance. This is not to say that there has not been solid research on Jewish life during the Third Reich (and Marion Kaplan's work is a strong example). In the past few years, there have also been important studies of German and German Jewish writing, poetry and prose, dealing with the Holocaust and with trauma more generally (see Eshel, *Zeit*; Schlant; Bower; Baer). However, much of the recent work done in German Jewish studies, in history, literature, and the arts, has begun to examine the period after 1945, not only as it stands in relation to the legacy of the Holocaust but also as it begins to move into a new, comparatively less burdened era.

Among the recent sociological and historical studies are those dealing with the various dilemmas faced by Jews during the decades after the war, such as Y. Michal Bodeman's *Jews, Germans, Memory: Reconstructions of Jewish Life in Germany* (1996), Lynn Rappaport's *Jews in Germany after the Holocaust: Memory, Identity, and German-Jewish Relations* (1997), and Michael Brenner's *After the Holocaust: Rebuilding Jewish Lives in Postwar Germany* (1997). In addition to the scholarship predominantly focused on Jewish cultural life in West Germany, there have been studies of German Jewish culture in the former East Germany (e.g., Ostow; Borneman and Peck). Finally, a burgeoning area of research has emerged in tandem with the spate of new literature, from short fiction and essays to poetry and novels, written by Jewish authors in both halves of Germany after 1989 (Gilman and Remmler; Gilman, *Jews in Today's German Culture*; Morris and Remmler) and in contemporary Austria (Lorenz). Given the steady stream of literary works published in Germany and Austria today, scholarship on the new generation of writers is apt to continue to flourish.

German Jewish Studies across the Atlantic

For the past two decades or so, interest in German Jewish literature and culture in the Federal Republic has remained steady, showing no signs of decline. Like their American counterparts, German scholars concentrating on this area of research have come from an array of university departments: *Germanistik*, history, political science, religion, and others. About the same time that the first scholarly volumes in German Jewish studies were published in the United States, Germany produced several of its own, often international, collaborative efforts. In 1985, Günther Grimm and Hans-Peter Bayerdörfer published a volume of essays, *Im Zeichen Hiobs: Jüdische Schriftsteller und deutsche Literatur im 20. Jahrhundert*, written by German, Australian, Israeli, and American scholars. A year later, the proceedings of a 1983 German-Israeli symposium, *Juden in der deutschen Literatur*, edited by Stéphane Mosès and Albrecht Schöne, were published by West Germany's premier trade press, Suhrkamp. These two early collections considered the diverse encounters between Germans and Jews in the literary and cultural sphere. In the meantime, German Jewish studies has gained even greater attention, both on the institutional level and in the public sphere in general.

One of the larger developments in transatlantic cooperation has come about as a result of the intense expansion of the field of Jewish studies in the Federal Republic of Germany both before and after the fall of the Berlin wall. Many of the recently established centers and institutes for Jewish studies in Germany, most notably the Moses-Mendelssohn Center in Potsdam and the new Berlin-based branch of the Leo Baeck Institute, emphasize German Jewish literary and cultural history in their research and curricular offerings. Moreover, the newly established chair of Jewish history and culture at the University of Munich, currently occupied by the leading historian of modern German Jewry, Michael Brenner, has provided abundant opportunities for scholars from around the world to participate in symposia, lectures, visiting fellowships, and summer seminars. Finally, in the years leading up to the Wende (literally, "the turn," used to designate the fall of the Berlin wall) and immediately following, journals such as *Babylon* and, slightly later, *Semit*, have offered a venue for scholarly debate among German and non-German academics and critics. Beyond the strict designation of academic Jewish studies, there has been important work done in German Jewish film and film theory (Koch, *Einstellung*), cultural and political criticism (Broder, *Erbarmen*), and archival genealogies and memoirs (Richarz). A relatively recent phenomenon, contributing to the wider reception of research by German-based scholars, has been the publication of translations and English renditions of their work. Among these are Dan Diner's *Beyond the Conceivable* (2000), Gertrud Koch's critical examination of Siegfried Kracauer (2000), and Henryk Broder's collection of essays, *To Each His Own* (forthcoming). French-based scholars of German Jewish culture have appeared in English as well (see Löwy; Traverso).

Contemporary Debates and the Future

In fall 2001, the *Chronicle of Higher Education* published an article titled "German Intellectuals, Jewish Victims: A Politically Correct Solidarity," written by Mark

M. Anderson, a Germanist at Columbia University. While attempting to draw parallels between the ostensible forces of political correctness manifest in the discourse on the Holocaust in Germany and in the current curricular changes in German studies in this country, Anderson made a number of controversial claims. He asserted that "American scholars have distorted the study of German culture" (B8); as a result, there has evolved what he calls "the power center of Benjamin, Kafka, and Celan" (B9). Owing to inordinate attention given to Hitler and the Holocaust, Anderson argues, German studies has had to accommodate—or, more in keeping with the rhetoric of the piece, to *compromi*se itself— to make up for this:

> To increase undergraduate enrollments, German professors here are obliged to reduce the canon of German literature to a tiny handful of teachable authors who often have a Jewish background. They are also forced to skew courses away from literature toward the study of persecution, exile, and genocide. (B9)

Soon after its publication, Anderson's article came up against a number of pointed critiques, which have insisted, among other things, that much of his argument is marred by inflammatory assertions and that the polemic he seeks to advance does not match the realities faced by most scholars and students. Yet, without going too far into the intricacies of the essay—and I for one recognize certain suggestive points as well as conspicuous shortcomings—it is possible to use the basic claims as a means for responding to the present situation. There is, admittedly, much interest in Kafka, Benjamin, and Celan today, but this interest seems a result less of the authors' Jewish background than of the availability of reliable translations and the applicability of their work to timely and enduring issues (this availability and applicability may be observed, at different times and to different extents, in such non-Jewish authors as Thomas Mann, Hermann Hesse, Bertolt Brecht, and Christa Wolf). Scholars have also expanded and enriched the study on these authors (e.g., Spector; Löwy; Eshel), while opening up the field to additional, less well known authors. Even with the increased focus on Hitler and the Holocaust, there has been a sizable amount of scholarship undertaken on areas that extend beyond that specific constellation: on German Jewish religious and philosophical figures and debates (Heschel; Batnitzky; Santner, *On the Psychopathology*; Mendes-Flohr); on Jewish culture in Weimar Germany (M. Brenner, *Renaissance*) and, more generally, on German modernism (Isenberg; Jonathan Hess); on the place of German Jews in medical history (Efron); on German Jewish periodicals (D. Brenner); on Yiddish (Grossman); and on Jewish women writers (Lorenz, *Keepers*).

If there has in fact been a reduction in the canon of German literature—and that remains open to debate—there has certainly been an expansion of the canon in German Jewish studies. Which does not mean that there are not possible dangers (e.g., parochialism and lack of openness) that could impede its continued expansion. Of course, it is still too early to predict how this subfield will establish itself as it matures. It does seem plausible, however, that there will be staples of study—genres, figures, periods, debates—while additional neglected areas of research enter the discussion. Finally, like other subfields, German Jewish studies will have to adjust to the divergent methodological transformations that take place in its midst; only then will it be able to keep up with the challenges it continues to face.

The Study of GDR Literature and Culture, 1970–90

DAVID BATHRICK

The Beginnings of an Academic Paradigm

It took a long time for the literature and culture of East Germany to become established as a field of inquiry in German studies. For much of the two decades following the founding of the German Democratic Republic (GDR) in 1949, the prevailing attitude toward culture produced in East Germany in American departments of German literature was similar to that of West German universities. Nurtured on the tenets of New Criticism and grounded in the autonomous status of art vis-à-vis the world of politics, American scholars who deigned to write about or teach literature officially promoted in the GDR tended to view it simply as state propaganda.

One important difference between West German and American Germanists during this time was that a significant number of the Americans were native Germans who had been driven into exile by the Nazis since their rise to power in January 1933. In the light of that experience, they tended to see the state-controlled production of GDR literature as another variant of the deformation of German culture due to totalitarian control that had forced them to leave Germany.

During the early 1970s a gradual change in attitude developed toward East German literature among American Germanists. This change was a consequence in part of the nascent detente between the East and West blocs globally, in part of the rapid expansion of GDR studies in the Federal Republic of West

Germany. In the 1960s scholars in both West Germany and the United States generally ignored the literature of East Germany as an institutional phenomenon and focused instead on a few isolated poetic voices who happened to be living there; the tendency moved in the opposite direction in the 1970s. "The literature of the GDR cannot simply be viewed immanently," wrote Peter Hohendahl and Patricia Herminghouse in 1974 and thereby articulated a call for contextualization, which was emblematic of methodological developments that were occurring more generally in American literary and cultural studies in the United States (Foreword 8). Applied more narrowly to the study of culture in the GDR, this contextualization entailed judging and interpreting individual works of literature according to the political guidelines and aesthetic norms of the official cultural policy of the East German socialist system as well as according to the larger comparative framework of German studies historically.

If one considers the authors and subjects in GDR studies that were being written about and taught in American German departments during the two decades before the fall of the wall in 1989, one finds that they were similar to those discussed in West German universities and in German programs of higher education in France, England, Italy, Canada, and Australia. The writers were Christa Wolf, Heiner Müller, Günter Kunert, Franz Fühmann, Anna Seghers, Irmtraud Morgner, Volker Braun, Brigitte Reimann, Peter Hacks, Christoph Hein. The topics were workers' literature, antifascism, women's literature, the role of the writer under socialism, oppositional literature, Jewish and Holocaust literature. The methodological questions related to theoretical debates about realism, Romanticism, the classical heritage, the search for subjectivity, the socialist public sphere, modernism, feminism, reception theory, and in the 1980s and 1990s postmodernism and poststructuralism.

In the United States, critical debates concerning the paradigms of a consciously socialist literature often helped generate challenges for a German studies that heretofore had limited its view of twentieth-century German literature to classics of the modernist canon by authors such as Rainer Maria Rilke, Thomas Mann, Heinrich Mann, Franz Kafka, Gottfried Benn, Ingeborg Bachmann, and Bertolt Brecht and to the New Critical methodologies of close reading deemed most appropriate to treat them. Thus as part of the larger intellectual sea change that was occurring in the humanities in the 1970s, scholars studying the literature of the GDR must also be seen in relation to those looking to promote neglected women writers, inaugurate the study of African American and other minority literatures, or teach popular-mass culture (film, media, popular literature). Like the methodological innovations in the profession as a whole, the call for contextualization for GDR studies inevitably required theoretical and methodological paradigms that would situate one's mode of analysis in a field of inquiry encompassed, however inadequately, by the terms *historical* and *interdisciplinary*.

Establishing an Institutional Framework

The establishment of GDR literature and culture as a subdiscipline in the evolving framework of German studies in the United States was accompanied and catalyzed by a number of institutional developments between 1970 and 1980. One early, important impulse was to introduce it as an area of study in its own right into the curricula of graduate programs in a number of prominent programs at the university level rather than simply treat isolated East German authors. The University of Wisconsin, University of Minnesota, Ohio State University, Washington University, Indiana University, University of Illinois, University of Pennsylvania, University of Massachusetts, and Cornell University all began to offer courses (graduate and undergraduate) in which East German writers were studied in the context of the socialist system. In addition, graduate students were encouraged to write dissertations on GDR topics, a number of which were published as important contributions to this embryonic but burgeoning field. John Flores's monograph *Poetry in East Germany*, Marc Silberman's study of the East German industrial novel (*Literature*), H. G. Hüttich's *Theater in the Planned Society*, and Arlene Teraoka's monograph on Heiner Müller (*Silence*) are but a few of such seminal works.

Another catalyst for the study of the GDR was the organization of conferences and workshops focusing on East German writers, along with seminar sessions and lectures at the annual meetings of the MLA, German Studies Association; AATG; Women in German; and the GDR summer symposia in Conway, New Hampshire. In the spring of 1974, the first major conference on GDR culture and theory was held at the University of Washington, where scholars from East and West Germany joined American colleagues for discussions. The results were published in a volume of essays (Hohendahl and Herminghouse, *Literatur* [1976]). Emphasis was placed on the exchange of ideas about the very different approaches to the central concerns involved in such study; some of the topics were the modernism debate in the GDR, the representation of women in East German novels, new trends in GDR literary theory, and the debate between the dramatic traditions of Bertolt Brecht and Friedrich Wolf. American participants such as David Bathrick, Jost Hermand, Herminghouse, Hohendahl, Frank Trommler, and Jack Zipes went on to play a key role in the development of the field. Comparing this conference and volume with a smaller conference held at Cornell and the volume that came from it at the beginning of the 1980s (Hohendahl and Herminghouse, *Literatur* [1983]) offers interesting insight into the increasingly critical attitude of American scholars toward the government of the GDR and its treatment of writers who failed to conform to official policies.

The annual meetings of the GDR symposium, held at a summer camp in Conway starting in 1975, established a more informal venue for American,

GDR, and West German scholars to present papers and discuss issues. While the prevailing posture of nonconfrontation was developed in the interest of intellectual détente, at times it prevented genuine critical exchange on such crucial issues as the repression of dissent or fundamental failures of the GDR regime. Nevertheless, the presentation and subsequent publication of papers on key subjects of mutual interest provided an important forum for the field as a whole. Similarly, a workshop held in Washington, DC, and sponsored by the American Institute for Contemporary German Studies in fall 1988 brought together leading scholars from the GDR, the Federal Republic, and the United States—and one GDR writer (Joachim Schädlich) who was living in exile—to discuss and compare the reception of GDR literature in all three countries. The frank and critical exchange was in many ways unprecedented; ironically it took place exactly one year before the collapse of the GDR.

A third major place for the support of GDR studies resided in journals, publishing houses, and archives, which communicate information, promote critical discussions, and distribute the work of scholars. The *GDR Bulletin*, which was established at Washington University in the mid-1970s, provided a valuable clearinghouse for the newest developments in GDR studies in East and West Germany and the United States. Of particular importance were the book reviews, conference reports, and interviews with leading GDR writers. Other journals in the field—*German Studies Review, German Quarterly, Monatshefte, New German Critique, Germanic Review, German Politics and Society, Women in German*, and *Basis*—regularly published articles as well as occasional special issues on the GDR. The first such special issue, done by *New German Critique* in 1974 (*Special Issue on the German Democratic Republic*), was an introduction to the field, and it was followed by issues devoted to the expulsion of Wolf Biermann, the work of Heiner Müller, and the collapse of the GDR in 1989. *German Politics and Society* published an issue entitled *The GDR at Forty* shortly before the wall came down; in the early 1990s *Germanic Review* published two special issues entitled *The End of GDR Literature*. Beginning in 1981, the organizers of the Conway conference published annually *Selected Papers from the New Hampshire Symposium on the German Democratic Republic*, edited by Margy Gerber.

A number of important works by American scholars of GDR literature were written in German and published in German publishing houses. Jay Rosellini's monographs on Volker Braun and Wolf Biermann, Silberman's study on the reception of Heiner Müller, Alexander Stephan's *Christa Wolf*, Dieter Sevin's study of Christa Wolf, Hohendahl and Herminghouse's above-mentioned conference volumes, and Christiane Romero's works on Anna Seghers are some examples. Particularly important for GDR studies in the 1970s and early 1980s was the extent to which the interchange of American and West German scholars was published in both the United States and the Federal Republic. In the United States, a number of presses have played a critical role in publishing works on the culture and literature of the GDR. The Peter Lang and Berghahn publishing houses have consistently made available major works concerning the GDR. University presses such as Wayne State, University of North Carolina, University of Nebraska, University of California, and Indiana University have series that are specifically devoted to German studies, and they include GDR culture and literature.

Finally, mention should be made of the rapid development in the 1980s of the study of GDR film. The recent establishment of the Deutsche Film Aktiengesellschaft Film Library and Archive by Barton Byg at the University of Massachusetts has considerably enhanced the presence of and access to these materials.

The Development of Reading Practices

While the struggle to establish GDR studies in the American academy was accompanied by a critique of the literary and critical canons prevailing in the *Germanistik* of the 1950s and 1960s, the emphasis on contextualization occasionally resulted in problematic approaches: scholars often did not question the political assumptions underlying their interpretive analyses. In the early 1970s, the sudden openness toward if not fascination with the newly discovered landscape of GDR literature was not accompanied by a critical inquiry of the GDR and its cultural creations. The born-again eagerness not to be anticommunist and the desire to view emergence of this literature and its ideas only in the premises of the GDR context at times entailed a suspension of one's evaluative position or even an apology for "necessary contradictions"— a stance that resembled the official cultural policy of the GDR itself. For instance, if a literary work was rejected for publication or partly censored in the GDR because of its deviation from the official aesthetic or thematic party line, some critics justified such decisions as historically necessary—that is, as the difficult but understandable means by which the socialist system was to ensure its development in the struggle to build a socialist revolution.

Such apologetic versions of the so-called contextual approach were challenged by counterreadings in the United States beginning in the late 1970s. This challenge demonstrates how discussion in GDR studies developed more nuanced and critical approaches to the literature and cultural policies of that state. It is important to stress that the evolution of scholars' critical positions also occurred in response to developments in the GDR itself. The emergence of a recalcitrant group of avant-garde writers and intellectuals in the GDR between the 1968 Soviet invasion of Czechoslovakia and the 1976 expulsion of the dissident poet Biermann (e.g., Müller, Morgner, Wolf, Braun, Kunert) had a significant impact on scholars' evaluation of the GDR itself. The often implicit critique of orthodox (Marxist-Leninist) notions of history and subjectivity in the poetic and theoretical work of GDR writers resonated with similar poststructuralist critiques of Marxism and other master narratives emerging in academic American journals such as *Critical Inquiry, Telos, New German Critique, October,* and *Social Text* in the 1980s, according to which it was important to recognize the primacy of language, discourse, and aesthetics in questions of political power and social change.

Similarly, the literature of GDR women writers (e.g., Wolf, Morgner, Kirsch) that questioned the instrumental, male prerogatives of the ruling regime was seen by many feminists in German studies to offer a theoretical bridge to discussions among American feminists in the 1970s. In this regard, the works of Christa Wolf in particular had a strong reception outside German studies in the United States. Wolf herself provided a fascinating interface between the competing epistemologies of Marxism and feminism. There is no question, feminists contended, that she stood firmly in the tradition of critical forms of Marxism in close proximity to thinkers like Bloch, Benjamin, and Brecht. But it was precisely her literary (aesthetic, linguistic) achievement that imbued her critical Marxism with female experience, an experience that unconsciously unmasked the limits of orthodox Marxism and its patriarchal underpinnings (see Bammer).

Beyond the Wall: A Brief Conclusion

Seen from the present post–Berlin Wall position, the American readings of the inner opposition in the GDR reveal the strengths but also the limitations of a critical strategy linked intellectually to and in discursive dialogue with the writers under investigation. The sustained aesthetic and theoretical critique of the prevailing ideology and its cultural policy was developed by dissident GDR writers and scholars from an Archimedean point—outside the ruling Marxist-Leninist paradigm—to generate a set of liberating, critical fantasies that would challenge the status quo. Certain American Germanists viewed this challenge to the canons of theory and literature by East German intellectuals as resonant with methodological and theoretical discussions in the institution of the humanities in the United States (see Bathrick, *Powers* 1–24). While this approach generated some very fine readings of works by Müller, Wolf, Seghers, Braun, Biermann, Hein, and Morgner, it also led to an American reception of GDR writers that sometimes placed them well outside of or even at variance with the GDR context.

For instance, Christa Wolf often pointed out that the western Marxist attempts of American feminists to appropriate GDR women writers like herself as mediators between feminism and Marxism involved a profound decontextualization of the work and thought of those writers. The point was that the moment an idea from one culture takes on another life in a different culture, it reflects more the values of the receiving culture and thereby misreads the original intention. But a misreading may be productive: often bringing to the surface aspects of an author's work that are either subordinate or repressed in the framework from which it comes.

While Wolf may have been naive to believe that cultural misreading can ever be avoided, her concerns did anticipate a problem that became egregiously apparent with the fall of the Berlin wall. The shock and in some cases disillusionment on the part of Western journalists and scholars at the extent to which these dissident writers revealed themselves to have been deeply embedded in the context of the GDR made it clear just how profoundly almost all scholars of GDR literature had been misreading all along. Revelations of these writers' cooperation with the Stasi or their abiding skepticism about forms of Western parliamentary democracy opened up aspects of their experience, identity, and basic allegiances that had not been visible or simply could not be seen in the black-and-white landscape of the cold war.

For scholars of GDR culture, the fall of the wall in 1989 has meant more than the end of a political or cultural system. It has also signaled the demise of a particular kind of interpretive certitude—but a chance to look anew as well. The interpretive paradigms based on a conflict between affirmative and resistant culture were clearly a part of a political framework in which literature was seen primarily as a medium for freedom of expression. That we are no longer bound to such coordinates and that archives are now available for greater scrutiny should free us to ask questions and generate readings that heretofore have not been possible.

5

Organizing
the Profession

∾

Edited by
PATRICIA HERMINGHOUSE

Introduction

Old jokes about the German penchant for forming and joining organizations aside, the historical record does reveal that this tendency has shaped Germanics in the United States in decisive ways. Most organizations came into being in response to specific situations in the evolution of the profession, from the opposition of the freethinking Lehrerbund founders to the authority of religious institutions over the teaching of German in the 1870s to the efforts of Women in German to open the profession to feminist scholarship a hundred years later. In addition to new publications that arose with the founding of these organizations, other journals came into being as outgrowths of an expanding research culture that sought new outlets for work in particular areas of specialization.

A century of organizational development has witnessed telling transformations in both the constituencies and missions of professional associations and publications in Germanics. Three main shifts have characterized the evolution of the profession as we at the beginning of the twenty-first century know it: (1) The early habitus of professional organizations as "gentlemen's clubs" of established male professors was concentrated in particular regions of the country, such as the Midwest with its large German ethnic population or the prestigious institutions of the Northeast. It has been succeeded by a much broader, consciously national—even international—orientation across lines of both gender and academic rank. (2) Larger changes in academic priorities have caused an ongoing shift of emphasis in professional life from concern with the teaching of the German language and literature to the public dissemination of

research. (3) The formerly excluded youngest members of the profession, graduate students, have not only come to be actively involved in the meetings and
publications of the profession; increasingly, they now organize graduate student
conferences and publish their own journals, to the point where concerns are
being raised about premature pressures for professionalization on scholars who
are still completing their formal training.

As Clifford Bernd shows in his introductory essay "Founding Professional
Organizations," it was not only the secular-minded German teachers of the
Lehrerbund who sought to organize in response to the sense of being beleaguered: the MLA, which has become the flagship organization for most postsecondary language and literature professionals in the United States, itself was
founded by professors of German and French in the Northeast who wanted to
challenge the hegemony of the classics over humanities education in the nineteenth-century curriculum.[1] Without daring to contest the place of Latin, they
suggested that the ability to read the classics of German (and French) literature
would also bring students closer to the ideas and ideals of antiquity. With this
argument, Bernd shows, the founders of the MLA positioned themselves as
advocates of modern language study for the reading of literary classics, whereas
the more ethnically oriented founders of the Lehrerbund championed pragmatic training in the use of the language for speaking and writing in contemporary life. The founding of the MLA and its journal *PMLA* in 1884, of *Modern
Language Notes* at Johns Hopkins University in 1886, of the *Journal of English
and Germanic Philology* at Indiana University, of *Americana Germanica* (later
German American Annals) at the University of Pennsylvania, along with the
founding of the Lehrerbund's *Pädagogische Monatshefte* in 1897 can be seen as
outgrowths of the American adoption of the model of the German research
university.

By the late nineteenth century, the Lehrerbund had come to recognize that
its affiliation with the freethinker movement was posing obstacles to its ability
to recruit membership in the American heartland. Abandoning its previously
adversarial relation to sectarian education, the Lehrerbund stressed instead uncritical identification with Wilhelminian Germany—a move that brought about
not only its demise in the xenophobic World War I era but also, by the end
of the war, the suspension of its journal, *Monatshefte*, which existed only as a
yearbook for most of the postwar decade. *German American Annals* likewise
ceased publication in 1919.

The dire situation that resulted from the anti-German sentiments of the
war years was addressed in a flurry of organizational activity in the second half
of the 1920s. The transfer of *Monatshefte*—which had been attempting to maintain its presence as a yearbook, as well as of the material assets of the Lehrerseminar—to the University of Wisconsin German department in 1927 enabled
the revival of the journal as a resource for teachers in 1928. But even before

Monatshefte reappeared, the *Germanic Review* had been brought into existence in 1926 by the Department of Germanic Languages at Columbia University as a journal that eschewed pedagogical topics and devoted its pages strictly to research in the Germanic languages and literatures. At the same time, the American Association of Teachers of German (AATG) was organized, and its publication, the *German Quarterly*, began to appear in 1928, with a focus somewhere between the language-teaching orientation of *Monatshefte* and the scholarly emphasis of *Germanic Review*. Despite concerns about the increased competition—competition among the new journals themselves as well as between them and the established ones, such as the *Modern Language Journal*—perusal of their pages reveals considerable overlap among their editors and authors, evidence that the crossover between pedagogical and scholarly publication was much more common then than now.

With the founding of the AATG—initially a regional organization, although its name suggested otherwise—the beleaguered profession finally had a vehicle for pursuing the interests of German teachers at all levels. But just at the point where the AATG's first president, Camillo von Klenze (Columbia University), was enunciating the importance of forging bonds between teachers and researchers, secondary schools and universities in this new organization, the MLA changed its statement of purpose from "the advancement of the study of the modern languages" to "the advancement of research in the modern languages and their literatures" (G. Stone 36). From its first meeting in 1934 in a Yale fraternity house until 1968, the AATG held its brief national meetings in conjunction with the MLA Annual Convention. Unsurprisingly, given this venue and its rituals, the level of participation by high school teachers and women was minimal (see Nagy, "Women").

Just as the profession appeared to be getting back on its feet in the early 1930s, the Great Depression and the rise of National Socialism in Germany posed new threats. While little could be done to counter the erosion in enrollments caused by a declining birth rate and a drop in the number of young people who could afford to attend college, the general record for this difficult era does reflect lessons learned and remembered from the World War I era. The number of Germanists who were willing to go out on a political limb by either endorsing or criticizing developments abroad—at least until the United States entered the war in 1941—was minimal; the great majority concentrated on improving the quality of language teaching and emphasizing the humanistic value of classical German high culture. As a result, AATG membership continued to grow and all extant journals survived this difficult era. Two Germanists, John A. Walz and Robert Herndon Fife, were elected by the profession at large to the presidency of the MLA during the period 1941–45.

This is not to say that the profession was not deeply affected by the years of National Socialism: the immigration to United States shores of German academics, both Jews and non-Jewish critics of the regime, brought with it heightened emphasis on research and scholarship. The shift—which gained further impetus from a second wave of academic emigration from postwar Germany—can be traced in both *Monatshefte* and the *German Quarterly*, which not without some controversy abandoned their focus on pedagogy for a more literary orientation. To the present day, however, the fall issue of *Monatshefte* remains one of the most important practical publications of the profession: it lists faculty members at most North American colleges and universities, presents information on hirings and promotions, dissertations completed, graduate and undergraduate enrollments; and occasionally contains surveys about various trends in the profession and clusters of articles on particular professional issues.

While the greater emphasis on literary scholarship became apparent in the major journals of the profession, a sense of crisis regarding the nation's ability to train students adequately in foreign language skills arose in the wake of the 1957 launch of the first Sputnik satellite by the Soviet Union. Renewed interest in foreign language competence resulted in a surge of federal funding and increased student enrollments at all levels, including graduate programs. As membership in both the AATG and MLA soared in the mid-1960s, dramatic expansion in the purview and range of services of both organizations led to new problems and tensions. In order to meet the needs of German teachers, the AATG began in 1968 to sponsor *Die Unterrichtspraxis*, a new journal focused on pedagogical matters at all levels of the curriculum. In the following year, the decades-long practice of holding the AATG annual meeting in conjunction with the MLA ended; the AATG entered into a new arrangement with the American Council on the Teaching of Foreign Languages, an organization founded by the MLA in 1967 in a move that signaled its willingness to reconsider its pointed aloofness from the concerns of language teaching since the early decades of the century. This change in venue enabled the AATG to offer a much richer program over several days; the meeting was thus much more attractive to the growing contingent of precollege members. But it was not until the 1980s that the presidency of the organization began to rotate between representatives of precollegiate and postsecondary levels. A traumatic interval in the 1970s, as the AATG was confronted with the consequences of insufficient oversight of its headlong rush into development and restructuring, had as its hard-won but fortunate outcome the high professionalism and active leadership of the organization as it exists today. *Die Unterrichtspraxis* currently has about twice as many subscribers among AATG members as does the *German Quarterly*.

Developments toward the end of the 1960s also brought about changes in the other major professional organization for American Germanists as challenges to the established order were raised with particular vehemence in the MLA. The emergence of feminist consciousness in the wake of the civil rights movement and the recourse to Marxist analysis—or at least rhetoric—in protests against the Vietnam War began to cause a stir in the American academy. At the same time, the unforeseen impact of reduced federal funding for language programs and widespread rebellion against the language requirements that had sustained strong enrollments put an end to the boom decade and led to the collapse of its robust job market. As hiring institutions raised expectations of candidates for employment and promotion and hiring procedures were formalized as a result of affirmative action legislation, the MLA—especially its annual meeting—was thrust into a much more crucial role in the professional life of academics. As the MLA Annual Convention became and has remained the site of the critical first interview stage of the hiring process, as well as an important venue for professional engagement of candidates with peers and potential employers, participation in it has expanded from somewhat more than 200 papers read in about 100 sessions in the mid-1960s to more than 2,000 presentations in more than 700 sessions in recent years. Graduate students now constitute about one-third of conference attendees and participate as elected representatives in the MLA Delegate Assembly and, most recently, on the Executive Council.

The dramatic transformation of the MLA also played itself out in a rapid series of other organizational developments in the 1970s, characterized by Sara Friedrichsmeyer in this volume section as a reorganization of the profession. New societies and journals responded to the need for forums for more specialized scholarly interests, which in turn were often a result of increased pressure for research activity and publication. Individual German departments sought to raise their profile by organizing annual or semiannual conferences, such as the Amherst Colloquia at the University of Massachusetts (since 1967), the Wisconsin Workshops at the University of Wisconsin (since 1968), and the International Symposia at Washington University (since 1972). Publication of the invited papers presented at these gatherings further contributes to the reputations of the sponsoring departments.

Most of the societies that were organized to encourage scholarship around a single writer—Lessing, Goethe, Brecht, for example—likewise have their institutional base in a sponsoring department. The Lessing Society, which also cooperates with institutions in Germany, has been associated with the University of Cincinnati since 1966; the International Brecht Society has since its founding in 1970 been affiliated mostly with the University of Wisconsin; the Goethe Society of North America has been with the University of California, Irvine, since 1979. Such societies usually have affiliated-organization status with the MLA, and they maintain Web sites, newsletters, and typically yearbooks rather than journals in their efforts to promote and present cutting-edge scholarship in their area of focus.

On a larger scale and having greater influence on the profession are two broadly based organizations that also arose in the 1970s, Women in German, which was founded in 1974, and the German Studies Association, which was established in 1984 as the successor to the Western Association for German Studies, founded in 1976. Each, in its own way, represents a uniquely North American response to the desire for change in the profession. From the beginning, Women in German has pursued a dual agenda: democratizing the profession, creating a more supportive professional environment for women and minorities, and furthering feminist scholarship in German literature and culture in the larger context of American academic feminism. It seeks to transcend the national borders of German scholarship and has in fact served as a model for similar, though less active, feminist organizations, such as Women in French and Feministas Unidas in the United States, Women in German Studies in the United Kingdom, and Frauen in der Literaturwissenschaft in Germany. In addition to organizing its own national conference, Women in German sponsors sessions at the national meetings of other major professional organizations (MLA, the German Studies Association, AATG); awards an annual dissertation prize and travel grants for graduate student research; maintains an active Internet discussion list; and publishes a thrice-yearly newsletter, with news, book reviews, and bibliographies, and a research-focused yearbook.

A product of the profession's interest in interdisciplinary approaches to teaching and research, the German Studies Association has sought to encourage interdisciplinary collaboration at its large annual conference, which is also notable for the number of participants from abroad (esp. in the social sciences), and through its dissemination of "Guidelines for Curricula in German Studies." In addition to its newsletter, the association has published the interdisciplinary journal *German Studies Review* since 1976. An annual prize for the best book in German studies, alternating between humanities and social sciences, is awarded in conjunction with the German Academic Exchange Service (DAAD [Deutscher Akademischer Austauschdienst]). Another annual prize has been established for the best book in any discipline that treats topics related to Nazi Germany and the Holocaust. A standing committee monitors and reports regularly on access to archives needed for work in this area.

An important move to interdisciplinarity was the founding of *New German Critique* in 1973. Unlike any of the other disciplinary journals discussed in this section, it pursued a policy of publishing only in English. This policy enabled it to address a much larger circle of scholars outside the immediate field of German studies. The journal has focused on cultural criticism—initially Frankfurt school thought—offering translations and analyses of developments in Continental theory, culture, and politics that often have implications for the American environment. Of all the journals in German studies, it has the most clearly recognizable political profile.

There is probably no richer resource for an examination of changing topics, methods, and debates in the profession than the various journals that have served the profession since the late nineteenth century—and those that have arisen more recently in response to new debates and shifts of focus. Contributors to this section have in many cases used that resource, although entire books could (and someday probably will) be written about some of the journals and organizations of our profession. The refereed journals and annual conferences profiled here have also played an increasingly important role in the shaping of academic careers. Many of the journals have responded to the growing importance of publication by instituting systems of anonymous or double-blind peer review, in which a submitted manuscript is evaluated by one or more experts in the field who do not know the identity of its author. In most cases, the author of the submission is also unaware of who has evaluated it. While such systems offer the opportunity to publish on the basis of the scholarly quality of the article rather than on the basis of the reputation or collegial connections of its author, editors occasionally question how well the system works.[2] Established scholars can avoid the process by submitting only directly solicited contributions, but younger scholars, who are expected to document that their work has been reviewed, are often frustrated by the slowness of the review procedure. As submissions increase in response to pressures to publish, even before completion of the PhD, editors are confronted with the need to find ever more reviewers for ever more manuscripts and with the difficulty of bringing to readers work done by the leading figures in the field. Just as troublesome for journals that offer book reviews is the problem of engaging qualified scholars who will submit reviews in a timely manner when the academic reward system accords so little value or prestige to this important task. These and other issues regarding the merits and timing of the anonymous review system, as well as the ethics of multiple submission, continue to be debated in heated sessions at professional conferences.

There are other problems on the near horizon: Faced with the burgeoning costs of journal subscriptions, especially in the sciences, which are more often produced by commercial publishers, libraries are reducing the number of journals to which they subscribe, thus depriving many humanities publications of much of their income. With the escalating use of the Internet and digitized research materials, the move from the familiar bound paper journal to electronic forms of publication is already taking place. The question of how to establish scholarly credentials accorded to online publications is still unresolved.

In time, new formats for the proliferating number of academic conferences may emerge. Younger members of the profession especially have begun to question the value of racing about the country, often several long weekends in a row, whether to listen to hurried readings of twenty-minute papers or to read their own work in such contexts. Beyond a growing number of smaller-format workshops on specialized topics, experiments with the distribution of papers online prior to the conference have shown some success, and electronic tele-conferencing is being tried, mostly in science disciplines. One can only spec-ulate what the profession's scholarly outlets will be in the next hundred years.

Notes

1 A good picture of the early involvement of Germanists with the MLA can be gleaned from the December 2000 Millennium issue of *PMLA* (*Special Millennium Issue*).

2 For a recent example of such questioning, see Carlos J. Alonso's comments on the extent to which *PMLA* has come to rely on solicited contributions.

Founding Professional Organizations, 1870–1920

The Lehrerbund and the MLA

CLIFFORD ALBRECHT BERND

The Lehrerbund

Der Nationale Deutschamerikanische Lehrerbund came into being in early August 1870 when one hundred teachers of German met in Louisville, Kentucky, to promote, according to their way of thinking, the best interests of German instruction in the United States (Wooley 359). The handwritten "Notes [in German] for a History of the Lehrerbund," preserved today in the basement of the Steenbock Memorial Library on the campus of the University of Wisconsin, Madison,[1] tell us why the federation was founded: to unite the teachers of German who were widely scattered throughout the nation, to free education from sectarian domination, and to abolish readings from the Bible and the singing of religious hymns in schools (archive note [1870]).

The goals proved to be, from the very start, the strength and weakness of the federation. By liberating education from any affiliation with religious institutions, pedagogy as well as German language and literature study could become objectives in their own right and hence receive increased emphasis. But the opposition that the Lehrerbund had to contend with from established churches remained formidable. Church-related schools had been, after all, the first to offer instruction in German in the United States, and it was in such religious institutions that the teaching of German continued to flourish most in the nineteenth century (Faust, "Vergangenheit" 247). In the archive notes (Jan. 1883) we read that half a million children in America were receiving instruction in the German language; the bulk of this instruction occurred in parochial schools operated by Catholic and Lutheran churches. In Little Germany in lower Manhattan, for instance, there were, during a good part of the second half of the nineteenth century, four Catholic parochial schools for non-English-speaking children of German immigrants and a similar number of schools attached to German Lutheran parishes. Yet only one nonsectarian school, sponsored by the Turn-Verein, offered a full-fledged elementary education in German (see Huebener, "German School" 14). According to the archive notes of January 1883 this preponderance of denominational over nonsectarian schools teaching German was typical. It was clear that at the time most teachers of German could not, because of their employment at church-affiliated institutions, belong to an organization that sought to divest the educational process of all religious control. Not surprisingly, E. O. Wooley observed that probably not more than a tenth of the eligible teachers of German in America ever belonged to the organization at any one time (359). They preferred instead to be members of local associations of German teachers, such as the particularly active Verein deutscher Lehrer von New York und Umgegend (see Leuchs).

But the Lehrerbund was not deterred by its inability to secure a large membership. It knew it had high ideals and continued to pursue them with vigor. It organized patriotic national gatherings of German teachers every summer in the various larger cities of the middle Atlantic and north central states, which were teeming with German immigrants. At these meetings, the federation appealed to the emotions of newly arrived Germans who, because of language and cultural barriers, had been alienated by the English-speaking population and confined in ghetto-like Little Germanys. Fiery speeches, German food, bands, and choral groups all did their share to help rally wide German American support for the cause of the Lehrerbund. As Wooley has said, even nonmembers of the association felt its stimulation (359). At all these boisterous gatherings the Lehrerbund never tired of stressing the importance of keeping the German language alive; of maintaining how essential for this purpose it was to have an adequate number of well-trained teachers of German; and, above all, of agitating for high-quality German teaching that would not be hampered by any restrictions imposed by denominational affiliations.

Largely because of the efforts of Peter Engelmann (1823–74) of Milwaukee, a forty-eighter who had become hostile to the collaboration of "throne and altar" in Germany and participated in the revolutionary uprisings there and who had become active in the freethinker movement in the United States, the Lehrerbund was established in 1878 as a German Teachers' Institute in Milwaukee, where future teachers of German could be trained under the freest possible conditions. Endowment funds solicited from affluent German Americans helped make this training possible (archive note [1881]). The federation also sponsored an educational journal, *Erziehungsblätter*, printed at the Freidenker Publishing Company in Milwaukee.

As the activity of the Lehrerbund increased, so did opposition to its goals from the churches (both Lutheran and Catholic). The Lutherans were the first to condemn openly the atheistic beliefs of the Lehrerbund. They established a rival Evangelischer Schul- und Erziehungsverein in Pennsylvania (archive note [1871]) in order to champion the necessity of a theologically based education. The German Lutheran Synod of Missouri, Ohio, and Other States organized three German teacher-training institutes (Meyer 46). At these institutions attention was given to reading Luther, not Goethe (O. Lessing 342); at the Lehrerbund seminary it was Goethe, not Luther.[2]

The Catholics struck the Lehrerbund closer to home. As a result of the initiatives taken by the Bavarian archbishop of Milwaukee, Michael Heiss (1818–90), and the Austrian friar Joseph Salzmann (1819–74), they founded a German Teachers' Institute right in Milwaukee—under the very noses, one could say—of the freethinking sages who were administering the Lehrerbund institute (archive note [1883]; Ludwig 453–54; Rainer 218–36). To make matters more difficult for the Lehrerbund, the Lehrer-Seminar zur Heiligen Familie, as the Catholic institute was called, enjoyed the financial backing of the king of Bavaria.

By 1889 the freethinker attitudes of the Lehrerbund had come under such heavy attack from church officials and conservative members who were teaching in public and parochial schools that the decision was reached to withdraw the federation's sponsorship of the radical *Erziehungsblätter* (archive notes [Jan., Mar., and Aug. 1889]). From that year on, the Lehrerbund became reluctant to be openly enthusiastic about anything except its Germanness.

A new journal was then published by the federation, the *Pädagogische Monatshefte* (later called *Monatshefte für deutsche Sprache und Pädagogik* and later *Monatshefte für deutschen Unterricht, deutsche Sprache, und Literatur*); the first issue appeared in 1899. No longer was there talk about "severing the connection between school and church" (archive note [1881]). The federation now solicited the cooperation of the entire body of German teachers, in religious as well as nonreligious institutions, "to join in one united effort to win for German in the schools that recognition which its importance in American culture demands" (Learned, "Lehrerbund" 11).

A new objective came into focus. By the turn of the century the flow of emigration from German-speaking lands declined and the Little Germanys gradually became smaller. No longer could a sufficient number of German teachers be recruited among those who were native speakers of German—native speakers either because they had been born abroad or because they had been brought

up in German-speaking homes in the German ghettos of urban America. The
Lehrerbund at the turn of the century felt it had the duty, therefore, to insist
that

> no teacher of German should permit his students to rest satisfied with a bare
> reading knowledge of German. Much less should any teacher venture, or any
> school board allow, a teacher to teach German without the ability to speak
> and write that language with reasonable facility. (Learned 14)

The Lehrerbund began to become more German than ever before. In 1912
the annual summer convention was held in Berlin. Four hundred members of
the federation sailed to Bremen on the German luxury liner *Großer Kurfürst*
and together went on a grand tour of twenty-eight German cities before as-
sembling in Kaiser Wilhelm's capital for their main meeting (Fick, "Zur Geschichte" 224).

As a consequence (how could it have been otherwise?), Wilhelminian patriotism among the federation's membership grew by leaps and bounds.[3] The
beginning of World War I brought the fervor to a peak. The first issue of the
federation's journal to appear after the outbreak of hostilities had, on its opening pages, the kaiser's "Proclamation to the German Nation." In the journal's
subsequent issues we read about the federation's sympathy for the "great and
holy" German war (309, in *Monatshefte* 15 [1914]); about the "outrageous in-
justice being done to Germany," the "justice of the German cause," the "lies"
against Germany, about the necessity of a German victory (1, 7, 34–35, and
42, in *Monatshefte* 16 [1915]), and many similar statements. One essay concludes
with the panegyric flourish "All hail the victory of German and Austrian arms
on the seas and below the seas, on land and in the air" (73).

Of course, such exuberant German patriotism had to lead to the demise
of the federation when America declared war on Germany and everything
German in April 1917. One year later, the Lehrerbund, faced with threats of
sedition charges, was forced to suspend its functions.

The MLA

The professional organization the MLA began thirteen years after the Lehrerbund was founded. Its first meeting was held at Columbia (then a college, not
a university) in New York City in late December 1883. Although the MLA turned
out to be an important organization, its history, at least in the early decades,
was less exciting and far less colorful than that of the Lehrerbund.

The forty founding members of the new association came together to realize one great objective: to make the study of German and French (the interest
in other modern languages came later) as important a factor of education in

America as Latin and Greek. Up to that time German and French were only electives at most colleges, whereas the ancient languages were requirements for graduation, indeed even for admission to college. Much debate ensued, and answers were not readily agreed on. The classics had been firmly established for a long time, especially Latin; Latin's primacy was not open to discussion for attendees at the early MLA meetings. But could German or French be substituted for Greek? Moreover, could the study of a spoken language, in which emphasis would have to be placed on the mastery of conversational skills, be allowed to replace the inestimable educational benefit of reading Homer, Plato, or Sophocles? Hjalmar Boyesen (1849–95), professor of German at Columbia, proposed these possibilities. But President Franklin Carter (1837–1919) of Williams College vigorously opposed the idea of discarding Greek (Cook xvii).

Debate continued almost endlessly, and the reader of accounts of the early MLA conventions gathers the distinct impression that the overriding tone of these meetings was one of Babylonian confusion. Apparently all that could be agreed on was that the association would continue to meet annually and that a publication, the *PMLA*, should be sponsored (see W. Parker). The general lack of consensus might have continued for a long time had it not been for another colleague who represented the field of German: Calvin Thomas (1854–1919). His importance for the early flowering of studies in modern languages has not yet been fully assessed, but one might claim that the MLA would never have realized its objective of putting the teaching of modern languages on an equal footing with the teaching of Latin and Greek had not his proposals carried greater weight than those of other attendees at MLA meetings.

With the power of expression for which Thomas was known (see the statement of Nicholas Murray Butler [1862–1947] in the introduction to C. Thomas's *"Scholarship"* [20]), he surpassed everyone else. He enjoyed other advantages over his colleagues. Among these were that he was a native English–speaking authority on modern languages and could address himself more effectively to the problems of their study than could his foreign-born colleagues (these, esp. in the field of German, were at the time in the majority); he had studied in Germany and could speak knowledgeably about German life and letters; and, most important, he had embraced the study of German literature from a solid educational basis in Greek literature. Indeed, he had majored in Greek at college, gone on to do graduate work in Greek at a German university, and had taught Greek before his interest in German literature was awakened.

As a scholar of both Greek and German, Thomas had the authority to claim that the choice between a modern language and Greek was not an either-or matter. To know the great Germans of the eighteenth century, he believed, was to know the Greeks (see C. Thomas, *"Scholarship"* 9). His argument proved to be convincing; he persuaded his colleagues that the study of Lessing, Goethe, and Schiller did not displace the Greek masters. The same argument applied to French literature: to know Corneille and Racine also meant to know the Greeks.

It followed that giving status to the study of the German (and French) classics by looking on them as a continuation and intensification of the Greek classics also meant "that it was not necessary to speak German [or French] at all, and that it was not worth while for a university to attempt such a conversational course" (W. Parker 16). German (and French) should be studied like Greek, through reading. What counted was German (and French) literature, and what held primacy in German (and French) literature was the study of the classical authors (Zeydel, "Die germanistische Tätigkeit" 240).

Thomas wielded an enormous influence as torchbearer of the German classics. He quickly became a member of the MLA Executive Committee and of the *PMLA* Editorial Committee. He became vice president of the association and then its president. He made perhaps his greatest impact when in 1896 he was appointed chairman of the Committee of Twelve, which set the direction in which the MLA would move for decades to come. The report of Thomas's committee, one hundred pages issued in 1899 (see C. Thomas, *Report*), made clear that the study of modern foreign languages could gain respectability on a par with Latin and Greek. Modern languages could become essential subjects in any college curriculum, if the emphasis was placed not on the acquisition of conversational skills but, instead, on reading literature as the most rewarding efflorescence of a language. This belief ran counter, of course, to the conviction of the Lehrerbund that spoken and written German were to be stressed; accordingly, the Lehrerbund was quick to raise its objections (see Rosenstengel), but these made no impression on the MLA.

After the report was issued and its recommendations adopted, the affairs of the MLA became, certainly for the next two decades, quiet and uneventful. We hear little of further feuding between the advocates of ancient and modern languages. We hear little about anything in this language association except the study of literature; papers at MLA meetings on philological topics became rarer. We hear little about the controversy on methods of teaching languages; with the importance attached to literature, reading was what counted most. As far as the study of literature itself was concerned, few Germanists attending MLA meetings up to 1920 seemed interested in giving or listening to papers on any topic other than Lessing, Goethe, and Schiller. For an observer in our time, the preponderance of papers on the eighteenth-century classics and the relative neglect of Germany's subsequent literature are striking. Even at the 1917 annual meeting, with America at war with Germany, the authority of the German classics, true to Thomas's precepts, was still unabashedly invoked. The presidential address in that year bore the title "The Idea of Progress from Leibniz to Goethe" (W. Parker 33).

Notes

1 National German-American Teachers Seminary general subject file, University of Wisconsin, Madison, Archives, ser. 7 / 14 / 10–2, box 3. I cite references as "archive note" for a given year. I am grateful to Cora Lee Kluge for making me aware of this unpublished material. I owe thanks, too, to Mary Devitt of the Max Kade Institute in Madison and Bernard Schermetzler, Archivist of the University of Wisconsin, Madison, for generously assisting me, far beyond the call of duty, in my research at the Steenbock Memorial Library.

2 See the Examination File of the Lehrerbund, University of Wisconsin Archives, ser. 7 / 14 / 10. Instruction in German literature between the Middle Ages and Goethe was omitted from the curriculum.

3 From 1907 to 1916 (with the exception of 1911) the Lehrerbund published annually in *Monatshefte* the names and addresses of its members. There were 306 members in 1907, 214 in 1908, 231 in 1909, 211 in 1910, 532 in 1912, 195 in 1913, 309 in 1914, and 384 in 1915–16. The sudden surge in membership in 1912 reflects, doubtless, the enthusiasm with which German teachers embraced the idea of sailing on a German liner for the summer convention held in that year in Berlin. The increase in membership that began in 1914 mirrors, surely, the wave of Wilhelminian patriotism that banded German Americans together in World War I.

History of the AATG

PATRICIA HERMINGHOUSE

If, as David Benseler, echoing Henry Schmidt, argues elsewhere in this volume, "Enrollments are the 'capital' of the academic enterprise of Germanics in the United States," by analogy it can be said that it was the specter of bankruptcy that underlay the controversial establishment of the American Association of Teachers of German (AATG) in 1926. The issues facing American Germanists at that time were those of survival, as members of the profession confronted the consequences of World War I: the 1918 demise of Der Nationale Deutsch-amerikanische Lehrerbund as the result of its own imprudent pro-German fervor in the war years (see Bernd's essay in this volume); the corresponding wave of anti-German sentiment in the American public; and the attendant decimation of enrollments, particularly at the secondary level, in states and school districts where patriotic anti-German sentiment had attained fanatic proportions. Throughout its history, with only a few exceptions when perceptions of American national interests were propitious for the teaching of German—during and after World War II and during the cold-war race for scientific and technological superiority, for example—the mission of the AATG has been shaped by the need to surmount the dwindling interest of American students in learning German. A recent *AATG Newsletter* registers a striking drop in AATG membership by more than a thousand (14%) in the period 1993–2000, with most of this attrition occurring at the postsecondary level (25%) and among student members (40%). The number of nonteaching members more than doubled in the same period ("AATG Membership").[1]

Whereas the erstwhile Lehrerbund had its principal base of support in the midwestern states, where there were large German-heritage populations, the initiative for the establishment of a new professional organization in the post-war years came from the New York City area, where William R. Price of the New York State Department of Education engaged heads of high school and college departments of German in a discussion of the need for a "professional body devoted exclusively to the interest of German teachers" (Liptzin, "Early History" 20). While high school teachers responded favorably, college teachers remained critical. Their critical attitude, however, did not preclude their assuming leadership functions in the new organization, which, as its first president explained, would "embrac[e] all teachers of German in every part of the country," at all levels of the educational system (Klenze 3). "Knowledge of German," the founders argued, should be integral to a national effort "to make American culture richer and more many-sided than any in history" (6). This was a time, they seemed to recognize, that could not afford a class division between teacher and researcher, or between school and university. In pursuit of their goals, members of the new association would promote the development of more modern and relevant textbooks, improvements in teaching method-ologies, and mutual professional support and self-renewal among teachers of German. In this effort, established professors at colleges and universities in New York City, such as E. W. Bagster-Collins (Teachers Coll., Columbia), Robert Herndon Fife (Columbia), F. W. J. Heuser (Columbia), Camillo von Klenze (Columbia), Sol Liptzin (Coll. of the City of New York), and Frank Mankiewicz (City Coll.)—most of whom were members of the all-male Verein deutscher Lehrer von New York—joined with members of the New York Chapter of High School Teachers, most of whom were women (Liptzin 21), to form the Metropolitan Chapter in December 1926. As Ellen Manning Nagy has pointed out, however, despite affirmations of solidarity, the presidency of AATG and the editorship of its journals were to remain in the hands of men, primarily university professors, for decades (see "Women"; tables 1 and 2 in the appendix; for other journals, see the table for Niekerk, "*Germanic Review*," and the table for Niekerk, "*New German Critique*"). What today might be termed the male bias of the organization was entirely typical of its time; it is nonetheless intriguing to discover that it was Henriette von Klenze, wife of the first AATG president, who as early as 1915 had presented a successful resolution to the MLA addressing the exclusion of female colleagues from the social network of the profession ("Women" 52). With the exception of some state language supervisors, it was not until the 1980s that secondary school teachers were elected to the presidency of the AATG.

Understandable as the impetus to form the new organization may appear in view of the dire situation of German teaching at the time, the attempt to organize language teaching along national lines was not peculiar to teachers of German: teachers of Spanish, whose enrollments were growing rapidly, had formed their own organization in 1917; teachers of Italian organized in 1922; and the American Association of Teachers of French was in the process of formation in 1926. All three organizations also established their own journals within a year or two of their founding. Meanwhile the MLA seemed to be distancing itself from the concerns of teachers, having dissolved its pedagogical section in 1902; by 1927 "without debate and almost without notice, the Association's official statement of purpose was changed from 'the advancement of the study of the modern languages' to 'the advancement of research in the modern languages and their literatures' " (G. Stone 36).

The first national meeting of the AATG took place in a fraternity house, in conjunction with the 1934 MLA Annual Convention, at Yale University. Until 1969, when the current practice of meeting with the American Council on the Teaching of Foreign Languages began, almost all subsequent meetings were also held at the MLA convention, as stipulated in the newly adopted AATG constitution. Compared with the elaborate program offerings of more recent decades, these were very modest affairs, consisting of a business session, meetings of some committees, a few lectures or a panel presentation, and a luncheon or dinner—sometimes highlighted by the singing of German songs! After the initial expansion of the founding Metropolitan Chapter into a quasi-national organization with the addition of four more chapters in New York State (1927) and one in Boston (1929), there was no growth in the number of chapters until a dozen more were formed, primarily in the German triangle of the Midwest (and one in southern California) in the period between 1936 and 1941.

Retrospectively, we may ask whether the commitment to meet in conjunction with the MLA did not actually serve to constrain the growth of the organization: the MLA was not a gathering central to the needs and interests of most high school teachers, nor were its venues—never farther west of the Mississippi than Saint Louis and never in the South—conducive to building a national constituency. Indeed, despite a desire he had expressed earlier that year to reach out to the central, western, and southern states, AATG president Alexander R. Hohlfeld worried in 1933 whether the location of that year's convention in Saint Louis would reduce attendance from the number seen at Yale ("Correspondence"). He recognized the need to respond to the threats posed economically by the Great Depression and politically by American isolationism:

> More than ever theorists and administrators are in search of possibilities for economy and curtailment. This challenge we can hope to meet successfully only if we unite our forces, first as language *men*, then as representatives of the modern languages, and finally as teachers of a special language. (Hohlfeld, "To the Members" 105; emphasis added)

At first glance, Hohlfeld's anxiety might seem surprising. The *German Quarterly* had been continually reporting satisfying growth in enrollments in German: approximately 25% for each year since 1927, for a total increase of 252% by 1932 ("Notes and News" [*GQ*] 145). It is hard to determine whether his concern about cutbacks in German programs was a residue of the World War I experience or prescience about things to come. At this point, the American English-language as well as the German-language press seem to have taken a wait-and-see attitude regarding developments in Germany, but as his predecessor Fife pointed out the previous year, the declining national birthrate had already begun to affect elementary school enrollments ("To the Members" 52). With one out of four American workers unemployed, young people were likely to attend and finish high school in greater numbers than before, but meeting the cost of college education was another matter.

When we peruse the official journal of the AATG for the 1930s, it is difficult to recognize high levels of concern about developments in Nazi Germany. Fife's 1932 assertion that "our methods will have to be adapted to American conditions," abandoning methods of instruction "which were developed to fit altogether different conditions from those which we have in America" (53), was a statement of pedagogical, not political principle. By 1936, however, concern was evident in AATG president Theodore Huebener's allusions to factors by which the study of German was "somewhat imperiled":

> Because of certain trends in the field of professional education and the repercussions here of the general state of political agitation in Europe, language study is more or less under fire in certain quarters; it therefore behooves those interested in this vital study, leaving aside more or less transient controversies, to stress more than ever in their studies and discussions fundamental and abiding values; specifically, among other things, it should be emphasized for the benefit of the general public that *Nazi* and *German* are not necessarily to be considered synonymous. (qtd. in "Secretary's Report" 96)

In December 1938, a cautiously worded resolution regarding the situation in Germany was presented to the annual meeting—and defeated. While declaring renewed faith in the "continuing value of many elements in German culture which have enriched the spiritual life of this country . . . [and] the ideals of tolerance, humanity, and individual freedom as represented in the works of Lessing, Goethe, and Schiller," the resolution also expressed "sympathy" at least for their colleagues, "those teachers in Germany who have suffered or are suffering from intolerance and fanaticism" (Feise 221). Disturbed by the defeat, the Executive Council proceeded to break down the resolution into its constitutive parts, which it submitted to the membership for a mail ballot. The four points on which 850 members were asked to vote were: an affirmation of "traditional and enduring values in German culture"; a pledge "to maintain

and defend the ideals of tolerance, humanity, and individual freedom"; a declaration of sympathy "with the oppressed minorities in Germany"; and a statement of belief "in defending and promoting those principles of American
democracy which make for peace and understanding." The ballot passed easily,
perhaps because the situation in Germany had in the meantime become clearer
than it was at the time of the December 1938 meeting; nonetheless, the third
point, referring to the situation of the "oppressed" in Germany, failed to gain
support among 30 of the 501 members who returned ballots (Feise). Susan
Pentlin's research into archival materials reveals further behind-the-scenes tensions that underlay the AATG's cautious attempt to remain unpolitical, including a 1933 dispute in the Metropolitan Chapter when "some Jewish
colleagues" allegedly attempted to "stampede the meeting" into passing a resolution that might be considered "anti-German" (231). Under the editorship
of Frank Mankiewicz, who had earlier been the object of anti-Semitic comments
in correspondence between some national officers and the New York Metropolitan Chapter (see Pentlin 230–34), the *German Quarterly* reflected a stance
more critical of events in Germany. Once the United States entered the war in
1941, it was, of course, easier to take such a stand. Yet even its publication of
Thomas Mann's address "An die Deutschlehrer Amerikas" in 1941, which spoke
of the political aberrations ("Verirrungen") in Germany, warned against con-
fusing Hitler's deeds with what is truly German:

> Even if the German present belongs to this vandal, neither the past nor the
> future are his, and the world of education would be much poorer if the study
> of German language and culture were expelled from it on such ephemeral,
> transient grounds. . . . The German language is the bearer and mediator of a
> great tradition, indispensable to any future, a glorious instrument, an organ,
> on which some of the richest fugues and most ennobling melodies of hu-
> manity have been sounded and will continue to sound, even in the confusion
> of these times. . . . Hitler [is] only a tool, used by the world will for the at-
> tainment of purposes and goals that lie far beyond his meager self-awareness.
> When these are attained, the tool will be discarded and quickly forgotten.
> These purposes and goals are the opposite of all forms of exclusiveness, in-
> tolerance, self-satisfaction, isolation, and narrow-mindedness. (67–68; my
> trans.)

In general the organization attempted to keep its political controversies
internal while publicly asserting the enduring humanistic values of German
culture and concentrating on improving the quality of the language-learning
experience. In support of the United States war effort, the national meetings
were canceled in 1942 and 1943.

Although little harmed by the war years, the AATG experienced very modest growth in the first postwar decade, having added only a few hundred mem-

bers since the end of the 1930s. In contrast with the number of metropolitan areas with sufficient numbers to support the founding of chapters in earlier years, most of the new chapters were formed on the basis of far-flung regions: the Pacific Northwest (3 states plus British Columbia) in 1948; the mountain plains (16 states) and northern New England (4 states) in 1953; south Atlantic (9 states) in 1957. This pattern changed dramatically with the advent of the Sputnik era in 1958. The ambitious national agenda for improving language teachers' competence as well as methods of delivery (see Schulz in this volume ["Pedagogical Issues"]) appears also to have spurred the formation of new AATG chapters. In the NDEA decade, 1958–68, membership almost quadrupled (from 1,300 to nearly 5,000), and twenty-six new chapters were founded, effectively doubling the number in existence in 1957. There was also a shift in the demographics of AATG membership as the number of high school teachers swelled to become the majority constituency. The system of organizing members into local and state chapters, whose elected presidents convene in the Assembly of Chapter Presidents at the annual meeting and elect their own representative to the AATG Executive Council, has played a key role in the AATG's ability to support German teachers in their own context. Chapters set their own programs and obtain support on a per capita basis from the national office. In the year 2000 there were sixty-one chapters.

Looking back on this era, Gerhard Weiss describes it as "the Golden Age of foreign language instruction, where people hopped from one cure-all [*allein-seligmachende*] method to the next, where money for all possible (and impossible) projects flowed into the coffers, and the NDEA with its various 'titles' saved even the weakest program" ("Presidential Address" 369; my trans.). The AATG expanded member services to include a newsletter; the Service Bureau, which loaned teaching materials—slides, tapes, maps, and so on—to teachers; the Teacher Placement Bureau, for members seeking positions at the secondary or college level; the FLES Promotion Center, to support the teaching of German in elementary schools; a battery of German achievement tests; and the National German Contest, to identify top-ranking students who had completed two or more years of high school German. The contest has grown in importance through the years and most recently involved more than 25,000 students competing for local chapters' nominations for the study trips to Germany that are sponsored by the German Pädagogischer Austauschdienst (*Study-Visit Grants*).

The demise of NDEA funding; increasing attacks on the college language requirement in the wake of the protest movements during the Vietnam War era, and growing frustration on the part of language teachers, who perceived a widening gap between their practical needs and the interests of the research elite, led to a sense of crisis. In 1967, under its secretary William Riley Parker, the MLA modified its decades-long aloofness from issues of language teaching by founding the American Council on the Teaching of Foreign Languages

(ACTFL). A National Symposium on the Advancement of the Teaching of German in the United States convened in December of that year and issued a call for action by the profession ("National Symposium"). Beginning in 1969, the AATG abandoned its long-standing pattern of meeting in conjunction with the MLA and moved to a late November date that coincided with the ACTFL meeting, a venue that was more attractive to the growing contingent of AATG members at the precollege level and that enabled the AATG to offer a much fuller program than was possible at the MLA convention.

In many ways, the function and operations of the AATG were decisively reshaped in the 1970s. Although the ambitious report of the National Symposium might appear to have catalyzed the explosion of activity that ensued, plans for some of these developments, such as the founding of *Die Unterrichtspraxis*, were in fact already under way. In retrospect, however, it can also be seen that in the headlong rush into expansion, the AATG lost oversight and control of its own affairs. Persuaded by the usefulness of the activities of the National Carl Schurz Association, an ethnic interest group, in promoting public support for German studies and providing motivation for students of German, the AATG became a partner in the formation of a new umbrella organization, the American Council on German Studies. This body was to coordinate and support financially the efforts of the National Carl Schurz Association and the AATG, as well as "any other organization which may seek to join it in the interest of promoting German studies in the United States; and to assist in the raising of the necessary financial support for these purposes" (Deeken 618). To this partnership the National Carl Schurz Association brought its journal, the *American-German Review*; a program of study tours to Germany; the Teaching Aid Project, which had already been supporting the *AATG Newsletter* sent by the AATG to all teachers of German, regardless of membership in the organization; and its sponsorship of the National Federation of Students of German, which by 1975 had over 25,000 student members in 844 clubs, organized into thirty state chapters, as well as its own publication, the *Rundschau*. From the pooled funds of these organizations, the American Council on German Studies was to contribute to programs that remained under the aegis of the AATG, such as the journals, the Service Center, chapter projects, and work-study programs in Germany like TAP V (the Teaching Aid Project 5, for prospective teachers of German). Some independent programs also came under the council's umbrella, including a teacher exchange program with Nordrhein-Westfalen. The private and governmental agencies from which the council sought funding included businesses in the United States and abroad and some West German sources, such as the embassy and the state of Nordrhein-Westfalen (for the teacher exchange).[2]

Yet, despite generous funding from the German embassy in 1971, the American Council on German Studies ran its enormous budget in deficit and became involved in attempts to develop revenue-producing operations, such as Education Services International, which sought to capture a market in travel, business, book marketing, and convention planning, including the large conventions of the National Federation of Students of German. With the council's administrative costs swelling with expenditures on such things as office refurbishment and a 1973 survey of American perceptions of Germany, which never was published, heated debates arose as AATG Executive Council members were confronted with proposed budget cuts in programs that provided services to students and teachers.[3] By 1973 it became obvious that German funding was ebbing.

In these years AATG membership reached record high numbers, but it remains unclear whether members realized that they had lost control of their own organization or how imperiled its very existence had become by the mid-1970s. The first official notice of the crisis did not appear until a September 1977 newsletter announcement that the American Council on German Studies board (composed of three representatives each from the AATG and the Natl. Carl Schurz Assn.) had terminated the services of its executive vice president, Deeken, who was also executive director of the National Carl Schurz Association as well as its assistant treasurer. Further, the terse announcement stated that the American Council on German Studies and the AATG had terminated all connections with Education Services International, a private corporation that shared facilities with the council, the AATG, and the National Carl Schurz Association at the administrative headquarters in Philadelphia (AATG Steering Committee). Three months later another announcement appeared under the rubric "Good News," reporting that although the German embassy had suspended indefinitely all funding to the council (and thus to AATG and the Natl. Carl Schurz Assn.), it had decided to provide direct funding to several AATG operations, such as the Testing and Awards program and the Chapter Presidents' Assembly. Furthermore, the student prizes it offered would be increased from 59 in 1977 to 67 for 1978.

By the end of the 1977–78 academic year, AATG president Edward Diller, in the first of several carefully worded messages that must have mystified those who were unaware of the crisis, reassured members that the AATG was "stronger than before" and would continue in its mission of providing services to teachers and students of German in the United States: "Our policies are determined by our constitution and the needs of our membership," he asserted, emphasizing that AATG was not affiliated with the National Carl Schurz Association, the National Federation of Students of German, or Education Services International. Further sketchy details were published in the fall of 1978, explaining that one year earlier, the AATG had faced not only the loss of all its funding but also a deficit of $50,000, which it had wiped out entirely by August 1978. "As at no time in the past, the AATG is a viable professional association, directed by its elected leaders and responsive to its individual members" ("Assessment" 2). All essential programs had been maintained, and, with the generous support of the Embassy of the Federal Republic of Germany, all publications continued on schedule. This pattern of targeted German funding and close supervision of disbursements continued until the association was once again on its feet. Despite whatever inhibiting effect that the association's desire to secure the support of "the donors" (i.e., German government agencies) may have had on some initiatives, German funding prevented the demise of the AATG in those difficult years. In fact, a new array of services was announced, including the Printed Materials Center, the Tape Depository, the AV-Media Center, and new programs abroad. In the process of staff reductions and the move of the national AATG office from Philadelphia to more modest quarters in nearby Cherry Hill, New Jersey, almost all records of the previous history of the association were lost. What was gained was a level of focus on its mission and a degree of professionalism and accountability in its operations that have characterized the AATG ever since.

Nor was this internal crisis the only challenge to the profession. Other larger developments, particularly in higher education, tended to complicate the identity of college and university Germanists as both teachers and researchers. Greatly increased expectations for publication and national visibility as criteria for tenure and promotion spawned a proliferation of specialized organizations, journals, and conferences, all of which currently compete for time, money, and commitment as venues for the development of individual reputations (see Friedrichsmeyer in this volume ["Role of Societies"]). Unable to do it all, Germanists are often faced with the need to make choices between what they perceive as their self-interest and the good of the profession, and various professional organizations have developed certain niches to respond to this need. In this more complex landscape, the AATG has come to represent primarily the pedagogical concerns of the profession, dealing with the crucial factors that determine whether students enter and remain in German programs. Among the many services available to AATG members are a Materials Center, which makes available a wide array of teaching aids, including materials from the Goethe-Institut Inter Nationes; summer seminars, many with stipends, for college and high school teachers; workshops on a variety of topics at regional and national meetings; a program of summer study opportunities for high school students, in addition to the PAD (Pädagogischer Austauschdienst) study trip prizes; an honor society for high school students, Delta Epsilon Phi, with 1,300 chapters; and an AATG electronic discussion list that enables teachers to share tips and information online and another list on available teaching positions at all levels. Less directly, members are served by the AATG's membership in the Joint National Committee for Languages / National Council for Languages and International Studies, which represents the interests of the profession to government agencies, and its affiliation with the Foreign Language Collaborative, the National Federation of Modern Language Teachers Associations, the American Council on the Teaching of Foreign Languages, and at the international level the Internationaler Deutschlehrerverband.

As the primary—if not the only—avenue of articulation between high school and college teachers of German, the AATG in the last decade has focused, among other things, on developing strategies that promote diversity by attracting members of minority groups to the learning and teaching of German, on increasing less advantaged students' opportunities for study abroad, and on educating teachers about the implications of the standards for linguistic and cultural competence that are increasingly being implemented at all levels nationwide. Locally and nationally, the AATG plays a central role for teachers of German at all levels who recognize the commonality of their needs and interests.

Notes

1 Another brief item in the same newsletter demonstrates a corresponding aging of the organization's membership. A statistical survey yields the following proportions of members in each age cohort: up to age 30, 9.8%; age 31–40, 18%; age 41–50, 26.6%; age 51–60, 30.7%; age 61–70, 9.8%; over age 70, 5.1% ("Aging AATG?").

2 This information is drawn from a 1971 "UP Porträt" of the council, which lists a council board of nine members: three from the AATG, three from the National Carl Schurz Association, and three at-large members. Hans Werner Deeken is listed as program director ("American Council on German Studies").

3 This information can be found in the bound volumes of unpublished AATG Executive Council minutes kept at AATG headquarters. Sincere thanks to AATG executive secretary Helene Zimmer-Loew for making these and other documents available and to David Benseler for assistance in reconstructing the saga of this era.

Appendix

Presidents of the AATG

Metropolitan

| 1927 | Camillo von Klenze | College of the City of New York |
| 1927–31 | E. W. Bagster-Collins | Teachers College |

National

1932	Robert Herndon Fife	Columbia University
1933	Alexander R. Hohlfeld	University of Wisconsin, Madison
1934	John A. Walz	Harvard University
1935	Albert W. Aron	University of Illinois, Urbana

1936	Theodore Huebner	Board of Education, New York, NY
1937	Frank H. Reinsch	University of California, Los Angeles
1938	Edward F. Hauch	Hamilton College
1939–40	Ernst Feise	Johns Hopkins University
1941	Lawrence M. Price	University of California, Berkeley
1942	George Danton	Union College, NY
1943–44	Gerhard Baerg	DePauw University
1945	Richard Jente	University of North Carolina, Chapel Hill
1946	John C. Blankenagel	Wesleyan University
1947	Curtis C. D. Vail	University of Washington
1948	Charles M. Purin	University of Wisconsin, Milwaukee
1949	Ernst Jockers	University of Pennsylvania
1950	Günther Keil	Hunter College, City University of New York
1951	Walter A. Reichart	University of Michigan, Ann Arbor
1952	C. R. Goedsche	Northwestern University, IL
1953–55	Werner Neuse	Middlebury College
1956–59	Alfred Senn	University of Pennsylvania
1960–63	John C. Kunstmann	University of North Carolina, Chapel Hill
1964–67	Karl-Heinz Planitz	Wabash College
1968–69	George J. Metcalf	University of Chicago
1970–71	Guy Stern	University of Cincinnati
1972–73	Margaret McKenzie	Vassar College
1974–75	Reinhold Grimm	University of Wisconsin, Madison
1976–77	Gustave Bording Mathieu	California State University, Fullerton
1978–79	Edward Diller	University of Oregon
1980–81	Adolph Wegener	Muhlenberg College
1982–83	Gerhard Weiss	University of Minnesota, Twin Cities
1984	Frank M. Grittner	Department of Public Instruction, Madison, WI
1985	Herta Stephenson	Saint Joseph's University
1986	Jermaine D. Arendt	Minneapolis Public Schools, MN
1987	Robert Di Donato	Massachusetts Institute of Technology
1988–89	Aleidine J. Moeller	Omaha Public Schools, NE
1990–91	Renate A. Schulz	University of Arizona
1992–93	Elizabeth Hoffmann	Nebraska Department of Education, Lincoln
1994–95	Keith O. Anderson	Saint Olaf College
1996–97	Thomas Keith Cothrun	Las Cruces High School, NM
1998–99	C. Lynne Tatlock	Washington University
2000–01	Elizabeth A. Smith	Plano Senior High School, TX
2002–03	Donna Van Handle	Mount Holyoke College

The Role of Societies and Conferences

SARA FRIEDRICHSMEYER

Throughout the history of the discipline, professional organizations have helped provide its contours, often suggesting and then sustaining directions for scholarly research. Articles elsewhere in this volume document the continuing influence of major organizations such as the AATG, the MLA, and the German Studies Association. There are others as well, such as the Society for German-American Studies, that have attracted a loyal membership, and yet others, many of them interdisciplinary, in which Germanists have had an ongoing if less marked presence, such as the American Society for Eighteenth-Century Studies. An additional and significant measure of the development of Germanics in the United States is the history of the professional groups that have been founded by Germanists and continue to draw their membership almost solely from within the discipline. After the AATG, most influential have been the societies that encourage scholarship relating to a particular canonical writer and the writer's times—among them the G. E. Lessing Society, the International Brecht Society, the Goethe Society of North America, the Kafka Society of America, the North American Heine Society, the American Grillparzer Society, and the International Herder Society. With the exception of the Lessing Society, which was organized in the 1960s during the heyday of Germanics, these societies were founded after 1970, following the collapse of language requirements and during a period of increased debates about the profession. Each was organized to address what its founders saw as the need for a forum beyond that offered by other national, regional, or international organizations. The MLA conferences, for example, did not offer what was perceived to be a sufficient number of small sections or forums for specific research interests. Societies could fill this need: once affiliated with the MLA or another organization, their members could meet and sponsor guaranteed sessions at national conferences. Pragmatic considerations were also important: institutional funding to attend a conference like the MLA was usually available only for the reading of a paper, hence the need for more presentation opportunities.

The founding of societies has been premised on the belief that scholarly interest in the seminal literary figures on which they focused would continue over time, albeit with varying intensity. Although the fortunes of various groups have fluctuated, most have indeed met this expectation. The more influential among them have created and maintained a presence in the field by supporting yearbooks and newsletters; arranging sessions at national meetings; organizing independent conferences; and, more recently, maintaining Web sites. Clearly, their organizational structures differ, and they were founded for different audiences, but together these professional societies have helped determine the directions the profession has taken since the watershed years of the late 1960s. To demonstrate in more detail their role and to illustrate their diverse structures and purposes, I profile here three groups—the Lessing Society, the Goethe Society of North America, and the International Brecht Society. These three exemplify the contributions of organizations that are similar but that, perhaps because they are relatively small or new, have exerted less influence on the field.

The Lessing Society was founded in 1966 at the University of Cincinnati, where it is still housed, to foster and support research on Gotthold Ephraim Lessing and the German Enlightenment.[1] With no German counterpart, the Lessing Society has aimed at bridging scholarship between the continents, a link that is ensured through a constitutional bylaw calling for society presidents to be elected alternately from Germany and the United States. The organization strives to maintain a presence in both countries in other ways as well. As an affiliate organization of the MLA and the American Society for Eighteenth-Century Studies, for example, the Lessing Society regularly sponsors sessions at both annual conferences and conducts its annual business meetings at the MLA. Equally as important to its members are its scholarly connections with both the Lessing Museum in Kamenz and the Lessing Akademie in Wolfenbüttel and the conferences organized by the society both here and in Germany. As part of an effort to assure continuity for new generations of scholars, graduate students from the University of Cincinnati can complete a six-week summer practicum at the Lessing Museum. That it introduces itself on its Web site in German (asweb.artsci.uc.edu/german/lessing)—the only society to do so—is in itself a statement indicating pride in its close ties to academic institutions in Germany.

Since 1969 the Lessing Society has supported the annual publication of the *Lessing Yearbook*, which contains articles and book reviews pertinent to the society's goals, and has also published several supplementary volumes; tables of contents of all its publications can be found on the society's Web site. The yearbook has an international editorial board and publishes articles in either German or English. Appearing originally with the Max Hueber Verlag and then until the mid-1990s with Wayne State University Press, the yearbook today, with a pressrun of a thousand, is published and distributed in Germany by Wallstein Verlag and is distributed in the United States by Wayne State University Press. Twice a year members of the society receive a newsletter, *Notes and Notices*, intended to help them maintain contact with one another and to inform them about the group's activities. Today the Lessing Society has over three hundred members, of whom at least one-third are in Germany.

Just as the organizational structure of the Lessing Society has in many ways served as a model for later societies (see Saine viii), so too the expansion of its research agenda is representative of the ways in which societies have evolved in response to new directions in the field. While the first yearbooks published primarily research on Lessing and his area of influence, the Lessing Society defines itself today not only as "eine wissenschaftliche Vereinigung, die Forschung zu Gotthold Ephraim Lessing und darüber hinaus zur Literatur der deutschen Aufklärung fördert und unterstützt" ("a scholarly organization that promotes and supports research on Gotthold Ephraim Lessing and also on the literature of the German Enlightenment") but, moreover, as a "Diskussionsforum für die Erforschung des 18. Jahrhunderts" ("forum for discussion of scholarship of the eighteenth century"). Its focus, as manifest also in its conferences and in the *Lessing Yearbook*, has thus expanded beyond Lessing to embrace his century and the entire culture that sustained him.

The International Brecht Society was founded in 1970 after positive responses to earlier Brecht sessions at MLA conventions. The society's institutional links are more flexible than some, but it is now associated with the University of Wisconsin, where it was founded. The society is "committed to maintaining Brecht as a living force in the theater as well as in the political and cultural arenas" (from its Web site: polyglot.lss.wisc.edu/german/brecht). In pursuit of its goals, the society organizes conferences here and abroad and sponsors sessions at the MLA. Twice yearly it publishes the newsletter *Communications*, which has grown from its original format as a small mimeographed brochure to a publication now described as a journal; it contains not only information about society activities but also substantive contributions. Book reviews and scholarly research appear in the *Brecht Yearbook*, published since

1982 in the United States, first by Wayne State University Press and more recently by the University of Wisconsin Press. Originally published by Suhrkamp Verlag from 1971 through 1973 as *Brecht Heute / Brecht Today* and from 1974 to 1980 as the *Brecht-Jahrbuch*, the yearbook has appeared annually, except in the 1980s, when its publication was less regular. Planned originally as a trilingual publication (German, English, and French) and for a time also soliciting articles in Spanish, the yearbook now publishes articles exclusively in German or English.

The society intentionally embraces a diverse membership, maintaining a home page on its Web site "as a service to scholars, critics, students, and theater people around the world who are interested in the works and thought of Brecht." Consequently, the Web site announces current productions of Brecht's plays and publications of interest to its members and maintains an archive for less-current material. It also provides a history of the Berliner Ensemble, a chronology of Brecht's life, information about translations of Brecht's works into English, and—reinforcing its goal of "facilitating international contacts and exchange"—even offers a link for suggestions. In addition to the tables of contents for its past yearbooks, similar to those provided by other societies, the site contains such helpful research tools as an alphabetical listing of all works by Brecht mentioned in a particular volume. The society thus exemplifies an organization in Germanics that reaches out to an international audience beyond academia. Its membership, numbering around two hundred, is international and multidisciplinary, academic and nonacademic.

The founders of The Goethe Society of North America envisioned a different, more specific type of membership. Because there exists in the Federal Republic of Germany a long-established Goethe Society, the American society, as its name signals, has always been intended primarily as a forum for scholars on this continent. Organized in 1979 and supported since its inception by the University of California, Irvine, it describes itself on its Web site (www .goethesociety.org/default.html) as an "organization dedicated to the encouragement of research on Johann Wolfgang von Goethe (1749–1832) and his age." The society has allied organization status with the MLA and also with the American Society for Eighteenth-Century Studies. It sponsors conferences here and abroad and since 1995 has published a newsletter, *Goethe News and Notes*, which is archived on the society's Web site. Since 1982 the society has supported the *Goethe Yearbook*, published generally at two-year intervals by Camden House and containing articles and book reviews that encompass the varying interests of the members. Titles of yearbook articles as well as those from special volumes can be found on the society's Web site.

In keeping with the organizational structure of the society, the first yearbook defined itself as an "outlet for the best of North American Goethe scholarship" (Saine vii). The direction of that scholarship has changed somewhat in the past few decades. Although the early volumes of the *Goethe Yearbook* are almost exclusively connected in some specific way to Goethe's writing, this has been less and less the case in recent volumes; the yearbook's most recent call for papers is a widely inclusive invitation for submissions in English or German "on Goethe, his works, his contemporaries, or the period 1770–1832 in general." With approximately 250 members, the society today stresses its distance from *Germanistik*, describing itself on its Web site as "a respected organ of eighteenth-century studies in diverse disciplines."

After decades of funding cutbacks throughout higher education in this country, most societies today have less institutional support than in earlier years; they are thus increasingly dependent on membership dues and on the resourcefulness of their leaders to find ways of securing financial stability. Yet their continuing existence and in some cases even vitality are proof that their members have indeed found ever new ways to adapt to the changing demands of academia.

By continuing to focus attention on new directions for research, these groups have been able to attract new members who are eager to work with a community of scholars on projects with the potential to affect positively the entire profession. The evolution of their research agendas is most convincingly documented by a comparison of recent yearbooks with earlier volumes. Pushed by the evolving scholarly interests of their members and always alert for good articles, the editors of these yearbooks have cast an ever wider net. While early volumes maintained a focus on the featured author and the methodologies were still largely reflective of traditional *Germanistik*, the thematic content and methodologies of later volumes are more diffuse and far more multi- or interdisciplinary. Rather than the linguistically or philologically based investigations that predominated in earlier publications, recent articles in fact incorporate an understanding of cultural contexts and a range of disciplinary approaches. Although there is no statistical way to measure the influence of the societies, it takes no great leap of the imagination to recognize that, by offering widely publicized forums for conference participation and well-regarded yearbooks for published papers, they have done much to cultivate interest in their particular areas of research and have helped to guide its expression.

Recognizing the importance of conferences for defining new areas of research and for bringing together scholars with similar interests, various departments in this country have established their own traditions of scholarly gatherings, some of which are now annual or biennial events. The Kentucky Foreign Language Conference, organized by faculty members from the University of Kentucky, has the most open structure and by far the longest history. Since its beginning in 1948, it has established itself as a well-known annual gathering for scholars of foreign literatures and cultures.[2] Throughout the first decade of its existence, the sessions at the Kentucky conference were devoted primarily to canonical writers; since the late 1960s, however, the conference has documented the same proliferation of scholarly interests that has been apparent throughout the profession. By the late 1970s it was sponsoring an increasing number of sessions that examined creative literature in interdisciplinary contexts; and by the 1990s its program was reflecting the often discussed explosion of the canon with a dramatic surge in attention to the works of women writers and writers from the GDR and to new areas of scholarly investigation, such as film, Holocaust literature, and transnational texts. Today, after some five decades of programming, the conference has garnered a niche in German studies: with its widely publicized calls for papers, its German sessions continue to offer to those throughout the profession—graduate students and faculty members at various stages of their careers—an annual forum for the presentation and discussion of scholarly papers. The conference has grown considerably over the years and provides with its relatively long history a look at the increasingly divergent interests that are combined in the discipline of Germanics.

Other departments have instituted smaller gatherings that are focused around a specific topic. The oldest are the Amherst Colloquia, initiated in 1967 by the Department of Germanic Languages and Literatures at the University of Massachusetts, Amherst. Originally an annual event, the colloquia now are generally held every other spring. They have from the beginning demonstrated interdisciplinary interests, with a distinct focus on literature in its social and cultural contexts. Colloquia topics have been predominantly from the late nineteenth or twentieth century and range from expressionism or Dada to well-known figures such as Rilke, Hesse, or Nietzsche.

The Wisconsin Workshops also have a long history. Sponsored by the Department of German at the University of Wisconsin, Madison, they have since their inception in 1968 offered an additional forum for the scholarly discussion of disciplinary and interdisciplinary topics. With recent themes such as "Günter Grass," "Heimat, Fatherland, Nation," and "Concepts of Culture," the annual workshops reflect the predominant interests of departmental faculty members in the literature and culture of the last half of the twentieth century.

Yet another regularly scheduled scholarly gathering is arranged by the Department of Germanic Languages and Literatures at Washington University. Designed as international symposia, these meetings have generally taken place in alternate years since 1972.[3] Symposia topics have varied widely, but with titles such as "Legitimationskrisen des deutschen Adels, 1200–1900" (1978), "Disenchantment of the World, 1200–1500" (1988), and "Science, Knowledge, and the Literature of the Early Modern Period" (1994), the symposia have demonstrated a more sustained concentration on literature and culture before 1750 than have the other conferences profiled here, a distribution reflecting the broad interests of departmental faculty members.

All three of these department-based gatherings bring together scholars from their home institutions with invited scholars from the United States and abroad.[4] Although they typically involve a small number of participants, their proceedings are made available to the wider profession through publication of the conference papers. Regardless of the terminology—symposium, workshop, or colloquium—these meetings reflect departmental responses to developments in the field. Because of their controlled size, they are flexible enough to offer a welcome forum for the exploration of new, even cutting-edge scholarly issues and theoretical approaches to literature and culture. Although their impact on the field as a whole is difficult to judge, it is certain that over the years they have helped create and solidify the reputations of their respective departments.

That the professional societies and the departmental gatherings considered here have continued their contributions over several decades is testimony to the commitment of the professionals who have shown themselves capable of creative responses to the changing research interests of their constituencies. That change must in turn be understood as influencing, and as influenced by, the larger developments that have so profoundly reshaped our field since the late 1960s, specifically the move toward a broadly defined German studies (see Friedrichsmeyer in this volume ["Reorganization"]). As these variously organized societies and conferences have responded to external pressures and to the changing realities of professional life in this country, they have helped give new contours to the study of German language, literature, and culture in the United States. At their best, they demonstrate how groups of dedicated scholars, despite their small numbers, have helped not only shape but also strengthen our discipline. Their continuing presence reflects a responsiveness to the needs of faculty members, students, and institutions in this country and thus argues for an understanding of Germanics in the United States as a field with increasingly fewer dependencies on *Germanistik* as traditionally practiced in the German-speaking countries.

Notes

1 For their help in collecting information about the societies, I thank Richard Schade of the Lessing Society, Siegfried Mews of the International Brecht Society, and Meredith Lee of the Goethe Society of North America. Quoted material pertinent to each society is taken from its Web site.

2 I thank Jeannine Blackwell for her analysis of the Kentucky Foreign Language Conference.

3 I thank Lynne Tatlock for her comments on this departmental undertaking.

4 In varying formats, information on these meetings is available on the Internet. For the International Symposia, see www.artsci.wustl.edu/~german/Isymposia.html; for the Amherst Colloquia, see www.umass.edu/germanic/id24.htm; for the current program of the Wisconsin Workshop, see polyglot.iss.wisc.edu/german/gradubook.htm.

The Emergence and Function
of Professional Journals

JOHN A. MCCARTHY

The oldest continuously published journals relevant for the history of Germanics are the *PMLA* (founded in New York in 1884–85), *Modern Language Notes* (founded at Johns Hopkins by A. Marshall Eliot in 1886), *Monatshefte* (founded in 1897 in Milwaukee by Max Griebsch as *Pädagogische Monatshefte*), and the *Journal of English and Germanic Philology* (founded in 1897 at Indiana Univ.). These journals can serve as a recording barometer of research trends. Other journals with shorter histories of publication, especially those from the early phase of Germanics in the United States, such as *Americana Germanica* (founded at Penn by M. D. Learned in 1897), are also rich sources of information about the objectives, concerns, and research agendas of Germanics. Journals that were founded later (e.g., *Modern Language Journal* [1916–17], *Germanic Review* [1926], *German Quarterly* [1928]) offer an insightful perspective on the history of journal activity, which becomes increasingly diversified and complicated with the founding of new outlets for publication in North America in the final third of the twentieth century. Here one thinks of the broadly based *Colloquia Germanica* (1967) as well as of the more specialized foci of the *Lessing Yearbook* (1967), *Die Unterrichtspraxis* (1968), *Brecht Yearbook* (1971), *New German Critique* (1973), the *Yearbook of the Goethe Society of North America* (1982), the *Women in German Yearbook* (1989), and *Herder Yearbook* (1992), not to mention the Canadian journals *Seminar* (1965) and *Mosaic* (1967) or even student-driven annual publications like *Focus on German Studies* (1994). It is particularly interesting that half these journals are institutionally based and supported, whereas the

351

other half are the official publications of special-interest groups. The proliferation of periodicals after 1970 corresponds to the changing profile of the professoriat, to its more diversified research agendas, and to the increased emphasis on publication in hiring and promotion decisions. Unfortunately, space does not permit an assessment of all the journals important to the history of Germanics in the United States. The history of these journals mirrors in many respects the history of Germanics itself (Henry Schmidt, "Wissenschaft" 75). Microhistories exist for the first one hundred years of *MLN* (McClain) and of the *Journal of English and Germanic Philology* (Guibbory and Kalinke), offering important information about their genesis and editorial policies. It would be useful to compare the editorial objectives of the later journals with those of the earliest ones, to compare them at their founding and again at decisive moments in their development. For example, A. Marshall Elliot, the first managing editor of *Modern Language Notes* (renamed *MLN* in 1964), proclaimed in the inaugural volume (Jan. 1886) that the journal was intended to be a "special organ of communication" for scholars and teachers working in the fields of English, German, and Romance languages. The editors hoped that these individuals might "express their opinions and have the benefit of frank and unbiased criticism" of their personal views on "literary or scientific subjects." They would also find critical assessments of the scholarly works and textbooks that were then appearing. Notable is the emphasis on shorter notes rather than longer articles in order to treat "a variety of subjects in little space."

In response to the perceived need for an outlet for scholarly research and critical debate, Marion Dexter Learned—who was the first to take a PhD in Germanics at Johns Hopkins—established *Americana Germanica* at Penn, publishing its inaugural volume in 1897. He secured a distinguished international board for the journal, which included thirty-three Germanists from Austro-Hungary, Belgium, England, Germany, and Scotland. Among them were Konrad Burdach, Max Koch, Jakob Minor, Franz Muncker, Bernhard Seuffert, Oskar Walzel, and Georg Wittkowski. The stated purpose was "to furnish a distinct medium for the publication of results obtained from the comparative study of the literary, linguistic, and other cultural relations between Germany and America" and to stimulate research on these connections on both sides of the Atlantic. The scope of *Americana Germanica* was intentionally broad, as it aimed to include reception and translation studies of German literature in America as well as studies of American literature in Germany. Dialect studies in the Germanic languages; investigations into "the cultural relations (exclusive of the literary and linguistic) of Germany and America, particularly folklore, manners, customs, industries and arts"; and "articles on the general field of Germanics written in America" were also welcome (*Americana Germanica* 1.1 [1897] v). In 1903 the title of the journal was changed to *German American Annals* (1903–19), and fifteen contributing editors from North America, who resembled a kind of who's who in Germanics at the time, were added. They were H. C. G. Brandt, W. Carruth, H. Collitz, Starr W. Cutting, Daniel K. Dodge, Albert B. Faust, Kuno Francke, Adolf Gerber, Julius Goebel, George A. Hench, W. T. Hewett, Alexander H. Hohlfeld, H. Schmidt-Wartenberg, Hermann Schoenfeld, Calvin Thomas, H. S. White, and Henry Wood (McCarthy, "Indigenous . . . Plant" 164–65). It is interesting to note that Learned, Hench, and Cutting all knew one another from their graduate student days at Johns Hopkins, where Henry Wood was their mentor.

The inaugural volume of 1897 offered contributions by leading American Germanists of the day. In addition to Learned and Daniel B. Shumway—who published "Ferdinand Freiligrath in America," "Pastorius's Bee-Hive" (both by Learned), and "The Verb in Thomas Murner" (Shumway)—the volume contained articles by Faust ("Charles Sealsfield's Place in Literature"), Francke ("Cotton Mather and August Hermann Francke") and a critical review of Francke's seminal *Social Forces in German Literature* by Schoenfeld. Articles by G. A. Mulfinger ("Lenau in Amerika"), T. S. Baker ("America as the Political Utopia of Young Germany"), and Karl Knortz ("Die Plattdeutsche Litteratur Nordamerika's") rounded out the volume. The scope both of the editorial statement as well as of the actual published essays underscores the desire to reach out to a North American audience and displays considerable independence from German *Germanistik* (see McCarthy, "Indigenous . . . Plant" 165.)

In volume 3, Learned published an editorial lauding the newly founded *Journal of Germanic Philology* (later the *Journal of English and Germanic Philology*) edited by Gustav E. Karsten in cooperation with Albert S. Cook, Horatio S. White, George A. Hench, and Georg Holz—Julius Goebel later became an editor. Of special note is Learned's comment that the initial numbers of the new journal give "ample evidence that the scientific method has taken root in American soil and will grow as a native plant" (*Americana Germanica* 1.3 [1897]: 106). In a footnote, Learned further explains that his own journal and Karsten's undertaking complement each other and "augur a new period in the history of Germanic studies in America" (105). While the *Journal of Germanic Philology* took English and German in general as the main goal and solicited contributions from Germany, *Americana Germanica* focused on the literary, linguistic, and cultural relations of Germany and America, with special emphasis on contributions by American Germanists. Both academic journals strove for a "scientific" treatment of issues, published in English or German, and had an international circulation (106).

The sketches of the *Monatshefte*, *German Quarterly*, *Die Unterrichtspraxis*, *Germanic Review*, and *New German Critique* in the following essays invite evaluation of critical turns in the publishing history of the profession in its journals.

Monatshefte

CORA LEE KLUGE

Monatshefte, the oldest continuously appearing American journal exclusively for German studies, was first published in December 1899 under the title *Pädagogische Monatshefte*. It was established with the support of the Herold Publishing Company of Milwaukee, when its predecessor, the *Erziehungsblätter*, succumbed to financial problems. Closely tied to the Nationales Deutschamerikanisches Lehrerseminar in Milwaukee (National German-American Teachers Seminary), the journal represented itself as the "Organen des Nationalen Deutschamerikanischen Lehrerbundes" (Journal of the National German-American Teachers Association). Typical monthly issues from the early years were approximately fifty pages. The contents included official reports of the association; short articles, often serialized, concerning both literary and pedagogical topics; book reviews; reports from correspondents in various cities; and editorials.

The history of the National German-American Teachers Seminary and of *Monatshefte* must still be written. Suffice it to say here that their existence in Milwaukee was jeopardized by the Germanophobia resulting from World War I; and after the events of 1917 and 1918, the seminary went into a period of dormancy from which it did not emerge. Its work was temporarily transferred to the University of Wisconsin, Madison, in 1927; in 1931, its entire assets, amounting to some $250,000, were transferred to Madison through a permanent arrangement. The seminary made it clear that the move was intended to further its interests—namely, the promotion of the teaching of German in America. The final terms of agreement between the seminary and the Regents of the University of Wisconsin stipulated, among other things, that the assets of the seminary should become a trust fund for the use of the Department of German in Madison to train teachers, especially those intending to teach German; that Max Griebsch (first editor of *Monatshefte*) should hold the position of National German-American Teachers Seminary Professor of German at the university; and that the publication of the *Monatshefte für deutschen Unterricht* should be continued under the auspices of the Department of German "as long as the teaching of German in American schools can be furthered by such a journal" ("Proposal" 3; see also Griebsch, "Das Nationale Lehrerseminar" 102).

Until December of 1918 (through vol. 19, number 10, of the series), the journal appeared ten times annually (monthly, excluding July and August). At that point, because of the anti-German sentiments in America, which had been documented in countless individual reports in *Monatshefte*, the journal took leave of its readers. It stated its intention to continue in the form of yearbooks and to resume monthly issues as soon as possible. The yearbook issues began in 1920; they continued through 1926–27. In January 1928, monthly issues resumed, beginning with volume 20, number 1. At that point, the place of publication became Madison. Since 1965, the publisher has been the University of Wisconsin Press. Between 1928 and 1955, eight monthly issues were published per year; from 1956 to 1965, it was seven; and since 1966, *Monatshefte* has, despite its name ("monthly magazine"), appeared as a quarterly.

Editors of *Monatshefte* and their years of service are as follows: Max Griebsch, 1899–1934; R. O. Roeseler, 1934–52; John D. Workman, 1952–72; Valters Nollendorfs, 1972–78, 1990–95; Reinhold Grimm, 1979–90; Cora Lee Nollendorfs (Kluge), 1996–2001; and Hans Adler, 2001–   . Through the years, the full title of the journal has also changed: *Pädagogische Monatshefte* (1899–1905); *Monatshefte für deutsche Sprache und Pädagogik* (1906–27); *Monatshefte für deutschen Unterricht* (1928–45); *Monatshefte für deutschen Unterricht, deutsche Sprache und Literatur* (1946–98); and *Monatshefte für deutschsprachige Literatur und Kultur* (1999–   ).

It is unlikely that the problems and concerns of German studies in America can be found anywhere in more complete fashion than in the pages of *Monatshefte*. For example, the journal's early volumes contain news of the National German-American Teachers Seminary and its course offerings; articles on the methods and principles of language teaching, such as the virtues of the natural method or the question of whether oral proficiency should be promoted; and numerous book reviews, especially of American textbooks for the teaching of German. A notice of the Deutsche Zentralstelle für internationalen Schüler-briefwechsel (German Central Office for International Pupils Correspondence) in Leipzig is designed to alert teachers of German to the possibility of pen pals for their pupils. A frequent topic of discussion is a comparison of teacher-training methods in Germany and America, with the clear implication that the seminary should strive to learn from what is going on in Europe. Membership lists of the Lehrerbund are published, and news of the MLA is included. There are numerous obituaries of professional leaders—many containing information not easily available elsewhere.

Problems concerning all aspects of teacher training in America are well documented, especially in the early years when *Monatshefte* was published in Milwaukee. The journal contains news about conferences on school issues throughout the United States and about school reforms throughout the world. One finds here, for example, a discussion of the pros and cons of corporal punishment in schools. There is a section called "Zeitschriftenschau," which offers short news summaries of pertinent items from major papers, both in the United States and abroad. The so-called feminization of American education is a topic of concern, with news that President Charles Eliot of Harvard has spoken against the hiring of married female teachers for the schools and a similar statement from a group of Catholic female teachers in Bavaria (from the column "Umschau" in *Monatshefte* 14 [1913] 303 and 17 [1916] 319).

When the journal first moved to Madison, the emphasis of its contents shifted only slightly. Numerous articles appeared on pedagogical topics, and reviews discussed textbooks suitable for classroom use. Beginning in 1930 (vol. 22), the catalog of the German Service Bureau in Madison—an organization that was established as a result of the agreement between the seminary and the University of Wisconsin—appeared on a regular basis. The function of the German Service Bureau was to assist schoolteachers of German by maintaining a wide range of teaching materials they could borrow on request.

In these and other ways, *Monatshefte* contributed year after year to the development and support of German studies in American secondary schools, colleges, and universities. The journal published statistical surveys of enrollment figures and trends, information concerning courses abroad, and textbook surveys. Bibliographies were added: for Goethe, for modern German literature, for Theodor Storm, for Gerhart Hauptmann, and so on. The years of World War II brought reports of curricular changes in German programs to meet the war emergency needs as well as reviews of military German courses and training for government translators. After the war, *Monatshefte* attempted to reestablish contact with Germanists in Germany through reports on German studies in Germany during the war, on book publishing in Germany, on the state of German libraries, and on other aspects of the situation there.

By the mid-1940s, *Monatshefte* was undergoing a change. Perhaps as a result of its connection with a department of German at a large university, particularly in an era when the number of American high schools offering the German language was declining, the focus of the journal turned away from matters of pedagogy and toward literary scholarship. Alexander R. Hohlfeld, himself a noted literary scholar, was dismayed. Having arranged the transfer of the assets and the work of the seminary to Madison, he felt obligated to see that the original agreement—which had stipulated that *Monatshefte*'s purpose should be to support the teaching of German in American schools—was remembered and upheld. Although retired from the University of Wisconsin's Department of German for nearly ten years, he engaged in a polemic with R. O. Roeseler, *Monatshefte*'s editor, which became so heated that the matter came to the attention (and ended up in files in the archive) of the university's administration.

Today *Monatshefte* has an established reputation as one of few American scholarly journals of German literature and culture. Its subscribers number approximately 850, about one-fourth of whom are in foreign countries and about three-fourths of whom are institutions and libraries. Its pedagogical interests have nearly been forgotten, yet it remains steadfast in its commitment to service to the profession—above all through its annual "Personalia" (first published in 1937), which lists members of departments and sections of German at universities and colleges throughout the United States and Canada and which since 1980 has included statistical information concerning new positions, promotions, enrollments, and other items. The journal also serves the profession through occasional discussions of professional issues. Since 1980, *Monatshefte* has been involved in the publication of the *Directory of German Studies*, which has appeared every five years, originally as a joint effort with the DAAD (German Academic Exchange Service) and, beginning with the 2000 edition, as a joint effort with the Max Kade Institute at the University of Wisconsin, Madison (Monatshefte / *Max Kade Institute Directory*).

From 1981 to 2000 *Monatshefte* published annually an average of twenty-two articles (of which 28% are in German, the rest in English), approximately ninety-seven book reviews, and several review articles. Over the same twenty-year period, twenty of the issues have been special issues, some dedicated to an individual author (Kafka, Heine, Thomas Mann, Christa Wolf, Libuše Moníková and Herta Müller, Brecht, Goethe), some to a field of interest (present trends, the late Middle Ages, Germanic linguistics, the history of German studies, German media, new historicism, German studies and the GDR, German American studies), some to a particular professional concern (graduate education, business German). A small "Texts and Documents" section under the supervision of Reinhold Grimm—featuring original, previously unpublished poems, prose texts, and interviews—was incorporated from 1980 through 2002. It has now been replaced by a column called "(Re) Readings–New Readings / (Wieder) Gelesen–Neu gelesen," which allows both younger and more experienced colleagues to comment on their readings of books influential for the development of German studies in the twenty-first century. Most scholarly articles have to do with German literature of the eighteenth through twentieth century. Close readings of individual literary texts have given way to modern theoretical approaches to literature and culture.

Monatshefte, unlike the *German Quarterly*, *German Studies Review*, and a number of other similar American scholarly journals in the field of German studies, is not attached to or supported by a professional organization and its membership. It is positioned to remain independent of political and scholarly agendas, trends, and influences. Admittedly, its editorial board has through the years consisted mainly—though recently not exclusively—of members of the Department of German at Madison. But the journal is independent and stable. It has subscribers around the world and considers submissions from colleagues everywhere and on a wide range of topics and approaches in the field of German studies.

Journals of the AATG

The *German Quarterly, Die Unterrichtspraxis*

PATRICIA HERMINGHOUSE

Although not the oldest of the major professional publications for Germanists in the United States, the *German Quarterly*, the official journal of the AATG, is generally viewed—in the United States and abroad—as the flagship journal of the profession. Established in 1927, with its first issue appearing in 1928, it was conceived as a journal that would promote the renewal of the teaching of German in the post–World War I era of crisis. While some prominent members of the profession, such as B. Q. Morgan, then editor of the well-established *Modern Language Journal*, questioned the wisdom of Germanists' attempting to go their own way at this time ("E Pluribus Unum"), the impulse for the newly established AATG—which was not yet a national organization—to have its own journal is understandable in the context of other contemporaneous developments: the American Association of Teachers of Spanish had been publishing *Hispania* since 1918, and the American Association of Teachers of French, newly organized, began its journal, the *French Review*, in 1927.

After the demise of the Germanophile Nationaler Deutschamerikanischer Lehrerbund in 1918 (see Bernd in this volume), its journal, *Monatshefte für deutsche Sprache und Pädagogik* (see Kluge in this volume ["*Monatshefte*"]) had ceased regular publication in 1918 and was preparing to reconstitute itself as *Monatshefte für deutschen Unterricht*, after several years of appearing as the *Pädagogisches Jahrbuch*. Concern that the new AATG journal would compete with *Monatshefte* during an already difficult time in the profession was expressed by both sides; efforts to collaborate and cooperate were, however, futile. Sol

Liptzin, who participated in the negotiations, reports that although the proposals were never ratified, "both Journals were to be made available to all members of the Association throughout the year 1928." The hope was that this arrangement would extend the influence of the AATG and support the vision of building a national membership ("Early History" 23).[1]

From 1928 to 1936, under its first editor, E. W. Bagster-Collins, who served concomitantly as AATG president from 1927 to 1931, the *German Quarterly* announced its purpose in a foreword to the first issue:

> While the *Quarterly* is intended primarily to be helpful in solving the problems of the classroom, the editorial staff is also keen to secure contributions that look beyond mere technique, that are informative in character or deal with broader questions of policy and organization of German instruction. (Foreword [*GQ*])

Sample copies were sent to teachers outside the New York metropolitan area, with the expressed hope that they would not only choose to subscribe to the journal but also pay an additional fifty cents for membership in the AATG and thus "hasten the day when the name given to the association will really apply" (1). With Frank Mankiewicz's succession of Bagster-Collins in 1937, the home of the journal remained in New York through 1941, moving from Teachers College of Columbia University to the School of Education of City College. The *German Quarterly* was not the only newly established journal for Germanists in that city: two years earlier, under its founding editor, Robert Herndon Fife (who served as AATG president in 1932), the *Germanic Review* (see the following essay in this volume, by Niekerk) had announced its arrival as a scholarly journal of the highest caliber, whose program "does not, of course, include pedagogical material" (Foreword [*GR*] 2).

Perusal of the *German Quarterly* in its early decades reveals that it remained true to its promised attention to issues relating to the teaching of German and to the restoration of that language as a subject of instruction in American schools. To this end, the second issue of the journal featured a discussion of the importance of learning German, "Shall German Be Taught in Our High Schools? A Symposium," in which sixty-one prominent United States businessmen, clergy, political figures, and scientists offered arguments for the contemporary and historical importance of the German language. Almost all articles in the journal dealt with strategies for the improvement of teaching, with testing, or with trends in language enrollment. The few articles on literature that appeared usually related to the teaching of these texts and were not characterized by attention to critical methodology or a developed scholarly apparatus. Book reviews, too, focused on textbooks and scholarly books in terms of their classroom usefulness. It is important to note, however, that contributors were very often the most highly recognized members of the profession, who were simultaneously publishing traditional literary scholarship in other venues. For them, the divide today between the production of knowledge and the dissemination of knowledge (see Tatlock in this volume) does not seem to have existed.

By 1932, AATG president Robert Herndon Fife was able to comment optimistically on "the restoration of German to school programs" ("To the Members" 52), and subsequent issues carried continuing good news about the growth in enrollments. There is a striking lack of commentary on developments in Germany during the National Socialist era. With the memory of the price that had been paid for the jingoistic *Deutschtümelei* ("Germanomania") of the World War I era still alive in the minds of most members of the profession, the *German Quarterly*'s continuing emphasis on topics relating to the needs of the American classroom teacher enabled the journal to avoid the pitfalls, and perhaps the moral necessity, of taking a stand on German developments. There were, on both sides, a few exceptions: Edmund K. Heller's Germanophile 1932 essay "Die Zukunft der deutschen Schrift" and, less naive, Theodore Schreiber's "Vom Fremdwort im deutschen Unterricht" a few years later, which railed against the use of such "minderwertig" ("inferior") and "unvölkisch" terms as *Ideal, Republik, Text*, and *Tourist* (162). After 1938, much sharper critiques, such as the articles by John A. Hess, did appear in the pages of the journal ("Free Speech" and "Volk"). While Erika Salloch does not entirely absolve the *German Quarterly* of charges of complicity in promulgating *völkisch* ideology as a result of its attempts during the National Socialist era to remain uncommitted by publishing the viewpoints of critics as well as admirers (267), the cautious neutrality of the journal, at least until the United States entered the war against Germany, was certainly related to pragmatic considerations. Even the "News and Notes" section reported almost exclusively on domestic matters. Thus there was little cause for surprise in 1944 when the editor Curtis C. D. Vail attributed the dearth of submissions on literary topics to the war ("Editorial Letter"). Much more surprising, at least in contrast with the present-day tendency of the profession to address current issues, is the near silence of the journal regarding the National Socialist period for almost a decade after World War II.

The war also had little effect on the relatively small number of articles by women. Although, as statistics developed by Ellen Manning Nagy demonstrate, the recruitment of men into military service and the postwar need for faculty members to cope with the influx of returning soldiers on the GI Bill resulted in notable increases in the number of women on the faculty, at least in the lower ranks (*Women* 101–15; tables 1–4), there was no corresponding increase in the proportion of them publishing in the *German Quarterly*, much less serving in editorial positions. Fifty years after its first issue in 1928 the journal finally had a female editor, Ruth K. Angress (Klüger), who also appointed women to the editorial board and instituted, to the chagrin of some established scholars, a policy of blind review of manuscript submissions. The increasing number of women in the profession, the rise of feminist consciousness, and the general formalization of decision-making procedures that followed in the wake of affirmative action legislation all contributed to the notable increase of articles by women in the journal. Nonetheless, it would be twenty years until another woman, Dagmar Lorenz, was appointed to edit the journal. In the more recently established (1968) *Die Unterrichtspraxis*, discussed below, women were first appointed to the editorial board by the editor Gerhard Weiss (1975–80), who was succeeded by Renate A. Schulz, the only female editor in the history of that journal to date (for complete lists of editors, see table 1 of the appendix following this essay).

The post–World War II years brought about a shift from the historically pragmatic focus of the *German Quarterly* to academic literary criticism, although the editors continued to express interest in pedagogical articles. Two decades after the war's end, despite the editor Robert M. Browning's cheerful 1966 report that "a happy balance has been reached in the publication of literary and pedagogical articles and reviews" (reported in "Minutes" 277), no issue of the journal contained more than one article related to the teaching of German. A year later, Browning's successor, Robert R. Heitner, declared that under Browning's stewardship the circulation of the *German Quarterly* had grown from 5,000 to nearly 7,000 and met "both the more parochial needs of the members of AATG, as the official periodical of the Association, and the broader demands of a scholarly journal, with worldwide recognition" ("New Editor's Greeting" 503). Heitner's choice of the word "parochial" suggests a possibly unreflected contradiction in his expressed intention "to encourage the submission of articles on pedagogical subjects," since he insists that such articles must not only meet the high standards of literary and linguistic scholarship but also succeed in "addressing and instructing colleagues and students all over the world—and future generations" (504, 505). No doubt the influx of the more internationally oriented European scholars who fled the Third Reich and the subsequent group of academic émigrés from reconstructionist Germany in the 1960s had influenced the push toward broader intellectual horizons as well as created a growing skittishness about the "pädagogische Provinz" (see Trommler, "Germanistik nicht als Nationalphilologie"), but was the place for the practical concerns of the classroom teacher about to be foreclosed?

To the contrary: in the late 1960s, a renewed sense of crisis about the loss of funding and declining enrollments in foreign language programs led to several important developments in support of the pedagogical enterprise. In 1967, the American Council on the Teaching of Foreign Languages was founded by the MLA and began publishing *Foreign Language Annals* in October of that year. Two months later, the National Symposium on the Advancement of the Teaching of German recommended "that the profession provide teachers of

German with many more pedagogical articles and more pedagogical information than is now the case" ("National Symposium" 134). In response, a new journal, *Die Unterrichtspraxis: For the Teaching of German*, was delivered to all AATG members in 1968. The founding editor, Eberhard Reichmann, of Indiana University, declared that this journal would be dedicated to the "improvement and promotion of the teaching of German" and "aimed at pedagogical interests from FLES to graduate school." It would have, he added, no "specific pedagogical party line" ("Introducing").[2] As if to illustrate the relevance of pedagogical matters across all levels of teaching in German, the first issue included an article on teaching graduate seminars in literature by two Harvard professors (Hatfield and Stein).

Two years later, *Die Unterrichtspraxis* officially became an AATG publication concerned, as the Executive Council emphasized, "with pedagogical and methodological subjects." Unwilling to establish "rigid lines of demarcation" between the focus of the *German Quarterly* and *Die Unterrichtspraxis*, the council merely affirmed, "The *Quarterly* [will] be free to continue its various departments as well as its book reviews both of pedagogical works and textbooks and of scholarly publications" (Metcalf 314). The quarterly remained "the official publication of the Association" but a few years later announced that, in the future, articles and reviews of a pedagogical nature would appear only in *Die Unterrichtspraxis*. While some journals have discontinued (or are considering discontinuing) their book review sections because of the difficulty of securing informed, timely reviews, both AATG journals have maintained the tradition, providing (in *Die Unterrichtspraxis*) evaluations of new textbooks and electronic media for classroom use and evaluating (in the *German Quarterly*) new scholarly works and editions that Germanists may wish to add to their personal library or request for their campus library. Given some institutions' insistence on published reviews of the work of candidates for promotion and tenure, the review sections of both these journals take on added importance.

Although there have been complaints about the "collegification" of *Die Unterrichtspraxis* (Letters 4–5), because its articles are predominantly authored by college and university faculty members, the journal does in fact serve the largest constituency of AATG members, the precollegiate teachers. When regarded together with the proliferation of specialized research journals in the profession since the 1970s, the policy initiated in 1996 that requires AATG members to choose which journal they wish to receive automatically with their membership dues and to pay an additional fee for the second journal would seem to separate AATG constituencies further: less than 25% of precollege instructors now subscribe to the *German Quarterly*, and only somewhat more than half the postsecondary members receive *Die Unterrichtspraxis*.

While a professor in a graduate seminar may feel little need for articles on teaching *der-die-das* and the foreign language teacher of French and German in a combined classroom of third- and fourth-year pupils may not find relevance in a psychoanalytic deconstruction of an eighteenth-century text, the one-journal option may effectively disengage both constituencies from discussions of import to the profession as a whole. Can a professor ignore without peril the implications of information presented in *Die Unterrichtspraxis* about standards for teachers and students of German being implemented at all levels or disregard discussions of strategies to remedy the underrepresentation of minorities in the classroom and strengthen the introductory-level enrollments on which the advanced seminar depends? Does a classroom teacher really have no stake in debates about the reorientation of German studies programs toward cultural studies approaches and the issues emerging in a newly multicultural Germany and its relation to its past? The AATG is the only association of its kind to publish two refereed journals (in addition to its newsletter) for its membership. Whether this remains an advantage or becomes a problem depends on whether members of the profession at all levels rediscover commonalities of purpose or increasingly pursue specialized interests.

Notes

Sincere thanks to Helene Zimmer-Loew, executive director of AATG, for her help in reconstructing the history of these journals and their editorships.

1 Another collaborative arrangement between *Monatshefte* and the *German Quarterly* was announced in 1937, whereby subscribers to either journal could obtain the other by payment of an additional $1.50 (Hauch 98).

2 Until it became an official journal of the AATG in 1970, the financial sponsorship of *Die Unterrichtspraxis* was shared by various funding sources. The first issue was published with support from the Stiftung Volkswagenwerk, "under the auspices of the American Association of Teachers of German by the Teaching Aid Project (TAP) at Philadelphia, PA" (i). Volume 1.2 (1968) added "and with the support of the Indiana Language Program" to its acknowledgments (inside cover). By the end of the year, AATG chapter presidents reported sufficient enthusiasm for the new journal, especially among high school teachers, that members at the annual meeting voted to make it "a publication of the Association, to be sent to each member besides the official publication, *The German Quarterly*," supported by a $2.00 increase in all members' dues (Metcalf 313). Acknowledgments in volume 2 indicate that in the transitional year (1969) the journal was "published by the National Carl Schurz Association in cooperation with the American Association of Teachers of German and with the support of the Indiana Language Program" (inside cover). By volume 2.2 mention of the Indiana Language Program was dropped, and with volume 3 *Die Unterrichtspraxis* became a journal published by the AATG (inside cover).

Appendix

Table 1

History of Editorship of *Die Unterrichtspraxis*

1968–71	Eberhard Reichmann	Indiana University, Bloomington
1972	Walter Lohnes F. W. Strothman	Stanford University
1972–75	Walter Lohnes	Stanford University
1975–80	Gerhard Weiss	University of Minnesota, Twin Cities
1980–85	Renate A. Schulz	University of Arkansas, Fayetteville University of Arizona
1985–88	David Weible	University of Illinois, Chicago
1988–94	George F. Peters	University of New Mexico, Albuquerque Michigan State University
1994–2000	Jürgen Koppensteiner	University of Northern Iowa
2000–	Jeff Mellor	University of Tennessee, Knoxville

Table 2

History of Editorship of the *German Quarterly*

1928–36	E. W. Bagster-Collins	Teachers College, Columbia University
1937–41	Frank Mankiewicz	City College, City University of New York
1942–45	Curtis C. D. Vail	University of Washington
1945–52	Edwin H. Zeydel	University of Cincinnati
1952–57	Stuart Atkins	Harvard University
1957–62	Werner Neuse	Middlebury College
1962–63	Thomas O. Brandt	Colorado College
1964	Adolf D. Klarmann	University of Pennsylvania
1964–67	Robert M. Browning	Hamilton College
1967–70	Robert R. Heitner	University of Illinois, Chicago
1970–77	William A. Little	University of Virginia
1978–83	Ruth K. Angress (Klüger)	University of California, Irvine Princeton University
1983–88	Henry J. Schmidt	Ohio State University, Columbus
1988–91	Paul Michael Lützeler	Washington University
1992–94	Reinhold Grimm	University of California, Riverside
1995–97	Marc A. Weiner	Indiana University, Bloomington
1998	Bernd Fischer Dagmar Lorenz	Ohio State University, Columbus
1999–2002	Dagmar Lorenz	University of Illinois, Chicago
2003–	Susanne Kord	Georgetown University

The *Germanic Review*

CARL NIEKERK

The *Germanic Review* started publication in 1926 and has always been published by the members of the Department of Germanic Languages at Columbia University. Over the years the format of the journal has remained remarkably consistent. I focus here on editorial statements and other indications of a change in editorial policy and examine four representative volumes (1935, 1955, 1975, and 1995) rather than attempt to locate trends and changes on the basis of all available issues. From the beginning, the core of the journal consisted of scholarly articles and a limited number of reviews that commented on a small selection of recently published scholarship; the aim clearly was not to provide a complete or representative overview of the literature. The editorial statement in the first issue emphasizes the need for a publication devoted solely to the study of the Germanic languages and their literatures, including "all of the Germanic dialects of the continent and the Scandinavian peninsula" (1–2, in 1 [1926]). The statement is indicative of a growing specialization by the language community, but it is also interesting for its refusal—possibly in response to this trend toward specialization—to limit itself to German alone. In volume 13 (1938) the subtitle "Devoted to researches dealing with the Germanic languages and literatures" was added to the title page. In contrast, *Monatshefte* (published since 1899) and the *German Quarterly* (since 1928) were limited to German. Only the *Journal of English and Germanic Philology* (since 1897) considers other Germanic languages and literatures.

Another motive for the founding of the new scholarly journal can be found in the editorial preface in the first issue of 1936, where the editors ask, "Have we in America developed anything original in methods of investigation or presentation in the fields of language and literature?" (2). In answer the editorial says only that the journal is proud of its tradition of publishing most of its contributions in English and indicates concern about a lack of interest in the linguistics and literature of the Middle Ages. While it is noteworthy that the issue of an autonomous American form of research in the Germanic languages is being discussed at this time, that the editors attribute the underrepresentation of medieval and linguistic submissions to a "lack of interest and opportunities in these subjects in American universities" (3) shows that the comparison with *Germanistik* based in Germany is still a decisive factor in the evaluation of the scholarship of American Germanics.

Dependence on developments in Germany is visible in an article by Ernst Jockers (Univ. of Pennsylvania): "Philosophie und Literaturwissenschaft." Jockers assumes the task of informing the American academic scene of a series of methodological developments in German literary scholarship over the past twenty years that all break with "the time-honored philological and historical-critical approaches to literature" (73). He attempts to introduce Dilthey's concept of Weltanschauung into literary studies. But his ambivalence about bringing philosophy into literary scholarship is evident in his stern warning, which extends half a page, that only those who can demonstrate their philosophical knowledgeability ("philosophischen Befähigungsnachweis" [171]) should undertake this type of research.

While Jockers acknowledges that the German program of the MLA has recently established a division concerned with methodological issues (77), all other contributions to the 1935 volume of the *Germanic Review* are based on philological and historical (particularly biographical) approaches. A number of articles touch on comparative issues (Anglicisms in German, Goethe on the German American stage, Nietzsche and George Sand). In keeping with the editorial goals, among the eighteen articles of 1935 are two contributions on Scandinavian literature (one of them a comparison of Ibsen and Hauptmann) and one that discusses medieval Dutch literature. The same diversity of interests characterizes the book review sections.

Contrary to expectations—especially in the period between 1941 and 1945—neither the authors nor the editorial team discuss the issue of a specifically American identity as an alternative to the development of the field in Germany. One could interpret this silence as a sign that the American scene had matured enough to become independent of developments in Germany. But it could also indicate that the editors and authors did not perceive a connection between their research and historical developments and that they considered art to be something essentially apolitical. The journal's statement that it was not interested in pedagogy does not explain its lack of interest in National Socialist culture. Exceptions are two contributions of 1946: Werner Richter's article on tendencies in contemporary scholarship, "Strömungen und Stimmungen in den Literaturwissenschaften von heute" (81–113, in 21 [1946]), which argues for more international cooperation and intellectual exchange as a response to the defeat of Germany and considers the consequences of that defeat for scholarship, and Leo Spitzer's etymological comments on the words *Nazi* and *Spezi* (114–17, in 21 [1946]). The minimal interest of the *Germanic Review* in political developments in Germany is confirmed by Magda Lauwers-Rech, who states that the journal is less relevant for her "because it was dedicated to pure research in German language and literature and did not deal with education" (5). Indeed, she rarely refers to the *Germanic Review*, and then mostly to book reviews.[1]

From 1945 to 1995 the journal published only two editorial statements, neither of which evinces any programmatic ambition. The editorial of 1953 (163–64, in 28) states the journal's intention to continue to exclude articles on the teaching of German. A note from the editors in the second issue of 1984 (42, in 59) reconfirms the journal's commitment to the study of German literature in its historical context and mentions linguistics and literary criticism as other areas of interest. One could interpret this lack of editorial interference as motivated by a basic allegiance to a notion of philology and to a concomitant belief that scholarship in the field of German did not need to change or rethink its foundations in order to argue its legitimacy.

Indeed, in many respects, the 1955 volume looks much like the one of 1935. Most articles are based on philological or a combination of historical and biographical research. Scandinavian languages and Dutch are present, linguistic topics are discussed, while interest in German classicism and in topics concerning older Germanic languages and literatures seems to have increased. The volumes immediately preceding 1955 demonstrate a substantial interest in contemporary authors who immigrated to the United States (Thomas Mann and Heinrich Mann, Franz Werfel). Two articles in 1955 display a political interest in German literature. Ludwig Marcuse writes about Heine and Marx (110–24, in 30), and Israel Stamm discusses Sturm und Drang and conservatism (265–81). This specifically political focus makes a clear break with an earlier tradition, and that break gradually intensifies.

Neither the 1975 nor the 1995 volume contains articles on Scandinavian or Dutch literature; in 1975, only one review of a study of Ibsen was published. In the second issue of 1984, the journal's subtitle "devoted to studies dealing with the Germanic languages and literatures" is dropped. An editorial statement declares in the same issue that the journal "will continue to publish the results of scholarly research in all periods of German literature from the medieval to the present, as well as articles of literary criticism and linguistics" (42, in 59).

In the mid-1990s the progress of scholarship is related to a rethinking of its theoretical basis. In comparison with the 1975 volume, where only one article had an explicitly theoretical basis—on Kantian aspects of Musil's writing (294–304, in 50)—the 1995 volume makes clear that theoretical reflection has become integral to analysis. This significance is particularly evident in the reviewed books, which are on philosophical topics, gender studies, aesthetic theory, popular culture, and musicology. The articles now reflect an interest both in specific topics and in broader theoretical reflection. In addition to a fair number of articles using philological or historiographic tools, the 1995 volume contains essays that employ gender studies (one on Ingeborg Bachmann, another on medieval texts), integrate Jewish studies (on Lili Körber), and deal with interdisciplinary topics such as the relation between literature and film (two pieces on film adaptations of books by Jurek Becker and by Peter Handke).

In 1996, another editorial statement further narrows the focus by describing the journal's task as a "forum for the exchange of critical studies of German literature, media, culture, and theory" (82, in 71); linguistics is removed from the topics of interest to the journal, while it is claimed that in its seventy years of existence "the *Germanic Review* has been a journal open to the diversity of methodological approaches that defines the ever-expanding theoretical horizon of German literary studies" (82). With a new editorial team in 1996, the emphasis on theory and interdisciplinary approaches intensified. The journal also received a new subtitle: *Literature. Culture. Theory.* The editorial team promises issues that will be more thematically focused. In recent years, the *Germanic Review* has devoted increased attention to Jewish culture, with articles on Mendelssohn, Benjamin, Kraus, and Kafka and special issues on Gershom Scholem (Goetschel and Roemer), and the theme "Writing in Jewish?" (Eshel, *Schreiben*). Other thematic issues—"German Dress Culture" (Purdy), "Evidence and the Insistence of the Visual" (Downing and Wild), and "Publishing Culture" (Werner) indicate a cautious move in the direction of German cultural studies.

These later volumes suggest that Germanists in the United States have been able to establish a link to developments in the American humanities and to emancipate their discipline from the shadow of *Germanistik* (i.e., from the type of intellectual mentoring that Jockers propagated in 1935). In this respect, the *Germanic Review* is representative of the development in the field of German studies as a whole. But the development of the journal over the seven decades of its existence also demonstrates that the achievement of its new identity has meant the exclusion of certain areas: Scandinavian and Dutch studies; linguistics; and, increasingly in recent years, medieval studies. At one point these areas were a constitutive part of the profession's self-definition. Because the excluded areas have their own publications, it could be argued that this loss is not a cause for concern. Paradoxically, the increased specialization in the field is accompanied by a broadening of the issues debated.

Note

1 I thank Meike Werner (Vanderbilt Univ.) for referring me to this useful and interesting work.

Appendix

History of Editorship of the *Germanic Review*

Year (Vol.)	Editor
1926 (1)	The Department of Germanic Languages of Columbia University, no individual editors named
1938 (13)	A. J. Barnouw (to 1965) Robert Herndon Fife (to 1958) Frederick W. J. Heuser (to Feb. 1961) Arthur F. J. Remy (to 1941) Otto P. Schinnerer (to 1942) Victor A. Oswald (to April 1945)
1942 (17)	add Carl F. Bayerschmidt (to winter 1984)
1945 (20)	add André von Gronicka (to 1962) (1968–77)
1946 (21)	add Marie E. Ledermann (later Marie L. Hall) (to 1956)
1947 (22)	add J. M. Stein (to Oct. 1958) add Henry Hatfield (to 1953)
1948 (23)	add Reginald Phelps (to 1949)
1949 (24)	add Helen M. Mustard (to Jan. 1969)
1953, Oct. (28)	add W. T. H. Jackson (to spring 1983)
1954, Oct. (29)	add Walter Silz (to winter 1981)
1955, Oct. (30)	add Benjamin Hunningher (to May 1964)
1957 (32)	add Walter H. Sokel (to 1967)
1961 (36)	add Alfred G. Steer (to 1965)
1962 (37)	add Joseph Bauke (to winter 1984)
1963 (38)	add Theodore Ziolkowski (to May 1964) (Mar. 1965–winter 1996)
1964, Nov. (39)	add Ernst Hoffmann (to 1965)
1965, Mar. (40)	add Peter Demetz (to 1969) add Heinz Politzer (to 1967) add Horst Weber (to 1966)
1966, Nov. (41)	add Carl S. Singer (to 1969)
1967 (42)	add J. W. Smit (to 1973)
1968 (43)	add Ludwig W. Kahn (to fall 1988)
1969 (44)	add Patricia Geisler (to Nov. 1969)
1969, Mar. (44)	add Wolfgang Paulsen (to fall 1990)

1970 (45)	add Klaus Schröter (to winter 1984) add E. Theodore Voss (to 1976, except Jan. and Mar. issues) add Walter Theurer (to 1977)
1974 (49)	add Brigitte L. Bradley (to winter 1990)
1975 (50)	add Neal Rendleman (to 1977)
1978 (53)	add James A. Schultz (to winter 1981) add John Cronin (to summer 1991)

1984, spring (59)	Executive editors:
	  add Inge Halpert (to winter 1996)
	  add Shelley Frisch (to summer 1991)
	  add Richard Koc (to fall 1984)
	Editorial board:
	  Brigitte Bradley (continuing)
	  Ludwig W. Kahn (continuing)
	  Wolfgang Paulsen (continuing)
	  Theodore Ziolkowski (continuing)
	  add Jerry Glenn (to winter 1996)
	  add Ingeborg Glier (to winter 1996)
	  add Alexander Stephan (to winter 1996)
	  add Hans Vaget (to winter 1996)
	  add David Wellbery (to winter 1996)
	  add Jack Zipes (to winter 1996)

1989 (64)	add Andreas Huyssen (editorial board)
1989, fall	Shelley Frisch listed as contributing editor add Frederick Lubich (to winter 1996) (book review ed.)
1991 (66)	add Russell Berman (to winter 1996) (editorial board)
1996, spring (71)	Andreas Huyssen the only continuing member of the editorial board add Harro Müller (executive ed.) add Willi Goetschel (book review ed.) add Mark Anderson add Dorothea von Mücke

New German Critique

CARL NIEKERK

Since its debut in 1974, *New German Critique* has been closely tied to the project of German studies.[1] Its articles mirror the diverse nature of this movement. The mirroring is particularly evident when one compares the journal with the *German Studies Review*, which started publication in the same decade (in 1978) and which, like *New German Critique*, also intended to broaden the scope of those working in the field of German. As the subtitle "An Interdisciplinary Journal of German Studies" makes clear, *New German Critique* offers a forum for interdisciplinary approaches. The *German Studies Review* does also but has relied heavily on contributions from literary scholars and historians who do not necessarily exemplify interdisciplinary work—in part because it is the journal of a professional organization, the German Studies Association, while *New German Critique* was begun by dedicated individuals who had their own specific ideas and interests. *New German Critique*, more successful in bridging the gap among different disciplines (philosophy, social theory, film studies, musicology) and in developing a dialogue among them, has anticipated and to a large extent shaped what by the 1990s was called German cultural studies. In 1995, it brought out a special issue on cultural history and cultural studies (65 [1995]).

In addition to its interdisciplinary agenda, three other components have been consistently important for the intellectual identity of the journal: an emphasis on critical theory and the relation between theory and practical analysis; an affiliation with the New Left, although not uncritical; an interest in minority questions, ethnicity, and gender. Because the journal has had this specific agenda, an analysis of its content can serve to identify changes in the academic left as well as in its own identity.

In the 1970s and to a lesser degree in the 1980s, the Frankfurt school dominated much of the theoretical debate in *New German Critique*—because of the journal's leftism and also because of the need to offer an alternative to orthodox Marxist approaches favored in the East without giving up the ambitions of social criticism. The rise and fall of interest in the Frankfurt school is evident in the relation between the journal and the Frankfurt school's most prominent contemporary representative, Jürgen Habermas. Between 1974 and 1980 the journal published twelve contributions on or by Habermas; from 1981 to 1985 the number is again twelve, and there is a special issue dedicated to Habermas (35 [1985]); between 1986 and 1990 only seven contributions by or on Habermas appeared; and between 1991 and 1995 eight contributions were associated with Habermas (four of them only marginally).[2] From 1996 through the first issue of 1999, Habermas is not mentioned. Similarly, in the leftist field emphasis has shifted gradually from figures like Herbert Marcuse and Ernst Bloch—embodiments of more activist forms of criticism, represented in the early volumes—to people, like Benjamin and Adorno (both the subject of special issues), who were more interested in critical theory as a form of cultural diagnosis.

"New French theory"—as it was called at the time (see Ryan)—was introduced by *New German Critique* in the winter 1979 issue (issue 16), which contains contributions on Lacan and Bataille, a contribution by Bataille himself (on the psychology of fascism), and an interview with Michel Foucault. Rainer Nägele's contribution on Lacan ("Provocation" 5–29) goes to great lengths to demonstrate the relevance of Lacan in the context of then-current Marxist debates. Nägele takes the unorthodox step of integrating the journal's editorial comments into a fictional dialogue, thereby providing unique insight into editorial practice. Some of these comments ask for simple clarification; others seek adequate representation or integration of positions articulated by Althusser and Habermas. One of the editorial remarks expresses concern that critical theory might be seen "as merely a pre-stage" rather than as part of a mutual dialogue—the editors see the dialogue as the "hidden bias" in Nägele's paper (28). A later response to Nägele's article wonders if the attitude behind the new French theory is "essentially depoliticized and aesthetic" and therefore just another way of "doing conventional or idealist literary criticism" (145, in 22 [1981]).

While the Frankfurt school clearly moves into the background after 1985, poststructuralism does not replace it in the pages of *New German Critique*—a development that may not be representative for the field of German studies in general. Similarly, a phenomenon like new historicism was discussed in the journal (Hohendahl, "New Historicism") but did not lead to a flood of essays claiming to use its methodologies. While theory remains an important topic in the journal in the 1990s, a pragmatic attitude seems to dominate. Theory in the 1990s does not imply a commitment to a specific set of epistemological principles. Rather, its function is to provide the analytic tools needed to tackle a problem, topic, or interdisciplinary issue.

From the journal's inception, the theoretical dimension was intertwined with a political agenda. In the early days, the editors' interest in a leftist program meant that the journal wanted to stimulate interest in the GDR and in Eastern Europe in general. This is most clearly pronounced in David Bathrick, Anson Rabinbach, and Jack Zipes's introduction to the second issue of *New German Critique*. There they present their project as enabled by but also critical of the New Left, which for instance had ignored the GDR.[3] Despite its leftist leanings, the journal was by no means uncritical of developments in Eastern Europe. Therefore at times the editors had to walk a fine line:

> It is evident that the political and social situation in the advanced capitalist countries influences developments in the GDR, and it is understood that a critique of the GDR that does not make clear its anti-imperialist and anti-capitalist assumptions can easily fall into a legitimation of anti-communism in the West. At the same time, recognition of this fact does not imply that a critical approach to the GDR is rendered impossible. (Bathrick, Rabinbach, and Zipes)

In other words, the journal desired to preserve a critical attitude toward East and West without being co-opted by the West.

A special issue on German unification (52 [1991]), which printed not only contributions by de Bruyn, Grass, Habermas, and Maron but also a piece by the archconservative Karl Heinz Bohrer, signaled the end of this tradition in several respects. Andreas Huyssen's contribution, "After the Wall: The Failure of German Intellectuals," thinks through the consequences of the collapse of the socialist East for Western intellectuals. The fierce debate surrounding Christa Wolf confirmed for Huyssen the close ties that still existed between aesthetic practice and politics in Germany. Writing that the "Wolf debate" indicates "the ending of a literary and critical paradigm," he notes discontinuities in cultural criticism and articulates the need for that criticism to rethink its premises: "The history of postwar German culture will have to be read in a different light" (143).

One could read this comment as a reflection on the necessity of turning to history in order to reevaluate one's ideological position. There are indications that *New German Critique* did precisely that. Certainly the journal has broadened its scope politically, especially since the late 1980s; this broadening is visible in contributions on Heidegger (45 [1988] and 53 [1991]) or on notoriously politically incorrect figures such as Ernst Jünger (59 [1993]) and Richard Wagner (69 [1996]). An interesting document in this context is Eric L. Santner's "The Trouble with Hitler: Postwar German Aesthetics and the Legacy of Fascism." In this essay, which mostly consists of a very ambivalent reading of some recent essays by Hans Jürgen Syberberg, Santner protests the inclination of postwar German aesthetics toward ideological investments and proposes instead a reorientation toward the realm of a nonideological form of aesthetic practice. He objects to the political contextualization of art in German cultural criticism that Huyssen still saw as a given.

Notwithstanding such occasional skeptical remarks regarding its political mission, *New German Critique* has not lost its interest in contemporary German society; that interest can be illustrated by pointing to another continuity in the journal's selections: the consistent foregrounding of issues of gender and ethnic identity. For example, volume 13 (1978) was designated a special feminist issue (see 83–177, in 14 [1978]). In 1980, three special issues on Germans and Jews appeared (issues 19–21), and issues 38 (1986) and 70 (1997) were dedicated to the same topic. In 1989, a special issue on minorities in German culture appeared (issue 46). In all these issues, the journal proved to be progressive and contributed substantially to an increased interest in these topics in German studies.

Without a doubt, *New German Critique* has functioned as a forum for innovative approaches and new topics, contributing thus to the cultural studies component in the German studies movement. Another significant trend in the journal is interdisciplinarity. The journal has increasingly referred to the application of methods from outside the field of German studies to aspects of German society, literature, and culture—a highly desirable integration of a specific American brand of German studies into the American academic curriculum. This development comes at a certain cost. While the early years of the *New German Critique* emphasized the introduction of (contemporary) German theory to an English-speaking audience, this objective gradually seems to have become less important. Exceptions are the special issue on Luhmann (61) and the special section on Habermas's discourse ethics (62), both in 1994. The special issue on Adorno (56 [1992]) contains some contributions on Adorno today but mainly locates him in a historical context. True interdisciplinarity should lead in both directions. Here too, the identity of German studies is a continual subject of discussion and reformulation.

Notes

1 *New German Critique* started publication at the German department of the University of Wisconsin, Milwaukee. Its editors were David Bathrick, Anson Rabinbach, and Jack Zipes. Andreas Huyssen was an associate editor; from the sixth issue on (fall 1975) he served as full editor. In addition to this editorial staff, the journal relied on a

widely varied and continually changing group of contributing editors. From the winter 1987 issue on, it was published by the Department of German Literature of Cornell University. The following scholars joined the editorial team: Helen Fehervary (spring 1977), Miriam Hansen (winter 1984), Peter Uwe Hohendahl and Biddy Martin (both winter 1992). From 1978 on, the journal has published, with increasing frequency, issues devoted to a specific topic.

2 These four contributions are responses to texts by Thomas F. Murphy III and Seyla Benhabib based on Habermas, and a response by Benhabib herself, in the special issue on Habermas and discourse ethics.

3 Criticism of the New Left may also have been inspired by the feeling that it was too intellectual and not practical enough to deal with socialism in its existing, everyday form. See Rorty 76–107 for a similar problematization of the "heirs of the New Left."

Appendix

History of Editorship of *New German Critique*

Year (Issue)	Editor
1974 (1)	David Bathrick
	Anson G. Rabinbach
	Jack Zipes
	Andreas Huyssen (assoc. ed.)
1975 (6)	Andreas Huyssen
1977 (11)	add Helen Fehervary to issue 55 (1992)
1984 (31)	add Miriam Hansen
1992 (55)	add Peter Uwe Hohendahl
	add Biddy Martin

The Reorganization
of the Profession after 1970

SARA FRIEDRICHSMEYER

Germanists in the United States have long expressed uneasiness about the academic study of their subject. Whereas, however, in past years most concerns were viewed as specific to German departments, today many are shared by higher education in general. Indeed, higher education in this country has been under almost persistent attack during the past three decades: from the political left in the late 1960s and early 1970s, and since the late 1980s predominantly from the right, with the brunt of the critique often focusing on such pursuits as the study of literature.[1] A decided stratification in the academy—in part a result of the democratization of the professoriat and the student body (Hunt, "Democratization")—and an increasing diversity of purpose among institutions have exacerbated the sense of crisis. In German departments these political and social pressures affecting academic study have taken on added urgency because of enrollment concerns magnified after the widespread abolition of foreign language requirements after 1968.[2]

The discipline has responded to all these pressures, perhaps not with as much decisiveness or in the specific ways that some would have wished, but the study of German language, literature, and culture in the United States today is markedly different from what it was in 1970, and the professional responses that have made it so are the focus here. A discipline that once accepted uncritically its status as *Auslandsgermanistik* (i.e., *Germanistik* as practiced outside the German-speaking countries) has by the beginning of this century emerged as one that is practiced at a considerable remove from *Germanistik* in Germany and is increasingly responsive to the needs of students and communities in this country.[3]

I concentrate here on the two organizations in the profession that in my judgment have been most instrumental in the shaping of a new disciplinary identity: Women in German and the German Studies Association. Both have provided their members with a forum for consciously and insistently partaking of larger discussions outside *Germanistik*, for becoming part of academic life in the United States, and at the same time for escaping what Jeffrey Sammons in 1989 described as the American "Niemandsland der Germanistik" ("no-man's-land of *Germanistik*") ("Germanistik"; see also Sammons, "Some Considerations"). Although the organizational impulses of each were and still remain to some degree distinct, they share a focus on interdisciplinary studies and on the cultural contexts in which literature is written, read, and critiqued.

Founded in 1974, Women in German can be viewed as part of the institutional development of feminism in this country and as part of an oppositional criticism in *Germanistik*.[4] Its organizing members came together with a mutual recognition of the need for engagement with other disciplines in the United States academy and with the mutual goal of making the field more inclusive—that is, to realize the democratic hopes of the 1960s. It was thus part of a movement for positive change, aimed at transforming society and the profession in socially responsible ways.[5] While its early goals included attracting more women to the field and enhancing career possibilities for those already in professorial ranks, it soon developed a professional identity as an organization desiring nothing less than a thorough revision of teaching and research agendas throughout the discipline.

The aspirations of the organizing members struck a responsive chord in the profession, and by 1977 Women in German had become an affiliate organization of the MLA, with several hundred members. Its mission and early successes soon made it a model for other feminist organizations, such as Women in Spanish and Portuguese (now known as Feministas Unidas) and for Women in French in this country,[6] and, unusual for an American organization, for Frauen in der Literaturwissenschaft in the Federal Republic of Germany (Lennox, "Feminist Scholarship" 163). Women in German has continued to expand and today has nearly 650 members from this country and abroad.

Over the years the organization has developed a number of ways to further its goals. Since 1976 it has organized its own annual meetings, usually around invited guests and their works—typically a German-speaking woman writer or filmmaker—or a specific theme. These conferences provide an opportunity for members to work together to develop new fields for scholarly research and to find effective ways of linking them with innovative pedagogical methodologies. The success of Women in German in exporting its interests to others in the profession must be credited at least in part to its members' willingness, even eagerness, to experiment with new approaches to its conferences. From the retreat concept of early years to the more traditional settings of recent meetings, members have tried to find new models for the annual meetings. The latest attempt at making the gatherings more interactive and less circumscribed includes making papers available on the organization's Web site before the conference and obviating the need for traditional lectures. Not coincidentally, this model promotes inclusiveness by making conference papers available to an audience far beyond those in attendance. A newsletter appearing three times a year and a dedicated electronic discussion list offer further opportunities for, and at the same time reflect the organization's fundamental commitment to, open and ongoing communication.

Women in German regularly sponsors sessions at MLA conventions as well as at national meetings of the German Studies Association and the AATG in order to articulate its members' concerns to the profession at large and to further explore other issues of importance to its members. Planning for the Women in German conferences and for sessions at other conferences has traditionally been a group process, with participants at the business meeting of one Women in German conference making decisions for the following year. Viewed by some as a positive example of feminist process and by others as an unnecessarily exaggerated form of democracy, these business meetings are designed to provide members with an opportunity to discuss openly the various pedagogical, curricular, and scholarly directions to pursue both at their own and at other disciplinary conferences.

With the launching of its yearbook in 1985, the organization responded to members' needs for a forum to advance a certain kind of research that was not yet embraced by the field at large and that today is defined as "feminist research in German literary, cultural, and language studies, including pedagogy, as well as on topics that involve the study of gender in various contexts" ("Notice"). The timeliness of this venture and its growing significance within the profession is evident. By 1990 a university press was publishing the yearbook, an international editorial board was guiding its policies, and the editors were receiving many more submissions than they could accommodate. In addition to refereed articles, the yearbook has in most years featured contributions from conference guests—original works, translations of original works, interviews, and essays, depending on the guest—to generate further discussion about the scholarly issues raised at the conferences.

Academic feminism in this country has always understood itself as transgressive of traditional disciplines, and that understanding is inherent in Women in German. Indeed, the title of the first conference—"Feminism and German Studies: An Interdisciplinary Perspective"—affirmed a defining focus that continues to the present. Other concentrations have gradually shifted over time. Paralleling the development of feminist literary studies in other disciplines, for example, the early exploration of the image of women in canonical literature gradually gave way to an archaeological search for forgotten women writers and to the reexamination of traditional definitions of literary history and genres. These efforts have been made concrete primarily in calls for curricular reforms and for the overhaul of the canon, and they continue to reverberate throughout the discipline. Although departments in this country have answered these calls in different ways and with varying degrees of enthusiasm, few have been able to ignore them.

Some three decades after its founding, Women in German continues to focus on refashioning research agendas and on achieving pedagogical and curricular reform. Its mission today, as formulated on its current Web site, is to provide "a democratic forum for all people interested in feminist approaches to German literature and culture or in the intersection of gender with other categories of analysis such as sexuality, class, race, and ethnicity." This mission is consistent with the organization's early aims, but changes have occurred. The increase in membership, for example, has brought attendant difficulties in maintaining certain feminist organizational principles. Although the organization functioned for over two decades without a president—a decision rooted in a resistance to the formation of hierarchies—the members recently, acting on the recommendations of the Steering Committee, voted to adopt a new structure, one headed by a president. Changing membership demographics too have brought new objectives: as members of the founding generation now near retirement, increased attention is being paid to the mentoring of graduate students and young assistant professors.[7] Although Women in German continues to offer constructive challenges to departments of German, the organization is less overtly ideological today; this shift reflects in part the interests of new generations of scholars who have entered the field as well as the integration of members and their aims into the profession. In fact, the members are increasingly assuming positions of leadership on campuses and in the profession, and the field has seen such a swell in the number of women graduate students and professors (though still at lower ranks), that attention has been somewhat apprehensively called to its "feminization" (V. Nollendorfs, "Out of Germanistik" 6–10).

In 1989, Sara Lennox observed that "gender is still not widely employed within *Germanistik* as a category of literary analysis" ("Feminist Scholarship" 158). Today, perhaps at least in part as a result of such prodding, the same can no longer be said. Although the issue of a feminist backlash must be taken seriously, it is still possible to conclude that major journals and conferences in our field, most graduate programs, and most departmental reading lists and course syllabi demonstrate at least nominal acceptance of the issues central to feminist studies.

The organization's influence can also be seen in the ways it has served as a conduit for introducing others in the profession to sophisticated theoretical approaches to literature and culture from outside the mainstream of *Germanistik*. The early scholarly engagement of Women in German members with poststructuralism, for example, and later with multiculturalism and postcolonialism helped profile these theoretical developments for the profession; their early work with Anglo-American and French criticism introduced issues involving identity that have led many in the field to rethink the categories defining national literature and even Germanness. Consistent with their interdisciplinary interests and their engagement with the various factors constituting individual and national identity, the organization's members have thus provided a strong and articulate voice in the move toward German studies[8] and, more recently, toward cultural studies.

In an assessment of the organization's role in moving the profession toward a disciplinary identity distinct from *Germanistik*, the coeditors of the organization's yearbook remarked in 1996 that those achievements were undertaken with varying degrees of intention. Whereas the desire for interdisciplinary alignments did and does not necessarily involve a conscious move toward an American Germanics, the 1994 adoption by the yearbook's editorial board of an all-English language policy did enforce such intent.[9] As the editors have stressed, the decision documented a "desire to be more intimately tied to academic institutions and discussions in this country where most of us live, study, and teach" (Friedrichsmeyer and Herminghouse, "Towards an American Germanics?" [1996] 239). Indeed, this ambition has been one of the fundamental intentions of Women in German and from the present vantage point can be seen as a guiding force that has helped shape not only the organization but also, in turn, the professional lives of its members.

As the pressures for change accelerated in the late 1960s, it was not only those interested in feminist studies who questioned the continuing efficacy of traditional disciplinary boundaries. It became clear to many that *Germanistik* as practiced in West Germany was no longer appropriate for the academy in this country and that the study of imaginative literature, if it were to attract student interest, would better be carried out in an interdisciplinary setting (see Hohendahl, "Interdisciplinary German Studies" 233–34). Some of the first attempts at reaching out to a diverse student population, such as area studies or literature-in-translation courses, did not employ interdisciplinary methodologies, nor were such teaching strategies incorporated into the early experiments with courses on film or those on Holocaust or GDR literature. Throughout the 1970s, however, many in the professoriat began to contemplate the possibility of new methodologies for contextualizing imaginative writing and soon were experimenting with working across disciplines. By the mid-1970s these interdisciplinary practices were being called German studies, and many took note of them as a way in which departments might be shaped in order better to serve an American student population.

In contrast to Women in German and its agenda for transforming the field, the German Studies Association originated out of a desire to strengthen the field by developing an interdisciplinary model for teaching and research. Oppositional critique was always acceptable but never de rigueur. Founded in 1984 as an outgrowth of the Western Association for German Studies, itself founded in 1976,[10] the original members of the German Studies Association came from history and literature departments—with scholars from literature departments forming a major constituency; more recently they have come from political science and economics as well. From the outset the kind of attention to imaginative literature encouraged by the association was distinct from that of *Germanistik* in the FRG, showing a concern for the pursuit of new methodologies and the desire for a new and more pragmatically focused discipline.

From its beginnings in 1976, the association has grown to include approximately 1,700 members from North America and abroad. In 2000 it announced itself as a "multi- and interdisciplinary association of scholars in German, Austrian, and Swiss history, literature, culture studies, political science and economics" and defined German studies as "a dynamic and growing field that provides a new paradigm for studying the record, experience, and legacy of the German-speaking peoples of Europe" (*Guidelines for Curricula*). Except for the welcoming of additional disciplines and the widening of its original scope, which was restricted to contemporary issues, this identity is consonant with the organization's origins.[11] Committed to a broad forum for interdisciplinary scholarship, the German Studies Association supports an annual conference that has approximately 150 sessions and publishes the *German Studies Review*. This journal appears three times a year and contains articles representing the numerous disciplinary and interdisciplinary allegiances in the organization as well as a significant number of reviews of books from those areas of interest.

In response to the rapid acceptance of interdisciplinary studies and subsequent attempts to integrate an interdisciplinary approach into departmental programs, the German Studies Association published in 1987 the *Guidelines for Curricular Organization at North American Educational Institutions*. Without prescribing any methodologies, the document provided curricular guidelines for institutionalizing German studies and for training graduate students in the United States accordingly. A 1998 revision, available on the organization's Web site, maintains this general concentration but places an even greater emphasis on teacher training and additional stress on the importance of language proficiency and the genuine practice of interdisciplinarity.[12]

Guidelines describes two forms in which German studies can be institutionalized, both derived from a summary of actual practices rather than from any prescriptive intent. The first type of program is one in which inter- or multidisciplinary work is carried out by Germanists who develop specialties in other disciplinary practices or work with scholars in ancillary fields, remaining dependent on the expertise available in their own institutions. The second, a more theoretical model that assumes the existence of something resembling a new discipline, is defined as "a shift from the philological focus of German *Germanistik* to a broader concentration on culture studies" (*Guidelines for Curricula*). Though initially viewed as a challenge to traditional practices and resisted in some quarters as faddish or ideologically driven, this second form of German studies now provides a disciplinary base for a number of new theoretical approaches, including film studies, ethnic and minority studies, queer studies, postcolonial studies, and cultural studies itself.[13] While the first type of German studies predominated in the organization's early years, the second is also now firmly established in a number of departments. Reinforcing the pragmatism and inclusivity of the German Studies Association, the latest guidelines argue for a merging of these two models.

Clearly, German studies is practiced in diverse ways. Indeed, its success is due in large part to its ability to accommodate such a wide variety of interests and practices under its increasingly capacious umbrella.[14] Whereas in 1974 A. Peter Foulkes could designate German studies as an "approximate equivalent" to *Deutschkunde*, as a phrase to describe "those programs which fall outside the scope of courses devoted principally to either language or literature" (530), Hohendahl in 1998 was able to refer to it as a "neutral term" for "the discipline that deals with German language and literature and, at least more recently, with German culture in general" ("Past" 76). In some variant or other, German studies is so integrated into departmental curricula today that it has been a factor in the preparation of most students trained in the past two decades.[15]

The success of the German Studies Association, however, has not masked certain concerns about German studies, concerns that apply to the interdisciplinary intents of Woman in German as well. Despite efforts to break down disciplinary boundaries, for example, genuinely interdisciplinary work remains difficult to do, as scholars continue to be trained in their own disciplinary methodologies.[16] Although many articles in the *German Studies Review* increasingly demonstrate a genuine inter- or multidisciplinary approach, others do not, and despite the efforts of organizers the disciplines also remain somewhat distinct at the association's conferences, often separated by topic and audience. Further, certain questions posed by scholars as early as the 1970s continue as points of discussion—for example, the role of imaginative literature and aesthetic issues in German studies or how much German-language study to require. Other concerns are voiced by those who, even while supporting the general thrust of interdisciplinary studies, have argued persuasively against the haste to abandon a disciplinary base;[17] they further warn that with our attention to interdisciplinary pursuits we are by our own volition decreasing the need for departments of literature or even for professionals trained in literary studies. Whether or not German studies has fulfilled expectations regarding increased enrollments also remains a subject of some controversy.

Although these concerns should not be minimized, it is clear that both the German Studies Association and Women in German have infused immense energy into the study of German literature and culture. But their very successes have also moved the discipline away from any methodological consensus and toward the creation of a field that now must thrive on its heterogeneity. While this flexibility has made it possible for increasing numbers of departments to experiment and develop the kind of programs best suited to their home institutions, the lessening of a firm disciplinary identity is not univocally applauded (see Ellis, *Literature Lost*, for a vehement critique). One of the underlying assumptions of most of the articles in the 1989 spring issue of the *German Quarterly*, Germanistik *as German Studies*, was the hope that some variant of German studies could provide the field with a disciplinary model and along with it a cohesive disciplinary identity. More than a decade later, although hopes for a unified methodology and a consistent identity have not vanished, there are far more reservations about the viability of such aspirations, especially in this era when higher education itself has become so multifaceted. The field seems increasingly to demonstrate a postmodern unwillingness to be captured by any single definition, so that any overarching vision of disciplinary identity is by necessity based on an affirmation of its very diversity. Perhaps our best hope is that the diversified discipline that Women in German and the German Studies Association have helped develop is strong enough and flexible enough to respond to the many challenges—whether in the form of a multicultural Germany or a unified Europe or, in institutional form, in the contours of the increasingly pragmatic United States academy—that will surely define the new century, indeed the new millennium, just as they have shaped the past three decades.

Notes

1 A number of recent studies have been published by university presses; see, for example, Kennedy; Kernan; Kolodny; Nussbaum; and Woodring. See also Delbanco; Honan.

2 The problem was articulated most aggressively by Van Cleve and Willson in 1993 when they described Germanics as "slowly sliding into oblivion" (foreword). See the authors' account of the enrollment crisis (1–13).

3 The notion of a distinct American branch of the field has been a theme—with variations—of many in the profession since the 1970s, notably Friedrichsmeyer and Herminghouse ("Toward an American Germanics?" [2001]); Hohendahl ("Germanistik in den Vereinigtan Staaten"); Lennox ("Feminismus"); McCarthy ("Double Optics"); Peck ("There's No Place"); Sammons ("Some Considerations"); Trommler

("Germanistik"); Weiner ("Letter"); and Ziolkowski ("Seventies"). On *Auslandsgermanistik*, see Hohendahl ("Past" 77) and Peck ("There's No Place" 183).

4 Some of the history of Women in German already exists, and I have made use of these sources: Friedrichsmeyer and Herminghouse ("Towards an American Germanics?" [1996]); Clausen and Friedrichsmeyer ("What's Feminism" and "WIG 2000"); Lennox ("Feminist German Studies," "Feminismus," "Feminist Scholarship"); and Martin ("Zwischenbalanz"). On oppositional criticism, see Henry Schmidt ("What Is Oppositional Criticism?"); see also Lennox's article in this volume.

5 As Martin put it in 1989, membership in the organization provided women at that time with "ein gewisses Vertrauen in die Möglichkeiten, den Beruf anders ausfüllen zu können, ein Bewußtsein, Teil eines kollektiven Projekts zu sein, die Zuversicht, daß unsere Arbeit auch in diesem Sinne gelesen und kritisiert wird und vor allem auch, daß wissenschaftliche Arbeit und politische Diskussionen entscheidend zur Veränderung der Wissens- und Machtverhältnisse in einer Institution wie der Universität beitragen können" ("Zwischenbalanz" 169; "a certain faith in the possibilities of practicing their profession in a different way, a consciousness of being part of a collective project, the confidence that our work will be read and critiqued from this perspective, and above all [the confidence] that scholarly work and political discussions can contribute decisively to a change in the relation between knowledge and power in an institution such as a university").

6 Both were established in 1978 as standing committees by the Women's Caucus of the MLA and encouraged to emulate the success of Women in German. Some of this history can be found in *Concerns: Newsletter of the Women's Caucus of the Modern Languages* (22–23, in 8.4 [1978]; 26–27, in 9.1 [1979]; 10–11, in 10.1 [1980]; and 31, in 10.2 [1980]).

7 This development has been addressed by Friedrichsmeyer and Herminghouse ("Generational Compact").

8 See Lennox ("Feminismus") for a view of feminism's influence on German studies.

9 Cf. Friedrichsmeyer and Herminghouse ("Towards an American Germanics?" [1996]). The professional dilemma of Germanists in the United States who conduct their professional lives predominantly in German has been written about in a variety of stylistic veins by, for example, Sammons ("Some Considerations"); Van Cleve and Willson (19–23); and Ziolkowski ("Seventies" 250–51).

10 I thank Gerald Kleinfeld for help in gathering information on the German Studies Association.

11 See the *Guidelines for Curricular Organization at American Educational Institutions* of 1987 for the stress on contemporary issues.

12 I thank Patricia Herminghouse for her comments on the difference between the 1987 and the 1998 version.

13 Others in the field have suggested a convergence between cultural studies and German studies under the rubric "German cultural studies," but the term has not yet gained wide acceptance. It has, however, gained some credibility with the 1997 publication of *A User's Guide to German Cultural Studies* (Denham, Kacandes, and Petropoulos). In their preface, the editors define German cultural studies as an interdisciplinary project that developed out of German studies as it has been variously practiced in the United States since the early 1970s and that is, they believe, an appropriate descriptor for a transformation that has already taken place (xi).

14 In stressing the association's pragmatic rather than theoretical focus, Trommler credits the Western Association of German Studies with providing "the peculiar form of a low-flying, yet goal-oriented pragmatism" that has guided the success of the German Studies Association ("Future" 212).

15 See for example *Monatshefte*'s 1995 "Special Survey" of German studies programs and courses, in which the editors write that recent dissertation titles indicate to scholars brought up in 1950s and 1960s "an almost total change in paradigm. Pure study of literature seems to be the exception now, rather than the rule" (360).

16 Lennox, herself a strong proponent of interdisciplinary work, has also acknowledged its inherent difficulties ("Feminist German Studies" 7–8).

17 In Hunt's succinct phrase, "Interdisciplinarity cannot live without the disciplines" ("Virtues" 1).

6

The Changing Profile of the Professoriat

~

Edited by
JOHN A. MCCARTHY

Introduction

When we look back over the history of our profession, a number of historical developments emerge as turning points: the establishment of graduate programs in the late nineteenth century, the high percentage of German speakers in the United States around 1900, the rise of an MLA culture, America's entrance into the Great War in 1917, the wave of highly educated émigrés in the 1930s fleeing fascism, the infusion of federal monies into the training of military personnel in the 1940s, the Sputnik shock of 1957 and the National Defense Education Act of 1958, the renewed influx of new immigrants in search of professional opportunities, the civil rights movement, the Vietnam War, and the end of the cold war. Each event or circumstance occasioned renewal, change, displacement, protest, or a search for continuity and legitimation. Calls for the Americanization of Germanics were heard around 1890 and 1990. These appeals peaked around 1990 with the publication of several important collections of position papers representing a broad spectrum in the professoriat (e.g., Benseler, Lohnes, and Nollendorfs; Trommler, "Einleitung"; Lützeler, Germanistik; McCarthy and Schneider; Roche and Salumets).

The following three essays on the changing profile of the professoriat from 1880 to 2000 provide detailed and differentiated perspectives on broad segments of those shifts, displacements, and attempts at reorientation. The increasingly narrower time lines in these essays are evidence of the professoriat's explosive growth (esp. around 1910 and after 1945), its increased Americanization, and finally its movement toward German studies after 1980

(Daemmrich; V. Nollendorfs, "Eine amerikanische Germanistik"). Taken together, the essays by Gisela Hoecherl-Alden, Meike Werner, and Arlene Teraoka provide an excellent introduction to the ways in which the profession has grown more complex, more gender-balanced, and more sensitive to—if not actually reflective of—minority issues. Together they represent an important introspective moment in the history of the profession. Two are objective, one personal in tone—personal because we are still in the third phase of this development. They mirror not only the changing profile of the professoriat but also its teaching and research agenda. (A clear distinction between profile and agenda cannot always be drawn.)

There are other introspective moments. One of the earliest is contained in Marion Dexter Learned's assessment of German studies and belletristic writing from 1898, "Germanistik und Schöne Litteratur in Amerika," in which he argued for the invigoration of American culture through a symbiotic engagement with some aspects of German culture while maintaining a specifically American pragmatic slant. That symbiosis was echoed in Albert B. Faust's *The German Element in the United States, with Special Reference to Its Political, Moral, Social, and Educational Influence* (1909). Evidence of such progress was seen in the generation of American-born and American-trained Germanists, but the anti-German hysteria of 1917 abruptly changed everything. Of the 318,000 students who had been moving through the educational system in 1915, only 14,000 remained in the classrooms in 1922 (Zeydel, "Teaching . . . to the Present" 361–62). This loss of students meant that positions at all levels of the educational hierarchy were cut. Programs were drastically reduced or eliminated. The result was an intellectual vacuum in higher education (Sammons, "Die amerikanische Germanistik" 109). Hoecherl-Alden sheds new light on this period.

In his assessment of 1978, Jeffrey Sammons explained that the Jewish émigrés from central Europe stepped into this gap, although it was not easy for them to find positions at colleges and universities. They infused the curriculum and the research agenda with new vigor and substance. While the exiles of the 1930s frequently pursued comparative topics and wrote for a North American audience (Remak; Trommler, "Recovering" 38–39), the later immigrants of the late 1950s and the 1960s tended to remain attuned to German *Germanistik* and to write almost exclusively in German. That trend led to what Sammons has called the invisibility and isolation of Germanists in the American academy (see also McCarthy and Schneider 46–52). Werner addresses these questions in her treatment of the period.

David Bathrick took a more radical approach in his 1976 contribution "On Leaving Exile: American *Germanistik* in Its Social Context," to the volume *German Studies in the United States: Assessment and Outlook* (Lohnes and Nollendorfs). That collection of essays was assembled in order to "define the specific situation, characteristics, and goals of the German-teaching profession in the

United States as compared to *Germanistik* in Germany" (*German Studies* 2; see also Bathrick, "Literaturkritik"). With the premise that American Germanics was based on a twofold separation—its discourse was separate from dominant discourses in the American academy and "the notion of literature [as] separate from the social matrix" in which it was created and received—Bathrick advocated the re-Americanization of Germanics with three steps: the implementation of a "dialectical materialist approach"; the rejection of "high-low dichotomy and the elimination of class, sex, and race bias"; and the opening of journals and organizations "to discussions around fundamental alternatives to prevailing practices" ("On Leaving" 254, 256–57). These very issues were championed by the German studies movement in the 1980s (without the fixation on Marxist criticism) and have evolved as the dominant model in Germanics. The ideological and thematic shift toward a radical questioning of the status quo and the perception of a need to Americanize the professoriat created opportunities for new voices in the profession (McCarthy, "Double Optics"; Hohendahl "Germanistik in den Vereinigten Staaten"). Teraoka's contribution in this section also addresses the topic and offers a few caveats.

Peter Uwe Hohendahl took a different tack in his 1998 essay "The Fate of German Studies after the End of the Cold War." Recalling the role of the Kentucky Foreign Language Conference in the immediate postwar years as a vehicle for reconsidering the shape of the discipline, he argued that the fate of foreign language departments fifty years later is part and parcel of a reconfiguration of university structure in general. The corporate model of the 1990s—unlike the "inefficient" departmental paradigm of the 1950s—was essentially a model of decentralization. The resultant emphasis on the need for "the flexibility and efficiency of the individual unit" would allow the German or foreign language department to take advantage of the proposed administrative drift toward collective corporate efficiency. Yet the streamlining of tasks in the academic setting is inherently flawed (Hohendahl 19–20). Heidi Byrnes also emphasized the practical aspects of the issues in her summary report of the future of German in the American educational environment ("Action Agenda"). This wider view—already apparent in the early phase of the discipline around 1900—emerged dramatically in the millennial issue of the winter 2000 *German Quarterly* (Lorenz), which was devoted to departmental structure, alternative practices, decentralization, Americanization, and so forth. The contributors reminded one of the connection between humanistic endeavors in general and German studies in particular and of the fact that the content of the discipline is more important than the form of its institutional organization (Strum 60, 63). The twelve brief position papers included in that millennium issue accurately mirror the profile of the professoriat at the end of the twentieth century. Simultaneously, the collective voices have begun to answer one of the pivotal questions about reading (or recovering) our past: "How has the field dealt with superimposed definitions of useful knowledge?" (Hohendahl, "How to Read" 11). Vital to this section of the volume is the additional, implicit question: How has the professoriat changed in response to those socially superimposed definitions of what is important?

The repercussions of these pressures on the discipline have begun to be analyzed. A longtime commentator on the shape of the profession, Valters Nollendorfs, gave the following diagnosis of more recent shifts in the professoriat and a prognosis for the future of the profession:

> I see in the present statistical trends in the profession—a growing feminization and increasing Americanization—a movement toward a much more public and open profession and a movement away from one that is dominated by a group of male expatriate high priests saying their incantations in German and demanding that the congregation respond in German. . . . But I also do not see in these trends the emergence of a unified American Germanics as a method or as a conviction. Personnel changes, exchanges, new specializations, proliferating teaching and research methodologies, indeed, new methods of instantaneous communication, distance learning, and research will inevitably bring about changes in our professional demeanor, approach, institutional structure, and politics. ("Present Trends" 53–54)

Renewed emphasis on second language acquisition and the professionalization of graduate student training has also prompted change in who gets hired and why (Nagy, "Patterns"; Glew). The general question now seems to be: What does it mean to be a Germanist today? (McCarthy, "Was heißt es, heute Germanist zu sein?"). In sum, the contributions of this section provide the historical context for contemporary issues of professorial profile in Germanics. They encompass the full range of possibilities from a "culture of elite literacy" to a "more democratic concept of professional citizenship" (Trommler, "Recovering" 34–35). But the reader of the essays in this section should bear two things in mind. First, one finds here mostly the names of distinguished Germanists, although most of us are not distinguished. Nor have all our predecessors been distinguished. By definition, only a few attain such status. Of the 1,388 faculty members listed in the 1999 "Personalia" of *Monatshefte*, only about three dozen (2.7%) are named in the essays that follow. Second, the focus tends to be on PhD-granting institutions, although they are outnumbered in North American higher education by non-PhD-granting ones. That focus skews our view of the extent of the democratization, feminization, and Americanization of the profession. Thus much of our history remains buried. We can recover it only when more studies of college and university departments become available (see Ziefle).

The Development of the Professoriat, 1880–1941

GISELA HOECHERL-ALDEN

Three distinct phases have shaped the German professoriat in roughly its first sixty years, from its institutionalization in the late nineteenth century until World War II. By the time the United States entered the war against Imperial Germany, the professoriat had become an integral part of American academe. The year 1917 marked a division between two factions that deeply influenced Germanists' self-perception during the Weimar Republic. The years from 1933 to 1941 are characterized by the professoriat's struggle to position itself with regard to Nazi Germany.

By 1850, mass immigration from Europe had brought a record number of German speakers to America. Numerous German-language newspapers highlighted German cultural developments and scientific innovations, and more than 9,000 Americans who had studied at German universities introduced German educational ideas to American universities (Herbst 1). Before the Civil War, American higher education had been organized around a Christian humanist tradition, aimed primarily at cultural conservation. Classical antiquity influenced the research methods while the Christian religion ruled campus life. After the Civil War, the reform debates revolved around rival concepts of higher education: differing notions of piety and discipline, the role of research, emerging liberalism, and questions of utility. Historians of education have established that American scholars returning from German universities had gained an appreciation for research and the importance of specialization. They had also acquired an academic code of conduct, which opposed dilettantism (Trommler,

"Germanistik" 874). The reform debate culminated in the establishment of the Johns Hopkins Graduate School of the Arts and Sciences during the centennial year of 1876. By combining the idea of a general humanistic education for undergraduate study with the more scientifically oriented graduate programs, the older English college tradition was merged with the German research institution to create a uniquely American university. As research gradually assumed a major function along with the duties of teaching and serving the needs of the community, the foundations for a potential division between theory and practice, between an emphasis on highly specialized scholarship and on excellence in broad-based teaching, were laid.

The establishment of German graduate departments all over the country elevated the study of language and literature to a new, more scientific level. Philology was regarded as an exact science of the underlying foundations and functions of language, and it was taught alongside the interpretation of the German literary canon. Dilettantes such as "theologians, lawyers, and men of many other professions could [no longer] become Germanists overnight" (Zeydel, "Teaching . . . through World War I" 34). According to Frank Trommler, interest in German as an academic subject developed with the growing number of instructors and students who needed to gain a better understanding of major scientific debates that were taking place in France and Germany. University presidents like Henry P. Tappan (Univ. of Michigan), Andrew Dickson White (Cornell), and Daniel Coit Gilman (Johns Hopkins) publicly pledged the inclusion of French and German as an integral part of a liberal and progressive education. By the end of the century most major universities had German departments with well-organized language, philology, and literature programs. Successful students of German philology and literature demonstrated that one did not have to go to Göttingen, Berlin, Heidelberg, or Leipzig in order to receive a thorough education in the humanities ("Germanistik" 867–69). In the university, the teaching of the German language was now relegated to the undergraduate college level, and teaching of advanced literary interpretation and philology had moved into the graduate domain. The needs of students were divided into two groups: some chose language instruction to be able to read publications in other fields; some pursued a humanistic education with an emphasis on philology, literature, and philosophy. While the first generations of German professors taught at every level, the need for specialization inherent in a research-oriented field would eventually divide the professoriat into graduate and undergraduate faculty members, into literary scholars or philologists and language pedagogues.

In the late nineteenth century, "the study of literature as such was new to the American academic world" (Spuler, "From Genesis" 159). Initially, literary criticism and philological research had been more incidental and personalized and often uncritically oriented toward German scholarship (159–60). Both administrative misconceptions about the value of studying modern languages and the lack of established role models presented a challenge for the newly emerging German professoriat. In the undergraduate curriculum, professors had to defend the inherent value of studying a living language while they felt growing pressure to conform to academic standards upheld by the sciences at the graduate school level. The sheer number of scholarly periodicals founded between 1884 and 1899 testifies to the increasing interest in scholarship on German philology and literature. Yet these periodicals often contain justifications, like that of German-born Julius Goebel, for establishing the study of German classics in general and Schiller in particular: to safeguard an aesthetic education in a classical sense by combining newer with older values that evolved from Latin and Greek ("Proposed Curriculum" 26). However, this line of reasoning remained essentially unsuccessful in changing prevailing institutional perceptions as the former exile Henry Remak noted nearly forty years later (176).

The establishment of American Germanics as an academic field was the result of enthusiasts of German literature and philosophy, not of philologists or literary critics. Before 1880, colleges and universities seldom employed more than one German lecturer or professor. At Harvard, for example, the Vormärz exile (Vormärz is a revolutionary, antimonarchical period in nineteenth-century Germany) Karl Follen and his successor, Henry Wadsworth Longfellow, are credited with institutionalizing German between 1831 and 1854. Their success stemmed from their enthusiasm for German literature and excellence in language teaching and not from professional training (Francke, *Deutsche Arbeit* 20–21; Zeydel, "Teaching . . . through World War I" 28–34). In fact, in reflecting on German influences in America and his position as a professor of German, the American-born and -trained Marion Dexter Learned (Pennsylvania) distinguished early on between intellectual influences of the Vormärz thinkers in the first part of the nineteenth century and educational influences after the Civil War. The nonacademic aspects of the profession become evident in the professoriat's attempts to create a professional image for itself in its fledgling discipline. German-born Kuno Francke, the first trained Germanist to teach at Harvard, proudly proclaimed himself the successor to Follen and others. As guardian of their legacy, he also likened his work as a German professor in the United States to that of a farmer, poised to till a largely uncultivated field (2–3, 5–8, 19–21). Francke was only one of many German-born academics who believed in the superiority of German culture and perceived the propagating of German culture in the predominantly Anglo- and Francophile American academe as a pioneering effort. In describing their work, some academics employed sacred imagery, figuratively embarking on a crusade to educate their American students through classical German ideas. There is no doubt that most of the members of the professoriat could identify with this rigorously authoritarian and elitist role the Germanists had created for themselves. Indeed, since both the German-born professors and their German-trained American colleagues generally came from wealthy, conservative, and Christian families, they were not averse to adopting the German image of the university professor as a spiritual leader. They became the academic mandarins that Fritz Ringer has described.

By the beginning of the twentieth century, the balance of power in university administrations was shifting rapidly. Successful businessmen had begun making large donations to higher education; in return, they took control of the universities' governing boards. Their monetary support for the sciences and economics reflects the growing pressures of an increasingly industrialized society in dire need of appropriately trained personnel (Hamilton 12–13). Furthermore, the prevailing isolationist attitude in American society in the late nineteenth and early twentieth century resulted in a general lack of interest in learning foreign languages, even among the new generation of more inward-oriented intellectuals. German professors embraced the idea of public service and frequently lectured to nonacademic audiences. Although the professoriat's efforts were geared, in part, toward members of the large German American communities, their speeches were often better received by their American audience. The professoriat quickly understood that the more recent immigrants were not interested in German high culture. In fact, Francke's near failure in garnering adequate financial support for his shrine to German culture, the Germanic Museum at Harvard, clearly symbolizes the rift that existed between academe and the vast majority of German Americans (Francke 54–55). Learned claimed that the predominantly uneducated German immigrants were responsible for the perception of German culture in the United States, and he appealed to the educated classes of Germany to support American Germanists in their efforts of mediation ("Lehrerbund"). Regardless of whether the members of the German professoriat were German-born, American-born native speakers, or of Anglo-American descent, their goals were the same. It was their style of discourse that distinguished them from one another.

I concur with John McCarthy's observation, made at the 1996 symposium "Shaping Forces in American Germanics," that focusing solely on the quasi-missionary zeal of these first German American Germanists, as Henry J. Schmidt ("Rhetoric" and "What Is Oppositional Criticism?") and Richard Spuler ("From Genesis") did, creates a biased image ("An Indigenous . . . Plant"). Highlighting only one aspect of their professional activities entails omitting another very important side of their work. The pragmatism prevailing at American universities ensured that even the most avid among American Germanists did not become a mere carbon copy of the German *Doktorvater* ("PhD adviser"). Follen had already understood that American Germanics, by its very nature of teaching the language as a vehicle for understanding the content, had to be different from its German sister discipline. Despite his short tenure at Harvard, he influenced the early development of an American German curriculum by publishing his *Deutsches Lesebuch für Anfänger* in 1826, which, apart from texts he considered canonical, also included grammatical explanations (Zeydel, "Teaching . . . through World War I" 28–34). In their attempt to disseminate German cultural values, leading Germanists wrote books they would not have written in Germany. In fact, Francke expressly stated that it was his desire for cultural mediation that led to the publication of his *Social Forces in German Literature* in 1896. His book, responding to the need to provide students with background information on German cultural and national developments, went on to become a staple of German instruction throughout the country. It was later also translated and published in Germany. In short, the image that the professoriat initially chose for itself as it became professionalized seemed to be first that of an educator in the classical sense and second that of a cultural mediator.

Until recently, most historical studies of the profession have ignored the contribution of female Germanists, although the first female Germanist to earn an American PhD and subsequently become a college teacher was Anne Irish in 1882 (Zeydel 45). In marked contrast with women in Germany, women in the United States participated in the development of Germanics from the beginning. Ellen Manning Nagy's study of two women teaching at Vassar College, the American-born Marian Whitney and the German-born Lilian Stroebe, reveals that they were dynamic innovators of teaching methodology for college German instruction, whose ideas remain influential today (*Women* 65–72). Stroebe's founding of the German Summer Language School at Middlebury College is a lasting contribution to American Germanics; the school has enabled students to become proficient in the language in a few months. Her innovative and highly successful approach to language instruction was not only largely responsible for the development of all Middlebury language schools but was also a model for the development of others in the country (Freeman, *Middlebury College* 20–29).

Nagy contends that even though women met the same educational and professional requirements as their male colleagues, their persistently low academic status at state universities and coeducational colleges suggests that they were judged by different standards. Female scholars rose to the top of their disciplines only in women's colleges. While the excellent reputation of the eastern women's colleges enhanced the status of female academicians, it seems unlikely that these same scholars could have risen to equivalent academic standing in the biased atmosphere of coeducational or all-male colleges (60–61). Their exclusion from elitist organizations such as the MLA placed women outside the professional network. Although American universities developed research-oriented graduate schools, women were often relegated to teaching at the college level. This division meant that most of their teaching and research was focused on the classroom and language pedagogy, the area in which women's contributions were most important and far-reaching (139–44). Although women also published on philology and literature, male Germanists, by virtue of their institutional affiliations alone, were not only more visible in the field but also played the more significant role as educators of the next generation of male and female PhDs. The increasing importance of research (as opposed to teaching), coupled with the fact that women published less on literature and philology, was a major factor in their continued marginalization. Excellence in teaching and pedagogical research was and still is considered of secondary importance in the giving of promotion and tenure.

Demographics for both male and female Germanists suggest that they adapted well to the conservative atmosphere of the universities at the turn of the century. Most of the German professoriat propagated the conservative bourgeois literary canon reflected in the scholarship from German universities, while their colleagues in the social sciences and economics began challenging capitalism. For advocating political reforms and the founding of labor unions, many social scientists and economists were dismissed from Cornell, Chicago, Wisconsin, Stanford, Brown, Pennsylvania, and other institutions. It was clear that university governing boards would suppress criticism of their ideologies. Eventually, concern among faculty members prompted the creation of the American Association of University Professors in 1915 (Hamilton 14–17). Meanwhile, World War I had broken out in Europe. The elitist, conservative mind-set, which had served the German professoriat well in its quest for academic respectability, had become suddenly dubious (see Hohendahl in this volume ["From Philology to the New Criticism"]). The German-born professors' attitude had always been suffused by German patriotism, and between 1914 and 1917 many professors, both heritage speakers and German-born, still felt secure in the prestige they had hitherto enjoyed. Though threats to the German-trained professoriat from all disciplines were numerous and public support for alternatives to war with Germany could be grounds enough for dismissal (Hamilton 12–16), some of the most astute and intelligent members of the German professoriat continued using intensely patriotic language to win sympathy for Imperial Germany. In 1917, when the United States entered the war, the backlash was immediate and immense (C. Nollendorfs, "First World War" 178; see also Benseler in this volume).

While his outspoken German patriotism cost the highly visible Francke his post in the German department, it is noteworthy that his equally candid colleagues Julius Goebel (Illinois) and Max Griebsch (Wisconsin) were able to retain their positions. The newly formed AAUP did not step in on their behalf. In fact, only two years after the publication of its "General Declaration of Principles of Academic Freedom" the association bowed to general pressure and agreed to wartime restrictions, as long as they did not jeopardize the intellectual independence of scholars (Hamilton 14–17). The German professoriat's integration in the MLA's network, however, provided important continuities and safeguarded, for example, Goebel's uncontested editorship of the *Journal of English and Germanic Philology* (Trommler, "Germanistik nicht als National-philologie" 875). The effect of such protection is evident also in examples of female professors like Bryn Mawr's Agathe Lasch, who had been stridently pro-German (Maas 469–73): they were unable to reestablish their positions in American Germanics because they were not members of a professional network.

Forced to reevaluate their position and redefine their role in the university, American Germanists fell into two camps regarding the survival of Germanics in American academe. The first group, whom I would term restorationists, continued to perceive themselves as representatives of classical German culture. The second group, the pragmatists, advocated an immediate, complete, and more practically oriented reorganization of the field. While the division did not run strictly along lines of national identity, most well-established German-born professors aligned themselves with the first faction. Articles published in *Monatshefte* by Griebsch ("Was wir wollen"), Ernst Voss, J. D. Diehl, and others between 1915 and 1922 summarize the scope of the discussion, while the language of publication clearly positions the authors in their respective camps: German for the restorationists, English for the pragmatists. Not only do these articles bear witness to the ideological metamorphosis the pragmatists underwent after 1917, but they also document several restorationist attempts to strengthen the elitist position of prewar years. The attempts of the American Germanists at regaining their former prestige parallel, in some ways, those undertaken by their colleagues at German universities during the Weimar years.

While the restorationists were mostly German-born academics, the pragmatists were diverse and included both male and female, German- and American-born, heritage and nonheritage speakers, Christians and Jews. For some, 1917 had brought about a drastic reorientation of their professional identity and values. The most prominent example is the German-born Alexander Hohlfeld of the University of Wisconsin. Trained in classical German literature, he believed in the uncontested value of a humanistic education. In 1901, he began building what was to become a German department of national importance. In 1914, as president of the MLA, Hohlfeld enthusiastically proclaimed the victory of specialized academic research over language pedagogy ("Light" lxxiii). But after 1917, Hohlfeld was in the forefront of those who emphatically advocated close cooperation of universities with German teachers in area schools and the professoriat's active role in teacher training. While his compatriots Goebel, Griebsch, Frederick Heuser (Columbia Univ.), and others hoped to regain prewar prestige without active intervention, Hohlfeld, Bayard Quincy Morgan (Stanford Univ.), Robert Herndon Fife (Columbia), and other established Germanists understood the need for reorientation if the profession was to survive. Whole departments became embroiled in the battle for the professoriat's future. Ideological positions were deeply entrenched and, as Cora Lee Kluge states, were clearly symbolized by the long-standing feud between Hohlfeld and the newly appointed editor of *Monatshefte*, Robert O. Röseler ("First World War" 190–91).

In the course of the 1920s, the next generation of Germanists joined the ranks of the pragmatists. The German-born Ernst Feise (Johns Hopkins) and the American-born heritage speakers Hermann Weigand (Yale) and Edwin Zeydel (Univ. of Cincinnati) were among those who had lost their positions in 1917 and had supported themselves in various ways outside American Germanics. During the interwar years they quickly rose to the top of their profession. In the meantime, Stroebe, whose Middlebury Summer Language School had been forced to close due to anti-German pressure in 1917, held on to her position at Vassar. Yet given the influx of qualified male PhDs during the postwar years, her focus on language pedagogy, and her position as faculty member in a women's college, she was not considered a viable candidate when the summer school reopened. Ernst Feise became her successor (Freeman, *Middlebury College* 106). Ironically, because of Middlebury's growing prestige, her excellence in teaching and pedagogy were no longer sufficient reasons to retain Stroebe as director. While numerous German-born and -trained women joined their American-trained female colleagues as Germanists in the interwar years, they remained largely invisible. Again, their invisibility was the result not of their lack of publications (Nagy, *Women* 113) but of their continued marginalization in their institutions, the profession, and its organizations. Eventually, the professoriat's efforts to redefine the discipline and its postwar responsibilities culminated in the establishment of another professional organization: the American Association of Teachers of German in 1926 (see Herminghouse in this volume ["History of the AATG"]). It followed the example of the American Association of Teachers of Spanish, which was founded nine years earlier. Although the new organization expressly included both secondary school and university teachers (Weiss, "From New York"), women were not equally represented (Nagy 116–20).

By the end of the 1920s, the professoriat had become active again, and most veterans of the 1917 purge, regardless of their ideological positions, had learned carefully to avoid politics. Hitler's ascent to power therefore placed American Germanists at a crossroads once again. In a document entitled "The German Teacher: Professor on the Spot," philologist W. Freeman Twaddell (Univ. of Wisconsin) characterized the professoriat's dilemma as twofold. On the one hand, professors wanted to safeguard their continued existence in academe; on the other, they feared the end of their professional ties to the country whose language and culture they were teaching. German-born professors also feared for their relatives. To avoid a repetition of their profession's turbulent history, several articles expounded the inherent value of studying

German and pointed out that *Hitler* and *German* were not synonymous (Bau-mann; Huebener, "Lernt Deutsch!"). In 1938, even Herbert Hoover beseeched the professoriat to continue teaching the language, since the Germans were developing "a new ideology of government, economics, and society" and chal-lenging the American "concepts of spiritual and intellectual liberty" (645). He concluded, "If other people had that insight which teaching the language can afford, it would give greater national security to our national ideals" (645–46). The *New York Times* seconded, by asking, "What better challenge to Hitlerism can there be than to get to know Lessing, Schiller and Goethe?" (Editorial; see also Hohendahl in this volume ["From Philology"]).

While the professoriat easily justified the teaching of German, it shied away from taking a public stand regarding Germany. In order to remain unobtrusively apolitical, neither American nor German-born Germanists joined the AAUP in its assertion that "the conditions of intellectual life in [Germany] are a matter of legitimate concern" in the wake of mass dismissals from German universities (Report). The question of whether or not American Germanists should openly denounce Hitler and the Nazi book burnings precipitated bitter quarrels in the New York chapter of the AATG. When Frank Mankiewicz, a well-respected, dynamic Germanist at New York's City College (Schueler, "In Memoriam") de-manded an open condemnation of Hitler's regime, a veritable flood of letters reached Hohlfeld, at that time president of the AATG. While the heated dis-cussion uncovered latent anti-Semitism among members of the professoriat, as a letter from Heuser to Hohlfeld indicates, Adolf Busse's (Hunter Coll.) descrip-tion of the event reveals that most of the Jewish Germanists voted in favor of abstaining from a public statement (Letter).

The prevailing atmosphere at the universities in the 1920s and 1930s was one of suspicion of political activism, and Germanists were well aware that the patriotism unleashed during World War I had set a precedent for considering teachers' treasonable utterances or attitudes a threat to national security. The growing fear of Communist indoctrination had made membership in a dubious political organization sufficient cause to place an academic's job in jeopardy. According to A. W. Coats, by 1936 twenty-one states and the District of Co-lumbia had reinstated the World War I practice of requiring loyalty oaths from their teachers. During the interwar years, there were numerous cases of arbitrary or unfair dismissal of university and college faculty members. There was ob-viously little more the association could do to protect the victims other than to publicize their cases in the *AAUP Bulletin* (138). When the openly leftist, European-born, Jewish Germanist Harry Slochower (Brooklyn Coll.) was among the first to publicly speak out against Hitler's regime, the more traditional venues of Germanist publication were closed to him (Vogt 50).

Although virtually powerless to affect change at American universities, the AAUP continued to protest infringements on freedom of speech in Nazi

Germany. The AATG and MLA remained carefully neutral. The years between 1933 and 1938 were marked by general unease, which fractionalized the professoriat. While the majority tacitly approved of the AATG's and MLA's silence, they differed in their opinions about course content. Some proposed ignoring Nazi Germany completely and went to great pains to circumvent the topic in their classrooms. Others, advocating its cautious inclusion into the curriculum, wanted to study the phenomenon. Certain Germanists' published reactions to the New Germany led scholars indiscriminately to accuse those authors of being Nazis (Pentlin; Salloch). Undeniably, the professors in question had voiced pro-German sentiments. But the adjective *Fascist* should be assigned prudently, reserved for those who were in fact Nazis. It has been established that Friedrich J. Hauptmann (Rutgers), Otto Koischwitz (Hunter Coll.), Heinrich Meyer (Muhlenberg Coll. and Vanderbilt), Hugo Schnuch (varying affiliations), Anna Schafheitlin (Kent State), and Matthias Schmitz (Smith Coll.) were promoting Nazi ideals on their respective campuses (Hoecherl-Alden, "Germanisten" 193–224, 233–49). Hauptmann and Koischwitz even returned to Nazi Germany. Because *Monatshefte* published the majority of articles about Nazi-sanctioned literature, Erika Salloch deduced that Wisconsin's German department was dominated by Nazi sympathizers (259), but she was merely echoing the exile community's belief during the 1930s (Heym 145). There is no doubt that Röseler and Charles Purin, in the 1930s, were if not pro-Nazi then at least ultranationalist and conservative (Hoecherl-Alden, "Germanisten" 225–49). Wisconsin was also the affiliation of such outspoken anti-Nazis as Hohlfeld and John D. Workman. But since Röseler was the editor of *Monatshefte* and Purin the editor of several questionable textbooks, it is not surprising that the opinion evolved that the department was pro-Nazi.

If Germanists were not of one mind when it came to dealing with Nazi Germany, it is clear that most members of the professoriat were not susceptible to the more blatant forms of Nazi propaganda actively targeted at them. Busse and Richard Jente (Washington Univ.) warned their colleagues that political representatives of Germany should not speak at academic meetings. In a letter to Hohlfeld, Jente maintained that "the German teachers in this country should have learned a lesson from what happened . . . during the war"; he concluded, "Only damage can be done by introducing politics into our work." Likewise, Albert Faust (Cornell) saw the introduction of Nazism into the classroom as a threat to the professoriat's continued existence (Jente 2–3).

Then as now, German teachers and professors wrote to Germany or German cultural institutions for materials, and some initially failed to recognize the more subtle forms of Nazi propaganda. For example, although Hohlfeld, Busse, and the Austrian-born Joseph A. von Bradisch (City Coll.) found Heinrich Roenneburg's pamphlets advertising study trips to the New Germany to be obvious propaganda, a more politically naive Germanist like Werner Leopold

(Northwestern Univ.) was not as skeptical; in 1935 he uncritically embarked on one of the advertised trips and even sung its praises afterward ("Reise"). As late as 1937, Charles Handschin (Miami Univ.) was among those who continued to react with disbelief and demonstrated incredible political naïveté when he advocated reading the statistical yearbook of the German Reich rather than paying heed to the anti-German American media ("Teaching"). But there are no grounds to accuse Handschin, Leopold, and others of being Nazi sympathizers. The same Leopold advocated the use of Erich Kästner's children's books for classroom use in 1937—he maintained that they were interesting for American students—and avoided any discussion of contemporary Germany and the fatal repetition of blind patriotism ("Realia").

A mixture of revulsion and admiration characterizes some of the articles published on the literature and culture of the New Germany. The Germanists' diverse reception of Hans Grimm's blatantly anti-Semitic and propagandistic novel *Volk ohne Raum* exemplifies this equivocation. Again, Hohlfeld, Busse, and others dismissed the book as Nazi propaganda almost immediately, while others, clearly impressed by the novel's unprecedented success in Germany, were not prepared to disregard it so readily. Even a scholar like George Danton (Union Coll.), who on another occasion had been openly critical of anti-Semitic tendencies at his own institution, enthusiastically endorsed the novel's introduction into a seminar on contemporary German culture. While Grimm's militarism, nationalism, expansionism, and anti-Semitism struck Danton as excessive, he dismissed them as "not rabid" (36) and causing no reduction in the book's overall pedagogical value. Danton was not alone. Both Röseler and West Virginia University's Victor J. Lemke advocated the inclusion of Nazi texts that they obviously admired. Conversely, their colleagues denounced Koischwitz's, Emil Jordan's (Rutgers Univ.), and Jane Goodloe's (Goucher Coll.) textbooks for revering certain aspects of Nazi culture and literature (Lenz; John Hess, "Volk" 6–7).

Germans and Anglo-Americans alike were initially struggling to come to terms with the developments in Nazi Germany. In fact, many Germanists, regardless of their heritage, seemed to have possessed a certain amount of political insensitivity, as an anecdote about Bayard Quincy Morgan illustrates. The Stanford Germanist invited not only his new colleague, the exiled writer-turned-German-professor Bernhard Blume, to his house for dinner but also the Nazi consul ("Auszüge" 113). The philologist Ernst A. Philippson (Univ. of Michigan), an exile himself, explained that

> the first years of the Nazi regime did not seem to be so terrible when seen from over here. Since notable figures like Gerhart Hauptmann, Guido Kolbenheyer, Wilhelm Schäfer, Josef Ponten, Agnes Miegel took a pro-Nazi stance and since some well-known anti-Nazis were pacifists, socialists, and /

or communists, naïve American observers tried to "understand." (Lauwers-Rech 40)

The professoriat's overall ambivalence and hesitation to condemn Nazism outright may have also stemmed from the fact that it felt great admiration for some of the German colleagues who had become Nazis in 1933. Professorial exchanges, which were instigated by Francke at the turn of the century, recommenced by 1928. Among the notable German scholars who had come to teach in the United States were the philologist Hans Naumann from the University of Frankfurt, whose year at Wisconsin was regarded as an "inspiration to American Germanists" (45, 221 in *Monatshefte* 20 [1928]). The Hebbel scholar Wolfgang Liepe, from Kiel, went to Harvard, while Karl Viëtor, from Giessen, spent a year at Columbia in 1931. In 1933, *Monatshefte* (25: 79) and the *German Quarterly* (6: 144) announced the illustrious Julius Petersen's visit to Stanford. Just a few years later, Liepe and Viëtor were both exiled in the United States, while Petersen and Naumann remained in the service of Nazi *Germanistik*.

Although the events of 1938 shattered any illusions regarding Hitler's intentions, neither German scholarly journals nor professional organizations reacted publicly when Austria joined the German Reich and the number of refugees rose dramatically. Even when President Roosevelt recalled his ambassador from Berlin after the November pogrom and America was protesting Nazi atrocities, most Germanists refrained from making public statements. They said nothing about Hitler and Nazi Germany in order not to jeopardize the generally positive attitude toward their profession on the eve of America's entry into World War II. They were soon faced with the consequences. At a time when even United States–trained PhDs were hard pressed to find suitable jobs in the severe economic crisis, the onslaught of foreign-trained PhDs fed the xenophobic tendencies in American academe. The Germanist Karl Arndt (Hartwick Coll.) complained that American universities had "become asylums for political irreconcilables and social misfits . . . exiled from their native land for political, usually Communistic, activities or opinions." At least for Arndt, fear of Communist infiltration seemed to outweigh anti-Semitism when he continued by asking, "Why not place some of our own American Jews before we establish professorships for Jews exiled from Europe?" (130). That a combination of xenophobia and anti-Semitism influenced the job market is indisputable. Yet, compared with other disciplines, the German professoriat included considerably more Jews among its ranks. It is also true that at some institutions highly qualified or experienced émigrés were preferred to local PhDs.

The professoriat's correspondence reveals that displaced Germanists frequently appealed to American colleagues they had come to know professionally during academic exchanges. When American Germanists could not help, the

Carl Schurz Memorial Foundation often succeeded in placing exiled Germanists at American universities (Gramm 114–28). The organization was instrumental in finding a position for Liepe at Yankton College in North Dakota, since Harvard had appointed Viëtor as Kuno Francke Professor in the meantime. Refugees were well aware of the difficulty of finding a suitable position even before they arrived in the United States. The half-Jewish baroque scholar Richard Alewyn had enjoyed a short but promising career in Heidelberg and could therefore expect his predicament to be known to his American colleagues. Like many others who could not be placed with the help of colleagues or the various Germanist organizations, Alewyn focused his hopes on the MLA. His notion of American academe and the types of appointments available to refugees is evident in his pessimistic description of the MLA convention as an "annual slave market" (Zelle 219; Zeller 268). Eventually his affiliation with Queens College made him one of the fortunate ones who were able to support their families with academic jobs. Alewyn's case demonstrates that fame and publications alone were not sufficient to secure European scholars a position in the more pragmatic American university system. In fact, as Twaddell explained in a letter to Robert Hutchins, president of the University of Chicago, Alewyn was considered unsuitable for a position at Wisconsin because the faculty had "heard the report that [he] was spectacularly unsuccessful as a teacher." In contrast, Martin Sommerfeld from the University of Frankfurt enjoyed a reputation as an excellent, patient, and tactful teacher who had rapidly adjusted to the American system. It was noted positively by Feise in his letter to Hohlfeld and was undoubtedly a decisive factor in Sommerfeld's placement first at Columbia University, then at Smith College.

Overall, American colleagues perceived most Germanists who had lost prestigious positions in Europe as arrogant (Lauwers-Rech 170). But the consensus among exiles teaching literary history was that only Viëtor had received an appropriate appointment (Blume 238). In fact, although Stuart Atkins later termed his death a loss for American academe, Viëtor himself seemed to have felt detached from if not disdainful of his fellow academicians, whom he regarded as relatively uneducated (Zelle 218). Displaying an attitude very similar to Francke's several decades earlier, he complained in a letter to his mentor, Julius Petersen, that abstract thinking was not one of the strengths of his American students and that he therefore needed to be quite elementary.

In retrospect, it is easy to classify certain refugees' adjustment problems as culture shock. On the whole, displaced academics found it difficult to adapt to the differences in status and workload as well as the fact that they had to teach everything from beginning language to advanced literature courses. Furthermore, the cosmopolitan Germanists often found their positions in small college towns, away from vibrant cultural centers like New York, doubly daunting. Henry Remak stated that it was a tragic paradox that these people who had been forced to leave their homes because they were regarded as non-German were now too German for America (180).

Given the distrust of leftist intellectuals, xenophobia, and the dismal job situation, it is not surprising that the diaries, autobiographies, and personal essays of several exiled Germanists have corroborated the established view that American Germanists generally did not extend a warm welcome to the refugees (Vordtriede 357; Schwarz, "Die Exilanten" 122–23). Contact between the exile communities and American Germanists were relatively infrequent. Because of sheer numbers and demographics, interactions between refugees and American academics predominantly occurred in the large East and West Coast cities and nearby universities. The German-born Anna Jacobson (Hunter Coll.), Sol Liptzin (City Coll.), John Whyte (Brooklyn Coll.), Gustave O. Arlt (Univ. of California, Los Angeles) and the New Jersey–born heritage speaker Harold von Hofe (Univ. of Southern California) were among those who raised funds to invite exiled colleagues and writers to talk at their institutions. Drawing on frequent incidents of cross-cultural miscommunication among exiles, their colleagues, students, and the administration firsthand, Whyte wrote an insightful book, *American Words and Ways*, that was intended as a guide to the refugees' successful adaptation to American academe. By illustrating differences in discourse, intellectual intensity, and dogmatism, he identified sharpness of tone and overly hierarchical thinking as the main reasons for the failure of the Germans.

The lack of outrage against profascist utterances in the profession can be partially explained by the politically charged atmosphere, in which the fear of Communism was greater than that of Nazism. The lack of outrage may also explain why many American Germanists ignored the growing number of exiles. During the 1930s, the professoriat had largely refrained from their language and culturally specific insights to influence American public opinion. Representing the other Germany of bourgeois classicism, Thomas Mann vindicated the exiles when he published in the *German Quarterly* an appeal to American Germanists to uphold those ideals. He also dealt the female professoriate another blow by addressing only the men who were so valiantly teaching German in adverse times (67). When it became evident that the United States was going to enter the war, the situation at the universities changed dramatically. Since the government now instituted Army Specialized Training Programs to train intelligence personnel, American women and both male and female Central European exiles were integrated into German departments all over the country.

Germanistik in the
Shadow of the Holocaust

The Development of the Professoriat, 1942–70

MEIKE G. WERNER

"Whether we know it or not—we stand as Germanists in the shadow of the Ettersberg and are in a bad situation. In bad situations, the chess champion Tartakower liked to say, bad moves come by themselves" (Eichner 216). With this almost melancholy insight, Hans Eichner concluded his contribution to a colloquium in 1991 "on the impact of German exiles in the field of *Germanistik* of their host countries" (Schmitz). His thoughts on the "Holocaust and *Germanistik*" simultaneously constituted a confession of failure and "an apology for my omission . . . for one doesn't see the Ettersberg from the Frauenplan and one forgets all too easily that they are close to one another" (Eichner 201 and 216).[1]

The Holocaust is the central event of the twentieth century, and, as Theodor Adorno has argued ("Erziehung" and *Negative Dialektik* 354–58), the vanishing point of modernity. As such, it has decisively changed the shape of Germanics. Even though in the first two decades after 1945 there was "a great deal of discussion about Weimar, but not much about Auschwitz" (Eichner 201), the immediate past, albeit in the form of an absence, shaped the professoriat in important ways.

That shaping was not straightforward. To understand the influence of the war and of the Holocaust on the profession in the period from 1942 to 1970, it is necessary to consider the composition of German departments both in the light of two separate waves of immigration and as the result of the interaction of recent immigrants with American-born Germanists. The first influx consisted of a younger generation of refugees, most of them Jewish, who arrived in the late 1930s and early 1940s. Often they came as teenagers and had begun but not completed their education in the universities of Central Europe. The second surge arrived in the 1960s, though some had started to arrive even earlier. Typically these refugees had received some of their university education in the German system. Almost exclusively from the Federal Republic, they too were deeply affected by what the historian Charles Maier has called Germany's unmasterable past (1). The second wave was a non-Jewish immigration.

For the development of the profession, both immigrations were a demographic fact of central importance (see Dowden and Werner). The first wave included, among many others, Eichner, Dorrit Cohn, Erich Heller, Ruth Klüger, Heinz Politzer, Henry Remak, Egon Schwarz, Walter Sokel, Guy Stern, and Harry Zohn. Peter Demetz, whom the Nuremberg Laws made into a "half Jew," survived the Nazi period in Prague but fled from the Communists in 1949; he should also be counted among this generation of refugees.

Though their individual plights were diverse, commonalities underlie their collective odyssey. Shaped by the arduous, often perilous experience of exodus and flight, many of them also endured the deprivations of internment camps and the uncertainties of temporary refuge: Heller in England, Remak in France, and Schwarz in South America. Others in this group served in the American armed forces, often with non-Jewish Germanists, and still others worked as manual laborers or in odd jobs (Müller-Kampel; Merrill and Cernyak-Spatz; Schmitz; Schwarz, *Keine Zeit*). In the 1940s and 1950s, however, most members of this contingency completed their education in the United States and secured positions in German departments across the country. Together with younger, American-born Germanists, they were a powerful force for the modernization of the study of German in the United States.

This modernization had already commenced under the aegis of Nazi refugees in the 1930s (Hoecherl-Alden, "Germanisten"). But most departments were still principally shaped by the old guard of Germanists, mainly of German American heritage, whose traditional image of Germany remained rooted in the Wilhelminian period (C. Nollendorfs, "First World War"; Henry Schmidt, "Rhetoric"). Cosmopolitan and urban—typically hailing from Berlin, Vienna, and Prague—the new generation could not have been more different. A sense of this difference can be gleaned from anecdotes about departmental life in the 1940s. Werner Vordtriede, for example, avoided the chair of the German department at Rutgers because the chair was in the habit of pulling him aside and discussing in an "idiotic sentimental way . . . beloved German matters" (174). In 1942, such encounters were concurrent with the genocidal apex of the Holocaust. For the chair, nothing much had changed; for Vordtriede, who was teaching Spanish then, everything had changed. With the same sense of estrangement, Peter Heller, who had fled from Vienna, described the German

Club at City College and at Columbia: "As had been customary in nationalistic fraternities in the early decades of our century," they still "struck a long dark table with a saber, learned to drink 'ex,' and sang 'Krambambuli' " (66).

From the vantage of the refugees, the line separating the German patriots from closet National Socialists was not always distinct (Eichner qtd. in "Auszüge" 114). In the faculty lounges across the United States, anti-Semitic remarks often punctuated a seemingly innocuous atmosphere of thoughtless joviality and unreflected nationalism. Hermann Weigand recalled these lapses in the Yale German department in the 1930s and 1940s. He remembered someone saying of a Jew, " 'He's a Yid.' Or: 'Er hat einen kleinen Webfehler,' meaning a Jewish grandmother, or so" (Henry Schmidt, "Interview" 288). Yale was no exception. German national and sometimes even National Socialist habits of mind pervaded many of America's German departments (Schwarz, "Die Exilanten" 122; Lauwers-Rech; Pentlin; Salloch).

These habits of mind attenuated the influence of German departments. In their résumé of the achievements and failures of Germanics between 1939 and 1946, Henry Hatfield and Joan Merrick caustically criticized the field's false sense of superiority and "intellectual isolation," which in turn undermined "what might have been its [Germanics's] greatest contribution . . . the interpretation of the German mind to a puzzled nation" (353–54). This task fell instead to journalists and historians.

National habits of mind also influenced the narrower field of what Germanists actually studied. Kafka, for example, did not count as a topic of legitimate scholarship. As a young doctoral student, Walter Sokel was quickly rebuked for his interest in Kafka. According to Sokel:

> Professor Henry Schulze in the Columbia German Department . . . pooh-poohed my project right away. "Comparing Kafka to E. T. A. Hoffmann does not make any sense," he decreed. "For one thing, there are no points of comparison, and besides the difference in literary rank between them precludes it." What he meant, of course, was that the crazy Jew from Prague was so immensely inferior that one could not consider him an academic subject. ("Embattled Germanistik" 195).

This state of affairs began to change with the Allied victory. When news about the death camps reached the American public, it rendered the anti-Semitism of the American academy unacceptable (Klingenstein), and the image of a "good old Germany" could no longer be sustained.

The change did not occur without tension or without anti-Jewish resentment (Guy Stern qtd. in "Auszüge" 117–18). And it was not always swift. In some places it did not occur until the late 1950s and early 1960s. One can see this delay in terms of texts taught. Works such as Storm's *Immensee*, Gerstäcker's *Germelshausen*, Heyse's *L'Arrabiata*, and Sudermann's *Frau Sorge* slowly lost their status on the reading list (Remak 176). The composition of departments also changed slowly. In the wake of professionalization and by force of retirement, many of the German nationalists gradually left the stage. But so too did such American-born, gentleman scholars as Robert Herndon Fife, who had for many years been chair of the Columbia German department and who in 1944 became president of the MLA (Heuser, "Robert Herndon Fife"). Born of well-to-do parents in Virginia, Fife had founded the *Germanic Review* and had been a champion of the idea that humanities scholars should develop a "really American school of criticism" ("Nationalism" 1286).

By the late 1950s, the intellectual constellation of German departments had changed, however, and even the work of someone as accomplished as Fife looked to the younger generation to be "solid and trustworthy, if often dull" (Hatfield, "Literaturgeschichte" 107). With a marked preference for the literature of the present, younger scholars embraced the "exceptional and risky" (Schwarz, *Keine Zeit* 256). They strove for a higher level of scholarly achievement and often presented their work with essayistic brilliance. In this, they respected the stricter standards set by the older refugees, men like Oskar Seidlin, Bernhard Blume, and Hans Sperber, who arrived in the 1930s and had by now begun to set the tone in German departments across the country, greatly influencing not only the second generation of refugees but also American-born Germanists. Also of great importance for the modernization of German departments, the American-born Germanists included scholars like Stuart Atkins, Henry Hatfield, Harold Jantz, Walter Silz, Blake Lee Spahr, Hermann Weigand, and Frank Wood, as well as younger scholars like Theodore M. Andersson, David Bathrick, Jeffrey Sammons, Theodore Ziolkowski, and Jack Zipes.

The collective influence of these scholars is more difficult to gauge. Fewer of them have written memoirs, and their stories are less dramatically narratives of displacement. Yet they accelerated the trend toward higher scholarly standards that developed in the postwar period. Partly, this acceleration had to do with the general change throughout the American academy, which underwent rapid professionalization in the 1950s, transforming American universities into unparalleled centers of scholarly innovation. Partly, these higher standards were a function of greater mobility; American-born Germanists could spend more time abroad in German manuscript collections (a few of these collections even made their way to the United States). Consequently, some of the best work of this generation consisted of studies of authors and their texts based on original investigation of correspondence, diaries, and manuscripts. These scholars also translated and wrote a number of important works on exiled authors, in particular Thomas Mann. Taken together, and perhaps for the first time, a significant group of American-born Germanists wrote books and articles in the field of German literature that could lay claim to fundamental originality.

External circumstances established the parameters in which the modernization of American German departments occurred (Zeydel, "Teaching . . . to the Present" 367–83). After the United States entered the war in 1941, there was a great demand for native speakers of German in the Army Specialized Training Programs (ASTP), in which American officers were given intensive language training to prepare them for the war effort in Europe. In the postwar period, the GI Bill of 1947, the onset of the cold war, and the Sputnik shock of 1957 encouraged the expansion of colleges and universities in general and foreign languages in particular. With the National Defense Education Act (NDEA) of 1958, the United States federal government provided another powerful financial impetus for the growth of foreign language departments, spending roughly $30 million by 1960. In order to supply the newly expanded language programs with faculty members, existing graduate programs were expanded and new graduate programs called into existence. For the field of Germanics, this development meant that the period from 1942 to 1970 was marked by considerably more auspicious employment opportunities as well as enhanced prestige for the humanities in general.

The change was not only quantitative. The influx of refugees, especially Jews from Central Europe, made American Germanics more cosmopolitan, more interdisciplinary, and more oriented to the present. This shift in turn altered not only the constellation of German departments but also the range of possible subject matters in the field of Germanics. But from the moment of the collapse in Europe, the field had been contested terrain. In a 1945 German-language essay published in *PMLA*, Karl Viëtor, a non-Jewish immigrant and Kuno Francke Professor of German at Harvard, argued for the return to a study of the purely aesthetic dimension of the German classical tradition. In Viëtor's opinion, American Germanists should "pass on to our barren times the timeless truths of the great authors and poets," for no less than "the survival of European culture was at stake" ("Deutsche Literaturgeschichte" 916). For Viëtor, the point of reference was still Europe, and more specifically Germany. In the same year, Leo Spitzer, a Jewish refugee teaching at Johns Hopkins, responded to Viëtor by arguing for a different approach. German literature departments, he maintained, had become "foreign enclaves" with little contact to other disciplines and with little influence on the life of the American academy (477). This isolation was one problem. A second was that, in Spitzer's words, "there was no criticism from the outside" (476). He envisioned an American Germanics that could revise "German axioms," bring a different perspective to the study of German literature, and flourish in the specifically American—and for him that meant cosmopolitan and comparative—context of American universities (477).

To some extent, American Germanists did in fact develop a criticism from the outside, even if it was not as comparative as Spitzer had hoped. In this endeavor, the refugees were again instrumental. As authors of dissertations, books, articles, translations, and course books, they edged out many of the minor figures of the older canon (e.g., Paul Ernst, Kolbenheyer, Miegel, Stehr, and Wiechert) and replaced them with the authors of modernist literature. The move proved momentous. Until the 1950s, few professors of German literature had thought the great authors of the twentieth century (save Gerhart Haupt-mann and Thomas Mann) to be worthy of academic study. Now Schnitzler, Hofmannsthal, Musil, Rilke, Hesse, Kafka, and the expressionists were placed at the center of study. Similarly, the refugees developed a veritable subfield for the study of exile authors: Richard Beer-Hoffmann, Stefan Zweig, Hermann Broch, Franz Werfel, Joseph Roth, and Thomas Mann.

The refugees also confronted the "deficit in cosmopolitan horizon" among the traditional Germanists with methodological innovation (Demetz, "150 Jahre" 176). Drawing from their personal background, a number of refugees, including Schwarz, Remak, Vordtriede, and Demetz, pursued explicitly com-parative topics. In this, they profited from the burgeoning American field of comparative literature, founded by two emigrant scholars of Romance lan-guages, Spitzer and Erich Auerbach, as well as by René Wellek. With Austin Warren, Wellek had published an epoch-making book, *Theory of Literature* (1949), which constituted a symbiosis of the innovations of the Prague lin-guistic circle with approaches to literature that privileged the analysis of form. The personal interest in modern literature also drew methodological sustenance from the New Criticism, then flourishing in American English departments, as well as from German text-immanent approaches to literature, which empha-sized the apolitical and aesthetic dimension of what Wolfgang Kayser called "das sprachliche Kunstwerk" ("the linguistic work of art") and Emil Staiger "die Kunst der Interpretation" ("the art of interpretation").

To subsequent generations, the emphasis on the intrinsic values of a work would seem apolitical (Berghahn, "Wortkunst"). But in the context of Ger-manics in the 1950s, it had two salutary effects. First, it liberated younger scholars from the chains of the pedantic and often positivist biographical ap-proaches of the old guard. Second, it freed them from the fetters of the synthetic and extrinsic method of German *Geistesgeschichte*. This method had appealed to the "soul of the German nation" in adjudicating the value of a literary work and thus had opened itself to contamination with National Socialist ideas. In this context, German literature became tainted as well. By emphasizing the intrinsic values of a work (values resistant to history) and by placing works of literature in a universal (and not a national) context, a younger generation of scholars sought to save the great works of German literature from the all-too-political tar brush of the recent past.

The methodological turn was deeply influenced by political considerations, even as it allowed young critics to escape politics. As the cold war deepened and the McCarthy era set in, this escape was especially welcome, since Jews and recent immigrants were often suspected of leftist sympathies. Lyman Bradley, the chair of German at NYU, had been imprisoned for refusing to cede information to the House Un-American Activities Committee concerning refugees and was subsequently fired from his tenured position. Similarly, Harry Slochower, who had taught at Brooklyn College, was fired in 1952 for alleged Communist activities (Hoecherl-Alden, "Germanisten" 464–69).

In this atmosphere, the question of one's Jewishness was also muted. Only recently have scholars begun to address this issue; the writings of Ruth Angress (Klüger) and Egon Schwarz (*Keine Zeit*) in the late 1970s represent initial forays. For many years, Harry Zohn, who had taught at Brandeis since 1951, seemed like an isolated beacon emphasizing the specifically Jewish tradition in German literature. In subtle ways, as David Suchoff has recently shown, there were others as well. In 1952 Erich Heller published *The Disinherited Mind*, a collection of essays on Burckhardt, Spengler, Nietzsche, Rilke, Kafka, and Karl Kraus. For a whole generation, Heller's concept of disinheritance opened a space for an approach to German literature and culture that attempted to overcome "the cultural setbacks of the last war" and therefore to bring Jewish authors back into the mainstream of the German literary and philosophical tradition (J. P. Stern qtd. in Suchoff 395). Reinforced by the exigencies of the cold war and by the threats of McCarthyism, public silence was the most prevalent response to the Holocaust. With the appearance of the *Disinherited Mind* this silence began, however tentatively, to crack. According to Suchoff, Heller's work evoked the Holocaust "by analogy" but without naming "the unparalleled catastrophe of modernity by its name" (395). Equally important was the work of Heinz Politzer, who came to the United States in 1947 via Israel. In his dissertation on Heine and Börne, completed in 1950, Politzer saw Jewish assimilation as a fundamental Jewish German paradox. But by 1962, with his publication of *Franz Kafka: Parable and Paradox*, Politzer universalized the dialectical tension of assimilation as a problem of identity central to the human condition *eo ipso* (Suchoff 399).

For this generation of refugees, the concept of a universal aesthetics was crucial to their identity as representatives of the "other Germany." Looking back, Remak valued these efforts as the preservation of "values in the foreign land that had been sullied at home" (190). The values that the refugees defended were the values of nineteenth-century, middle-class culture: classical aesthetics and high art conceived, not without arrogance, in contrast to American mass culture. In later years, this stance would be criticized as aesthetically conservative, as a nostalgic and timid preference for Goethe over Lessing, Thomas Mann over Döblin or Brecht. But in the immediate postwar years, this preference—the values it represented and the institutional battles fought in its name—was a starting point for an intellectually rejuvenated, increasingly cosmopolitan Germanics in the United States.

The intensification of contacts to Germany through travel, exchange

Table 1

The Expansion of German Departments, in Faculty Positions

University	1942 Total (tenured)	1959 Total (tenured)	1969 Total (tenured)
Harvard	10 (4)	10 (4)	12 (7)
Yale	9 (5)	11 (6)	14 (6)
Columbia	11 (6)	19 (6)	21 (9)
Stanford	8 (4)	7 (6)	13 (7)
Wisconsin	10 (6)	11 (7)	22 (14)
Ohio State	9 (4)	12 (6)	22 (9)
Indiana	8 (1)	10 (6)	31 (18)
Berkeley	11 (8)	17 (11)	19 (10)

(Source: *Monatshefte*)

programs, and guest professorships paved the way for a second wave of immigration. This wave arrived in the wake of the Sputnik shock and consisted of two groups. The first group comprised people who had already completed their doctorates at a German university: scholars such as Sigrid Bauschinger, Ernst Behler, Klaus Berghahn, Michael Curschmann, Reinhold Grimm, Karl S. Guthke, Jost Hermand, Peter Uwe Hohendahl, Andreas Huyssen, Wulf Köpke, Kurt Mueller-Vollmer, Katharina Mommsen, and Frank Trommler. The second group comprised academics who had begun their education in Germany and completed it in the United States: Erhard Bahr, Anton Kaes, Paul M. Lützeler, Ursula Mahlendorf, Rainer Nägele, Hans Vaget, and many others. Their combined impact on the field was greater than that of the refugees from the Third Reich. This impact was partly a matter of sheer numbers. Without the Sputnik shock and the wave of immigration, the expansion of German departments in the 1960s could not have taken place. That expansion proved substantial, as table 1 suggests.

German departments in traditional private universities increased in size, but the most dramatic increases were in large state universities, and, to some extent, the intellectual center of gravity of the study of German literature shifted in the late 1960s from Harvard and Columbia to places like Madison, Ohio, Indiana, and Berkeley.

In other ways, however, the structure of the professoriat looked remarkably similar to what it was in earlier times. For one, the percentage of women, especially in tenured positions, remained embarrassingly small. By 1969, the German departments at Harvard and Yale had yet to tenure a woman; Stanford, Ohio State, and Indiana had one tenured woman on their respective faculties.

NYU had three women: two associate professors and a full professor. But NYU was an exception. Most women who had made a career in Germanics taught at four-year women's colleges. These women included, among many others, Louise G. Stabenau at Barnard, Erika M. Meyer at Mount Holyoke, Hilde D. Cohn at Swarthmore, Lilian L. Stroebe and Ruth J. Hofrichter at Vassar, and Marianne Thalmann at Wellesley (Nagy, *Women*).

The national composition of German departments also remained largely the same. Ethnic minorities continued to be underrepresented, though this imbalance was not a problem of German alone. More important, the emigrants from German-speaking lands continued to dominate departments. Although there has not been a systematic or quantitative study of this question, impressionistic evidence suggests that Germanics remained what Wulf Köpke has called an "Einwandererwissenschaft" ("Germanistik" 63; "immigrant science").

But unlike earlier refugees, the new immigrants took leave of Germany and its intransigent educational system voluntarily. As Köpke put it, many of them "rubbed up against the traditional *Ordinarien* university, where independence of judgment and conduct often blocked the path to a university career, or they became impatient with the long hard road to the *Habilitation*" (57). Thus it was not the United States per se that drew most of these young academics but, rather, professional opportunities. For a smaller group, the search for their "other" fathers may have also been a motivating factor. "For the Germanists who began their academic careers in the United States in the sixties," Trommler recently recounted, "there was a generation of established emigrants who were intellectually of special interest, among them Heinz Politzer, Bernhard Blume, Erich Heller, Henry Remak, and Hans Eichner" (Trommler qtd. in "Auszüge" 115). These men exerted a pull on young German scholars wishing to escape the institutional and intellectual confines of Germany in the early 1960s. Hinrich Seeba, for example, was drawn to Berkeley by the possibility of working with Heinz Politzer ("Cultural Poetics" 1). The attraction may have reflected a sense that there was something amiss in the field of German literature in Germany. In this context, it bears remembering that Germanists did not publicly discuss, until the Germanistentag of 1966, the complicity of the field in the policies of National Socialism. The problem, however, inhered not only in the field's complicity but also in its methodological backwardness. Conversely, a number of émigré scholars cultivated innovative literary analysis beyond anything found at German universities (Trommler qtd. in "Auszüge" 115). Still, and precisely in its emphasis on its critical distance from Germany, the second wave of immigrants remained in language, method, and scholarly style beholden to the Federal Republic of Germany. Most of the new immigrants also published in German. Conversely, ties to the Federal Republic often implied a distanced relation to the host nation and institution.

This distance powerfully influenced the field. For one, it meant the continued modus of "splendid isolation" of Germanics both in the American academy and in the broader American literary public (Lange, "Thoughts" 10). Since its first mention in Fife's MLA address in 1944 ("Nationalism"), the topos of "splendid isolation" was never completely free of the charge of German preponderance in the field (Henry Schmidt, "What Is Oppositional Criticism?"; Van Cleve and Willson 19–23). On the one hand, Germans had invigorated the study of German literature intellectually. On the other, as the more caustic critics pointed out, there were not a few in this wave of immigrants who resembled "mediocre guest workers content to rest at the level of their Gymnasium education" (Trommler, "Einleitung" 31).

In their attempts to confront the past, both generations of immigrants, those who had fled Nazi Germany and those who came to the United States in the 1960s, shared something: their lives and their careers had been shaped by National Socialism. Yet the way in which the past affected the profession was never simple. For the generation of Germanists in the 1960s, the Eichmann trial in Jerusalem in 1961 and the Auschwitz trials in Frankfurt in 1963 were historical episodes of great moment. So too were the American civil rights movement and the demonstrations against the Vietnam War. Coupled with the deepening politicization and democratization of the universities, these historical forces framed the experience of the new immigrants as well as that of American-born Germanists now coming of academic age. These developments brought an end to Germanics as traditionally conceived (Sander, "Wohin treibt"; H. Mayer; Mueller-Vollmer, "Differenzierung" 152–56).

As in the past, the challenge to reflect critically on scholarly methods did not occur without a struggle. But text-immanent (*werkimmanent*) approaches to literature gradually ceded ground to critical, contextual, and often highly political agendas that appropriated the language of sociology, psychoanalysis, and Marxism. As Jost Hermand argued in his influential work *Synthetisches Interpretieren* (1968), the new direction would entail a democratizing pluralism of method. For young scholars in the 1960s, the new approach opened normative possibilities and broadened the spectrum of what might be studied. Political literature, especially left-liberal or socialist, made its way into the canon. Brecht and Seghers, not Mann and Werfel, were suddenly at the center of twentieth-century literature. One studied Lessing and Wieland with renewed vigor, but also the young Jacobins, the revolutionaries of the Vormärz, Young Germany, and the literature of exile. Against an earlier generation's insistence on the value of elite culture, the 1960s generation took on popular literature as a legitimate object of academic study.

But the change was more than just a broadening of the category of acceptable texts. This wave of immigration also brought the theorists of the Frankfurt school with it, in particular Max Horkheimer and Adorno, Georg Lukács and Herbert Marcuse (and later Walter Benjamin). At home among the "critical left," the 1960s generation eagerly consumed the classics of a peculiarly German version of cultural Marxism (e.g., Ernst Bloch, Siegfried Kracauer, Hans Mayer, Peter Weiss), from which one could deduce a socially transformative role for culture generally and Germanics specifically. Their ideological proclivities reflected the specific valences of their confrontation with their German past. For this generation, what marked and marred the middle years of the twentieth century was not anti-Semitism per se and not totalitarianism. Rather, Nazism was but a variant of fascism. The concept of fascism served a seminal function, for it allowed the 1960s generation to construct the Third Reich as a product of the contradictions of capitalism and—more germane for their culture critique—of the commercialized mass culture of advanced capitalism (which the United States epitomized). In the eyes of leading Germanists like Hermand, the concept of fascism demonstrated that a critical continuity existed between the Nazi period and the Federal Republic (not to say the United States). Consequently, political action, especially in the cultural realm, meant the continuation of an antifascist struggle.

The theoretical coordinates of the new immigrants had considerable bearing on the study of literature. If the refugees of the 1940s and 1950s eschewed the instrumentalization of literature for political purposes, the new Germanists of the late 1960s often applauded literature, however mediocre its formal contents, that served the class struggle, undermined oppressive regimes (unless those regimes were socialist), and pointed up contradictions in society.

The new direction established itself in an institutional context. The central public forums that reshaped the field included the Wisconsin Workshops organized by Reinhold Grimm and Hermand at Madison, the conferences at Washington University in Saint Louis, and the conferences organized by Wolfgang Paulsen at the University of Massachusetts, Amherst. In 1970, for example, the Wisconsin Workshop was organized around the topic "Klassik-Legende"—a polemical thrust clearly directed against the older generation.

The differences between the two generations should not be exaggerated. There were members of the younger generation, like Trommler and Seeba, who were also drawn by the theoretical work of the older generation and who served as mediators between the two. Moreover, there were plenty of immigrants who came to the United States for professional opportunities, and many of them watched the methodological struggles from the sidelines. Finally, a new generation of Germanists, either born or raised in the United States, also entered the field in the 1960s. Some, like Sander Gilman, have even had a large impact on the field, though not until the 1980s. Despite these caveats, the line dividing the two waves of immigration was sharp, often impermeable, and formative for the field of Germanics in the late 1960s.

The line was sharp because the division concerned the past and who claimed it. From the conclusion to one of Hermand's recently published review articles, one can sense just how barbed this division sometimes seemed. According to Hermand, it was

> less the exiles, who still stood under the shock of experience and who sought cultural reassurance among the literary masterworks of the past, and more the second generation, who communicated to the American public an impression of what it means to be a Leftist and/or a Jew—and for this reason to be driven into exile. ("Germanistik" 745)

The second generation was with few exceptions not Jewish, and the appropriation of the status of the Jew as pariah must in this context remain problematic, especially when directed against the first generation of exiles, Jews being prominent among them. Here the politics of identification reveals a great deal. "Between us and Weimar lies Buchenwald," Richard Alewyn famously put it in his inaugural address in 1949 (686). Buchenwald's geographic proximity to Goethe's Weimar became a metonym for the relation of literature to the immediate past. Like all tropes, metonyms are neither innocent nor without ambivalence. Buchenwald was not an extermination camp, and so it could not easily direct attention to the full dimension of the catastrophe. Yet the Holocaust cast a deeper shadow on the first generation of exiles than some representatives of the second generation have allowed, even if the silences of the first generation were in retrospect conspicuous. For the second generation, Buchenwald was also important. A concentration camp prominent in antifascist mythmaking, Buchenwald was a site where, at least initially, the Nazis incarcerated and killed more political prisoners than Jews. It was therefore a place where one could imagine the persecution of German antifascists in conjunction with the Jewish Holocaust. In this sense too, Buchenwald was not Chelmno, Belzec, Sobibor, Majdanek, or Auschwitz.

Note

1 The Frauenplan is the location of Goethe's house in Weimar. Ettersberg is the site of the Buchenwald concentration camp.

Democratization of the Profession

Women and Minorities in German, 1971–2000

ARLENE A. TERAOKA

Democracy, at least in principle, is a form of government based on representation. It embodies the idea of political, social, or even economic equality. It is defined by the absence or disavowal of hereditary or arbitrary class distinctions or privileges. The use of the word *democratization* with regard to German studies of the last three decades of the twentieth century implies that we have moved toward a faculty profile that reflects the face of graduate education in our field at the very least, if not the face of American higher education or of the general population of the United States. Further, *democratization* projects an image of a profession historically held together by a telos of German nationhood (Hohendahl, "Past" 78) and now open to diverse goals, constituencies, methods, and concerns. I doubt anyone would question, publicly at any rate, that this is the German studies to which we aspire. The issue is whether and to what extent the process of democratization has actually occurred.

As one of only a handful of women in German who also belong to a racial minority, I'd like to begin with some facts about my own history in German studies, which coincides nearly exactly with the decades of our self-proclaimed democratization. Are tales such as mine simply token success stories that belie the premises of their own success? Or do they represent a new or emerging professional profile for German studies in this country?

I entered Yale University in the fall of 1972. Yale had begun to accept women undergraduates in 1969; it was also actively recruiting Asian Americans and other minorities. I was one of about three hundred women in a freshman class still big enough to fulfill Yale's promise to produce its thousand male leaders a year. As was the trend at colleges and universities across the country, there was no foreign language requirement in effect. Of the thirty-seven courses I took as an undergraduate, mostly in literature and philosophy, eight were taught by women. Strikingly, half the women faculty members with whom I studied were in German. Of the six courses I took in German literature, three were taught by female instructors (one later became an assistant professor), one was taught by a male African American assistant professor, and one was taught by the department's sole female full professor, who had recently been hired from Germany.

I did my graduate work at Stanford from 1976 to 1983. This was the period in which the field of German expanded into areas such as GDR literature, women's literature, and film. I would eventually write my dissertation on an East German playwright and identify myself as a specialist in GDR studies. The overwhelming majority of graduate students in my department were women. But our graduate faculty consisted of seven male professors, one female full professor from Germany (do we begin to detect a pattern?), and one female adjunct who taught language courses; at the nonprofessorial rank there were four lecturers, three of whom were women. I would be hard-pressed to name texts by women that I was required to read; it wasn't much, if anything at all, beyond Mme de Staël's *De l'Allemagne*, Droste-Hülshoff's *Die Judenbuche*, and a poem by Catharina Regina von Greiffenberg. We read with profit, in a course introducing us to the field of German literary studies, the work of Emil Staiger, René Wellek, Roman Jakobson, and E. D. Hirsch, Jr. In my last year of dissertation work, Sara Lennox visited Stanford and offered a course on the women's movement, but my own graduate course work, both in and outside the department, was completed with male faculty members, except for the course on teaching methods.

In 1983 I began a tenure-track position as assistant professor at the University of Washington. The department was 70% tenured and 80% male. The one tenured woman (definitely a pattern) was Diana Behler, who served as department chair. In 1985, in order to ease my bicoastal commute, I left Washington for a tenure-track position at Princeton University. There, the only other woman, and again the only tenured woman (let us call it a rule), in the German department was its chair, Ruth Angress, who would resign the next year. In my first two years at Princeton, two other female assistant professors were hired; we were the most junior members of the German faculty and taught mostly language courses. Two of us were in commuting marriages, and our departures from campus were taken as indications of our lack of commitment. All three of us resigned before coming up for tenure.

In 1989 I moved to a tenured associate professorship at the University of Minnesota. There I found a powerful feminist colleague and friend in Ruth-

Ellen Boetcher Joeres. The department as a whole accommodated my needs as I became the mother of two children. After four years, my spouse was hired, as the result of a national search. (I am aware of the gender-based privileges that have worked at times to my advantage and that many others cannot ply.) In 2000 over 40% of the faculty in German at Minnesota—three of seven full professors and all three assistant professors—were women. To bring this story to a temporary close, in that year I became the first woman chair in the hundred-year history of my department and probably the first minority woman chair of a German PhD program in this country.

Did the face of the profession change from the mid-1970s, when I studied German literature at Yale, to the end of the twentieth century, when women in German were established as senior professors and department chairs, as deans, and even as provosts in their universities? When the question is put in these terms, the answer is yes. But I can't help but wonder whether this perception is based on the achievements of a relatively small group of women and whether this sentiment is expressed primarily by members of the professoriat who speak from positions of distinction. The case for democratization is less clear-cut when we look at large-scale statistics and at our lower and nonprofessorial ranks rather than at individuals or even individual programs. My history in German studies, in other words, may be more an anomaly than an indication of discipline-wide structural and attitudinal change.

The canonical historical account of German studies in the United States goes, in broad strokes, like this. For decades the field was defined and dominated by native German male émigrés (Bathrick, "On Leaving"; Henry Schmidt, "What Is Oppositional Criticism?").[1] Beginning in the 1930s, talented refugees from both the political left and right cultivated a study of German literature that sought to promote humanistic ideals and a classical vision of German culture unsullied by national politics. Their preoccupation with the interpretation of canonical texts and with valued traditions of the German past led to a new eminence of German literary scholarship in this country; it also led to the cultural and social isolation of Germanists in the changing American university. Then the social and political upheaval brought by the civil rights movement, the Vietnam War, and the women's movement, resulting in the establishment of academic disciplines such as women's studies, ethnic studies, and Afro-American studies, forced a critical remodeling of German literary studies as well. German departments in the 1970s, faced with declining enrollments caused by the widespread elimination of foreign language requirements, expanded their offerings to include cultural history and literature in translation. The profile of the profession was reshaped by a generation of politically committed American scholars who moved beyond the German national literary canon into areas such as GDR literature, Jewish literature, women's literature, and film—specializations that distinguish the discipline even today from

Germanistik in Germany. Organizations such as Women in German (est. 1974) and the German Studies Association (1976) and journals such as *New German Critique* (1973) solidified the change. Indeed, the shift in the profession that began in the early 1970s was so momentous that scholars taking stock of the field in the 1990s could speak in broad terms of our "feminization," "Americanization," and "democratization" (Friedrichsmeyer and Herminghouse, "Towards an American Germanics?"; Lennox, "Feminisms"; V. Nollendorfs, "Out of *Germanistik*"; Kacandes 20–21).

My discontent with this narrative is that it is compelling in limited contexts. (McCarthy expresses reservations and cautions as well ["Double Optics"].) There are in fact more American-born or American-trained scholars in German departments across the country; there are more women, in both prominence and number, in the field; and the profile of scholarship in German studies is more diverse, in the theories it adopts and in the materials it investigates, than ever before. Yet the disproportionate hiring of women PhDs in nonprofessorial positions, the virtual absence of minority faculty members, and the continued dominance of native German scholars all point to a troubling continuity rather than to a change in the direction of democratization and openness.

To begin, as we all know, the field of German has faced falling enrollments nationwide over the last three decades; this is probably the single most important factor affecting the curriculum, the staffing, and the stature of the field. After reaching a peak in the late 1960s, German-language enrollments sank from about 200,000 in 1970 to 96,000 in 1995 (Brod and Huber [1997]). The MLA's fall 1998 survey showed a further decline of 7.5% since 1995, at a time when institutions reported a record-high total of registrations in ancient and modern languages ("MLA's Fall 1998 Survey"). German has suffered greater losses over the last thirty years than any of the other leading modern foreign languages.

Interestingly, the halving of German enrollments has had only a moderate effect on faculty positions. The "Personalia" information reported by *Monatshefte* indicates a steady increase in the number of German departments between 1971 and 1999 and a fluctuating number of faculty positions (around 1,500) that peaked in the early 1990s and declined 18% between 1992 and 1999 (see app., table 1). Notably, the profile of the profession according to faculty rank has remained relatively constant over the last two decades: since the early 1980s, tenured professors have made up about 65% of the faculty in German departments, tenure-track assistant professors have accounted for another 20%, and temporary or nonprofessorial faculty members have constituted the remaining 15%.

The *Monatshefte* listings indicate that women have made progress in achieving proportional (or, rather, a less disproportional) representation. In 1999 one in three tenured professors was a woman, compared with one in nine in 1971; in 1999 women held half of all tenure-track positions, up from one-fourth of assistant professorships in 1971. Overall, their numbers in tenured and tenure-track faculty positions doubled: women occupied 17% of these ranks in 1971 and 38% in 1999. (See B. Huber, "Women," on the underrepresentation of women at the full professor level in modern languages throughout the 1980s.) However, when compared with the increased percentages of PhD degrees and of nonprofessorial positions awarded to women over this same period, the progress is less impressive. In 1971 women earned 35% of PhDs and made up 42% of nonprofessorial faculty and 21% of faculty overall; in 1999 they earned 61% of PhDs, held 75% of nonprofessorial positions, and comprised 43% of total German faculty. In other words, relative to their representation among finished PhDs, women have made little if any progress as faculty members: they are being hired in the same low proportions relative to their availability and disproportionately in lower-paid non-tenure-track positions, now as they were nearly three decades ago.[2] Their progress in actual numbers might in fact coincide more with the decrease in the number of men earning PhDs—97 in 1971, only 29 in 1999—than it does with any attitudinal change in the profession. It was numbers similar to these that led Gretchen Wiesehan to speak in the late 1980s of the "myth of feminization" in our field that "fosters complacency by promising women that the process of improvement is already under way" (28). Indeed, as she points out, "this so-called trend is not supported by the employment data" (29).

Also frustrating is the slow pace of improvement in our gender profile. In the 1980s, men made up two-thirds of German faculty; throughout the 1990s, they remained steady at about 60%. In the two decades from 1980 to 1999, the proportion of women increased from 28% to 43% of German faculty. At this rate of change—15% over twenty years—it would take another two decades for women to attain the 60% of faculty positions proportional to their current 60% of degrees earned. To take another measure: tenured men made up 43% of German faculty in 1971, 50% of German faculty in the 1980s, and about 45% of German faculty throughout the 1990s—a small overall change in their representation and institutional dominance over the last three decades. Discontent and frustration are expressed as well in different essays regarding the resistance of German studies to change (Kuhn; Fries qtd. in McCarthy, "Double Optics" 2; Joeres). There is a noticeable split in the field between Germanists who celebrate a sense of progress and those who vent criticism. In what follows I suggest an explanation for this paradox.

In the light of these slow-changing baselines, I suspect that the perceived feminization, Americanization, or democratization of German studies is more accurately a top-down phenomenon. That is, these changes occur most visibly among faculty members at the top of the field rather than among the far larger numbers of faculty members in lower-level positions, in lower-ranked departments or institutions, and in undergraduate German-language programs.

My first supporting data follow in a distinguished but unorthodox tradition initiated by Jeffrey Sammons and continued by Henry Schmidt. In 1976, in an essay criticizing the "invisibility" of German scholars in American scholarly life, Sammons presented the results of a private experiment in which he listed the twenty outstanding Germanists in North America, the selection based on "their creativity, their productivity, and their accomplishments on the forward edge of scholarship in our field" ("Some Considerations" 17). Fourteen of the 20, and 8 of the 10 in the top half of the list, he discovered, habitually wrote in German and published abroad. A decade later Schmidt offered similar evidence of the dominance of German immigrants in the discipline: in his private lists of the most prominent Germanists in the United States, native Germans accounted for 75% of the top 12, 71% of the top 24, and 60% of the top 104. All but one (92%) of the first 12, 88% of the top 24, and 83% of the 104 leading Germanists were men ("Wissenschaft" 71). My own lists, which follow Schmidt's by another decade, include one woman and 4 Americans among the 10 leading German studies scholars. Of 30 top scholars, 8 are women and 14 were born in the United States; of 100 scholars, 42 are women and 49 were born in the United States.

Assuming some sort of useful judgment on the part of the three people possessed to produce such lists, we can indeed observe a changing profile of German studies. Where for two decades three out of four of the dominant scholars in the field had been native Germans, the 1990s brought American-born scholars into prominence, in numbers nearly equal to those of native Germans. Where women made up slightly over 10% of the leading faculty members through the 1980s, their representation among 30 distinguished names is now more than doubled. However, there is still only one woman included in two of the three lists of the ten to twelve most prominent scholars in the field (Sammons offers no information on gender distribution), and the percentage of women scholars among the top 30 in my current list (27%) falls significantly below the 43% of women among German faculty members as a whole reported in *Monatshefte* in 1999. In short, women are still not present in representative numbers at the most distinguished levels of our field; there are indeed more women at the top, but there are still too few of them. This finding suggests that our perception of the feminization of German studies rests disproportionately on the presence of a group of women scholars who have gained professional recognition but who, in sheer numbers, remain a minority in the field.

We can survey the top in a different way, following another distinguished example, this time that of Jeannine Blackwell, who compiled data on faculty members at the top twenty degree-producing programs in German in 1983 ("Turf Management"; see app., table 2). Blackwell showed that in the early 1980s, at a time when women were earning over half the PhDs in German, they made up 13% of full professors, 22% of associate professors, and 39% of assistant professors in the top German graduate programs in the country. My later numbers for these departments show a 100% increase in women at the tenured ranks: women made up 26% of full professors and 46% of associate professors in these programs in 1998. Further, between 1983 and 1998, tenured faculty lines in the top departments were reduced by 9%, with losses borne largely by men. The number of tenured men fell 27% over the fifteen-year period, while women in the tenured ranks nearly doubled their number. Even with these shifts, however, tenured men outnumbered tenured women in 1998 by a factor of two (130 to 61). The greatest losses were incurred by men at the associate professor level, where their number decreased 41% (from 49 to 29) at the same time that the number of women associate professors increased nearly 80% (from 14 to 25). While the presence of women in tenured ranks grew considerably—feminization at the top—the numbers for assistant professors present a regressive picture. Over the same fifteen-year period, the number of tenure-track positions in the top programs decreased 19%, affecting the hiring of men and of women in equal proportion. At the same time, the number of nonprofessorial positions increased slightly, with a higher proportion of these positions occupied by women in 1998 compared with 1983. The only growth at the lower ranks, in other words, has been for women hired in nonprofessorial positions. This is not a new trend or one specific to German. Bettina Huber reports that "63% of the total growth in faculty numbers [in the modern languages] between 1970 and 1985 was due to increases in the number of part-time employees"; further, these employees were "disproportionately likely to be women" ("Women" 60).

Table 3 in the appendix provides information on the distribution in 1998 of men and women in top departments according to their country of birth. This categorizing raises a contentious point, since this one factor does not do justice to the complexities of biography and self-identity among German studies faculty members. Nonetheless, country of birth and native language have a bearing on how scholars and their careers are judged and promoted in the profession at large (on this point, see Hohendahl, "American-German Divide"; Tatlock, "Response"); consider especially our insistence on native or near-native fluency as a prerequisite for academic employment. In this context, it is notable that faculty members in the top programs tend to be more "American" than German studies faculty members nationwide. Of 234 faculty members, 57% (133) were born in the United States; it is 51% nationally (Van Cleve and Willson 90). Further, American men dominate the top programs: 40% of the 234 professors are American males, 81% of whom are tenured and 62% of whom are tenured at the full professor rank. German-born men make up the next largest group overall, with 21% of faculty positions, 63% of which are at the full professor rank; in the top ten graduate programs, 78% of the German men are full professors.

American-born women constitute only 17% of the professorial faculty in the top programs, spread relatively evenly over the three ranks. The number of German-born women professors is roughly half that of the American-born women, but they are clustered at the full professor rank. The smallest constituency is the group of faculty members born in countries other than the United States, East and West Germany, Switzerland, and Austria (8.5% of the total); two-thirds of them are women. In sum, in the major PhD-granting programs in German as a whole, two-thirds of the faculty are men; one-third were born in a German-speaking country, and, of these, two out of five are German men at the rank of full professor; finally, one out of every four faculty members in these departments is an American male at the rank of full professor. If we wish to speak of the Americanization of German studies, we should remind ourselves that, at least in terms of the profile of our professoriat, the phenomenon is both hierarchical and gender-specific: it applies most fittingly to senior men in top programs.

Of the 58 positions in the top departments at the rank of assistant professor, 62% are held by men, which shows a continuing disproportion in gender representation among new hires. Of the assistant professorships, 31% are held by American men, 21% by German men, 19% by American women, 9% by German women, and 10% by foreign persons born in non-German-speaking countries. In terms of new hires in prestigious departments, American women are outnumbered by American men and are hired in numbers on par with those of German men. Assuming equal rates of tenure success and maintenance of faculty lines, these figures suggest that German-born faculty members, the majority of them men, will continue to constitute a third of the faculty in the top echelon of our profession. (German men outnumber German women by 3:1 at the full professor rank and by more than 2:1 at the assistant professor level.) To cite further evidence of the continued strength of the native German presence in our field: Huber reported in 1993 that native speakers accounted for 28% of graduate students in German and that 65% of graduate courses in German departments were taught in the target language ("Recent and Anticipated Growth" 29).[3] This continuing commitment to the ideal of the native German may well be a factor in our abysmal record of minority recruitment, to which I now turn.

In 1990, AATG president Renate Schulz convened an ad hoc committee to examine the status of minorities in German; three years later, the organization established a standing committee on the recruitment and retention of minorities in the field. In its mission statement the ad hoc committee affirmed "the diversity of our citizenry" and recognized the responsibility of the AATG "to ensure the study of German by a diverse American population taught by a profession whose members themselves reflect the racial and ethnic composition of our nation" (Peters et al. 97). But the available numbers show an enormous gap between this goal and the present reality. There is a striking discrepancy between our ideal of demographic diversity and the hiring practices of our discipline, which continue to measure its candidates, perhaps unaware of the bias that using this criterion promotes, against the standard of native fluency. As Lee Wilberschied and Jean-Louis Dassier point out, the native or near-native ideal defines cultural assimilation or socialization in the target language and society as a prerequisite for success. In the light of the treatment often accorded to minorities in German society, this prerequisite places a difficult if not unconscionable obstacle in the path of nonwhite students hoping to enter the field.

Summarizing the results of the 1992 AATG membership survey, Schulz reported that an overwhelming 98% of all respondents—37% of whom were college and university faculty members—listed themselves as white ("Profile" 227). Only 16 German teachers and faculty members identified themselves as African American, 10 as Native American, 9 as Asian or Pacific Islander, 4 as Hispanic, and 23 as "other"—for a total of 62 minority individuals (1.8%) among 3,465 respondents. (Here and elsewhere I use the ethnic-racial categories of the study I am discussing.) Further, the lack of racial diversity among German faculty members was mirrored in the lack of diversity in German classrooms, where at best minority students made up less than 10% of enrollments for half our teachers (232). This pattern stands in sharp contrast to the racial makeup of the general population. As George Peters points out, in the mid-to-late 1980s blacks and Hispanics made up about 20% of the United States population, approximately 14% of undergraduate students, 8% of graduate students, 8% of college and university faculty members, and 6% of postsecondary faculty members in English and foreign languages—compared with 0.6% for German teachers at all instructional levels (6; see also Huber, "Incorporating"). In the mid-1990s, minorities made up 36% of United States public elementary and secondary school students, 26% of undergraduates, 16% of graduate students, 9% of PhDs in the humanities awarded to United States citizens, 13% of full-time college and university faculty members, and 24% of full-time instructional faculty and staff members in foreign languages (*Minorities in Higher Educ.*, tables 6, 19, 20; *Digest of Educ. Statistics* [1999], tables 45 and 229)—this in contrast to an estimated 1–2% of minority faculty members in German studies.

Robert Fikes, Jr., lists 32 black Germanists earning PhD degrees between 1920 and 2000, with 24 earning degrees since 1971. The high point for minority PhDs occurred in the 1970s, with 13 black Germanists completing their graduate degrees and receiving academic appointments; in contrast, only 11 PhDs were granted to black Germanists in the 1980s and 1990s. Of the 24 black Germanists since 1971, 14 are listed in either the 1995 *DAAD / Monatshefte Directory* or the 1999 *Monatshefte* "Personalia" rolls, only 4 of them with PhDs from the 1980s or 1990s. For information on other minority groups in German studies, I gathered names from eight professional colleagues, all of them interested in minority issues in German. The result was a list of 9 minority faculty members in PhD-granting German programs (5 African Americans, 3 Asian Americans, 1 Hispanic), 4 minority faculty members in German programs granting a BA or MA (3 African Americans, 1 Asian American), and 4 faculty members (all African Americans) whose research falls in German studies but who work in departments other than German. The cumulative list of minority faculty members from Fikes's and my informal survey yields 14 African Americans, 4 Asian Americans, and 1 Hispanic in German; this total of 19 represents 1.4% of the 1,388 faculty members listed in the *Monatshefte* rolls in 1999, a figure not much different from the 2% for minority faculty members in German reported by Demetz in 1982 ("Report" 947).

To put these data in another perspective: reports in *Monatshefte* in 1979 and 1984 provided numbers for minorities enrolled in German graduate programs in the United States and Canada. Of 88 graduate programs responding to the 1979 survey, 20 departments listed 34 minority students: 5 blacks, 23 Asians or Pacific Islanders, 4 Hispanics, and 2 American Indians or Alaskans ("Graduate Programs" 310). Higher numbers were reported five years later for 99 programs, with 16 blacks, 16 Asians or Pacific Islanders, 14 Hispanics, and 1 American Indian or Alaskan enrolled, for a total of 47 minority graduate students in German (V. Nollendorfs and Arness 330). Although Valters Nollendorfs and Carol Arness write that "minorities do not seem to have made major inroads among our professional ranks" (330), the numbers they report are surprisingly high. With 679 master's candidates and 477 doctoral students in German in 1983–84 (312), the 47 minority students constituted 4.1% of the graduate population in German in the early 1980s. What happened to them? Perhaps they were concentrated in MA-only programs; perhaps they never entered, or were not successful in, the nationwide applicant pool for faculty positions. The available data suggest that minorities are, or were, present in our graduate programs, but it is clear that they are not becoming professors of German.

The CIC's 1999 *Directory of Minority PhD and MFA Candidates and Recipients* further documents the absence of minorities among PhD students in competitive programs in German. The directory lists American Indians, African Americans, Mexican Americans, Puerto Ricans, Hispanic Americans, and Asian Americans (this last group only in humanities and social sciences) who are United States citizens and who completed or expected to complete the PhD or MFA degree between 1998 and 2000, in the Big Ten universities and the

University of Chicago. Over a quarter (61, or 27%) of the 222 minority students listed are in fields in the humanities; a third (21, or 34%) of the minority graduate students in humanities are in language, literature, or cultural studies; and none are in German. This fact means that over a three-year period from 1998 to 2000 not one minority student earned a PhD in any of the PhD programs in German in the CIC consortium—these include programs at the University of Chicago, University of Illinois, Indiana University, University of Michigan, University of Minnesota, Ohio State University, and the University of Wisconsin. The CIC data, even in such small numbers, indicate that minority students pursue PhDs and do not shun the humanities for more lucrative fields. Furthermore, the 21 minority doctoral students in literature or cultural studies are not consistently enrolled along ethnic or racial lines—that is, with Hispanics in Spanish or Latin American literature or Asian Americans in Chinese or Japanese.[4] We cannot put forth or accept crass materialist or, worse, "Blut und Boden" ("blood and soil") explanations for the absence of minority students in German. According to statistics published by the United States Department of Education, 13% of PhDs conferred in foreign languages and literatures in 1995–96 were earned by scholars from racial and ethnic minority groups (*Digest of Educ. Statistics* [1999], table 271). But where is our 13% minority population among PhD students in German? Were the numbers in German to correspond to numbers in foreign languages and literatures as a whole, the 87 completed PhDs in German in the United States in 1998 would have included 6 Hispanics, 4 Asian Americans, and 1 black—11 minority PhD recipients in this year alone.

Democratization? Americanization? Feminization? The profile of the German studies professoriat in this country has changed considerably in terms of gender and national origin over the last three decades: there are indeed more women (though not in representative numbers at the top) and more American-born scholars (though disproportionately male ones) in the field. The Americanization and feminization of German studies are hierarchical phenomena. To ignore differences among ranks when describing the increased presence of women or to ignore gender differences in discussing our evolving Americanization is to mask the inequities that still shape our profession. Let us not, to repeat Wiesehan's warning, be lulled into complacency in the belief that improvement is under way. As for the continued absence of minorities in our field, I have no further words. Diversity in German has meant curricular reform at best, not demographic movement. Thus, I can celebrate with others the increased (but still too small) numbers of prominent women in German. I am happy to be working in a department that employs more than one tenured woman. And I am gratified to note an increased scholarly interest in minority literature in Germany. As a minority person, however, I find my field still the lonely place that it has always been.

Notes

1 I wish to acknowledge the expert work of my research assistant Alison Guenther-Pal, who collected the materials needed for this study and formatted my statistical data; any errors in the data I present are my own.

2 The ratio of the percentage of women faculty to the percentage of women PhDs (see table 1) was 6:10 (21:35) in 1971 and 7:10 (43:61) in 1999; the ratio of the percentage of women in nonprofessorial positions to the percentage of women PhDs was 6:5 (42:35) in 1971 and still 6:5 (75:61) in 1999.

3 See also Bullivant's expression of shock at the number and dominance of native Germans in American departments of German.

4 The CIC list includes, for example, an Asian American in classics, an Asian American in seventeenth-century French literature, and an African American specializing in nineteenth-century French poetry.

Appendix

Table 1

United States German Faculty Members by Rank and Gender, 1971–99

	1971	1975	1980	1984	1988	1992	1996	1999
Total departments	187	185	226	267	264	331	344	333
Total faculty	1,573	1,354	1,462	1,585	1,540	1,693	1,464	1,388
Faculty by rank (%)								
tenured	48	57	62	65	66	63	66	65
tenure-track	33	30	26	21	20	20	20	22
other	19	13	12	15	14	17	14	14
Representation of women (%)								
in total faculty	21	23	28	33	36	40	40	43
in tenured faculty	11	14	17	21	24	28	30	33
in tenure-track faculty	24	28	41	45	46	55	52	54
in tenured and tenure-track faculty	17	19	24	27	29	35	35	38
in non-tenure-track faculty	42	54	63	72	78	64	71	75
in total PhDs awarded	35	44	51	52	49	65	58	61
tenured in total faculty	6	8	11	13	16	18	20	21
Representation of men (%)								
in total faculty	79	77	72	67	64	60	60	57
tenured in total faculty	43	49	51	51	50	45	46	43

Source: The *Monatshefte* "Personalia" from 1971 to 1999

Table 2

Male and Female Faculty Members at the Top Twenty PhD-Producing Programs in German, 1983 and 1998

A. Ratio of Male to Female (M/F) by Professorial Rank

University ranked by number of PhDs, 1985–94 (rank in 1983)	Full		Associate		Assistant		Other	
	1983	1998	1983	1998	1983	1998	1983	1998
1 Wisconsin (4)	10/2	9/2	2/0	1/3	4/1	1/2	1/4	0/2
2 UC Berkeley (7)	8/1	9/3	3/1	0/1	3/1	1/0	2/0	0/0
3 Texas (8)	7/2	6/2	6/0	6/2	2/2	2/2/1*	0/0	0/1
4 Princeton (13)	4/1	6/1	2/0	1/0	3/1	1/2	0/1	1/0
5 Harvard (3)	3/2	5/2	0/0	0/1	4/1	1/0	1/3	2/3
6 Yale (9)	4/1	3/2	0/4	0/0	4/0	4/1	0/0	3/4
7 Cornell (18)	9/1	5/3	0/0	1/1	2/1	1/0	1/3	1/5
8 Minnesota	6/1	4/2	2/1	4/1	3/0	0/3	2/0	0/0
9 UCLA (16)	8/0	6/2	0/0	0/1	3/1	1/0	0/1	2/2
10 Johns Hopkins (15)	2/1	4/0	0/0	0/1	2/2	0/1	2/1	1/1
11 Pennsylvania (14)	4/0	3/1	1/0	1/0	1/1	1/1	2/3	0/6
12 Washington U (20)	4/0	3/2	0/1	2/0	3/1	2/2	0/0	0/0
13 Michigan (10)	11/0	4/0	1/1	2/2	3/2	6/2	0/0	0/1
14 Stanford (1)	5/1	3/1	1/0	0/0	1/0	1/2	3/3	3/2
15 U of Washington (5)	4/1	6/3	5/0	1/1	2/2	0/2	0/0	0/0
16 North Carolina (17)	5/1	4/0	1/0	0/3	1/2	2/1	1/1	0/0
17 Ohio State (11)	6/1	2/2	4/4	2/3	2/2	2/1/1*	0/0	0/1
18 Virginia (19)	3/0	4/3	5/0	2/1	3/4	2/0	0/3	0/1
19 Illinois (12)	6/1	3/2	3/2	1/1	1/3	4/0/1*	0/0	1/0
20 Chicago	4/0	5/0	6/0	2/1	0/0	1/0	0/1	0/2
Indiana (2)	13/0	6/2	4/0	1/1	0/2	4/1	1/2	0/1
NYU (6)	2/2	1/1	3/0	2/1	0/1	1/1	1/1	1/0

*Persons whose gender I cannot determine.

B. Summary by Professorial Rank

	Full		Associate		Assistant		Other	
	1983	1998	1983	1998	1983	1998	1983	1998
Total men/women at the German Top 20	128/19	101/36	49/14	29/25	47/30	38/24	17/27	15/32
% women at the German Top 20	12.9	26.3	22.2	46.3	39.0	38.7	61.4	68.1
% women in German at all US institutions	16.3	26.1	24.9	38.8	46.5	50.5	68.1	70.9
% faculty at the German Top 20	44.4	45.7	19.0	18.0	23.3	20.7	13.3	15.7
% faculty in German at all US institutions	35.6	39.6	28.9	26.0	21.8	23.3	13.6	11.1

Sources: Blackwell, "Turf Management"; the *Monatshefte* "Personalia" in 1983 and 1998. Totals do not include visiting faculty members. The listing of institutions by order of number of PhDs in German granted 1985–94 is based on *Monatshefte* 89 (1997): 389–90; Indiana and NYU do not appear in these data.

Table 3

Faculty Members by Rank, Gender, and Country of Birth at the Top Twenty PhD-Producing Programs, 1998

	Men				Women			
Rank	Native German	USA	Other	Unknown	Native German	USA	Other	Unknown
Full professor	31	58	5	0	11	16	5	1
% of total (n = 127)	24.4	45.7	3.9	0.0	8.7	12.6	3.9	0.8
Associate professor	6	18	1	1	6	12	3	2
% of total (n = 49)	12.2	36.7	2.0	2.0	12.2	24.5	6.1	4.1
Assistant professor	12	18	2	4	5	11	4	2
% of total (n = 58)	20.7	31.0	3.4	6.9	8.6	19.0	6.9	3.4
Total number	49	94	8	5	22	39	12	5
Total % (n = 234)	20.9	40.2	3.4	2.1	9.4	16.7	5.1	2.1

Sources: The *Monatshefte* "Personalia" in 1998; the *DAAD / Monatshefte Directory of German Studies* of 1995

7

Sociopolitical Dimensions

Edited by

CORA LEE KLUGE

Introduction

It should be obvious, and yet one forgets: the approach, content, purpose, and goals of German studies in the United States are not the same as those of *Germanistik* in German-speaking countries, and, for that matter, they are not necessarily the same as those of German studies in any other country. Furthermore, one should not assume that the nature and purpose of German studies in America have remained constant through the many years since American German studies began or that their evolution is dependent solely on developments intrinsic to the field. At any given time, they are conditioned by a wide variety of external factors: the societal and political circumstances of the United States, the societal and political circumstances of the German lands whose cultural traditions are being transmitted, the American educational context of German studies programs, the United States and Germany's changing cultural and political relations, and Germany's *Kulturpolitik*. These factors lie at the heart of the interchange between the German and American communities that has shaped German studies in America over the years. The three contributions in this section of the volume address that interchange and elucidate both the American and the German circumstances that helped give a particular profile to American German studies.

Brent Peterson's essay concentrates on the American circumstances of the early years, roughly 1850–1920. The United States was a new country welcoming large numbers of immigrants, and newcomers founded German communities in many parts of America, with German schools, German newspapers,

German churches, and German organizations. At the end of the nineteenth century, people of German background constituted the largest single ethnic group in the country. Many new settlers and citizens from German-speaking areas harbored hopes of maintaining their German language, culture, values, and communities in America. Yet, as Peterson argues, American German studies was not a product of these immigrant communities; nor was it of particular interest to them. There was a surprising lack of connection between the large numbers of German immigrants and the study of German in their new homeland.

Peterson attributes much of this disconnect to German American diversity. He advances the thesis that what divided the immigrants of German heritage may have been stronger than what united them: their different religious beliefs, their various dialects, many of which were not mutually understandable; their differing views of which German traditions were worth preserving and why. He shows, for example, that the family journal *Die Abendschule* (Saint Louis) argued in 1860 that the German language should be learned in America so that immigrants and their descendants could read Luther's works in the original German and spurned numerous great examples of German culture as immoral, whereas *The Golden Signpost* (Cleveland) argued in 1881 that German should be learned precisely because of the superiority of such cultural masterpieces (Brancaforte).

By the end of the nineteenth century, great numbers of American college and university students were learning German. But Peterson insists that this interest was neither because of their ethnic background nor because of the appeal of German studies per se; students were attracted by the reputation of German universities for graduate studies. High enrollment figures for the study of German—at the University of Wisconsin 9.5% of all student credit hours in Letters and Science for the academic year 1915–16 were taught in the Department of German—as well as the success and popularity of German houses and German clubs were the result of students' desire to use German to further their academic interests, no matter what their field of study. During this era, not only college and university students but also their German teachers were for the most part not members of the German American community.

The deleterious effect of World War I on German language and culture in the United States has been well documented. But the war conditions and attitudes were not alone to blame for the decline. To be sure, as Peterson points out, a large number of German journals and newspapers ceased to publish, but we should remember that small English-language newspapers were also disappearing from the scene in the same period, as smaller communities of whatever ethnicity could no longer maintain their self-sufficiency and independence. The number of schools where German was the language of instruction was also declining, but then second- and third-generation immigrants were more likely to be fluent in English than their parents had been. As educators were pointing out well before the United States entered World War I—at least since the first few years of the twentieth century—German was on its way toward losing its foothold at all levels of the education system except the college level, and enrollment strength in German departments at this level continued for the most part not to come from German Americans.

Hinrich Seeba looks at the subject from a different point of view. Instead of concentrating on the sociological situation in which German studies first developed in the United States, he investigates reciprocal influences between Germany and America, especially the influence of German cultural policy. He begins with remarks on developments of the last few years, such as Germany's increasingly commercialized and internationalized foreign cultural policy, suggesting that these developments may undermine support of academic programs that are based on the concept of national cultures. He then presents a historical overview of German foreign cultural policy as it has influenced the development of American German studies through the years.

Seeba separates academic from political approaches to cultural policy, international from national views of cultural studies. Contributions before World War I to cultural transfer came, from the German side, from academic circles— for example, through the work of the German cultural historian Karl Lamprecht, whose interests lay in cultural mediation and understanding between peoples. Another early key figure in the development of German-American cultural relations was Friedrich Althoff, director of the Hochschulabteilung (College and University Department) of the Prussian Ministry of Culture (1882– 1907). Althoff assisted in efforts to found the Germanic Museum at Harvard and, even more important, in efforts to develop exchange professorships between German and American universities, such as those that involved well-known figures like Eugen Kühnemann and Kuno Francke.

Standing in sharp contrast with such cultural policies, whose goal was to internationalize and foster cooperation, were the strident, nationalist views of the Deutschamerikanischer Nationalbund, which insisted on the superiority of German culture. More research, including basic research, needs to be done into the nature and role of this organization and also of the smaller association of teachers, the Nationaler Deutschamerikanischer Lehrerbund. Their strident and loudly proclaimed nationalist pro-German stance was undoubtedly responsible for some of America's well-documented Germanophobia in the World War I era. However, we need more information concerning their size, their members, their activities, and their influence—on American attitudes in general and on German studies programs.

After World War I, Weimar Germany turned cultural representations abroad—which had previously been an academic matter—into a political priority, establishing the Kulturabteilung des Auswärtigen Amtes (Cultural Department of the German Foreign Service) (1920) as well as student exchange programs. The Weimar period saw the founding of organizations such as the Alexander von Humboldt Stiftung and the Deutscher Akademischer Austausch-dienst (DAAD [the German Academic Exchange Service]). But the Third Reich effectively terminated cultural understanding, curtailing and then putting an end to exchange programs and finally reducing cultural transfer to the exodus of German-speaking refugees as exiles to America.

The picture Seeba presents is completed with developments since the end of World War II. Almost immediately, German studies programs in America and American studies programs in Germany were created with the help of German agencies, in the hope of achieving international conciliation. The DAAD's New York office, under the directors Peter Ebel, Manfred Stassen, We-digo de Vivanco, and Heidrun Suhr, not only supported exchanges but also helped promote—through programs, conferences, and summer seminars—the development of German studies as a newly conceived discipline of cultural discourse, whose goal was "a new, theoretically refined, critical approach to German culture." The centers of excellence or centers for German and European studies, established with German assistance beginning in the early 1990s at several American universities, became an important next step. Today American German studies, now a discipline involving both humanists and social scien-tists, is far different from what it was. American Germanists are not engaged in an imitation of *Germanistik* from abroad; instead they have defined a specific cultural approach and have created a self-sufficient and independent field. They use their distance from Germany to identify cultural difference, and they em-phasize the otherness of German culture as a means of understanding their own.

In the third essay of this section, Stassen, the longtime head of the DAAD office in New York and later senior fellow in residence at the American Institute for Contemporary German Studies in Washington, DC, addresses more nar-rowly the topic of the relation between the field of German studies in the United States and foreign organizations, focusing on the years after World War II. Like Seeba, he points out that before the end of World War I there was no German political-governmental support of German culture in the United States—only support from academia. In the aftermath of each of the World Wars, Germany devoted funds to the representation abroad of German culture (*auswärtige Kulturpolitik*), driven not only by the desire to change its image in the world and to bring about international reconciliation but also by the need to reestablish scientific and cultural ties. Thus publicly funded but legally pri-vate agencies such as the DAAD and the Alexander von Humboldt Stiftung were created during the Weimar Republic and reconstituted in the early 1950s. That these agencies were not to be under government control or even guidance made them acceptable to members of American academia, including German émigrés. Today, the Goethe House, the DAAD office in New York, the German

Historical Institute, and a number of other German foundations are partners of Americans involved in German studies.

Stassen outlines in some detail the role such German agencies have played in supporting German studies in the United States. His comments provide a historical perspective on the backgrounds and ties of different supervising agencies, including the Ständiger Ausschuß Deutsch als Fremdsprache (Standing Committee on German as a Foreign Language), which oversees the various foreign language projects and programs of the Goethe Institutes, InterNationes, the Zentralstelle für das Auslandsschulwesen (Central Office for Schools Abroad), and DAAD; the DAAD and the Alexander von Humboldt Stiftung, which provide summer language courses ("Hochschulsommerkurse"), initial graduate research grants (short-term grants or "Kurzstipendien"), one-to-two-year dissertation and postdoctoral research grants ("Jahresstipendien"), research grants for the Leo Baeck Institute in New York or appropriate institutes in Germany, and such faculty development grants as research grants to German institutions; guest lectureships to enable German scholars to visit German departments in the United States; and stipends for junior faculty members to visit the Center for Contemporary German Literature (Washington University) or the American Institute for Contemporary German Studies (Washington, DC).

Finally, Stassen turns to the role the DAAD has played in curricular and methodological initiatives for innovation in American German studies. He extends and adds detail to Seeba's statement, especially in areas that concern the movement toward interdisciplinarity and the definition and development of a specific *Auslandsgermanistik* ("German studies abroad"). He lists a number of new activities and endeavors that Germany's foreign cultural policy began funding during the 1980s, despite fiscal constraints in the German government, including guest lectureships and endowed chairs; awards; grants for team-taught courses; prizes for best books or articles; the *DAAD/Monatshefte Directory of German Studies*; the German studies syllabus database; and, since 1990, the creation of German and European studies centers. Stassen provides us with a view of the interaction of American Germanists and German agencies for cultural policy over the last several decades. Through the success of their joint efforts, German studies in the United States has changed. It is becoming a model for *Auslandsgermanistik* in other lands and is even affecting the discipline of *Germanistik* in Germany itself.

One new development urgently demands consideration. It is becoming evident that German programs today are appealing to students whose major interest is another field, such as business, economics, political science, or law. Even our German majors are increasingly in fact double majors: their main interest in German studies is in learning the German language. At the same time, an unfortunate by-product of the new interdisciplinary German studies programs, which, as Stassen confesses, were to some extent going to necessitate that beginning instruction would be in English, is that occasionally German studies now does not get much beyond English-language courses. Thus the disconnect of which Peterson writes is perhaps emerging once again. Are our programs appealing to our natural clientele? Who are the students on whose enrollments our departments depend? What is their interest in our courses? Are the graduate programs in German studies preparing future members of the profession to teach these students and answer their needs? What is the relation between instruction in the German language and our graduate-level programs and our research in German studies? When we have grappled more successfully with questions concerning the sociopolitical dimensions behind German studies in the United States, both historically and for the present time, we may be closer to understanding our role and function as American Germanists.

Opportunities Forgone

Sociopolitical Dimensions of
German Studies in the United States

BRENT O. PETERSON

Once its practitioners decided what to study and why, the academic study of German in the United States should have enjoyed a huge, built-in audience; German professors should have been poised for cultural and institutional success. By the end of the nineteenth century Germans constituted the largest single ethnic group in the country, and these millions of first- and second-generation speakers of German maintained a vast cultural apparatus: newspapers, magazines, publishing houses, and libraries; theater and choral groups, innumerable clubs and congregations of various faiths and denominations; and political organizations, labor unions, and gymnastic societies—to mention only the most prominent representatives of German American life. These German men and women were a fiercely literate agglomeration of origins and interests. Part of the difficulty of determining the relation between those interests and German studies rests on our incomplete understanding of German American diversity. In all likelihood that diversity lies at the root of the disconnect between this potential audience and the development of the discipline in the United States.

Although the first German immigrants arrived in North America in 1689, mass migration was a nineteenth-century phenomenon. Approximately five million Germans left their various homelands in the years 1830–1900, and another million arrived before World War I. The German waves peaked in 1854 and again in 1883, for reasons connected with both the German and American economies—namely, too few opportunities in Europe, coupled with the hope of re-creating Old World communities in America. Essentially, the immigrants were farmers, craftsmen, and their families, who hoped to re-create the lives they had left behind. To be sure, the Revolution of 1848 sent some politically and culturally prominent Germans abroad, and there were always some religious migrants, but their numbers were statistically insignificant. The great bulk of German immigrants before World War I were forced from their homes by the pressures of economic and social change. Once here, they settled, in large part, inside the triangle bounded by Milwaukee, Cincinnati, and Saint Louis, where they remained and gradually accepted both the norms and language of the English-speaking majority. Nowadays, except for a few culinary survivors, some linguistic fallout, and the odd, attenuated festival, that once-vibrant German American culture has disappeared. The 1930s saw another trickle of Germans, including prominent figures in science and the arts, but by and large they did not seek out the disappearing culture of America's Germans. Migration from Germany after World War II was similarly modest, and many of the prewar intellectual migrants returned to Europe. During the 1960s and 1970s a number of the Germans who shaped American German studies came from Germany, but they were few and their home was the university rather than the country's German community. This essay concentrates on the formative period, roughly 1850–1920, because it was then that Germanists failed to forge a link to a larger German American public that might have supported them. Of course, that failure was mutual, as not only potential leaders but also followers misunderstood and ignored the other side.

To begin, it is a mistake to regard German Americans as a homogeneous group. Until 1871, people migrated from Prussia, Bavaria, Saxony, and the roughly three dozen other German territories in Central Europe, places where half the population owed allegiance to a different government than the one that had ruled them before 1815, when Napoleon and the Congress of Vienna redrew the map. People one could call Germans also came from the Austro-Hungarian Empire, from Switzerland, Russia, France, and Liechtenstein. More important, these Germans spoke a dizzying array of mutually incomprehensible dialects, and they were also divided along religious, class, gender, and political lines. Although they usually settled with or near other Germans who were like them in language and culture, migrants to the United States probably became German Americans in part by learning standard German. In addition to English, they needed a German lingua franca to communicate with neighbors in the ethnic enclaves they inhabited. Standard German also gave immigrants access to high and low literatures and the press, which is where they gradually learned the store of information necessary for them to become German Americans, if indeed that was their primary identity. They nevertheless remained divided confessionally; this means that German Catholics and German Jews only occasionally joined members of various German Protestant groups for events such as a celebration of German unification in 1871. Thus, had academic Germanists wanted to address *the* German Americans, the task might have overwhelmed an already burdened professoriat.

Contrary to accepted wisdom about the existence of a German *Kulturnation*, German Americans actually harbored conflicting attitudes not only about religion and politics but also toward the monuments of German literary culture. On the one hand, *Die Abendschule*, a family journal published in Saint Louis and aimed primarily at conservative Lutherans, warned its readers in 1860 against the classics, including Goethe (see Hilarious). Even a work as benign as the great one's "Heideröslein" could distract unsuspecting believers from essential questions of immortality and redemption. To be sure, *Die Abendschule*'s subscribers learned something of United States and German history; they were introduced to developments in science and industry; and they read pious novels, poems, and short stories. However, the real reason behind the magazine's impeccable German was to maintain doctrinal purity by refusing to translate Luther's works into English, where they might be misunderstood. For such readers, German was the language of worship, and the pastors who served them needed German as a part of their seminary training and then to preach. *Germanistik* had little purchase on such an audience.

At the other extreme, *The Golden Signpost,* an immigrant guide that appeared in Cleveland in 1881, gave its readers almost exactly the opposite advice. After claiming, from the standpoint of a diminishing number of native speakers that "our language, German, is one of the oldest, purest, and most cultivated of the living languages and surpasses most modern languages in richness and strength, in malleability and suppleness," the author advocates learning German for cultural rather than practical reasons:

> In order to imbue the rising generation with love for a language in which people such as Lessing, Schiller, or Goethe wrote, one must open up to them the inexhaustible wellspring of beauty which this language contains and let them drink from it. . . . If the German generation born here only learns to speak and read German without becoming familiar with the magical profound spirit of the German language, then they will naturally only use it when they are forced to do so, or when they see their advantage in so doing. (337–38)

Such sentiments might have played into the hands of professional Germanists, but along with its filiopietistic bombast the passage also raises some difficult issues for anyone interested in the study of German at the end of the nineteenth century. To begin, the undertone is defensive, almost fearful, as if German Americans were already anticipating the decline in the language that would bedevil its adherents for most of the twentieth century and beyond. Mere usefulness threatens the language's spirit; it reduces German to a means of commerce or social interaction and undermines any genuine German identity. Unfortunately, the argument also confines real knowledge to an ethnic ghetto, while it simultaneously ignores most of the texts that German Americans actually read and wrote. Thus, the opening provided by this potentially sympathetic guidebook turns out to be surprisingly narrow.

Strangely enough, these diametrically opposed examples mirror tensions in the academic community as teachers and professors struggled to define what it was they studied and taught, for whom, and why. Writing from near the summit of the profession, W. T. Hewett, a professor of German language and literature at Cornell, addressed the "aims and methods of collegiate instruction in modern languages" in the inaugural issue of *PMLA* in 1884. After a dismissive reference to increasing exchange among nations—that is, to the practicality of language study—Hewett claims, "These tendencies are separate from any questions touching on the usefulness of the study of modern languages as a method of discipline and the culture which is to be obtained from contemporary literatures" (25). By "modern" he means French and German, while "contemporary" refers to works produced after the heyday of Greek and Latin—for example, Goethe and Schiller. Hewett wants to relegate instruction in these languages to the public schools, and he is careful to point out, probably in a defensive gesture, that it need not be at the expense of other subjects, if teachers use their time more efficiently. Furthermore, German can be learned in private schools or from one of the more than two million native speakers residing in the nation's cities, towns, and villages. This solution makes life easier for prospective applicants to Cornell, but Hewett never mentions the possibility that some of these German Americans might also be interested in his work. Here, he draws a distinction between speaking ability and the real object of language learning, namely, "the study of the thoughts of an author, and the intellectual enlargement and expansion which comes from it" (34). If college instructors waste too much time on conversation, "will not valuable time which should be spent in the study of the literature necessarily be consumed in the process, and the result be that the student is left the proud master of a few sentences but without any literary knowledge?" (31). Except that Hewett addresses a different audience, his is precisely the argument contained in *The Golden Signpost.*

One needs to look a bit deeper to find *Die Abendschule*'s position in *PMLA*, but the listing of college language teachers included in the inaugural volume contains tantalizing hints about a divergence from Hewett's high-minded agenda ("List"). The list includes 616 college instructors, representing 273 institutions of higher education in 36 states. Of the instructors listed, 216 teach German, although the actual number may have been higher, because some appear in the category "modern languages." That slippage makes all the more impressive the fact that 35% of the total are identified as German instructors.

Since the MLA was unable to find anyone in either Alabama or Arkansas, the named German teachers range, alphabetically by school, from Professor Albin Putzker of the University of California, Berkeley, to Professor William H. Rosenstengel at the University of Wisconsin, Madison. The colleges named are smaller, less prestigious schools; but on a positive note, German instruction formed part of the regular offerings at colleges where a century later it was threatened or had already been dropped. Judging by demographics and geography, widespread instruction in German had little to do with the country's German American population and was also largely unrelated to German literature. A far more compelling explanation for the spread of German through the educational landscape of North America concerns Germany's own university system and its function both as a training ground for American PhDs and as a model for graduate education in the United States.

This country's first real university, Johns Hopkins, based itself on the University of Berlin, hoping that it would no longer be necessary for Americans to travel to Germany for advanced study in the sciences or to work in disciplines that had been invented or transformed there during the nineteenth century (e.g., history, sociology, and philology). Germany also led the world in theology, but none of these disciplines required the study of German literature. Thus, when in 1876 Hopkins hired Hermann Brandt, its first German instructor, his duties were those of an assistant who provided scholars and their students with the tools they needed for their work. It is indicative that his publications included a German grammar for high schools and colleges (1884), a beginning reader (1889), a scientific reader (1897), and a teaching edition of Lessing's *Nathan* (1895). By 1884 Brandt had moved to Hamilton College in New York, where he taught both French and German, a typical combination. In fact, the vast majority of the German teachers listed that year gave instruction in German and some other language—mostly French but sometimes Greek, Latin, Italian, or Spanish. Many of these people seem to have acquired enough German to teach it, perhaps by doing advanced work in Germany, but they were not Germanists. Thus, the roster contains professors of natural science and German, professors of philosophy and German, professors of mathematics and German, and two men whose specialties were bookkeeping and German. Even more common were theologians who also offered German instruction, 31 by my count, and the list is dotted with people like Reverend J. Franklin Heitland, professor of Greek and German at Trinity College in North Carolina, and Reverend A. S. Yerbe, professor of Greek and acting professor of German at Heidelberg College. The Saint Francis College's Brother DeSales Witmer appears as professor of geometry, algebra, drawing, differential and integral calculus, German literature, astronomy, surveying, and engineering. Only 84 of the 216 instructors taught German exclusively—that is, 39% of the total.

Not everyone on the list has a title, but instructors outnumber professors. Wellesley's Elizabeth H. Denis, professor of medieval languages and art, was one of a very few women and one of only two female professors. Evelyn Darling, professor of French, German, and English at Antioch, was the other. In all, 185 men vastly outnumber the 31 women. Vassar's Fräulein Minna Hunkel's German title stands out; most of her colleagues had to make do with "Miss" or "Mrs." Finally, the ranks of German teachers in the MLA of 1884 contain surprisingly few German names. In fact, given the country's huge German-speaking population, German Americans are conspicuous by their absence.

Space permits a look at only a few prominent members of the profession, but the results are revealing. Cornell's Hewett was born Waterman Thomas Hewett in Miami, Missouri. The location could be German American, but his name and his mother's maiden name, Parsons, cast doubt on that theory. By contrast, Hopkins's Hermann Brandt was born in Vilsen, Germany, and came to the United States as a seventeen-year-old in 1867. That makes him German American, but not from an established community. So, too, did one of the early proponents of German American literary studies, Julius Goebel of the University of Illinois, come from Germany. He was born in Frankfurt am Main in 1857 and emigrated once he completed his PhD in 1882. However, another early proponent of things German American, Marion Dexter Learned, was born in Dover, Delaware, in 1857. His mother's maiden name, Griffith, was as little Germanic as his surname, and Learned's PhD was from Johns Hopkins. Again, the disconnect with America's German Americans seems obvious.

To find German Americans in large numbers one has to look at secondary or even primary rather than postsecondary education. In communities where German was the first language, often true in the Midwest, the availability of German-language schools remained an important issue until well into the twentieth century. There, German had to compete not only with English but also with Greek and Latin in curricula designed to prepare students for college. In a sense, the issue again becomes classical versus modern foreign language training, with the important difference that German had a large, built-in constituency, buoyed by religious educators, who could often count on parents' support for parochial schools with instruction in the native language of German Catholics and Protestants. German-language freethinker schools also existed in places like Milwaukee. However, relatively few if any of these students would have gone on to higher education or aimed to become professors of German.

A quasi-institutional connection among German teachers at all levels came into being with the founding of the journal *Monatshefte* (initially *Pädagogische Monatshefte*) in 1899.[1] Although the journal was subtitled *Journal for German-American Schools*, the initial list of contributors contained professors from Johns Hopkins, Indiana University, Harvard, the University of Chicago, the University of Oregon, Cornell, the University of Wisconsin, Columbia, the University of Pennsylvania, Vanderbilt, and Swarthmore, along with high school teachers, principals, and superintendents. The editor understands his mission as preserving the German language and literature, and with them the German spirit, not only for those who have inherited it from their parents, but to conquer a larger area in the firm belief that it will prove fruitful for the development of our great nation. (Griebsch, "Was wir wollen" 2)

That optimism lasts for less than ten pages, until Learned begins his history of German teaching in the United States by saying, "It is characteristic of the American people as an English speaking nation to ignore forms of modern culture which are not expressed in the English language" ("Lehrerbund" 10). Learned counsels compromise. No sensible American, he argues, can object to German culture

> *found in those German communities which represent the highest culture and most liberal ideas.* It is in the German communities representing the *uneducated classes* that we find the German element so objectionable, not only to the English population, but to the better German classes as well. (13)

It would become a hard battle, and the first skirmish came long before World War I.

Already in March of 1900, *Monatshefte* reported attempts in Chicago and Cincinnati to reduce or perhaps even eliminate German from the public schools, ostensibly to save money (Griebsch, Editorial [1901] 1). In September 1901, Learned warned of "a completely new problem knocking on the doors of our elementary schools, the problem of Spanish." Showing remarkable prescience, he continued, "No one believes that Spanish could become the language of the United States, but everyone who understands the situation knows Spanish will play an important role in American culture in the course of the twentieth century" ("Deutsch" 291). Learned argued historically, using the accomplishments of Germans in America to advocate German's continued status as a cultured language in America, and he pointed to its usefulness in business and the sciences. He nevertheless admitted that German parochial schools were disappearing, that German sermons were giving way to services in English, that German newspapers were merging with one another and losing their influence, and that German clubs of all sorts were fighting in vain against their English counterparts. Lamenting the decline in German and wondering what to do about it were standard fare among Germanists at the beginning of the twentieth century. Almost from its beginning German was a discipline in crisis. In part, commentators reacted to the post-1880 new immigration, consisting largely of migrants from southern and eastern Europe; they saw it undercutting the privileged position that German enjoyed in the public school curriculum as well as at colleges and universities. If not yet in Spanish, these more recent immigrants could legitimately want their children schooled in Italian, Russian, or Yiddish.

To survive, German would have to succeed despite the country's German American population, not because of it. As Hans Fröhlicher argued:

> The goal of German language instruction in American high schools and colleges cannot consist primarily in training philologists, just as it cannot be learning a foreign language as a means of conversation, maintaining a separate German cultural sphere [abgesonderten Deutschtums], or simply memorizing names, dates, titles, and epochs from literary history. (144)[2]

The only goal left was the traditional civilizing mission of German high culture, which was precisely what *The Golden Signpost* had advocated for German Americans, but the intended audience had come to include all students in America rather than those whose ethnicity supposedly predisposed them in the direction of German. For Germanists at the turn of the century the danger was losing the Americans without gaining or keeping the Germans. The situation would soon worsen.[3]

Criticism of Germany and German politics rose to new heights once war began in Europe, and Germanists soon realized that they would have to counter such opinions if their discipline was to survive. One of their most prominent representatives, Harvard's Kuno Francke, responded to the critics in October 1914, in an essay in the *Atlantic Monthly* ("Kaiser"). As an indication of the climate he faced, the magazine prefaced his article as follows: "Striving to maintain our impartiality in the face of what seem to us arguments of incontrovertible strength, we have invited the following paper from Professor Francke" (566). In other words, the editors had more or less made up their minds against Germany, but they were still willing to listen to a divergent view. Thus Francke, consciously or not, wrote in narrow limits. For example, he makes no effort to minimize Germany's role in the war's outbreak, admitting "there can be no question that German ascendance of the last half century has been its ultimate cause," but he refuses to blame German society as a whole. Instead he attempts to limit guilt to "the one grave defect of imperial Germany: the arrogance and overbearing of the military and bureaucratic class." Otherwise, he terms Germany "the best governed country of the world. . . . Indeed, the Emperor on the one hand, the Socialist party on the other, are the two most unimpeachable witnesses to the passionate German zeal for good government." Having nominated this unlikely pair of champions, he asks rhetorically, "What country is there in which the drama, the opera, and the orchestra exert as deep and noble an influence as in Germany?" (566, 569, 568–69, 570). Clearly, the implications are, first, that Germany is no worse and in some regards better than Europe's other powers and, second, that the emperor, the socialists, and members of the cultural elite could right whatever had gone awry. The argument would soon lack all purchase, as Germany and German culture came to represent in the American mind murderous warmongering rather than the noble spirit of Goethe and Schiller.

Contrary to popular belief, German did not disappear from the United States during World War I. It came under attack, but we need to remember that both as a language taught in schools and as an academic discipline German had entered the twentieth century in a weakened state, having only just come into its own at the end of the nineteenth. Nevertheless, the entry of the United States into the war against Germany in April 1917 marked a new stage in the language's difficulties. Soon prominent people throughout the country were calling for strict controls on all German-language publications and activities to prevent spies from undermining the war effort, and the demands included the elimination of German from school curricula. Since proponents of continued German instruction were widely viewed as self-serving or disloyal, Frank C. Barnes decided to query businessmen, scientists, educators, and government officials for a report that he published in the *Modern Language Journal*. His respondents ranged from Charles Steinmetz, the chief engineer for General Electric, to Charles W. Eliot, the former president of Harvard University, and their views were just as varied. At one extreme, L. H. Baekeland, a Belgian chemist living in Yonkers, reported, "It would have been much better for the world at large if the majority of the German literature had never existed" (188). At the other, W. A. Noyes, a chemist at the University of Illinois, "writes most emphatically that it is not wise to discontinue or discourage the study of the German language . . . [because] to scientific men the language will be indispensable in the future as it has been in the past" (195). Most of Barnes's sample took a middle ground, but even here voices such as Nicholas Murray Butler, the president of Columbia University, provided evidence of how much damage the war had done to the perception of German.

As an indication of how dire the situation had become in both practical and intellectual terms, a 1919 article from the *Modern Language Journal* should suffice. It bears a prescient and familiar title, "The Outlook for German." The anonymous author uses Chicago's Hyde Park High School as an example and notes that the enrollment in German remained constant at roughly 20% of the student body from September 1914 through June 1917. That proportion fell to 4% by June 1919; even more troubling, that year's enrollment consisted solely of advanced classes, as no beginners' section had garnered the requisite number of students since February 1918. The author nevertheless expects German to return to the curriculum "when judgment supplants hysteria," and he or she advances a number of reasons why German will again outstrip French and Latin (26). As usual, the article mixes high-minded praise for the products of the German spirit, albeit in a language that we find embarrassing today, with thoroughly practical concerns. Although the arguments differ little from those that supported the study of other modern languages, German remained a threatened discipline, caught as it was between ethnicity, high culture, and practicality—practicality for the sciences in particular, where it remained an important *Hilfswissenschaft* ("auxiliary science or tool"). The future seemed both open and threatening, in large part because the academic premise behind *Germanistik* had never become clear.

The postwar period witnessed both a minor revival of German and continued difficulty in coming to terms with the mission behind studying it. On the one hand, journals such as *Die Abendschule* regained many of their prewar subscribers, and the magazine did not cease publishing until 1940, when it went out of business for demographic rather than political reasons. Its history was similar to that of other journals and newspapers that continued to exist but were consolidated as publishing became a larger business. On the other hand, German-language publishing in the United States had been declining at least since 1900, and it became increasingly difficult to define just what a German magazine or newspaper offered beyond the language. Once the number of new German immigrants slowed to a trickle and once the second and third generations of German Americans ceased speaking German, the need for a separate press disappeared. Likewise, German churches and their parochial schools went out of existence. The net result was to leave the field of *Germanistik* with precisely that public that most of its practitioners had wanted to serve in the first place. The demise of the German American community as a vibrant, German-speaking culture also meant there was no further guilt by association, which had proved so dangerous during World War I; the absence of that guilt made it easier for Germanists to remain apolitical until the 1960s.

Throughout this rather long period of decline, German-American literary relations followed a parallel course, again for reasons that had little to do with either the German community in the United States or the position of German in the academy. American transcendentalists and others knew German philosophy, and the German classics were widely available in translation. In fact, translating works from German seems to have been something of a cottage industry in the United States, sponsored by commercial interests and executed by people without scholarly pretensions. For example, Mrs. Chapman Coleman and her daughters (as the title pages rather injudiciously indicate) produced an eighteen-volume set of Louise Mühlbach's historical novels that can still be found in hundreds of libraries throughout the United States (Kurth-Voigt and McClain). The twenty volumes of *The German Classics of the Nineteenth and Twentieth Centuries* (1913–14) appeared under Francke's august editorship, but their orientation was also extra-academic. By contrast, the one hundred volumes of Continuum's German Library seem to be a last-ditch effort to keep a broader selection of texts available in English for classroom use. While a few programs attempt to increase their undergraduate enrollments by appealing to heritage Germans, the profession retains the same orientation it had from the start. To a surprising degree the study of German in the United States has risen, fallen, and now muddles on with barely a glance toward a group that could have provided a vast public and that did serve, albeit later and largely without recognition, as a source of German professors. The history of German studies and German American communities remains characterized by misunderstandings and missed opportunities.

Notes

1 The list of "gewonnene Mitarbeiter" can be found on pages 4 through 9. This journal began, in part, to make up for the loss of an earlier journal, *Erziehungsblätter* (Educational Papers) that the publisher had canceled for lack of profits. The editor claims the new journal will succeed if it garners one-fourth of the country's 12,000 German teachers.

2 For another version of the same argument see Hohlfeld, "Die Zukunft."

3 Charles M. Purin chides Germans for their lack of confidence and for their willingness to accept foreign customs and languages ("Deutscher Sprachunterricht").

Cultural Exchange

The Historical Context of German *Kulturpolitik* and German Studies in the United States

HINRICH C. SEEBA

At the end of the twentieth century, the inflationary use of the term *culture* was as much an indication of the demise of culture—and the confusion about what cultural identity meant in the age of globalization and how it could be used—as it was a century earlier, when the concept of foreign cultural policy emerged from similar invocations of culture and the concurrent cultural pessimism. The so-called cultural turn, which has defined the theoretical and methodological discourse of the humanities and social sciences in the last two decades, is operating in a cultural vacuum, where culture, frequently employed as "incidental ornament for the economy" (Gentz; "schmückendes Beiwerk für die Wirtschaft"), can easily be reinterpreted as a mere vehicle of global marketing.

German studies in the United States is indebted conceptually to the global cultural turn and institutionally to the local interplay of politics, economics, and culture in cultural policy. The first, more theoretical aspect is framed by debates among American intellectuals as the transnational, multilateral objectives of cultural studies; the second, more historical aspect is framed by political and economic concerns as international, bilateral arrangements between Germany and the United States. The historical aspect is central to the following exploration of the influence of Germany's foreign cultural policy on the concept of German studies in the United States.

At this time, German cultural representation is characterized by corporate involvement (with increasing funds) on the one hand and political influence (with decreasing funds) on the other. The German government spends 3.5 billion marks (out of a total budget of more than 800 billion) annually on cultural affairs (Deweke), including 1.1 billion marks on projects abroad, while German industry makes annual investments abroad of 42 billion marks (Leonhard 21). Industrialists rather than intellectuals are now leading the call for the government to improve the educational system and the exhibition of German cultural interests abroad. Thus the chair of the influential culture club of the industrialists, the Kulturkreis des BDI (Bundesverband der Deutschen Industrie [Federal Organization of German Industry]), Arend Oetker, suggested improving foreign cultural policy by giving large-scale international trade fairs like the Expo 2000 in Hannover a more cultural image and making it "both entertaining and simultaneously culturally meaningful" (42; "unterhaltsam und zugleich kulturell wertvoll"). Such references to cultural values (and their commercial benefit) may indicate an emerging acceptance of cultural parameters of political and economic development. Critics of the recent German obsession with "Spaßgesellschaft" ("society governed by fun") claim that such invocations of culture as a tool for business are simply empty formulas that can serve many sponsors.

If culture is endangered by commercialization, its politicization can be considered another threat. Traditionally, cultural policy in Germany is handled at two levels: predominantly at the domestic level, which constitutionally is the responsibility of the sixteen federal states; to a lesser extent, as foreign cultural policy, which is the responsibility of the federal government. But the delicate balance of state and federal priorities began to shift in 1993, when the European Union usurped from the national governments some important cultural decisions such as the regulation of copyrights. In 1998, the newly elected chancellor Gerhard Schröder appointed the first state minister of culture, Michael Naumann, to oversee and coordinate the many (and often competing) organizations involved in cultural affairs. This new post has a new parliamentary equivalent in the Bundestagsausschuß für Kultur und Medien (Parliamentary Committee for Culture and Media). Together, they mark the trend toward political centralization of cultural decisions. A recently published memorandum on the reform of cultural politics in Austria ("Weißbuch zur Reform der Kulturpolitik in Österreich"), which calls for the creation of a central ministry of culture in Vienna, is indicative of the continuing erosion of the cultural autonomy of the federal states (Kulturhoheit der Länder) in both Germany and Austria (Keller).[1] According to the general secretary of the Goethe Institute, Joachim Sartorius, this trend, which has been advocated by the foreign minister, Joschka Fischer, could undermine the relative independence of government-funded cultural organizations and compromise the independence that grants the necessary latitude for innovative ideas and critical views.

Domestically, where on average only 1% of the state budgets in Germany is committed to cultural affairs (according to Evelies Mayer, the former minister of science and art in the state of Hesse), the lobby to prevent further reductions in the support of cultural institutions such as universities, theaters, museums, libraries, and orchestras is weak and ineffective. Internationally, the effects of cutbacks, though hardly noticed in Germany, are even more alarming, because foreign cultural policy has traditionally relied on the assumption that political and economic advances of German interests had to be accompanied, if not anticipated and prepared, by generous cultural efforts abroad. In the aftermath of the Third Reich and the Holocaust, it has been important for West Germany and, since 1990, for united Germany to create a positive image as a modern democratic and socially just society, which is based on a great cultural tradition. This immensely moral effort also happened to be good for business. While economic development in Germany was organized nationally (in a worldwide competition among industrial nations rather than among international corporations), the institutions involved in the advancement of German interests have benefited from and often contributed to the rampant instrumentalization of German culture. While it may be desirable to internationalize culture, de-nationalization also carries risks for the future of universities if they are forced to compete as a business in the global market of ideas. Especially programs in the humanities that are based on the concept of a national culture, language, and literature will face increasing challenges (see Hohendahl, "Fate" 18).

When budget cutbacks are considered, foreign cultural policy is often targeted first because of a lack of resistance. Even before the financial crisis of the late 1990s, the budget of the Goethe Institute had already been drastically reduced. The Deutsche Welle, the single most important German outreach program in worldwide radio and television, was projected to lose 89 million marks between 1999 and 2003 and to lay off more than five hundred employees; close six radio stations in Eastern Europe, Japan, and South America; and discontinue the popular TV show *Schauplatz Deutschland*. When the very existence of Deutsche Welle was called into question in the summer of 1999, the protest in Germany was hardly heard beyond the small group of affected employees. When eleven Goethe Institutes were slated for closing in September 1999—in Chania, Nicosia on Crete, Patras, Costa Rica, York, Toulouse, Genoa, as well as in Vancouver, Seattle, Ann Arbor, and Houston—German taxpayers were not immediately affected; they were little concerned about German lecture series and art exhibits in distant places and about methods and institutions involved in *Deutsch als Fremdsprache* ("German as a foreign language").

German resistance to educational reforms modeled on the American university system shows a fear of reverse colonialism. Many Germans suspect that the brain drain of the 1950s and 1960s, when Germany lost many scientists, such as the physicist and 1961 Nobel Prize winner Rudolf Mössbauer, to better equipped and less bureaucratically entangled American universities, is taking its toll on the next generation. American-trained scientists and scholars have become critical of German culture and are suggesting what is widely perceived as American solutions to the obvious crisis of the educational system in Germany. As these suggestions often resemble Wilhelm von Humboldt's university model, the irony of such cultural transfer is not lost on critics from both sides of the Atlantic (see Seeba, "Klassische Bildung"). If there are traces of anti-Americanism among younger German intellectuals (Herzinger and Stein; Diner, *Verkehrte Welten*) and misgivings about American elitism, there is also an unspoken fear of an inversion of conventional stereotypes, whereby Germans would be seen as caricatures of Americans—materialistic, unsophisticated, intellectually soft, physically aggressive, ambitious without real drive, intent on instant gratification, and obsessed with pop culture—while Americans would assume the image Germans strove after, that of a powerful cultural elite with a political mission for the world.

The scientific and political communities on both sides of the Atlantic have had a history of ups and downs, but they have been affected more by persistent attempts to confront cultural difference than by stereotyping. From the first visiting professors and exchange students to today's centers for German and European studies, scholars and politicians have collaborated for nearly one hundred years to design and establish foreign cultural policy and to promote German studies.

The development of German studies as a discipline has been facilitated by the German Academic Exchange Service (DAAD [Deutscher Akademischer Austauschdienst]), which is funded by the Foreign Ministry. The DAAD office in New York (under the consecutive directors Peter Ebel, Manfred Stassen, Wedigo de Vivanco, and Heidrun Suhr) was the most visible American outpost of Germany's foreign cultural policy; in the late 1970s it helped major German departments lead the way in changing the discipline from interpretation of literary masterworks in the manner of the New Critics to the poetics of cultural discourse and new historicism. Germany's foreign cultural policy of the last two decades has encouraged the cultural turn in Germanics and a new, theoretically refined, critical approach to German culture. Ranging from the Interdisciplinary Summer Seminars in German Studies, which started in Berkeley in 1979, to the critical review one decade later at the DAAD Conference in Tempe, Arizona, in January 1989, German Studies in the USA: A Critique of *Germanistik*? (see *German Studies*), and to similar conferences in Washington, DC, Nashville, Boulder, and Madison, these DAAD-sponsored programs and conferences did not include a single Germanist from Germany. It is ironic that German studies, though largely German-sponsored, has become an exclusively American affair. It was even discussed as a challenge to German *Germanistik* at an international DAAD conference in Germany in 1995 (see Seeba, "German Studies"). More recently, the American model of German studies and its emphasis on positionality is beginning to appeal to Germanists in other, non-German cultures.

The institutional success of German studies as a paradigm for the study of cultural difference is partly due to a shift in German foreign cultural policy. The shift was prepared in 1970, when Chancellor Willy Brandt's parliamentary state secretary in the Foreign Ministry, the liberal sociologist Ralf Dahrendorf, formulated the ground rules for foreign cultural policy (Witte). The shift was reinforced on the national level with the report of the parliamentary commission on foreign cultural policy ("Bericht der Enquete-Kommission 'Auswärtige Kulturpolitik' des Deutschen Bundestages" [1975]) and on the international level with UNESCO's decision at a conference in Mexico City (1982) to recognize the vast disparities in cultural identities and to support local cultures (Seib).

The liberal tendencies of Germany's foreign cultural policy during the last thirty years are a reminder that the very concept as it was first discussed in 1912 came from academic, not political, circles. Its nationalist variant was manifest by German Americans in the United States, while its internationalist interpretation originated in Germany. The term "nationale Kulturpolitik" ("national cultural policy") was a common slogan among more than two million members of the chauvinist Deutschamerikanischer Nationalbund before World War I. One of their prominent activists was the Germanist Julius Goebel, who had taught at Johns Hopkins, Stanford, and Harvard from 1885 to 1908, before he became professor of German at the University of Illinois, Urbana. Goebel's mission, as expounded in a public lecture in New York City on 27 May 1912, was the aggressive dissemination of what he believed to be the superior German culture in the United States. To him, "national cultural politics in the strongest and most noble sense" ("Die deutsche Bewegung" 4; "nationale Kulturpolitik im höchsten und edelsten Sinne") was meant to interact with and direct the developing American culture along the guidelines of German culture: "What is culture? To us Germans culture means, in the final analysis, true and superior humanity, rooted in the native soil of our folkish culture" (4; "Was ist Kultur? Für uns Deutsche bedeutet sie im letzten Grunde wahres, höheres, im Mutterboden unserer Volksnatur wurzelndes Menschentum"). Promising salvation through German humanism, Goebel propagated cultural separatism to counter what he despised as the Zionist notion of the melting pot and proposed instead the establishment of an institute for German culture modeled on the Berlin Academy of Sciences (10). Goebel's ideas were too extreme to gain political support in either Germany or the United States. Other German-born scholars such as the Harvard professors Hugo Münsterberg and Kuno Francke, who kept their distance from the nationalist agenda of the Nationalbund, were more successful in improving the institutional context for an integrative rather than supremist cultural policy.

A nationalist approach to the new concept of cultural politics (*Kulturpolitik*) was the exception in Germany. Even Ludwig Stein (1859–1930), a philosopher who gave up his professorship in Bern to move to Berlin and to purchase the troubled journal *Nord und Süd*, stated in his first editorial of January 1912, which was programmatically entitled "Kulturpolitik," that national imperialism was nothing but a vehicle "toward cultural imperialism, that is, the permanent domination of the white race on our planet" (9–10; "zum Kultur-Imperialismus, d.h. zur endgültigen Herrschaft der weißen Rasse auf unserem Planeten"). But he considered such racist support of Western (rather than merely German) culture an essential contribution to international—that is, European—conciliation (Bruch 125).

In contrast to "national cultural politics" ("nationale Kulturpolitik"), the more common term "foreign cultural politics" ("auswärtige Kulturpolitik") did not originate in nationalist circles; it was not introduced as a vehicle of colonialist discourse. Instead, it came from an untimely commitment to international understanding and comparative methodologies before World War I. The concept was suggested by a cultural historian rather than by state authorities. Karl Lamprecht (1856–1915), who had taught at the University of Leipzig since 1891, coined the term as the title of a public lecture he gave in Heidelberg on 7 October 1912 to the Verband für internationale Verständigung (Association for International Understanding). Founded in the previous year as an academic effort to help ease political tensions through international law, this association had attracted famous scholars such as Max Weber, Ernst Troeltsch, Georg Simmel, Adolf von Harnack, Paul Natorp, and Hermann Cohen. Amid the nationalist fervor that would eventually lead to war, the occasion of the lecture was programmatic: Lamprecht's talk ("Über auswärtige Kulturpolitik") was a plea for universal (rather than national) cultural history and an attempt to secure an institutional framework by appealing to national politics: "Can our nation today still refrain from the development of a foreign cultural policy in the broad sense?" (809; "Kann sich nun unsere Nation heute noch von der Entwicklung einer breiten äusseren Kulturpolitik dispensieren?"). What appeared to be a plea for the promotion of national interests through culture was in fact a strategy to employ political means for Lamprecht's academic agenda:

> Thus, the theoretical foreign cultural politics easily turns into a universal cultural history; and only a clear understanding of the latter can lead to the fully successful execution of the former. (810–11)

> So wird denn die theoretische äussere Kulturpolitik ohne weiteres zur universalen Kulturgeschichte: und erst ein klares Verständnis der einen lässt die völlig erfolgreiche Durchbildung der andern erhoffen.

Although Lamprecht was more popular in the United States than in Germany, where his internationalist and materialist orientation was generally disliked and rejected by his colleagues, he proved to be an advocate and effective agent of international, especially German-American, communication. For instance, he served beginning in 1902 as counselor to the Department of Historical Research in the Carnegie Foundation and visited many American universities, among them Columbia, Harvard, Yale, Johns Hopkins, Pennsylvania, Chicago, Stanford, and Berkeley, to preach the gospel of universal and cultural history.

It was in fact in Lamprecht's name and in view of his anti-idealist approach to history that the American school of new history was formed, an almost forgotten precursor of new historicism and similarly dedicated to discursive contextualization. One of its major proponents was James H. Robinson, who in 1919 would become the first director of the famous New School for Social Research and thus prepare a haven for the next wave of cultural transfer, where many Jewish intellectuals who had escaped Nazi Germany found their first academic refuge (see Seeba, "Interkulturelle Perspektiven" and "New Historicism"). Robinson invited Lamprecht to New York in 1904 to give a series of lectures on the occasion of Columbia University's hundred and fiftieth anniversary (Lamprecht, *What Is History?*), just before the Germanist Ernst Richard started his own lecture series, also at Columbia, on German cultural history (see the syllabus of this course in *Activities*; see Richard). Now programmatically called interdisciplinary, the crossover between German literature and history was common practice at the time.

Lamprecht's plea for foreign cultural policy was largely based on his experience in the United States. It was the beginning of his attempt to give political muscle to his project of cultural history at the international level. He turned to Chancellor Theobald von Bethmann Hollweg (1856–1921), whom he knew from his school years at Schulpforta, and urged him in a letter of 19 May 1913 "to establish a complete program for a German foreign cultural politics" (Bruch 147–48; "für eine deutsche auswärtige Kulturpolitik ein wirkliches volles Programm aufzustellen") and thus to enhance the "idea of conciliation" ("Gedanke der Völkervereinigung") (147). Bethmann Hollweg's answer, in a letter of 21 June 1913, is a telling document of the German difficulty with self-identity as a nation. He remarked with surprising candor and restraint: "We are not yet that far along. We are not yet certain and aware enough about our culture, our inner nature, and our national ideal" (149–50; "Wir sind noch nicht so weit. Wir sind unserer Kultur, unseres inneren Wesens, unseres nationalen Ideals nicht sicher und bewußt genug"). First it was necessary "to prepare our people for the new task" (150; "daß unser Volk zu der neuen Aufgabe geweckt werde"). Although he emphasized that this project lacked broad public support and was merely an academic rather than a political concern, the chancellor nevertheless took Lamprecht's initiative into the political arena. On 5 August 1913 he issued a decree to the Ministries of the Interior, Foreign Affairs, and Finances that ordered the three respective secretaries to explore possibilities for an "orderly promotion of German culture abroad" (Bruch 152; "planmäßige Förderung deutscher Kultur im Auslande")— for ethical as well as for economic reasons. But this first official attempt at German foreign cultural policy was doomed, at least until the end of World War I, because of bureaucratic resistance in the Foreign Office and the lack of coordination among competing branches of the government.

The chancellor's caution may also have been guided by constitutional constraints. The states were reluctant to cede all their influence in cultural policy to the central government in Berlin. If there was any concern that the number of American students studying at German universities had dropped from 1,088 in 1880 (when a German degree practically ensured an academic career in the US) to only 338 in 1912 (when English and French universities had lifted their barriers against American applicants), such educational concerns belonged to the responsibility of the German states. It is here that foreign cultural policy had already been at work locally, while it could not get off the ground nationally.

Friedrich Althoff (1839–1908), director of the Division of Higher Education (Hochschulabteilung) in the Prussian Ministry of Culture from 1882 to 1907, conducted a very successful foreign cultural policy *avant la lettre*. His successor from 1920 to 1933, Friedrich Schmidt-Ott (1860–1956), called him "Germany's first great politician for culture" (253; "der erste große Kulturpolitiker Deutschlands"). Althoff's importance for German-American cultural relations was even celebrated with an honorary degree from Harvard University in 1906. Kuno Francke (1855–1930)—the German-born Germanist at Harvard University who held the position created in 1830 for the very first Germanist in the United States, Karl Follen—was assisted by Althoff in his efforts to found the Germanic Museum at Harvard; it opened in November 1902 and in 1950 was renamed the Busch-Reisinger Museum. Althoff built on the German support for the museum and developed a larger project for an exchange of German and American professors. As Francke relates in his memoirs, *Deutsche Arbeit in Amerika* (1930), in March 1902 Althoff stormed into the first meeting of Francke's museum committee, which included Adolf von Harnack, Friedrich Paulsen, Wilhelm von Bode, Heinrich Wölfflin, and Ernst von Wildenbruch, who were gathered in the Berlin Kunstgewerbemuseum (today Martin Gropius-Bau), only to declare the museum project

> a relatively insignificant affair compared to the need to send German scholars to American universities for regular lecture series and thus to create continuing intellectual ties between the two countries. (46)

> eine verhältnismäßig unbedeutende Sache verglichen mit der Notwendigkeit, deutsche Gelehrte zu regelmäßigen Vortragszyklen an amerikanische Universitäten zu entsenden und so ein dauerndes geistiges Band zwischen den beiden Ländern zu knüpfen.

This anecdotal moment happened at a time when the founding president of Cornell University, Andrew D. White, was United States ambassador in Berlin (from 1897 to 1902) and thus a shining example of the interaction of politics and the academy, and when the first German ambassador in Washington, DC (from 1897 to 1903), Theodor von Holleben, also was making cultural diplomacy his top priority.

The annual exchange of professors began in 1905 and involved Harvard University, Columbia University, and Berlin. A number of luminaries participated, such as the literary scholars Eugen Kühnemann (1906–07) and William H. Schofield (1907–08), the art historian Paul Clemen (1907–08), the psychologist Hugo Münsterberg (1910–11), the historians Eduard Meyer (1909–10) and Archibald C. Coolidge (1913–14), the music historian Max Friedländer (1910–11), the philosopher and winner of the 1908 Nobel Prize in literature Rudolf Eucken (1912–13), the cultural historian and president of Berkeley Benjamin I. Wheeler (1909–10), and the psychologist and founder of Ganzheitspsychologie ("holistic psychology") Felix Krüger (1912–13).

Eugen Kühnemann (1868–1946) was the most effective among the German participants in advancing cultural political diplomacy. Even before serving as an exchange professor in 1908–09 to replace Francke, who was on sabbatical, he toured American cities in 1905–06 under Althoff's aegis, giving popular lectures on German culture to develop a base for future foreign cultural policy in the German American community (Kühnemann 149–63). Perhaps the most popular German Germanist in the United States, he was later appointed the first Carl Schurz Memorial Professor at the University of Wisconsin (1912–13).

The exchange agreements were meant to cover the whole spectrum of German academic culture and to promote both intellectual exchange and intense social contacts. Behind all these efforts there was also a shared commitment to comparative cultural history as it was personified best by Lamprecht on the German side and by Francke on the American side: Lamprecht became director of the Institut für Universal- und Kulturgeschichte (Institute for Universal and Cultural History) at the University of Leipzig in 1908; Francke's position was renamed professor of German cultural history in 1905. The two men strove to bring political history and social movements together with intellectual, artistic, and literary developments and to examine them as expressions of national identity (see Hohendahl in this volume ["From Philology"]). Lamprecht and Francke, who openly admitted his "Abhängigkeit" ("dependence") on Lamprecht (23), developed an early concept of German studies as we know it today. Through their involvement in the nascent phase of German foreign cultural policy they established a new academic paradigm. Although they were sentimentally patriotic, they cultivated an outsider's critical perspective that later became essential to German studies.

Weimar Germany turned cultural representation abroad, which until 1914 had been handled mainly as an academic affair, into a political priority in order to improve its international standing. The first central administrative agency to deal with foreign cultural policy was instituted in 1920 as the Division of Culture in the Ministry of Foreign Affairs (Kulturabteilung des Auswärtigen Amtes); it was directed first by Friedrich Heilbron and then by Hans Freytag (Düwell). This government step launched a new administrative effort in the cultural exchange between Germany and the United States. At this time, the Alexander von Humboldt Stiftung (founded in 1925) and the Deutscher Akademischer Austauschdienst (DAAD, German Academic Exchange Service, so named in 1931) were the most important agencies to promote student exchanges with American universities. Adolf Morsbach (1890–1937), who directed the Akademischer Austauschdienst from its inception in 1927 and its successor organization, the DAAD, from 1931 to 1934, was most successful in reorganizing foreign cultural policy. His reform plan of March 1934 allowed the centralizing of the various activities without compromising the independence of the agencies involved (Laitenberger, "Organisations- und Strukturprobleme" 79–86). However, the official DAAD program, which was formulated by the political scientist Arnold Bergsträsser (1896–1964) in 1930 (58–80), could not rekindle the intensity of intellectual collaboration of Americans and Germans before the war. The methodologies of the time were not favorable to cultural criticism. In the United States, the emerging New Criticism concentrated on the formal analysis of isolated masterworks; in Germany, the predominant *Geistesgeschichte* ("history of ideas") explored philosophical issues in the tradition of German idealism (Seeba, "Zum Geist- und Strukturbegriff"). There was little interest in bringing together American and German scholars, historians and Germanists. The postwar professorial exchange between Harvard and Berlin dwindled to just one scholar, the art historian Adolph Goldschmidt, and the exchange with Columbia to only two visiting professors, the Germanists Paul Merker (1931) and Karl Viëtor (1931–32).

But there was a new emphasis on the exchange of students. The success of that exchange, as documented in Klaus Mehnert's report of 1930 on his year in Berkeley, was short-lived, however, because of the political situation. The number of German students supported with a fellowship for the United States climbed from 13 in 1924–25 to 66 in 1930–31, but after Hitler assumed power, the number dropped to 48 in 1933-34 and to 39 in 1934–35 before it picked up again to reach 79 in 1937–38, when German students were expected to serve as emissaries of the Third Reich. The sharply decreasing numbers of United States students in Germany is even more striking. While in the winter semester 1932–33 there were still 800 American students in Germany, their number fell to 540 in the following semester, to 369 in the summer semester of 1934 (a drop of 53.9%), and to 252 in the summer semester of 1938 (Laitenberger, *Akademischer Austausch* 267–68). Americans had always constituted the largest contingent of foreign students in Germany, but ten years of exchange, from 1923 to 1933, were far too few to make up for the time and the goodwill lost in World War I. The advent of Nazi ideology and its implementation in a totalitarian state would forever change the American perception of German culture.

Cultural policy in the United States had been largely left to private initiative. Only in 1938 was the State Department's Division for Cultural Relations opened in response to aggressive propaganda from Germany and Italy (Dexheimer 127–28). In the Third Reich, the centralization and ideological control of all agencies led to an awkward competition among central agencies. Foreign cultural policy became a bone of contention when the Ministry of Propaganda (under Josef Goebbels) was created in March 1933 and the Ministry of Culture (under Bernhard Rust) in May 1934, both of which competed with the Foreign Office (under Konstantin von Neurath and, from Feb. 1938, under Joachim von Ribbentrop) for control of foreign cultural policy. The administrative and political tangle, however, left some room for maneuvering. Until a decree of 30 October 1937 from the Foreign Office mandated the institution of cultural attachés in all German embassies and consulates, it was often left to the DAAD offices in London, Paris, or Rome to take care of German cultural affairs locally.

The situation in the United States was much more difficult. The Röhm revolt of June 1934, in whose aftermath the president of the DAAD, Morsbach, was arrested and sent to a concentration camp, was a turning point for public opinion in the United States toward Germany. Cultural representation of Nazi Germany had little chance in a country that was becoming the main refuge for many intellectuals, writers, and artists escaping from German tyranny. The plan for a DAAD office in New York, which had been charted by Morsbach as early as 1930, did not become reality until 1938, and even then against the explicit advice of both the German consulate in New York and the embassy in Washington, DC. Called the German University Service, the DAAD office was closed by United States authorities after only six months because its director, Georg Rettig, was suspected of ties to the German secret police (Laitenberger, *Akademischer Austausch* 123–29). The Germanist Bernhard Blume, a German exile who taught at Mills College in Oakland, California, from 1936 to 1945, relates in his memoirs how he had to convince the president of his college that the blond, blue-eyed exchange student Gretchen Schmidt, who was everybody's favorite teaching assistant because she seemed so full of enthusiasm for America, was practically a secret agent; on her return to Germany, as it turned out, she published an ideologically charged invective against America, based on her experience at Mills (Blume 222–23).

Ironically, the representation of German culture in the United States was left to those deemed un-German, mostly Jewish exiles who, like Blume, had escaped from Germany in 1933 after the "law for the restoration of civil service"

("Gesetz zur Wiederherstellung des Berufsbeamtentums") of April 1933 excluded all Jews from public positions. Estimates suggest that there was a total of 500,000 German-speaking exiles, among them 1,100 to 1,500 professors, who had made up 15% of the professoriat in Germany at the time (Strauss 10). Most of the exiled scholars eventually came to the United States, where the Emergency Committee in Aid of Displaced Scholars; the Refugee Scholars' Fund; and the American Council for Scholars, Artists, and Writers helped them with the first phase of integration. According to one source, no fewer than fifty-six Germanists who had taught at German universities were forced into exile (Möller 91). Many ended up teaching German at United States colleges and brought new and less academic perspectives to the study of German culture. Literature was no longer the only form of cultural representation; often the visual (in art, film, and architecture) inspired the exiles' critical analysis (see Seeba, "Zwischen den Kulturen"). Among the exiles who went on to help shape the discipline from 1935 to 1985 are distinguished critics such as Richard Alewyn, Dorrit Cohn, Hans Eichner, Erich Heller, Ruth Klüger, Franz H. Mauthner, Wolfgang Paulsen, Heinz Politzer, Egon Schwarz, Oskar Seidlin, Walter H. Sokel, Guy Stern, Marianne Thalmann, Werner Vordtriede, and Harry Zohn (Strauss and Röder). The enormous exodus eventually returned the power of cultural policy to the academy, where it had been located before World War I. Once again, it was at the universities that the American image of German culture was cast and upheld against political tyranny and cultural barbarism.

The conceptual opposition of the good cultural past and the bad political present, however, also had its downside when it was extended beyond the end of the Third Reich. What had been valid as an oppositional gesture until 1945 now tended to ignore the political and social context of the postwar years, even in literature. It reinforced the dichotomy of culture and politics, which had been part of the German ideology. The division of good past and bad present, of culture and politics, proved so persistent that a work as recent as E. D. Hirsch's acclaimed educational canon, *Cultural Literacy: What Every American Needs to Know* (1987), represents German culture with many famous composers and philosophers but German politics exclusively with the villains of the Third Reich. Obviously, the image of Germany divided into cultural idealism and political barbarism is hard to overcome.

While East Germany (GDR) had no foreign cultural policy to speak of with regard to the United States, postwar West German foreign cultural policy was faced with the difficult task of reconnecting German culture with the political present and convincing the American public that Germany had changed and become a reliable democratic ally. The task of restoring confidence in postwar Germany and its cultural tradition relied on views that were to become the conceptual basis of German studies. The very term "German studies," which was first used in 1948, was motivated by the same ethos: an intercultural perspective to advance respect for alterity. It was one of the few exiles who returned to Germany soon after the war, the Germanist Alewyn (1902–79), who instituted the first program in German studies under this very name. In a move similar to that of Hugo Münsterberg, who had temporarily returned from Harvard to Berlin in 1908 to organize the first American Institute at the University of Berlin, Alewyn left Queens College in New York in 1948 to establish at the University of Cologne not only an American Institute, which he codirected, but also a Summer School for German Studies (using the English name!); the mission was "to familiarize foreign students beyond the study of the German language and literature with German history, politics, and culture" (Alewyn in a letter of 15 Sept. 1948, qtd. in R. Weber 251; "die ausländischen Studenten über das Studium der deutschen Sprache und Literatur hinaus mit deutscher Geschichte, Politik und Kultur vertraut machen"). Only three years after the war, the institutional crossover of Germans studying American culture and Americans studying German culture was reflecting the shifting perspectives on cultural difference. Against the background of the Holocaust, the implicit hope for international conciliation—the claim that had explicitly informed Lamprecht's introduction of the term "auswärtige Kulturpolitik" in 1912—motivated this first reference to intercultural German studies in 1948.

If there was a convergence of interests in German foreign cultural policy and in German studies in the last decades of the twentieth century, this correlation in direction, concepts, and methods does not suggest that German studies was a mere instrument of German politics. German studies is in no way an affirmative tool; rather, it is much more critical than most of the exiles in their nostalgic ambivalence toward Germany ever were. An intellectual distance from Germany is more noticeable in the United States than in most other countries, where the memory of the Holocaust is not as much alive. Initiatives in foreign cultural policy could easily be misinterpreted as attempts at damage control—a suspicion that was raised when Chancellor Helmut Kohl's counselor on German-American affairs, the political scientist and expert on German identity formation Werner Weidenfeld, first introduced the idea of "centers of excellence" at a conference of the German Studies Association in Philadelphia in 1988. But if some early critics feared that these centers, which were established in the early 1990s at Berkeley, Harvard, and Georgetown and were soon called centers for German and European studies, might promote, in the interest of the German government, a rosy view of German culture, they were proved wrong. The centers have developed into outstanding exchanges not only between German and American scholars but also between scholars of the various disciplines involved in German studies, in both the humanities and social sciences. In the tradition of the Frankfurt school, they highlight the conflict between instrumental and critical concepts of culture and draw attention to those aspects of German culture that played a fateful role in the preparation, justification, cover-up, and expurgation of the Holocaust.

The cultural turn in the humanities and social sciences has given the construct called "German culture" a more clearly defined face, but it also has put more distance between Germany today and its American observers. Whereas German foreign cultural policy in the beginning tended to serve mainly German Americans who tried to reaffirm their German identity in America, the new partners are Americans and, in some cases, former students of exiles or descendants of Holocaust survivors, who instead of looking for their roots are anxious to find and define cultural difference, using the otherness of German culture as an example to reflect on their own alterity. This new attitude of American students of German culture may eventually find its counterpart among Germans who look at themselves to find the difference within. The former president of the Alexander von Humboldt Stiftung Reimar Lüst remarked:

> Our foreign cultural policy should be framed by domestic cultural politics of understanding foreign traditions, mentalities, and civilizations. This means, however, to become more curious and linguistically more competent toward other cultures, which are in the process of presenting themselves globally with increased confidence. (48)

> Unsere auswärtige Kulturpolitik muß begleitet werden von einer nach "innen" gerichteten Kulturpolitik des Verstehens fremder Traditionen, fremder Mentalitäten und Zivilisationen. Das aber heißt: neugieriger und sprachfähiger zu werden gegenüber anderen Kulturen, die im Begriff sind, sich mit zunehmender Deutlichkeit global zu artikulieren.

In other words, only as a model of looking at cultural difference (self-) critically may German studies, like *auswärtige Kulturpolitik*, have a chance to survive in the age of globalization.

Note

1 See also the situation in Switzerland, where Pro Helvetia—founded in 1938 as part of "geistige Landesverteidigung" to withstand the propaganda of Nazi Germany and fascist Italy—is the only government-funded agency that represents Swiss culture both at home and abroad.

Relations with Foreign Organizations

MANFRED STASSEN

Relations between American Germanists and foreign organizations are many and diverse. Like agencies in the Federal Republic of Germany, agencies in the former German Democratic Republic (GDR), Austria, and Switzerland have played an important role in promoting German language and culture and supporting United States academic pursuits, but they cannot easily be incorporated into this analysis, because of differences in the history and cultural interaction between these countries and the United States. Therefore, my remarks concentrate solely on the role and contributions of funding agencies in the Federal Republic.

German organizations had been established to develop relations with foreign scholars of German before members of the profession in the United States themselves expressed a need for them. A German national foreign cultural policy (*auswärtige Kulturpolitik*) had become necessary because of Germany's cultural and scientific isolation resulting from World Wars I and II. Its focus was to promote the German language abroad; to support research by scholars from other countries; and to facilitate the incorporation of that research into the cultural fabric of Germany, particularly its literary, philosophical, and social-scientific tradition. The research support was intended to advance scholarship but also to enhance other diplomatic efforts to build confidence among and reconcile relations with the family of civilized nations after the two catastrophic and barbaric experiences that originated in Germany. (For the beginnings of *auswärtige Kulturpolitik*, see Seeba in this volume.) The agencies that were created in the Weimar Republic were reconstituted in the early 1950s to carry out these support programs. They were conceived as independent and as free as possible of governmental tutelage and direction (*staatsfern*). *Auswärtige Kulturpolitik* is thus more than, and essentially different from, *kulturelle Außenpolitik* ("cultural foreign policy"). It is precisely this autonomy (*Staatsferne*) that made these organizations politically acceptable to and culturally compatible with United States academia in general and with the Germanists in particular, many of whom were German émigrés.

The German Academic Exchange Service (DAAD [Deutscher Akademischer Austauschdienst]) was established in Berlin in 1925 and refounded in 1950 in Bonn—in both instances with the help of the Institute of International Education in New York as a mediating agency (*Mittlerorganisation*) between the state and the university community. Its legal status was private, but it was publicly funded and served as a testimony to the policy of decentralized pluralism in the management of foreign cultural affairs. In the seventy-five years of the DAAD's existence, under very different governments, its status has not changed, except for a twelve-year hiatus during totalitarian Nazi rule, and it has continued to receive increasing political and financial support, even in times of financial crunches and budget deficits. The same holds true for the two other significant German agencies, the Alexander von Humboldt Foundation and the Goethe Institute. The location of the institute's headquarters in Munich underscores the decentralized, federalistic spirit of German foreign cultural policy.

Perhaps the largest and most significant contribution Germany ever made to the promotion of German-inspired scholarship and German philology in American academia did not involve funding agencies. It was the involuntary transfer of German Jewish and other German brain power to the United States during World War II and in the immediate postwar period. This contribution did not enjoy German support; in fact, for many years after the war, teachers at American universities who still held a German passport were categorically excluded from participation in the funding schemes of most German organizations.

It is a sobering thought for these funding agencies today that very little organized German support of things German seems to have been offered or deemed necessary until after World War I. The newly founded Johns Hopkins and Stanford universities had been set up along German models in 1876 and 1892, respectively; there were many German immigrants who kept scores of German-language newspapers alive in all major American cities; and, as early as 1911, Middlebury College started its first model German Language Summer School for American students—all without support from Germany.

In 1957 the Goethe House New York, a branch of the Goethe Institute, was founded by German Americans interested in supporting German language and culture, and in 1971 the DAAD opened its branch office for North America in New York. Today, many other German organizations, such as the German Historical Institute and the United States offices of the political foundations affiliated with the five parties represented in German Parliament, are partners of American scholars of German studies. With the reduction in American funding for foreign language, culture, and area studies programs over the past decades, these partnerships have proved essential for the support of the profession, especially its relatively new focus, interdisciplinary German studies.

The records of who and what was supported by the DAAD from 1925 to 1945 were destroyed during World War II. Even for the immediate postwar period, the records are incomplete. Therefore, my analysis here proceeds typologically rather than chronologically, according to the kinds of support offered over the years; I give the underlying policies and policy changes of each. A distinction is made among the support to promote German-language study in American high schools and universities, support for traditional German philology, and support for more recent Germanics and interdisciplinary German studies. In all their activities, German funding agencies cooperate closely with relevant American partners, such as the AATG, Women in German, and the German Studies Association.

Cooperation in Promoting German as a Foreign Language ("Deutsch als Fremdsprache")

Even though nearly sixty million Americans trace their roots to Germany and hundreds of thousands of American soldiers have been stationed in Germany since the end of World War II, it has not been easy to promote the German language in American schools and universities. The German *Mittlerorganisationen* for foreign cultural policy have established a special United States chapter of the Standing Committee on German as a Foreign Language (Ständiger Ausschuß Deutsch als Fremdsprache [StADaF]) to coordinate all language-related activities of the German funding agencies in the United States: the Goethe Institute, InterNationes, the Central Office for German Schools Abroad (Zentralstelle für das Auslandsschulwesen), and the DAAD.

While the role of the DAAD is reserved for the tertiary sector (from the junior year on in colleges and universities) and the role of InterNationes for the development and distribution of textbooks and other instructional material to teachers of German, the main responsibility for the promotion of the German language rests with the language divisions of the Goethe Institutes (currently in ten major US cities) and with the foreign language policy and curriculum advisers ("Fachberater") of the Central Office for German Schools Abroad (who are currently assigned to the relevant departments of state education departments in six states).

These advisers are sent by their German school authorities to state school boards in areas where there is a heavy concentration of German-language teaching on the high school level. Their task is to lobby for more courses on German language and civilization in the curricula, introduce state-of-the-art didactic methodologies and instructional materials, and promote strategies for teacher education ("Lehrer Aus- und Fortbildung"). Their work is a significant factor in motivating and building the next generation of university students of German and German studies.

The Goethe Institute's activities in the high school sector are directed primarily toward working with the teachers. Seminars on a variety of themes, including instructional technologies and the production of teaching materials, are offered (and funded) at regular intervals; and fellowships are offered for teachers of German at all levels for participation in summer-school programs in the United States and in Germany. The German American Partnership Program supports forty-five partnerships between United States and German high schools. Through jointly sponsored workshops and other ventures, there is a continuous exchange of information on all aspects of foreign language instruction between the Goethe Institute and the American Association of Teachers of German and its regional branches.

Cooperation in Promoting Germanics (German Philology) at Universities and Colleges

While the Goethe Institute reinforces the efforts of American high schools and colleges to motivate and prepare American pupils and undergraduates for the study of German and Germanics at the tertiary level, the DAAD and the Alexander von Humboldt Foundation concentrate on offering support to beginning graduate students and PhD candidates on the one hand and to postdoctoral scholars and faculty members on the other.

Fully funded scholarships and fellowships for participation in summer language courses ("Hochschulsommerkurse"), initial graduate research ("Kurzstipendien" ["short-term grants"]), and one-to-two-year dissertation and postdoctoral research ("Jahresstipendien") in Germany are intended to help build a highly qualified corps of university professors and scholars of Germanics. The goal is to offer to prospective university-level teachers of German the opportunity to spend a significant period of time in German archives and libraries, to consult with German colleagues, and to get firsthand exposure to the country of their future expertise.

In recognition of its special responsibility to Jewish scholars in the United States—and to scholarship on the social, communal, and intellectual history of German-speaking Jewry—the DAAD offers special research grants for research at the Leo Baeck Institute in New York and at relevant research institutes in Germany.

While neither the DAAD nor the Alexander von Humboldt Foundation interfere with the choice of topics and methodologies proposed by the applicants for their fellowships, a conscious effort is made to select the best applicants for these privileged opportunities. Undoubtedly the choices made have shaped the profile of American departments of German.

The number of fellowships offered annually to future American Germanists has dropped significantly over the past twenty years. This drop is a function of three factors: there is a limited number of new faculty openings in the field; a limited number of new faculty members are needed annually to reproduce the field; and many departments continue to recruit native speakers for faculty positions. Considerations of this sort notwithstanding, the DAAD and the foundation continue to support individual scholarly excellence in the field.

In addition to this support for students, there are a number of alumni relations programs that enable former fellowship holders to keep in touch with their host institution, with the DAAD or the foundation, and with Germany in general.

Scholars at major research universities or prestigious liberal arts colleges are self-directed and often have at their disposal the funds they need to carry out their research anywhere in the world. Experience has shown, however, that for certain individual research projects or projects undertaken together with a German counterpart, the DAAD Study Visit Research Grants are a welcome incentive and can frequently be arranged in conjunction with a sabbatical leave. Certainly, in selecting the research projects to be funded—a process in which noted American representatives of the field have assisted—the DAAD has had a hand in guiding major research trends.

The Alexander von Humboldt Foundation Senior Award and the DAAD Jacob und Wilhelm Grimm Preis for scholars of Germanics are not fellowships but rather marks of distinction reserved for the leaders in the field, in recognition of their life's work.

The DAAD also provides opportunities for curricular and methodological interaction between United States and German Germanists through the support of short-term guest lecturerships of up to six months. These are intended as a contribution to the internationalization of instruction in Germanics and German studies.

Further, junior faculty members have the opportunity to compete for DAAD-supported summer residency grants to be used at the Center for Contemporary German Literature at Washington University and at the American Institute for Contemporary German Studies in Washington, DC. These grants are an effort to encourage young American scholars to focus on the culture of the past fifty years of postwar Germany, including the former GDR.

Cooperation in Promoting Interdisciplinary German Studies

In the late 1970s, modest bilateral consultations and workshops took place between American teachers of German language and literature (Germanics) and the DAAD about the future of the discipline and the perceived need for thorough curricular reform. Special issues of *Monatshefte* and the *German Quarterly*, which were funded with considerable support from Germany; a series of DAAD occasional papers on German *Landeskunde* and *Deutschlandstudien*; and the creation and rapid evolution of the Western Association for German Studies into the nationwide German Studies Association were a direct outcome of these debates.

With the growing awareness that aggressive action was needed to maintain interest in Germany, German culture, and German language among the next generation of American students, a task force consisting of representatives of the German Studies Association and Women in German was formed in the early 1980s, and an action program was formulated. The DAAD office of New York also made a number of decisions that helped shape the American debate and encouraged individual college and university departments to test innovative curricular and organizational structures. Foremost among these new ideas was the notion that Germanics as a hitherto largely philological discipline would stand to profit from engaging other disciplines and their perspectives on a common subject, namely, all things German. It was further recognized that doing Germanics in the United States would henceforth have to be essentially different from doing *Germanistik* in Germany. It was understood that interest in German language and culture could best be stimulated with information about Germany as a modern country and European partner of the United States. This stimulation of interest would entail creating alliances among teachers and scholars from different disciplines, including instruction in English, and adding subjects that went beyond the domain of the humanities. To offset the reproach of dilettantism, new didactical practices had to be introduced, such as collaborative teaching with faculty members from other disciplines.

The debate about the canon in the humanities may have helped the gradual transformation of traditional Germanics into an open field of interdisciplinary discourses. However, the financial crisis in the language departments limited the implementation of the recommendations that the task force on German studies had elaborated in 1985. Assistance was needed. Since the DAAD had been actively involved, it developed the requisite expertise and gained the trust of the American academic community for its support programs.

In the mid-1980s, Germany's foreign cultural policy was not free of financial constraints, but despite German reluctance to spend more money on cultural matters, a number of factors helped the DAAD claim the resources needed to bring about this paradigm shift in the support of matters German in America: the recognition of the advent of a "successor generation" to the German émigrés in American academe and to the old hands in American politics who had known Germany (and many of them German) very well, mostly through personal experiences in the war and the immediate postwar era. There was a concern that the new generation had to be groomed carefully in the wake of the growing irritations between a superpower and an ally in the process of political emancipation and, eventually, in the face of German unification.

Some of the DAAD and Alexander von Humboldt Foundation programs that had a measurable effect on this paradigm shift in Germanics in America were:

the award, to outstanding young scholars, of the Bundeskanzler Fellowships through the foundation

the introduction of jointly sponsored and financed German Studies Guest Lecturerships (currently 8) and endowed chairs (currently 4) through the DAAD

the introduction of DAAD postgraduate seminars on selected German studies topics, in collaboration with the University of California, Berkeley; Cornell University; and the University of Chicago

DAAD grants for team-taught courses in German studies

annual prizes for best articles, books, and German studies syllabi, in collaboration with the German Studies Association

the creation of a *German Studies Syllabi* database, in collaboration with Cornell University

the creation of a *German Studies Faculty Directory* database and publication, in collaboration with *Monatshefte*

support for the Humanities Program and the Documentation Center of the American Institute for Contemporary German Studies

The benefits from this paradigm shift were manifold; the discipline of Germanics was challenged to move in response to the changes occurring around it.

Cooperation in Promoting German and European Studies Centers

The changing realities of the transatlantic relation in the wake of the end of the cold war and the beginning of European integration led to the recognition that German studies in a North American context needed to be couched in the larger framework of European studies. At the same time, the need to focus on a national effort to produce academically trained United States experts for the coming interaction with Europe on a qualitatively new level was acutely felt. And it was recognized that a number of different skills, for different careers, must be promoted.

In 1990, the DAAD created so-called centers of excellence for the training of future United States leaders in the transatlantic European dialogue with the United States, in which Germany would play a major role. Today, five such centers for German and European studies exist in the United States. They receive DAAD support for the first ten years of their existence, after which their programs are to continue with funds raised independently.

While each center has its unique profile and emphasizes different projects and approaches, they are all interdisciplinary and undertake comparative research projects in the humanities and social sciences to support young academics, and they all provide a forum for discussions on contemporary German and European issues while encouraging the use of the German language on a sophisticated level. The centers form a network of cooperation and consultation among themselves and with other similar centers in the world (Birmingham, England; Montreal-York, Canada; Paris-Lyon, France; Wroclaw, Poland; Sofia, Bulgaria; Amsterdam, Netherlands; Tokyo, Japan). Special synergies are achieved through joint appointments of faculty members to the centers and relevant departments of the host universities.

When one looks back on some twenty years of close cooperation between departments of German, Germanics, and German studies in the United States and German agencies for the promotion of things German, it seems fair to say that through joint intellectual efforts, but also through joint funding, the landscape of the discipline and of the profession was significantly changed. In many ways, the United States development and the current status quo are models for the discipline of *Auslandsgermanistik* in other countries. There are signs that even *Inlandsgermanistik* in Germany is being affected.

Closing Remarks

Reflections on Writing
a History of German Studies
in the United States

FRANK TROMMLER

Can one write a history of German studies in the United States since the nineteenth century that is both a comprehensive account of the institutional developments and a window into American-German intellectual relations? As one reads the impressive, almost overwhelming material in this volume, the question might not come as a surprise. It arises from the assessment of the various elements of the professional discipline of German, elements that draw on many aspects of the culture of the American academy, thereby raising interest in larger, intercultural issues. But the question also results from the apparent disconnect between the history of an academic discipline that follows a certain pedagogical and linguistic mission and the wider world of cultural bridge building across the Atlantic. Underlying the question is the understanding that this vast body of new information about an old discipline needs to be contextualized in the American educational system as well as in the dialogue between American and German cultural elites.[1]

The editors and contributors of this volume are aware of this understanding and have tried to insert references to those contexts wherever possible, though few are as outspoken as Jeffrey Sammons in his critical observations on the marginality of the discipline since the watershed year of 1917. As the function of such a handbook is determined primarily by the usefulness both of the individual articles and of their organization in coherent clusters, the question of contextualization takes a backseat. Yet the creation of a comprehensive analysis of a discipline will not well serve a fruitful rethinking of the discipline's future without a look outside. The difficult charge is to foster the retrospective view for the process of rethinking the discipline's survival in the twenty-first century without locking the analysis into a mere affirmation of institutional legitimacy.

Still, one cannot put the second step before the first. Only after the various narratives have been put side by side can the discipline's contributions be historically situated and evaluated in the light of today's concerns. The following remarks attempt to lay out some of the venues for historical contextualization. By looking at the wider arena of the intellectual exchange between Americans and Germans since the early nineteenth century, at the interconnections with the sizable German immigrant group, and at the relation with German *Germanistik*, I hope to provide some criteria for an evaluation of the past course of the profession and its future options. By way of a conclusion, I sketch out the place of German in the recent transformations of the academy in general and the study of foreign languages in particular.

American-German Intellectual Relations

When did German studies function as a window into American-German intellectual relations? Considering the last two centuries of an initially fairly close, later dramatically discontinuous exchange between the two nations, one is tempted to answer: As long as it was not institutionalized in academic confines. Though provocative, this response helps us focus on the most fruitful period of German-American intellectual relations, when the study of German language, literature, philosophy, and science was central to American elites: the nineteenth century. While the fact that the German research university became the model for the transformation of the American college into a modern university was never totally forgotten (Hofstadter and Metzger 367–412), German influences in other areas, in particular in the emergence of an American national literature, were similarly incisive yet lost favor with intellectual historians, at least since the anti-German agenda in this country during World War I. Only specialists remembered that New England transcendentalists learned to forge the first genuine American intellectual movement as students of German literature and philosophy, of Goethe, Schiller, Herder, Lessing, Kant, and the Romantics (Bauschinger). Awakened by Mme de Stael's *De l'Allemagne*, which was translated in 1814, the New England intelligentsia found in Germany a model for their own endeavors to generate an aesthetic culture. Based on Herder's concept of the modernity and authenticity of national cultures, they saw as their task "to foster American genius, and by independent literary criticism, instruct and guide the public taste" (qtd. in Nye 241; see Mueller-Vollmer, "Translating" 89).

Of course, attending the universities of Göttingen and Berlin helped create intellectual sparks, as in the cases of Edward Everett (professor of classics at Harvard and teacher of George Ripley and Ralph Waldo Emerson), George Ticknor (the first professor for Romance philology and literature at Harvard), and George Bancroft (the founder of American historiography), whose 1824 call in the *North American Review* for studying German authors found a resounding response in the following decades. The veneration of Goethe and Schiller—the "cult of classicism" (Buckley)—did not originate in the classrooms of colleges, which were often led by clerics who abhorred the paganism of certain German men of letters, especially Goethe. Harvard College was the exception, thanks to Karl Follen, a German political refugee who assembled a very intelligent *German Reader for Beginners* (1826) with excerpts from Lessing, Schiller, Novalis, Goethe, Wackenroder, and August Wilhelm Schlegel (Brumm 150–51)—also thanks to Henry Wadsworth Longfellow, who promoted the vision of Germany, the Romantic country, that inspired generations of American students to go to Germany and learn its language.

In contrast, the academic study in the newly established graduate programs of Johns Hopkins, Yale, Cornell, University of Pennsylvania, Columbia, and other universities after 1876 contains all the elements of serious scholarship but conveys little of this public fascination with the Romantic and idealistic spirit of German literature. If one looks for a lively public exchange with Germany at this time, one finds it in the realm of science, pedagogy, and—most enthusiastically—in music, not in literature. Though the reading public took note of the more recent German writers (Tatum; Mullen), the academicism of the engagement with German literature indicates a qualitative change in the relation. As indicated by Peter Uwe Hohendahl in the introduction, there was still, among Germanists like Kuno Francke and Marion Dexter Learned, a sense of a mission for American *Germanistik*, a sense of contributing guidance "to the development of a truly national literature in America" (Learned, "Lehrerbund" 13). Seen in the context of the nineteenth century, however, this missionary spirit is a faint echo of the emphatic emulation of the German model with which the transcendentalists and their contemporaries elevated literature as a crucial contributor to the creation of a national culture.

As a consequence, one needs to understand the academic pursuit of German, strongly regulated by the newly imported principles of German *Wissenschaft* and the dominance of the philological paradigm, both as an advancement and as an expression of a specialization that does not come without cultural presumptions toward the world outside the academy. Certainly, most of the energy was directed toward teaching and analyzing the foreign language, and in a multilingual society this work seemed close enough to everyday life. How far that work progressed in the hierarchy of higher education became apparent with the founding of the Modern Language Association in 1883 against the resistance of the classical philologists who had dominated college curricula. Yet the preceptorial spirit and rhetoric that came with the German scientific connection penetrated the teaching of both language and literature. It benefited from America's newly achieved sense of full participation in the manifestations of high culture, which Lawrence Levine and Michael Kammen have brilliantly documented for the late nineteenth century (Levine; Kammen). But this advancement as part of the new buildup of American cultural and scientific prowess in reflection if not imitation of European models also made the German academic enterprise dependent on the fortunes of this process. When the authority of German *Wissenschaft* and academic culture, which had provided strong support for this enterprise, was challenged in World War I and when the symbolism of the German language as a tool for social and intellectual cultivation appeared to have been exaggerated, even unwarranted, fortunes turned, leaving the discipline exposed and without recourse. Not having been able to become much of a player in the intellectual dialogue between the two cultures, American Germanics was still visible enough to serve as a lightning rod for the aggressive self-confirmation of American identity. While the story of the invention of the enemy for America's international self-assertion has been explored (Trommler "Inventing"), one should not overlook the backlash effect of the ambitious pursuit of cultural mastery with the help of another culture.

Except for the Aspen Convocation at the anniversary of Goethe's birth in 1949, arguably the largest public festivity in the United States in honor of a German writer since World War I, American Germanists remained at the margins of the intellectual discourse between the two cultures. The only larger forum where Germanists effectively negotiated the high standing of German culture was the MLA. Its community of language and literature specialists, whose organizational growth owed much to Germanists, recognized academic distinction beyond political sentiments. It facilitated that special moment when its president, Robert Herndon Fife, a professor of German at Columbia, presented his address in 1944, at the height of the war with Germany, under the title "Nationalism and Scholarship."[2] Unsurprisingly the MLA, after shedding much responsibility for language pedagogy and its advocacy during World War I, had turned into a rather elitist organization. Beyond its confines, however, the German profession became used to a certain isolation. Henry Hatfield and Joan Merrick's 1948 critique of the failure of the profession to interpret "the German mind to a puzzled nation" summed up that isolation (354).

In fact, during Hitler's reign over Germany and Austria, whose effect on the profession has been thoroughly examined (Hoecherl-Alden, "Germanisten"; Lauwers-Rech), it was an exiled writer from Germany who became a national authority in interpreting the German mind for Americans. Thomas Mann, whose public appearances as a celebrated speaker against Hitler and as the author of *Doktor Faustus* were not particularly welcomed by German departments, reinstated for a short moment literature as a window to the other country for a broad American audience. When other refugee writers and academics—from Franz Neumann to Hannah Arendt and Paul Tillich—opened far-ranging debates about Germany's descent into barbarism, only a few Germanists participated in a visible way, among them Werner Richter, the former undersecretary of the Prussian Ministry of Education, who wrote a sobering yet insightful and realistic book on the problems of reeducating the Germans after the war (*Re-educating Germany*). It was all the more reassuring that the Aspen Convocation in 1949, which brought together musicians and politicians but also luminaries like Ortega y Gasset, Albert Schweitzer, Stephen Spender, Thornton Wilder, and Ernst Robert Curtius, gave Germanists a prominent place. Among them, Barker Fairley, Hermann Weigand, and Ludwig Lewisohn discussed Goethe's humanistic vision for a newly emerging postwar world. It might have been the last time that a literary writer—the quintessential representative of the German mind—was celebrated as a great catalyst for the problems of a world in shambles. Victor Lange remarked that the convocation became "beyond its immediate purpose of honoring Goethe, a remarkably revealing mirror of our own thinking" ("Goethe Convocation" 33).

The Ethnic Nexus

Contextualizing the history of German in the United States with the expansion and contraction of the German ethnic group appears at first to be of rather marginal importance. The volume does little to correct this assumption, reflecting the prevailing aversion of Germanists to any association with the rituals and celebrations of German Americans, which usually congeal into the stereotype of beer-drinking lovers of sauerbraten and sentimental German group singing. The aversion has at least three well-founded reasons. First was the impact of both the anti-German hysteria of World War I and the shunning of things German in view of the Holocaust, whose perpetrators made the concept of Germanness unfit for public consumption. Second, the association with German Americans tends to make American Germanists ill at ease, as they are used to pursuing the study and teaching of German as an activity whose legitimacy is clearly recognized as professional, not ethnic. Third, closely related to this attitude is repugnance for the low or outmoded intercourse with German culture and literature that has been associated with this community since the nineteenth century.

Yet the reasons for rethinking this relationship are manifold and in no way merely antiquarian.[3] Historians and Americanists have begun to move beyond the self-serving stereotypes about German Americans that have led to a reconfiguration of the notions of culture, immigration, and assimilation (Conzen, "Phantom Landscapes" and "Political Myths"; Sollors, *Multilingual America;*

Kazal, "Revisiting Assimilation" and *Becoming*). That German immigrants represent the largest ethnic group in the United States should prompt us to take a more than fleeting look at the group's traceable influence as the other on the formation of an American cultural identity in the nineteenth century and at the fact that for German Americans culture was the only truly dominant factor in their self-definition. In the words of the foremost historian of German American ethnicity, Kathleen Conzen:

> What unity Germans [in the United States] had ever possessed was always cultural: they were united in fair degree by commitment to a lifestyle, a language, and a common cultural heritage, but divided by religion, region, occupation, and class. ("Political Myths" 128)

This role of culture was not unknown among American Germanists before 1917; on the contrary, some of the most remarkable contributions of the profession focused on intercultural studies, without exclusively concentrating on literature. The most prominent Germanist in this field was Oswald Seidensticker, who with Friedrich Kapp in New York and Heinrich Rattermann in Cincinnati established the academic study of Germans in America after 1867 at the University of Pennsylvania, where his successor, Marion Dexter Learned, expanded scholarship with the leading journal *German American Annals*. The journal was to document the cultural and scholarly commitment of the National German-American Alliance, which was founded in 1901. Aside from this function the journal is a rich source of scholarship on German Americans in the nineteenth century. The most comprehensive study on this subject, *The German Element in the United States, with Special Reference to Its Political, Moral, Social, and Educational Influence*, was published by the Cornell Germanist Albert B. Faust in 1909. In his efforts to build a museum of German art and culture at Harvard, Kuno Francke focused strongly on the German American community, which applauded his plan but was, except for the brewer Adolphus Busch in Saint Louis, not particularly eager to invest substantial money in it.

While the academic institutionalization of the study of German profited from the high standing of German scientific culture, it also gained momentum from the fact that, thanks to the mass immigration and the ascendancy of Germans in the ranks of social and cultural elites since the arrival of the forty-eighters, German functioned as a second language in the public sphere in a way that is often compared with that of Spanish nowadays. What this success meant in terms of literary publication and reception has recently been made evident by the Harvard Americanist Werner Sollors and his Longfellow Institute: among the 120,000 imprints published in the United States in foreign languages that he found in the Harvard University system, German titles accounted for more than 25,000, making German by far the largest single language group. Note also the 5,000 German newspapers and periodicals that Karl Arndt and

May Olson listed in their volume *The German-Language Press in the Americas, 1732–1955.*

The projection of ethnic homogeneity that has surrounded the German immigration group needs to be revised in favor of a more porous, dialogic concept. The traffic of people, books, and cultural practices across the Atlantic reached enormous proportions in the nineteenth century, with German speakers in newspapers, colleges, and the professions moving back and forth between the two countries. This exchange lost momentum in the twentieth century, especially in the 1930s and 1940s when the mostly Jewish refugees from Nazi Germany were cut off from their land of birth. Though usually not inclined to return, many German Jews maintained a strong intellectual attachment to German humanism, becoming cultural mediators during and after World War II. The movement across the Atlantic gained new intensity with the immigration wave of more than 300,000 Germans after World War II, which included, in the 1960s and 1970s, numerous Germanists. For more than a century, American Germanics has replenished its ranks with native-born Germans whose acculturation presents valuable clues to this interconnectedness.

The patterns of merging American and German approaches in the daily work of departments have always been highly developed, though little studied. The two approaches were a source of tension yet also a much cherished and debated feature of the departments' intercultural appeal. How much that feature corresponded with certain cultural practices of German American communities can be seen in the maintenance of German theater performances that brought academic and ethnic communities together. While German American communities in the nineteenth century could afford professional German theaters in larger cities like New York, Philadelphia, Cincinnati, and Baltimore (Guthke), in the twentieth century German departments continued to project the central role of theater in German culture with festive lay performances both of serious plays like *Faust, Wilhelm Tell, Der zerbrochene Krug, Woyzeck,* or *Mutter Courage* and lighter fare like Franz and Paul Schönthan's *Der Raub der Sabinerinnen* or comedies by Dürrenmatt.

On the larger scale, future research of the nexus of American Germanics with the fortunes (or ill fortunes) of the immigrant group of Germans will shed light on the special dynamics of certain periods: the interconnectedness of the decrease in German immigration—and subsequent loss of public influence— in the late nineteenth century with the institutional buildup of the academic study of German; the effects of the immigration wave after World War II and the institutional expansion of German in high schools and colleges in the 1960s and 1970s. This contextualization might help develop a sharper picture of the present and future shape of a considerable part of the student constituency, especially in the Midwest, where both the German heritage speaker and the heritage of German speakers still supply a sizable clientele. A sober look at the utilitarian and less cultural attitudes toward German and Germany among younger German Americans whose parents or grandparents came to the country after World War II will contribute to more sensitive recruitment strategies.

The Relation with German Germanistik

Close relations with German *Germanistik* have always been part of the self-definition of the institutionalized study of German in the United States. Departments on the graduate level were established to keep American students from studying overseas, and they emphasized their closeness to the German model. This similarity was welcomed by the university presidents and administrators, who learned to foster the new spirit of scholarly inquiry over the routines of the religion-and-classics-based college education for young gentlemen. They rarely committed themselves to direct imitations of German structures and curricula—not even at the first German-style university, Johns Hopkins—but helped institute a German scientific attitude, which, in the words of the sociologist Edward Shils,

> meant no trifling, no self-indulgence, getting on with the job. It was uncongenial to false pride and all-knowingness. Specialization was quite consistent with the secularized Protestant Puritanism of the quarter of the century which preceded the First World War. (186)

New and often shocking was the application of this attitude to the humanities. Germanists took a prominent position with their devotion to the spirit of philology, which paralleled the historians' zeal for archival sources. Both disciplines offered a kind of apprenticeship that proved the need of the academic study of their subjects, though that study lacked broader appeal among college educators. At the 1896 MLA meeting, Calvin Thomas, a Germanist at Columbia, distinguished between the philologists who engaged in painstaking analysis and the "the literary men" who were stronger in delivering engaging talks about literature (Graff 94). The dominance of philology notwithstanding, the stature of the "literary men" remained attractive, as it had been the norm among nineteenth-century literary critics and helped reconnect German, English, and Romance departments with the larger public also in the new century. In his study of the history of English departments, Gerald Graff has pointed to the waning of the philological paradigm that was used to legitimize the need for the specifically academic study of languages and literatures. He illuminates how the concept of literary criticism emerged after World War I "as a common cause of diverse groups who sought an alternative to the research model that would close the yawning gap between investigators and generalists" (121).

In the debate whether German studies in the United States followed a path that distinguished itself from that of German *Germanistik*, Graff's observations are of extreme importance. The steps that led from Thomas's "literary men," who included the most intriguing and celebrated mediator of German literature in the nineteenth century, Bayard Taylor, to the literary critics of the 1930s, 1940s, and 1950s, who honed the mastery of well-written, circumspect interpretations, are indeed qualitative. Yet they display a continuity in their strongly reader-based, readable analyses that allow us to distinguish the American tradition on its own terms. While this volume shows the reflection of German methodologies since the 1880s, especially in the sections "Approaches and Methods" and "Research in Historical Perspective," it leaves the study of this American continuity, which is based on an acculturation that is different from reading German literature and has a different relation with the audience inside and outside the classroom, to future scholarship.

What is clearly presented as an American form of Germanics is the development of German studies under the auspices of interdisciplinarity, cultural studies, and minority studies since about 1980. In turn, the two preceding waves of distancing practices vis-à-vis German *Germanistik* are marked by their German origins: first, the influx of mostly Jewish refugees who tried to reconnect American Germanics with comparative and world literature, as expressed in Leo Spitzer's answer to an article by Karl Viëtor in 1945 and in books that became academic best sellers in the 1950s, like Erich Heller's essay volumes *The Disinherited Mind* and *"The Artist's Journey into the Interior"*; second, the influx of younger German Germanists in the 1960s and 1970s, who learned to reconnect the discipline with the new spirit of political and social commitment that had penetrated the German university in the late 1960s. Some of the most unsettling debates about what the role of American Germanics was in the era of Hitler and the Holocaust took place between members of these two groups, whose generational differences also mirrored changing attitudes to literature in general, as could be seen in English and foreign language departments at that time. Raising the question of what the classical tradition of German literature had meant during the 1930s and 1940s in the United States reflected some of the confrontations between students and professors at German universities yet did not lead to a thorough analysis in the larger frame of German culture in the United States (Henry Schmidt, "What Is Oppositional Criticism?"; Rey, "Offener Brief").

Since the 1980s German studies has generated a scholarly dynamic that is based on methods and theories of the American academy and internalizes the German study object as the other. The centrality of German *Germanistik*, which dominated the transatlantic exchange for a long time, has given way to a consciously American discipline that at times even claims intellectual leadership in the reevaluation of German literature and literary scholarship. This discipline has been particularly fruitful in the area of women's and minority studies in

German. In general, temptations to make such a claim have grown in recent years, given the catalytic role that the American academy has assumed in mediating theories in their travel from continent to continent and culture to culture. What has been scarcely addressed in this development is whether departments, increasingly caught by the lack of interest and enrollments, are in the process of abandoning a thorough understanding of the rich history of German literature and language from the Middle Ages through the Reformation, Baroque, and Enlightenment to the nineteenth and twentieth centuries. A retrospective look at the history of German in the United States shows that its academic institutionalization has always been a rather precarious operation, surviving in many shapes and structures. It has always existed in a larger network of cultural and intellectual forces and cannot be masterminded by one theory, one action plan, one understanding of what the study of German language and literature is good for.

Ironically, the reality of globalization also works against generalizing images of the other culture. The need for regional or individual understanding articulates itself everywhere—with or without the reflection of multiculturalism. The new Americanization of German studies gives a clear signal for this need, and it should be understood side by side with the redefinition of a specific German *Germanistik*. This redefinition might (and should) result in new transatlantic dialogues on the uniqueness *and* multifacetedness of German language and literature, thus enriching and differentiating our understanding of the intellectual presence of a rather heterogeneous though central European region. At the same time, the Americanized discipline, in its current projection of American perspectives, especially those of United States multiculturalism, should not repeat what educated Germans did in the nineteenth century when they projected their generalizing concept of (high) culture onto America: they criticized the other culture for not being like their own.

German Studies in the American Academy

A final look at the standing of German in the American academy profits greatly from the assembled wisdom of this volume. These essays illuminate the many transformations not only of the teaching and research methods of a national literature, of its institutional support and functioning as well as of its professional identity, but also of the study of literature in general and that of foreign literature in particular. Assessing the rich material with regard to these transformations, one cannot overlook the increasingly methodological awareness of the need to define and fortify the work of criticism with knowledge of the foreign culture—especially in the period since the 1960s, in which English assumed the role of a lingua franca in science, politics, business, and communication.

Since the late nineteenth century, when the scholarly study of foreign languages and literatures was institutionalized as part of building the American research university, there has not been such an energetic recasting of the study of foreign cultures as in the last third of the twentieth century. While German, particularly with philology and the ethos of *Wissenschaftlichkeit*, occupied a prominent place in the professionalization of the humanities after 1880, it was less visible in the reforms a hundred years later. German participated in the three main areas of activity with different intensity. First, it took an active, even leading role in the pedagogical reforms under the auspices of applied linguistics, which led to the establishment of standards for teaching foreign languages, an achievement that gave foreign languages—after the devastating report of the President's Commission on Foreign Language and International Studies in 1979—much-needed legitimacy in the institutions of higher learning (*Standards* [1999]; President's Commission). Second, German participated actively though in a way less oriented toward the transitions in other disciplines, especially English, in what has been termed the cultural (or culturalist) turn in literary studies since the 1970s. While the discipline reflected the new cultural studies, with which English departments learned to transform themselves from stalwarts of high culture to mediators of the much-debated multiculturalism, it conceptualized the cultural mainly as a device for revamping the interpretive approach to a national literature. In concrete terms: with the organizational and intellectual spread of German studies, the profession of German found a new frame of reference for the contextualization of its literary works in their national and linguistic boundaries. Third, the least visible contribution of Germanics occurred in the realm of theoretical discourse, which literary critics were able to endow with an aura of authenticity usually reserved for literary works. Here English, French, and comparative literature departments, with the help of new travel networks of stars and ministars, forged new hierarchies of literary studies in which literature tended to become a platform for staging theory as an event. Although much of poststructuralist theory was rooted in German philosophy, especially Nietzsche and Heidegger—the conservative critic Allan Bloom, in his 1987 jeremiad about the demise of the American university, was eager to blame poststructuralism on German immigrants (141–56)—German scholars, if they engaged in theory, usually maintained, with intermittent invocations of Benjamin and Habermas, the exegesis of the texts of the Frankfurt school as a cautionary tale against Nietzschean antirationalism.

This abbreviated summary leaves no illusion about the small turf on which the discipline has been working. What the overly aware contributors to this volume neglect is that between the two reform periods at the end of the nineteenth and twentieth centuries European foreign languages enjoyed a stable period of integration in the American university. Although the events of World

War I can be rightly described as a break with the preponderance of German among the foreign languages in the United States, they do not indicate a departure from the embrace of Europe as a main source of American cultural identity. The war only shifted that preponderance from German to French— without, by the way, providing the additional support and privileges that the members of French departments hoped for in the 1920s and 1930s. As indicated in regard to the self-confident role of the MLA as the guardian of academic high culture, the individual departments of national literatures were woven into the fabric of liberal arts education. At times they reached out into the public discourse on national issues yet usually were content to perform their functions well in a society that did not hold academic pursuit in particularly high esteem. Thanks to the cold war, which moved higher education into the limelight and triggered an unprecedented stream of financial support for the teaching of foreign languages and cultures, the European connection held considerable weight, reinforced by the Vietnam debacle, long into the 1980s.

While the initial reaction to the demise of the European connection in the 1990s was to blame it on the end of the cold war, a long-term view that takes into account the shifts in the academy helps us see developments that weakened the academic embrace of European cultures years before. When the journal of the American Academy of Arts and Sciences, *Daedalus*, in 1997 devoted a special issue entitled "American Academic Culture in Transition: Fifty Years, Four Disciplines" (see Bender and Schorske), it distinguished, in the articles on literary studies, a clear split between the earlier period of Eurocentrism and the current period of a multicultural agenda. The historian Thomas Bender stated:

> The ambitious, white, male, Europe-oriented, and quite privileged culture of major research universities that had taken its style and intellectual agenda from the 1950s could not sustain itself through the last quarter of the twentieth century. (24)

A few years earlier, the MLA had provided a survey of the new agenda, *Redrawing the Boundaries: The Transformation of English and American Literary Studies* (1992), edited by Stephen Greenblatt and Giles Gunn. This survey delineated the turn from literary studies as a humanistic discipline with a unifying mission to a discipline of illuminating, crossing, and redesigning boundaries (4). On a deeper level, Greenblatt and Gunn's book confirmed the end of the universalism that the study of French and German literature had once made so stimulating for Americans in the search for their own cultural universalism. It called off the claim of universalism in literature in general as it empowered boundaries of, in the term of the 1970s and 1980s, difference or *différence*. That this shift does not privilege English literature—though English departments have created new intellectual capital from it—was made evident by Robert Scholes, who summed up the change: "Literature which once represented universal values is now seen as representing values that are more local, historical, connected to particular times and places, to particular groups and their interests" (21).

The contrast to the celebration of Goethe as a "cosmopolitan humanist" at Aspen after World War II, in which Bender saw an attempt "to heighten the stature of American culture," could not be greater (19). Foreignness is now the key to the truth value of literature, though preferably in English, not in another language. The foreignness that once was approached through the learning of the other language in order to establish the universality of the humanistic message beyond all boundaries is now the guarantor of identity in contradistinction to universalist claims. It had better be articulated in English to sustain partiality and identity. It is hardly surprising that Scholes concludes, "English is now a foreign literature in a (relatively) familiar language." American literature has taken its place. "The literature of this foreign country, England, now requires formal preparation in the background of English history and culture, just as the study of French literature requires the study of France" (21). The question has become, Is it worth the effort? What do the national literatures of Europe offer to those who look for a reflection of their minority status, their identity in opposition to universalist claims? The draw of postcolonialist studies might help redefine the draw of these literatures.

As German, apart from mediating a business- and technology-oriented competitor, keeps the European share of American self-reflection cognizant of some of the most powerful challenges of the twentieth century, the social, political, and gender-related contextualization of language and literature in the confines of this European culture helps provide professional identity. While there is less glamorous intellectual avant-gardism than in the discipline that straddles two or three literatures, comparative literature, there is more coherence in the constant revisiting of the other culture both as geographic and historic entity and as a generator of alterity. What's more, the tension between the elevation of literature as the primary pursuit and the study of cultural productions and discourses of all sorts, which lies at the heart of every literary discipline, seems to tear less deeply into the professional coherence of German than of comparative literature, as the critical reaction to the Bernheimer report (Bernheimer) showed in the mid-1990s. As Denis Hollier stated in his enlightened introduction to the unusual and much acclaimed *New History of French Literature*, "Literature's production and consumption remain for the most part shaped by the nonuniversality of languages, framed by the experience of frontiers" (xxi). Tracing the dialectic of national and universalist tendencies in literature since the eighteenth century, Hollier defined the enterprise of literary historiography as a constant confirmation and overcoming of frontiers that gives a French literary history written outside France particular intellectual momentum.

Unlike French, the American discipline of German has not (yet) come together to produce a conceptually innovative literary history that reflects both sides of the border. But it has come together in many other, carefully organized ways, instituting forums for younger professionals to get recognition and feedback; attracting substantial financial support from German-speaking countries; devising strategies for the increasing needs of professional self-reflection and improvement; and, most inspiring, reinterpreting many areas of German literature and culture in unprecedented ventures. After all, this volume, devised to provide information about the history of the profession, already shows, with its broad array of contributors from many fields and specializations, a high degree of integration and awareness. Those qualities seem an effective prerequisite for the further well-being of the discipline.

Notes

1 The best and most comprehensive work on this dialogue, Henry Pochmann's *German Culture in America: Philosophical and Literary Influences, 1600–1900,* does not explicitly go into the history of German departments.

2 The *PMLA Special Millenium Issue* in 2000 recognized the significance of the lecture and reprinted it in excerpts (Fife, "Nationalism").

3 For a more extensive discussion of this much neglected topic, see my "Literary Scholarship."

David Bathrick is Jacob Gould Schurman Professor of German Studies and Theatre, Film, and Dance at Cornell University. His publications include *The Dialectic and the Early Brecht* (1976), *Modernity and the Text* (coedited with Huyssen; 1989), and *The Powers of Speech: The Politics of Culture in the GDR* (1995). He is a cofounder and coeditor of *New German Critique* and is currently finishing a book on the Holocaust and film.

David Benseler is Emile B. de Sauzé Professor of Modern Languages and Literatures and professor of German at Case Western Reserve University. He is coeditor of *Teaching German in America: Prolegomena to a History* (1988) and *Teaching German in Twentieth-Century America* (2001). He continues to work in the history of the profession. His current project is "Dissertations in German Studies from 1861 to the Present."

Russell A. Berman is Walter A. Haas Professor in the Humanities in the Departments of German Studies and Comparative Literature at Stanford University. Some of his books are *The Rise of the Modern German Novel: Crisis and Charisma* (1986) and *Enlightenment or Empire: Colonial Discourse in German Culture* (1998). He is currently working on a study of literary autonomy and social change.

Clifford Albrecht Bernd is professor of German at the University of California, Davis. He is author of "World War I as a Shaping Force in American Germanics" (2001), *Theodor Storm: The Dano-German Poet and Writer* (2003), *Poetic Realism in Scandinavia and Central Europe* (1995), *German Poetic Realism* (1981), and *Theodor Storm's Craft of Fiction* (1966).

Jeannine Blackwell is professor of German and women's studies at and dean of the Graduate School of the University of Kentucky. She is president of Women in German. Her research centers on women's fiction, fairy tales, and autobiography from 1500 to 1900. She is coeditor of *Bitter Healing: German Women Writers, 1700–1830, The Queen's Mirror: Fairy Tales by German Women Writers, 1780–1900,* and *Cultural Contentions in the Early Modern Era* (1995).

Sara Friedrichsmeyer is professor of German and head of the Department of German Studies at the University of Cincinnati. A former coeditor of the *Women in German Yearbook*, she is author of *The Androgyne in Early German Romanticism* (1983) and coeditor of *The Enlightenment and Its Legacy* (with Becker-Cantarino; 1991) and *The Imperialist Imagination: German Colonialism and Its Legacy* (with Lennox and Zantop; 1998).

Francis G. Gentry is professor emeritus of German at the University of Wisconsin, Madison, and Pennsylvania State University. He is coeditor of *The Nibelungen Tradition: An Encyclopedia* (2002) and editor of *A Companion to Middle High German Literature to the Fourteenth Century* (2002). He is currently editing "A Companion to Hartmann von Aue."

Donald Haase is chair of the Department of German and Slavic Studies at Wayne State University. He is editor of *The Reception of Grimms' Fairy Tales: Responses, Reactions, Revisions* (1993), Joseph Jacob's *Fairy Tales and More Fairy Tales* (2002), and *Fairy Tales and Feminism: New Approaches* (forthcoming). He is currently at work on the fairy tale in war, exile, and the Holocaust.

Jost Hermand is William F. Vilas Research Professor of German Studies in the Department of German at the University of Wisconsin, Madison, and honorary professor of the Humboldt University in Berlin. He is author, with Richard Hamann and Frank Trommler, of *Cultural History of Germany in Eight Volumes* (1959–88); *History of Germanistik* (1994); and *Zuhause und anderswo: Erfahrungen im kalten Krieg* (2001). He is currently writing a book under the title "Nach der Postmoderne: Eine alternative Ästhetik."

Patricia Herminghouse is Karl F. and Bertha A. Fuchs Professor Emerita of German Studies in the Department of Modern Languages and Cultures at the University of Rochester. She is coeditor of *German Feminist Writing* (2001), *Women in German Yearbook* (1995–2001), and editor of *Ingeborg Bachmann and Christa Wolf: Prose and Drama* (1998). Her "Feminist Doctorates and Careers in Germanics, 1980–2000," coauthored with David Benseler, appears in *Women in German Yearbook* 19.

Gisela Hoecherl-Alden is assistant professor of German in the Department of Modern Languages and Classics at the University of Maine, Orono. She is author of articles on German scholars in the United States and the role of women in Germanics in the first half of the twentieth century. She is coauthor of the elementary textbook *Deutsch heute*. She is working on the Holocaust and Nazism in recent German films.

Peter Uwe Hohendahl is Jacob Gould Schurman Professor of German and Comparative Literature and director of the Institute for German Cultural Studies at Cornell University. Among his publications are *The Institution of Criticism* (1982), *Reappraisals: Shifting Alignments in Postwar Critical Theory* (1991), and *Prismatic Thought: Theodor W. Adorno* (1995). One of his current projects is the fate of the humanities and the present crisis of the university.

Noah Isenberg teaches German and film studies at Wesleyan University. He is author of *Between Redemption and Doom: The Strains of German-Jewish Modernism* (1999) and editor and translator of Arnold Zweig's *The Face of East European Jewry* (2004). He is currently writing a book on the cinema of Edgar G. Ulmer and editing a volume on Weimar cinema.

Irene Kacandes is associate professor of German studies and comparative literature at Dartmouth College. She is author of *Talk Fiction: Literature and the Talk Explosion* (2001) and coeditor of *A User's Guide to German Cultural Studies* (1997). She is coediting *Teaching the Representation of the Holocaust* for the MLA. Her current research focuses on violence in the Weimar Republic.

Cora Lee Kluge is professor of German at the University of Wisconsin, Madison. She is editor of Christian Essellen's *Babylon* (1996) and *Teaching German in Twentieth-Century America* (with Benseler and Nickisch; 2000) and author of articles on Schiller, Droste-Hülshoff, German American studies, and the history of the profession. She is currently working on an anthology of German American literature, 1850–1914.

Sara Lennox is professor of Germanic languages and literatures and director of the Social Thought and Political Economy Program at the University of Massachusetts, Amherst. She is editor of *The Imperialist Imagination: German Colonialism and Its Legacy* (with Friedrichsmeyer and Zantop; 1998) and *Feminist Movements in a Globalizing World* (with Roth; 2002). She is currently working on a book about Ingeborg Bachmann.

John A. McCarthy teaches German and comparative literature at Vanderbilt University. His research interests extend to the history of Germanics, the institutionalization of literature, and philosophy and literature. He is author of *Crossing Boundaries* (1989) and coeditor of *The Future of Germanistik in the USA* (1996). His forthcoming book is *Remapping Reality: Nietzsche, Goethe, Grass*.

Wolfgang Natter teaches German studies, geography, and cultural and social theory at the University of Kentucky. He is coeditor of *Objectivity and Its Other* (1995) and *The Social and Political Body* (1996) and author of *Literature at War, 1914–1940: Representing the "Time of Greatness" in Germany* (1999). He is currently researching epistemological and substantive spaces of globalization in the nineteenth and twentieth centuries.

Carl Niekerk is associate professor of German at the University of Illinois, Urbana. He is author of *Zwischen Naturgeschichte und Anthropologie: Lichtenberg im Kontext der Spätaufklärung* (2004) and articles on eighteenth-century German literature, twentieth-century Austrian literature, and theory. He is currently working on "Gustav Mahler, the Idea of a German National Culture and the Avant-Garde."

Brent O. Peterson is associate professor of German at Lawrence University. He is author of *Popular Narratives and Ethnic Identity* (1991) and articles on history and historical fiction, middlebrow culture, and reading German American literature. He is currently finishing work on a book "History, Fiction, and Germany: Writing the Nineteenth-Century Nation."

Simon Richter is associate professor in the Department of Germanic Languages and Literatures at the University of Pennsylvania. He is author of *Laocoon's Body and the Aesthetics of Pain* (1992), coeditor of *Unwrapping Goethe's Weimar* (2000), and editor of the *Goethe Yearbook*. His research and teaching interests concern eighteenth-century literature and culture, gender studies, and film.

Orrin W. Robinson is professor of German studies at Stanford University and Christensen Chair and Director of Stanford's Introduction to the Humanities Program. He is author of *Whose German?: The ach/ich Alternation and Related Phenomena in "Standard" and "Colloquial"* (2001), *Clause Subordination and Verb Placement in the Old High German* Isidor *Translation* (1996), and *Old English and Its Closest Relatives: A Survey of the Earliest Germanic Languages* (1992).

Jeffrey L. Sammons is Leavenworth Professor of German Emeritus at Yale University. He is author of *Ideology, Mimesis, Fantasy: Charles Sealsfield, Friedrich Gerstäcker, Karl May, and Other German Novelists of America* (1998) and *The Shifting Fortunes of Wilhelm Raabe: A History of Criticism as a Cautionary Tale* (1992). He is currently working on "Friedrich Spielhagen: Novelist of Germany's False Dawn."

Renate A. Schulz is professor of German studies and former director of the Interdisciplinary PhD Program in Second Language Acquisition and Teaching at the University of Arizona. She has published widely on the learning and teaching of foreign languages. She is a past president of the AATG (1990 and 1991) and former editor of *Die Unterrichtspraxis* (1980–85). Her special interests include the role of explicit grammar teaching in foreign language learning, language assessment, and teacher development.

Hinrich C. Seeba is professor of German at the University of California, Berkeley. He is author of books on Hofmannsthal (*Kritik des ästhetischen Menschen* [1970]) and Lessing (*Die Liebe zur Sache* [1974]) and coeditor of Kleist's works for Deutscher Klassiker Verlag (1987–91). His special interests are the cultural contexts of literary and visual representation, Wissenschaftsgeschichte, and academic emigration.

Manfred Stassen is former director of the DAAD office for North America in New York and visiting professor of German studies and letters at Johns Hopkins University. He is author of *Heidegger: The Man, The Method, The Message* (2003). He is currently working on "Nationalökonomie und Literatur: Die epistemologischen Differenzen der frühen Kapitalismuskritik (Marx, Goethe, Balzac)" and "Mésalliances philosophiques: Hannah Arendt / Martin Heidegger et Simone de Beauvoir / Jean-Paul Sartre."

Lynne Tatlock is Hortense and Tobias Lewin Distinguished Professor in the Humanities at Washington University. She has published widely on German literature and culture from 1650 to the 1990s with a concentration in the late seventeenth century and the nineteenth century. She is currently working on a translation of Justine Siegemund's *The Court Midwife* (1690).

Arlene A. Teraoka is professor of German and chair of the Department of German, Scandinavian, and Dutch at the University of Minnesota, Minneapolis. She is author of *East, West, and Others: The Third World in Postwar German Literature* (1996) and *The Silence of Entropy or Universal Discourse: The Postmodernist Poetics of Heiner Müller* (1985). Her special interests are contemporary German literature, cultural theory, and German intellectual history.

Frank Trommler is professor of German and comparative literature at the University of Pennsylvania. In 1995–2003 he directed the Humanities Program of the American Institute of Contemporary German Studies and edited the series Contemporary German Culture. He is author of *Sozialistische Literatur in Deutschland* (1976) and *Die Kultur der Weimarer Republik* (with Hermand; 1978), editor of *Germanistik in den USA* (1989), and coeditor of *The German-American Encounter* (2001).

Gerhard Weiss is Distinguished Teaching Professor of German (emeritus) in the Department of German, Scandinavian, and Dutch at the University of Minnesota, Minneapolis. He is author of *Begegnung mit Deutschland* (with Charlotte Anderson; 1970) and *In Search of Silk: Adam Olearius's Mission to Russia and Persia* (1983). He is currently working on social issues in Berlin as reflected in literature.

Meike G. Werner is assistant professor of German at Vanderbilt University. She is author of *Moderne in der Provinz: Kulturelle Experimente im Fin de Siècle Jena* (2003) and coeditor of *Romantik, Revolution & Reform: Der Eugen Diederichs Verlag im Epochenkontext 1900–1949* (1999), *German Literature, Jewish Critics* (2002), and *Karl Korsch: Briefe 1908–1939* (2001).

❦ WORKS CITED ❦

"AATG Membership Declines since 1993–94." *AATG Newsletter* 36.1 (2000): 2.

AATG Steering Committee. "Dear AATG Member." *AATG Newsletter* 13.1 (1977): 1.

"The AAUP's 'General Declaration of Principles,' 1915." *American Education: A Documentary History*. Vol. 2. Ed. Richard Hofstadter and Wilson Smith. Chicago: U of Chicago P, 1961. 861.

About the Society. Soc. for Germanic Linguistics. U of Wisconsin Dept. of German. 21 Apr. 2003 <http://german.lss.wisc.edu/~sgl/about.html>.

ACTFL Proficiency Guidelines. Yonkers: ACTFL, 1986.

The Activities of the Germanistic Society of America, 1904–1910. Vol. 4. New York: Pubs. of the Germanistic Soc. of Amer., 1910.

Adelson, Leslie A. *Making Bodies, Making History: Feminism and German Identity*. Lincoln: U of Nebraska P, 1993.

"Adjustment of the College Curriculum to Wartime Conditions and Needs." *German Quarterly* 17 (1944): 112–19.

Adorno, Theodor W. "Erziehung nach Auschwitz." *Erziehung zur Mündigkeit*. 7th ed. Frankfurt: Suhrkamp, 1981. 88–104.

———. *Negative Dialektik*. Frankfurt: Suhrkamp, 1966.

"The Aging AATG?" *AATG Newsletter* 36.1 (2000): 2.

Alewyn, Richard. "Goethe als Alibi." *Hamburger Akademische Rundschau* 3 (1949): 685–87.

Allardyce, Gilbert, et al. "The Rise and Fall of the Western Civilization Course." *American History Review* 87 (1982): 695–743.

Almstedt, Hermann. "The Merits of the Direct Method." *Monatshefte* 16 (1915): 81–88.

Alonso, Carlos J. "Editor's Column: Lost Moorings—*PMLA* and Its Audience." *PMLA* 116 (2001): 9–15.

Alter, Maria P. *A Modern Case for German*. Philadelphia: AATG, 1970.

Altschul, Arthur. "Lehrproben zum deutschen Unterricht nach konkreter Methode." *Monatshefte* 5 (1904): 108–11.

———. "Über die natürliche Methode im deutschen Unterricht." *Monatshefte* 4 (1903): 322–32.

Alwall, Ellen. *Der Dichter im Schulbuch: Die Auswahl von Dichtern in deutschen Lesebüchern, 1875–1964*. Stockholm: Almqvist, 1993.

"The American Council on German Studies." *Die Unterrichtspraxis* 4.2 (1971): 139.

Anderson, John. *The Architecture of Cognition.* Cambridge: Harvard UP, 1983.

Anderson, Mark M. "German Intellectuals, Jewish Victims: A Politically Correct Solidarity." *Chronicle of Higher Education* 19 Oct. 2001: B7–10.

Andress, Reinhard, et al. "Maintaining the Momentum from High School to College: Report and Recommendations." *Die Unterrichtspraxis* 35 (2002): 1–14.

"Die Anfänge der Frauenbewegung." *Frauenjahrbuch 1.* Frankfurt: Roter Stern, 1975. 10–18.

Angress, Ruth K. "The Woman's Perspective." Other Perspectives on the Study and Profession of Germanics Forum. MLA Annual Convention. Saint Francis Hotel, San Francisco. 28 Dec. 1975. Pub. as "German Studies: The Woman's Perspective." Lohnes and Nollendorfs, *German Studies* 247–51.

Appelt, E. P. "Das Grammophon im Sprachunterricht." *Monatshefte* 20 (1928): 166–69.

Apple, R. W., Jr. "Beyond Wursts: Renaissance in Eastern Germany." *New York Times on the Web* 29 July 1998. 2 Apr. 2003 <http://query.nytimes.com/search/advanced>.

Army Specialized Training Program. Spec. issue of *German Quarterly* 17 (1944): 165–240.

Arndt, Karl J. R. "Should Americans Teach Foreign Languages?" *School and Society* 27 (1935): 127–30.

Arndt, Karl, and May Olsen, eds. *The German-Language Press in the Americas, 1732–1955.* New York: Saur, 1980.

Arnim, Gisela von. *Märchenbriefe an Achim.* Ed. Shawn C. Jarvis. Frankfurt: Insel, 1991.

Arnim, Gisela von, and Bettina von Arnim. *Das Leben der Hochgräfin Gritta von Rattenzuhausbeiuns.* Ed. Shawn C. Jarvis. Frankfurt: Insel, 1986.

Aschheim, Steven E. *Brothers and Strangers: The East European Jew in the German and German Jewish Consciousness, 1800–1923.* Madison: U of Wisconsin P, 1982.

Ashcroft, Bill, Gareth Griffiths, and Helen Tiffin, eds. *The Empire Writes Back: Theory and Practice in Post-colonial Literatures.* London: Routledge, 1989.

"An Assessment." *AATG Newsletter* 14.1 (1978): 1–2.

Atkins, Stuart. "Karl Viëtor (1892–1951)." *Germanic Review* 26 (1951): 171–72.

"Auszüge aus der Diskussion zum Vortrag von Guy Stern." Schmitz 109–18.

Babbitt, Irving. *Literature and the American College: Essays in Defense of the Humanities.* Boston: Houghton, 1908.

Baer, Ulrich. *The Remnants of Song: Trauma and the Experience of Modernity in Charles Baudelaire and Paul Celan.* Stanford: Stanford UP, 2000.

Bagster-Collins, E. W. "Beobachtungen auf dem Gebiete des fremdsprachlichen Unterrichts." *Monatshefte* 10 (1909): 216–28.

———. Rev. of *Experiments and Studies in Modern Language Teaching,* by Algernon Coleman. *German Quarterly* 8 (1935): 43–46.

———. "Underlying Principles and Aims of Present-Day Modern Language Teaching." *German Quarterly* 5 (1932): 161–72.

Bahlsen, Leopold. "Die deutsche Lektüre an den amerikanischen Schulen." *Monatshefte* 4 (1903): 165–76.

Bammer, Angelika. "The American Feminist Reception of GDR Literature (with a Glance at West Germany)." *GDR Bulletin* 16.2 (1990): 18–24.

Bancroft, George. "Life and Genius of Goethe." *North American Review* 19 (1824): 303–25.

Barkin, Kenneth. "Bismarck in a Postmodern Age." *German Studies Review* 18 (1995): 241–51.

Barner, Wilfried. "Literaturgeschichtsschreibung vor und nach 1945: Alt, neu, alt/neu." Barner and König 119–49.

Barner, Wilfried, and Christoph König, eds. *Zeitenwechsel: Germanistische Literaturwissenschaft vor und nach 1945*. Frankfurt: Fischer, 1996.

Barnes, Frank C. "Shall German Be Dropped from Our Schools?" *Modern Language Journal* 2 (1918): 187–202.

Baross, Zsuzsa. "Poststructuralism." Makaryk 158–59.

Barry, Peter. *Beginning Theory: An Introduction to Literary and Cultural Theory*. Manchester: Manchester UP, 1995.

Bartle, Andrea, et al., eds. *"In Spuren gehen . . .": Festschrift für Helmut Koopmann*. Tübingen: Niemeyer, 1998.

Basilius, H. A. "Concerning the Objectives and Methodology of the Second Year." *German Quarterly* 13 (1940): 177–88.

Bathrick, David. "Literaturkritik als Kulturkritik: Marxistische Tendenzen in den USA?" Trommler, *Germanistik* 122–46.

———. "On Leaving Exile: American *Germanistik* in Its Social Context." Lohnes and Nollendorfs, *German Studies* 252–57.

———. *The Powers of Speech: The Politics of Culture in the GDR*. Lincoln: U of Nebraska P, 1995.

Bathrick, David, Anson Rabinbach, and Jack Zipes. "Editor's Introduction." *Special Issue on the GDR. New German Critique* 2 (1974): 2–3.

Batnitzky, Leora Faye. *Idolatry and Representation: The Philosophy of Franz Rosenzweig Reconsidered*. Princeton: Princeton UP, 2001.

Baumann, Carl. "Why Study Foreign Languages?" *Modern Language Forum* 21 (1936): 33–34.

Bauschinger, Sigrid. *Die Posaune der Reform: Deutsche Literatur im Neuengland des 19. Jahrhunderts*. Bern: Francke, 1989.

Bayerschmidt, Carl F. "The Department of Germanic Languages." *A History of the Faculty of Philosophy, Columbia University*. Ed. Jacques Barzun. New York: Columbia UP, 1957. 221–35.

Beck, Ulrich. *What Is Globalization?* Oxford: Blackwell, 2000.

Beerbaum, Alfred. "German in Our American Elementary Schools: A Report on the Experiences of the Dependents Schools in Postwar Germany." *German Quarterly* 27 (1954): 150–58.

Belgum, Kirsten. *Popularizing the Nation: Audience, Representation, and the Production of Identity in* Die Gartenlaube, *1853–1900*. Lincoln: U of Nebraska P, 1998.

Bender, Thomas. "Politics, Intellect, and the American University, 1945–1995." *Daedalus* 126.1 (1997): 1–37.

Bender, Thomas, and Carl Schorske, eds. *American Academic Culture in Transition: Fifty Years, Four Disciplines*. Princeton: Princeton UP, 1997.

Benhabib, Seyla. "Reply to Sterba and Young." *New German Critique* 62 (1994): 111–89.

Bennington, Geoffrey. "Postal Politics and the Institution of the Nation." Bhabha, *Nation* 121–37.

Benseler, David. "The Upper Division Curriculum in Foreign Languages and Literatures: Obstacles to the Realization of Promise." Silber 186–99.

Benseler, David P., Walter F. W. Lohnes, and Valters Nollendorfs, eds. *Teaching German in America: Prolegomena to a History*. Madison: U of Wisconsin P, 1988.

Benseler, David P., Craig W. Nickisch, and Cora Lee Nollendorfs, eds. *Teaching German in Twentieth-Century America*. Madison: U of Wisconsin P, 2001.

Benseler, David P., and Renate A. Schulz. "Methodological Trends in College Foreign Language Instruction." *Modern Language Journal* 64 (1980): 88–96.

Berdahl, Daphne. "Dis-membering the Past: The Politics of Memory in the German Borderland." Denham, Kacandes, and Petropoulos 309–31.

Berghahn, Klaus L. "New Historicism." *Monatshefte* 84 (1992): 141–47.

———. "Wortkunst ohne Geschichte: Zur werkimmanenten Methode der Germanistik nach 1945." *Monatshefte* 71 (1979): 387–98.

Bergsträsser, Arnold. *Sinn und Grenzen der Verständigung zwischen Nationen*. Munich: Duncker, 1930.

Berman, Russell A. "The Concept of Culture in Culture Studies Programs." *Monatshefte* 74 (1982): 241–46.

———. *Cultural Studies of Modern Germany: History, Representation, and Nationhood*. Madison: U of Wisconsin P, 1993.

Berman, Russell A., and Elizabeth Bernhardt-Kamil. "From German 1 to German Studies 001: A Chronicle of Curricular Reform." *Die Unterrichtspraxis* 32 (1999): 22–31.

Bernd, Clifford. "World War I as a Shaping Force in American Germanics." Benseler, Nickisch, and Nollendorfs 58–68.

Bernhardt, Elizabeth B. "Retrospective and Prospective Views on Foreign Language Teaching Methodologies." Stanford U. 2 June 1999.

Bernheimer, Charles, ed. *Comparative Literature in the Age of Multiculturalism*. Baltimore: Johns Hopkins UP, 1995.

Bertram, Mathias, ed. *Deutsche Literatur von Lessing bis Kafka*. Berlin: Digitale Bibliothek, 1998.

Bettelheim, Bruno. *The Uses of Enchantment: The Meaning and Importance of Fairy Tales*. New York: Knopf, 1976.

Bhabha, Homi K., ed. *Nation and Narration*. London: Routledge, 1990.

———. "Of Mimicry and Man: The Ambivalence of Colonial Discourse." *The Location of Culture*. New York: Routledge, 1994. 85–92.

———. "Postcolonial Criticism." Greenblatt and Gunn 437–65.

"A Bibliography of Publications by Jack Zipes on Fairy Tales, Fantasy, and Children's Literature." *Jack Zipes and the Sociohistorical Study of Fairy Tales*. Spec. issue of *Marvels and Tales: Journal of Fairy-Tale Studies* 16 (2002): 132–39.

Blackwell, Jeannine. "Control-Alt-Delete: Reshaping Germanics Publication in the Age of Electronic Reproduction." Benseler, Nickisch, and Nollendorfs 192–210.

———. "Fractured Fairy Tales: German Women Authors and the Grimm Tradition." *Germanic Review* 62 (1987): 162–74.

———. "Turf Management; or, Why Is the Great Tradition Fading?" *Monatshefte* 77 (1985): 271–85.

Blancké, Wilton W. "General Language as a Prognosis of Success in Foreign Language Study." *German Quarterly* 12 (1939): 71–80.

Bledsoe, Robert, Bernd Estabrook, J. Courtney Federle, Kay Henschel, Wayne Miller, and Arnim Polster, eds. *Rethinking Germanistik: Canon and Culture*. New York: Lang, 1991.

Bloch, Ernst. *The Principle of Hope*. 3 vols. Trans. Neville Plaice, Stephen Plaice, and Paul Knight. Cambridge: MIT P, 1995.

Bloom, Allan. *The Closing of the American Mind: How Higher Education Has Failed Democracy and Impoverished the Souls of Today's Students*. New York: Simon, 1987.

Bloomfield, Leonard. *Outline Guide for the Practical Study of Foreign Languages*. Baltimore: Linguistic Soc. of Amer., 1942.

Bluhm, Lothar. *Grimm-Philologie: Beiträge zur Märchenforschung und Wissenschaftsgeschichte*. Hildesheim: Olms, 1995.

Blume, Bernhard. *Narziß mit Brille: Kapitel einer Autobiographie*. Ed. Fritz Martini and Egon Schwarz. Heidelberg: Lambert Schneider, 1985.

Bodemann, Y. Michal, ed. *Jews, Germans, Memory: Reconstructions of Jewish Life in Germany*. Ann Arbor: U of Michigan P, 1996.

Bodensieck Tyre, Anne. "The Status of German in Some Universities, Colleges, and High Schools." *Monatshefte* 26 (1934): 109–12.

Boeckh, Philip A. *Encyklopädie und Methodologie der philogischen Wissenschaften*. Leipzig: Teubner, 1877.

Borneman, John, and Jeffrey M. Peck. *Sojourners: The Return of German Jews and the Question of Identity*. Lincoln: U of Nebraska P, 1995.

Bottigheimer, Ruth B. *Fairy Godfather: Straparola, Venice, and the Fairy Tale Tradition*. Philadelphia: U of Pennsylvania P, 2002.

———, ed. *Fairy Tales and Society: Illusion, Allusion, and Paradigm*. Philadelphia: U of Pennsylvania P, 1986.

———. *Grimms' Bad Girls and Bold Boys: The Moral and Social Vision of the Tales*. New Haven: Yale UP, 1987.

———. "One Hundred and Fifty Years of German at Princeton: A Descriptive Account." Benseler, Lohnes, and Nollendorfs 83–98.

Bourgeois, Joseph E. "German on Television in Cincinnati." *German Quarterly* 32 (1959): 43–48.

Bovenschen, Silvia. *Die imaginierte Weiblichkeit: Exemplarische Untersuchungen zu kulturgeschichtlichen und literarischen Präsentationsformen des Weiblichen*. Frankfurt: Suhrkamp, 1979.

———. "Über die Frage: Gibt es eine weibliche Ästhetik?" *Ästhetik und Kommunikation* 25 (1976): 60–76.

Bower, Kathrin M. *Ethics and Remembrance in the Poetry of Nelly Sachs and Rose Ausländer*. Rochester: Camden, 2000.

Brancaforte, Charlotte Lang, ed. *The Golden Signpost: A Guide to Happiness and Prosperity*. Trans. Thomas Colin. Madison: Max Kade Inst. for German-Amer. Studies; U of Wisconsin P, 1993.

Brandt, Hermann C. G. "How Far Should Our Teaching and Textbooks Have a Scientific Basis?" *PMLA* 1 (1884–85): 57–60. Rpt. in Graff and Warner 28–33.

Brantlinger, Patrick. "Cultural Studies versus the New Historicism." *English Studies / Culture Studies: Institutionalizing Dissent*. Ed. Isaiah Smithson and Nancy Ruff. Urbana: U of Illinois P, 1994. 43–58.

Breiner-Sanders, Karen E., Pardee Lowe, Jr., John Miles, and Elvira Swender. "ACTFL Proficiency Guidelines—Speaking (Revised 1999)." *Foreign Language Annals* 33 (2000): 13–18.

Brenner, David A. *Marketing Identities: The Invention of Jewish Ethnicity in "Ost und West."* Detroit: Wayne State UP, 1998.

Brenner, Michael. *After the Holocaust: Rebuilding Jewish Lives in Postwar Germany*. Princeton: Princeton UP, 1997.

———. *The Renaissance of Jewish Culture in Weimar Germany*. New Haven: Yale UP, 1996.

Brenner, Michael, and Derek J. Penslar, eds. *In Search of Jewish Community: Jewish Identities in Germany and Austria, 1918–1933*. Bloomington: Indiana UP, 1998.

Brinkmann, Richard, Kennosuke Ezawa, and Fritz Hackert, eds. *Germanistik International: Vorträge und Diskussionen auf dem internationalen Symposium "Germanistik im Ausland" vom 23. bis 25. Mai 1977 in Tübingen*. Tübingen: Niemeyer, 1978.

Brod, Richard. *Survey of Foreign Language Course Registrations and Student Contact Hours in Institutions of Higher Education*. New York: MLA, 1974.

———. *Survey of Foreign Language Course Registrations in Institutions of Higher Education*. New York: MLA, 1996.

Brod, Richard, and Bettina Huber. "Foreign Language Enrollments in United States Institutions of Higher Education, Fall 1990." *ADFL Bulletin* 23.3 (1992): 6–10.

———. "Foreign Language Enrollments in United States Institutions of Higher Education, Fall 1995." *ADFL Bulletin* 28.2 (1997): 55–61.

Brod, Richard, and Elizabeth B. Welles. "Foreign Language Enrollments in United States Institutions of Higher Education, Fall 1998." *ADFL Bulletin* 31.2 (2000): 22–29.

Broder, Henryk. *Erbarmen mit den Deutschen*. Hamburg: Hoffmann 1993.

———. *To Each His Own: A Jew in the New Germany*. Ed. Sander Gilman. Champaign: U of Illinois P, forthcoming.

Broemel, G. F. "From the Diary of a High School Teacher of German." *Monatshefte* 1 (1899): 13–18.

Bronsen, David, ed. *Jews and Germans from 1860 to 1933: The Problematic Symbiosis*. Heidelberg: Winter, 1979.

Brubacher, John S., and Willis Rudy. *Higher Education in Transition: A History of American Colleges and Universities, 1636–1968*. 4th ed. New Brunswick: Transaction, 1997.

Bruch, Rüdiger von. *Weltpolitik als Kulturmission: Auswärtige Kulturpolitik und Bildungsbürgertum in Deutschland am Vorabend des Ersten Weltkrieges*. Paderborn: Schöningh, 1982.

Brumm, Ursula. "Charles Follen: Kultureller Mittler bei den amerikanischen Transzendentalisten." Hebel and Ortseifen 146–56.

Buchwalter, Grace M. "High Schools Teach German Too." *German Quarterly* 20 (1947): 145–48.

Buckley, Thomas L. "The Bostonian Cult of Classicism: The Reception of Goethe and Schiller in the Literary Reviews of the *North American Review, Christian Examiner,* and the *Dial* (1817–1865)." Elfe, Hardin, and Holst 27–40.

Bullivant, Keith. "The Americanization of German Studies: The Curriculum." McCarthy and Schneider 105–10.

Bürger, Christa. "Die soziale Funktion volkstümlicher Erzählformen—Sage und Märchen." *Projekt Deutschunterricht*. Ed. Heinz Ide. Vol. 1. Stuttgart: Metzler, 1971. 26–56.

Burt, Marina K., Heidi Dulay, and Mary Finocchiaro, eds. *Viewpoints on English as a Second Language*. New York: Regents, 1977.

Busse, Adolf. "Die Lehrerbildung in den Vereinigten Staaten." *Monatshefte* 13 (1912): 315–23.

———. Letter to Alexander Hohlfeld. 19 Apr. 1933. Memorial Lib. Archives. U of Wisconsin, Madison.

Butler, Judith. "Against Proper Objects." Weed and Schor 1–29.

———. *Bodies That Matter: On the Discursive Limits of Sex*. New York: Routledge, 1993.

———. *Gender Trouble: Feminism and the Subversion of Identity*. New York: Routledge, 1989.

Byrnes, Heidi. "An Action Agenda for German Studies in the Twenty-First Century." McCarthy and Schneider 162–64.

———. "How Visible Are We Now?" McCarthy and Schneider 46–52.

Cadzow, Hunter. "The New Historicism." Groden and Kreiswirth 534–40.

Carter, Erica. *How German Is She? Postwar West German Reconstruction and the Consuming Woman*. Ann Arbor: U of Michigan P, 1996.

Case, Sue-Ellen. *The Domain-Matrix: Performing Lesbian at the End of Print Culture*. Bloomington: Indiana UP, 1996.

Castells, Manuel. *The Power of Identity*. Oxford: Blackwell, 1997.

Chaucer, Geoffrey. *The Canterbury Tales*. Trans. Neville Coghill. *The Riverside Chaucer*. 3rd ed. Ed. Larry D. Benson. New York: Houghton Mifflin, 1987. 3–328.

———. *Life and Times*. CD-ROM. Primary Source Media, 1995.

"A Checklist for Self-Study for Departments of Foreign Languages and Literatures." *Chairing the Foreign Language and Literature Department, Part 2*. Ed. Elizabeth B. Welles and David Goldberg. Spec. issue of *ADFL Bulletin* 32.3 (2001): 122–29.

CIC (Committee on Institutional Cooperation). *Directory of Minority PhD and MFA. Candidates and Recipients*. University Park: Center for Minority Graduate Opportunities and Faculty Development, Pennsylvania State U, 1999.

Cioffari, Vincenzo. "The Influence of the Language Institute Program—Past, Present, and Future." *Modern Language Journal* 46 (1962): 62–68.

Classen, Albrecht, ed. *Medieval German Voices in the Twenty-First Century: The Paradigmatic Function of Medieval German Studies for German Studies*. Amsterdam: Rodopi, 2000.

Clausen, Jeanette, and Sara Friedrichsmeyer. "What's Feminism Got to Do with It? A Postscript from the Editors." *Women in German Yearbook* 7 (1991): 169–73.

———. "WIG 2000: Feminism and the Future of Germanistik." *Women in German Yearbook* 10 (1994): 267–72.

Coats, A. W. "Economists, the Economics Profession, and Academic Freedom in the United States." Hanson 124–55.

Coenen, F. E. "An Excellent Reading Method." *German Quarterly* 11 (1938): 139–41.

Coffman, George R. "The Mediaeval Academy of America: Historical Background and Prospect." *Speculum* 1 (1926): 5–18.

Coleman, Algernon. *The Teaching of Modern Foreign Languages in the United States*. New York: Macmillan, 1929.

Collitz, Hermann. *Das schwache Präteritum und seine Vorgeschichte*. Göttingen: Vandenhoeck, 1912.

Confino, Alon. *The Nation as a Local Metaphor: Württemburg, Imperial Germany, and National Memory, 1871–1918*. Chapel Hill: U of North Carolina P, 1997.

Conrady, Karl Otto. "Leseliste für das Studium der neueren deutschen Literaturwissenschaft." *Einführung in die Neuere deutsche Literaturwissenschaft*. Ed. Conrady. Reinbek: Rowohlt, 1966. 111–33.

Conzen, Kathleen. "Phantom Landscapes of Colonization: Germans in the Making of a Pluralist America." Trommler and Shore 7–21.

———. "Political Myths and the Realities of Assimilation." *A Heritage Deferred: The German-Americans in Minnesota*. Ed. Clarence A. Glasrud and Diana M. Rankin. Moorhead: Concordia Coll., 1981.

Cook, William. "The Selection, Which Every Teacher of a Modern Language Should Make, of Subjects to Teach." *Proceedings at New York: December 29, 30, 1884. PMLA* 1 (1884):xv–xx. *JSTOR* 28 Apr. 2003 <http://www.jstor.org/search>.

Cooper, William A. "Status of the Direct Method in the Western States, As Revealed at the N.E.A. Meeting in Portland." *Monatshefte* 18 (1917): 243–45.

Consetino, Christine. "Frau und Staatsbürger in Volker Braun's Schauspiel *Tinka*." *Women in German Symposium*. Miami U, Oxford. 24 Sept. 1977.

Crew, David F. "Who's Afraid of Cultural Studies? Taking a 'Cultural Turn' in German History." Denham, Kacandes, and Petropoulos 45–61.

Crosland, Maurice, ed. *The Emergence of Science in Western Europe*. New York: Science History Pubs., 1976.

Curme, George O. *A Grammar of the German Language*. New York: Macmillan, 1905.

Cutting, Starr W. "Einige Prinzipien des Sprachunterrichts." *Monatshefte* 1 (1900): 14–21.

———. "Some Defects in the Teaching of Modern Languages in College and University." *Monatshefte* 5 (1903): 38–46.

Czaplicka, John, Andreas Huyssen, and Anson Rabinbach. "Introduction: Cultural History and Cultural Studies: Reflections on a Symposium." *New German Critique* 65 (1995): 3–17.

DAAD Special Issue. German Studies Review 13 (1990): 1–185.

Daemmrich, Horst. "Die Germanistik in den Vereinigten Staaten: Studium und Forschung." *Colloquia Germanica* 3 (1969): 316–32.

Dainat, Holger. " 'Wir müssen ja trotzdem weiterarbeiten': Die *deutsche Vierteljahrsschrift für Literaturwissenschaft und Geistesgeschichte vor* und nach 1945." Barner and König 76–100.

Danton, George. "Hans Grimm's *Volk ohne Raum*." *Monatshefte* 27 (1935): 34–38.

Dapprich, Emil. "Die Methoden des modernen Sprachunterrichts." *Monatshefte* 1 (1899): 33–36.

Davis, Boyd H., and Raymond K. O'Cain, eds. *First Person Singular: Papers from the Conference on an Oral Archive for the History of American Linguistics (Charlotte, NC, 9–10 March 1979)*. Amsterdam: Benjamins, 1980.

Decker, W. C. "Tests and Examinations." *German Quarterly* 1 (1928): 74–80.

Deeken, Hans W. "The AATG and Its Partners." *German Quarterly* 42 (1969): 618–19.

de Lauretis, Teresa. "Queer Theory: Lesbian and Gay Sexualities: An Introduction." *Differences: A Journal of Feminist Cultural Studies* 3.2 (1991): iii–xvii.

Delbanco, Andrew. "The Decline and Fall of Literature." *New York Review of Books* 4 Nov. 1999: 32–38.

Demetz, Peter. "150 Jahre Germanistik: Jubiläumsbetrachtungen statt eines Nekrologs." *Neues Forum* 14 (1967): 176–82.

———. "Report of the Commission on the Future of the Profession, Spring 1982." *PMLA* 97 (1982): 940–58.

Denecke, Ludwig. "Grimm, Wilhelm Carl." Ranke et al. 6: 186–95.

———. *Jacob Grimm und sein Bruder Wilhelm*. Stuttgart: Metzler, 1971.

Denham, Scott, Irene Kacandes, and Jonathan Petropoulos, eds. *A User's Guide to German Cultural Studies*. Ann Arbor: U of Michigan P, 1997.

Deweke, Klaus. Statement. *Internationale Politik* 51.3 (1996): 46.

Dexheimer, Wolfgang. "Die deutsch-amerikanischen Kulturbeziehungen seit den zwanziger Jahren." Düwell and Link 126–40.

"Dialogue." *News from Women in German* 15 May 1975: 3.

Di Donato, Robert. "Ausbildung des Deutschlehrers in den Vereinigten Staaten von Amerika um die Jahrhundertwende." *Zeitschrift für Kulturaustausch* 35 (1985): 180–89.

Diehl, J. D. "Adjusting Instruction in German to Conditions Imposed by the War." *Monatshefte* 19 (1918): 128–34.

Digest of Education Statistics. Natl. Center for Educ. Statistics, US Dept. of Educ. Washington: GPO, 1999.

Diller, Edward. "Dear AATG Member." *AATG Newsletter* 13.4 (1978): 1.

Dillon, John B., Barbara L. Hinrichsen, and Thea L. Lindquist, comps. *The Frances Ellis Collection of North American German Textbooks: A Preliminary Catalogue of Holdings in the Department of Special Collections.* Madison: General Lib. System, U of Wisconsin, Madison, 1998.

Diner, Dan. *Beyond the Conceivable: Studies in Germany, Nazism, and the Holocaust.* Berkeley: U of California P, 2000.

———. *Verkehrte Welten: Antiamerikanismus in Deutschland: Ein historischer Essay.* Frankfurt: Eichborn, 1993.

"Dissertations in Progress." *Monatshefte* 41 (1949): 52–55; 58 (1966): 258–67.

"Doctoral Dissertations." *Monatshefte* 80 (1988): 344–46; 90 (1998): 533–36; 91 (1999): 526–29.

"Doctoral Dissertations, 1977–78." *Monatshefte* 70 (1978): 287–90.

Doderer, Klaus. "Das bedrückende Leben der Kindergestalten in den Grimmschen Märchen." *Klassische Kinder- und Jugendbücher: Kritische Betrachtungen.* Weinheim: Beltz, 1969. 137–51.

Doherty, Robert L. "Foreign Language Study at the United States Service Academies: Evolution and Current Issues." Diss. Columbia U, 1983.

Doughty, Catherine, and Jessica Williams. *Focus on Form in Classroom Second Language Acquisition.* Cambridge: Cambridge UP, 1998.

Dow, James R., and Hannjost Lixfeld, eds. and trans. *German* Volkskunde: *A Decade of Theoretical Confrontation, Debate, and Reorientation, 1967–1977.* Bloomington: Indiana UP, 1986.

Dowden, Stephen D., and Meike G. Werner, eds. *German Literature, Jewish Critics: The Brandeis Symposium.* Rochester: Camden, 2002.

Downing, Eric, and Christopher Wild, eds. *Evidence and the Insistence of the Visual.* Spec. issue of *German Review* 76 (2001): 99–191.

Du Bois, W. E. B. *The Souls of Black Folk.* New York: New Amer. Lib., 1969.

Düwell, Kurt. "Die Gründung der Kulturpolitischen Abteilung im Auswärtigen Amt 1919/20 als Neuansatz." Düwell and Link 46–61.

Düwell, Kurt, and Werner Link, eds. *Deutsche auswärtige Kulturpolitik seit 1871: Geschichte und Struktur: Referate und Diskussionen eines interdisziplinären Symposiums.* Köln: Böhlau, 1981.

Ebert, Robert P., Oskar Reichmann, and Klaus-Peter Wegera, eds. *Frühneuhochdeutsche Grammatik.* Tübingen: Niemeyer, 1993.

Editorial. *New York Times* 11 Apr. 1938: 22.

"Editors' Introduction." *New German Critique* 2 (1974): 2–3.

Editor's Preface. *Modern Language Notes* 1 (1886): 2.

Edwards, J. David (executive director of the Joint Natl. Committee for Langs.). Telephone conversation with David Benseler. 14 Sept. 1999.

Efron, John M. *Medicine and the German Jews: A History.* New Haven: Yale UP, 2001.

Eggert, Hartmut, Ulrich Profitlich, and Klaus R. Scherpe, eds. *Geschichte als Literatur: Formen und Grenzen der Repräsentation von Vergangenheit.* Stuttgart: Metzler, 1990.

Eichner, Hans. "Der Blick auf den Ettersberg: Der Holocaust und die Germanistik." Schmitz 199–216.

Eiselmeier, J. "Der amerikanische Volksschullehrerstand und seine Besoldung." *Monatshefte* 3 (1902): 221–27.

———. "Ein Beitrag zur Lehrerbildungsfrage." *Monatshefte* 19 (1918): 183–89.

———. "The Training of the Teacher of German." *Monatshefte* 9 (1908): 3–6.

Elfe, Wolfgang, James Hardin, and Günther Holst, eds. *The Fortunes of German Writers in America: Studies in Literary Reception*. Columbia: U of South Carolina P, 1992.

Elling, Barbara. "Career Alternatives for Students of German." Lohnes and Nollendorfs, *German Studies* 233–46.

Elliott, A. Marshall. Editor's preface. *Modern Language Notes* 1.1 (1886): 1. *JSTOR* 30 Apr. 2003 <http://www.jstor.org/browse/01496611?config=jstor>.

Ellis, John M. *Literature Lost: Social Agendas and the Corruption of the Humanities*. New Haven: Yale UP, 1997.

———. *One Fairy Story Too Many: The Brothers Grimm and Their Tales*. Chicago: U of Chicago P, 1983.

Emerson, Oliver Farrar. "The American Scholar and the Modern Languages." *PMLA* 24 (1909): lxxiii–cii.

The End of GDR Literature. Spec. issues of *Germanic Review* 67.3–4 (1992): 98–134, 146–80.

Eshel, Amir, ed. *Schreiben auf Jüdisch? / Writing in Jewish?* Spec. issue of *Germanic Review* 75 (2000) : 91–167.

———. *Zeit der Zäsur: Jüdische Dichter im Angesicht der Shoah*. Heidelberg: Winter, 1999.

Farrer, W. V. "Science and the German University System, 1790–1850." Crosland 179–92.

Faust, Albert Bernhard. *The German Element in the United States, with Special Reference to Its Political, Moral, Social, and Educational Influence*. Vol. 2. New York: Houghton, 1909.

———. "Vergangenheit und Zukunft der deutschen Sprache in Amerika." *Monatshefte* 17 (1916): 233–50.

Fehervary, Helen. "Women and the Aesthetics of the Positive Hero in the GDR." Women in German Symposium. Miami U, Oxford. 27 Sept. 1977.

Fehervary, Helen, Renny Harrigan, and Nancy Vedder-Shults. Foreword. *New German Critique* 13 (1978): 3–4.

Feise, Ernst. "Report on Referendum." *German Quarterly* 12 (1939): 221–22.

Feise, Ernst, and Harry Steinhauer, eds. *German Literature since Goethe: Part 1: The Liberal Age, 1830–1870*. Boston: Houghton, 1958.

———. *German Literature since Goethe: Part 2: An Age of Crisis, 1870–1950*. Boston: Houghton, 1959.

Fessenden, Patricia K. "More than a Question of Numbers: Women Deputies in the German National Constituent Assembly and the Reichstag, 1919–1933." Women in German Symposium. Miami U, Oxford. 24 Sept. 1977.

Fick, H. H. "Erfolgreicher Deutschunterricht in amerikanischen öffentlichen Schulen." *Monatshefte* 10 (1909): 229–37.

———. "Zur Geschichte des Nationalen Deutschamerikanischen Lehrerbundes." *Monatshefte* 19 (1918): 217–25.

Fife, Robert H. "Nationalism and Scholarship." *PMLA* 59 (1944): 1282–94; 115 (2000): 1841–43.

———. "Some New Paths in Teaching German." *German Quarterly* 1 (1928): 7–17.

———. "To the Members of the American Association of Teachers of German." *German Quarterly* 5 (1932): 51–53.

Fikes, Robert, Jr. "African-Americans Who Teach German Language and Culture." *Journal of Blacks in Higher Education* 30 (2000–01): 108–13.

Finkelstein, Norman G. *The Holocaust Industry: Reflections on the Exploitation of Jewish Suffering.* London: Verso, 2000.

Fleischhauer, Wolfgang. Rev. of *Leid: Studien zur Bedeutungs- und Problemgeschichte, besonders in den grossen Epen der Stauferzeit,* by Friedrich Maurer. *Modern Language Notes* 69 (1954): 586–94.

Flores, John. *Poetry in East Germany.* New Haven: Yale UP, 1971.

Fohrmann, Jürgen. *Das Projekt der deutschen Literaturgeschichte: Entstehung und Scheitern einer nationalen Poesiebeschreibung zwischen Humanismus und Deutschem Kaiserreich.* Stuttgart: Metzler, 1989.

———. "Von den deutschen Studien zur Literaturwissenschaft." Fohrmann and Voßkamp 1–14.

Fohrmann, Jürgen, and Wilhelm Voßkamp, eds. *Wissenschaftsgeschichte der Germanistik im 19. Jahrhundert.* Stuttgart: Metzler, 1994.

Follen, Charles. *German Reader for Beginners / Deutsches Lesebuch für Anfänger.* 3rd ed. Boston: Simpkins, 1843.

———. *The Works of Charles Follen.* Vol. 5. Boston: Hilliard, 1841.

Foreword. *Germanic Review* 1 (1926): 1–3.

Foreword. *German Quarterly* 1 (1928): 1–2.

"Forum: Forty-One Letters on Interdisciplinarity in Literary Studies." *PMLA* 111 (1996): 271–311.

Foulkes, A. Peter. "Some Speculations on the Future of German Departments in the United States." *German Quarterly* 47 (1974): 525–43.

Francke, Kuno. *Deutsche Arbeit in Amerika: Erinnerungen.* Leipzig: Meiner, 1930.

———. *"German Ideals of To-Day" and Other Essays on German Culture.* Boston: Houghton, 1907.

———. *Glimpses of Modern German Culture.* New York: Dodd, 1898.

———. "The Kaiser and His People." *Atlantic Monthly* Oct. 1914: 566–70.

———. "Modern Ideas in the Middle Ages?" *PMLA* 6 (1890): 175–84.

———. *Social Forces in German Literature.* New York: Henry Holt, 1897.

Frank, Roberta. "The Unbearable Lightness of Being a Philologist." *Journal of English and Germanic Philology* 96 (1997): 486–513.

Frank, Ted E. "Die Anfänge des Deutschunterrichts an den öffentlichen Schulen Amerikas: Eine Studie über das Buch *Der amerikanische Leser* von 1854." *Zeitschrift für Kulturaustausch* 35 (1985): 171–79.

Fratzke, Dieter, and Wolfgang Albrecht, eds. *Deutsch-amerikanische Aufklärungskultur in Cincinnati/Ohio: 38 Kamenzer Lessing-Tage 1999.* Kamenz: Bautzen, 1999.

Freeman, Stephen A. *The Middlebury College Foreign Language Schools, 1915–1970: The Story of a Unique Idea.* Middlebury: Middlebury Coll. P, 1975.

———. "What Constitutes a Well-Trained Modern Language Teacher?" *Modern Language Journal* 25 (1941): 293–305.

Friedrichsmeyer, Sara, and Jeanette Clausen. "What's Missing in New Historicism or the 'Poetics' of Feminist Literary Criticism." *Women in German Yearbook* 9 (1994): 253–58.

Friedrichsmeyer, Sara, and Patricia Herminghouse. "The Generational Compact: Graduate Students and Germanics." *Women in German Yearbook* 11 (1995): 223–27.

———. "Toward an American Germanics? Feminism as a Force for Change." Benseler, Nickisch, and Nollendorfs 89–97.

———. "Towards an American Germanics? Editorial Postscript." *Women in German Yearbook* 12 (1996): 233–39.

Friedrichsmeyer, Sara, Sara Lennox, and Susanne Zantop. *The Imperialist Imagination: German Colonialism and Its Legacy.* Ann Arbor: U of Michigan P, 1998.

Fries, Marilyn S. "Zur Rezeption deutschsprachiger Autorinnen in den U.S.A." *Weimarer Beiträge* 39 (1993): 410–46.

Fröhlicher, Hans. "Über Ziele und Lehrmittel des deutschen Unterrichts an Sekundarschulen und Gymnasien." *Monatshefte* 2 (1901): 138–44.

Fürbeth, Frank, et al., eds. *Zur Nationalgeschichte und Problematik der Nationalphilologien in Europa: 150 Jahre erste Germanistenversammlung in Frankfurt am Main (1846–1996).* Tübingen: Niemeyer, 1999.

Fuss, Diana, ed. *Inside/Out: Lesbian Theories, Gay Theories.* New York: Routledge, 1991.

Gaede, William Richard, and Daniel Coogan, eds. *Stimmen der Zeit: A Selection of Contemporary German Prose and Verse.* 1957. Rev. ed. New York: Henry Holt, 1963.

Gallagher, Catherine. "Marxism and the New Historicism." Veeser 37–48.

Gay, Peter. *Freud, Jews, and Other Germans: Masters and Victims in Modernist Culture.* New York: Oxford UP, 1978.

Gay, Ruth. *The Jews of Germany: A Historical Portrait.* New Haven: Yale UP, 1992.

———. *Safe among the Germans: Liberated Jews after World War II.* New Haven: Yale UP, 2002.

The GDR at Forty: The Perils of Success. Spec. issue of *German Politics and Society* 17 (1989): 1–106.

Geertz, Clifford. "Thick Description: Toward an Interpretive Theory of Culture." *The Interpretation of Cultures.* New York: Basic, 1973. 3–30.

Geiger, Roger L. *To Advance Knowledge: The Growth of American Research Universities, 1900–1940.* New York: Oxford UP, 1986.

Gemünden, Gerd. " 'Der Unterschied liegt in der Differenz': On Hermeneutics, Deconstruction, and Their Compatibility." *New German Critique* 48 (1989): 176–92.

Gentry, Francis G., and Christopher Kleinhenz, eds. *Medieval Studies in North America: Past, Present, and Future.* Kalamazoo: Medieval Inst. Pubs., 1982.

Gentz, Manfred. "Sammlung DaimlerChrysler." *Berliner Zeitung* 14 Oct. 1999: 14.

"German Enrollment in American Institutions of Higher Learning." *German Quarterly* 7 (1934): 129–44.

"German Enrollments in American Institutions of Higher Learning, 1936–37." *German Quarterly* 11 (1938): 8–9.

"German Enrollments in Fifty-Nine American Universities and Colleges and in Seven American Preparatory Schools, 1935–38. *Deutscher Nachtwächter* 10 (1938): 1, 3. *German Quarterly* 12 (1939): 16–17.

German Histories: Challenges in Theory, Practice, and Technique. Spec. issue of *Central European History* 22.3–4 (1989): 227–457.

Germanistik as German Studies. Spec. issue of *German Quarterly* 62 (1989): 139–288.

Germans and Jews. Spec. issues of *New German Critique* 19 (1980): 3–165; 20 (1980): 3–186; 21 (1980): 3–145.

German Studies in the USA: A Critique of Germanistik? Proc. 19–22 Jan. 1989. Tempe: Consortium for Atlantic Studies, Arizona State U; DAAD, 1989.

Gerstner, Hermann. *Brüder Grimm in Selbstzeugnissen und Bilddokumenten.* Reinbek: Rowohlt, 1983.

Geyer, Michael, and Konrad Jarausch. "The Future of the German Past: Transatlantic Reflections for the 1990s." *Central European History* 22 (1989): 229–59.

Gibbons, Michael, Camille Limoges, Helga Nowotny, Simon Schwarzman, Peter Scott, and Martin Throw, eds. *The New Production of Knowledge: The Dynamics of Science and Research in Contemporary Societies.* London: Sage, 1994.

Gibson-Graham, J. K. *The End of Capitalism (As We Knew It)*. Oxford: Blackwell, 1996.

Gilbert, Sandra. *Final Report of the MLA Committee on Professional Employment*. New York: MLA, 1997.

Gillespie, Gerald. "The Graduate Curriculum: Notes on What's Right/Wrong with It." McCarthy and Schneider 91–98.

Gilman, Sander L. *Jewish Self-Hatred: Anti-Semitism and the Hidden Language of the Jews*. Baltimore: Johns Hopkins UP, 1986.

———. *Jews in Today's German Culture*. Bloomington: Indiana UP, 1995.

———. "Why and How I Study the German." *German Quarterly* 62 (1989): 192–204.

Gilman, Sander L., and Karen Remmler, eds. *Reemerging Jewish Culture in Germany: Life and Literature since 1989*. New York: New York UP, 1994.

Gilman, Sander L., and Jack Zipes, eds. *Yale Companion to Jewish Writing and Thought in German Culture, 1096–1996*. New Haven: Yale UP, 1997.

Glew, Elizabeth. "Where Do We Stand Now? Language Program Direction As Reflected in the MLA *Job Information List*." *Die Unterrichtspraxis* 33 (2000): 18–23.

Goebel, Julius. "Die deutsche Bewegung in Amerika: Rückblicke und Aussichten." Goebel, *Der Kampf* 1–13.

———. *Das Deutschtum in den Vereinigten Staaten von Nord-Amerika*. Munich: Lehmann, 1904.

———. "German Classics as a Means of Education." *PMLA* 1 (1884): 156–69.

———. *Der Kampf um deutsche Kultur in Amerika: Aufsätze und Vorträge zur deutsch-amerikanischen Bewegung*. Leipzig: Dürrsche Buchhandlung, 1914.

———. "Notes on the History and Principles of Hermeneutics." *Journal of English and Germanic Philology* 17 (1918): 602–21.

———. "A Proposed Curriculum for German Reading." *Modern Language Notes* 2 (1887): 22–26.

———. Rev. of *The German Classics from the Fourth to the Nineteenth Century*, by F. Max Muller and F. Lichtenstein. *Modern Language Notes* 2 (1887): 166–67.

———. "Rudolf Hildebrand." *Modern Language Notes* 9 (1894): 171–75.

———. *Über tragische Schuld und Sühne: Ein Beitrag zur Geschichte der Aesthetik des Dramas*. Berlin: Duncker, 1884.

———. "Wilhelm Dilthey and the Science of Literary History." *Journal of English and German Philology* 25 (1926): 145–56.

Goetschel, Willi, and Nils Roemer, eds. *Theme Issue on Gershom Scholem*. Spec. issue of *Germanic Review* 72 (1997): 2–92.

The Golden Signpost: A Guide to Happiness and Prosperity. Madison: Max Kade Inst. for German-Amer. Studies, U of Wisconsin, 1993. Trans. of *Der goldne Wegweiser: Ein Führer zu Gluck und Wohlstand*.

Goldhagen, Daniel J. *Hitler's Willing Executioners: Ordinary Germans and the Holocaust*. New York: Knopf, 1996.

Goodman, Al. "Scraping Away at the 'Black Legend' of a Spanish King." *New York Times* 1 July 1998, late ed., final: E2+.

"Good News." *AATG Newsletter* 13.2 (1977): 1.

Gowa, Ferdinand. "Present Trends in American and German Criticism." *Germanic Review* 28 (1953): 99–112.

"Graduate Programs: From the 1970s into the 1980s: Special Survey." *Monatshefte* 71 (1979): 298–334.

Graff, Gerald. *Professing Literature: An Institutional History*. Chicago: U of Chicago P, 1987.

Graff, Gerald, and Michael Warner, eds. *The Origins of Literary Studies in America: A Documentary Anthology*. New York: Routledge, 1989.

Gramm, Hanns, ed. *The Oberlaender Trust, 1931–1953*. Philadelphia: Carl Schurz Memorial Foundation, 1956.

Green, Mary Jean. "Marketing Strategies for a New Economy: Can We Sell French without Selling Out?" *Studies in Twentieth Century Literature* 26 (2002): 22–32.

Greenblatt, Stephen. "Towards a Poetics of Culture." Veeser 1–14.

Greenblatt, Stephen, and Giles Gunn, eds. *Redrawing the Boundaries: The Transformation of English and American Literary Studies*. New York: MLA, 1992.

Greenlaw, Edwin. *The Province of Literary History*. Baltimore: Johns Hopkins UP, 1931.

Griebsch, Max. Editorial. *Monatshefte* 8 (1907): 321–22.

———. Editorial. *Pädagogische Monatshefte* 1.4 (1900): 1–2.

———. "Das Nationale Lehrerseminar zu Milwaukee." *Monatshefte* 22 (1930): 97–103.

———. "Warum die direkte Methode?" *Monatshefte* 17 (1916): 293–301.

———. "Was wir wollen." *Monatshefte* 1 (1899): 1–3.

———. "Zur Methodik des deutschen Unterrichts." *Monatshefte* 22 (1930): 167–74; 23 (1931): 12–17, 41–46, 77–82; 24 (1932): 187–94; 26 (1934): 43–47.

Grimm, Günther, and Hans-Peter Bayerdörfer, eds. *Im Zeichen Hiobs: Jüdische Schriftsteller und deutsche Literatur im 20. Jahrhundert*. Königstein: Athenäum, 1985.

Grimm, Hans. *Volk ohne Raum*. 1926. München: Langen, 1932.

Grimm, Reinhold, and Jost Hermand, eds. *Die Klassik-Legende*. Frankfurt: Athenäum, 1971.

Groden, Michael, and Martin Kreiswirth, eds. *The Johns Hopkins Guide to Literary Theory and Criticism*. Baltimore: Johns Hopkins UP, 1994.

Grossberg, Lawrence, Cary Nelson, and Paula A. Treichler, eds. *Cultural Studies*. New York: Routledge, 1992.

Grossman, Jeffrey A. *The Discourse on Yiddish in Germany from the Enlightenment to the Second Empire*. Rochester: Camden, 2000.

Gruenberg, Elsa. "The Status of the Teaching of German in the State of Missouri." *German Quarterly* 8 (1935): 37–40.

Grueningen, John Paul von. "The Problem of Outlining Objectives." *Monatshefte* 28 (1936): 216–23.

Grumann, Paul H. "The Question of Methods." *Monatshefte* 18 (1917): 281–84.

Guerin, Wilfred L., et al., eds. *A Handbook of Critical Approaches to Literature*. 4th ed. New York: Oxford UP, 1999.

Guibbory, Achsah, and Marianne E. Kalinke. "*JEGP* at One Hundred Years." *Journal of English and Germanic Philology* 96 (1997): 481–85.

Guidelines for Curricula in German Studies at Universities and Colleges in North America. German Studies Assn. 10 Apr. 2003 <http://www.g-s-a.org/curric.html>.

Guidelines for Curricular Organization at American Educational Institutions. Tempe: German Studies Assn., 1987.

Guillory, John. *Cultural Capital: The Problem of Literary Canon Formation*. Chicago: U of Chicago P, 1993.

Guthke, Karl S. "Weimar im Wilden Westen: Schiller auf der Bühne der Vereinigten Staaten." Bartle et al. 157–77.

Haase, Donald. "Feminist Fairy-Tale Scholarship: A Critical Survey and Bibliography." *Marvels and Tales: Journal of Fairy-Tale Studies* 14 (2000): 15–63.

———. "German Fairy Tales and America's Culture Wars: From Grimms' *Kinder- und*

Hausmärchen to William Bennett's *Book of Virtues*." *German Society and Politics* 13.3 (1995): 17–25.

——, ed. *The Reception of Grimms' Fairy Tales: Responses, Reactions, Revisions*. Detroit: Wayne State UP, 1993.

——. "Television and Fairy Tales." Zipes, *Oxford* 513–18.

Haber, Samuel. *The Quest for Authority and Honor in the American Professions, 1750–1900*. Chicago: U of Chicago P, 1991.

Haenicke, Diether H. "Graduate Education: Review and Outlook." *Monatshefte* 77 (1985): 258–61.

Hagboldt, Peter. "Achievement after Three Quarters of College German As Measured by the American Council Alpha Test, Form B." *German Quarterly* 2 (1929): 33–43.

Hall, Robert A. *A Life for Language: A Biographical Memoir of Leonard Bloomfield*. Amsterdam: Benjamins, 1990.

Hall, Stuart. "Cultural Studies and Its Theoretical Legacies." Grossberg, Nelson, and Treichler 277–94.

——. "The Emergence of Cultural Studies and the Crisis of the Humanities." *October* 53 (1990): 11–23.

Hamacher, Werner. "Das Beben der Darstellung." Wellbery [1985] 149–73.

Hamacher, Werner, Neil Hertz, and Thomas Keenan, eds. *Responses: On Paul de Man's Wartime Journalism*. Lincoln: U of Nebraska P, 1989.

Hamilton, Neil. *Zealotry and Academic Freedom: A Legal and Historical Perspective*. New Brunswick: Transaction, 1995.

Hancock, Charles, ed. *Teaching, Testing, and Assessment: Making the Connection*. Lincolnwood: Natl. Textbook, 1994.

Handschin, Charles H. *Elf neue Erzählungen*. New York: Prentice, 1930.

——. *Methods of Teaching Modern Languages*. Yonkers: World, 1923.

——. "Teaching German Civilization." *German Quarterly* 11 (1937): 61–70.

Hanson, W. Lee, ed. *Academic Freedom on Trial: A Hundred Years of Sifting and Winnowing at the University of Wisconsin*. Madison: U of Wisconsin P, 1998.

Hänssler, William. "Modern German Literature in the High School." *Monatshefte* 12 (1911): 138–45.

Haraway, Donna. *Primate Visions: Gender, Race, and Nature in the World of Modern Science*. New York: Routledge, 1989.

——. *Simians, Cyborgs, and Women: The Reinvention of Nature*. New York: Routledge, 1991.

Hart, James M. *German Universities: A Narrative of Personal Experience*. New York: Putnam, 1874.

Hart, Jonathan, and Terry Goldie. "Post-colonial Theory." Makaryk 155–57.

Hatfield, Henry C. "Literaturgeschichte—mit Maßen." Unseld 106–10.

——. *Thomas Mann: An Introduction to His Fiction*. London: Owen, 1952.

Hatfield, Henry C., and Joan Merrick. "Studies of German Literature in the United States, 1939–1946." *Modern Language Review* 43 (1948): 353–92.

Hatfield, Henry C., and Jack M. Stein. "Graduate Seminars in German Literature: Some Procedures." *Die Unterrichtspraxis* 1.1 (1968): 77–81.

Hatfield, James T. "The Teaching of German at Northwestern University." 54 pp. in ts. Evanston, 1939.

Hauch, Edward F. "Secretary's Report of the Annual Meeting of the American Association of Teachers of German (1937)." *German Quarterly* 11 (1938): 98–103.

Hebel, Udo J., and Karl Ortseifen, eds. *Transatlantic Encounters: Studies in European-American Relations.* Trier: Wissenschaftlicher, 1995.

Hedge, Frederic Henry. *Hours with German Classics.* Boston: Roberts, 1886.

Heffner, R.-M. S. "The Reading Objective and the Reading Method." *Monatshefte* 30 (1938): 367–75.

Heitner, Robert R. "The New Editor's Greeting to the Subscribers, Members, and Authors." *German Quarterly* 40 (1967): 503–05.

Helbig, Louis F. "German Studies as Culture Studies: The Bloomington Model." Lohnes and Nollendorfs, *German Studies* 47–55.

———, ed. *German Studies in America.* Bloomington: Inst. of German Studies, 1978.

Held, David, et al. *Global Transformation.* Palo Alto: Stanford UP, 1999.

Heller, Edmund K. "Die Zukunft der deutschen Schrift." *German Quarterly* 5 (1932): 188–94.

Heller, Erich. *"The Artist's Journey into the Interior" and Other Essays.* New York: Harcourt, 1976.

———. *The Disinherited Mind: Essays in Modern German Literature and Thought.* London: Bowes, 1952.

Heller, Jean. *Otto Heller.* Saint Louis: n.p., 1962.

Heller, Peter. "Ambivalence and Nostalgia." Merrill and Cernyak-Spatz 57–71.

Helt, Richard C., and David J. Woloshin. "Where Are We Today? A Survey of Current German Teaching Methods in American Colleges and Universities." *Die Unterrichtspraxis* 15 (1982): 110–15.

Hench, George A., ed. *Der althochdeutsche Isidor: Facsimile-ausgabe des Pariser codex nebst critischem texte der Pariser und Monseer bruchstücke: Mit einleitung, grammatischer darstellung und einem ausführlichen glossar.* Strassburg: Trübner, 1893.

Henke, Burkhard, Susanne Kord, and Simon Richter, eds. *Unwrapping Goethe's Weimar: Essays in Cultural Studies and Local Knowledge.* Rochester: Camden, 2000.

Hepp, Jean. "Über natürliche Methoden beim Lehren neuer Sprachen." *Monatshefte* 1 (1899): 7–12; (1900): 2–5.

Herbst, Jürgen. *The German Historical School in American Scholarship: A Study of the Transfer of Culture.* Ithaca: Cornell UP, 1965.

Hermand, Jost. "Germanistik." Krohn et al. 736–46.

———. *Geschichte der Germanistik.* Reinbek: Rowohlt, 1994.

———. *Synthetisches Interpretieren: Zur Methodik der Literaturwissenschaft.* Munich: Nymphenburg, 1968.

Herminghouse, Patricia. "Retreat Discussion." *Women in German Newsletter* 9 (1976): 6.

Herminghouse, Patricia, and Magda Mueller, eds. *Gender and Germanness: Cultural Productions of Nation.* Providence: Berghahn, 1997.

Hertz, Deborah. "Madame de Staël's Counterparts: Literary Salons in Berlin, 1800." Women in German Symposium. Miami U, Oxford. 24 Sept. 1977.

Herzinger, Richard, and Hannes Stein. *Endzeit-Propheten oder Die Offensive der Antiwestler: Fundamentalismus, Antiamerikanismus und Neue Rechte.* Reinbek bei Hamburg: Rowohlt, 1995.

Heschel, Susannah. *Abraham Geiger and the Jewish Jesus.* Chicago: U of Chicago P, 1998.

Hess, John A. "Free Speech and the Nazi Press." *German Quarterly* 11 (1938): 191–95.

———. "The Problem of Third-Year College German." *German Quarterly* 15 (1942): 119–26.

———. "Volk und Führer." *German Quarterly* 11 (1938): 4–7.

Hess, Jonathan M. *Germans, Jews, and the Claims of Modernity.* New Haven: Yale UP, 2002.

Heuser, Frederick W. J. Letter to Alexander Hohlfeld, carbon copy to B. Q. Morgan. 14 Mar. 1933. Memorial Lib. Archives. AATG File. German. Box 1. U of Wisconsin, Madison.

———. "Robert Herndon Fife." *Germanic Review* 23 (1948): 85–90.

———. "Shall German Be Taught in Our High Schools? A Symposium." *German Quarterly* 1 (1928): 53–67.

Hewett, W. T. "The Aims and Methods of Collegiate Instruction in Modern Languages." *PMLA* 1 (1884–85): 25–36.

Heym, Stefan. "Eine kleine deutsche Chronik: USA." *Das Wort* 3.8 (1938): 144–46.

Hilarious, G. "An Göthe." *Die Abendschule* 7.1 (1860): 1.

Hildebrand, Janet E. "Methods for Teaching College German in the United States, 1753–1903: An Historical Study." U of Texas, 1977. UMI, 1983.

Hirsch, E. D., Jr. *Cultural Literacy: What Every American Needs to Know.* New York: Houghton, 1987.

Hoecherl-Alden, Gisela. "Cloaks and Gowns: Germanists for the United States' War Effort." *Yearbook of German-American Studies* 32 (1997): 143–51.

———. "Germanisten im 'Niemandsland': Die exilierten Akademiker und ihre Wirkung auf die amerikanische Germanistik (1933–1955)." Diss. U of Wisconsin, Madison, 1996.

Hoenigswald, Henry M., ed. *The European Background of American Linguistics: Papers of the Third Golden Anniversary Symposium of the Linguistic Society of America.* Dordrecht: Foris, 1979.

Hoesterey, Ingeborg. "Postmodern Bricoleurs: The New Syncretism in German Studies." *German Studies Review* 14 (1991): 587–96.

Hofstadter, Richard, and Walter P. Metzger. *The Development of Academic Freedom in the United States.* New York: Columbia UP, 1955.

Hohendahl, Peter U. "The American-German Divide." McCarthy and Schneider 19–28.

———. "Bürgerliche Literaturgeschichte und nationale Identität: Bilder vom deutschen Sonderweg." Kocka 200–31.

———. "The Fate of German Studies after the End of the Cold War." *ADFL Bulletin* 29.2 (1998): 18–21.

———. "Germanistik in den Vereinigten Staaten: Eine Disziplin im Umbruch." *Zeitschrift für Germanistik* 3 (1996): 527–35.

———. "How to Read Our Professional Past: A Modest Proposal." Benseler, Nickisch, and Nollendorfs 3–15.

———. "Interdisciplinary German Studies: Tentative Conclusions." *German Quarterly* 62 (1989): 227–34.

———. "Nationale Ausdifferenzierungen der Germanistik: Das Beispiel der USA." Schönert 357–81.

———. "The New Historicism." *New German Critique* 55 (1992): 87–104.

———. "The Past, Present, and Future of *Germanistik.*" *Stanford Humanities Review* 6.1 (1998): 76–87.

———. "A Return to History? The New Historicism and Its Agenda." *New German Critique* 55 (1992): 87–104.

Hohendahl, Peter U., and Patricia Herminghouse. Foreword. Hohendahl and Herminghouse, *Literatur und Literaturtheorie* 7–9.

———, eds. *Literatur der DDR in den siebziger Jahren.* Frankfurt: Suhrkamp, 1983.

———, eds. *Literatur und Literaturtheorie in der DDR.* Frankfurt: Suhrkamp, 1976.

Hohlfeld, Alexander R. "Anthologien deutscher Lyrik." *Monatshefte* 13 (1912): 196–214.

———. "Correspondence." *German Quarterly* 6 (1933): 187–88.

———. "Die direkte Methode und die oberen Unterrichtsstufen." *Monatshefte* 18 (1917): 248–52.

———. "Light from Goethe on Our Problems." *PMLA* 29 (1914): lvii–lxxxvi.

———. "To the Members of the American Association of Teachers of German." *German Quarterly* 6 (1933): 103–05.

———. "Die Zukunft des deutschen Unterrichts im amerikanischen Unterrichtswesen." *Monatshefte* 6 (1905): 238–45.

Hollier, Dennis, ed. *A New History of French Literature.* Cambridge: Harvard UP, 1989.

Hollingsworth, Ellen J., and Rogers Hollingsworth. "Major Discoveries and Biomedical Research Organizations: Perspectives on Interdisciplinarity, Nurturing Leadership, and Integrated Structure and Culture." Weingart and Stehr 215–44.

Holub, Robert C. "Graduate Education in German: Past Experience and Future Perspectives." McCarthy and Schneider 35–45.

———. *Reception Theory: A Critical Introduction.* London: Methuen, 1984.

———. "Rewriting the Canon Revisited." Bledsoe, Estabrook, Federle, Henschel, Miller, and Polster 21–26.

Holzmann, Albert W. "A Suggested German Reading List." *Monatshefte* 40 (1948): 406–10.

Honan, William H. "The Ivory Tower under Siege." *New York Times* 4 Jan. 1998, Educ. Life Supp., late ed., sec. 4A: 33.

Honig, Lucille, and Richard Brod. *Foreign Languages and Careers.* New York: MLA, 1979.

Hoover, Herbert. "Herbert Hoover on Languages." *Modern Language Journal* 22 (1938): 645–46.

Howells, William D. *My Literary Passions.* New York: Harper, 1895.

Huber, Bettina J. "Incorporating Minorities into Foreign Language Programs: The Challenge of the Nineties." *ADFL Bulletin* 21.2 (1990): 12–19.

———. "Recent and Anticipated Growth in Foreign Language Doctoral Programs: Findings from the MLA's 1990 Survey." *ADFL Bulletin* 25.1 (1993): 15–35.

———. "Today's Literature Classroom: Findings from the MLA's 1990 Survey of Upper-Division Courses." *ADE Bulletin* 101 (1992): 36–60.

———. "Women in the Modern Languages, 1970–90." *Profession 90.* New York: MLA, 1990. 58–73.

Huber, Philipp. "Mündliche Erteilung des deutschen Unterrichts in den Anfangsklassen unserer öffentlichen Schulen." *Monatshefte* 4 (1903): 75–81.

Huebener, Theodore. "The German School of the New York Turn-Verein." *American-German Review* 16.6 (1950): 14–15.

———. "Lernt Deutsch!" *Monatshefte* 27 (1935): 294–96.

———. "Will Our Educational Standards Continue to Decline?" *German Quarterly* 12 (1939): 1–2.

Hunt, Lynn. "Democratization and Decline? The Consequences of Demographic Change in the Humanities." Kernan 17–31.

———. "Virtues of Disciplinarity." *Eighteenth-Century Studies* 28 (1994): 1–7.

Hüttich, H. G. *Theater in the Planned Society: Contemporary Drama in the German Dem-*

ocratic Republic in Its Historical, Political, and Cultural Context. Chapel Hill: U of North Carolina P, 1976.

Huyssen, Andreas. *After the Great Divide: Modernism, Mass Culture, Postmodernism.* Bloomington: Indiana UP, 1986.

———. "After the Wall: The Failure of German Intellectuals." *New German Critique* 52 (1991): 109–43.

Hymes, Del. *On Communicative Competence.* Philadelphia: U of Pennsylvania P, 1971.

"Imperialism." Def. 2. *Merriam-Webster's Collegiate Dictionary.* 10th ed. 1993.

Isenberg, Noah. *Between Redemption and Doom: The Strains of German-Jewish Modernism.* Lincoln: U of Nebraska P, 1999.

Ittner, Robert T. "Implications of the Armed Forces' Language Program." *German Quarterly* 17 (1944): 176–82.

Jagemann, H. C. G. von. "Das Rüstzeug eines Lehrers des Deutschen." *Monatshefte* 3 (1902): 261–68.

Jäger, Ludwig, ed. *Germanistik: Disziplinäre Identität und kulturelle Leistung: Vorträge des deutschen Germanistentages, 1994.* Weinheim: Beltz, 1995.

James, Dorothy. "Bypassing the Traditional Leadership: Who's Minding the Store?" *Profession 1997.* New York: MLA, 1997. 41–53.

Jarvis, Shawn C. "Trivial Pursuit? Women Deconstructing the Grimmian Model in the *Kaffeterkreis.*" Haase, *Reception* 102–26.

Jarvis, Shawn C., and Jeannine Blackwell, eds. and trans. *The Queen's Mirror: Fairy Tales by German Women, 1780–1900.* Lincoln: U of Nebraska P, 2001.

Jay, Martin. *The Dialectical Imagination: A History of the Frankfurt School and the Institute of Social Research, 1923–1950.* Boston: Little, 1973.

———. *Permanent Exiles: Essays on the Intellectual Migration from Germany to America.* New York: Columbia UP, 1986.

Jelavich, Peter. *Berlin Cabaret.* Cambridge: Harvard UP, 1993.

———. "Contemporary Literary Theory: From Deconstruction Back to History." *Central European History* 22 (1989): 360–80.

Jenny, Florence G. "A Survey of the Preparation of Teachers of German in the High Schools of the United States." *Monatshefte* 19 (1918): 121–27, 146–53.

Jente, Richard. Letter to Alexander Hohlfeld. 27 Sept. 1933. Memorial Lib. Archives. AATG-File. German. Box 1. U of Wisconsin, Madison.

Jockers, Ernst. "Philosophie und Literaturwissenschaft." *Germanic Review* 10 (1935): 73–97, 166–86.

Joeres, Ruth-Ellen B. " 'Language Is Also a Place of Struggle': The Language of Feminism and the Language of American Germanistik." *Women in German Yearbook* 8 (1992): 247–57.

Johnson, Barbara. *A World of Difference.* Baltimore: Johns Hopkins UP, 1987.

Jones, George Fenwick. "The Function of Food in Medieval German Literature." *Speculum* 35 (1960): 78–86.

Jones, J. B. E. "Richtlinien für die Auswahl des Lesestoffes." *Monatshefte* 16 (1915): 169–76.

Joos, Martin, ed. *Readings in Linguistics: The Development of Descriptive Linguistics in America since 1925.* Washington: Amer. Council of Learned Soc., 1957.

Kacandes, Irene. "German Cultural Studies: What Is at Stake?" Denham, Kacandes, and Petropoulos 3–28.

Kaes, Anton. *Deutschlandbilder: Die Wiederkehr der Geschichte als Film.* Munich: Text + Kritik, 1987.

————. *From Hitler to Heimat: The Return of History as Film*. Cambridge: Harvard UP, 1989.

————. "New Historicism and the Study of German Literature." *German Quarterly* 62 (1989): 210–19.

Kaes, Anton, Martin Jay, and Edward Dimendberg, eds. *The Weimar Republic Sourcebook*. Berkeley: U of California P, 1994.

Kahn, Lothar. *Mirrors of the Jewish Mind: A Gallery of Portraits of European Jewish Writers of Our Time*. New York: Yoseloff, 1968.

Kambas, Chryssoula. "Germanistik: Eine Disziplin oder eine Gruppe von Disziplinen? Gemeinsamkeiten und Tendenzen zur Verselbstständigung." Jäger 56–68.

Kammen, Michael. *American Culture, American Tastes: Social Change and the Twentieth Century*. New York: Knopf, 1999.

Kaplan, Marion A. *Between Dignity and Despair: Jewish Life in Nazi Germany*. New York: Oxford UP, 1998.

Karell, Linda K. "Career Possibilities in Administration; or, How That Job Helped Me Get This One." *Profession 1998*. New York: MLA, 1998. 208–15.

Karsten, Gustav E. *The Study of Modern Languages (German, French, Spanish, Italian, Norwegian, and Danish) at the University of Illinous, 1906–07*. Urbana: U of Illinois Dept. of Mod. Langs., 1906.

Kayser, Wolfgang. *Das sprachliche Kunstwerk: Eine Einführung in die Literaturwissenschaft*. 1948. Bern: Francke, 1978.

Kazal, Russell A. *Becoming "Old Stock": The Waning of German-American Identity in Philadelphia, 1900–1930*. Ann Arbor: UMI, 1998.

————. "Revisiting Assimilation: The Rise, Fall, and Reappraisal of a Concept in American Ethnic History." *American Historical Review* 100 (1995): 437–71.

Keller, Rolf. "Wände einreißen und Durchblick schaffen: Auswärtige Kulturpolitik— besser unter einem Dach?" *Zeitschrift für Kulturaustausch* 49.2 (1999): 6.

Kelley, Bruce M. *Yale: A History*. New Haven: Yale UP, 1974.

Kelly, Louis G. *Twenty-Five Centuries of Language Teaching*. Rowley: Newbury, 1969.

Kennedy, Donald. *Academic Duty*. Cambridge: Harvard UP, 1997.

Kenngott, A. M. "Answers to Questions concerning the Direct Method." *Monatshefte* 16 (1915): 13–17.

Kernan, Alvin, ed. *What's Happened to the Humanities?* Princeton: Princeton UP, 1997.

Kiefer, Arthur. "Der deutsche Unterricht und der Lesestoff in der Hochschule." *Monatshefte* 7 (1906): 105–08.

————. "Report on the Present Status of Instruction in German in the High Schools of Ohio." *Monatshefte* 9 (1908): 136–39.

Kim, Karl H. S., Norman R. Relkin, Kyoung-Min Lee, and Joy Hirsch. "Distinct Cortical Areas Associated with Native and Second Languages." *Nature* 10 July 1997: 171–74.

Kirschbaum, Erik. *The Eradication of German Culture in the United States, 1917–1918*. Stuttgart: Heinz, 1986.

"Klassenbibliothek." *Monatshefte* 8 (1907): 303.

Klein, Julie T. "A Conceptual Vocabulary of Interdisciplinary Sciences." Weingart and Stehr 3–24.

Kleinsasser, Robert C. "Foreign Language Teacher Certification: Quo Vadis?" *Die Unterrichtspraxis* 27 (1994): 45–55.

Klenze, Camillo von. "The American Association of Teachers of German." *German Quarterly* 1 (1928): 3–6.

Klingenstein, Susanne. *Jews in the American Academy, 1900–1940*. New Haven: Yale UP, 1991.

Kneale, J. Douglas. "Deconstruction." Groden and Kreiswirth 185–92.

Koch, Gertrud. *Die Einstellung ist die Einstellung: Visuelle Konstruktionen des Judentums*. Frankfurt: Suhrkamp, 1992.

———. *Siegfried Kracauer*. Trans. Jeremy Gaines. Princeton: Princeton UP, 2000.

Kocka, Jürgen, ed. *Bürgertum im 19. Jahrhundert: Deutschland im europäischen Vergleich*. Munich: DTV, 1988.

Koischwitz, Otto, and Archer W. Hurd. "Experimental Application of the Interpretative Reading Method." *Monatshefte* 27 (1935): 92–96.

Kolbe, Jürgen, ed. *Ansichten einer künftigen Germanistik*. Munich: Hanser, 1969.

Kolodny, Annette. *Failing the Future: A Dean Looks at Higher Education in the Twenty-First Century*. Durham: Duke UP, 1998.

Köpke, Wulf. "Germanistik als eine deutsch-amerikanische Wissenschaft." Trommler, *Germanistik* 46–65.

———. "Lifting the Cultural Blockade: The American Discovery of a New German Literature after World War I: Ten Years of Critical Commentary in the *Nation* and the *New Republic*." Elfe, Hardin, and Holst 81–98.

Kramsch, Claire. *Language and Culture*. Oxford: Oxford UP, 1998.

Krashen, Stephen D. "The Monitor Model of Adult Second Language Performance." Burt, Dulay, and Finocchiaro 152–61.

Krashen, Stephen D., and Tracy D. Terrell. *The Natural Approach: Language Acquisition in the Classroom*. New York: Pergamon, 1983.

Krause, Carl A. "Discussion on: Present Conditions and the Direct Method." *Monatshefte* 11 (1910): 308–10.

———. "The Teaching of Grammar by the Direct Method." *Monatshefte* 13 (1912): 178–84.

———. "What Prominence Is to Be Assigned to the Work in Speaking the Foreign Language?" *Monatshefte* 11 (1910): 39–43.

Krauss, P. G. "Suggested Methods and Materials for Teaching German in Elementary Schools." *German Quarterly* 29 (1956): 239–50.

Krohn, Claus-Dieter, et al., eds. *Handbuch der deutschsprachigen Emigration, 1933–1945*. Darmstadt: Primus, 1998.

Kruckis, Hans-Martin. "Goethe-Philologie als Paradigma neuphilologischer Wissenschaft im 19. Jahrhundert." Fohrmann and Voßkamp 451–93.

Krug, Joseph. "Die Fortbildung des Lehrers im Amte." *Monatshefte* 1 (1900): 2–14.

Kufner, Herbert L. *The Grammatical Structures of English and German*. Chicago: U of Chicago P, 1962.

Kuhn, Anna. "Canon as Narrative: A Feminist Reading." Bledsoe, Estabrook, Federle, Henschel, Miller, and Polster 91–104.

Kühnemann, Eugen. *Mit unbefangener Stirn: Mein Lebensbuch*. Heilbronn: Salzer, 1937.

Kurth-Voigt, Lieselotte E., and William H. McClain. "Louise Mühlbach's Historical Novels: The American Reception." *Internationales Archiv für Sozialgeschichte der deutschen Literatur* 6 (1981): 52–77.

Kuttner, B. "Die berufliche und finanzielle Stellung des Elementarlehrers." *Monatshefte* 3 (1901): 90–93.

———. "Wertschätzung und Lehrmethoden der deutschen Sprache." *Monatshefte* 2 (1901): 185–92.

Kuzniar, Alice A. "Cross-Gendered Cross-Cultural Studies and the German Program." McCarthy and Schneider 122–30.

——. Introduction. Kuzniar, *Outing* 1–32.

——, ed. *Outing Goethe and His Age*. Stanford: Stanford UP, 1996.

——. *The Queer German Cinema*. Stanford: Stanford UP, 2000.

Kyes, Robert L., ed. *The Old Low Franconian Psalms and Glosses*. Ann Arbor: U of Michigan P, 1969.

Lacey, Kate. *Feminine Frequencies: Gender, German Radio, and the Public Sphere, 1923–1945*. Ann Arbor: U of Michigan P, 1996.

Lafayette, Robert C., ed. *National Standards: A Catalyst for Reform*. Lincolnwood: Natl. Textbook, 1996.

Laitenberger, Volkhard. *Akademischer Austausch und auswärtige Kulturpolitik: Der Deutsche Akademische Austauschdienst (DAAD), 1923–1945*. Göttingen: Musterschmidt, 1976.

——. "Organisations- und Strukturprobleme der auswärtigen Kulturpolitik und des akademischen Austauschs in den zwanziger und dreißiger Jahren." Düwell and Link 72–96.

Lämmert, Eberhard. "Auszüge aus der Diskussion zum Vortrag von Guy Stern." Schmitz 116–17.

Lamprecht, Karl. "Über auswärtige Kulturpolitik." *Deutsche Revue* Dec. 1912: 277–86. *Ausgewählte Schriften: Zur Wirtschafts- und Kulturgeschichte und zur Theorie der Geschichtswissenschaft*. By Lamprecht. Ed. Herbert Schönebaum. Aalen: Scientia, 1974. 809–20.

——. *What is History? Five Lectures in the Modern Science of History*. New York, 1905.

Lange, Victor. "The Goethe Convocation at Aspen." *American-German Review* 15.6 (1949): 33–34.

——. "The History of German Studies in America: Ends and Means." Benseler, Lohnes, and Nollendorfs 3–16.

——. "Thoughts in Season." Lohnes and Nollendorfs, *German Studies* 5–16.

Larson, Magali Sarfatti. *The Rise of Professionalism: A Sociological Analysis*. Berkeley: U of California P, 1977.

Lauwers-Rech, Magda. *Nazi Germany and the American Germanists: A Study of Periodicals, 1930–1946*. Literature and the Sciences of Man 2. New York: Lang, 1995.

Learned, Marion D. "Deutsch gegen Englisch, oder Deutsch neben Englisch?" *Monatshefte* 2 (1901): 290–93.

——. "Germanistik und Schöne Litteratur in Amerika." *Monatshefte* 2 (1901): 97–107.

——. "The Lehrerbund and the Teachers of German in America." *Monatshefte* 1 (1899): 10–16.

——. *The Life of Francis Daniel Pastorius: The Founder of Germantown*. Philadelphia: Campbell, 1908.

——. "The President's Address: Linguistic Study and Literary Creation." *PMLA* 25 (1910): xlvi–lxv.

——. "Walthersage." *PMLA* 7 (1892): i–iv, 1–208.

——. "When Should German Instruction Begin in the Public Schools?" *Monatshefte* 3 (1901): 86–89.

Lee, James, and Albert Valdman, eds. *Form and Meaning: Multiple Perspectives*. Boston: Heinle, 2000.

Lefebvre, Henri. *The Production of Space*. Trans. Donald Nicholson-Smith. Oxford: Blackwell, 1991.

Leland, Charles G. [Hans Breitmann]. *Memoirs*. New York: Appleton, 1893.

Lemke, Victor J. Rev. of *Deutsches Leben,* by E. P. Appelt and A. M. Handhardt. *Monatshefte* 33 (1941): 48.

Lennox, Sara. "Feminism and New Historicism." *Monatshefte* 84 (1992): 159–70.

———. "Feminisms in Transit: American Feminist Germanists Construct a Multicultural Germany." Milich and Peck 77–92.

———. "Feminismus und German Studies in den USA." *Zeitschrift für Germanistik* 3 (1996): 561–74.

———. "Feminist German Studies across the Disciplines: Introduction to Grossmann, Ferree, and Cocks." *Women in German Yearbook* 12 (1996): 1–9.

———. "Feminist Scholarship and Germanistik." *German Quarterly* 62 (1989): 158–70.

———. " 'Der Versuch, man selbst zu sein': Christa Wolf und der Feminismus." *Die Frau als Heldin und Autorin: Neue kritische Ansätze zur deutschen Literatur.* Ed. Wolfgang Paulsen. Bern: Francke, 1979. 217–22.

Lenz, Harold. Rev. of *Reise in die Literatur,* by Otto Koischwitz. *Monatshefte* 31 (1939): 154.

Leonhard, Elke. "Mehr Effizienz, bitte!" *Zeitschrift für Kulturaustausch* 49.1 (1999): 19–22.

Leopold, Werner F. "Polarity in German Literature." *Journal of English and Germanic Philology* 29 (1930): 420–33.

———. "Realia, Kulturkunde, and Nationalism." *Monatshefte* 29 (1937): 17–24.

———. "Reise durch Deutschland, 1935." *Monatshefte* 27 (1935): 299–300.

Lessing, Gotthold Ephraim. *Nathan der Weise: Ein dramatisches Gedicht in fünf Aufzügen.* Ed. and introd. H. C. G. Brandt. New York: Henry Holt, 1895.

Lessing, O. E. "Die Zukunft deutscher Bildung in Amerika." *Monatshefte* 17 (1916): 337–47.

Letters to the Editor. *Die Unterrichtspraxis* 20 (1987): 4–6.

Leuchs, Fritz A. H. "Die Geschichte des Vereins deutscher Lehrer von New York und Umgegend." *German Quarterly* 8 (1935): 50–59.

Levine, Lawrence W. *Highbrow/Lowbrow: The Emergence of Cultural Hierarchy in America.* Cambridge: Harvard UP, 1988.

Lewis, David L. *W. E. B. DuBois: Biography of a Race, 1868–1919.* New York: Henry Holt, 1993.

Lindenberger, Herbert. "The Comparative Perspective." Other Perspectives on the Study and Profession of Germanics Forum. MLA Annual Convention. Saint Francis Hotel, San Francisco. 28 Dec. 1975.

———. *The History in Literature: On Value, Genre, Institutions.* New York: Columbia UP, 1990.

Liptzin, Solomon. "Early History of the A.A.T.G. (1926–1931)." *German Quarterly* 12 (1939): 20–23.

———, ed. *From Novalis to Nietzsche: Anthology of Nineteenth-Century German Literature.* 1929. 2nd ed. New York: Prentice, 1958–59.

Liskin-Gasparro, Judy E. "Assessment: From Content Standards to Student Performance." Lafayette 169–96.

———. *ETS Oral Proficiency Testing Manual.* Princeton: Educ. Testing Service, 1982.

"List of Colleges and of Their Modern Language Professors." *PMLA* 1 (1884): lv-xcvii. *JSTOR.* 3 Apr. 2003 <http://www.jstor.org/browse#Language+&+Literature>. Path: PMLA; Modern Language Association of America: Proceedings; Proceedings at New York; Back Matter; Select Another Page.

Littmann, Ulrich. *Partners—Distant and Close: Notes and Footnotes on Academic Mobility between Germany and the United States of America, 1923–1993.* Bonn: DAAD, 1997.

Logan, Gerald E. "Observations about the High School Laboratory." *German Quarterly* 35 (1962): 309–17.

Lohnes, Walter F. W. "Advanced Placement and the Future of German Teaching." *German Quarterly* 38 (1965): 415–26.

———. "The Training of German Teachers in the United States." *Die Unterrichtspraxis* 2.2 (1969): 69–76.

Lohnes, Walter F. W., and Valters Nollendorfs, eds. *German Studies in the United States: Assessment and Outlook.* Madison: U of Wisconsin P, 1976.

———. Introduction. Lohnes and Nollendorfs, *German Studies* 1–4.

Loiseaux, L. A. "Proceedings for 1910: Report of the Committee of Fifteen." *PMLA* 26 (1911): xii–xvii.

Lorenz, Dagmar C. G., ed. *Contemporary Jewish Writing in Austria.* Lincoln: U of Nebraska P, 1999.

———. *Keepers of the Motherland: German Texts by Jewish Women Writers.* Lincoln: U of Nebraska P, 1997.

———, ed. Millennial Issue. *German Quarterly* 73.1 (2000): 1–83.

Lorenz, Dagmar C. G., and Gabriele Weinberger, eds. *Insiders and Outsiders: Jewish and Gentile Culture in Germany and Austria.* Detroit: Wayne State UP, 1994.

Löwy, Michael. *Redemption and Utopia: Jewish Libertarian Thought in Central Europe.* Trans. Hope Heaney. Stanford: Stanford UP, 1992.

Ludwig, M. Mileta, Sr. *Right-Hand Glove Uplifted: A Biography of Archbishop Michael Heiss.* New York: Pageant, 1968.

Lüst, Reimar. "Defizite der deutschen auswärtigen Kulturpolitik." *Internationale Politik* 51.3 (1996): 43–48.

Lützeler, Paul M., ed. Germanistik *as German Studies: Interdisciplinary Theories and Methods.* Spec. issue of *German Quarterly* 62 (1989): 139–234.

———, ed. *Der postkoloniale Blick: Deutsche Schriftsteller berichten aus der Dritten Welt.* Frankfurt: Suhrkamp, 1997.

———. *Schriftsteller und "Dritte Welt": Studien zum postkolonialen Blick.* Tübingen: Stauffenburg, 1998.

Maas, Utz. "Die vom Faschismus verdrängten Sprachwissenschaftler—Repräsentanten einer anderen Sprachwissenschaft?" *Die Künste und die Wissenschaften im Exil, 1933–1945.* Ed. Edith Böhne and Wolfgang Motzkau-Valeton. Gerlingen: Schneider, 1992. 445–502.

MacLeod, Catriona. "Floating Heads: Weimar Portrait Busts." Henke, Kord, and Richter 65–96.

Maddox, Lucy, ed. *Locating American Studies: The Evolution of a Discipline.* Baltimore: Johns Hopkins UP, 1999.

Maier, Charles S. *The Unmasterable Past: History, Holocaust, and German National Identity.* Cambridge: Harvard UP, 1988.

Makaryk, Irena R., ed. *Encyclopedia of Contemporary Literary Theory: Approaches, Scholars, Terms.* Toronto: U of Toronto P, 1993.

Makins, Christopher. *The Study of Europe in the United States: A Report to the German Marshall Fund of the United States.* 1998. 21 Feb. 2003 <http://www.eurunion.org/infores/studyof/studyof.htm>.

Malkiel, Yakov. "Aspirations, Organization, Achievement." Hoenigswald 107–19.

Malone, Kemp. "In Memoriam: James Wilson Bright, 1852–1926." *Modern Language Notes* 41 (1926): v.

Mann, Thomas. "An die Deutschlehrer Amerikas." *German Quarterly* 14 (1941): 67–68.

Maren-Grisebach, Manon, ed. *Methoden der Literaturwissenschaft*. Munich: Francke, 1998.

Marks, Peter. "A Parody of the Past Becomes a Tribute." *New York Times on the Web* 15 July 1998. 2 Apr. 2003 <http://query.nytimes.com/search/advanced>.

Martin, Biddy. *Femininity Played Straight: The Significance of Being Lesbian*. New York: Routledge, 1996.

———. "Zwischenbalanz der feministischen Debatten." Trommler, *Germanistik* 165–85.

Maurer, Friedrich. *Leid: Studien zur Bedeutungs- und Problemgeschichte, besonders in den grossen Epen der staufischen Zeit*. Bibliotheca germanica 1. Bern: Francke, 1951.

Mayer, Evelies. Personal conversation with Hinrich Seeba. Berlin. 26 Sept. 1999.

Mayer, Hans. "Deutsche Literaturwissenschaft heute." *Germanic Review* 45 (1970): 163–78.

Mayer, Michael A., ed. *German-Jewish History in Modern Times*. 4 vols. New York: Columbia UP, 1996–98.

McCarthy, John A. "Double Optics: The Americanization of Germanistik—the Germanization of Americans." McCarthy and Schneider 1–13.

———. " 'An Indigenous and Not an Exotic Plant': Toward a History of Germanics at Penn." Benseler, Nickisch, and Nollendorfs 146–72.

———. "Was heißt es, heute Germanist zu sein? Antworten eines amerikanischen Germanisten." Fratzke and Albrecht 127–57.

McCarthy, John A., Herbert Rowland, and Richard Schade, eds. *Lessing International: Lessing Reception Abroad*. Lessing Yearbook 32. Göttingen: Wallstein, 2001.

McCarthy, John A., and Katrin Schneider, eds. *The Future of Germanistik in the USA: Changing Our Prospects*. Nashville: Vanderbilt UP, 1996.

McCaughey, Robert A. *International Studies and Academic Enterprise: A Chapter in the Enclosure of American Learning*. New York: Columbia UP, 1984.

McClain, William H. "Criticism as Institution: One Hundred Years of German Studies in *MLN*." *Modern Language Notes* 102 (1987): 419–36.

McClintock, Anne. "The Angel of Progress: Pitfalls of the Term 'Post-colonialism.' " Williams and Chrisman 291–304.

———. *Imperial Leather: Race, Gender, and Sexuality in the Colonial Context*. New York: Routledge, 1995.

McFalls, Laurence. "Living with Which Past? National Identity in Post-Wall, Postwar Germany." Denham, Kacandes, and Petropoulos 297–308.

McGlathery, James M., ed. *The Brothers Grimm and Folktale*. Urbana: U of Illinois P, 1988.

———. *Fairy Tale Romance: The Grimms, Basile, and Perrault*. Urbana: U of Illinois P, 1991.

———. *German and Scandinavian at Illinois: A History*. Urbana: U of Illinois, 1990.

McVeigh, Joseph G. "The Undergraduate Curriculum: What's Right/Wrong With It?" McCarthy and Schneider 57–64.

Mehnert, Klaus. *Ein deutscher Austauschstudent in Kalifornien*. Stuttgart: Veutsche, 1930. Rpt. in *Amerikanische und russische Jugend um 1930: Neudruck zweier Frühwerke*. By Mehnert. Stuttgart: Deutsche, 1973. 11–106.

Mendes-Flohr, Paul. *German Jews: A Dual Identity*. New Haven: Yale UP, 1999.

Mensel, Ernst H. "Some Aspects of Modern Language Teaching in This Country." *Monatshefte* 15 (1914): 128–34, 162–68.

Merrill, Charles S., and Susan E. Cernyak-Spatz, eds. *Language and Culture: A Tran-

scending Bond: Essays and Memoirs by American Germanists of Austro-Jewish Descent. New York: Lang, 1993.

Metcalf, George J. "A Report by the President of AATG." *German Quarterly* 42 (1969): 313–15.

Meves, Uwe. "Zum Institutionalisierungsprozeß der deutschen Philologie: Die Periode der Lehrstuhlerrichtung." Fohrmann and Voßkamp 115–203.

Meyer, Frederick. "Audiator et altera pars!" *Monatshefte* 18 (1917): 43–49.

Mieder, Wolfgang, ed. *Disenchantments: An Anthology of Modern Fairy Tale Poetry.* Hanover: UP of New England, 1985.

———. "Survival Forms of 'Little Red Riding Hood' in Modern Society." *International Folklore Review* 2 (1982): 23–40.

———. *Tradition and Innovation in Folk Literature.* Hanover: UP of New England, 1987.

Mildenberger, Kenneth W. "The Consequences of Prudent Affluence." *Modern Language Journal* 49 (1965): 349–53.

Milich, Klaus J., and Jeffrey M. Peck, eds. *Multiculturalism in Transit: A German-American Exchange.* New York: Berghahn, 1998.

Miller, J. Hillis. "The Critic as Host." *Deconstruction and Criticism.* Ed. Harold Bloom et al. New York: Seabury, 1979. 217–53.

Miller, Wallis. "Schinkel and the Politics of German Memory: The Life of the Neue Wache in Berlin." Denham, Kacandes, and Petropoulos 227–56.

Millett, Kate. *Sexual Politics.* New York: Doubleday, 1970.

Minert, Roger P. "Factors Influencing Enrollment in Public High School German Courses: Results of a National Survey." *Die Unterrichtspraxis* 25 (1992): 173–83.

Minorities in German Culture. Spec. issue of *New German Critique* 46 (1989): 3–208.

Minorities in Higher Education, 1997–98. Washington: Amer. Council on Educ., 1998.

"Minutes of the Thirty-Third Annual Meeting." *German Quarterly* 39 (1966): 276–83.

"Mission Statement." *Women in German.* 1 May 2003 <http://www.womeningerman.org/>.

MLA Guide to the Job Search. New York: MLA, 2000.

"MLA's Fall 1998 Survey Shows Increase in Foreign Language Enrollments in United States Colleges and Universities." *MLA Newsletter* 31.4 (1999): 1–2.

Möller, Horst. *Exodus der Kultur: Schriftsteller, Wissenschaftler und Künstler in der Emigration nach 1933.* Munich: Beck, 1984.

Monatshefte / Max Kade Institute Directory of German Studies: Departments, Programs, and Faculties in the United States and Canada, 2000. Ed. Katherine Ebel, Alan Ng, and Cora Lee Nollendorfs. Madison: U of Wisconsin P, 2001.

Montrose, Louis A. "Professing the Renaissance: The Poetics and Politics of Culture." Veeser 15–36.

Moore, Suzanne S., and David P. Benseler, comps. and eds. *A Comprehensive Index to the* Modern Language Journal, *1916–1996.* Boston: Blackwell, 2000.

Moore, Wilbert E., with Gerald W. Rosenblum. *The Professions: Roles and Rules.* New York: Sage Foundation, 1970.

Morgan, Bayard Quincy. "After the War: A Blueprint for Action." *German Quarterly* 17 (1944): 241–43.

———. "E Pluribus Unum." *Modern Language Journal* 11 (1927): 485–88.

———. "In Defense of Translation." *Modern Language Journal* 1 (1917): 236–40.

———. "A Memorandum on the 'Intensive' Course in a Foreign Language." *German Quarterly* 16 (1943): 199–201.

———. "New Hope for Learners of German." *Monatshefte* 30 (1938): 454–56.

Morize, André. *Problems and Methods of Literary History: With Special Reference to Modern French Literature*. Boston: Ginn, 1922.

Morris, Leslie, and Karen Remmler, eds. *Contemporary Jewish Writing in Germany*. Lincoln: U of Nebraska P, 2002.

Morris, Leslie, and Jack Zipes, eds. *Unlikely History: The Changing German-Jewish Symbiosis, 1945–2000*. New York: Palgrave, 2002.

Morrow, Ralph E. *Washington University in St. Louis: A History*. Saint Louis: Missouri Historical Soc., 1996.

Moses, Stéphane, and Albrecht Schöne, eds. *Juden in der deutschen Literatur*. Frankfurt: Suhrkamp, 1986.

Mosse, George L. *Confronting the Nation: Jewish and Western Nationalism*. Hanover: UP of New England, 1993.

———. *German Jews beyond Judaism*. Bloomington: Indiana UP, 1985.

———. *Germans and Jews: The Right, the Left, and the Search for a "Third Force."* New York: Fertig, 1970.

Moulton, William G. *A Linguistic Guide to Language Learning*. New York: MLA, 1966.

———. *The Sounds of English and German*. Chicago: U of Chicago P, 1962.

Mueller, Magda. "Germania Displaced? Reflections on the Discourses of Female Asylum Seekers and Ethnic Germans." Herminghouse and Mueller 276–89.

Mueller-Vollmer, Kurt. "Differenzierung oder Auflösung? Der Weg der US-Germanistik seit 1964." Jäger 150–63.

———. "Translating Transcendentalism in New England: The Genesis of Literary Discourse." Mueller-Vollmer and Irmscher 81–106.

Mueller-Vollmer, Kurt, and Michael Irmscher, eds. *Translating Literatures, Translating Cultures: New Vistas and Approaches in Literary Studies*. Stanford: Stanford UP, 1998.

Mullen, Inga E. *German Realism in the United States: The American Reception of Meyer, Storm, Raabe, Keller, and Fontane*. New York: Lang, 1988.

Müller, Siegfried H. "Report on the Proceedings of the Television Committee, A.A.T.G." *German Quarterly* 28 (1955): 89–95.

Müller-Kampel, Beatrix, ed. *Lebenswege und Lieblingslektüren österreichischer NS-Vertriebener in den USA und Kanada*. Tübingen: Niemeyer, 2000.

Musumeci, Diane. *Breaking Tradition: An Exploration of the Historical Relationship between Theory and Practice in Second Language Teaching*. New York: McGraw, 1997.

Nägele, Rainer. *Echoes of Translation: Reading between Texts*. Baltimore: Johns Hopkins UP, 1997.

———. "The Provocation of Lacan." *New German Critique* 16 (1979): 5–29.

Nagy, Ellen M. "Patterns in Advertising: What New Professionals Should Know." *Die Unterrichtspraxis* 33 (2000): 14–17.

———. "Women and the AATG." Nagy, *Women* 39–54.

———. *Women in Germanics, 1850–1950*. New York: Lang, 1997.

"National Symposium on the Advancement of the Teaching of German in the U.S." *Die Unterrichtspraxis* 1.1 (1968): 132–36.

"Das Nationale Deutschamerikanische Lehrerseminar." *Pädagogische Monatshefte* 2.7 (1901): 252–53.

Natter, Wolfgang. "Disciplining Boundaries." McCarthy and Schneider 111–21.

———. "Über Identität, Global-Regionalismus und Globalisierung von unten: Kentucky, eine Fallstudie." *Comparativ* 13.2 (2002): 93–129.

Nelson, Cary, Paula A. Treichler, and Lawrence Grossberg. "Cultural Studies: An Introduction." Grossberg, Nelson, and Treichler 1–22.

Nemec, Friedrich, and Wilhelm Solms, eds. *Literaturwissenschaft heute. 7 Kapitel über ihre Praxis*. Munich: Fink, 1979.

Neuse, Werner. "Lesefertigkeit und direkte Methode." *Monatshefte* 24 (1932): 217–20.

Newell, William, ed. *Interdisciplinarity: Essays from the Literature*. New York: College Board, 1998.

Newton, Judith Lowder. "History As Usual? Feminism and the 'New Historicism.' " Veeser 152–67.

Nickisch, Craig W. "German and National Policy: The West Point Experience." Benseler, Lohnes, and Nollendorfs 76–82.

Nietzsche, Friedrich. Aphorism 188. *Jenseits von Gut und Böse*. 1886. Ed. Giorgio Colli and Mazzino Montinari. Munich: Deutscher Taschenbuch, 1988. 110. Vol. 5 of *Kritische Studienausgabe*.

Nollendorfs [Kluge], Cora L. "Deutschunterricht in Amerika im Schatten des Ersten Weltkrieges: Öffentlich-offizielle Verfahrensweisen und gesellschaftliches Gebaren." *Zeitschrift für Kulturaustausch* 35 (1985): 190–99.

———. "The First World War and the Survival of German Studies." Benseler, Lohnes, and Nollendorfs 176–95.

———. "Special Survey: To Whom and to What End Do We Teach German?" *Monatshefte* 89 (1997): 386–91.

Nollendorfs, Valters. "Eine amerikanischere Germanistik: Entwicklungen im amerikanischen Deutschstudium in den 70er und 80er Jahren." *Zeitschrift für Kulturaustausch* 35 (1985): 230–36.

———. "Out of *Germanistik*: Thoughts on the Shape of Things to Come." *Die Unterrichtspraxis* 27 (1994): 1–10.

———. "Present Trends and Future Directions of American Germanics." McCarthy and Schneider 53–56.

Nollendorfs, Valters, and Carol A. Arness. "Graduate Programs: Looking toward the 1990's." *Monatshefte* 76 (1984): 311–31.

"Notes and News." *German Quarterly* 1 (1928): 148–54; 2 (1929): 27–32, 67–72, 111–15, 164–68; 6 (1933): 188–91.

"Notes and News." *Modern Language Journal* 4 (1920): 192.

"Notice to Contributors." *Women in German Yearbook* 1 May 2003 <http://www.womeningerman.org/pubs/yearbook/yearbook.html>.

Novick, Peter. *The Holocaust in American Life*. New York: Houghton, 1999.

Nussbaum, Martha C. *Cultivating Humanity: A Classical Defense of Reform in Liberal Education*. Cambridge: Harvard UP, 1997.

Nutz, Maximilian. "Das Beispiel Goethes: Zur Konstituierung eines nationalen Klassikers." Fohrmann and Voßkamp 605–37.

Nye, Russel Blaine. *The Cultural Life of the New Nation, 1776–1830*. New York: Harper, 1960.

Oetker, Arend. "Fruchtbare Wechselwirkungen: Auswärtige Kulturpolitik und die deutsche Wirtschaft." *Internationale Politik* 51.3 (1996): 39–42.

Omaggio Hadley, Alice. *Teaching Language in Context*. Boston: Heinle, 1986.

Osterle, Heinz D. "Historicism, Marxism, Structuralism: Ideas for a German Culture Course." Helbig, *German Studies* 11–66.

Ostow, Robin. *Jews in Contemporary East Germany: The Children of Moses in the Land of Marx*. New York: St. Martin's, 1989.

Ott, Ulrich. *Amerika ist anders: Studien zum Amerika-Bild in deutschen Reiseberichten des 20. Jahrhunderts*. Frankfurt: Lang, 1991.

"The Outlook for German." *Modern Language Journal* 4 (1919): 24–28.

Oxford, Rebecca L., and Madelyn E. Ehrmann. "Second Language Research on Individual Differences." *Annual Review of Applied Linguistics* 13 (1993): 188–205.

Pan, David. "The Crisis of the Humanities and the End of the University." *Telos* 111 (1998): 69–106.

Parker, Clifford S. "The Training of Language Teachers in the Secondary Schools of New Hampshire." *Modern Language Journal* 19 (1935): 401–24.

Parker, William R. "The MLA, 1883–1953." *PMLA* 68 (1953): 3–39.

Peck, Jeffrey M. " 'The British Are Coming! The British Are Coming!' Notes for a Comparative Study of Institutions." Benseler, Lohnes, and Nollendorfs 271–84.

———. "There's No Place like Home? Remapping the Topography of German Studies." *German Quarterly* 62 (1989): 178–87.

Pehlke, Michael. "Aufstieg und Fall der Germanistik—von der Agonie einer bürgerlichen Wissenschaft." Kolbe 18–44.

Pelz, Bill. "Revolutionary Women in Imperial Germany." Women in German Conf. Miami U, Oxford. 25 Sept. 1976.

Pencil Vania. "Zum nächsten Lehrertage." *Monatshefte* 2 (1901): 221–24.

Pennell, Elizabeth R. *Charles Godfrey Leland: A Biography.* 2 vols. Boston: Houghton, 1906.

Pentlin, Susan L. "German Teachers' Reaction to the Third Reich." Benseler, Lohnes, and Nollendorfs 228–52.

"Personalia—1938–1939." *Monatshefte* 30 (1938): 396–403.

Peters, George F. "Dilemmas of Diversity: Observations on Efforts to Increase Minority Participation in German." *ADFL Bulletin* 25.2 (1994): 5–11.

Peters, George F., et al. "Report and Recommendations of the AATG Committee for the Recruitment and Retention of Minorities in German." *Die Unterrichtspraxis* 26 (1993): 97–98.

Petrey, Sandy. "When Did Literature Stop Being Cultural?" *Diacritics* 28.3 (1998): 11–22.

Pfanner, Helmut F. *Exile in New York: German and Austrian Writers after 1933.* Detroit: Wayne State UP, 1983.

Pfeffer, J. Alan. "Realia in American Modern Language Instruction." *German Quarterly* 10 (1937): 1–11.

Piel, Sara Elizabeth. "Present Trends in Foreign Language Requirements." *German Quarterly* 24 (1951): 12–16.

Pino, Barbara Gonzalez. "Helping Language Teacher Candidates Achieve Proficiency at the U of Texas at San Antonio." Dallas. 21 Nov. 1999.

"Placements in Non-academic Jobs." *Monatshefte* 71 (1979): 305–06.

Pochmann, Henry. *German Culture in America: Philosophical and Literary Influences, 1600–1900.* Madison: U of Wisconsin P, 1961.

"Politics in Poetry: The Search for a Radical German Tradition." *Times Literary Supplement* 30 Apr. 1971: 489–91.

Politzer, Heinz. *Franz Kafka: Parable and Paradox.* Ithaca: Cornell UP, 1962.

———. "Studies on Jewish Contributors to German Literature: Heine and Börne." Diss. Bryn Mawr Coll., 1950.

Politzer, Robert L. *Teaching German: A Linguistic Orientation.* Waltham: Blaisdell, 1968.

President's Commission on Foreign Language and International Studies. *Strength through Wisdom: A Critique of US Capability: A Report.* Washington: GPO, 1979.

Prewitt, Kenneth. "Presidential Items." *Items* 50.2–3 (1996): 31–40.

Price, W. R. "Results of the Examinations for Approval for Oral Credit: The Licensing of Teachers of Modern Languages." *Modern Language Journal* 4 (1920): 345–47.

Programs of the Annual Kentucky Foreign Language Conference. U of Kentucky Archives, 1948–99.

Prokop, Manfred. "A Survey of the State of German Studies in Canada." Roche and Salumets 233–61.

Prokosch, Eduard. *A Comparative Germanic Grammar.* Philadelphia: Linguistic Soc. of Amer.; U of Pennsylvania, 1939.

"Proposal of the Regents of the University of Wisconsin to the National Teachers' Seminary of Milwaukee." Ser. 7/14/10-2, Box 10, Univ. Archives, U of Wisconsin, Madison.

Purdy, Daniel, ed. *German Dress Culture.* Spec. issue of *Germanic Review* 72 (1997): 163–230.

Purin, Charles M. "Deutscher Sprachunterricht und bewusstes Deutschtum." *Monatshefte* 9 (1908): 42–46, 71–76, 104–07.

———. "German in the Colleges and Universities of Wisconsin." *Monatshefte* 22 (1930): 81–85.

———. "The Training of Modern Foreign Language Teachers in the Light of Investigations." *Modern Language Journal* 13 (1928): 15–20.

———. *The Training of Teachers of the Modern Foreign Languages.* New York: Macmillan, 1929.

Rabinbach, Anson, and Jack Zipes, eds. *Germans and Jews since the Holocaust: The Changing Situation in West Germany.* New York: Holmes, 1986.

Radosavljevich, P. R. "Eine Skizze aus der Experimental-Pädagogik." *Monatshefte* 15 (1914): 168–70.

Rainer, Joseph. *Doctor Joseph Salzmann: Ein Lebensbild.* 2nd ed. Saint Francis: Saint John's Taubstummen-Anstalt, 1903.

Ranke, Kurt, et al., eds. *Enzyklopädie des Märchens: Handwörterbuch zur historischen und vergleichenden Erzählforschung.* 6 vols. Berlin: de Gruyter, 1977–99.

Rankin, Jamie. "Hit or Miss, or Missing: The Role of Second Language Acquisition Research in Language Teacher Training." *Die Unterrichtspraxis* 27 (1994): 18–27.

Rappaport, Lynn. *Jews in Germay after the Holocaust: Memory, Identity, and German-Jewish Relations.* New York: Cambridge UP, 1997.

Rauch, Irmengard. *The Old Saxon Language: Grammar, Epic Narrative, Linguistic Interference.* New York: Lang, 1992.

Readings, Bill. *The University in Ruins.* Cambridge: Harvard UP, 1996.

Reichert, Herbert W. "Conventional Textbooks in the Foreign-Language Telecourse." *German Quarterly* 32 (1959): 34–42.

———. "Translation and the Reading Objective." *German Quarterly* 21 (1948): 175–84.

Reichmann, Eberhard. "Introducing the *Unterrichtspraxis*." *Die Unterrichtspraxis* 1.1 (1968): 1.

———, ed. *The Teaching of German: Problems and Methods.* Philadelphia: Natl. Carl Schurz Assn., 1970.

Reinhardt, Kurt F. "Basic Principles in Literary History and Literary Criticism." *Journal of English and Germanic Philology* 30 (1931): 383–91.

Reinharz, Jehuda, and Walter Schatzberg, eds. *The Jewish Response to German Culture: From the Enlightenment to the Second World War.* Hanover: UP of New England, 1985.

Reiter, Rayna R., ed. *Toward an Anthropology of Women.* New York: Monthly Review, 1975.

Remak, Henry H. H. "Deutsche Emigration und amerikanische Germanistik." Schmitz 173–90.

Report. *AAUP Bulletin* 19 (1933): 302.

Report of the Commissioner of Education for 1897–98. Washington: US Bureau of Educ., 1899.

"Report of the Committee of Twelve of the Modern Language Association of America." *Report* 1391–433.

"Report of the Committee on a Four Years' Course in German for Secondary Schools." *Monatshefte* 7 (1906): 71–76.

Rey, William H. "Offener Brief an Henry J. Schmidt." *Monatshefte* 80 (1988): 297–99.

Rheinberger, Hans-Joerg. *Toward a History of Epistemic Things.* Stanford: Stanford UP, 1997.

Rich, Adrienne. "Compulsory Heterosexuality and Lesbian Existence." *Signs* 5 (1980): 631–60.

Richard, Ernst. *History of German Civilization: A General Survey.* 2nd ed. New York: Macmillan, 1913.

Richarz, Monika, ed., *Bürger auf Widerruf: Lebenszeugnisse deutscher Juden, 1780–1945.* Munich: Beck, 1989.

Richter, Dieter, and Johannes Merkel. *Märchen, Phantasie und soziales Lernen.* Berlin: Basis, 1974.

Richter, Simon. "Help from the Devil in Boosting Course Enrollments." *Chronicle of Higher Education* 14 July 2000: A56.

———. "The Ins and Outs of Intimacy: Gender, Epistolary Culture, and the Public Sphere." *German Quarterly* 69 (1996): 111–24.

Richter, Werner. *Re-educating Germany.* Trans. Paul Lehman. Chicago: U of Chicago P, 1945.

———. "Strömungen und Stimmungen in den Literaturwissenschaften von heute." *Germanic Review* 21 (1946): 81–113.

Ringer, Fritz K. *The Decline of the German Mandarins: The German Academic Community, 1890–1933.* Cambridge: Harvard UP, 1969.

Rippley, La Vern J. "Ameliorated Americanization: The Effect of World War I on German-Americans in the 1920s." Trommler and McVeigh 217–31.

———. "German Assimilation: The Effect of the 1871 Victory on Americana-Germanica." Trefousse 122–36.

Risser, Nancy A., et al. *Humanities PhDs and Non-academic Careers: A Guide for Faculty Advisers.* Evanston: Committee on Institutional Cooperation, 1983.

Robinson, Orrin W. *Clause Subordination and Verb Placement in the Old High German Isidor Translation.* Heidelberg: Winter, 1997.

Roche, Jörg, and Thomas Salumets, eds. *Germanics under Construction: Intercultural and Interdisciplinary Prospects.* Munich: Iudicium, 1996.

Roesch, Lydia. "Der völkische Dichter und seine nationale Sendung im neuen Deutschland." *Monatshefte* 29 (1937): 158–60.

Röhrich, Lutz. *Märchen und Wirklichkeit.* Wiesbaden: Steiner, 1979.

Rölleke, Heinz. *"Wo das Wünschen noch geholfen hat": Gesammelte Aufsätze zu den Kinder- und Hausmärchen der Brüder Grimm.* Bonn: Bouvier, 1985.

Romero, Christiane Zehl. *Anna Seghers: Eine Biographie, 1900–1947.* Berlin: Aufbau, 2000.

———. *Anna Seghers: Mit Selbstzeugnissen und Bildokumenten.* Reinbek bei Hamburg: Rowohlt, 1993.

Rorty, Richard. *Achieving Our Country: Leftist Thought in Twentieth-Century America.* Cambridge: Harvard UP, 1998.

Röseler, Robert O. Rev. of Langenscheidt's *Deutsche Lesehefte. Monatshefte* 29 (1937): 89.

Rosellini, Jay. *Volker Braun.* Munich: Beck, 1980.

———. *Wolf Biermann.* Munich: Beck, 1992.

Rosenberg, Ralph P. "American Doctoral Studies in Germanic Culture: A Study in German-American Relations, 1873–1949." *Yearbook of Comparative and General Literature* 14 (1955): 30–44.

Rosenstengel, W. H. "Bericht des Zwölferkomitees der 'Modern Language Association of America.' " *Monatshefte* 1.4 (1900): 10–13; 1.5 (1900): 26–29; 1.6 (1900): 20–22.

Rowland, Herbert. "Lessing in American Magazines in the Nineteenth Century." McCarthy, Rowland, and Schade 269–81.

Rubin, Gayle. "Thinking Sex: Notes for a Radical Theory of the Politics of Sexuality." Vance 267–319.

———. "The Traffic in Women: Notes on the 'Political Economy' of Sex." Reiter 157–210.

Rudolph, Frederick. *The American College and University: A History.* New York: Knopf, 1962.

Ruplin, Ferdinand A., and John R. Russell. "A Type of Computer-Assisted Instruction." *German Quarterly* 41 (1968): 84–88.

Ryan, Michael. "New French Theory in *New German Critique.*" *New German Critique* 22 (1981): 145–61.

Ryder, Frank G. "The Present and Future Shape of Graduate Programs." Lohnes and Nollendorfs, *German Studies* 121–27.

Said, Edward W. *Orientalism.* New York: Random, 1978.

Saine, Thomas P. Preface. *Goethe Yearbook.* Vol. 1 Columbia: Camden, 1982. vii–viii.

Salloch, Erika. "Traces of Fascist Ideology in American Professional Journals." Benseler, Lohnes, and Nollendorfs 253–70.

Sammons, Jeffrey L. "The American Perspective." Other Perspectives on the Study and Profession of Germanics Forum. MLA Annual Convention. Saint Francis Hotel, San Francisco. 28 Dec. 1975.

———. "Die amerikanische Germanistik: Historische Betrachtungen zur gegenwärtigen Situation." Brinkmann, Ezawa, and Hackert 105–20.

———. "Germanistik im Niemandsland." Trommler, *Germanistik* 104–20.

———. "*Germanistik* in the Academy; or, The Invisible Lodge." *German Studies* 13–18.

———. Rev. of *Synthetisches Interpretieren,* by Jost Hermand." *German Quarterly* 43 (1970): 98–101.

———. "Some Considerations on Our Invisibility." Lohnes and Nollendorfs, *German Studies* 17–23.

———. "Were German-Americans Interned during World War II? A Question concerning Scholarly Standards and Integrity." *German Quarterly* 71 (1998): 73–77.

Sander, Volkmar. "Doctorates Awarded in German, 1965–1989." *Monatshefte* 82 (1990): 319–23.

———. "Figures and Trends Updated." *Monatshefte* 72 (1980): 235–44.

———. "Wohin treibt die Germanistik?" *Germanic Review* 45 (1970): 179–87.

Santner, Eric L. *On the Psychopathology of Everyday Life: Reflections on Freud and Rosenzweig.* Chicago: U of Chicago P, 2001.

———. *Stranded Objects: Mourning, Memory, and Film in Postwar Germany.* Ithaca: Cornell UP, 1990.

————. "The Trouble with Hitler: Postwar German Aesthetics and the Legacy of Fascism." *New German Critique* 57 (1992): 5–24.

Sartorius, Joachim. Statement. *Zeitschrift für Kulturaustausch* 48.3 (1998) : 11–12.

Schade, Richard E. "*Jahrhundertwenden*: The Centenary of the Department of Germanic Languages and Literatures, U of Cincinnati." *German Quarterly* 73 (2000): 299–307.

Scheck, Ulrich. "Deutschunterricht an der Queen's University von 1870 bis 1945: Eine Fallstudie zur Germanistik in Kanada." Timm 80–104.

Schenda, Rudolf. *Volk ohne Buch: Studien zur Sozialgeschichte der populären Lesestoffe.* Frankfurt: Klostermann, 1970.

Scherer, George A. C. "The Use and Misuse of Language Laboratories." *German Quarterly* 38 (1965): 335–44.

Scherer, George A. C., and Michael Wertheimer. "The German Teaching Experiment at the U of Colorado." *German Quarterly* 35 (1962): 298–308.

Scherer, Wilhelm. *Geschichte der deutschen Literatur.* 1880–83. 7th ed. Berlin: Weidmann, 1894.

Schiller, Friedrich. *Über die ästhetische Erziehung des Menschen: in einer Reihe von Briefen.* Projekt Gutenberg-DE. 9 June 2003 <http://www.gutenberg2000.de/schiller/erziehng/erziehng.htm>.

Schlant, Ernestine. *The Language of Silence: West German Literature and the Holocaust.* New York: Routledge, 1999.

Schmidt, Henry J. "Interview with Hermann J. Weigand (1892–1985)." Benseler, Lohnes, and Nollendorfs 285–92.

————. "The Rhetoric of Survival: The Germanist in America, 1900–1925." Trommler and McVeigh 204–16. Benseler, Lohnes, and Nollendorfs 165–75.

————. "What Is Oppositional Criticism? Politics and German Literary Criticism from Fascism to the Cold War." *Monatshefte* 79 (1987): 292–307.

————. "Wissenschaft als Ware und als Selbstbehauptung: Die institutionellen Grundlagen der amerikanischen Germanistik." Trommler, *Germanistik* 66–83.

Schmidt, Hugo. "A Historical Survey of the Teaching of German in America." Reichmann, *Teaching* 3–7.

Schmidt-Ott, Friedrich. "Anfänge deutscher Kulturpolitik im Auslande." *Zeitschrift für Politik* ns 3 (1956): 252–58.

Schmidt-Wartenberg, H. M. "Ein Tiroler Passionspiel des Mittelalters." *PMLA* 5 (1890): i–xi, 1–127.

Schmitz, Walter, ed. *Modernisierung oder Überfremdung? Zur Wirkung deutscher Exilanten in der Germanistik der Aufnahmeländer.* Stuttgart: Metzler, 1994.

Scholes, Robert E. *The Rise and Fall of English: Reconstructing English as a Discipline.* New Haven: Yale UP, 1998.

Schönert, Jörg, ed. *Literaturwissenschaft und Wissenschaftsforschung.* Stuttgart: Metzler, 2000.

Schreiber, Theodore. "Vom Fremdwort im deutschen Unterricht." *German Quarterly* 8 (1935): 160–68.

Schueler, Herbert. "Foreign Language Teaching under the Army Specialized Training Program." *German Quarterly* 17 (1944): 183–91.

————. "In Memoriam: Frank Mankiewicz." *German Quarterly* 15 (1942): 1–4.

Schultz, Hans-Dietrich, and Wolfgang Natter. "Imagining Mitteleuropa: Conceptualizations of 'Its' Space in and outside German Geography." *European Review of History* 10 (2003): forthcoming.

Schulz, Renate A. "Foreign Language Teacher Development: *MLJ* Perspectives, 1916–1999." *Modern Language Journal* 84 (2000): 496–523.

————. "Methods of Teaching German in the United States: A Historical Perspective." Benseler, Lohnes, and Nollendorfs 55–75.

————. *Options for Undergraduate Foreign Language Programs: Four-Year and Two-Year Colleges.* New York: MLA, 1979.

————. "Profile of the Profession: Results of the 1992 AATG Membership Survey." *Die Unterrichtspraxis* 26 (1993): 226–52.

Schulz, Renate A., et al. "Professional Standards for Teachers of German: Recommendations of the AATG Task Force on Professional Standards." *Die Unterrichtspraxis* 26 (1993): 80–96.

Schwarz, Egon. "Die Exilanten und die heutige amerikanische Universität." Schmitz 119–29.

————. *Keine Zeit für Eichendorff: Chronik unfreiwilliger Wanderjahre: Mit einer Nachschrift 1991 und einem Essay von Hans-Albert Walter.* Frankfurt: Büchergilde Gutenberg, 1992.

"26. Generalversammlung des Nationalen Deutschamerikanischen Lehrerseminar-Vereins." *Pädagogische Monatshefte* 5.7–8 (1904): 213–23.

"Secretary's Report of the Annual Meeting of the American Association of Teachers of German." *German Quarterly* 10 (1937): 95–98.

Sedgwick, Eve Kosofsky. *Between Men: English Literature and Male Homosocial Desire.* New York: Columbia UP, 1985.

————. *Epistemology of the Closet.* Berkeley: U of California P, 1990.

————. "Gender Criticism." Greenblatt and Gunn 271–302.

Seeba, Hinrich C. "Cultural Poetics: Academic Emigration and Intercultural Criticism: On the Role of Jewish Critics in Exile." Dowden and Werner 1–22.

————. "German Studies in Amerika: Ein interdisziplinäres und interkulturelles Modell der Kulturtheorie." *Reformdiskussion und curriculare Entwicklung in der Germanistik.* Ed. Günter Blamberger et al. Bonn: DAAD, 1995. 27–37.

————. "Interkulturelle Perspektiven: Ansätze einer vergleichenden Kulturkritik bei Karl Lamprecht und in der Exil-Germanistik." *German Studies Review* 16 (1993): 1–17.

————. "Klassische Bildung: Ein deutscher Begriff im amerikanischen Kontext." *Humanismus und Menschenbildung: Zur Geschichte, Gegenwart und Zukunft der bildenden Begegnung der Europäer mit der Kultur der Griechen und Römer.* Ed. Erhard Wiersing. Essen: Blaue Eule, 2001. 432–47.

————. "New Historicism und Kulturanthropologie: Ansätze eines deutsch-amerikanischen Dialogs." *Historismus am Ende des 20. Jahrhunderts: Eine internationale Diskussion.* Ed. Gunter Scholtz. Berlin: Akademie, 1997. 40–54.

————. "Zum Geist- und Strukturbegriff in der Literaturwissenschaft der zwanziger Jahre: Ein Beitrag zur Dilthey-Rezeption." *Literaturwissenschaft und Geistesgeschichte 1910 bis 1925.* Ed. Christoph König and Eberhard Lämmert. Frankfurt: Fischer Taschenbuch, 1993. 240–54.

————. "Zwischen den Kulturen: Wissenschaftsemigration und German Studies." *Der Exodus aus Nazideutschland und die Folgen: Jüdische Wissenschaftler im Exil.* Ed. Marianne Hassler and Jürgen Wertheimer. Tübingen: Attempto, 1997. 304–24.

Segebrecht, Wulf. *Was sollen Germanisten lesen? Ein Vorschlag.* Berlin: Schmidt, 1994.

Sehrt, E. H., and Taylor Starck, eds. *Notkers des Deutschen Werke nach den Handschriften neu herausgegeben.* Halle (Saale), Ger.: Niemeyer, 1933– .

————, eds. *Notker-Wortschatz: Das gesamte Material zusammengetragen.* Halle (Saale), Ger.: Niemeyer, 1955.

Seib, Walter. "Zur Weltkulturdekade." *Die Weltdekade für kulturelle Entwicklung, 1988–1997: Eine Informationsschrift.* Ed. Hans-Dieter Dyroff. Bonn: Deutsche UNESCO-Kommission, 1989. 5–30.

Seidlin, Oskar. *Essays in German and Comparative Literature*. Chapel Hill: U of North Carolina P, 1961.

———. "The History of the Department of German of the Ohio State University: On the Occasion of the University's Centenary." Ohio State U, Columbus. 1969.

———. "Das Humane und der Dichter." *Monatshefte* 32 (1940): 333–38.

Sevin, Dieter. *Christa Wolf: Der geteilte Himmel: Nachdenken über Christa T.* Munich: Oldenbourg, 1982.

Seyhan, Azade. Introduction. *New German Critique* 46 (1989): 3–9.

———. *Representation and Its Discontents: The Critical Legacy of German Romanticism*. Berkeley: U of California P, 1992.

———. *Writing outside the Nation*. Princeton: Princeton UP, 2000.

"Shall German Be Taught in Our High Schools? A Symposium." *German Quarterly* 1 (1928): 53–67.

Shea, Victor. "New Historicism." Makaryk 124–30.

Shears, Lambert A. "The Approach to the Study of German Literature." *Modern Language Journal* 7 (1922–23): 26–28.

Shils, Edward. "The Order of Learning in the United States from 1865 to 1920: The Ascendency of the Universities." *Minerva* 16 (1978): 159–95.

Showalter, Elaine. "Feminist Criticism in the Wilderness." *The New Feminist Criticism: Essays on Women, Literature, and Theory*. Ed. Showalter. New York: Pantheon, 1985. 243–78.

———. "Review Essay: Literary Criticism." *Signs* 1 (1975): 435–60.

Silber, Ellen, ed. *Critical Issues in Foreign Language Instruction*. New York: Garland, 1991.

Silberberg, Betty. "Die Schwierigkeiten der deutschen Sprache für Ausländer und Mittel zu deren Bekämpfung." *Monatshefte* 2 (1901): 200–05.

Silberman, Marc. *Heiner Müller*. Amsterdam: Rodopi, 1980.

———. *Literature of the Working World: A Study of the Industrial Novel in East Germany*. Bern: Lang, 1976.

Silz, Walter. *Early German Romanticism: Its Founders and Heinrich von Kleist*. Cambridge: Harvard UP, 1929.

Simon, Paul. *The Tongue-Tied American: Confronting the Foreign Language Crisis*. New York: Continuum, 1980.

Siskel, Gene. " 'Ragtime': Milos Forman's Loving Salute to America." *Chicago Tribune* 27 Dec. 1981, sec. 6: 16+.

Slaughter, Sheila, and Larry L. Leslie, eds. *Academic Capitalism: Politics, Policies, and the Entrepreneurial University*. Baltimore: Johns Hopkins UP, 1997.

Slepack, Donna. "A Comparative Analysis of Sex Role Stereotyping in Children's Readers: USA vs. GDR." Women in German Conf. Miami U, Oxford. 25 Sept. 1976.

Smith, Phillip D., Jr. *A Comparison of the Cognitive and Audiolingual Approaches to Foreign Language Instruction*. Philadelphia: Center for Curriculum Development, 1970.

Sokel, Walter H. "Embattled Germanistik: Part of an Intellectual Autobiography." Dowden and Werner 186–205.

———. *The Writer in Extremis: Expressionism in Twentieth-Century German Literature*. Stanford: Stanford University P, 1959.

Sollors, Werner, ed. *Multilingual America: Transnationalism, Ethnicity, and the Languages of American Literature*. New York: New York UP, 1998.

Spaethling, Robert. "The Germanist as Educator in the First Two Years of College Teaching." Lohnes and Nollendorfs, *German Studies* 168–75.

Spanhoofd, A. Werner. "Psychologische Grundlage für die Methoden des Unterrichts in den modernen Sprachen." *Monatshefte* 9 (1908): 237–43.

Special Issue on Culture Studies. Spec. issue of *German Quarterly* 69 (1996): 367–472.

Special Issue on the German Democratic Republic. Spec. issue of *New German Critique* 2 (1974): 1–168.

Special Millennium Issue. PMLA 115 (2000): 1714–2096.

"Special Survey: German Studies Programs and Courses." *Monatshefte* 87 (1995): 360–66.

Spector, Scott. *Prague Territories: National Conflict and Cultural Innovation in Franz Kafka's Fin de Siècle.* Berkeley: U of California P, 2000.

Spencer, Samia L., ed. *Foreign Languages and International Trade: A Global Perspective.* Athens: U of Georgia P, 1987.

Spiker, Claude C. "The Foreign Language Teacher as a National Asset in Reconstruction." *Modern Language Journal* 6 (1921): 65–73.

Spitzer, Leo. "Deutsche Literaturforschung in Amerika." *Monatshefte* 37 (1945): 475–80.

Springer, Otto. "Intensive Language Study as a Part of the College Curriculum." *German Quarterly* 17 (1944): 224–40.

Spuler, Richard. "From Genesis to Convention: Literary Criticism as a German-American Institution." Benseler, Lohnes, and Nollendorfs 155–64.

———. *Germanistik in America: The Reception of German Classicism, 1870–1905.* Stuttgart: Heinz, 1982.

Staël, Germaine de. *De l'Allemagne.* Ed. Simone Belayé. Vol. 1. Paris: Garnier-Flammarion, 1968.

Staiger, Emil. *Die Kunst der Interpretation.* Zürich: Atlantis, 1951.

Standards for Foreign Language Learning: Preparing for the Twenty-First Century. Yonkers: ACTFL; Natl. Standards in Foreign Lang. Educ. Project, 1996.

Standards for Foreign Language Learning in the Twenty-First Century: Including Chinese, Classical Languages, French, German, Italian, Japanese, Portuguese, Russian, and Spanish. Lawrence: Natl. Standards in Foreign Lang. Educ. Project; Allen, 1999.

Starck, Taylor, and J. C. Wells, eds. *Althochdeutsches Glossenwörterbuch: Mit Stellennachweis zu sämtlichen gedruckten althochdeutschen und verwandten Glossen.* Heidelberg: Winter, 1971– .

"Statistical Retrospective: 1980–1999." *Monatshefte* 91 (1999): 537–39.

Stein, Ludwig. "Kulturpolitik." *Nord und Süd* 36 (1912): 9–16.

Stein, Mary Beth. "Coming to Terms with the Past: The Depiction of *Volkskunde* in the Third Reich since 1945." *Journal of Folklore Research* 24 (1987): 157–85.

———. "How Big Is Our Subject? Brokering Disciplinary and National Cultures." *Journal of Folklore Research* 36 (1999): 149–55.

———. "Wilhelm Heinrich Riehl and the Scientific-Literary Formation of *Volkskunde*." *German Studies Review* 24 (2001): 461–86.

Stephan, Alexander. *Christa Wolf.* Munich: Beck, 1976.

Stern, Guy. "Deutsch-jüdische Exilanten bei der amerikanischen Aufklärung—mit einem Exkurs über den Beitrag zukünftiger Germanisten." Schmitz 85–104.

Stone, George W. "The Beginning, Development, and Impact of the MLA as a Learned Society." *PMLA* 75 (1958): 23–44.

Stone, Priscilla. "The Remaking of African Studies." *Africa Today* 44 (1997): 179–84.

Strauss, Herbert A. "Wissenschaftsemigration als Forschungsproblem." Strauss, Fischer, Hoffmann, and Söllner 9–23.

Strauss, Herbert A., Klaus Fischer, Christhard Hoffmann, and Alfons Söllner, eds. *Die Emigration der Wissenschaften nach 1933. Disziplingeschichtliche Studien.* Munich: Saur, 1991.

Strauss, Herbert A., and Werner Röder, eds. *The Arts, Sciences, and Literature.* Munich: Saur, 1983. Vol. 2 of *International Biographical Dictionary of Central European Emigrés, 1933–1945.*

Strich, Fritz. *Deutsche Klassik und Romantik, oder Vollendung und Unendlichkeit.* Munich: Meyer, 1922.

Stroebe, Lilian L. "The Teaching of German Literature in College." *German Quarterly* 1 (1928): 120–31.

Strolle, Jon (associate provost for Executive and Special Programs, Monterey Inst. of Intl. Studies). Telephone conversation with David Benseler. 14 Sept. 1999.

Strum, Arthur. "German Studies and the Crisis of Humanistic Work." *German Quarterly* 73 (2000): 45–66.

Study-Visit Grants to Germany for AATG Members. AATG. 27 Feb. 2003. 28 Apr. 2003 <http://www.aatg.org/programs/index.html>. Path: DAAD Study-Visit Grants for 2003.

Suchoff, David. "Jüdische Kritik in der amerikanischen Nachkriegsgermanistik." *Weimarer Beiträge* 39 (1993): 393–409.

Sullivan, Constance. "The Corporatized Research University and Tenure in Modern Language Departments: Notes from Minnesota." *Profession 1999.* New York: MLA, 1999. 86–95.

Swender, Elvira, and Greg Duncan. "ACTFL Performance Guidelines for K-12 Learners." *Foreign Language Annals* 31 (1999): 479–91.

A Symposium on Intensive Civilian Courses in German Spec. issue of *German Quarterly* 19 (1946): 1–112.

Tatar, Maria, ed. *The Classic Fairy Tales.* New York: Norton, 1999.

———. *The Hard Facts of the Grimms' Fairy Tales.* Princeton: Princeton UP, 1987.

Tatlock, Lynne. Introduction. *From a Good Family.* By Gabriele Reuter. Trans. Tatlock. Rochester: Camden, 1999. xvi.

———. "Response to Hohendahl." McCarthy and Schneider 29–34.

Tatum, John H. *The Reception of German Literature in U.S. German Texts, 1864–1918.* New York: Lang, 1988.

Teraoka, Arlene. *East, West, and Others: The Third World in Postwar German Literature.* Lincoln: U of Nebraska P, 1996.

———. *The Silence of Entropy or Universal Discourse: The Postmodernist Poetics of Heiner Müller.* New York: Lang, 1985.

Tewarson, Heidi. "The Woman Question in the Early Work of Alfred Döblin." Women in German Symposium. Miami U, Oxford. 24 Sept. 1977.

Thomas, Calvin. *Report of the Committee of Twelve of the Modern Language Association of America.* Boston: Heath, 1901.

———. *"Scholarship" and Other Essays.* New York: Henry Holt, 1924.

Thomas, Ursula. "Mark Twain's German Language Learning Experiences." Benseler, Lohnes, and Nollendorfs 133–43.

Thrall, William Flint, and Addison Hibbard. *A Handbook to Literature.* Ed. C. Hugh Holman. New York: Odyssey, 1960.

Timm, Eitel F., ed. *Challenges of Germanistik: Traditions and Prospects of an Academic Discipline. / Germanistik Weltweit? Zur Theorie und Praxis des Disziplinrahmens.* Munich: Iudicium, 1992.

Tomorrow's Teachers: A Report of the Holmes Group. East Lansing: Holmes Group, 1986.

Traverso, Enzo. *The Jews and Germany: From the "Judeo-German Symbiosis" to the Memory of Auschwitz.* Trans. Daniel Weissbort. Lincoln: U of Nebraska P, 1995.

Trefousse, Hans L., ed. *Germany and America: Essays on the Problems of International Relations and Immigration.* New York: Brooklyn Coll. P, 1980.

Trommler, Frank. "Einleitung." Trommler, *Germanistik* 7–43.

———. "The Future of German Studies; or, How to Define Interdisciplinarity in the 1990s." *German Studies Review* 15 (1992): 201–17.

———, ed. *Germanistik in den USA: Neue Entwicklungen und Methoden.* Opladen: Westdeutscher, 1989.

———. "Germanistik nicht als Nationalphilologie: Die Entwicklung des Faches in den USA." Fürbeth et al. 863–78.

———. "Inventing the Enemy: German-American Cultural Relations, 1900–1917." *Confrontation and Cooperation: Germany and the United States in the Era of World War I, 1900–1924.* Ed. Hans-Jürgen Schröder. Providence: Berg, 1993. 99–125.

———. "Literary Scholarship and Ethnic Studies: A Reevaluation." *German? American? Literature? New Directions in German-American Studies.* Ed. Winfried Fluck and Werner Sollors. New York: Lang, 2002. 25–40.

———. "Recovering the History of Germanics in the United States: An Exploration." Benseler, Nickisch, and Nollendorfs 26–41.

———. "Updating German Studies in the New Century." *German Studies Association Newsletter* 26.2 (2001): 47–54.

Trommler, Frank, and Joseph McVeigh, eds. *America and the Germans: An Assessment of a Three-Hundred-Year History.* Vol. 2. Philadelphia: U of Pennsylvania P, 1985.

Trommler, Frank, and Elliott Shore, eds. *The German-American Encounter: Conflict and Cooperation between Two Cultures, 1800–2000.* New York: Berghahn, 2001.

Turner, Steve. "What Are Disciplines? And How Is Interdisciplinarity Different?" Weingart and Stehr 46–65.

Twaddell, W. Freeman. "The German Teacher: Professor on the Spot." Aug. 1938. W. Freeman Twaddell File. German. Box 15. Ts. Memorial Lib. Archives. U of Wisconsin, Madison.

———. Letter to Robert Hutchins. 7 Dec. 1938. Alewyn File. German 7/14/2. Box 1: Memorial Lib. Archives. U of Wisconsin, Madison.

Twarog, Leon. "Foreign Language Recommendations of the President's Commission and the JNCL Resolutions on Language in American Education: An Analysis." *Modern Language Journal* 64 (1980): 303–10.

Tyre, Ann B. "Increase Percentages in German in Various Universities, Colleges, and High Schools for the Last Two Biennia." *Monatshefte* 25 (1933): 42–47.

Unseld, Siegfried, ed. *Wie, warum und zu welchem Ende wurde ich Literaturhistoriker? Eine Sammlung von Aufsätzen aus Anlaß des 70. Geburtstages von Robert Minder.* Frankfurt: Suhrkamp, 1972.

Vail, Curtis C. D. "Editorial Letter." *German Quarterly* 17 (1944): 40–42.

——— "Language Learning and Scientific Method." *German Quarterly* 21 (1948): 143–52.

"Values, Objectives, Methods, and Materials of the Two-Year College Course in German: The Report of the Association's Committee." *German Quarterly* 21 (1948): 203–21.

Van Cleve, John, and A. Leslie Willson. *Remarks on the Needed Reform of German Studies in the United States.* Columbia: Camden, 1993.

van Coetsem, Frans, and Herbert Kufner, eds. *Toward a Grammar of Proto-Germanic.* Tübingen: Niemeyer, 1972.

Vance, Carole S., ed. *Pleasure and Danger: Exploring Female Sexuality.* Boston: Routledge, 1984.

VanPatten, Bill. "Attending to Form and Content in the Input: An Experiment in Consciousness." *Studies in Second Language Acquisition* 12 (1990): 287–301.

Veeser, H. Aram, ed. *The New Historicism*. New York: Routledge, 1989.

"Verhandlungen der 29. Jahresversammlung des Nationalen Deutschamerikanischen Lehrerbundes: Cleveland, Ohio, 5.–9. Juli 1899." *Pädagogische Monatshefte* 1.1 (1899): 17–23.

Veysey, Laurence R. *The Emergence of the American University*. Chicago: U of Chicago P, 1965.

Viëtor, Karl. "Deutsche Literaturgeschichte als Geistesgeschichte: Ein Rückblick." *PMLA* 60 (1945): 899–916.

———. Letter to Julius Peterson. 12 Feb. 1939. 66.1143/7: Deutsches Literaturarchiv, Marbach.

Viëtor, Wilhelm. Der Sprachunterricht muß umkehren: *Ein Pamphlet aus dem 19. Jahrhundert neu gelesen*. Ed. Konrad Schröder. München: Hueber, 1984.

Vogt, Silvia. "Zwischen Demokratie und Anti-Intellektualismus: Untersuchungen zur amerikanischen Germanistik, 1939–1945." Diss. New York U, 1994.

Vordtriede, Werner. *Das verlassene Haus: Tagebuch aus dem amerikanischen Exil, 1938–1947*. Munich: Hanser, 1975.

Voss, Ernst. "Zum Weltkriege." *Monatshefte* 16 (1915): 69–73.

Wadepuhl, Walter, and Bayard Quincy Morgan. *Minimum Standard German Vocabulary*. New York: Crofts, 1934.

Walz, John A. *German Influence in American Education and Culture*. Philadelphia: Carl Schurz Memorial Foundation, 1936.

Wartenberg, Dorothy. "A Critical Look at *Brigitte*." Women in German Conf. Miami U, Oxford, 25 Sept. 1976.

"Was in den Volksbibliotheken gelesen wird." *Monatshefte* 13 (1912): 25–26.

Watts, Michael. "African Studies at the Fin de Siecle: Is It Really the Fin?" *Africa Today* 44 (1997): 185–92.

Weber, Regina. "Zur Remigration des Germanisten Richard Alewyn." Strauss, Fischer, Hoffmann, and Söllner 235–56.

Weber, Sam. *Demarcating the Disciplines*. Minneapolis: U of Minnesota P, 1986.

Weed, Elizabeth, and Naomi Schor, eds. *Feminism Meets Queer Theory*. Bloomington: Indiana UP, 1997.

Weigand, Hermann. *The Modern Ibsen: A Reconstruction*. 1925. New York: Dutton, 1960.

———. *Thomas Mann's Novel* Der Zauberberg. New York: Appleton, 1933.

———. "Zu Otto Ludwigs *Zwischen Himmel und Erde*." *Fährten und Funde: Aufsätze zur deutschen Literatur*. Bern: Franke, 1967. 120–38.

———. "Zu Otto Ludwigs *Zwischen Himmel und Erde*." Weigand, *Fährten* 120–38.

Weigel, John C. "The Reorganization of Teachers' Training in German in Our Colleges and Universities." *Monatshefte* 17 (1916): 16–20, 34–44.

Weimar, Klaus. *Geschichte der deutschen Literaturwissenschaft bis zum Ende des 19. Jahrhunderts*. Munich: Fink, 1989.

Weiner, Marc A. "From the Editor." *German Quarterly* 69 (1996): v–ix.

———. "Letter from the New Editor of the *German Quarterly*." *AATG Newsletter* 30.1 (1994): n.p.

Weingart, Peter. "Interdisciplinarity: The Paradoxical Discourse." Weingart and Stehr 25–42.

Weingart, Peter, and Nico Stehr, eds. *Practising Interdisciplinarity*. Toronto: U of Toronto P, 2000.

Weisbuch, Robert. Foreword. *The Humanities Ph.D. and Careers outside the Academy: A Convening Organized by the Woodrow Wilson National Foundation Conference,*

22–24 October 1998. 12 Mar. 1999 <http://www.woodrow.org/conferences/phd/forword/htm>.

———. *Unleashing the Humanities: The Doctorate beyond the Academy.* 12 Mar. 1999 <http://www.woodrow.org/conferences/phd/agenda/htm>.

Weisert, John J. "Foreign Languages as Mental Discipline: A Survey." *German Quarterly* 12 (1939): 61–70.

Weiss, Gerhard. "From New York to Philadelphia: Issues and Concerns of the American Association of Teachers of German between 1926 and 1970." Benseler, Lohnes, and Nollendorfs 215–27.

———. "Presidential Address." *German Quarterly* 61 (1983): 366–73.

Weiss, Gerhard H., and Walter F. W. Lohnes. "The National Defense Language Institutes: A Benchmark in the Training of Teachers of German." Benseler, Nickisch, and Nollendorfs 185–91.

Wellbery, David, ed. *Positionen der Literaturwissenschaft: Acht Modellanalysen am Beispiel von Kleists* Das Erdbeben in Chili. 1985. 3rd ed. Munich: Beck, 1993.

Wellek, René. *American Criticism, 1900–1950.* London: Cape, 1986. Vol. 6 of *A History of Modern Criticism.*

———. *Concepts of Criticism.* Ed. Stephen G. Nichols. New Haven: Yale UP, 1963.

Wellek, René, and Austin Warren. Preface. Wellek and Warren, *Theory* 7–9.

———. *Theory of Literature.* 1949. 3rd ed. New York: Harcourt, 1963.

Wenger, Luke. "The Medieval Academy and Medieval Studies in North America." Gentry and Kleinhenz 23–40.

Werner, Meike, ed. *Publishing Culture: Cultural Studies and the History of Books in Modern Germany.* Spec. issue of *Germanic Review* 76 (2001): 283–348.

Whitney, William D. *A Compendious German Grammar.* 6th ed. New York: Henry Holt, 1888.

Whyte, John. *American Words and Ways, Especially for German Americans.* New York: Viking, 1943.

———. "On the Use of Phonograph Records in the Teaching of German Pronunciation." *German Quarterly* 4 (1931): 170–74.

Wiegman, Robyn, ed. *The Future of American Studies.* Spec. issue of *Cultural Critique* 40 (1998): 1–234.

Wiesehan, Gretchen. "The Myth of the Feminization of Germanistik." Bledsoe, Estabrook, Federle, Henschel, Miller, and Polster 27–30.

Wiggins, Grant. "Toward More Authentic Assessment of Language Performance." Hancock 69–85.

Wilberschied, Lee, and Jean-Louis P. Dassier. "Increasing the Number of Minority Foreign Language Educators: Local Action to Meet a National Imperative." *Modern Language Journal* 79 (1995): 1–14.

Wilhelm II. "Proclamation to the German Nation." *Monatshefte* 15 (1914): 229–30.

Williams, Patrick, and Laura Chrisman, eds. *Colonial Discourse and Post-colonial Theory: A Reader.* New York: Columbia UP, 1994.

Willing, Matthew H. "Present Trends in the Secondary School Curriculum and Their Implications for the Teaching of Modern Foreign Languages." *Monatshefte* 29 (1937): 275–84.

Winter, Joseph. "Der deutsche Unterricht in den New Yorker Schulen." *Monatshefte* 11 (1910): 179–83.

Wischkaemper, Richard. "Die neuen Sprachunterrichtsmethoden." *Monatshefte* 18 (1917): 129–35.

Witte, Barthold C. "Die Kulturabteilung des Auswärtigen Amtes im Schnittpunkt innenpolitischer Impulse." *Zeitschrift für Kulturaustausch* 31.2 (1981): 239–45.

Woldmann, Hermann. "Welche gemeinschaftlichen Ziele sollte der Unterricht im Deutschen unter den verschiedenen Schulsystemen haben?" *Monatshefte* 6 (1905): 264–67.

Wolf, Ernst. "Hilfsmittel für den Unterricht in der modernen Sprache." *Monatshefte* 10 (1909): 2–5.

———. "Lehrplan für die deutschen Klassen in der Hochschule von Saginaw, E. S., Mich." *Monateshefte* 2 (1901): 206–09.

Woodring, Carl. *Literature: An Embattled Profession.* New York: Columbia UP, 1999.

Wooley, E. O. "Five Decades of German Instruction in America." *Monatshefte* 36 (1944): 359–70.

Zantop, Susanne. *Colonial Fantasies: Conquest, Family, and Nation in Precolonial Germany, 1770–1870.* Durham: Duke UP, 1997.

Zelle, Carsten. "Emigrantengespräch: Ein Brief Richard Alewyns an Karl Viëtor." *Euphorion* 84 (1990): 213–27.

Zeller, Bernhard, ed. *Klassiker in finstren Zeiten, 1933–1945: Eine Ausstellung des Deutschen Literaturarchivs im Schiller-Nationalmuseum Marbach am Neckar.* Vol. 1. Stuttgart: Klett, 1983.

Zeydel, Edwin H. "Die germanistische Tätigkeit in Amerika, 1918–1926." *Euphorion* 29 (1928): 239–46.

———. "The Teaching of German in the United States from Colonial Times through World War I." Benseler, Lohnes, and Nollendorfs 15–54.

———. "The Teaching of German in the United States from Colonial Times to the Present." *German Quarterly* 37 (1964): 315–92.

Ziefle, Helmut. "Historical Forces, German Departments, and the Curriculum in Small Liberal Arts Colleges in the Midwest." Benseler, Nickisch, and Nollendorfs 173–91.

Zimmer-Loewe, Helene. "German Enrollments in American Schools and Colleges." Personal communication to David Benseler. Oct. 2000.

Ziolkowski, Theodore. *The Novels of Hermann Hesse: A Study in Theme and Structure.* Princeton: Princeton UP, 1965.

———. "The Seventies: Verweile doch! Du bist so schön!" *Monatshefte* 72 (1980): 245–53.

Zipes, Jack, ed. *Beauties, Beasts and Enchantments: Classic French Fairy Tales.* New York: New American Lib., 1989.

———. "Breaking the Magic Spell: Politics and the German Fairy Tale." *New German Critique* 6 (1975): 116–36.

———. *Breaking the Magic Spell: Radical Theories of Folk and Fairy Tales.* New York: Methuen, 1984. Rev. ed. Lexington: UP of Kentucky, 2002.

———. *The Brothers Grimm: From Enchanted Forests to the Modern World.* New York: Routledge, 1988.

———, ed. *The Great Fairy Tale Tradition: From Straparola and Basile to the Brothers Grimm.* New York: Norton, 2001.

———. "Might Makes Right: The Politics of Folk and Fairy Tales." Zipes, *Breaking* [1984] 20–40.

———, ed. *The Oxford Companion to Fairy Tales.* Oxford: Oxford UP, 2000.

———, ed. *Spells of Enchantment: The Wondrous Fairy Tales of Western Culture.* New York: Viking, 1991.

———. "The Struggle for the Grimms' Throne: The Legacy of the Grimms' Tales in the FRG and GDR since 1945." Haase, *Reception* 167–72.

———. "Toward a Theory of the Fairy Tale Film." *Happily Ever After: Fairy Tales, Children, and the Culture Industry*. New York: Routledge, 1997. 61–87.

———, ed. *The Trials and Tribulations of Little Red Riding Hood*. 2nd ed. New York: Routledge, 1993.

———, ed. *Victorian Fairy Tales: The Revolt of the Fairies and Elves*. New York: Methuen, 1987.

Zohn, Harry. *Wiener Juden in der deutschen Literatur*. Tel Aviv: Olamenu, 1964.

Dufner, Max, 42
Duke, Washington, 36
Duncan, Greg, 208
Dürrenmatt, Friedrich, 484
Dutch studies, 367, 368, 369
Düwell, Kurt, 465

Early German Romanticism (Silz), 223
East Germany. *See* German Democratic
    Republic (GDR)
Ebel, Peter, 442, 459
Ebert, Robert P., 288
Ebner-Eschenbach, Marie von, 130, 133,
    148, 150
Eckhoff, William J., 262
education theory, and language instruc-
    tion, 187, 200
Edwards, J. David, 109
Efron, John M., 305
Eggert, Hartmut, 246
Ehrlich, Edith, 149
Ehrmann, Madelyn E., 210
Eichendorff, Joseph von, 270, 271
Eichmann, Adolf, 418
Eichner, Hans, 409, 410, 411, 417, 467
Eighteenth-Century Studies (journal), 265
Einen Jux will er sich machen (Nestroy),
    59
Eiselmeier, J., 119, 120, 121
elementary schools
    foreign languages in, 199, 207, 337
    German classes in, 193, 195, 200,
        325–26, 335
    minorities in, 429
    religion in, 325–27
    teacher training for, 193, 326–27,
        363–64
Eliot, Charles William, 67, 100, 356, 453
Elling, Barbara, 51, 89n3
Elliott, A. Marshall, 351, 352
Ellis, Frances H., 126
Ellis, John, 296, 385
Ellis Collection, 126–34
Emerson, Oliver Farrar, 94
Emerson, Ralph Waldo, 32, 480
Emory University, 43
employment patterns, in German stud-
    ies, 83–89, 141
    See also faculty members; Germanists
Engelmann, Peter, 326
English studies
    and critical theory, 488
    and emergence of literary criticism,
        485
    and feminism, 242
    and foreignness, 490

history of, 1, 220
impact on Germanics of, 3, 8–9, 29,
    213, 382
and linguistics, 286, 291
and multiculturalism, 488
and poststructuralism, 274
and scientific methodology, 212,
    215, 221
    See also New Criticism
enrollments, in German programs
    contemporary drop in, 1, 3, 14, 49–
        50, 78, 93, 104–05, 115, 116,
        207, 362, 378, 385n2, 423, 424,
        487
    efforts to increase, 18, 39–41, 63,
        109, 110, 115, 362–63, 382, 383,
        385, 423
    factors influencing, 39, 47, 95, 115,
        138
    graduate-level, 34, 35, 40–41, 93, 115
    importance of, 107–08, 111, 115,
        116–17, 138, 332, 364, 424
    and Jewish studies, 305
    and language study, 95
    late-nineteenth-century, 114
    long-term decline in, 96, 105–06,
        117
    after Sputnik, 47, 48, 61–62, 76, 108–
        09, 320
    statistical data on, 40, 115–16, 320,
        356
    WWI-era, 11, 12, 39, 40–41, 58, 109,
        112–13, 114, 335, 360, 361, 392,
        441
    WWII-era, 42–43, 104, 110, 114
Enzyklopädie des Märchens (Ranke), 295,
    298
Equal Opportunity Employment Act
    (1972), 66
Ernst, Paul, 268, 414
Erziehungsblätter (journal), 327, 354
Eshel, Amir, 303, 305, 369
Estabrook, Bernd, 63
ethnic studies, 376, 384
    See also German Jewish studies; Jews;
        minorities
Eucken, Rudolf, 464
Europe
    as context for German studies, 15–
        16, 40, 176, 476–77, 487, 490
    United States cultural connections
        to, 488–89
Everett, Edward, 218, 480
exchange programs
    for faculty members, 8, 31, 47, 406,
        415–16, 463, 464, 465

State Department, United States,
Division for Cultural Relations, 466
State University of New York (SUNY),
44–45, 47, 49
Steakley, James, 273
Stegemeier, Henri, 42, 43
Stehr, Hermann, 268, 414
Stehr, Nico, 183n1, n6
Stein, Hannes, 459
Stein, Jack M., 43, 149, 363
Stein, Ludwig, 461
Stein, Mary Beth, 294, 298
Steinhauer, Harry, 149
Steinmetz, Charles, 453
Stephan, Alexander, 236, 270, 310
Stern, Guy, 410, 411, 467
Stern, J. P., 415
Stone, George W., 319, 334
Stone, Priscilla, 183n2
Storm, Theodor, 129, 130, 138, 148,
356, 411
Straparola, Giovan Francesco, 297
Strauss, Herbert A., 467
Strich, Fritz, 221, 223
Stroebe, Lilian L., 103, 399, 402, 417
Strolle, Jon, 109
Strum, Arthur, 393
Struthmann, Friedrich Wilhelm, 41
structuralism, 15, 61, 231, 238, 247,
260, 269
American, 289
See also poststructuralism
student movement, United States, 231
study-abroad programs, 31, 47, 87, 207,
341, 344, 356, 468
Nazi sponsorship of, 404–05
See also exchange programs
Suchoff, David, 415
Sudermann, Hermann, 130, 411
Suhr, Heidrun, 442, 459
Suhrkamp (publisher), 304, 346
Sullivan, Constance, 89n1
Summer Seminars in German Studies,
459
Swaffar, Janet, 46
Swarthmore College, 43, 48, 50, 417,
450
Swender, Elvira, 208, 211n3
Swiggett, Glen Levin, 262
Switzerland, cultural initiatives in,
469n1, 470
Syberberg, Hans Jürgen, 376

Taine, Hippolyte Adolphe, 219
Tappan, Henry P., 396

Tartakower, S. G., 409
Tatar, Maria, 297, 298
Tatlock, Lynne, 18, 25–26, 143, 148,
361, 427
Tatum, John Hargrove, 480
Taylor, Bayard, 219, 486
teacher training
of college teachers, 122
current concerns about, 209
for elementary schools, 193
in foreign languages, 201
FRG-funded support for, 473
NDEA support for, 202
overview of, 93, 119–24
proposals for, 45, 383
reading lists for, 144
and specialization, 147–48
teaching
intrinsic rewards of, 72–73, 74
second-class status of, 66–68, 80, 85
See also faculty members; foreign
language courses; German
language
teaching assistants (TAs), 42, 43, 44, 45,
46, 94, 111, 114, 141
Teaching of German: Problems and Methods, The (Reichmann), 203
technology, instructional, 191, 200–01,
207
Telos (journal), 233, 312
tenure system, 68, 69, 74, 82, 82n1, 88,
95, 181, 340, 363, 400, 416–17
Teraoka, Arlene, 15, 85, 250–51, 309,
392, 393, 421–23
Terrell, Tracy, 206
testing, standardized, 199, 202–03, 205–
06
Tewarson, Heidi, 238
Texas, University of, 43, 122, 290
textbooks
for children, 97, 126, 236
college-level, 48, 99, 134, 204, 399,
480
development of, 333
FRG funding for, 472
graded, 202
in high schools, 145–48
historical overviews of, 93, 96, 125–
34
images of Germany in, 96, 125, 130,
131, 143, 146
literary selections in, 128, 129–30,
132, 133
and Nazi propaganda, 405
publishers, 133–34